D1272524

The SAGE Handbook of
MEDIA STUDIES

The SAGE Handbook of
MEDIA STUDIES

Editor-in-Chief

JOHN D. H. DOWNING
University of Illinois, Carbondale

Associate Editors

DENIS McQUAIL
University of Southampton

PHILIP SCHLESINGER
University of Sterling

ELLEN WARTELLA
University of California, Riverside

SAGE Publications
Thousand Oaks ■ London ■ New Delhi

For information:

Sage Publications, Inc.
2455 Teller Road
Thousand Oaks, California 91320
E-mail: order@sagepub.com

Sage Publications Ltd.
1 Oliver's Yard
55 City Road
London EC1Y 1SP
United Kingdom

Sage Publications India Pvt. Ltd.
B-42, Panchsheel Enclave
Post Box 4109
New Delhi 110 017 India

Printed in the United States of America on acid-free paper.

Library of Congress Cataloging-in-Publication Data

The SAGE handbook of media studies / edited by John D. H. Downing, Denis McQuail, Philip Schlesinger, Ellen Wartella.
    p. cm.
Includes bibliographical references and index.
ISBN 0-7619-2169-9 (cloth)
   1. Mass media—Handbooks, manuals, etc. I. Downing, John.
P90.S18 2004
302.23—dc22

2004007121

04 05 06 07 08 09 10 9 8 7 6 5 4 3 2 1

Acquiring Editors:	Margaret H. Seawell and Julia Hall
Editorial Assistant:	Jill Meyers
Project Editor:	Claudia A. Hoffman
Copy Editor:	Gillian Dickens
Typesetter:	C&M Digitals (P) Ltd.
Indexer:	Kathy Paparchontis
Cover Designer:	Janet Foulger

CONTENTS

ACKNOWLEDGMENTS

I would like to thank all the contributors to this volume; my fellow-editors; Margaret Seawell and Julia Hall, Acquisitions Editors at Sage California and London, and Claudia Hoffman, Project Editor at Sage California; Caroline Frith, editorial assistant, and doctoral candidate at the University of Texas, Austin; my former faculty and staff colleagues, friends and students in the Radio-Television-Film Department at UT-Austin; my current faculty and staff colleagues, friends and students in the College of Mass Communication and Media Arts at Southern Illinois University, Carbondale, in particular Dean Manjunath Pendakur; my partner of many happy years, Ash Corea; and our daughters.

I dedicate this volume to the memory of Dr Marjorie Ferguson, journalist, researcher, teacher, formerly of *Woman* magazine, the London School of Economics and the University of Maryland, whose intellectual perspicacity, personal warmth and sardonic wit served as a model for researchers in media, and beyond.

—John Downing
Global Media Research Center,
Southern Illinois University

OVERVIEW OF THE HANDBOOK

◆ Denis McQuail

◆ *Identifying the Field*

The field of communication and media studies is far from unique in having uncertain boundaries, a mixed history, and an unclear future path of development. In putting together this volume, the editors have implicitly presented a certain view of the field, based on their own judgments of significance and relevance. This introduction is not a collective effort but the view of one editor, describing and reflecting on the various strands and components that contribute to the story but that may be combined in different ways and with different degrees of emphasis. This is at least consistent with a central tenet of communication theory—namely, that there can be no unique or fixed version of any supposed reality.

There is no doubt that communication and media study is an aspect of reality, objectified in programs of study and research, books, journals, associations of professionals, degrees and diplomas, and so forth. But even without appealing to the intrinsic uncertainty of message encodings and decodings, it is obviously extremely various in what it covers and where its emphasis might lie. There is little point in trying to reduce this ultimate diversity to any central definition of the "field." Where it has been attempted (as by Berger & Chaffee, 1987, in what was in some respects a forerunner of this book), it is likely to claim precedence for a partial view of the field. But there is some point at the start of this collection in seeking to map out contours and parameters, if only to provide readers with some idea of the interconnections between chapters and of the thinking that led to choosing topics and authors.

Such histories of the field that have been written do largely agree on finding the origin of the field in the phenomenon of *mass communication,* which was first labeled as such in the 1930s. The primary focus of attention was the then new mass media of film, phonograph, and radio that appeared in the industrialized world (primarily Europe and North America) between 1895 and 1920. Newspaper and magazine publishing had a much longer prehistory but only became a true mass medium towards the end of the 19th century. By 1950, these media had been joined by television, and all could be treated within much the same frame of reference. They all shared the same capacity to reach and appeal to the majority of a national population on a more or less continuous basis, with a potential for various consequences of great significance from various perspectives. The central focus in this early phase was on various "effects" and models, and theories of mass media as well as research designs were shaped accordingly. The "dominant paradigm" of (mass) communication research treated the media message as a powerful (and scarcely avoidable) stimulus that could lead to predictable responses in behavior, attitudes, and opinions on a society-wide basis (Gitlin, 1978; McQuail, 2000).

This version of the phenomenon of mass communication that was established by mid-century was one that appealed to sociologists and also to a wide range of would-be communicators, especially advertisers, politicians, and governments seeking control by persuasion and information. At the same time, it alarmed another set of interests, especially educators and moral guardians fearful of harmful effects on the young and impressionable, as well as social theorists with varying value positions and members of cultural elites foreseeing a debasement of values. Theoretical opponents of mass communication (few were in favor) ranged from conservative thinkers who deplored the fragmentation of society and the decay of institutions of cohesion and order (church, school, nation, family)

to liberals and social critics who saw in the mass media a force for hegemony and total control by an established order, whether statist or capitalist.

The influence of external (neither media nor academic) interests in defining the field has not always been benign. It has given recurrent support to banal and primitive notions of the processes at work in communication. It has also resulted in needless repetition of research, especially where one "mass medium" succeeds another and gives rise to much the same notions of effect. Political or commercial motives and judgments often trump scientific perspectives and prevent objective assessment. On the other hand, the need to operate in a context of public concern and political sensitivity heightens the excitement of research and forces those in the field to face up to questions of objectivity, value implications of research, and critical purpose.

It can be understood, from these brief remarks, that the study of media and communication was powerfully driven in its early years by influential and vocal forces outside the academy and in the public domain, more so than by the inner logic of any single established discipline. In fact, the rise of communication as a branch of theory and research coincided with the emergence of the social sciences (especially sociology and psychology), and for the most part, it was their way of thinking and methods that were adopted for purposes of inquiry. On this matter, national histories tend to be divergent. The United States can be credited as the first main home of the new branch of inquiry, although it is worth noting that the formal study of the newspaper was already established in Germany at the turn of the 20th century under the name *Zeitungswissenschaft,* or newspaper studies (Hardt, 1979; Rosengren, 2000), and there are direct links with subsequent American media research, especially the work of Robert Park (Turner, 1967). The German diaspora during the Nazi period reinforced the continental influence in

America just as it impoverished the German tradition (Averbeck, 2001). World War II had the effect of consolidating U.S. "hegemony" of the field (Tunstall, 1977), as well as reinforcing the individualist and effect-centered paradigm.

Inevitably, this potted early history does not do justice to many details and byways of intellectual history. A more general notion of a "science of human communication," not focused on mass media as institutions and broad social effects, was also emerging from the 1920s onwards, based on the work of psychologists of learning, sociologists working on small groups and having interpersonal interactions in various settings, and students of speech and rhetoric. Not least important were proposals for a field of cybernetics, which opened the way for research in computer and information studies (Wiener, 1948). However, for the most part, these alternative pathways have not flowed strongly into the "mainstream" of media study as it has developed, although they have contributed to a contemporary profusion of subfields that also carry the term *communication* in their titles. The selection of content for this book has been guided by a continuing tradition of mass media study that starts out as described, although it has evolved and become internally differentiated to encompass a wide range of intellectual positions.

The diversification of paradigms is explored further below, especially with reference to the decay of the "dominant" social scientific paradigm. However, in one way or another, our implicit identification of the field, in terms of subject matter at least, still links it with the operation of institutionalized media in the public sphere and with considerations of collective and longer term consequences for society. In some respects, the field is still about mass communication, and on a superficial inspection, most of the topics that are named in chapter titles would be recognized and understood by an informed reader of 50 years ago. However, as noted later, mass communication itself has changed and comprises only a part of the spectrum of communication activities under study.

◆ Alternative Points of Entry

The diversity that is concealed by long familiar topic names is exhibited in more than one way. One has to do with the route by which one comes to problematize media and communication in the first place. There are different motivations at work and different aspects of the reality of the media phenomenon to be highlighted. There are many ways of describing the various approaches to media and schools of thought, but most explanatory power seems to derive from looking at different disciplinary or thematic perspectives on much the same subject matter. The perspectives chosen for elucidation in this introduction focus selectively on certain aspects of the larger "media problematic." Along with different priorities come differences of method and of style of inquiry. There is no possibility or even need to be exhaustive in seeking to cover the field, but we have tried to represent the most important issues and lines of enquiry, as they seem to us. The descriptions that follow are intended to provide a framework that will help to make interconnections between the work of our contributors and provide a shared context.

TECHNOLOGY OF COMMUNICATION

The various forms of media have all been grouped together above under the collective term *mass media* because they seem to share at least the capacity to disseminate large amounts of the same information and stimuli from a central point to peripheries and to countless individual receivers. This apparent common property conceals significant differences in the type of content that different media can carry, in the relations established between senders and receivers, and in the type of experience that characterizes the audience experience. Different media can be defined according to different kinds of criteria (social, psychological, physical), but the most salient difference is that of type of technology, even if the matter is very complex, with any given technology having several relevant dimensions of difference. For present purposes, we can say, nevertheless, that a technology perspective opens a wide range of questions, including the basic one of *degree* of determination from a given type of technology to uses and consequences when applied (Schement & Curtis, 1995).

Indeed, the development of the field has been affected in various ways by debate about technological determinism. Proponents of a certain technological determinism, starting most famously with Canadian scholars Innis (1950) and McLuhan (1964) in regard to television, are inclined to see successive new media as each opening a new era with quite different but broad social consequences. McLuhan's work provided the foundation for various formulations of "medium theory" (see Meyrowitz, 1985) that have sought to distill the implications of a given technology as it has been applied for the communicative relations it sustains and, ultimately, the social effects that might be expected. In our time, computer-based digital media, especially as they are being institutionalized in the Internet, are also regarded as heralding a new era, effectively engendering a communications revolution with many and still unpredictable consequences. Thoughts along these lines give further support to the idea that we are now entering the phase of a new "Information Society" (see Webster, 2003, for a critical account) that is replacing the postindustrial society.

The essential nature and likely consequences of the so-called new media (see Chapters 6 and 7, this volume) are still being explicated and evaluated, but there is no doubt that there are significant differences from the "old" or traditional mass media. The new media are much more productive and flexible and more accessible to more people as senders and receivers. They have an interactive capacity quite unlike that of mass media and are able to disseminate rapidly and cheaply on a very large scale. We are at the stage when technological capacity has still to be translated into institutional reality and a clear pattern of use. The new media are hailed as personally and socially liberating by their advocates, but pessimists still suspect that they will be largely incorporated into an industrial and commercial imperium, with global ramifications, that does not value their liberating potential as much as their profitability. Technological determinist theories are of little help in resolving this argument because they can sustain both optimism and pessimism. There is no substitute for the systematic observation and assessment that is already taking place within the field of media and communication (Lievrouw & Livingstone, 2002).

Media as Text

The most visible and (until recently) lasting evidence of processes of media communication at work has been the texts that are produced and disseminated in vast quantities (see Chapters 5 and 20, this volume). Early students of the media were drawn to examine this evidence for clues to possible effects and also motives of originators. Much of the early theory of mass communication was based on simple ideas drawn from the evidence recorded in words, sounds, and pictures (Berelson, 1952; Holsti, 1969), coupled with some assumptions about direct effects. Media texts were seen as repetitive and persuasive, carrying deeply encoded messages in support of, or deviant from, the established order; they were also judged as to their conformity with or distortion of a social reality. George Gerbner and colleagues (see Signorielli & Morgan, 1990) wrote of "message systems" that carried powerful and consistent messages to media audiences, with "cultivating" effects. Critical attention to such theorizing, derived especially from audience reception research (see Chapters 8 and 11, this volume), led to the recognition that media texts "as transmitted" are only part of the story because in the process of "decoding," many variant texts are produced by readers according to individual differences and social and cultural contexts.

In a parallel development, the texts of media were taken up for analysis from a linguistic perspective and subjected to semiological analysis with a view to disclosing their hidden as well as overt meanings (Barthes, 1967). The main purpose was not to study effects but to shed light on the culture in which such texts were produced and read, as well as to advance the "science of signs." There are many variants and branches of textual analysis, with many now operating in the separate disciplinary field of discourse studies, although they are still relevant for the study of media. Important in what is sometimes called the "linguistic turn" of media research (Jensen & Jankowski, 1991) is the possibility (perhaps necessity) of treating media texts as coextensive with and similar to many other very different kinds of "text," including conversations, photographs, film, displays, designs, architecture, performances, and so on. In this volume, Holden (Chapter 22) gives an account of research on advertising texts, and Zuberi (Chapter 21) looks at different aspects of music as a communicative form. The concept of intertextuality captures the idea of a web of forms of meaning connecting media experiences with the rest of experience. It also helps in grappling with the "texts" that characterize the latest mass medium, that of the Internet, warning us against trying to reduce these to some conventional model derived from the old mass media. The overt component of interactivity in the production of texts, as well as the hybridity of forms, is a challenge for contemporary analysis.

Power and Politics

Of the perennial issues that have drawn public as well as scholarly attention to the media, none is more potent than that of the relation between media and politics (see Chapter 16, this volume). The perception of the mass media as a tool of propaganda, in both the national as well as the international arena, exerted a strong influence on the founding of the field. For the most part, the term *propaganda* was first invoked in a negative sense to denigrate the communicative efforts of one's opponents (Jowett & O'Donnell, 1999) or to label the *misuse* of the mass media (usually by demonized foreign regimes, especially communistic or fascist) for the ends of party or state. In nominally free and democratic societies of the mid- to later 20th century, the mass media were expected to play a supportive but somewhat subordinate role in the political process by informing and advising citizens about electoral choices and providing a two-way channel of communication between citizens and government (see Chapter 17, this volume). This "service" to the democratic society would ideally be provided without undue imbalance or distortion and in a responsible and journalistically objective manner.

This textbook ideal was rarely to be found in practice, and the media were often embroiled in public controversy for their failure to live up to many aspects of the role, according to the perception of many actors in the public sphere. The media were variously accused of following the prejudices of their wealthy owners, failing to inform the public adequately either through neglect or sensationalist practices. Broadcasting regimes were constructed in many countries to secure compliance with public and political expectations (see Chapter 23, this volume). In many countries, some limits were set to press concentration, and in some cases, support was given to the press to ensure its democratic functioning. Latterly, the institutional arrangements for such purposes have weakened.

Media have become bigger and more international businesses, with less interest in their role in domestic politics and more inclined to follow consumer demand wherever it leads than political wishes or democratic theory. The ensuing "crisis of public communication" that is allegedly upon us has an additional and relatively novel component. The belief in the power of media to deliver positive results to political campaigners and the intensity of efforts to gain beneficial access to the media have never been stronger, even though mass interest in media coverage of politics has seemed to decline. The new component consists in a shift from direct persuasion by argument or exhortation and advocacy to the skillful management of information in all its forms, especially when it comes as "news," which carries expectations of reliability and retains some trust on the part of the public. The study of political communication is now a very broad field of inquiry that requires attention to not only traditional objects of study, such as election campaigns, but also the economic ties that link media with political power, as well as law, regulation, and policy as they affect the freedoms and obligations of media in relation to political actors. As Wasko reminds us (see Chapter 15, this volume), many of the fundamental issues in the territory of exercising power in society can best be handled in terms of a political economic approach that takes account of the unequal distribution of resources, especially ownership and control of the means of media production and distribution.

MEDIA USE AND EFFECT

The large territory identified by this summary heading lies at the heart of the earliest maps of the field, as indicated above. The earliest reasons for studying media stemmed from practical concerns of the media industry to know about their audience and market or those of would-be communicators to plan their strategies, as well as from fears of harmful social and individual effects as perceived by observers (although not on the whole by those mainly observed—namely, media audiences). There is no need to say much at this point because the ground is either familiar or well covered in several chapters in this book, especially those by McDonald (Chapter 9), Kitzinger (Chapter 8), Holden (Chapter 22), MacBeth (Chapter 10), and Smith, Moyer-Gusé, and Donnerstein (Chapter 26), but a few key points need to be underlined.

Firstly, there is the matter of media use as a form of behavior and time use, the sheer volume of which has continued to provoke surprise and sometimes even alarm. The reading of books, magazines, and newspapers was often looked down on in earlier times, more because of the content than the time devoted to it. This changed with audiovisual media and especially television, for which reliable evidence began to place watching television as a time use second only to sleeping or working for many in the industrialized world. The notion of *addiction* has been floated from time to time to apply to media use, even though the degree of attraction hardly justifies the term. After surprise and alarm came the search for reasons for this exceptional investment of time, even if much of it replaced doing nothing and other pastimes of earlier ages. The explanations that have emerged from research are in fact highly varied, showing media use to have no single meaning and to be linked to many other aspects of social circumstances and lifestyles.

Secondly, in respect of media industries and their aspirations to stimulate and manage demand for their product, it cannot be claimed that research into media use has delivered many reliable tools for this purpose. Although accurate estimation of past "exposure" or use behavior has improved, despite increasingly complex patterns of choice in a multimedia environment, audience likes and dislikes, in addition to media successes and failures, still remain largely outside the range of prediction and explanation. Media use is still more determined by users than by suppliers of content, and the manipulation of demand is more art than science. There are, nevertheless, certain constants stemming from the relatively fixed contours of social structure, known distributions of tastes, and ingrained habits and routines that help to reduce the potential disorder and allow an overall view of territory to be arrived at. These remarks reflect different positions that have been taken up by students of media, separating the proponents of control from critics of a system whose ultimate goal is to deliver consumers to advertisers (see Chapter 22).

A third set of comments is called for in relation to the "fearful" perspective on media. Firstly, it should be acknowledged that the media institution is not primarily in the business of causing harm to individuals and society. For the most part, the reverse is true. It aims to provide information and "harmless" entertainment and to make channels available for diverse other communicative services. When harm is feared, leaving aside time-wasting and displacement effects, it stems mainly from unintended or unpredictable harm from certain content or from inappropriate exposure on the part of vulnerable categories of people to content that is in itself justifiable. This does not exclude the possibility of certain kinds of serious (though not physical) injury being experienced by individuals directly or indirectly or that of injurious acts being stimulated by some media message. In light of these remarks, it is not surprising that most research attention has focused on the media environment of children and young people, who are both vulnerable to harm and may be caught up accidentally in the audience for inappropriate content (see Perse, 2000).

We should also keep in mind that *harm* has to be defined in terms of values and standards and that many potentially harmful effects from media are unrelated to crime, violence, aggression, bad language, and antisocial behavior, the staple ingredients of past research agenda. These include matters of systematically distorting or neglecting the truth, whether or not by design; fostering prejudice; and causing offence on a variety of grounds, including gender, race, politics, religion, nationality, and so on. Although such matters can and have been

investigated in the tradition of empirical inquiry into audience and effects, a much broader approach is called for than is available within the original empirical research tradition that centers on "who said what to whom and with what effect." We have to investigate ethical issues and become informed about relevant norms and values, cultural standards, and beliefs (see Chapter 1, this volume).

Questions in the area of possible harm from media cannot be framed without deploying clear ideas of what the media's freedoms and responsibilities are in the sphere of content at issue. They cannot be answered without taking account of the cultural context of production and reception of media. Inquiry into possible harm from media has to take place with an awareness of the mixed and conflicting imperatives driving the media as a whole. These include, on one hand, a range of normative purposes or communicative ideals that are appropriate to the creative and informative role of media and, on the other hand, the material and commercial purposes that drive media firms and organizations (and those they service) and also motivate many individuals working in media.

FEMINIST MEDIA THEORY

Media research from a feminist perspective made its appearance during the 1970s and has had a significant impact on subsequent development of the field. The main driving force was the women's movement itself, seeking to put right numerous inequalities in society between women and men. The relevance of the media for this research issue stemmed initially from a view of the media as a powerful socializing force that was currently largely directed at sustaining the subordinate position of women but might potentially improve it. Attention focused most on the widespread representation of women and the role of women in inferior terms in fiction, news, and advertising (Tuchman, Daniels, & Benet,

1978). Essentially, the media were seen as reinforcing stereotyped perceptions of the role of women that held back progress. As a matter of fact, it was also apparent that most media were owned and managed by men, and media content of all kinds was produced by men (often for women).

Both early and late, media research has reflected particular concerns on the part of women about the quality of media content and especially about its potential role in provoking violence against women or spreading degrading and offensive images of women, especially in various forms of pornography. Women have also often been in the forefront of demands that media should respect the interests of children and other vulnerable groups. Although the question of media pornography and its effects has been a matter of contention within the women's movement itself and in the assessment of media effects (Perse, 2001), there is a general public sentiment that favors the concerns of women in these matters, as described, despite implications for freedom of the media.

Beyond the question of role portrayal and offensive content, the range of attention widened considerably (see Van Zoonen, 1994) to embrace the proposition that media made by women might be fundamentally different and speak more satisfactorily to women's experience. It was also thought necessary to represent the perspective of women as audiences much more effectively, especially by qualitative and ethnographic study of the female audience for popular content largely directed at women (e.g., soap operas).

In fact, all forms of audience experience could claim to need a more adequate interpretation in terms of feminist perspectives (see Chapters 11 and 12, this volume). There has been a proliferation of work on these and other themes, although most feminist-inspired media research has reflected a predominant interest in audiences and content. More recently, the appearance of new media, especially the Internet, has given rise to new issues about

the involvement of women as users and the implications for a number of the issues raised above. Although the fields of women's and gender studies have gained their own independence since the earliest gender-related media research, they have retained a key place as subfields within the discipline of media and communication.

CULTURAL ISSUES

Communication and culture are inextricably mixed, as are media studies and cultural studies. Several contributions in this book, notably that by Hermes (Chapter 12), shed light on the complexities of this interrelationship. Simple attempts to draw a consistent line between the two by distinguishing a sphere of the cultural from matters of structure (media and social) are not very viable, although they serve some very limited purposes. It is possible, for instance, to regard all media texts as "cultural" products and apply methods of cultural analysis to unpack their putative or attributed meanings (see Chapter 20, this volume). But this opens up the need to take account of the "culture" (in other senses) of producers and receivers, crossing the line that has been drawn.

In simpler times, it was thought possible to examine the "cultural role" of the media by identifying some types of content as more "cultural" than others (e.g., drama, fiction, and music) or by distinguishing some content as more culturally valuable (e.g., "art," classical music, and traditional or regional art or performance). In the latter mode, the distinctions made between "high culture" and "popular culture" were applied to the role of mass media (typically viewed as carriers of popular culture). Such lines of inquiry did little more than express and reinforce cultural preconceptions or ended in tautology.

When the source of definition of cultural value was not derived from class or social hierarchy but from ethnicity, locality, or differences of taste as such, some more progress could be made in investigating the relation between media and culture. For instance, when the debates about media "imperialism" that erupted in the 1970s posed the problem of media as global disseminators of Western, consumerist, or commercial media culture to the detriment of older, indigenous, and arguably more authentic local cultures (and languages), it became possible to pose and investigate the issues arising. At least it was possible to identify relevant cultural artifacts (in media texts of words, music, or film), state clear criteria of preference, and empirically investigate relevant media flows. Although the debates have cooled, the theme remains a lively one in various parts of the world—it is an issue not only between North and South but also within nation–states, where cultural diversity is adhered to as a value (see Chapter 3, this volume).

However, the main transformation in the study of media cultural issues did not arrive by the "globalization" route but by the decomposition of the notion of "popular" and its reassembly in terms of relevance to everyday life and closeness to cultural and social experience. In essence, there was a popular revolt (although not led by the people) that rejected the hierarchical notion of *popular* as synonymous with *inferiority* (in cultural as well as social terms). The story of the revalidation of the popular has often been told by its critics as well as its advocates, but when the dust has dispersed, it can be seen that the study of popular media, including their meaning and use, has been largely redefined if not actually taken over by an entirely different tribe in a different territory to that being described here (see Fiske, 1987). The effective takeover was carried from a variety of perspectives, including the feminist, the socially subversive, and that of the true aficionado of the popular. Putting it crudely, the fans took over the study of popular culture from the accountants, classifiers, and number crunchers. The mainstream study of media was largely initiated by social scientists and carried (still perhaps) without any necessary

affection for much of what media are doing. Where there was deep interest, it was likely to be in news and journalism.

There is another essential component to this account, however, although it is not offered as an alternative. In the late 20th century, similar social and theoretical influences affected the humanities as well as the social sciences. The traditional humanistic and literary branches of inquiry for which the study of "culture" had long been the primary goal also turned their attention to popular cultural forms, formerly disregarded as without merit. Something similar happened in relation to anthropology, the other main traditional "owner" of the study of culture and of everyday life. Media use practices and popular cultural content opened up a new frontier for anthropological exploration, with many new subcultures and rich flora. These trends both exposed the limited capacity of the social sciences to study media culture and also removed much of the subject matter to other branches of the academy.

An Industrial and Commercial Perspective

Several different topics appear under this heading, but the main point is to highlight the material and economic character of the media institution as distinct from its sociological, cultural, and political aspects, which played the main role in getting the study of media and communication started and defined it as pertaining to the social sciences and humanities. Of course the media, from the first books and newspapers, were commercial enterprises, requiring capital, labor, and other material resources of production and distribution. It is also fairly clear that the steep path of innovation and development of media technology has been driven more by economic forces than by considerations of perceived societal or consumer needs. There are exceptions to this generalization when it comes to the actions of states in securing strategic communication resources or, exceptionally, when engaged in certain programs of political control.

Firstly, economic interest in media has increased steadily, as media businesses have steadily grown and diversified and become a core component of the whole information sector. Media software (culture and content) have come to be seen a key to the expansion of hardware manufacturing, and more and more links are made between media and other fields of commercial activity and consumption, including leisure, sport, travel, finance, and many other personal services. Not least, advertising continues to be regarded as another key to general economic control and over an expanding area (see Chapter 22, this volume). The "media industrial sector," if it can be identified as such, is not just at the mercy or behest of other powerful economic interests, as perceived in earlier critical media theory. It is one of those sources of power in its own right. This does not invalidate the critical point but changes the manner in which problems have to be formulated and introduces new issues. Our selection of content gives particular attention to the place of the film industry in 20th-century media (see Chapters 24 and 25, this volume).

This affects certain themes of inquiry that have long been represented in the field and adds to their importance. One such theme concerns the nature of media work. The sociology of news production (see Chapter 19, this volume) has long provided insights into the requirements and consequences of production constraints and routines, especially in relation to news making, typically with the "newsroom" of a traditional newspaper or television station as the context. Many findings are still relevant, but the organization of all kinds of media work (distribution and production) has been and is being changed drastically by new technology and forms of control and organization of work— not least through the expansion of the workforce and change in its composition, with new skills, trades, and professions.

Secondly, there are implications, arising for similar reasons, for traditional "media economics" (see Chapter 14, this volume). In earlier times, the media were of less interest to economists, and economics was (or appeared) somewhat peripheral to media work and organization. It sometimes seems now that it is economics rather than technology or social purpose that provides the main dynamic of media activity. Not only the expansion and diversification of media economic activity is of relevance but also their steadily increasing internationalization. Although the media seem to remain primarily national in terms of structure and organization, the markets for many media products are more and more global (see Chapter 3, this volume). Another factor in current changes is the convergence of different forms of media, either for technological reasons (especially digitization) or for reasons of market synergy. Media economics in its earlier days tended to treat each medium separately, as if having a self-contained market. However, the whole character and structure of media markets is undergoing profound changes for these and other reasons, requiring a major reconceptualization.

Thirdly, new conditions briefly described have consequences for the relations between media and governments, especially as represented in frameworks of policy, law, and regulation. One feature is that governments no longer have the same capacity as they once had to control media within national frontiers or to secure frontiers against "invasion," although geography and language may still do this effectively. The Internet is the chief example of a medium that seems essentially ungovernable (see Lessig, 1999), although this may change. In fact, the general trend has been for a withdrawal of direct government regulation of media, where it existed. Governments prefer to leave details to self-regulation by media industries, which have an interest in orderly markets, and concentrate on forms of regulation that will increase media economic activity and, where possible, the national share of economic rewards. On the whole, this is interpreted as maximizing the freedom of market forces. However, there remain strategic and political interests in retaining controls (e.g., in relation to infrastructure and also increasingly to address crime and terrorism). This leads in the direction of international agreements and conventions rather than national law making. These trends are likely to reduce freedom of communication on the Internet and to remove relevant decisions further from democratic control.

Last, but not least, media industry change has implications for various aspects of media professionalism. As noted, the very nature of media professions has been changing, although the issues to be faced have a certain constancy, especially where they concern the freedom and obligations of professionals within the media. *Freedom* here means freedom to choose lines of work, publication, and production, which does not seem likely to be advanced by the predominant media industry trends outlined. On the other hand, "new media" potentially open up new channels without the same barriers to entry, and the very expansion of media may widen or increase opportunities for free expression and creativity within the mainstream media (see Chapter 7, this volume). The reference to "obligations" refers especially to ethical constraints that apply to what individual media people do, with regard to possible effects on other individuals and on the society or community, as well as to intrinsic values of truth and decency. Such matters have always been problematic, and it remains to be seen how they are being affected by current changes.

Normative and Ethical Perspectives

A number of the debates and lines of inquiry already referred to entail larger issues of social theory and ethics. Although media research has proceeded pragmatically to investigate specific questions and build limited or middle-range theories, there have been some efforts to deal with fundamental questions concerning the basic justifications for the general operation of media in the large social context. These questions do not usually trouble the media very much, but even they at times refer to some larger purpose, according to which they may be regarded as essential to the working of society and able to claim certain rights and privileges. The large issues of social theory concern especially the claim of media to freedom (from government and law) to operate freely and to publish what they want as long as they do not break other laws, whether the media have some obligations to serve the public good and what the public good might consist of, and how, if at all, a society might hold its media to account for its activities.

Normative issues arise at different levels, particularly that of the media system, the media organization, and the individual communicator. Moreover, they arise in different relationships: between media and government or society, between a medium and some other social organization, and between media (as an organization or individual) and a single person. These complexities mean that diverse systems and types of norms and ethics have to be deployed for different purposes. In fact, the operation of media is not very systematically governed by norms and ethics for a variety of reasons, one being the freedom claimed for expression and publication, which media often see as threatened by too much control. Although there are certain expectations from the audience about minimum standards on sensitive issues (e.g., concerning sex and violence), most media content and uses of media do not give rise to normative and ethical considerations.

The questions raised have been dealt with in the past according to different theoretical traditions. As far as relations between media and society are concerned, the main "normative theory" tradition was first exemplified in the publication titled *Four Theories of the Press* (Nerone, 1995; Siebert, Peterson, & Schramm, 1956), which proposed generally that prescriptions for how the media *ought* to behave derive in practice essentially from the nature of the social and political system that is in place at a given time. The historical analysis of the book describes a progression from authoritarian times in which the media (press) was controlled by government and expected to follow its dictates to a libertarian age in liberal democracies, where there are no requirements and no limitations beyond what the rights of other individuals require. Debate about the usefulness of this theoretical approach has largely degenerated into an argument between advocates of complete freedom (of the market) as a means of meeting the communication needs of society and advocates of public intervention designed to meet these needs in conditions where market forces are not performing well for democratic purposes. These interventions have mainly been designed to treat the threat from economic control and intervention as equal to the threat from government and to ensure that a media system has the structural diversity that will deliver the variety of content that a free society should have.

A range of other theoretical ideas or proposals for media governance "in the public good" is available. Oldest amongst them are principles derived from the theory of electoral democracy, according to which citizens should have the freedom to express their ideas and communicate them to others, as well as the freedom in practice to receive not only ideas but relevant information about candidates and policies on which to make informed choices. These principles set minimum standards for a media system and indicate where action might be needed to remedy deficiencies, with the necessary legitimacy to overcome claims to total freedom. Democratic theory also provides a source for a number of prescriptions about media activity, including the expectation that they will act as a check and a means of public accountability.

A quite separate tradition of media theory can be found in functionalist media sociology from its earliest formulations. Even if functionalism is no longer well regarded, it is hard to escape entirely from some of the

formulations it offered concerning the various roles of the media in society, based on claims of necessity for the social order. These included functions of information provision (or surveillance of the environment) for purposes of warning and guidance; the advisory, guidance, opinion-forming function for citizens; the "platform" function for expressing opinion and advocating social goals; the socially cohesive or unifying function for society and community under conditions where the pursuit of purely individual goals is overly dominant; the function of transmitting social and cultural norms (or socialization); and diversion and entertainment. Elements of these ideas continually resurface in debates about standards of contemporary media performance.

Without exhausting the alternative bases for deriving norms for assessing media or for media to derive their own goals, we should recognize the part played by professionalism in setting and holding to certain standards. The drive towards professionalism in news journalism began in the early 20th century, with varying motivations, but a common agreement was that news exists to serve the interest of the public (or audience) and should set certain minimum standards of quality of performance and ethical integrity. As to the first, the primary quality would be adherence to truth in the form of objective (factual, reliable, accurate, and neutral) news information. Ethical standards are more varied but at least involve a commitment not to cause harm by publication to individuals or society, unless a higher "public interest" made it unavoidable. Some other media professions have developed relevant versions of their ethical responsibilities.

This sketchy account is designed to illustrate the place that normative and ethical theory occupies in the larger range of inquiry. It is called for wherever critical assessment or accountability of the media at different levels is called for, wherever the purposes of media are at issue, and wherever law, policy, or regulation of media is under consideration. We should also recall (see Chapter 4, this volume) that norms governing media can vary considerably according to media structure and culture.

COMMUNICATION AND SPATIAL LOCATION

Early communication theorists reflected on the links between communication and the identity of, and attachment to, particular geographical and social locations, especially those of nation, region, and community (variously defined). The general basis for reflection was that communication was both necessary to identity with place and also a means of enlarging the scope of identity or incorporating newcomers into existing space. Communication could also create new types of identity. These ideas were applied to the situations of migrants, to the possibilities for resisting the alienating effects of big cities. They also came into issues of national identity, patriotism, and international relations.

The emergence of new nations and processes of decolonization or reconstruction after war or revolution have entailed decisions about the structure of media. Historically, media developed within national societies and often had their base of operation at a metropolitan center. But there are numerous past and present models and degrees of structural diversity of media in terms of nation, region, and locality (see Chapters 2, 4, 13, and 18, this volume). Questions that arise for media research and policy, inter alia, concern the role of media in supporting local and regional cultures and forms of association within larger national units. The rise of successive new media (community television, local radio, satellites and cable, video, and now the Internet) plays a part in the definition and working out of these issues.

In the general history of the field, most prominence has been given to the part played by media in the process of globalization, partly because it has been a politically loaded issue. Essentially, it refers to various dimensions of convergence between nations and regions. The world has been made "smaller" by increasing ease of travel, by economic and trade flows, and by communications media that ensure that much of the world enjoys much the same diet of news, advertising, entertainment, spectacle, and gossip, despite entrenched differences in standards of living and other inequalities. Although the media have often been attributed a key role in the ongoing globalization process, this role has been subject to much debate and criticism.

Media globalization was first explicated uncritically as part of the process of the "modernization" of traditional societies in the aftermath of World War II. The media would bring literacy and the message of free elections and free markets, as well as the incentives to consume and break away from the constraints of traditionalism (Lerner, 1958). They would be both innovations in themselves as well as the means of diffusing innovations. This optimistic view took little account of the real economic, political, and cultural barriers to global mass communication. Even the technologies were not adequate to their predicted uses.

Optimism was succeeded by the severe critique of the central notion that Western (especially American) mass media must be good for those at the receiving end in other countries and cultures. On the contrary, it was argued that such one-way exports were vehicles for cultural and economic imperialism, including ideological subversion of local opposition. Alternative visions of a world of more balanced international communication between North and South were advanced, not least in the context of UNESCO proposals for a New World Order of Communication (McBride, 1980). Globalization was pronounced as undesirable in communication, as in a number of other areas, especially the economic sphere, even though the reality of some elements of a shared media culture cannot be denied.

Research has shown that there is no simple process of assimilation into a dominant global culture. There are many barriers on a global scale to such a process and many sources of resistance. Original cultures do not have to be surrendered in exchange for novelties; variant forms of culture can be tolerated, and new or hybrid forms of foreign models emerge and flourish. Even so, the debate ebbs and flows, and we need to be reminded (as we are by Sreberny in Chapter 4, this volume) that the situation is different from place to place and perceived as more or less problematic according to local circumstances.

◆ Dilemmas and Choices of Approach

No reader of this book is likely to need reminding that the field of media and communication is diverse not only in subject matter but also in purposes and methods of inquiry. This diversity is represented in this book by the varied styles and manners of discourse of different authors, as well as by differences in how topics are problematized and in forms of evidence that are adduced. To some extent, this diversity is entailed in the varied character of the topics, some calling for description and interpretation, others for precise and reliable evidence. Even so, it is worth calling attention to some of the basic divisions in the field that do stem not only from a sensible division of labor but sometimes also from fundamental differences of philosophy and epistemology.

A rather obvious point is that the field now has quite a long history, and its accumulated body of theory and evidence reflects, much as do sedimentary layers, the considerable changes that have taken place over decades in the humanities and social sciences more generally. Some of the shifts of priority and approach might be accounted as fads and fashions or as temporary reflections of events in the "real world," such as war, civil unrest, economic depression, and changes in political ideology. It is inevitable

and proper that the study of media should be engaged by "reality" in this way and also adapt to more fundamental changes in society and the world environment. In this connection, the larger process of economic and cultural globalization, the growing inequality of the world, the emancipation of women, and the rise of new social movements, for example, have to be attended to. They can independently affect media content, structure, and use and are experienced by way of the media. Whether the media can influence them, in turn, is at least a question to be considered.

Returning to the dilemmas of inquiry, we can find some guidance from the experience of other disciplines. Rosengren (1983), for instance, adapted a classification of schools of sociology to map out the main types of media theory. His scheme involved two main dimensions, with one representing opposed conceptions of science and the other assumptions about society. The first contrasted a "subjective" with an "objective" approach, whereas the second distinguished a view of society as in need of regulation and control from one that favored radical change. This gives rise to four main paradigms for communication theory.

One of these is a *functionalist* paradigm (objective evidence and a regulated society). This emphasizes the positive contribution of media to the existing social order and favors empirical, quantitative research. This largely corresponds to the "dominant paradigm" referred to at the outset. The second is an *interpretive* paradigm (a subjective or descriptive approach to a regulated, orderly society). This is represented in communication research by using qualitative methods to investigate cultural issues of meaning and content. The third paradigm, *radical-humanist* (subjective approach favoring radical change), is reflected in a critical-cultural approach to media that uses interpretive methods to expose the hegemonic role of media or to advance the aspirations and perspectives of the powerless in terms of class, race, or gender. The fourth paradigm, the *radical-structural* approach, looks at the media as a material, especially political-economic, force in society that has to be investigated in its concrete manifestations (i.e., with reference to patterns of ownership and control, market power, political connections) and by objective methods of analysis applied to reliable data.

This scheme helps to make clear the main kinds of interrelation between the alternative approaches that are exposed in the history of the field and exist as choices for contemporary researchers. In simple terms, we can choose more or less quantitative or qualitative methods, or combinations of both. We can also be inclined to conduct research for socially or culturally critical purposes in respect of the existing order, or we can do work that makes the system function more effectively. As the scheme presented makes clear, however, there is no necessary correspondence between critical intention and type of method. Different forms of science can serve the same purpose.

Rather apart from the above, we should also take account of a more general division within the field that shows up in all the paradigms. This can be described as a socio-centric versus a media-centric approach to various topics in the field. In its most basic formulation, a socio-centric approach assumes that media are themselves a product of society and that their structures, activities, and effects can only be explained in terms of underlying social forces affecting the context of their operation and their individual users. A media-centric approach is prepared to view media as potentially independent influences on individuals and on societies. There is, of course, scope for the view that media and society are continually interacting, making this choice purely schematic. Even so, leaving aside the question of the direction of effect, it remains the case that many researchers are drawn to the media as their primary object of interest, whether as technology, content, sphere of work, or organizational structure. Others prefer to approach media by way of relevant political, economic, social, or psychological factors. The editors have taken no position on these choices for purposes of this reader, and the whole range of assumptions can be found in one form or another in the pages that follow.

◆ Forces for Change

Although at the start of this overview, emphasis was placed on the continuity of many themes, especially those that arise from apparently essential aspects of mass communication, there are evident changes under way. For some observers, these are sufficient in degree and kind to warrant a claim that the age of mass media has passed. The advent of computerization (and its essence in digitization) has undermined or bypassed the original core industrial process of mass production and dissemination from center to periphery, from the few to many. Ever since communication satellites and computer networks came into the service of the media, a step change in the media phenomenon has been proclaimed. It no longer has to be a process of one-way transmission but can also be interactive. It is no longer so limited to the local or national territory. It no longer has to be "massive" either in terms of uniformity of content or the mass attention of the public. It is fragmented, diverse, and ever changing to suit the needs of senders and consumer-receivers. In many developed countries, the level of material welfare has reached a point where there are much larger resources available for investment and consumption of communication goods. The media no longer have to be dominated by a few massive media providers, nationally or internationally.

However, the possibilities for change are not the same as the reality of change, and we are back at the starting point of weighing the extent to which technology has really caused a revolution. On the side of the "public," there continue to be reasons for continuing the old patterns of mass consumption of much the same informational and cultural goods. For different reasons, the same holds good for institutional communicators and for the media industries themselves in "industrial societies" that have not yet fundamentally changed. We hope we have assembled arguments and evidence for these and other issues to be debated in an informed way.

◆ References

Averbeck, S. (2001). The post-1933 emigration of communication researchers from Germany. *European Journal of Communication, 16*(4), 419–450.

Barthes, R. (1967). *Elements of semiology*. London: Jonathan Cape.

Berelson, B. (1952). *Content analysis in communication research*. Glencoe, IL: Free Press.

Berger, C. R., & Chaffee, S. H. (Eds.). (1987). *Handbook of communication science*. Beverly Hills, CA: Sage.

Fiske, J. (1987). *Television culture*. London: Routledge Kegan Paul.

Gitlin, T. (1978). Media sociology: The dominant paradigm. *Theory and Society, 6*, 205–253.

Hardt, H. (1979). *Social theories of the press: Early German and American perspectives*. Urbana: University of Illinois Press.

Holsti, O. R. (1969). *Content analysis for the social sciences and humanities*. New York: Addison-Wesley.

Innis, H. (1950). *Empire and communication*. Oxford, UK: Clarendon.

Jensen, K. B., & Jankowski, N. (1991). *A handbook of qualitative methodologies*. London: Routledge.

Jowett, G., & O'Donnell, V. (1999). *Propaganda and persuasion* (3rd ed.). Thousand Oaks, CA: Sage.

Lerner, D. (1958). *The passing of traditional society*. New York: Free Press.

Lessig, L. (1999). *Code: And other laws of cyberspace*. New York: Basic Books.

Lievrouw, L. A., & Livingstone, S. (Eds.). (2002). *Handbook of new media: Social shaping and consequences of ICTs*. London: Sage.

McBride, S. (1980). *Many voices, one world*. Paris: UNESCO.

McLuhan, M. (1964). *Understanding media*. London: Routledge.

McQuail, D. (2000). *Mass communication theory*. London: Sage.

Meyrowitz, J. (1985). *No sense of place*. New York: Oxford University Press.

Nerone, J. C. (Ed.). (1995). *Last rights: Revisiting four theories of the press*. Urbana: University of Illinois Press.

Perse, E. (2001). *Media effects and society*. Hillsdale, NJ: Lawrence Erlbaum.

Rosengren, K. E. (1983). Communication research: One paradigm or four? *Journal of Communication, 33*(3), 185–207.

Rosengren, K. E. (2000). *Communication: An introduction*. London: Sage.

Schement, J., & Curtis, T. (1995). *Tendencies and tensions of the information age*. New Brunswick, NJ: Transaction.

Siebert, F. S., Peterson, T., & Schramm, W. (1956). *Four theories of the press*. Urbana: University of Illinois Press.

Signorielli, N., & Morgan, M. (Eds.). (1990). *Cultivation analysis*. Newbury Park, CA: Sage.

Tuchman, G., Daniels, A. K., & Benet, J. (Eds.). (1978). *Hearth and home: Images of women in mass media*. New York: Free Press.

Tunstall, J. (1977). *The media are American*. London: Constable.

Turner, R. H. (Ed.). (1967). *On social control and collective behavior*. Chicago: University of Chicago Press.

Van Zoonen, L. (1994). *Feminist media studies*. London: Sage.

Webster, F. (2003). *Theories of the information society* (2nd ed.). New York: Routledge.

Wiener, N. (1948). *Cybernetics*. Cambridge: MIT Press.

PART I

PROLEGOMENA

1

ETHICAL AND NORMATIVE PERSPECTIVES

◆ Clifford Christians

Media ethics is an important branch of professional ethics. Recognizing the power of mass communications in today's global world, occupations in the media are now included with such professions as medicine, law, business, and engineering under the purview of applied ethics. Although the media have been roundly criticized for more than a century,[1] the exponential growth in media ethics did not occur until it began rising in parallel during the 1980s with the growth of professional ethics as a whole. In line with the other professional fields, more monographs and books on media ethics were produced in this decade than had been published in total since the beginning of the 20th century.

From 1978 to 1980, the Hastings Center of New York carried out the most extensive study ever done of the status, problems, and possibilities for teaching professional ethics in American higher education. Funded by the Carnegie Foundation, the results were published in a series of volumes and monographs that have defined the field of applied and professional ethics ever since. The Hastings project included empirical analyses and teaching strategies. It made recommendations about course goals, evaluation, indoctrination, and teacher preparation (e.g., Callahan & Bok, 1980). And the results are evident everywhere. The Association for Practical and Professional Ethics began in 1991 and now publishes its own book series. Journals such as the *International*

Journal of Applied Philosophy, Ethical Perspectives, and *Professional Ethics* deal with generic issues, and virtually all the professions now have their own journals, books, and courses on ethics as well. Interest groups within academic associations and centers for ethics and society are commonplace. Research universities are including practical ethics courses within their general education curriculum and in professional programs. Graduate studies typically include courses in the ethics of scientific research and ethical standards in social science methodology. Liberal arts colleges reflect similar dynamics, introducing courses in bioethics and the ethics of health care, ethics in government, social work ethics, computer ethics, and so forth. The dramatic growth in research, teaching, and interest among media professionals and academics has been unrelenting as well. MacDonald and Petheram (1998, pp. 257–349) list more than 200 research centers and academic departments around the world committed to media ethics.

◆ *Developing Credible Theory*

As a subset of professional ethics, media ethics, in terms of its logic and rationale, is bilingual. It combines theory with actual events and real-life dilemmas. Even the most sophisticated media ethics retains an interest in concrete moral judgments, in the way ethical decision making actually functions in media practice. But integrating particular knowledge into general ethical theory is considered crucial as well. Work in the larger world of applied ethics demonstrates that if description of actual morality becomes the exclusive aim, the results are superficial moralism. If abstract theory dominates, the conclusions are out of touch with reality. Therefore, as professional ethics develops itself into a field of philosophy with its own identity, it insists on the interactive character of theory construction, with principles and practice building on one another dialogically (cf. Almond, 1995; Kearney & Dooley, 1999, chaps. 3–5). Stephen Toulmin (1988) has assisted the enterprise by demonstrating that issues from the bedside, newsroom, and parliament have always dominated the history of philosophy, and applied ethics is restoring that vision. The reissuing of Henry

Sidgwick's (1898/1998) *Practical Ethics,* with an articulate defense of its intellectual significance by Sissela Bok, signals this trend toward professional ethics as a scholarly enterprise with its own subject matter.[2]

There have been intellectual gains in the middle range—on conflict of interest, promise keeping and contractual obligation, paternalism and client autonomy, indoctrination, reform of institutional structures, and vocation. Media ethics has made important advances on the ethics of distributive justice, confidentiality, and deception. However, theory in applied ethics generally and media ethics in particular continues to be a major challenge. Applying ethical principles to specific cases is often busywork, descriptive and functional in character. Students are typically taught to choose among practical alternatives without knowing how to consider ethically the right course of action. They can unravel specific conundrums, but the theory that equips them to deal with similar situations later is often too obscure to have any intellectual payoff. In the first half of the 1980s, the material was largely atheoretical. Media ethics was often defined as descriptive in character, and taking seriously a complex professional arena seemed to demand war stories rather than abstractions. However, most of today's classroom texts, as well as some anthologies, include a section on theory. On occasion, book-length studies in media ethics now develop a philosophical framework. But the concept of theory as pedagogically meaningful, as well as theory as fundamental to the normative character of communication ethics, remains woefully underdeveloped. The long-term future of the field depends on the common language of theory, not as an abstract authority but as something that assists us in thinking more systematically on our own. Going beyond classical theorists without forgetting them and welcoming theory as empowering provocateur are central to making significant progress on media ethics' complicated agenda at present.

Developing a credible normative ethics in media studies faces a formidable obstacle. Given the dual character of professional ethics, the morality of the practitioners' world interacts with the philosophical framework of academics. On one side of the equation, the conventions and guidelines of media practice are basically utilitarian. In print and broadcast journalism, public relations, advertising, and entertainment, the modus operandi is self-consciously or superficially determined by consequences. In news and editorial departments, advertising agencies, and media companies, the overarching appeal is to serve the majority and benefit the greatest public good with the least possible harm. John Stuart Mill's treatise on political freedom in 1859, *On Liberty,* and his *Utilitarianism* in 1861 work in and through each other, as does the natural affinity today in democratic life toward determining the morally right alternative by the greatest balance of good over evil (Mill, 1859/1975, 1861). Mill contended that happiness was the sole end of human action and the test by which all conduct ought to be judged. With later utilitarians expanding the notion of pleasure, assessing rightness or wrongness in terms of the total amount of value is a definite guideline for aiding our ethical choices. A utility calculus fits hand-in-glove with the press's zeal for

the public's right to know, as well as with the commitment in public relations and advertising to provide clients with the maximum benefits at the least cost. For the entertainment industry, utility resonates with capitalism's supply and demand and an institution's risk-benefit calculations. Moreover, the utility principle does not presume commands from heaven or a universe of natural laws and brings together disparate segments of a diverse society. The press's actions in Watergate, for instance, were considered appropriate by most people; the public saw the pain inflicted on a few as proper because the overall consequences for the many were beneficent.

Although the utilitarian perspective is powerful and happiness is an end few would wish to contradict, utilitarianism does present serious difficulties for theory formation in media ethics at this juncture. It depends on making accurate measurements of the consequences, when in everyday affairs, the results of our choices are often blurred, at least in the long term. In addition, utilitarians view society as a collection of individuals, each with his or her own desires and goals. Thus, institutions and structures are not analyzed in a sophisticated manner, and an atomistic, procedural view of democracy is presumed. Moreover, the principle of the greatest public benefit applies only to societies in which certain nonutilitarian standards of decency prevail. And on a deeper level, there is mounting criticism of utilitarianism's commitment to an exceptionless norm as determining all ethical judgments. As a matter of fact, consequentialism in its various forms is intellectually appealing in the same way scientific theories are—a single principle constitutes all moral judgments. In the longstanding conflict over love or justice as the highest good, for example, the balance of pleasure over pain becomes the standard by which to adjudicate them in specific situations. However, the appealing exactness of this one-factor model represents a "semblance of validity" by leaving out whatever cannot be calculated (Taylor, 1982, p. 143).

In some media situations, consequences are a reliable guide. But practitioners usually find themselves confronting more than one moral claim at the same time, and asking only what produces the most good is too limiting. In the full range of human relationships, we ordinarily recognize that fulfilling promises, preventing injury, providing equal distribution, and relieving distress are moral imperatives. But utilitarianism as a single-consideration theory renders irrelevant other moral demands that conflict with it. In some of the most crucial issues we face at present, utility is not an adequate guide—for understanding distributive justice, diversity in popular culture, violence in television and cinema, truth telling, digital manipulation, conflict of interest, and so forth. We face the anomaly that the ethical system most entrenched in the media industry is not ideally suited for resolving its most persistent headaches.

Insisting on a rigorous version of rule-utilitarianism is one alternative.[3] The best types of utility are not the same as expediency, nor are they a simple matter of ends justifying the means. A sophisticated model of utilitarianism emphasizing long-term consequences will eliminate many of the media's day-to-day quandaries and provide critical leverage over against the quasi-utility that is typically invoked at present. However, based on a century of experience with utilitarian rationalism and its fluorescence as media ethics has grown over the past two decades, it is arguable that an ethics of duty is a more compelling means of moral decision making for the media professions.[4] Duty responds to a broader range of human experiences and relations. Duty recognizes that responsible actions are necessary to keep the human community humane. For Emmanuel Levinas (1981), for instance, our duties to others are more fundamental to human identity than are individual rights. Oxford's W. David Ross (1930) has developed the most influential critique of utilitarianism within philosophical circles and establishes prima facie duties as a compelling

alternative, in which reparations, fidelity, justice, noninjury, gratitude, and self-improvement are given centrality. An ethics of duty provides a critical framework for checking our common inclinations toward majoritarianism rather than having our theory and practice slide into one another. Therefore, in terms of the overall task of developing a theoretically credible media ethics, the most promising direction is a deontological one.

◆ Medium- and Genre-Specific Issues

With constructing a credible theoretical foundation as the overarching task, our work in media ethics can be divided into three main branches according to the standard functions of communication systems in democratic societies—reporting news, promoting products and services, and entertaining. In capitalist societies, however, practitioners of journalism, advertising, and entertainment often belong to the same corporation and encounter all three media areas directly or indirectly in their work. And with the convergence of media technologies into digital formats, cyberspace is a current concentration point for dealing with media ethics. Three of the important issues described below represent each of the media genres—truth (news), sexism (advertising), and violence (entertainment). Two pressing issues are selected from the new technologies (just distribution and hate speech). Together, they illustrate the challenge of moving particular problems from their generally utilitarian orientation to duty ethics instead.

TRUTH

The press's obligation to truth is a standard part of its rhetoric. High-minded editors typically etch the word on cornerstones and on their tombstones. Virtually every code of ethics begins with the newsperson's duty to tell the truth under all circumstances. Credible language is pivotal to the communications enterprise. As the norm of healing is to medicine, justice to politics, and critical thinking to education, so truth telling is the occupational norm of the media professions.

Living up to this ideal is virtually impossible, even for those who idolize it. Seeking the truth in newsgathering and producing the truth in newswriting is complicated by budget constraints, deadlines, editorial conventions, and self-serving sources. Journalism is often referred to as "history in a hurry"; providing a precise, representative account can rarely occur under such conditions. Meanwhile, sophisticated technology generates unceasing news copy so that journalistic gatekeepers must choose from a mountain of options, often without the time to sift through the intricacies of truth telling. Agreeing on visual accuracy in a digital world has been impossible even among competent professionals of good will.

Rather than Band-Aids to cover the sore spots and bleeding, a believable concept of truth is the primary need. Truth is typically shriveled down to accurate facts and neutrality. During a formative period for the media in the 1920s, a dichotomy between facts and values dominated Western thinking. Genuine knowledge was identified with the physical sciences, and the objectivity of physics and mathematics set the standard for all forms of knowing. Journalistic morality became equivalent to unbiased reporting of neutral data. Presenting unvarnished facts was heralded as the standard of good performance. The best news mirrored reality. Objective reporting was not merely a technique, but withholding value judgments was considered a moral imperative.

This mainstream view of truth as accurate information is too narrow for today's social and political complexities. A more sophisticated concept is truth as disclosure. Already in 1947, the famous Hutchins Commission Report on *A Free and Responsible Press* (Commission on Freedom of the Press, 1947) called for this alternative. It advocated a deeper definition of the press's mission as "a truthful, comprehensive and intelligent account of the day's events in a context which gives them meaning." Forsaking the quest for precision journalism does not mean imprecision but precision in disclosure and authenticity—in getting to the heart of the matter. To replace newsgathering rooted in empiricism, fiction and fabrication are obviously not acceptable substitutes.

In terms of disclosing the meaning, reporters will seek what might be called "interpretive sufficiency." They recognize that no hard line exists between fact and interpretation; therefore, truthful accounts mean adequate and credible interpretations rather than first impressions. The best journalists will ensure the news story's deeper reading by understanding from the inside the attitudes, culture, language, and definitions of the people and events they are actually reporting. In the process of weaving a tapestry of truth, reporters will attempt to reduce as much as possible the distance between the concepts of social science and those of the particular news context itself. Their disclosures will ring true on both levels; that is, they will be theoretically credible and realistic to those being covered. The truth of authenticity unveils the inner character of a series of events. They generate an insightful picture that gets at the essence of the matter. Rather than reducing social issues to the financial and administrative problems defined by politicians, the news media ought to disclose the depth and nuance that enables readers and viewers to identify the fundamental issues themselves.[5]

ADVERTISING AND GENDER

Companies in the United States spend $200 billion a year on advertising. Its effects are controversial, but would the $1 million to produce a Super Bowl commercial and the $1.5 million to air it be spent if advertising had no impact? When

Victoria's Secret paraded models in lingerie across the screen for 30 seconds during the 1999 Super Bowl, 1 million people logged onto the Web site promoted in the ad. In the standard calculations, average Americans see more than 3,000 ads per day and spend more than 3 years of their lives watching commercials. Advertising is pervasive, using all media, making itself inescapable, and intruding on our privacy. As George Gerbner (1994) puts it,

> For the first time in human history, most of the stories about people, life, and values are told not by parents, schools, churches, or others in the community who have something to tell, but by a group of distant conglomerates that have something to sell. (p. 389)

If the advertising industry can persuade us to buy products or particular brands, it can surely influence the way we think. Given its size and power, as privatization and the market principle expand around the world, advertising will be controversial—and one longstanding issue is its exploitation of women. In the Middle East, for instance, "as for privately owned Arab satellite channels, global consumerism is clearly manifest in the array of advertisements and video clips featuring Arab women who, interestingly enough, conform more to a Western archetypal beauty ideal than to an Arab one" ("The Power of Advertising," 2001, p. 9). Similarly in China,

> Advertising not only sells goods but also identity. . . . The White female has become the prime fetish in a new Chinese symbolic universe, governed not by class struggle and resistance to imperialism, but by the symbolic exchange of a globalized commodity culture. (Johansson, 1999, p. 377)

The United Nations Commission on the Status of Women has named advertising as the world's worst offender in perpetuating the image of women as sex symbols and therefore an inferior kind of human being (www.un.org/womenwatch/daw/csw/index.html). As Sut Jhally (1989) says, "Never in history has the iconography of a culture been so obsessed or possessed by questions of sexuality and gender." Life is rich and varied, but "there is no sense of scale in advertising"; it capitalizes on and feeds the overemphasis on sex in our lives while "underemphasizing other important things (friendship, loyalty, fun, the love of children, community)" that define human relationships (Kilbourne, 1999, p. 265). Advertising as a form of communication seeks its audience, and explicit sex attracts attention. Calvin Klein has set the standard for proving it works. Undergarments or the lack of them in Calvin Klein's ads from 1980 to 1995 captured an audience and aroused controversy. The CK Jeans campaign since 1995 ("nothing between me and my Calvin's"), lascivious perfume ads, and preschool children in designer underwear have positioned Klein with the appealing image as daring rebel to the majority of its customers. Along with the windfall of media publicity, Klein's jean sales have doubled already in the first year (Ivinski, 2000, pp. 108–115).

The critique of advertising's portrayal of women falls along three lines: their objectification, deformation of human sexuality, and what Jean Kilbourne calls "the hypersexualization of girls" ("The Power of Advertising," 2001, p. 6).

The first pressing concern about advertising's image of women is their objectification. Women and their body parts are used to sell every product imaginable. Objectifying and dismembering create second-class citizens of those used to serve someone else's interest.

Cathy Shepherd of the Caribbean Association for Feminist Research and Action (CAFRA) describes the issue in these terms for the Caribbean media:

> Locally, alcohol advertising consistently portrays women as sex objects who exist for the viewing and consuming pleasure of men. . . . Many males learn to see

women as a pretty package, something to behold, but not necessarily to respect. ("The Power of Advertising," 2001, p. 6)

The Media Monitoring Project in South Africa drew the same conclusion about its advertising industry in 1999: "Women are exhibited in social roles for the benefit of entering and providing pleasure to men" ("The Power of Advertising," 2001, p. 6). Erving Goffman (1978) demonstrated in *Gender Advertisements* that the poses and language of advertising teach us the superiority (often disdainful) of males and the subservience of women.

A second issue in gender and advertising revolves around the corrupting of relationships.

> Most of us yearn for intimate and committed relationships that will last. . . . But we are surrounded by advertising that yokes our needs with products and promises that things will deliver what in fact they never can. . . . All too often our market-driven culture locks people into adolescent fantasies of sex and relationships. And there is a connection between the constant images of instant sexual gratification and passion and the increasing burden on marriage and long-term lovers . . . Of course, all these sexual images aren't intended to sell sex . . . but shopping. This is the intent of the advertisers—but an unintended consequence is the effect these images have on real sexual desire and real lives. (Kilbourne, 1999, pp. 25, 77, 268)

In subtle but excessive form, products no longer are a means to a noble end but the end itself. Advertisements encourage us to develop an identity with and loyalty to the products themselves. They turn "lovers into things and things into lovers" and nurture "passion for products rather than our partners. . . . In the world of advertising, lovers grow cold, spouses grow old, children grow up and move away—but possessions stay with us and never change" (Kilbourne,

1999, pp. 77, 94). In this climate, abuse is inevitable. "It is difficult, perhaps impossible, to be violent to someone we consider an equal human being, but it is very easy to abuse a thing" ("The Power of Advertising," 2001, p. 7).

Third, advertising images demean and trivialize girls. Columnist Ellen Goodman contends that the fashion and advertising worlds help to produce "another generation of girls growing up in painfully hostile relationships with their own bodies" (quoted in Christians, Fackler, Rotzoll, & McKee, 2001, p. 179). Ads by and large create ultra-slender role models with silky hair and flawless skin. "Stunning creatures," writes Don Kaul, "but thin, painfully, excrutiatingly thin. It's the modern equivalent of foot binding" (quoted in Christians et al., 2001, p. 180). One study found that women's magazines contained "ten times as many advertisements and articles promoting weight loss as men's magazines—corresponding exactly to the ratio of eating disorders in women versus men" (Jacobson & Mazur, 1995, p. 75). As Carol Gilligan and other social critics have pointed out in recent years,

> Adolescent girls in America are afflicted with a range of problems, including self-esteem, eating disorders, binge drinking, date rape and other dating violence, teen pregnancy, and a rise in cigarette smoking. Teenage women are engaging in far riskier health behavior in greater numbers than any prior generation. (Kilbourne, 1999, p. 129)

"We need to take the obsession with thinness and eating problems as seriously as we take drug problems and treat them as public health problems, not as individual pathologies" ("The Power of Advertising," 2001, p. 9). For advertising, girls are a montage of perfume, clothing, and bodies. In this form, they are "extremely desirable to advertisers because they are new consumers, are beginning to have significant disposable income, and are developing brand loyalty that might last a lifetime. Teenage girls spend over $4 billion annually on cosmetics alone" (Kilbourne, 1999, p. 132).

Given the complexity of advertising's exploitation along these three lines, the argument that sexually explicit advertising is morally offensive has little to recommend it. Nudity, erotica, and racy language indeed do affront tastes and are legitimately labeled soft-core pornography. Advertising is not generally interested in artistic realism or authentic sensuality as are high-minded writers and producers in entertainment. In that sense, advertising's sexism rightly offends the virtuous. But opposing it on the basis of embarrassment or offensiveness carries little public clout. It easily dissipates into debates over whose morals are under attack. Most advertisers, for example, see wider latitude in standards among the younger audience they are aiming to reach and, in fact, welcome objections from parents. In addition, the moral offensiveness argument is too easily dismissed by those who do not want restrictions on free speech.

In terms of ethics, the fundamental issue is discrimination based on gender. Subordinate images of women hinder their chance of equal opportunity; depictions of subordination perpetuate subordination. Advertising's exploitation of women violates their human rights as a class. The world of male dominance and female submission is dehumanizing in principle. Women as sexual turn-ons or, more blatantly, as objects for conquest and possession face unacceptable discrimination. Civil equality is virtually impossible to achieve when a multi-billion-dollar industry promotes inequality. Rather than arguing from offended tastes, women's rights cuts a wider swath. It is a broad, compelling basis for moving forward constructively.

Women's rights links advertising and gender with the longstanding problem of sexism in the media as a whole. Instead of being scandalized by advertising's sex appeals per se, the ethical challenge is acting against discriminatory culture, actions, and

policies in news reporting, entertainment media, interactive information systems, and public relations as well as advertising. We need the leverage of human rights to make a difference not only in consumer culture but also in popular culture and in the citizen culture represented in the press. In this major component of media ethics—that is, the ethics of representation—the master principle is gender inclusiveness. And in terms of gender parity, the goal is to clarify and critique and transform the media's role in reproducing and reinforcing patterns of discrimination against women in society. In addition to examining the limited role of women in decision making and media production, the ethics of representation focuses on the deficiencies in the way women are symbolized and imagined in all media forms beyond advertising (see "New Age, New Agendas," 2001, p. 4). What William Bird concludes regarding South Africa is true of industrialized countries across the globe: "The most pressing needs . . . are to reinvent and reformulate advertising in line with a democracy and constitution which enshrines human rights" ("The Power of Advertising," 2001, p. 6).

With sexism embedded in our culture and social order, the broader agenda needs the persistent and thoughtful attention of media professionals everywhere. Even if media behavior is improving in particular cases, without institutional, representational, and structural reform, a long and entrenched history will not be permanently changed.

TELEVISION VIOLENCE

Few issues command as much attention from media reformers as violence in television and film. In the United States, for example, studies have shown that by high school graduation, the average 17-year-old will have seen 18,000 murders on TV. From the horrific shootings at Columbine High School in the spring of 1999 to similar tragedies in other states and countries since then, teenagers who slaughter their classmates and teachers and then kill themselves are linked by debate or research to the culture of violence in which they live. Although "the U.S. leads the world in the prevalence of violence on television . . . findings indicate that television shown in all parts of the world contains a great deal of violence," including a high percentage of guns as weapons, indifference to brutality, and consequences only in hints or not shown at all (Potter, 1999, pp. 56, 59). "Gun-related deaths increased more than 60% from 1968–1984, and this problem is now considered a public health epidemic by 87% of surgeons and 94% of internists across the United States" (Potter, 1999, p. 1). America has been a violent society since its birth in the Revolutionary War, but now there is more anxiety about it than ever.

In the past 15 or so years, a remarkably cavalier, vicious, wanton, and senseless pattern of violence entered society and the American psyche. Drive-by shootings and gangbanger crimes, fueled by a trade in handguns and crack cocaine, has ushered in fears of an epidemic of violence we may not fully comprehend. The violence panic of this time . . . seems much more to surround children and youth, as both the victims and the perpetrators of violence. (Wartella, 1996, p. 3)

The opposition of media industries and combat-hardened libertarians to the censors of violence can be summarized around four claims:

♦ Artistic freedom and aesthetic integrity demand a laissez-faire approach. The government has no business policing writers and directors.

♦ Violence is a social and historical problem, not the result of violent television or films. To think otherwise is the same as blaming John Wayne for the Vietnam War.

♦ Boundaries between news and entertainment programming are artificial. Television news-magazine shows, for instance, are hungry for visual material that will generate revenue-rich audiences. All of the free marketplace arguments that traditional news has enjoyed are now applied equally to entertainment programs. The public apparently wants the pleasure of being aroused, and the industry wishes "to use the violence formula to build audiences and thus maximize their profits. . . . Violence is harmless entertainment and it is okay to pursue selfish ends" (Potter, 1999, p. 163).

♦ No direct effects can be documented or proved. Indirect effects are the consequence of living one's life in a world of mediated messages and cannot be made the basis of criminal prosecutions.

This last argument against curtailing violence on television has long been the most persistent and persuasive. However, the no-effects conclusion is not credible any longer. "Evidence of a causal relationship between media violence and real violence has been accumulating for at least 40 years." Certainly, "violent behavior is a complex, multivariable problem, formed of many influences." And "violence in the media may not be the most important contributor to violence in the real world." But "it is surely one of the multiple, overlapping causes" (Wartella, 1996, pp. 3–4). Meta-analyses during the 1990s of literally hundreds of studies on media violence "demonstrated a causal link between viewing televised violence and real-life aggression with some of the strongest effects observed among younger children" (Wilson, Smith, et al., 2002, p. 6). The same conclusion was verified by research for the American Medical Association, the National Centers for Disease Control and Prevention, and through the exhaustive multiyear

National Television Violence Study (1994–1998) (Wilson, Colvin, & Smith, 2002, pp. 36–57; Wilson, Smith, et al., 2002, pp. 9–31).[6] In James Potter's (1999) review of the research—with the caveat that the effects process is highly complex—he is certain of both immediate and extended consequences from televised violence. In the short term, fear and habituation occur, but "increased viewer aggression" is most strongly supported also. And likewise for long-term effects, "we can conclude that exposure to violence in the media is linked with long-term negative effects of trait aggression, fearful worldview, and desensitization to violence" (Potter, 1999, p. 42).

Violence is a serious ethical issue because it violates the persons-as-ends principle. In Immanuel Kant's standard formulation, we must treat all rational beings as ends-in-themselves and never as means only. In Judeo-Christian *agape* and feminist relational ethics, violence contradicts Other-regarding care. Gratuitous cheapening of human life to expand ratings, in terms of Aristotle's teleological model, is a reprehensible misuse of human beings as means to base ends. From the persons-as-ends perspective, there is a special interest in the sexual violence so common in music video, horror movies (especially slasher films), pornographic literature, videocassettes, and the commercials promoting them. Sadistic, bloodthirsty torture in a sexual context is a particularly offensive form of dehumanization.

In complicated cases with several layers of meaning and disagreements among legitimate parties such as with television violence, Aristotle's mean enables us to think ethically and avoid doctrinaire moralism. With temperance the cardinal virtue for the Greeks through which all others flowed, moral virtue in Aristotelian terms is a middle state determined by practical wisdom.[7] Humans who are not fanatics or eccentrics but of harmonious character, over a career of moral growth, develop acuity in their perceptions and a disposition to reason wisely. And those of such integrated traits of character apply their practical wisdom, in this case, to televised violence and locate the "mean between two vices, that which depends on excess and that which depends on defect" (Aristotle, 1947, 1107A). With censorship—the evil of defect—and gratuitous, sensational violence without restraint—the evil of excess—practical wisdom (*phronesis*) identifies aesthetic realism as the middle state. The path of equilibrium and harmony is artistically genuine violence, programs of artistic integrity. Violence, physical and psychological, is in itself not amenable to a center but contradictory of humans as ends in themselves. *Artistic* representations of violence, however, admit of a virtuous middle state such as exemplified in *Holocaust, Schindler's List, Gandhi, Amistad, Roots, The Pianist,* and *The Day After.* And consistent with aesthetic proportion are the several middle-level solutions worth pursuing—media education, an effective classification and ratings system, v-chip technology, reflective writers and producers, media criticism, informed network executives voluntarily reducing violence, publicly appointed monitors and congressional pressure, a violence index, and so forth.

Media ethics can contribute to understanding media violence by delineating responsibility. Nonutilitarian ethics always takes seriously the matter of who should be held accountable. The important question then becomes whether producers of violent entertainment can dismiss their responsibility by claiming to give the public what it wants. Are only parents culpable for the television programs their children watch, or do advertisers and networks carry obligations also? If so, in what proportions? Does the person with greatest technical expertise have the greatest moral liability? How can paternalism that downgrades laypeople and informal social networks in the decision-making process be avoided? When is the state or the courts the final adjudicator? In professional ethics generally and media ethics specifically, clarifying accountability is an important safeguard against the human penchant for evading culpability. The ongoing challenge for media ethics, then, is establishing the appropriate levels of responsibility among the principal players in media violence: producers and writers, actors, network executives, the public, and politicians. In meeting this challenge, communication ethics will make a unique contribution to understanding media violence and offer sure-footed guidance in dealing with it.

DISTRIBUTIVE JUSTICE

A host of ethical issues are already obvious as global media empires take shape. Some are new moral problems, such as digital manipulation. Other longstanding issues are being transformed. Privacy, surveillance, deception, gender discrimination, and ethnic diversity are more complicated than ever.

But the centerpiece ought to be the ethics of justice. A social ethics of justice should be up front at the vortex of the information revolution. Only a sophisticated view of social justice can respond adequately to the new world information order. Justice is the normative foundation on which to base regulatory standards for international communication.

The overriding question of justice is accessibility. In terms of the principle of just distribution of products and services, media access ought to be allocated to everyone according to essential needs, regardless of income or geographical location. Comprehensive information ought to be ensured to all parties without discrimination.

In contrast, the standard conception among privately owned media is allocating to each according to ability to pay. The open marketplace of supply and demand determines who obtains the service. A prominent role is assigned to free choice. Consumers are considered to be at liberty to express their preferences and to select freely from a variety of competing goods and services. The assumption is that decisions about allocating the consumers' money belong to them alone as a logical consequence of their right to exercise their own social values and property rights without coercion from others. From this perspective, commercial companies are not considered charitable organizations and therefore have no obligation to subsidize the information poor.

An ethics of justice in which distribution is based on need offers a radical alternative to the conventional view. Fundamental human needs are related to survival or subsistence. They are not frivolous wants or individual whims or desserts. Agreement is rather uniform on a list of most human necessities—food, housing, clothing, safety, and medical care. If we cannot provide them for ourselves because of the finitude of our circumstances, they nonetheless remain as essential goods. Everyone is entitled without regard for individual success to that which permits them to live humanely.

The electronic superhighway cannot be envisioned except as a necessity. Communications networks make the global economy run, they give us access to agricultural and health care information, they organize world trade, and they are the channels through which the United Nations and political discussion flow—through them, we monitor war and peace. Therefore, as a necessity of life in a global order, the information system ought to be distributed impartially, regardless of income, race, religion, or merit.

But there is no reasonable likelihood that need-based distribution will ever be fulfilled by the marketplace itself. Technological societies have high levels of computer penetration, and nonindustrial societies do not. Digital technology is disproportionately concentrated in the developed world, and under the principle of supply and demand, there are no structural reasons for changing those disproportions. Around 75% of the world's users are in selected Asian countries (Japan, Korea, Taiwan, Singapore, and the Hong Kong region), Europe, and the United States. Only .01% of the population in Africa has computers, and in India, 1 out of 50,000 uses the Internet. Finland has more Internet hosts than all of Latin America. Even in wired societies, the existence of Internet technology does not guarantee it will reach its potential as a democratic medium. There is a direct correlation between per capita gross national product (GNP) and Internet distribution. In the United States, for example, 80% of those households with incomes of $75,000 have computers; only 6% do of those with incomes of $15,000 or less.

Universal diffusion driven by profits is unlikely. There are no grounds for supposing that the geography of the digital world will be fundamentally different from that of the offline world. There is no technological fix. The history of the communications media indicates that they follow existing political and economic patterns; inequities in society lead to inequities in technology. An ethics of justice requires that we intervene through legislation, government policy, and public ownership to implement open access. Our approach to media institutions should be modeled after schools, which we accept as our common responsibility, rather than determined by engineers or by profits alone.

Given the realities of international politics and limited resources, the need-based principle of justice must be supplemented by the similar treatment formula. In the actual distribution of services under suboptimal conditions, the principle of similar treatment for similar cases calls us to honor the equal distribution of limited services for all. If providing an entire range of expensive technologies for everyone is impossible, it is unjust for a few to be equipped with sophisticated systems and the rest given only minimal service or none at all. If we accept the case for equal access, it is more just to discriminate in terms of categories of service rather than between the information rich and poor. All homes, for instance, could have fire and police view-data communications capability, rather than some being served by every convenience and others receiving no benefits. The formula of similar treatment for similar cases modifies the application of a need conception of justice to address the real world of constraints. But

the goal of equal access to essential services remains due to its moral significance. To realize it only in part is better than jettisoning the formula because of difficulties in implementing it within an environment characterized by resource limitations.

Distributive justice earlier produced a social responsibility framework for broadcasting, as well as a professional ethics of social responsibility for newspapers and magazines. The guideline is informed citizenship, that is, the public learning the day's events in a context of meaning. For telecommunications, the just distribution principle yields the norm of equitable access, with data transmission, telephony, and legal and postal services available to everyone following equivalent standards.

But social responsibility for broadcasting and journalism and equitable access for telecommunications are guidelines in a national setting. They presume and serve explicit political entities. In the digital age—rooted in computers, the Internet, satellites, and the World Wide Web—ideally all types of persons will use all types of media services for all types of audiences. Therefore, the normative guideline ought to be universal access, based on need. And universal service is the Achilles heel of new technologies driven by invention, engineering, and markets. As the economic disparity between rich and poor continues to grow, a structurally defined information underclass exacerbates the problem under the patina that information and education are the pathways to equality. Without intervention into the commercial system on behalf of distributive justice, we will continue to divide the world into the technologically elite and those without adequate means to participate.

HATE SPEECH ON THE INTERNET

Hate groups are on the rise, boosted by the Internet. In 1995, former Ku Klux Klan (KKK) leader Don Black established Stormfront, the first White supremacist site on the World Wide Web. As access to the Internet became less expensive and creating Web pages much simpler, the number of Web sites and people visiting them has grown exponentially.

Mirroring this growth, bigoted Web sites have grown dramatically also, with more than 2,200 such sites promoting hate, which have been identified in the 2001 Report of the Simon Wiesenthal Center (www.wiesenthal.org; see www.adl.org). "In the past, hate was promoted through crude graffiti and mimeographed pamphlets." Low-class mailings to a few hundred were always difficult. But "these days, slick Web sites devoted to hate are available for a potential audience of millions" (Lauterman, 1999, p. 1).

Today's Ku Klux Klan is more fragmented than at any time since World War II, but its many factions are using the World Wide Web for revitalization. The Southern Poverty Law Center has identified 200 active KKK sites at present. They maintain and defend "the superiority of the White race" and warn "against miscegenation of the races." Jews are vilified as Satan's people, and immigration is condemned as an "uncontrolled, outrageous, and unprecedented plague." In addition, the number of Web sites for the National Association for the Advancement of White People (NAAWP), founded by former Klan leader David Duke, has mushroomed and energized the so-called "Klan without robes" (www.adl.org/main_internet).

Numerous neo-Nazi Web sites promote the anti-Semitic racism of Adolf Hitler's Nazi party. According to the Anti-Defamation League, the National Alliance is the most prominent overtly Hitlerian organization in the United States today, and its Web site includes transcripts of anti-Semitic radio broadcasts, scathing articles from its *National Vanguard* magazine, and a catalog of more than 600 books. Jews are blamed for inflation, media brainwashing, and government corruption, with Blacks depicted as criminals and rioters. Books and speeches by Hitler, Joseph Goebbels,

and the American neo-Nazi George Lincoln Rockwell are displayed and promoted. A host of the sites are devoted to Holocaust revisionism, denying the murder of Jews in World War II. In addition, many neo-Nazi skinheads such as the Oi! Boys and Hammer Skin Nation have Web sites saturated with racist hard rock music (www.adl.org/main_internet).

The Web sites of religious groups are flourishing too. Congregations of Christian Identity are virulently racist and anti-Semitic. Today's Jews are not descended from Old Testament Jews but are Satan's creation. Jews and Blacks are enemies, a virus seeking to destroy "the purity of the Aryan (White) race." The World Church of the Creator (WCOTC) calls non-Whites physiologically inferior, subhuman "mud people." Vicious drawings brutalize Jews and Blacks, and a WCOTC Kids Web site promotes White supremacy in children's terms. The site for White Aryan Resistance (WAR) preaches "your races as your religion" and rails with others against the "non-White birthrate," "massive immigration," and "racial intermarriage." Other religious sites are anti-Catholic and anti-Muslim or violently anti-abortion. Alex Curtis's Nationalist Observer Web site features his "Tribute to Jewry," that is, "Jew York City" decimated by an atomic bomb (www.adl.org/main_internet).

Most organizations that monitor Internet hate activity do not advocate censorship. Education is seen as more effective than trying to silence the bigots. The Southern Poverty Law Center publishes a comprehensive "Community Response Guide" on ways to combat hate. The Anti-Defamation League, as a tool for parents, provides a software filter that blocks hate sites. The Simon Wiesenthal Center advocates that Internet service providers follow the lead of newspapers, which traditionally have rejected advertising judged offensive. David Goldman, founder and director of HateWatch, a Web-based educational resource organization to combat online bigotry, wants knowledgeable citizens to speak up. He summarizes the general conclusion of most observers that ignorance and apathy "allow this poison to grow" (Lauterman, 1999, p. 7).

Whereas with most moral problems in the media, some ethical theories are more appropriate than others, hate speech on the Internet is contradicted by all major theories without exception. Even consequentalism speaks without ambiguity about it. For Aristotelian virtue ethics, vitriolic hatred is patently a vice. Kant's principle that humans ought to be treated as ends in themselves does not tolerate physical or psychological abuse. In utilitarian ethics, White supremacy–Black inferiority produces too much harm and benefits only a misguided few. The advocacy of hate speech, as well as any actions based on it, violates John Rawls's first principle guaranteeing maximum equal liberty for all. And obviously Internet hatred, as in real life, is the polar opposite of agape's Other-regarding care. This condemnation across the theoretical board suggests that all personal, educational, and policy efforts to combat it are permissible, even mandatory, but obviously short of revengeful and aggressive means that contravene good ends.

◆ Generic Concerns

Some important ethical problems cut across all three functions, media technologies, and organizational structures. Two of the most urgent, with the greatest potential impact, are cultural diversity and democratization.

CULTURAL DIVERSITY

Indigenous languages and ethnicity have come into their own. Sects and religious fundamentalists insist on recognition. Culture is more salient these days than countries.

Muslim immigrants are the fastest growing segment of France's population, and longstanding policies of assimilation have not been credible. Thirty thousand Navajos live in Los Angeles, isolated from their native nation and culture. The nomadic Fulani search for good pasture throughout sub-Saharan West Africa and are held together by clan fidelity, but their political future hangs in the balance. Hasidic Jews in the Williamsburg community of Brooklyn, New York, live under constant threats to their safety. The Detroit area has 200,000 people of Middle Eastern descent; 1,500 small grocery and retail stores in the vicinity are owned by a subculture of Chaldean Christians with roots in Iraq. More than 30% of the information technicians working for mammoth Microsoft come from India. At the turn of the 20th century, 80% of the immigrants to the United States emigrated from Europe. Starting in the 1960s, the majority has come from Asia, Latin America, and developing countries in Africa. And rather than the melting-pot Americanization of the past century, immigrants now insist on maintaining their culture, religion, and language. With identity politics the dominant issue in world affairs after the cold war and ethnic self-consciousness a source of social vitality, social institutions, including the media, are challenged to develop a healthy cultural pluralism.

To comprehend the new demands of cultural diversity, we must give up an individualistic morality of rights for a social ethics of the common good. A commitment to cultural pluralism makes sense when the community is understood to be axiologically and ontologically prior to persons. Human beings in this communitarian perspective do not disappear into the tribe, but their identity is constituted organically; persons depend on and live through the social realm. Our selfhood is not fashioned out of thin air. We are born into a sociocultural universe where values, moral commitments, and existential meanings are both presumed and negotiated (Schutz, 1967, chap. 2). Social systems precede their occupants and endure after them. Indeed,

Socrates argued playfully that he could not be responsible for ruining the polis or free to save it because the polis educated him.

In communitarian ethics, morally appropriate action intends community. Unless my freedom is used to help others flourish, my own well-being is negated. Fulfillment is never achieved in isolation but only through human bonding at the epicenter of social formation. Contrary to the 18th-century dualism between thinker and agent, reason and will, we know ourselves primarily as whole beings in relation. There are no singular selves split into mind and body pursuing an isolated identity across time. Humans survive and develop through interaction with others and not from isolated introspection or private experience. Thus, communitarian democracy argues that an atomistic political liberalism operating with an aggregate of individual pursuits cannot yield a comprehensive approach to the age of diversity. Because the social nature of human life has been underdeveloped in classical liberal theory, it lacks the intellectual resources to articulate a multicultural society. In communitarianism, moral agents are understood to need a context for assessing what is valuable. What is worth preserving cannot be determined in isolation but ascertained only within specific social situations in which human identity is nurtured. The public sphere is conceived as a mosaic of distinguishable communities, a pluralism of ethnic identities and world-views intersecting to form a social bond but each seriously held and competitive as well. At its origin three centuries ago, liberal political philosophy found traditional communities unproblematic and saw the intellectual challenge as defining individual autonomy. While coming to grips with liberty and expanding its scope conceptually and governmentally, liberal societies have tended to rely on a dualism of two orders—liberty in the public arena of involved citizens undergirded by moral values in the sphere of family and peers. However, instead of paying lip service to the social nature of the self while presuming this

divide, communitarian democracy interlocks liberty and communal well-being as both inscribed in the social organism.[8]

For linking communal values with the political ideals of freedom and equality, only democratic models of community are appropriate. Some forms of association are authoritarian and gender biased. Occupational groups or fans supporting a local baseball team are not communities in the sense that one's self-identity is derived from the whole. The Ku Klux Klan is driven by racial supremacy. Some ethnic communities are sexist. Thus, Carole Pateman (1989) advocates participatory democracy as the normative core of community formation. In her perspective, social contract theory, from John Locke to Rawls, argues for voluntary consent but actually demands acquiescence. Liberal arguments for freely created obligation obscure the nature of the political obedience involved; otherwise, "it would strip the liberal democratic state of a major portion of its ideological mantle" (Pateman, 1989, p. 70). Participatory democracy alone is appropriate to community formation. Civil associations bound together by a network of beliefs and values are only possible through active participation in articulating the common good and mutuality in implementing it.

Communitarianism as the basis for cultural pluralism enables us to move beyond melting-pot homogeneity and replace it with the politics of recognition. Amy Gutmann's (1994) question gets to the heart of the matter: "Is a democracy letting its citizens down, excluding or discriminating against us in some morally troubling way, when major institutions fail to take account of our particular identities?" (p. 3). In what sense should our specific cultural and social features as African Americans, Asian Americans, Native Americans, Buddhists, Jews, the physically disabled, or children publicly matter? Should not our public institutions treat us as free and equal citizens without regard to race, gender, or religion and ensure only that democratic citizens share an equal right to political liberties and due process? Charles Taylor (1994, pp. 25–73) considers the issue of recognizing multicultural groups politically as one of the most urgent and vexing on the democratic agenda at present, and the equalitarian social philosophy of classic democratic liberalism cannot accommodate it. Beneath the rhetoric is a fundamental philosophical dispute that Taylor calls the "politics of recognition." As he puts it, "Nonrecognition or misrecognition can inflict harm, can be a form of oppression, imprisoning someone in a false, distorted, and reduced mode of being. Due recognition is not just a courtesy we owe people. It is a vital human need" (Taylor, 1994, p. 26). This foundational issue regarding the character of cultural identity vis-à-vis equal rights needs resolution for cultural pluralism to come into its own.

Dialogic relations are the heart of the communitarian paradigm, and from a dialogical perspective, recognition is not a supercilious pursuit. As Taylor (1994) argues,

We become full human agents, capable of understanding ourselves, and hence of defining our identity, through our acquisition of rich human languages of expression. But we learn these modes of expression through exchange with others. People do not acquire the languages needed for self-definition on their own. Rather we are introduced to them through interaction with others who matter to us. . . . My own identity crucially depends on my dialogical relations with others. . . . In a culture of authenticity, relationships are seen as the key loci of self-discovery and self-affirmation. (pp. 32, 34, 36)

Language is the marrow of community, the public agent through which our identity is realized. Persons are displayed, made accessible, nurtured, and integrated into social units through symbol, myth, and metaphor. Our constitutive relations as humans are linguistic. Symbols cannot be isolated in our cranium. The lingual dimension forms an organic whole with our deepest humanness, and its vitality or oppression inevitably conditions our well-being. Our first existential order is the symbolic theater we call culture, and therefore our human identities inscribed in culture matter to us.

Therefore, while requiring political neutrality in government affairs, communitarian democracy simultaneously insists that public institutions further particular cultural values. Michael Walzer (1994, pp. 11–12) distinguishes two kinds of liberalism: Liberalism 1 is committed to a neutral state and the strongest possible version of individual rights. In Liberalism 2, the state promotes the survival and flourishing of particular cultures and religions. Should there be multicultural societies of Liberalism 2, Liberalism 1 would be chosen through a democratic process. However, both versions are possible at the same time. Amy Gutmann recommends correctly that we see these conceptions as two strands within a single paradigm of liberal democracy—one that requires state neutrality in such areas as religion "but not in others, such as education, where democratically accountable institutions are free to reflect the values of one or more cultural communities as long as they also respect the basic rights of all citizens" (Walzer, 1994, p. 12). Within this model, the democratic institutions of communications are challenged to develop policies and practices that take seriously the politics of recognition based on a dialogic social philosophy.

Consistent with this framework, Robert Entman and Andrew Rojecki (2000) indicate how the race dimension of cultural pluralism ought to move forward in the media. Race in 21st-century United States remains a preeminent issue, and their research indicates a broad array of White racial sentiments toward African Americans as a group. They emphasize not the minority of outright racists but the perplexed majority. On a continuum from comity (acceptance) to ambivalence to animosity and then racism, a complex ambivalence most frequently characterizes the majority. "Whites bring complicated combinations of assumptions, misinformation, emotional needs, experiences, and personality traits to their thinking about race" (Entman & Rojecki, 2000, p. 21). They may believe, for example, that Blacks face discrimination and merit aid but argue against welfare spending for Blacks out of a suspicion of government programs. They do not "generally harbor deep-seated fears or resentment, . . . but also sometimes lose their patience over racial issues" (p. 33). Correcting White ignorance and dealing with ambiguities appear to hold "considerable promise for enhancing racial comity" (p. 21). The reality is, however, that ambivalence shades off into animosity most easily and frequently. In Entman and Rojecki's interviews, "the media serve as resources for perpetuating racial animosity." Personal experiences of Black effort and achievement tend to be discounted "in favor of television images, often vague, of welfare cheats and Black violence." Unfortunately, interviewees did not draw "on television or other media for evidence that pulled them toward comity" (Entman & Rojecki, 2000, p. 28). Overwhelming in the White majority experience are

> media images of Blacks on welfare, of Black violence on local news, and of crude behavior—open sexuality and insolence—in entertainment television. The mediated experience rises just above a critical threshold where these ambivalent respondents say they do know better intellectually, from coming into contact with a variety of Black people who offer compelling evidence to the contrary, but nevertheless feel themselves taken in by the flood of images. . . . The habits of local news—for example, the rituals in covering urban crime—facilitate the construction of menacing imagery. (Entman & Rojecki, 2000, p. 34)

The media are not enhancing racial understanding among those most open to it. They are "tipping the balance toward suspicion and even animosity among the ambivalent majority of Americans" (p. 44). Unfortunately, the media do not serve this important swing group for moving forward and changing policy and institutions toward cultural pluralism.

Democratization

How can the global media, entertainment empires, international wire services, and cyberspace fulfill their democratic potential? Ethicists are always concerned about ends, aims, and goals. Therefore, an important question is whether educational and information services will be primary in the technologically sophisticated media systems of the 21st century. Worldwide news operations open windows on politics everywhere. Technologies such as the interactive Internet give people a voice and connect users directly without professionals or gatekeepers in between. They are democratic tools in principle—hence the concern that the new media serve the people's needs rather than those of special interest groups or the market's. "I have some reservations," Ellen Goodman (1993) writes,

> about an information superhighway roaring through my front door. For one thing, . . . this highway is not heading for the library; it's heading for the marketplace. [Automobile] highways took people from Main Street to the Mall. The information highways hope to turn our homes into domestic versions of the Great Mall of America in Minneapolis. Has anybody asked for this? . . .The superhighways are promoting, indeed betting on, superspending. (p. 15)

Five hundred online channels are technically feasible. Will they tangibly improve the quality of education, broaden our political horizons, or make public policy alternatives more understandable? Can a complicated enterprise overcome the contradiction between an antidemocratic, media-centered professionalism and a citizen-centered ethics?

The social narrative we call news is an agent of political deliberation. In deliberative democracy, the public must press their claims "in terms accessible to their fellow citizens"; they must "reason beyond their narrow self-interest" and use arguments that "can be justified to people who reasonably disagree with them" (Gutmann & Thompson, 1996, pp. 55, 2; see also p. 255). The media, in other words, facilitate the process of negotiation over the social, political, and cultural agenda. In terms of the deliberative democracy entailed by the dialogic social ethics advocated here, citizens engage one another in normative terms, that is, on both practical matters *and* social vision. Social conflicts are a major component of democratic life, and in deliberative politics, they remain the province of citizens rather than usurped by judicial or legislative experts. Affirmative action, environmental protection, health policy, global warming, gun control, incarceration, arms trade, and welfare reform raise moral conflicts that the public themselves must negotiate. When agreement is not forthcoming, channels of continued interaction are kept open by acknowledging "the moral standing of reasonable views" opposed to our own (Macedo, 1999, p. 123). This approach is more pluralistic than Habermas's discursive account and more substantive than Rawls's liberal neutrality allows (Bohman, 2000, pp. 4–15).

Public life cannot be facilitated in technical terms only, but professionals must speak of moral issues in appropriately moral discourse. When journalists, for example, investigate government policies that are vacuous or unjust, they must do so in terms of common values that have broad acceptance in the community as a whole. Our widely shared moral intuitions—respect for the dignity of others, for instance—are developed through discourse within a community.

In this sense, media professionals participate in the citizens' ongoing process of moral articulation. In fact, culture's continued existence depends on identifying and defending its normative base. Therefore, public texts must enable us "to discover truths about ourselves"; narratives ought to "bring a moral compass into readers' lives" by accounting for things that matter to them (Denzin, 1997, p. 284). Communities are woven together by narratives that invigorate their common understanding of good and evil, happiness and reward, the meaning of life and death. Recovering and refashioning moral discourse helps to amplify our deepest humanness and to provide the soil in which democracy can flourish.

Most democratic theorists since Rousseau have considered deep moral conflicts intractable. As Bohman (2000) notes, "Moral and epistemic diversity often go hand in hand" (p. 86). Differences in moral outlook are entangled in different assessments of the evidence, varying data, and disagreements over appropriate public language. In these instances, "Appeal to a common human reason can still fail to produce agreement even when agents are not irrational" (p. 86). And Rawls's "method of avoidance" in such cases is typically counterproductive. Certainly, pragmatic devices such as a "gag rule" or "self-binding" device to remove some issues from public discussion do not entail deliberation but contradict it (p. 74). Therefore, a dynamic and pluralistic framework does not seek a singular, impartial standpoint that all citizens are expected to endorse (Rawls, 1993, p. 217). Rather, the media facilitate a public discourse that takes all interpretations into account, without aiming toward the convergence of an abstract point of view. No single norm of reasonableness is presupposed, and deliberation goes beyond trade-offs and making concessions that compromise our beliefs. In a pluralist democracy, "Agents can come to an agreement with one another for different publicly accessible reasons. . . . The ideal of public reason . . . permits rather than denies or avoids, moral conflict and differences in democratic politics" (Bohman, 2000, pp. 83–84). In terms of the democratization promoted by the contemporary media, citizens' values and conceptions of the good life put up for public debate "provide an expanded framework for deliberating about differences" (p. 92). When the terms of debate are widened beyond the values of individual rights, and moral disagreements are articulated in public communications, a larger universe of discourse can emerge, or, at a minimum, the various sides can learn to tolerate one another's position.

◆ *Conclusion*

The utilitarian ethics that dominates the media professions needs to be replaced by a sophisticated deontological theory. The building blocks in constructing such a theoretically credible media ethics are moving the specific conundrums in the field away from their utilitarian orientation.

In the process of restructuring media ethics in nonutilitarian terms, this normative composite must become explicitly cross-cultural in character. As true of professional ethics generally, media ethics ought to be repositioned as a comparative domain. The media ethics canon has been largely Western, gender biased, and monocultural. The field of the future must be international, gender inclusive, and multicultural. The global reach of communication systems and institutions requires a broadband ethics commensurate with its scope.

The ethics of individualistic rationalism has presumed political neutrality but is now more clearly understood as a "fighting creed." It is not a "meeting ground for all cultures" but expresses "one range of cultures, quite incompatible with other ranges" (Taylor, 1994, pp. 62–63). The traditional ethics of reason is entangled with the West's democratic liberalism in presuming its neutrality while actually imposing its own logic, fueled by a colonialism of intellectual and political superiority—thus the revolution in perspective toward a diversified comparative ethics with a level playing floor rooted in equal respect for all cultures. Replacing a one-way monologic ethics with a collaborative media ethics in the interactive, transnational mode is "by no means unproblematic and involves something like an act of faith" (Taylor, 1994, p. 66). The claim is that human cultures have something important to say to all human beings, a starting hypothesis that must be validated concretely. This presumption does not require of us "preemptory and inauthentic judgments of equal value, but a willingness to be open to comparative . . . study of the kind that displaces our horizons in the resulting fusions" (Taylor, 1994, p. 73). With its roots in language, culture, dialogue, and identity-in-relationship, media ethics has the opportunity to set the cross-cultural standard for all of applied and professional ethics.

◆ *Notes*

1. The first use of *ethics* by press critics was in July 1889. Garcia (1989) terminates her examination of journalistic standards in the United States at this date, citing it as the transition from everyday procedures to a more reflective period focusing on ethical precepts.

2. Ethics is normally distinguished into three parts: descriptive ethics, normative ethics, and meta-ethics. Descriptive ethics accounts for actual moral practices, beliefs, and traditions of particular persons or groups. It avoids moral judgments. In approach, it belongs to the social sciences. Normative ethics and meta-ethics are encompassed within moral philosophy. Meta-ethics examines the means and uses of moral terms, analyzes moral discourse and reasoning, and establishes the foundations on which moral judgments are made. Normative ethics examines moral arguments for the justice or injustice of

societies and institutions. It studies which classes of conduct are right or wrong, good or bad, and worthy of praise or blame (Kagan, 1998). Professional ethics, with its interaction of theory and practice, considers itself a type of normative ethics.

3. Richard Brandt (1963) and J. O. Urmson (1953) constructed a rule utilitarianism that confronted the weaknesses in emphasizing acts. In this view, we should judge rightness and wrongness not by the consequences of specific acts but by the consequences of their becoming a general rule. The question is not which action yields the greatest utility but which rule does. The principle of utility is still the standard, but at the level of rules rather than individual judgments. If one household waters its lawn in a drought, there are no discernible consequences, but rule utilitarians make a broadly applicable rule based on the results that suppose everyone did. Most critics of utility see little practical difference between act and rule utilitarianism because only maximum human happiness determined by counting one by one has intrinsic value in both versions.

4. For a detailed review of utilitarian rationalism from 1890 to the present, see Christians (2000).

5. For elaboration, see Denzin (1997, chaps. 8–9).

6. For a complete bibliography of television violence research, see Wilson, Colvin, and Smith (2002, pp. 57–60); Wilson, Smith, et al. (2002, pp. 32–53); and Potter (1999, pp. 257–285). The *National Television Violence Study* (1996–1998) was published in three volumes.

7. In Aristotle's own words, the principle is this: "Virtue, then, is a state of character concerned with choice, lying in a mean, that is, the mean relative to us, this being determined by a rational principle, and by that principle by which the man of practical wisdom would determine it" (Aristotle, 1947, 1107a).

8. *Communitarianism* is understood here as a social philosophy developed by Charles Taylor, Michael Sandel, Carole Pateman, and others as an alternative to egalitarian democracy (such as Richard Rorty's procedural version). When Amitai Etzioni uses the term for a political movement, it bears the same discontinuity with communitarian political theory as the Democratic Party does with the term *democracy*.

◆ References

Almond, B. (1995). *Introducing applied ethics.* Oxford, UK: Blackwell.

Aristotle. (1947). *Nicomachean ethics.* New York: Modern Library.

Bohman, J. (2000). *Public deliberation: Pluralism, complexity and democracy.* Cambridge: MIT Press.

Brandt, R. (1963). Toward a credible form of utilitarianism. In H. N. Castaneda & G. Nakhnikian (Eds.), *Morality and the language of conduct* (pp. 107–143). Detroit, MI: Wayne State University Press.

Callahan, D., & Bok, S. (1980). *Ethics teaching in higher education.* New York: Plenum.

Christians, C. (2000). An intellectual history of media ethics. In B. Pattyn (Ed.), *Media ethics: Opening social dialogue* (pp. 15–45). Leuven, Belgium: Peeters.

Christians, C., Fackler, M., Rotzoll, K., & McKee, K. (2001). *Media ethics: Cases and moral reasoning* (6th ed.). New York: Longman.

Commission on Freedom of the Press. (1947). *A free and responsible press.* Chicago: University of Chicago Press.

Denzin, N. K. (1997). *Interpretive ethnography: Ethnographic practices for the 21st century.* Thousand Oaks, CA: Sage.

Entman, R. M., & Rojecki, A. (2000). *The Black image in the White mind: Media and race in America.* Chicago: University of Chicago Press.

Garcia, H. D. (1989). *Journalistic standards in nineteenth-century America.* Madison: University of Wisconsin Press.

Gerbner, G. (1994, July). Television violence: The art of asking the wrong question. *The World and I,* pp. 384–397.

Goffman, E. (1978). *Gender advertisements.* Cambridge, MA: Harvard University Press.

Goodman, E. (1993, October 25). Driving ourselves crazy on America's high-tech highway. *Chicago Tribune,* sec. 1, p. 15.

Gutmann, A. (1994). Introduction. In A. Gutmann (Ed.), *Multiculturalism: Examining the politics of recognition* (pp. 3–24). Princeton, NJ: Princeton University Press.

Gutmann, A., & Thompson, D. (1996). *Democracy and disagreement.* Cambridge, MA: Harvard University Press.

Ivinski, P. A. (2000). I see London, I see France, I see Calvin's underpants. In S. Heller (Ed.), *Sex appeal: The art of allure in graphic and advertising design* (pp. 108–115). New York: Allworth.

Jacobson, M. F., & Mazur, L. A. (1995). *Marketing madness.* Boulder, CO: Westview.

Jhally, S. (1989). *Advertising, gender and sex: What's wrong with a little objectification?* (Working Paper No. 29). Evanston, IL: Center for Transcultural Studies.

Johansson, P. (1999). Consuming the other: The fetish of the Western woman in Chinese advertising and popular culture. *Postcolonial Studies, 2*(3), 377–388.

Kagan, S. (1998). *Normative ethics.* Boulder, CO: Westview.

Kearney, R., & Dooley, M. (Eds.). (1999). *Questioning ethics: Contemporary debates in Philosophy.* New York: Routledge.

Kilbourne, J. (1999). *Can't buy my love: How advertising changes the way we think and feel.* New York: Simon & Schuster Touchstone.

Lauterman, C. (1999, May 7). www.i.hate. *Chicago Tribune,* sec. 2, pp. 1, 7.

Levinas, E. (1981). *Otherwise than being or essence.* The Hague, the Netherlands: Martinus Nijhoff.

MacDonald, B., & Petheram, M. (1998). *Keyguide to information sources in media ethics.* London: Mansell.

Macedo, S. (Ed.). (1999). *Deliberative politics: Essays on democracy and disagreement.* New York: Oxford University Press.

Mill, J. S. (1861). *Utilitarianism.* London: J. M. Dent & Sons.

Mill, J. S. (1975). *On liberty.* New York: W. W. Norton. (Original work published 1859)

National Television Violence Study (3 vols.). (1996–1998). Thousand Oaks, CA: Sage.

New age, new agendas. (2001). *Media and Gender Monitor, 8,* 4. Accessed from mdn@wacc.org.uk

Pateman, C. (1989). *The disorder of women: Democracy, feminism, and political theory.* Stanford, CA: Stanford University Press.

Potter, W. J. (1999). *On media violence.* Thousand Oaks, CA: Sage.

The power of advertising. (2001). *Media and Gender Monitor, 8,* 5–10. Accessed from mdn@wacc.org.uk

Rawls, J. (1993). *Political liberalism.* New York: Columbia University Press.

Ross, W. D. (1930). *The right and the good.* Oxford, UK: Clarendon.

Schutz, A. (1967). *The phenomenology of the social world.* Evanston, IL: Northwestern University Press. (Original work published 1932)

Sidgwick, H. (1998). *Practical ethics: A collection of addresses and essays.* New York: Oxford University Press. (Original work published 1898)

Taylor, C. (1982). The diversity of goods. In A. Sen & B. Williams (Eds.), *Utilitarianism and beyond.* Cambridge, UK: Cambridge University Press.

Taylor, C. (1994). The politics of recognition. In A. Gutmann (Ed.), *Multiculturalism: Examining the politics of recognition* (pp. 25–73). Princeton, NJ: Princeton University Press.

Toulmin, S. (1988). The recovery of practical philosophy. *The American Scholar, 56,* 337–352.

Urmson, J. O. (1953). The interpretation of the moral philosophy of J. S. Mill. *The Philosophical Quarterly, 3,* 33–39.

Walzer, M. (1994). Comment. In A. Gutmann (Ed.), *Multiculturalism: Examining the politics of recognition* (pp. 99–103). Princeton, NJ: Princeton University Press.

Wartella, E. W. (1996, November). *The context of television violence.* Paper presented at the Speech Communication Association, San Diego, CA.

Wilson, B. J., Colvin, C. M., & Smith, S. L. (2002). Engaging in violence on American television: A comparison of child, teen, and adult perpetrators. *Journal of Communication, 52*(1), 36–60.

Wilson, B. J., Smith, S. L., Potter, W. J., Kunkel, D., Linz, D., Colvin, C., et al. (2002). Violence in children's television programming: Assessing the risks. *Journal of Communication, 52*(1), 5–35.

2

THE LONG AND WINDING ROAD OF ALTERNATIVE MEDIA

◆ Alfonso Gumucio Dagron

SNAPSHOTS

◆ A torn poster on a wall reads *La Lutte Continue* (The Struggle Goes On). Paris, France, May 1968.

◆ "Release our husbands from prison or we will not stop our hunger strike," shouts a miner's wife, live, on Radio La Voz del Minero (Miners' Voice Radio). Siglo XX, Bolivia, June 1967.

◆ Performers from an ACT-UP street theatre group distribute fake U.S. $10 bills on Wall Street with the added caption: "White heterosexual men can't get AIDS . . . Don't bank on it." New York, United States, 1988.

◆ In the basement of a church during the Pinochet dictatorship, a group of Chilean families watches the latest video news produced by Teleanálisis and distributed underground through unions and churches. Santiago, Chile, September 1976.

◆ Text messages calling for a public demonstration are multiplied through cellular phones. Manila, Philippines, 2001.

◆ Dozens of women demonstrate with their heads covered by white scarves with the printed photographs of their disappeared children and husbands. Buenos Aires, Argentina, any Thursday.

- ◆ Addressing its programmes to many thousands of war refugees from Burundi and Rwanda, Radio Kwizera (Radio Hope) is a response to Rwanda's former hate radio station Mille Collines (Thousand Hills), which had been a principal agent in inciting the previous year's genocide. Ngara, Tanzania, 1995.

- ◆ Raised high on a wooden pole, the six cone speakers of Maragusan Audio Tower warn the community against companies that are using motorized chainsaws to illegally cut trees in the valley. Davao del Norte, Philippines, 1997.

- ◆ *Hermano soldado, no dispares a tu padre* (Brother soldier, don't shoot your father), reads a large graffito on the adobe wall at a mining camp. Huanuni, Bolivia, 1981.

- ◆ At an international press conference, the Kayapó Indians show a video they made exposing how the construction of a dam at Altamira would affect their lands. They made the cover of *Time* a month later. Brasilia, Brazil, early nineties.

- ◆ Hanging high on the façade of the University of San Andrés, jobless workers from the mines put themselves on crosses to protest against being fired. La Paz, Bolivia, 1985.

◆ The Urgency of Being Alternative

The word *alternative* is provocative. It went out of fashion during the years following the fall of communist bureaucracies and the end of the bipolar division of the world, but it is coming back in again, driven by the creative force of freedom activist movements that, after bringing down the Berlin Wall, decided to assault the ramparts of globalisation. If we think of it, *alternative* is a beautiful word; it may save our values and reaffirm our identities. How can we not expect it to "alter" the current state of things? How can we live with our conscience in peace if we do not oppose the current global organisation of human life and propose alternatives to it?

Coming from Bolivia and having experience in developing communication programmes for social change there, as well as in Mexico, Nicaragua, Guatemala, Haiti,

Nigeria, and many other locations of the global South, my perspectives on media and media studies are different from some contributors to this volume. Having studied filmmaking in France intensively for 3 full years at IDHEC (Institut de Hautes Etudes Cinématographiques), the national film school, also differentiates my analyses from solely scholarly ones. From where I stand, academic research needs a much richer vision to be more global and much more closely tied to actual needs and practice. I see media studies at their best as focusing on a challenge to how the world is, not simply on explaining it.

Thus, we have to begin by recognising that the most unbelievable situations have become our stale tough daily bread that we eat without a blink. Values have been drained dry. We look but we don't see, we read but we don't learn, and we know, but what we know is diluted by trepidation and a desire to hang on to our comforts. We tolerate many situations that violate our principles and ideals. We watch the world being shaped as a nightmare, but most of us don't react.

Many countries in the world—North and South, East and West—spend four or five times more on their military forces than on education and health programmes combined (www.globalsecurity.org). In poor and rich countries, the defense budget is often larger than the entire welfare budget. Education and health problems are far from being solved, but the armies of the world always have modern deadly weapons, just in case. This commerce only benefits the countries that produce and sell weapons, a huge business led by the United States in the name of freedom, democracy, and free trade. In the name of globalisation.

Globalisation is another word for wiping out the world's borders and permitting huge financial speculation and all kinds of horrendous trade. Never before have we seen such an increase in the traffic of weapons, hard drugs, religious art, fake pharmaceuticals, radioactive materials, human organs, girls and boys for prostitution, archaeological artifacts, live wild animals, babies for adoption, immigrants (South to North), and nuclear garbage (North to South).

We live with a dominant political discourse that is hypocritical. How can we not be alternative to it? The United States provided weapons to the Taliban to get rid of the Soviet-supported Afghan leadership; once the Russians were out, the Taliban were redefined as repressive and cruel. The United States put Chilean dictator Pinochet in place in 1973 and trained torturers to squash the Chilean movement for democracy; 20 years later, Pinochet found himself on his own, no longer useful as strongman, trying to survive the international humiliation of house arrest and being defined as mentally incompetent to stand trial. The United States is responsible for the largest amount of emissions of greenhouse effect gases in the world but opposes and blocks the implementation of the Kyoto Protocol, an international convention to limit their consequences for climate change. Palestinians are forbidden to buy weapons and Iraq to develop nuclear weapons, but Israel can buy as many as it wants from the United States and has a nuclear arsenal. The United States has military bases in Japan, Italy, Germany, Spain, and a long list of other countries in the world, including Cuba, at Guantánamo. How about a small Cuban—or French, or Russian, whatever—military base on U.S. territory? Teenagers kill their schoolmates in U.S. schools, but the government opposes vehemently any serious moves, nationally and internationally, to control handgun use. The United States has been the largest producer and distributor of landmines, some of them shaped as toys, designed to attract children, but it has refused to join the international ban on landmines. It is also the only major country that has not ratified the International Convention for the Rights of the Child.

The world is upside down. *Patas Arriba (Upside Down: A Primer for the Looking-Glass World)* is the theme and title of a book by Uruguayan social analyst Eduardo Galeano (1998/2001), who shows with irony and biting wit how we have all become so used to the most grotesque and unbelievable distortions that we have become accomplices in the lies. The book is required reading to understand why we *have* to be alternative in the world as it currently is.

There is no protective measure against strongly globalising media trends. In a world surrounded by several thousand communication satellites, there is no shield that can wall off a culture against the culture globalisation brings with it. However, if this is impossible, the development of alternatives remains the only chance of counterbalancing its impact. We only want a fair exchange between cultures. There are many examples in history of cultures that have disappeared under the influence of other cultures, but also cultures that are the result of interaction and exchanges. The terms of exchange are obviously very uneven today, and that is why globalised Western culture is widely perceived as a gigantic project aiming to wipe out the rest of the cultures—European, Chinese, Arab, Latin American, and indigenous land-based peoples—and not only the so-called "weak cultures." For Henry Kissinger, former U.S. secretary of state and national security adviser, speaking in 1999, "What is called globalisation is really another name for the dominant role of the United States."[1]

Countries may "preserve" some of their traditions as folklore, just to prevent losing them completely. But we know that folklore is culture without oxygen. Folklore is a dead organ that you keep in formaldehyde or a dead animal that a taxidermist stuffs with sawdust: The eyes are dull, and the whole thing is stiff and rigid.

Live cultures have much to interject into the ongoing dialogue between cultures, to prevent the dialogue from becoming a monologue by the stronger party—the speaker that doesn't listen and only imposes its free-market fundamentalism. However, many alternative voices can be heard in many parts of the world, even as the monologue continues. The market-forces monologue continues like a sermon in a cathedral, but while the preacher continues preaching, many other murmured conversations are taking place, with alternative contents and meanings. And the cathedral doesn't belong to the priest, though he may feel it is his. So even though all of us, wretched delinquents that we are, may speak quietly inside, we voice our views noisily outside its walls.

Demonstrators and activists periodically express their anger and opposition to the drive to impose a single worldwide model of society that aims to establish the rule of rich countries over poor ones and to put an end to human priorities and cultural diversity. They are fighting for a world that is not "upside down." Their attitude is alternative to conformism and has inspired new alternative communication activism, which is why this introduction has been necessary to understand what follows.

ROOTED IN SOCIAL MOVEMENTS AND THE PROCESSES OF SOCIAL CHANGE

Just as commercial media are tightly linked to the health of business, and state or government media depend so much on the power structure, the very life of alternative media is tied to social struggle and social movements. Alternative media, as well as the paradigms that they oppose, establish a mutual relationship with the process of social change: They nurture social change as much as they feed from it. Alternative media are bonded to social movements and are seldom sustainable if detached from them. The dialectical relation between social struggles and the need of a voice to express them is a characteristic of alternative media. And this is true at the many levels of the process of social change.

Alternative media became "visible" in Europe and North America during the 1960s and 1970s because during those decades, it was fashionable to be a rebel with or without a cause. The rebel category included a very broad range of movements worldwide. In the United States alone, Black Panthers, hippies, anti–Vietnam War protestors, and pro-choice and other social network activists contributed to stir up in the public sphere debates on racism, violence, drugs, war, and abortion, among others. Every single movement felt the necessity to develop its own media, alternative to mainstream media. (However, alternative radical media existed much earlier in history, as can be seen in the Protestant Reformation, the English Civil War, and the American and French revolutions.)

There are "Third Media," as there is a Third World—"Third Media" that have been always distinct both from the First Media (dominant, capitalist, multinational, private sector driven) and the Second Media (media financed by socialist, communist, or/and leftist political parties). The Third Media have no organic relations with political parties but are in their flesh and bone a part of social movements. There is a permanent dialogue and interaction between social movements and media that support social changes. Nonetheless, in the final analysis, the independence of alternative "Third Media" is their main characteristic. This independence could be found 50 years ago in the first miners' radio station of Bolivia and today in the media initiatives supporting the autonomous movement of protesters against globalisation (Seattle, Prague, Washington, D.C., Genoa, and elsewhere).

Let me give two instances, one from Brazil, which ran from the 1890s through the 1960s, and the other from the famous political upheaval in Paris during May and June 1968.

In the northeast of Brazil, we can see an example that helps us to understand the evolution from a very basic form of communication to a more sophisticated one—namely, the *cordel*. (A *cordel* consists of a few very small sheets of paper, with illustrations and elementary captions, strung together on a little piece of cord.) The *literatura de cordel* originated in 1890, only a couple of years after the abolition of slavery, and was initially based on oral transmission of information that gradually evolved into a communication art form. Singers and storytellers used to travel from one marketplace or a local popular festival to the next, often improvising their tales and informative accounts according to their audience. In the Brazilian *sertão* (the arid hinterland of the northeast), this was the only source of public information for more than 50 years. These popular poets and storytellers—journalists, reporters, effectively—would gather news about events taking place in one town and narrate them in another town or ranch. They wrote their news in verse, carefully crafting rhyming poems. At some point, the storytellers started producing 8- or 16-page summaries, poorly printed, but well enough to keep the information or gossip in circulation. In the absence of any other source of news, these pamphlets were the newspaper, radio, and theatre.

Over the years, small *folhetos* (pamphlets), which recorded local happenings and were sold to the literate few, became more sophisticated and included images that were printed using woodblock carvings crafted by very creative artists. Used truck tires soon replaced wood as a material for creating the prints. In the 1950s, the traditional oral *literatura de cordel* met up with modern printing techniques, and the booklets became even more popular; thousands of copies were printed of each pamphlet. National and international events continued to be portrayed, including oppositional views to mainstream media and hegemonic culture. In the 1960s, when the military took power in Brazil, censorship was imposed on mass media and any form of communication. The creators of *folhetos* managed to bypass censorship through the invention of all kinds of demons and monsters typical of religious themes, but a blurred allusion to the generals.

In May 1968 in Paris, low-cost and rudimentary silk-screen techniques were instantly put in service of the student revolt. The collection of posters issued during the uprising are now classic images of simple, creative, and direct alternative communication. Art students exercised their talent and contributed to express the collective messages that the crowds shouted behind the barricades. When Daniel Cohn-Bendit—the most publicized leader of the revolt—was labelled by the government as an "undesirable foreign extremist" and deported to Germany, a poster was immediately produced with his face and the words *Nous Sommes Tous Indésirables* (We Are All Undesirables). To highlight the unexpected linkages between the students' revolt and many factory workers' grievances, a series of posters presented images of factories occupied by the workers, as well as slogans such as *Brisons Les Vieux Engrenages* (Let's Bust Up the Daily Grind) and *Salaires Legers, Chars Lourds* (Light Wages, Heavy Tasks). Mainstream media were particularly targeted in some posters. One showed a bottle of poison and read,

Presse, Ne Pas Avaler (The Press: Do Not Swallow). Another, showing a riot policeman, read, *La Police Vous Parle Tous Les Soirs à 20 Heures* (Prime Time News Straight From Police HQ). *La Radio Ment* (Radio News Lies), read another one. (Both these last are free translations.) This telescoped period of social unrest was enough to produce a very intensive and creative alternative communication flow, truly representative of the social movement at that time.

THE STRAWBERRY

Alternative media include community radio and television, press, and a wide range of communication activities. *Alternative media* refers to communication experiences that emerged as a need to counterbalance the state and/or commercial mass media. They have been defined as opposing established media channels, though their creation often only aims to offer a different perspective and more access. They have quickly been labelled as part of the leftist movement, subversive and revolutionary, and demonised by their more hostile detractors as destabilizing "democratic" society (read "the ordered routines of electoral politics") and threatening the "free media" (read "corporate media"). They have also been dismissed by many within the progressive movement as local, of limited impact, anarchic, and short-lived.

Readers might expect this chapter to offer a nice precise definition of alternative media. A tight definition is the strawberry on top of the academic research cream cake. Sadly, alternative communication seems allergic to that strawberry. The reason is simple: It is an ongoing process; nobody has a manual for it, a how-to recipe. When somebody attempts to promote a recipe to convert the process into a Step 1 and Step 2, then the spirit is lost, gone. In my own view, alternative communication is in essence participatory communication, and the alternative spirit remains as long as the

participatory component is not minimized or excluded.[2] Over the years, some definitions actually "freeze" the understanding of living and constantly evolving processes. One of the reasons why researchers have difficulty classifying alternative media is because of their free spirit, which generates multifaceted experiences refusing to be catalogued. Those who are actually involved in alternative communication initiatives may not be able to define or even name their own activity as alternative media, but they know very well what they are doing and how the process works.

We shouldn't really mind seeing the cake with lots of strawberries on top. Definitions are merely an attempt to create a common language, which is good. However, at the level where each experience is being built on a daily basis, tight definitions are *ni frio ni caliente* (neither cold nor hot), meaning they are irrelevant to the process. This should actually worry researchers, as it leads to a larger question: How useful is research to those being researched?

Another wave of alternative communication deals with citizens' rights and is an attempt to recognize the numerous interests within communities that have developed in large urban areas of the Third World through several decades of intensive migration from rural areas. It emerges in communities made up of people deprived of their land and forced to join the city poor. Urban communities often create their own means to express a culture that is suffering from adaptation stress and deprivation. The most recognizable forms of popular media and popular art are the result of the communities' need to have a voice and presence. Usually, they do not correspond to a well-structured programme that has laid out long-term objectives and a set of clearly defined activities. They are mostly the consequence of a desire to rehearse the community's cultural identity, for the purpose (which may not be spelled out explicitly) of giving a kind of proof of existence: We are here; we too are part of the big picture.

Alternative media can be an alternative to the absence of any other channels of information and communication. The first radio station on Kiribati (Christmas Island) was created in the context of silence; people did not even own radio sets because there was no radio station. By extension, silence can also signify the emptiness of relevant content in existing media. Small rural communities in the Philippines raised poles with cone speakers on top, creating community audio-towers, because existing media did not respond to any of their real needs. In the centre of Guatemala City, La Voz de la Comunidad (The Community's Voice) radio station was created to address the problems of just a couple of poor neighbourhoods in a deep ravine. It too started as a cone-speaker system before it was upgraded with a small transmitter.[3] To take a particularly clear example, Radio Kwizera (*kwizera* means *hope* in Kiswahili), near the Tanzanian refugee camps of Ngara at the border of Rwanda and Burundi, was created in response to the hate radio station Mille Collines, which in 1994 had been a prime tool in organizing the genocide. Radio Kwizera has an audience of waves of refugees who come and go across the border, hundreds of thousands, but it also transmits to the rural population living near the borders of Tanzania, Rwanda, and Burundi.

Radio is no doubt the alternative medium that has made the most widespread impact globally over the past 50 years. Since the early 1950s, several thousand community radio stations emerged, particularly in Latin America. During the 1970s, a similar phenomenon developed in Europe; the *radios libres* or "free radio" exploded in Italy and France, though the stations were mostly soon tamed to the point that they disappeared or became commercial stations. This is no surprise if we consider that the Salvadoran guerrilla Radio Venceremos (Radio We Will Win) became a mainstream commercial station after the peace accords were signed in the 1990s, and even its name was changed to

"R.V." to avoid any political meaning. Africa and Asia have been experimenting with community radio since the early 1990s, and South Africa has taken the leadership with appropriate legislation to protect it. I will return to radio later.

The alternative press, perhaps with less direct impact than alternative radio, is very common within the labour movement and is growing very quickly to be Internet based, as is radio itself. Radio, television, press, Internet, and the other media have been used for alternative and independent journalism, revitalizing the whole practice of alternative and activist reporting and taking it away from the false paradigm of "objectivity" towards an explicit commitment to social change. Although alternative media have grown faster in certain regions of the world, they have the potential to emerge in any social, cultural, and political context where there is a need for a voice to represent people and not only the economic or political interests of a powerful minority.

Alternative communication is often understood as "opposed to." Undeniably, many of the independent communication projects that emerged over recent decades were a reaction against hegemonic and vertical models of social and economic development under the umbrella of the U.S. "modernization" paradigm. When, in the 1960s and 1970s, the opposed "dependency" paradigm of development gained force in Latin America and soon in the rest of the world, participatory communication became alternative as opposed to the mainstream media that promoted modernization through the so-called diffusion of innovations. Even the United Nations Educational, Scientific, and Cultural Organization (UNESCO) became an important player in analysing the inequalities that existed in the world of information and communication. The 1978 McBride (1980) report, despite its diplomatically phrased language, was clear about the need to promote a new world information order where other voices would have the opportunity to be heard.

UNESCO promoted regional news agencies in Africa, Asia, and Latin America to counter balance the handful of news agencies that controlled and still control 80% of the information flow in the world. This search to rebalance for diversity in information and global access to communication technologies prompted the U.S. government to pull out of UNESCO from 1984 to 2002, proclaiming as it did so that UNESCO was actually fostering the reverse, a clampdown on the freedom of journalists.

Despite these smokescreens and blackmail, alternative media have flourished. *Horizontal, dialogic, participatory, communitarian, radical, popular,* or *alternative* are just some of the names used to refer to communication initiatives that often did not have a clear plan but were definitely the work of people finding their way out of the hegemonic media system and building their own capacity to communicate. According to the various attempts to define each word, some of the new experiences could be both communitarian and dialogic, participatory and popular, or horizontal and alternative. It didn't really matter. Communities involved in the actual experiences didn't use the labels that much.

As distinct from hegemonic and mainstream media, alternative media are not dependent on technology, at least not what we generally understand by technology: electronics, machines, and other of the kind. A pencil or can of paint are great pieces of technology, if we look at them as inventions that favor human advancement. What a person learning to write can do with a pencil is almost magic and certainly is revolutionary. Paint has been the vehicle for many of the most alternative popular expressions: graffiti, posters, and body paint, among others. The variety of tools and the combinations of tools and actions reveal that the communication *process* is more important than the infrastructure and the technology. To put it in other words, alternative communication is about software, not hardware. Institutions, technology, and messages are less important than *the participatory process, the capacity building within the community, and the ownership by a social movement.* Owning the hardware, the video equipment, the computers, and the like is important for alternative media projects but not their essence. The ideological software is what really matters: a shared vision of the future, a deep consciousness about current struggles, and a clear memory of the winding road collectively journeyed in the past.

Size and Significance

Friends and critics alike tend to minimize the importance of alternative media (too small, too local, too boring, too narrow, too marginal, too militant, too extreme, too underfunded). These attempts to analyse alternative media through the mass media lens are doomed to failure. If anything, alternative media are closer to nonformal education and grassroots cultural struggles than to mass media information channels. We cannot productively use the parameters and criteria of dominant media to measure alternative media. The success or failure of alternative media cannot be measured by numbers and percentages of audience or income but in terms of the ability for opening dialogue in the public sphere, be it at the community level or through existing social networks.

Though small and not necessarily always radical in terms of confronting the power structure and the hegemonic culture, alternative media have often suffered repression, to the point that one could almost measure their importance by the attempts to silence them. Many examples support this idea. How often did the Bolivian army attack and destroy the miners' radio stations since their creation in the early 1950s? How assiduously did the Soviet state track down and punish the writers and distributors of underground *samizdat?*[4] How energetically did the FBI in the cold war try to repress tiny-circulation dissident newspapers, the civil rights movement, and the movement against the Vietnam War? How vigorously did the apartheid (White supremacist) South African government try to stamp out African opposition communications?

Being local is not the same thing as being marginal. A local school has never been considered marginal. What is acceptable for schools should also be accepted for alternative media: A primary responsibility *is* to serve the local constituency. It makes more sense to compare alternative media with schools rather than with mainstream radio, journal, or television. Nobody ever would dare to question that a school *only* benefits 300 or 500 children because everyone knows that in global terms, the educational process is the result of thousands of schools working in parallel. If only this perspective could be applied to alternative media, a more intelligent understanding of them might emerge.

Growth, expansion, and other criteria based on large numbers are key to hegemonic media, not necessarily to alternative media. If we are dealing with social change for development, we do not apply market concepts to schools, libraries, or hospitals. In terms of alternative media, there is no need to desperately yearn for huge audiences, just to compete with mainstream media on their own terms and avoid the stigma of marginality. The ideal situation for alternative media is not suddenly multiplying their users by millions and covering geographical areas that go far beyond their constituency. The ideal is the multiplication of alternative media channels, each one founded on the bedrock of process/participation. There is no point in alternative media becoming global if, on their way to multiplying their audiences, they sacrifice the participatory process, the dialogue, and debate. This is precisely the story of Radio Sutatenza, the first ever community radio station in Latin America. In 1947, it was an alternative media channel for the farmer communities surrounding the Tenza Valley in Colombia; however, several years later, it became the largest national educational radio network and lost the alternative spirit that had made the station so special when it started.

The aspiration of any alternative media movement should be to reach its constituency. For the Bolivian miners' radio stations, that meant the miners and their families, as well as the farmers who lived in surrounding areas and the citizens of nearby small towns. If the stations were also heard in the capital, La Paz, or in Denmark, fine, as long as that audience did not modify the content of programming. In Latin America and Africa, I have visited community radio stations where station managers seemed very proud because a listener from Germany or Canada sent them a postcard with an encouraging message, as if that was the best proof of their achievement as a community media instrument.

Alternative media with a global scope— if any—should logically be dealing with global issues. An example would be the monthly French publication *Le Monde Diplomatique,* now available in half a dozen languages, which has consistently exposed the fallacies and perils of neoliberal globalisation. We recognize this characteristic in the very energetic alternative media movement that emerged after the Seattle anti-globalisation struggles and has been growing and getting better organized through successive worldwide demonstrations. The Internet, in particular, has helped anti-globalisation alternative media to become a global phenomenon. However, the movement is not global because of the Internet but because it deals with global issues. The Internet is only another communication vehicle and still to be shaped. Few movements use the Internet as much as the Korean alternative media movement, which is intimately linked with the independent labor movement there. Nonetheless, its main thrust is to address national issues, and the Internet is an instrument that allows them to do this in Korean, except for some pages they translate into English to solicit international solidarity.

Thus, anyone asserting that alternative media are fine *but* their coverage is too limited geographically or in terms of users does not understand what alternative media really are. The comparisons between mass media and alternative media serve no other purpose than labelling alternative media as unthreatening to commercial media, having a limited social impact, and being short-lived.

The requirement that alternative media should ensure wide coverage and continuously expand has much to do with a distorted concept of sustainability. The new wave of telecentres or telecottages, for example, is now under scrutiny from many friends and foes who would like to exact from these recently installed experiences a certificate of "self-sustainability." It is enough in some poverty-bureaucrats' minds for a telecentre to automatically be classified as sustainable and "successful" if it makes money, regardless of its real impact on social change or its contribution to social organization or cultural development.

What is it in alternative media that makes its comparison with mainstream media so intuitively compelling for many people? The fact that alternative media may often use similar instruments (radio and television equipment, air waves, technical staff) does not put both in the same category. Commercial aviation and military aviation both use planes, but any straightforward comparison will be defeated by the fact that their purposes are different. Military aviation cannot be evaluated by the number of passengers transported in a year, the income generated, or the quality of food provided in-flight.

ALTERNATIVE VOICES INSIDE THE FORTRESS?

Independent cinema during the 1960s developed in parallel to social movements in Europe, the United States, Latin America, and Africa. Frustrated by what they felt was their disadvantageous marginality, many independent directors tried to enter the film industry to change it from within. French filmmaker Jean-Luc Godard once observed in response that their attempt to take over the fortress of mainstream cinema ended with them taken prisoner inside. Alternative media, as well as occasional access to mainstream media, need to be separately defined. The fact that from time to time mainstream media generously open up so outsiders may debate critical issues doesn't mean much. The fragility of this access is permanent. You don't own the freedom to communicate; you are just graciously tolerated until you cross the fine line or until the fine line moves closer to you.

For example, the Federation of African Media Women of Zimbabwe (FAMWZ) spent a lot of energy on a project that aimed to pave the way towards community radio. The Mugabe government had no intention of tolerating the establishment of community media but offered FAMWZ the possibility of using airtime at one of the national radio broadcasters. Selected community women received training to coordinate radio listening clubs in rural areas of Zimbabwe. These activists received a cassette recorder to tape the opinions of women that often addressed questions to government bureaucrats. These questions were then addressed to the respective civil servants who would, in turn, respond. Both questions and answers were edited and aired during a 1-hour weekly programme on national radio. Considering the fact that there was no community radio in the country, this was an interesting option, at least better than nothing. It was a small but significant opening up of debate and dialogue in the national public sphere and an example of flexibility of government-controlled media. However, the honeymoon didn't last long; several months before the March 2002 national elections, the minister of information suspended the programme "until further notice."

Examples of occasional access to mainstream media are abundant in both industrialized and developing countries. Both public media and commercial media claim to contribute to the democratization of media by offering programme slots for expressing pluralistic views. These access experiences are unthreatening to mainstream media, are merely cathartic, often demobilize social networks, and contribute to consolidating the public image of a particular mass media firm as democratic and pluralistic. Be it independent journalists who express their strong progressive views on editorial pages or individuals from impoverished sectors of society who feel better when they can complain and shout into a microphone, the fact is that linkages with social movements are absent, which is why their expressions are tolerated. Mainstream media and hegemonic ideology have the capacity to absorb these isolated moments and even polish their image with them.

Once distant from social movements, many expressions of independent communication are just outbursts of individuals' creativity, with no connection to social change, only to reinvigorated artistic expression. When I was a film student in Paris in the early 1970s, a new post-'68 wave of rejection of bourgeois art was dominant among progressive intellectuals. The leading film magazine, *Cahiers du Cinéma,* for example, refused to publish any photographs, with the argument that film stills were a bourgeois form of expression. So the film magazine went on publishing only text for a couple of years, often very boring and written by hard-line leftists (who some years later returned with relief to their repressed passion for film images). In that context, one of the Film Department professors at the leftist Vincennes University campus did an experimental film where, for about 40 minutes, the only thing on the screen was a still shot of a woman's open vagina. While this image continued nonstop, a voice-over made intelligent observations that I forgot as soon as I left the screening.

Was this rebellious individual's "alternative" expression a form of alternative communication or just a way of revisiting the surrealists or Andy Warhol under the influence of the French students' uprising? The acid test is the depth of a dissident communicator's involvement with a social movement. The May '68 rebels had effectively

used graffiti, as well as magnificent silk-screen posters and other handmade communication resources, and their connection with the revolt was clear: A social movement produced those anonymous messages. When they became the expression of individuals, they lost the power to stir up debate in the public sphere, and the individuals' desire to scandalize was actually a hidden, maybe not fully conscious, attempt to replace the elite with a new one, or at least to introduce new artistic fashions. The enormous acceptance that installation art has today in galleries and museums is an index of how ready the art establishment is to absorb and domesticate.

Ephemeral Tools, Lasting Symbols

Fleeting alternative communication activism and long-term alternative media process are different; the latter implies the establishment of permanent alternative media channels that can deal with a variety of issues, whereas the former is like a punch—concentrated, direct, and right to the intended target. One is definitely more participatory than the other and helps to build organizational capacity to communicate; the other sometimes even has a second-level impact through mainstream media, breaking thus the confines of the initially very localized audience. Most examples of fleeting or ephemeral alternative communication pivot on one main idea and are often characterized by their direct visual and semantic impact, their almost bare-hands technology, and their emergence during periods of political repression. Several authors have concentrated on describing particular examples, in almost every region of the world, and have included songs, graffiti, jokes, bumper stickers, hairstyles, quilts, fabrics, and dress, among other forms of alternative communication.[5] The difficulty is that the borders are often blurred between the alternative communication function and the artistic, institutional, commercial, or personal significance of the messages.

If we take written graffiti as an example, we can find from "I love you, Maria" to "Burn, burn, burn," as well a "Vote for El Compadre" to "We sell puppies, give us a call." Which of the four meets the criteria of alternative communication? Painted graffiti are also difficult to classify. We know that graffiti were originally a way for youth groups in poor neighbourhoods to mark their territory, as well as to express their taste for music and generally the counterculture they represent. Nowadays, graffiti have evolved into a full-blown artistic expression, taken from subway walls to respectable museums. They are a well-thought-out and well-executed art form, often encouraged by municipalities to decorate neighbourhood schools or abandoned buildings. Are they alternative communication or "just art"? Art communicates, but we risk losing our focus if we are too inclusive.

A similar blurred distinction can be observed in dress codes. The way people carry their key chains may signify one thing for gay groups in California and nothing at all for gay groups in Europe. Certain symbols are ways of communicating alternative ways of life, but they don't necessarily pertain to alternative communication. Women in Africa wear printed fabrics with images and messages commemorating a particular event, and they create songs to celebrate a marriage, a political demonstration, or the visit of a government official. Carnivals in many countries are a vehicle to mock those in power through characters wearing clothes and makeup that the public can easily identify. Even if these take place completely outside of mainstream media, how much of them can be included within the examples of alternative communication? Could we draw the line at the point where oppositional social movements inspire alternative communication activism?

Graffiti can be one of the best examples of alternative communication related to social movements, which have enormous impact when they take the public sphere by assault. It is May 1968 in Paris that leaps to mind as a particularly attractive example, both because of the relation to a powerful social movement and because of the amazing creativity displayed. Slogans such as *Soyez Réalistes, Demandez L'Impossible* (Be Realistic, Demand the Impossible), *Il Est Interdit D'Interdire* (Prohibitions Are Hereby Prohibited), and *L'Imagination Prend Le Pouvoir* (The Imagination Is Seizing Power), among others, were the anonymous—but also collective—expression of the reigning anger and hope. They didn't last long in terms of actual production of contents and display on the walls of Paris, but the impact is still felt today.

Graffiti remain an important expression of alternative media, even during the apparently peaceful times of liberal democracy. Mujeres Creando (Women Creating), a very active Bolivian feminist group during the late 1990s, intervened in the public sphere by sparking debate on gender discrimination, writing on the walls of La Paz such imaginative poetic statements as the following:

Mujer	Woman
ni sumisa	neither submissive
ni devota	nor devoted
libre, linda y loca	free, pretty and wild
De hacerte la cena	From making your supper
de hacerte la cama	from making your bed
se me fueron las ganas	I lost the desire
de hacerte el amor	to make love to you
Detrás de una mujer feliz	Off behind a happy woman
hay un machista abandonado	there's a deserted macho.

The *long-term* symbolic impact of ephemeral communications such as these demands to be understood and acknowledged.

Without that step being taken, it will be difficult, for example, to grasp accurately the remarkable power wielded by the Mothers of the Plaza de Mayo in Buenos

Aires through their very effective communication strategies. These mothers, of those disappeared by the 1976–1983 military regime, wore diapers as scarves while demonstrating every Thursday since 1977 in May Square, sometimes with the printed images on their headgear of their lost children or husband. Their elementary act asserting maternity and care was a powerful symbol that, over the years, succeeded, despite being publicly defined by the military and other citizens as the demented ranting of obsessive women, in encouraging participation, dialogue, and debate—a splendid example of nontechnological alternative media.

The Mothers of May Square started demonstrating against all the odds. The context couldn't have been more dangerous for them—on one hand, a fascist military dictatorship capable of doing the "magic" of disappearing 30,000 people and, on the other hand, domesticated, self-censored, and fearful mainstream media, blind to any of the obvious signs of repression and state terror.[6] Like the drop of water that over time carves a hole in the rock, the Mothers of May Square continued their demonstrations at the same place and the same time, even after the military left power by the back door, and *still* continued until, nearly 25 years later, some of the military were imprisoned on kidnapping[7] charges (because they could not be tried for the murders).

In Bolivia, the Asociación de Familiares de Detenidos Desaparecidos (ASOFAMD, the Association of Family Members of Disappeared Prisoners) used life-size human profiles cut out of corrugated cardboard to publicly demonstrate for justice. Each mother, brother, or relative of a victim held the cardboard profile, which often also included a photo of the victim or a poem. This group of relatives-turned-human rights activists organized their demonstration in different squares and streets, in front of the Parliament or the Government Palace, wherever their presence would signify that the memory of those who were killed and buried without trace

is alive. In Bolivia too, in 1985, when the government closed down the loss-making national mining companies and left thousands of workers without jobs, "crucifixions" became a quite common alternative communication tool. Jobless miners would attach their arms and legs to a large crucifix high on the façade of the university or another public building and stay there many days until their demands were heard. It was a very powerful image to see their bodies hanging above the heads of passersby, night and day. In Christianized cultures, it is difficult to think of a more potent symbol of injustice.

Theatre has provided a broad array of experiences, urban and rural, most of which owe to Bertolt Brecht's approach. Street theatre has a few notable representatives, such as Brazilian Augusto Boal, but mostly it has developed all over the world in small groups that have not theorized much about their own work but, nonetheless, had a cultural and political multiplier effect. Very much following Boal's street theatre but also nurturing it,[8] Teatro Nuevos Horizontes was active during the 1950s and 1960s in Bolivian mining camps. Led by libertarian Líber Forti—a former printer born in Argentina—Nuevos Horizontes contributed to the organizational struggle of miners in northern Potosí. Performances were mounted without props, often on a truck, and lighted by the lamps on miners' helmets. The repertoire included not only plays committed to the reality of social struggles in Bolivia but also adaptations of leading Latin American playwrights and even great theatre classics. Bolivian miners were known for their thirst for cultural activities, and drama was also a tool for promoting consciousness on political issues.

Mime and performance art groups conduct a guerrilla-type of theatre activism. Fleeting as it may seem, its impact may be enormous via the (unenthusiastic) amplification provided by mainstream media. The ACT-UP experience in the United States is a key example. Beginning in 1987, the AIDS

Coalition To Unleash Power disrupted many mainstream "normal" events with its "politically incorrect" messages bringing attention to the struggles surrounding AIDS. This was particularly important in the Reagan era, when the establishment was very loathe, to say the least, to deal with the AIDS issue. When both the president and Cardinal O'Connor stated their opposition to advertising condoms, one of the ACT-UP groups erupted on Wall Street and in St. Patrick's Cathedral, scandalizing the immaculate consciences of stockbrokers and pious Christians. On Wall Street, they distributed fake dollar bills with the following message: "White heterosexual men can't get AIDS . . . Don't bank on it." They also disrupted a mass celebration in St. Patrick to protest O'Connor's attacks on homosexuality. The fact that ACT-UP was a coalition of groups resulted in widespread activity, a rich diversity of communications, and sustainability over time.[9]

The sustainability of alternative media, or the headaches of sustaining them, is an issue often manipulated to minimize their importance or their long-term impact. Well, maybe some alternative media activism has no intention in the first place to be sustainable or well established. Examples of this "compact" alternative media activism, valid through a limited period of time and for specific purposes, are abundant but poorly reported, in part, because of their highly intangible character. The audiocassettes with the sermons of Ayatollah Khomeini that circulated underground undermining the power of the shah of Iran, the clandestine video news bulletins produced and distributed through unions and churches during the Pinochet dictatorship in Chile, and, more recently, the cell phone text messages calling for public demonstrations in the Philippines (see Coronel, 2001) are some examples of this intensive and evanescent alternative media activism.

Thus, we have to acknowledge the fact that, notwithstanding the illusory objective of finding a permanent niche inside mainstream media, sometimes mainstream media may briefly amplify alternative communications. We also need to admit how hard it is to draw tidy lines between these diverse forms of alternative communication. For example, street theatre or popular theatre may be fleeting or ongoing. A single play to sensitise people to a particular issue may correspond to the fleeting type of activism, but the establishment of a network of theatre groups as a counterhegemonic communication channel would certainly belong to the category of long-term alternative communication processes. Both can be participatory at different levels: The performance-focused drama group engages with people, prompting them to interact with performers, whereas the process-oriented theatre channel may, over time, absorb people from the community as actors or scriptwriters.

Radio as Alternative Medium

Although radio in affluent nations has become basically a music medium, with just a few stations broadcasting inventive and significant popular artists, in most of the world, it is a crucial force, not least in nations with low literacy rates. I will focus here on a typical process of development of a community radio station and then illustrate a little from the experience of Latin America's most striking example of alternative radio over the past 50 years—namely, the Bolivian tin miners' stations.

In the development of community radio stations, phase one, for most of them—at least those that are not the initiative of a church or a nongovernment organization (NGO)—starts with very humble means, such as a pair of cone speakers and a karaoke amplifier. Their programming may sound at first like an analogue of First World music radio: music, music, and music, all day long. Nevertheless, there is much more to it. In the first place, it is their own station that is airing the music through the cone speakers or through a small FM transmitter. Second, it is the music they like, not the music that is programmed elsewhere. It doesn't mean that the music itself will be entirely different—though it generally is—but it means that people know they can request the music they want. I have learned to value these small stations that fill their programming with music because I know the process that comes next.

Next, in phase two, people visit the radio station to make specific requests and send short dedications to family and friends. It is not an exaggeration to state that the sense of local ownership of a community radio station starts from the moment anyone can send and receive his or her name through the airwaves: "I would like to dedicate this song to my best friend, on his birthday. With love, from Nicté." The breaking of the sound barrier, a social breakthrough, is what this means, socially speaking.

A third phase starts with short messages that allow the community to be better informed on community happenings. For example, "We are sad to announce the death of Mr. López, who passed away at the age of 68. He was one of the brave leaders of our community and founder of this radio station. We send our condolences to his family. He will be buried tomorrow at . . ." Or, "The free vaccination day will be held in our community next Thursday, just in front of our station, all day. All children below 2 years should attend. Mothers, do not forget the vaccination card." A usual message in community radio stations in rural areas deals with the reception of correspondence: "Ms. Aida González, Mr. José Chavajay, Mr. Felipe Morales. . . . Please drop by the radio station to pick up letters recently arrived." The radio station can simultaneously be the post office and an occasional health centre.

Information on social happenings will gradually include other topics of community interest. In the next phase, the radio station starts playing an organizing role, and community leaders will use it for the purpose of advancing the community. "We have learned that the municipality is planning to create a large reservoir for garbage only 1 kilometre from our neighbourhood.

If the project thrives, it will have a negative impact on the health of our families." And next, "A community meeting will be held tonight to elect the members of a delegation that will represent us and discuss with the municipal authorities the issue of the garbage site." The radio station is already serving the purpose (not declared, not sought at the beginning) of contributing to better organize the community and empower it to face challenges.

Microphones start getting out of the small building of the station in phase five. "The delegation of our community visited the deputy mayor and expressed our concerns. This is how Mr. Zapeta, a member of our delegation, described the meeting. . . ." Very soon, the radio station will send a reporter to interview the deputy mayor or other authorities and will open the microphones to anyone from the community to express what he or she thinks about a particular issue. The concept of a "reporter" is naturally born: someone who has to take a cassette recorder outside and question people, leaders, the community teacher, or outsiders who somehow relate to the community life. The "news" programme is built with all these bits and pieces that relate to the community. The essence is to distribute the information formerly held by a few leaders. From now on, leaders will report to the community through the radio station, and the station microphones will be present at community meetings, sometimes transmitting them live for several hours. Boring? Not for a community whose future depends on so many external forces.

Phase six will naturally expand the station's influence, both by improving the signal (often, new equipment is bought or obtained through donations) and incorporating new actors into the programming exercise. The schoolteacher will become responsible for a weekly educational programme, a nurse living in the area will be invited to conduct a health and nutrition segment, the leader of the community youth club will talk about sport, and the local priest will take advantage of a slot to talk about human values and faith. While visiting Radio Tubajon on the island of Surigao, north of Mindanao in the Philippines, I was present for an interesting exercise of pluralistic democracy: Around the same table, leaders from six different religious confessions were discussing the station's religious programming for the next 6 months.

Many community radio stations have evolved over the years to become important region-wise, which means transcending the scope of the village or urban community initially served to a larger audience. This can be an improvement, if participatory standards are maintained, *or can be a defeat,* if the radio station's programming has begun to respond to commercial or institutional agendas but no longer to community needs.

In the best scenario, phase seven marks the station's transformation into an integral communication and culture project that supports social development. Social organizations in the community participate in strategic decisions and programming. The station's influence expands to education, health, environment, and other areas of development and social change. Similarly, the miners' radio stations in Bolivia started with community messages, local music, and sports events before they discovered their potential as the voice of the miners' unions. Miners' organizations strengthened as their radio stations conveyed unifying voices that promoted debate on national issues and not union issues alone.

The Bolivian miners' radio stations had an enormous advantage over other similar alternative labour media projects. The Bolivian miners' struggle was deeply enriched by the fresh winds of the anarchist movement. The anarchist ideals that travelled from Europe to Argentina from the beginning of the 20th century prevented the miners' movement from being shaped too much by Leninist principles of organization. Bolivia's unions were, for many decades, a shining example of openness and balance between various political forces, something very unlikely to happen in other Latin American countries. In any important union

meeting, Trotskyists, Communists, Maoists, anarchists, and nationalist leaders sat together to struggle for common goals defined by the mechanisms of the workers' democratic participation, not by political parties' agendas. This explains why there was always only one union at the grassroots level, one miners' federation at the national level, and a single Central Obrera Boliviana (COB, Bolivian Workers' Congress) grouping all the other federations of workers, farmers, teachers, miners, students, artisans, and other associations. This same spirit was embedded in the management of miners' alternative media and is one very important reason for the development and sustainability of the radio stations over five decades. Typically, the Leninist type of organization claims to be able to unify workers, but in this case, it was the libertarian influence that had this impact, despite several attempts by the most dogmatic political parties—the Communists and the Trotskyists—to fragment the unions.

Independent Film and Video: Our Image, Our Memory

Video has been considered by many the "poor relative" of film and television industries and has been perceived as a marginal attempt to compete with commercial networks. The privatisation of television in Third World countries has only impoverished its contents. At least state-owned networks attempted to promote cultural and educational programmes, whereas commercial television is so dependent on advertising that it has to fill the daily schedule only with what "sells." The cost of running a television station condemns to a short life most independent projects that aim to promote culture or social issues. Even in industrialized nations, public broadcast stations have a hard life. A few attempts were made in Latin America during the 1960s and 1970s to establish alternative television stations, but none was successful over the years. At one point, each university in Bolivia had its own television channel offering cultural programming, debates, and news from a different perspective. But as soon as commercial licenses were accessible through bidding and cable stations entered the market, most university television channels faded away.

A similar process is taking place in countries of Asia and Africa at the beginning of this century. In Namibia, a country with only brief experience of community radio, a small private television station was installed at Rehoboth, 100 kilometres from Windhoek, in a community of *bastas*,[10] a racially mixed group long discriminated against by both Blacks and Whites. The station operated for a couple of years (1996–1998) from a garage, with a mix of VHS and 8-mm old cameras. What was interesting about this station is that it addressed issues that no other media in the country had ever addressed: the particular history of the *basta* community. This was done through a programming that paid especial attention to rescuing the cultural traditions and memory of the elders through interviews and open microphones.

Independent filmmakers and video makers have managed to build over the years a strong alternative to the emptiness of commercial television, thus creating not only alternative ways of producing and distributing film and video but also contributing with a different content and aesthetics. Independent video networks managed to survive—despite people's tastes having been greatly moulded by commercial television and cable networks—by revealing a social reality seldom seen on television. As technology became more affordable and easier to manipulate, video grew as a separate communication tool, with its own advantages over television.

Before video cameras became lightweight, technologically advanced, and very affordable, independent filmmakers were expressing similar social concerns through Super 8 film. I was personally involved with the *Taller de Cine Super 8* (Super 8 Workshop) of the Central Sandinista de Trabajadores (CST)[11] in Nicaragua, which later became a video unit. During the first year after the Sandinista Revolution, in 1980, the role of communication was crucial to sustain people's activism. At the *Taller,* a group of young workers was trained as filmmakers and started documenting important economic issues that the revolution had to face, such as the reactivation of factories abandoned by their owners who had fled to Miami or the promotion of corn as an alternative to wheat, which was previously imported from the United States. This project was personally supported by Comandante Modesto, the minister of planning, but it did not benefit from support by INCINE (Instituto Nicaraguense de Cine) the National Film Institute, whose resources were focused on producing prestigious feature films for export. The example shows that even in power, you can still be alternative to the hegemonic political culture and ideology. The Sandinistas may have won the war in 1979 and dominated government, but they were still alternative in a country where the dominant ideology had not disappeared and was only silent in the shadows—not to mention the aggression by the contras, supported by the U.S. administration.

Many innovative participatory video experiences have developed all over the world—Maneno Mengi in Tanzania, Video SEWA in India, the Kayapó Indians in Brazil, Televisión Serrana in Cuba, CESPAC in Perú, and Video & Community Dreams in Egypt, among others.[12] Video as a participatory tool has been the guiding vision of Maneno Mengi, a group based in Zanzibar. Maneno Mengi (*many words* in Kiswahili) specializes in low-cost digital video production, in support of social development initiatives. Its work has benefited fishing communities as well as farmers. Maneno Mengi uses the video camera as a "mirror" for communities to scrutinize their problems and find solutions. The entire process can last for several months: The camera participates in community discussions, and the recorded segments are shown again and again to the community or to relevant authorities to support an environment of social change. When changes are already taking place, the material is edited, mostly as a summary of the whole process. Community representatives participate in the editing sessions, which are simplified with the use of laptops with editing software. Maneno Mengi emphasizes the process rather than the video products themselves.

Video SEWA (India) is another experience that shows the participatory potential that video can unleash. It started in 1984 through Martha Stuart, who conducted a video training workshop in Gujarat for mostly illiterate market women from the Self-Employed Women's Association (SEWA). Among the achievements of this experience is the fact that women with almost no formal education were capable of assimilating the video tool, and their role in society changed as a result. The women who produced these tapes can conceptualise a script, film, record sound, and edit, though many of them cannot find the tape on the shelf when they need it, as they cannot read. Screening videos has become an important part of workers' education classes at SEWA. Watching tapes helps new members feel a connection with the larger movement. For the 1991 census, Video SEWA produced *My Work, Myself*, a 15-minute programme addressed to Gujarati women, which reached an audience of approximately half a million through cassette playbacks and was broadcast on state television. Others are training videos about oral rehydration therapy or building smokeless stoves.

The innovative uses of alternative and independent video can be categorized in three distinct perspectives, whereby (a) the process *before* the video product is essential, (b) the video product is the objective, and (c) the emphasis is on the process *after* the video product is completed, meaning the way the video is distributed and screened. These distinctions are not too rigorous in reality, but they allow us to better understand the strengths of each perspective.

Maneno Mengi, for example, puts the accent on the process of making the video, not in the product that results. Video SEWA could be an example of how the three perspectives are balanced. TV Maxambomba and TV Viva in Brazil, as well as Teleanálisis in Chile, are examples that show the impact of video; they are outstanding because of the way they relate to audiences.

Teleanálisis folded long ago. Nonetheless, it had an enormous social impact in Chile during the Pinochet dictatorship, as an alternative for the news systematically censored by the regime. Camera people went out risking their own lives to record people's demonstrations, political repression, and a variety of social problems; the material was edited in secret and copied to VHS cassettes, which were distributed through clandestine unions, religious organizations, and community groups. In Brazil, TV Viva and TV Maxambomba operate in a different context, a democracy where media are owned by the most influential economic media groups in Latin America, such as TV Globo. Both TV Viva (Recife) and TV Maxambomba (Rio de Janeiro) offer the marginalized neighbourhoods another image of their country, one that takes into account the problems, the needs, and, overall, the expression of the local community. Despite their names, neither is a television station. In streets and open places, TV Viva and TV Maxambomba deploy their giant screens to project video shows that attract people by the hundreds. They are public entertainment and at the same time educational; viewing is no longer a passive activity. The video production touches on all kinds of issues: politics, health, sexuality, unemployment, education, Black culture, citizens' rights, and the environment. Humour is an important ingredient. Cuban independent video production groups have multiplied since the early 1990s and now have their own national festival. Televisión Serrana is, in that context, an alternative communication experience because it takes place in rural areas, in a country where the government still has a strong hold on media. Televisión Serrana looks at the social situation of the farmer population and provides an opportunity for local communities to voice their concerns and aspirations. Particularly successful items are the video-letters, mostly by children and addressed to other children in Cuba and the world.

The potential of video within the framework of an interactive and dialogic process is huge. The instant playback of video is one of its empowering qualities; it enables continuous participation and feedback.

Indigenous Media

Ethnic and indigenous movements in Latin America have enriched the landscape of alternative communication. Most of the 4,000, maybe more, community radio stations air in indigenous languages and address the needs of the Aymara, Quechua, or Maya indigenous population. A news agency, Pulsar, provides needed support to the regional network of community radio through special programming and news. Independent indigenous video has also blossomed, as well as community theatre and other forms of grassroots communication.

The example of the Kayapó Indians in Brazil is just one among many. In 1985, Monica Frota, a young Brazilian photographer and filmmaker, started a video project with the Kayapó. Initially, the Kayapó used video for the preservation of the cultural memory of the community and recorded their rituals. In a second stage, video was used to communicate among villages and their chiefs, enabling relatives to see each other after many years. Soon, they also started to exchange political speeches and document their protests against the Brazilian state. The political dimension of the project was a logical development; the Kayapó showed a high level of understanding of how media interacted with public opinion. Their image as "hi-tech" Indians quickly gained the first pages of important newspapers, including a *Time* magazine

cover, when they denounced the construction of a hydroelectric dam that would flood their land. The Kayapó became much more self-conscious about their own "culture" as an important component of their identity as a social group and a valuable political resource, although in some cases, they reinvented the content of that culture to appeal to nonindigenous allies. The appropriation of video tools by the Kayapó strengthens the notion that people can govern their own history, as long as they can control their own representation.

Audiocassette forums have been undertaken in countries such as Venezuela and Mexico. In 1983, the Tosepan Titataniske cooperative,[13] based in Cuetzalan del Progreso, a town in the state of Puebla, adopted the cassette forum to increase the participation of small villages and local cooperatives. Decisions were increasingly being taken by a small group of leaders who lived nearby, whereas cooperatives farther away had no one to represent them. The solution to use audiocassettes to communicate among cooperatives was reached after conducting a brief survey of the local media landscape, which showed that the farmers had no access whatsoever to the provincial capital radio stations, and the cooperatives had no means to fund one themselves. The solution had to be at a very low cost.

A communication process was established in various steps. The survey showed that most rural families had audiocassette recorders but were only using the radio feature. A "monthly audio bulletin" on cassette tapes[14] started, produced by young "correspondents" appointed by their communities and briefly trained in general principles of communication and audio-reporting. Various sessions were held to establish priority issues, and the correspondents drafted a list of themes related to the management and lack of democratic participation at the central cooperative. After preparing half-hour news with interviews and comments and copying the news bulletin onto the 44 original cassettes, correspondents had to return to their cooperatives and make sure that everyone would listen to the cassettes. They were instructed to tape new interviews and short reportages on Side B about problems or events in their community. The correspondents would reconvene a month later, with 44 half-hours of community news, to produce another bulletin, this time with information on each respective village. However, the main community leaders tolerated this initiative rather than supporting it. They did not perceive it as essential for the development of their community, or maybe they did not like the participatory approach. Community democracy is not always welcomed by traditional leadership.

ULTRARIGHTIST ALTERNATIVE MEDIA

Although less important in numbers, there are also "alternative media" that serve small groups on the extreme right. For the same reasons—opposing commercial and state media that do not represent their views—hate groups have used alternative media to convey racist and violent messages. Neo-Nazi groups early on took advantage of the Internet to promote their philosophy. Another example already mentioned is Radio Mille Collines, an independent station that, during the civil war in Rwanda and Burundi, encouraged massive killings by Hutus of Tutsis and any Hutus associated with them.

Today, there also is a global network of more than 700 Christian fundamentalist television cable stations: These are now powerful channels, moving millions of dollars across borders and influencing simultaneously people in Asia, the United States, or Southern Africa. Religious alternative media today are also formed by many small radio stations owned by new sects—mostly little known—spread in rural areas of Latin America, Africa, and Asia, damaging the social tissue of poor urban and rural communities with messages that exploit people's discontents, suggesting either violence or blind faith as solutions.

◆ Conclusions

I have not been in any community, even the most poor and isolated, where there is no manifestation of communication or art. Every time I have had the opportunity to spend some time in a village, I've found the heartbeats of communication and artistic expression. Otherwise, it would mean that there is no culture, and that is simply unthinkable. Culture is always there and is manifest in many ways. I just have to ask if someone has a musical instrument, and instruments will show up, most of them made locally by local craftsmen. In a matter of minutes, a band can start playing because it already knows the local songs, the rhythm, and the accords. The same thing will happen with drama and local dances: Costumes will be unfolded and masks will be proudly brought out, as local traditions will be represented. This happens almost throughout rural communities.

Alternative participatory communication develops naturally within communities in the world, though often the main actors will not be aware of the alternative value of their work. Perhaps we, communicators who often remain external to people's experiences, are not ourselves equipped to see what is part of an oppositional alternative expression and what is not. Our own limited concepts about alternative media as oppositional to mainstream media may not allow us to recognize other forms of alternative communication that play an oppositional role to whatever is hegemonic in the political, cultural, and social context.

I am thinking, for example, of the woodcuts I have seen in Papua New Guinea, carved by artists in communities along the Sepik River. These woodcuts describe an incredible variety of daily scenes, with characters performing tasks such as hunting, fishing, cooking, or travelling on the river. An initial analysis may conclude that the woodcuts are a way to preserve the memory and history of the tribe, as if writing a book for future generations. Are these everyday-life descriptions an example of oppositional alternative media? In some way they are, because they are a significant statement against oblivion and an expression of attachment to traditional values that modernity and newly introduced technology are already changing. But there is more to it. Some of the most ancient woodcuts—not those that are now made for tourists—depict scenes of wars and confrontations between tribes or against the domination of a tribe by a neighbouring clan. Even if we may not fully understand the codes implicit in the carvings, it is certain that they express a political point of view and thus are oppositional or alternative to whatever may have been the dominant point of view at the time they were created. Our own limits and the lack of other supporting documents do not allow us to better understand them as a form of alternative communication. A similar thing would happen if, in the distant future, all supporting information and analysis about the May 1968 revolts in Paris had disappeared, and we could only find some of the posters that were produced in those days. Would we be able to learn anything from them or to classify them as oppositional without knowing more about their context?

Alternative media and participatory communication are possibly the only means that our world has to preserve and strengthen the diversity of cultures, languages, images, and artistic expressions that make each community unique and rich. By promoting participation and ownership of media, communication contributes to build strong identities, independence of thought, and societies that are democratically organized and represented. It is an alternative to the tidal wave of globalisation that aims to wipe out cultural borders and differences and convert our world into a single society of passive and domesticated consumers.

◆ Notes

1. Speaking on the topic "Globalisation and World Order," at the Independent Newspapers Annual Lecture, Trinity College, Dublin, Ireland, October 12, 1999.

2. We could also question the word *media*. *Media* denotes that the lens through which alternative communication is regarded is the lens of mass information channels, which already poses the issue the wrong way. Also, the word suggests technology rather than the human act of communicating. However, it seems to work for most English-speaking readers, and because I am not overly picky about definitions, we will use it here.

3. For more information on this and other participatory communication experiences in Latin America, Asia, and Africa, see *Making Waves* (Gumucio Dagron, 2001).

4. *Samizdat* was a made-up Russian word meaning "self-published" that underground dissidents created to describe their typed, single-spaced, no-margins, no-graphics, carbon sheet–copied, hand-to-hand distributed writings. All officially printed media, of which there was a flood, were stamped *gosizdat,* meaning government published. We know who won.

5. *Radical Media* (2001), by Downing, Villarreal Ford, Gil, and Stein (2001), provides a good overview of all these forms.

6. Some of those seized were pregnant; after they had delivered their children, they were murdered, and their infants were given to torturers and others in the conspiracy to bring up. The Argentinean feature film *The Official Story* (1985) is one of several addressing this monstrous story.

7. A shameless *Ley del Olvido* (literally, "law of oblivion") was negotiated between the military and the new civilian rulers to try to hide forever the responsibility of the armed forces for the massive killings, disappearances, tortures, and kidnappings of the victims' children.

8. Brazilian theatre activist Augusto Boal (1974/2001, 1998) mentions this in his writings.

9. More on this in Downing et al.'s (2001) *Radical Media.*

10. The word derives from *bastards.*

11. A joint project between the Sandinista Workers Federation (CST) and the Ministry of Planning, under the umbrella of the Economic Literacy Campaign.

12. The reader can learn more about these in *Making Waves* (Gumucio Dagron, 2001).

13. Producers of coffee and black pepper.

14. The main investment in equipment and supplies for this project consisted of 44 blank audiocassettes and batteries.

◆ References

Boal, A. (1998). *Legislative theatre: Using performance to make politics*. London: Routledge.

Boal, A. (2001). *Theatre of the oppressed*. London: Pluto. (Original work published 1974)

Coronel, S. (2001). The media, the market and democracy: The case of the Philippines. *Javnost/The Public, 8*(2), 109–124.

Downing, J., Villarreal Ford, T., Gil, G., & Stein, L. (2001). *Radical media: Rebellious communication and social movements*. London: Sage.

Galeano, E. (2001). *Upside down: A primer for the looking-glass world*. New York: Picador. (Original work published as *Patas Arriba: La Escuela del Mundo al Revés*, 1998)

Gumucio Dagron, A. (2001). *Making waves: Participatory communication for social change*. New York: The Rockefeller Foundation. (Also available in Spanish: *Haciendo Olas* and French: *Ondes de Choc*)

McBride, S. (Ed.). (1980). *Many voices, one world*. Paris: UNESCO.

◆ Additional Sources

Academy for Educational Development (AED). (2001). *What works? A blast from the past*. Washington, DC: Author.

De Zutter, P. (1986). *¿Cómo Comunicarse con los Campesinos? Educación, Capacitación y Desarrollo Rural* [How to communicate with peasants? Education, training and rural development]. Lima, Peru: Editorial Horizonte.

Fox, E. (Ed.). (1989). *Medios de comunicación y política en América Latina. La lucha por la democracia* [Media and politics in Latin America: The struggle for democracy]. México D.F.: Ediciones Gustavo Gili.

Fraser, C., & Restrepo-Estrada, S. (1998). *Communicating for development: Human change for survival*. London: I. B. Tauris.

Freire, P. (1973). *¿Extensión o comunicación? La concientización en el medio rural* [Extension or communication? Awakening of critical consciousness in the rural environment]. México D.F.: Siglo XXI Editores.

Gumucio Dagron, A. (1981). *El cine de los trabajadores* [Workers' cinema]. Managua: Central Sandinista de Trabajadores.

Gumucio Dagron, A. (1994). *Popular theatre*. Lagos: UNICEF.

Gumucio Dagron, A., & Cajías, L. (Eds.). (1989). *Las Radios Mineras de Bolivia* [The miners' radios of Bolivia]. La Paz: CIMCA-UNESCO.

Habito-Cadiz, M. C. (1994). *Communication and participatory development*. Laguna: University of the Philippines, Los Baños.

Hornik, R. (1988). *Development communication: Information, agriculture and nutrition in the Third World*. New York: Longman.

Moemeka, A. (1994). *Communicating for development: A new pan-disciplinary perspective*. Albany: State University of New York Press.

Pasquali, A. (1976). *Comunicación y cultura de masas* [Communication and mass culture]. Caracas: Monte Ávila Editores.

Prieto Castillo, D. (1999). *La comunicación en la educación* [Communication in education]. Buenos Aires: Ediciones Ciccus La Crujía.

Quebral, N. C. (1988). *Development communication*. Laguna: University of the Philippines, Los Baños.

Rockefeller Foundation. (1999). *Communication for social change: A position paper and conference report*. New York: Author.

Rodríguez, C. (2001). *Fissures in the mediascape: An international study of citizen's media.* Cresskill, NJ: Hampton.

Servaes, J. (1999). *Communication for development: One world, multiple cultures.* Cresskill, NJ: Hampton.

Simpson-Grinberg, M. (1986). *Comunicación alternativa y cambio social* [Alternative communication and social change]. Puebla: Editorial Premia.

White, S. K. (with Nair, S., & Ascroft, J.) (1994). *Participatory communication: Working for change and development.* London: Sage.

3

GLOBALIZATION, SUPRANATIONAL INSTITUTIONS, AND MEDIA

◆ John Sinclair

As the 20th century entered its closing decade, the concept of globalization became ever more seen and heard as "a key idea by which we understand the transition of human society into the third millennium" (Waters, 1995, p. 1) but with ever-decreased precision of meaning. At least in the humanities disciplines and social sciences relevant to media studies, one reason for this was that globalization was more than a new concept—it marked nothing less than a fundamental shift in the scope of their paradigm, as academic disciplines adjusted their focus to look beyond their former unit of analysis, the nation-state. Previously, to talk about "a society" or "a media system" meant a more-or-less self-contained national society and its media system—American, British, Canadian, and so on. The concept of globalization was adopted as it became necessary to see each nation-state and its various systems—cultural as well as economic and political—in a world context, a new reality in which supranational institutions were having their influence in shaping national structures and processes to an extent never quite known before.

Thus, although the concept has gone on to become associated primarily in everyday discourse with the global economic and political interdependency brought about by such supranational institutions as the World Trade Organization (WTO) and the World Bank, there has also developed a vigorous discourse about globalization in the sphere of culture and media. This embraces theory, research, and public policy, as they confront the issues of identifying and understanding the structures and processes through which supranational media institutions exert their influence on national cultures and media systems, as well as the conditions under which those cultures and systems can transcend their boundaries and assert a global influence in turn.

As will be explained, these issues are not entirely new, having first arisen in the 1970s in a worldwide debate about "cultural imperialism." However, that was very much within the context of a world structured by the cold war. In the much less dichotomized and more fluid and pluralistic "New World Order"—that is, the post–cold war era that emerged after the collapse of the communist nation-states at the turn of the 1990s—the unity and representativeness of national cultures has been called into question, especially given the large-scale movement and settlement of peoples across national borders. And at the same time, most national media systems have become more internationalized, both in their content and in their ownership and control, due largely to the liberalization of trade, the deregulation of national markets, and the inroads of foreign capital.

As well as these "real-world" developments that have made globalization so central an issue, there are certain social and cultural theorists whose work has demanded attention be given to globalization in media studies. Although some of these are theorists of globalization as such, others are more inclined to view globalization in the context of other wider or longer term historical processes—notably, the spread of modernity, or modernization, from Europe to the rest of the world. The first section of this chapter will consider some of these theorists.

◆ Theorists of Globalization

One of the most influential theorists of globalization has been Arjun Appadurai (1990), widely quoted for his innovative use of the suffix -*scape* to generate a series of visual metaphors to conceptualize the various "flows" of people (ethnoscapes), media (mediascapes), technology (technoscapes), capital (finanscapes), and ideas (ideoscapes) that constitute globalization. Importantly, Appadurai argues that these flows are "disjunctive" (i.e., they operate independently of each other); for example, it is not as if technology and capital are necessarily driving the globalization of media. This marks an important departure from more traditional critical approaches to be considered below, such as political economy and dependency theory, which have their roots in Marxism. Appadurai notes that such theorists have tended to put much more emphasis on the trend to cultural *homogenization* in the theoretical debate on globalization, particularly in the form of "Americanization." Others— more postmodernist theorists like himself— see that trend as being much more in tension with its opposite, *heterogenization*; that is, the proliferation of cultural fusion or "hybridity," which occurs as global influences become absorbed and adapted in a host of local settings.

Consistent with a long tradition in communication studies, which goes back to Harold Innis and the "Toronto Circle" (Tomlinson, 1999, pp. 152ff), much globalization theory emphasizes the evident triumph over time and space that has been brought about by converging media and communication technologies in the global era. Social theorists such as Joshua Meyrowitz (1985) have drawn attention to the consequent "disembodiment" and spatial displacement of mediated social relations and behavior. These same phenomena are conceived more broadly by Appadurai (1990) and others—notably, Néstor García Canclini (1995)—as *deterritorialization*. To give one significant example, international satellite television allows people to receive daily news from their countries of origin, even when they live far away from them, so "home" retains a virtual reality (Morley, 2000).

In a more elaborate theoretical framework, such technological mediation is an instance of what Anthony Giddens (1990) calls "time-space distanciation," which, along with *disembedding* and *reflexivity*, constitute the dynamic modes through which the institutional mechanisms of modernity have become global. These mechanisms are the spread of the capitalist nation-state, especially under the auspices of the transnational corporation, and the rise of a military order and an industrial division of labor on a global scale. Communications media facilitate these processes because of the way they overcome space and time, which thus allows individuals to free themselves from physical constraints and also to see themselves in, and adapt to, a global context, regardless of where they are. Similarly, Roland Robertson (1992), another of the "high" theorists of globalization, defines it in terms of "the compression of the world" and "the intensification of consciousness of the world as a whole" (p. 8). Unlike Giddens and the "world-systems" theorist Immanuel Wallerstein (1990), Robertson believes that globalization is a long-term process that actually predates modernity, whereas David Harvey (1989) is more a theorist of postmodernity rather than of globalization. Nevertheless, taking his cue from Marx's idea of the "annihilation of space by time," Harvey agrees that the process of what he calls "time-space compression" is crucial to the social changes of our era.

The differences between these various theorists are less important in this context than their similarities. Clearly, though without discounting their disagreements, they have all identified the control of space and time as the defining abstract principle behind globalization. The media are central to this control, not only for their technological transcendence of space and time as such but also for the interconnectedness inherent in communications, especially in their capacity to give individuals access to global networks. The internet is the most obvious manifestation of this, but a more media-based example would be interactive subscription television. Manuel Castells (1996) has been particularly influential in drawing attention to this dimension with his concept of the "space of flows," which underlies the global "network society." Spatial location still matters, says Castells, but only in terms of the relation of a place to other locations in the patterns of global flow (whether of capital, goods, people, information, etc.). John Tomlinson (1999) sees such interconnectedness as the principal fact about globalization, calling it "complex connectivity," but also emphasizes complexity as a defining characteristic in itself. Mike Featherstone (1995) goes further, arguing that the cultural complexity and "spatial relativization" wrought by globalization mark the transition of modernity into postmodernity.

Michael Richards and David French (1996, pp. 33–34) provide a helpful conceptual framework for thinking about globalization, dividing it into three dimensions: structural, ideological, and empirical. First, there are the stratospheric political-economic structures of supranational businesses and organizations, including not just the obvious transnational corporations but also a whole range of intergovernmental and nongovernmental organizations. Next, there is the ideological dimension of globalization, propagated by the global media and such corporate interest groups as the World Economic Forum. Finally, there is the empirical dimension of globalization, as "a process which can be observed." In the next section, the globalization of the media will be considered in light of the first and last of these categories. Before moving on to that, however, it is worthwhile to acknowledge some of those theorists who have helped shape the critique of globalization as an ideological phenomenon.

In a widely quoted article, Marjorie Ferguson (1992) lists a series of ideological "myths," or self-serving beliefs about globalization, propagated by the interests that benefit from it. These include the idea that "bigger is better" (as in the case of corporate mergers) and that "more is better" (such as more television channels). Another influential critic is Doreen Massey (1994), who reminds us that there is a "power geometry" to globalization, meaning that there are winners and losers, or globalizers and the globalized. She argues that although physical location in space might now matter less, location in social hierarchies, notably class and gender, continues to be determinant. That is, globalization is a highly relative phenomenon, but the ideological discourse about it talks as if everyone on the planet is both participating in and benefiting from it. Appadurai (1990) makes much the same critical point when he says, "One man's imagined community is another man's political prison" (p. 295). Especially if he's a woman.

◆ Supranational Institutions and the Media

Returning now to the framework set out by Richards and French (1996), this section will outline the different categories of transnational institution as they are relevant to the media and focus on the transnational or, more properly said, global media corporations. It will then refer to some particular

cases and outline the main empirical trends evident in the expansion and formation of these historically quite recent institutions.

Whereas the 19th century produced a world dominated by nation-states, the 20th century saw the advent of international institutions set up to coordinate the common interests of national governments on a world scale, such as the United Nations (UN) and its agencies. Most of these have been dedicated ostensibly to peaceful purposes and world development, even if, in reality, they have been a site of conflict between various alignments of national interests. The United Nations Educational, Scientific, and Cultural Organization (UNESCO) is a classic case, and one with strong relevance to the media, as will be outlined in the next section. More significant for the recent advance of globalization in economic and political terms have been new global institutions such as the World Bank and the WTO. Both of these began under the auspices of the UN, but they have gone on to become powerful global agencies in their own right, often criticized for pursuing an agenda identified with the rich countries and the global corporations. Also found at the supranational level is a wide range of international nongovernmental organizations (NGOs) set up on a public interest basis to achieve developmental, health, environmental, and charitable purposes, such as the Red Cross. Included here as well are organizations such as Amnesty International and Greenpeace, which often confront the interests of national governments and global corporations alike.

The global corporations are privately owned institutions with their roots in large nationally based companies that became "transnational corporations," mainly in the 1960s and 1970s, and subsequently globalized themselves. That is, they became more complexly interpenetrated with other companies and more decentralized in their operations—no longer necessarily controlled by a head office located in their country of origin and now part of a movement toward "disorganized capitalism" (Lash & Urry,

1994). Most obviously, this category includes long-established consumer goods companies whose products are made and marketed worldwide, such as Coca-Cola and Ford. Their relevance for the media is in their capacity as the advertisers from which the corporate media derive their income. They are predominantly "American" but not exclusively so: British, Dutch, and French companies, many with their origins in colonial times, are also in this category, and they have been joined more recently by Asian companies, notably Sony. Indeed, it has been Sony that explicitly developed the strategy of *glocalization,* the tailoring of global products for differentiated local markets (Robertson, 1995). In this process, the fusion of homogenization and heterogenization is finely managed so that the products appear in the marketplace without the evidence of their ultimate national provenance in Japan (Iwabuchi, 2000).

Sony is a significant case for two other reasons: First, it was Sony that brought home the reality of globalization in the United States when it acquired Columbia TriStar film and television interests and CBS Records in that country in 1989. This showed dramatically that globalization was more than just something that U.S.-based companies did to the rest of the world but that the United States itself was subject to the forces of globalization. Second, Sony exemplifies a particular kind of global corporation, a media company that enters the media field from a basis in industrial manufacturing—in its case, looking for "synergy," or cross-stimulation, in the horizontal integration of its media "hardware" and "software" divisions. Other examples have a less direct connection between their manufacturing and media activities, such as Westinghouse's ownership of the U.S. and global television operations of CBS Broadcasting before it merged with Viacom. Others again have had a base in financial or commercial services such as advertising: Two European examples this time are Silvio Berlusconi's Mediaset in Italy and Havas in France (Herman & McChesney, 1997).

However, the global media companies with the greatest size, complexity, and profile have been built on the basis of the media industries themselves. The rapid growth of these entities over the closing decades of the past century needs to be understood in terms of the ideological and structural shift toward privatization and economic liberalization of trade and investment that characterized this era, as well as a range of technological developments, particularly the trend to the convergence of media with telecommunications. These factors made possible great transformations in the regulation of media industries, such as those that permitted the wide-scale privatization of the television systems of most nations of Western Europe in these decades, to take a significant example, or the advent of private ownership of international television satellites. Indeed, television is the medium that has been most transformed by globalization but also the one that is most deeply implicated in facilitating globalization as a cultural process. For that reason, television will be the medium most often referred to in the analysis presented in this chapter.

News Corporation can be regarded as an archetypical model of how the new regulatory mood and technological developments became business opportunities that could be exploited. Although News has its origins and still dominates the press in Australia, it has become a high-profile, vertically and horizontally integrated media conglomerate with a truly global character, albeit strongly identified with the person of its chair, Rupert Murdoch. It has a history of risk and debt-prone but strategic international acquisitions—first of press interests in the United Kingdom and United States and then network television in the United States and international film production and distribution based in the United States (Twentieth Century Fox), followed by the extension of its satellite television interests from the United Kingdom and Europe to all of Asia and Latin America (Herman & McChesney, 1997, pp. 70ff).

However, at the stratospheric level at which global corporations make mergers, achieve their integration and synergies, and establish their economies of scale and scope, Murdoch has complained that News Corporation is a relative "minnow." Indeed, News ranked fifth amongst the corporations that make up the first of the two tiers into which Herman and McChesney (1997) classified the global media corporations towards the end of the 1990s, in accordance with their volume of sales. Heading that list was Time-Warner, followed by Disney, Bertelsmann (the largest European-based media corporation), and Viacom. This order still remained the same after Viacom's merger with CBS in 1999, although Sony would be the biggest of all if total revenue (i.e., including its electronic products division) were counted (Thussu, 2000, pp. 126–127). After that, the top tier became rounded out with Universal (formerly owned by the Canadian distiller Seagram but later merged with PolyGram and the French conglomerate Vivendi); Liberty Media, following the merger of TeleCommunications, Inc. with American Telephone & Telegraph (AT&T); and General Electric, owner of the leading U.S. and global television network NBC. A second tier consisted mainly of U.S. newspaper and information service companies, plus several European media groups—notably, Pearson and Reuters in the United Kingdom; Kirch in Germany; Reed Elsevier in the Netherlands; Havas, Hachette, and Canal Plus in France; Prisa in Spain; and Mediaset in Italy. However, it is significant that Televisa of Mexico, Globo of Brazil, Clarín of Argentina, and Grupo Cisneros of Venezuela were also found at this level, together with Asian companies such as TVB International of Hong Kong and the Modi Group of India (McChesney, 2000).

The presence of European, Latin American, and Asian corporations in these lists should make it clear that the biggest of them all, Time-Warner, which merged with the internet company America Online (AOL) in 2000, is not necessarily typical, in that not all global media corporations have emanated from the United States. However, Time-Warner is very much an American affair. Even before the merger with AOL, Time-Warner's 1996 merger with Turner Broadcasting had given it Cable News Network (CNN), the world's leading cable news service, enabling synergies with Time-Warner's own channels such as HBO through its cable service provision activities (Thussu, 2000). National origins apart, the kind of convergence of traditional and new communications media evident in the AOL Time-Warner merger, like the fusion of cable and telecommunications interests in the Liberty Media deal with AT&T, probably indicates the direction future agglomerations will take. The merging of cable, satellite, and internet services can be expected to intensify in the future, particularly with the technological advantages of digital television and the commercial advantages of addressable interactive subscription services on a direct-to-home basis.

◆ From Cultural Imperialism to Global Culture

Much of the history of international communication research, cultural critique, and policy debate over recent decades can be understood as a response to the rise of all of these types of corporations, to the structure of relations between them and their national governments, and to the social and cultural effects attributed to them. Most influentially, there has been the critical discourse of *cultural imperialism*, especially that associated with the work of Herbert Schiller and Armand Mattelart, which not only established itself as an anchoring point in communication and cultural theory but also helped to articulate the demands of the developing countries—collectively known at the time as the "Third World"— for what they called a "New World Information and Communication Order"

(NWICO). This section will focus on the debate around cultural imperialism, as it was a watershed both for the theoretical critique of the media and for the internationalization of media policy issues, played out as they were in the forum of a major supranational intergovernmental organization, UNESCO. Furthermore, echoes of this debate continue to be heard in current discourse about the phenomenon of *global culture,* to be considered further in the next section.

The issues in the debate, in one of its most systematic formulations, can be narrowed down to *media imperialism,* which ranged from the transfer of news values and journalistic training, through advertising and consumption patterns, to film and television entertainment (Boyd-Barrett, 1977). These were all seen as means by which the West (but especially the United States) could exert ideological influence on the Third World, an issue taken in the context of the cold war structure of international relations at the time. Although theorists such as Oliver Boyd-Barrett recognized the fundamental importance of the implantation of Western institutional structures and organizational models in the developing countries, the heat in the debate was generated more by the content of the media and its supposed power to determine or at least exert influence over thought and behavior. These influences were inferred from the bias inherent in international news reporting sourced from the West, or the "consumerist" values and lifestyle models discernible in television series and movies imported from the United States.

Much of the critique emanated from Western Marxist scholars interested in the political and economic functions attributable to culture and the media. This was "the dominant ideology thesis" (Abercrombie, Hill, & Turner, 1985) writ large on an international scale: the view of capitalist culture as a homogenizing ideological force, with the media as its Trojan horse. In the United States, Herbert Schiller took up the metaphor of imperialism, initially in his *Mass Communications and American*

Empire (1969), which traced out the political economy of the connections he saw between U.S. government foreign policies, the overseas activities of U.S. corporations, and the cultural role he attributed to the media in facilitating and legitimizing them. In Europe, Armand Mattelart and his collaborators became articulate and active theorists working within this same paradigm, although with an acknowledged debt to Latin American dependency theory, a much more sociologically subtle variant (Mattelart, 1980). Western empirical research provided evidence for the case—notably, large-scale comparative studies, supported by UNESCO, of television import and export patterns (Nordenstreng & Varis, 1974; Varis, 1984) and other work on the key gatekeeping role of the Western news agencies (Boyd-Barrett, 1980).

With the process of decolonization and the creation of new independent nations that had followed World War II, the UN and its agencies had soon found themselves not only split by the cold war division between capitalist and communist blocs but also having to accommodate a host of new members. For their part, these nations pursued their common interests both outside the UN, meeting as the Nonaligned Movement, and inside, as a voting bloc, sometimes called the Group of 77. It was in these forums that the concept of cultural imperialism began to figure in their debates about how to obtain a more equal status with the world powers and to achieve more autonomous economic development. The diffusion of Western models of life and cultural values through the media, secured through UNESCO's commitment to the liberal principle of the "free flow" of information across borders, became seen as an obstacle to these objectives. Drawing explicitly on the rhetoric of cultural imperialism, these countries came to demand a "New World Information and Communication Order" as instrumental to their larger objective of a "New International Economic Order."

Although they were successful in having a UNESCO Commission report in their favor and in winning a vote in support of "a free and balanced flow" as UNESCO's new principle, this was at the cost of, first, the United States, in 1985, and, a year later, the United Kingdom, withdrawing from UNESCO. These withdrawals followed acrimonious and often sham debates over several years about the freedom of the press, on one hand, versus the rights of governments to control information flows on the other. For the United States and the United Kingdom, this debate often was reduced to the ideological struggle of capitalism versus communism, but it was also about an issue on which they were outnumbered (Roach, 1997). The United Kingdom rejoined in 1997, but the United States only in 2002. The absence of two such major powers over so many years significantly weakened UNESCO because it undermined not only the organization's legitimacy and representativeness but also its finances, given the reduced revenue base UNESCO could use without the substantial contributions of these countries. The NWICO outcome provides a limit case of how far a supranational organization, even with ostensibly benign purposes, can truly serve as a global forum, where debate is "highly circumscribed and ultimately limited by the existing distribution of global economic power" (Tomlinson, 1991, p. 16).

◆ *Global Culture: Another Layer of Complexity*

With the wisdom of hindsight, the NWICO issue now appears as a response of the world of nation-states as they adjusted to the internationalization of the media in the post–World War II era, structured, on one hand, by the inequalities between the old imperial nation-states and the new postcolonial ones and, on the other, by the dichotomous politics of the cold war. Indeed, it is not accidental that the rise of the discourse of globalization coincided with the collapse of the latter as a structuring principle. However, so far as culture and the media were concerned, this discourse also sought to identify a number of other developments. In this light, Peter Golding (1994) has summarized the trends associated with the emergence of a global culture: firstly, the decline of the nation as a cultural force (as well as an economic and political one), relative to supranational influences; secondly, the growth of organizations and affiliations not only above the nation-state but also below it, that is, at a more local level; thirdly, the "syndicalization of experience," in the form of globalized consumer goods; and finally, the role of dominant world languages in the diffusion of a global culture. This can serve as a useful framework here to discuss the concept of global culture.

CULTURE AND THE NATION

Setting aside for the moment the debate about the alleged decline of the nation-state as an economic and political force, the nation as a cultural force is seen to be in retreat for two reasons. Firstly, the massive increase in the movement of people across borders caused by globalization has resulted in much more culturally and linguistically pluralistic populations in each nation-state. This means that nation-states are much less culturally homogeneous than they once were, or at least believed themselves to be, and also that their diverse populations can retain much stronger ties to the culture and language of their original homeland than to the nation where they now live. Secondly, this situation has led to the concept of national culture falling into disrepute, as national culture now is criticized as the preferred culture of the dominant strata, not the nation as a whole. "Culture is a multilayered phenomenon; the product of local, tribal, regional or national dimensions, which is anything but a single national culture" (Richards & French, 1996, p. 30). In the era of globalization, this has important theoretical implications for the traditional concept of culture itself, rooted as it has been in terms of the "organic" way of life of a certain people fixed in a certain place. "Culture" now seems more about people on the move (Clifford, 1992), a form of adaptation to displacement and changing circumstances, and always "hybrid" rather than "pure" (Nederveen Pieterse, 1995).

Although there continue to be many different forms of population movement, ranging from that of expatriate corporate executives to asylum-seeking refugees, most discussion of the phenomenon has focused on the substantial minorities established throughout the world as a result of the great diasporas, both those of the past as well as those of the present. These include such massive dispersals of people as the historical transplantation of Africans into the Americas and then, for many, from there to Europe; the flows of Chinese into Southeast Asia and elsewhere from the late 19th century onwards; and the spread of communities of Indians into the Pacific, Africa, and the Middle East, and later to Europe and North America. These people include not just wage-earning workers and professionals but also financial and industrial capitalists who have formed institutional linkages such as the "Overseas Chinese" and the "Non-Resident Indians" (Kotkin, 1992). Karim (1998) has even suggested that these globally dispersed communal networks can be thought of as effectively a "third tier" of supranational connections, after those of the global organizations and nation-states. These diasporas form global cultural markets for news and entertainment media in their own language, "geolinguistic regions" that international satellite services can reach on a "global narrowcasting" basis, regardless of the economics of the breadth and depth of their distribution across the world (Cunningham & Sinclair, 2001). This is the deterritorialization of culture of which the theorists speak: residents of a nation able to maintain cultural identifications brought from outside that nation and no longer obliged to assimilate themselves to a national culture.

At the same time, the national cultures that progressive critical theorists once sought to defend against being swamped by cultural imperialism now stand exposed as the ideological constructions through which the dominant forces in each nation-state legitimize and perpetuate their domination in terms of gender, ethnicity, and class (Tomlinson, 1991, pp. 68ff). Thus, along with movements based on gender and sexual preference, global migration has brought to the fore social differences that once were suppressed under the weight of national culture. This leads us back to the second trend identified above by Golding (1994)—that is, the disintegration of national cultural identities and social organization in favor of more heterogeneous identities, which, although local in character, are able to communicate with their counterparts in other countries. Nation-states are thus said to be losing their cultural authority over their own populations at the same time as their economic and political sovereignty is being compromised by pressures from the supranational level (Papastergiadis, 2000, pp. 76ff).

CULTURAL HOMOGENIZATION

Of more immediate relevance to the media is what Golding (1994) calls the "syndicalization of experience." This can be taken to mean the spread of globally branded consumer goods around the world and, by extension, a whole modern culture of consumption and the commercial popular culture that is integral to it. Just as cultural imperialism theorists once railed against the "export of consumerism" (Schiller, 1979, p. 24) and "cultural synchronization" (Hamelink, 1983), globalization theorists have conceived of a "global culture" but with the important difference that they do not fear global culture as an irresistible force of homogenization. Nevertheless, the concept of cultural imperialism is like the return of the repressed in Freud or the unwelcome party guest thrown out of the front door, only to sneak around and come in the back. That is, despite more than a decade of criticism, some of the assumptions behind cultural imperialism get smuggled back into the debate around global culture.

Cultural imperialism and its related discourses became discredited for a number of reasons (Tomlinson, 1991). It ascribed an irresistible omnipotence to external powers and their cultural influence, without taking account of either the empirical impact of that supposed influence on the populations of the countries believed to be affected or the way that such influence actually might be sought after and mediated by social strata in those countries themselves. In other words, it tended to equate economic power with cultural effects, interpreting the undeniable presence of foreign cultural products as self-evident "proof" of their influence. Ironically, this only reinforced the myth of an all-powerful United States, particularly when it was argued that the U.S. government and its corporations, for both ideological and commercial reasons, were deliberately seeking to obtain such influence.

Furthermore, cultural imperialism theory assumed not only that media audiences in the affected countries would absorb the same ideological meanings in the same way as just so many "cultural dupes" but that the alien messages would drive out whatever previous values, beliefs, and worldviews were held by these people. Finally, there was the "anthropological melancholy" (Papastergiadis, 2000, p. 109) with which the cultures of the subjected countries were regarded. Like the 19th-century myth of the "noble savage," Third World national cultures were reified and romanticized as authentic, pristine, and fragile. Cultural imperialism critics sought to keep them that way by defending them, whether they liked it or not, against the corrupting influence of modernization from the United States in particular and the West in general.

Although there is always the danger of backsliding into these assumptions and the

ad absurdum positions they lead to, the best formulations of global culture—or, better said, the globalization of culture—have tried to stake out more secure ground for themselves. In contrast to the simple dualistic worldview of cultural imperialism, Tomlinson (1999) urges that the complexity of globalization be grasped as a first principle: "Lose the complexity and you have lost the phenomenon" (p. 14). Similarly, in contrast to cultural imperialism theory's ultimately comforting belief in cultural influence as a deliberate strategy, for whom there is someone to blame, globalization theory makes an existential leap to the view that no one is in control. Tomlinson (1997, p. 189) cites Giddens's metaphor of the Hindu "juggernaut," an unstoppable but unwieldy idol-bearing cart, quite capable of crushing its devotees.

MULTIPLE LEVELS OF CULTURAL IDENTITY

Instead of the homogeneous mass of victims conceived of by cultural imperialism theory, or even the integrated, rational individual of modern Western thought, it is the deterritorialized, decentered subject of postmodernism that now best enables us to confront the globalization of culture as the complex, out-of-control process that it is. Postmodern theory's conception of the individual subject as composed not of one single and relatively constant identity but, rather, of multiple identities that become mobilized within different cultural discourses is consistent with understanding cultural identity in a world where people are on the move, where there are cultural affiliations at various levels, and in which the cultural ties of nationhood are becoming ever less credible and binding.

Stuart Hall (1992) argues that now people are more inclined to assert their various identities at the same levels as we saw were described by Golding (1994)—that is, "below" the nation, such as the province or neighborhood, and also "above" it, on the scale of what Hall calls the "global post-modern." He means by this the way in which the flows of goods, services, and media messages across borders facilitate global consumption. This is exemplified as much by the proliferation of Indian restaurants in the United Kingdom as it is by young Asians wearing jeans (Hall, 1992, pp. 302–303). The resultant implosion of older notions of traditional and modern, East and West, produces cultural fusions that are viewed as incongruous by academics in the West, what might be called the "Thai boxing by Moroccan girls in Amsterdam" syndrome (Nederveen Pieterse, 1995, p. 53). The point is that the globalization of culture presents people with a mélange of cultural and consumption choices that they never had when their cultural imagining was defined by the limits of their national media system and, furthermore, leaves them with very few rules as to how their choices might be combined. In this sense, a postmodern *decollecting,* or the selective disembedding of cultural goods from their traditional context, is the counterpart of deterritorialization (García Canclini, 1995, pp. 223–228).

The idea that people can have more than one cultural identity at the same time or, rather, cultural affiliations existing at different levels might seem commonsensical now, but it took postmodernism's challenge to the "dominant ideology thesis" in the 1990s before this could begin to be theorized in the context of the globalization of culture. Of equal importance was the recognition that the process of globalization was also one of regionalization and that the regions concerned existed both above and below the nation-state or at both macro and micro levels. Thus, a person was, for example, Welsh, Catalan, or Bavarian at the same time as he or she was, respectively, British, Spanish, and German, as well as, of course, European. The several crisscrossing levels of structural organization fostered by globalization could thus be seen to correspond to cultural identifications: transnational (or global), international,

macro-regional, national, micro-regional, municipal, and local (Nederveen Pieterse, 1995, p. 50). These multiple levels were usefully applied to the analysis of the globalization of television in particular, with the important addition, to be returned to below, of geolinguistic region (Sinclair, Jacka, & Cunningham, 1996; Straubhaar, 1997).

They also have the advantage of treating the local as a level in its own right in the whole global-local dialectic, rather than constantly conflating local with national culture (Sreberny-Mohammadi, 1991).

Above all, by thinking of the production, circulation, and consumption of cultural products as occurring at the interlocking series of levels just described, with cultural identities corresponding to each level, we are able to put the concept of global culture into a more credible perspective. Rather than a universal force for homogenization, global culture becomes, rather, one more level at which certain kinds of cultural forms can circulate around the planet. For example, Boyd-Barrett (1997, p. 15) refers to the "global popular," meaning a globally marketed cultural product of a certain kind, such as a blockbuster movie from Hollywood like *Titanic* or the global release of the latest CD from Madonna. These products receive maximum publicity and marketing support on a global scale and are distributed through complex hierarchies of channels, ensuring the products reach local cinemas and stores in almost in the same way that Coca-Cola is brought to some of the remotest villages of the world. Yet it is crucial to appreciate that although this material might assert its own level of cultural influence, there is no reason to believe that it thereby drives out other identities, especially those based on ethnicity and religion. Cultural identity is not a zero-sum game. As Marjorie Ferguson (1993, p. 4) once rather understatedly observed, global commercial popular culture—"jeans, theme parks, fast food, CNN"—is a "surface" phenomenon, which does not reduce the "deep" realities of cultural difference but just adds "another layer of complexity" to understanding the process of identity formation.

Between the global popular and the national levels of cultural production and consumption are the international and the macro-regional. For the purposes of this analysis, the international can be thought of as culturally connected, whereas the macro-regional refers more to physically and politically connected space. Thus, American and English television programs are seen in Australia, Canada, and New Zealand (and, to a very small extent, vice versa) because of the colonial and ethnocultural relationships between those markets and the common language that they share, whereas the countries of Europe form a common market for television only on the basis of the European Union as an economic and political entity, despite linguistic and cultural differences.

To take another example, to watch a Brazilian *telenovela* in Portugal is international, but to watch a game show from elsewhere in Europe is macro-regional. We shall see that this distinction easily collapses into the concept of geolinguistic region, but it is useful to the extent that it takes account of cultural and linguistic similarities and differences as "market forces" in the international trade in media goods and services. It is in this context that Joseph Straubhaar (2000) identifies "cultural proximity" as a factor facilitating such exchange, as in the former example just given, whereas Colin Hoskins and his colleagues see how a "cultural discount" can hamper it (Hoskins & Mirus, 1988; Hoskins, McFadyen, & Finn, 1998), as in the latter. That is, cultural and linguistic similarities are often more decisive than geographical location and physical distance in forming international markets for cultural products. This is particularly true of television in the age of the transnational satellite, which not only can distribute signals across whole world regions, without regard to national borders, but actually transforms the export trade in television from being about the sale of rights to broadcast individual programs to

the sale of programming packaged into channels offered as continuous services.

It is the national, micro-regional, and more local levels that are the ones seen to be vulnerable to being swamped by global media. Clearly, there are vast differences in how nations are placed with regard to this problem. As noted, many national media systems are facing a crisis of legitimacy as far as their role in fostering national culture is concerned, particularly in the case of national broadcasters. Similarly, national cinema industries, where they exist, struggle to maintain themselves in the face of the massive competitive advantages of Hollywood. On the other hand, it is at the micro-regional and local levels below the nation that some of the most inventive cultural hybridization or "creolization" is taking place and the greatest resistance to globalization is found. Carlos Monsiváis's (1994) anecdotes are emblematic here, such as the Mexican villagers who included Freddy Kruger from *Friday the 13th* and other movie characters in their Easter parade.

As far as television in particular is concerned, it appears that passing through an initial stage of foreign dependence to a maturity of the national market is, if not universal, then certainly a common pattern. Crucial in this transition is the growth of not just the national audience size but also domestic program production. Now that many countries have had almost 50 years of television, the evidence indicates that audiences come to prefer television programming from their own country and in their own vernacular or, if that is not available, from other countries that are culturally and linguistically similar (Straubhaar, 1997). This is most significant in light of the fact that it was the apparent domination of television by foreign content that inspired much of the cultural imperialism debate. On the other hand, it should also be said that there is a marked tendency to stratification in television, particularly in those regions that have digital, direct-to-home (DTH) subscription services. Such services carry global content, for those with a taste and the money for it, whereas national and local terrestrial free-to-air television services are much more in tune with popular culture at those levels (Sinclair, 1999, pp. 166ff).

GEOLINGUISTIC REGIONS

As we have seen, a geolinguistic region is defined not necessarily by its geographical contours but more in a virtual sense, by commonalities of language and culture. Most characteristically, these have been established on the basis of the world languages propagated by historical relationships of colonization, as has been the case with English, Spanish, Portuguese, and French. However, in the age of international satellites, geolinguistic regions have also come to include perhaps quite small but, more significantly, remote and dispersed pockets of users of particular languages on a global scale. This is most often where there have been great diasporic population flows out of their original countries, such as the Chinese and Indians noted earlier. In other cases, geographical proximity still matters, such as the unique case of the Spanish-speaking minorities of diverse origin who inhabit the United States, who are integrated in particular ways with the larger geolinguistic media markets of Latin America.

At the cultural level, these regions can be thought of, to some extent, as a globalized equivalent of what Benedict Anderson (1991) famously called the "imagined community" of the nation, that is, where a common print culture and language provided an inclusive sense of belonging. In their economic dimension, they can be understood in terms of what the classical economists called "comparative advantage," now more often referred to as "competitive advantage." Hoskins and McFadyen (1991) use this concept to explain the traditional dominance of the United States in media production. In addition to the "first mover" advantages accruing from the exploitation of new technologies as they become available, U.S. producers enjoy economies of

scale and scope attributable to their "unique access to the largest market" (Hoskins & McFadyen, 1991, pp. 209–212)—that is, to the largest English-speaking nation in a world in which English is "the language of advantage," with the English-speaking world being the largest and richest world-language community (Collins, 1990, p. 211). English has the further advantage of being the world's most widely spoken second language (Crystal, 1997), which is both an effect and a cause of the preeminence of the United States in the world's audiovisual trade.

Although language is an obvious although taken-for-granted element in the globalization of media markets in the English-speaking world, it is instructive to see how significant it is in similar ways in other geolinguistic regions, at least in the case of television. Thus, the major television corporations of Mexico and Brazil dominate the program export trade in the Spanish and Portuguese geolinguistic regions because their home markets are the largest in those respective regions (Sinclair, 1999). "Greater China" forms the world's largest geolinguistic region, in which programs are traded between the People's Republic of China (Mainland) and the Republic of China (Taiwan), despite their political differences (Man Chan, 1996), and Hong Kong remains a major center for all kinds of audiovisual production and distribution, serving the Chinese diaspora as well. In addition to exporting television programs and packaged cultural products such as videos, both the state-owned China Central Television and the private TVB International transmit satellite services available to millions of Chinese around the world (Sinclair, Yue, Hawkins, Kee Pookong, & Fox, 2001). For the Arabic-speaking world, the main equivalent service is the London-based Middle East Broadcasting Centre, while Al-Jazeera, based in Qatar, specializes in independent news for the region (Thussu, 2000, pp. 208–212).

India also has both state (Doordarshan) and private (Zee) international satellite services for its diaspora but provides an interesting case in which the liberalization of television has meant a boost for "local" languages, emerging from their former suppression by a dominant national language. Despite fears of "cultural invasion," which greeted the advent of Star TV and CNN at the beginning of the 1990s, by the end of the decade, it was Indian satellite-to-cable channels that had secured the allegiance of the audiences. Most striking has been the proliferation of dozens of channels in the regional languages. These are languages with tens of millions of speakers, such as Tamil and Bengali, quite large enough to commercially sustain more than one channel in that language. Thus, it is the massive size of these geolinguistic micro-regions, larger than many nations, that allows them to escape the dull compulsion of media economics that usually militates against broadcasting in minority languages and so favors world languages. Yet, also most significant in the Indian case is the fact that these channels allow the speakers of those languages to escape the former hegemony of Hindi, which undermines the traditional "nation-building" role of television in India and instead fosters a degree of cultural pluralism that the nation- state would never have wanted (Sinclair & Harrison, 2000).

◆ Globalization, Regionalization, and Cultural Trade

Referring to the whole debate about the impact of homogenizing and heterogenizing global forces on culture, Ferguson (1993) declares,

> For national cultural policy-makers and film and TV producers, such seemingly arcane issues translate into pragmatic questions of market access, industry control, product demand and supply, where relevant legal and commercial questions are those of copyright law,

import regulation, foreign ownership, product support and audience preference. At the level of bi-lateral and multilateral trade negotiation . . . McLuhan's global village vision dissolves into hard bargaining about who wins and who loses from cultural trade deals. (p. 7)

A focus on the regional tendencies within globalization not only helps to make the processes involved more comprehensible but also identifies further kinds of supranational organization that have a bearing on the media industries—namely, regional trading blocs and international trade organizations. The paradigm case of how trade agreements can consolidate regions and produce a new level of governance beyond the nation-state is the European Union (EU), for that has now evolved into a unique "politico-communicative" entity, much more than a trading bloc (Schlesinger, 1999). In the Americas, the significant agreements are the North American Free Trade Agreement (NAFTA), based on the United States, Canada, and Mexico, and Mercosur, in the cone of Latin America. In Asia and the Pacific Rim, there is the much looser organization for Asia Pacific Economic Cooperation (APEC). Each of these exists, although to a highly variable extent, to foster free trade on a regional basis, and that includes the removal of protection for national media industries.

At the global level, a series of rounds of international negotiations under the auspices of the UN General Agreement on Trade and Tariffs (GATT) culminated in agreements in 1995 that set up the WTO and committed signatories to the liberalization of trade in services. Although the agreements did not include the media as such, they were very much concerned with telecommunications. Given the considerable degree to which media and telecommunications are converging, for example, in satellite and cable television, the General Agreement on Trade in Services (GATS) of 1995 does therefore have an indirect interest in the media trade, whereas the WTO is committed to the eventual removal of trade barriers across all sectors.

Even before the establishment of the WTO, the two organizations in charge of the international coordination of telecommunications services—the International Telecommunications Union (ITU) and INTELSAT, the satellite agency—underwent measures that strengthened private ownership in them and diminished their public service responsibilities. They became committed to the pursuit of open markets in telecommunications (Thussu, 2000, pp. 84ff). This is very much to the benefit of the global media corporations that have a vested interest in free trade. At around the same time, the United States was putting direct pressure on the many nations of the world, including Canada and Australia, which have various policies—subsidies, screen quotas, import levies, and the like—to bolster their national cultural industries against market dominance by high-quality but low-cost media products and services from countries with comparative advantages in media trade, which overwhelmingly in practice means the United States.

The United States refuses to accept that these countries might have these schemes as a means of protecting cultural identity, saying that that is merely a cloak for economic protectionism. However, although the "free-flow" principle is now truly back on the international agenda, this time in the WTO rather than UNESCO, several of the countries involved have resisted tenaciously. Indeed, France's leadership of European dissent on this issue almost upset the conclusion of the GATT in 1994. As well as having various protective measures for its national media industries, France at one stage was seeking to lead Southern European and Latin American countries in the cultivation of a "Latin audiovisual space" to counteract that of the English-speaking world. France, of course, is the center of its own geolinguistic media empire, based on the French colonial system that once extended from Africa to

Asia, the Pacific, and the Caribbean (Mattelart, Delcourt, & Mattelart, 1984).

For its part, Europe introduced a "Television Without Frontiers" directive in 1989, aimed at not only coordinating regulation throughout the EU but also fostering EU and national production within member states. Although the scheme is not very effective, the EU continues to hold its ground, at least with the rhetoric of the cultural identity issue (Thussu, 2000, pp. 179–180). Given the ideological tide towards free trade and the complexities of convergence, together with the fact that for most countries, their audiovisual industries are not as important to them as that sector is to the United States, it is possible that protection in the media sector ultimately will be traded off to achieve trade liberalization across the other sectors where they want it to happen.

◆ Conclusion

For all the apparent inevitability of globalization—the rise to power of the global corporations, the fluid movement of media and people across borders, the drive to free trade—the supranational institutions have not yet overtaken the nation-state. It remains the effective unit of economic, political, and sociocultural authority in the world, even if it now finds itself in constant struggle with the supranational institutions above it, as well as a plurality of social and cultural differences that have opened up below it. Although there undoubtedly has been a relative loss of its sovereignty and legitimacy as an institution over the past century, like Mark Twain, the nation-state is still here to say that rumors of its death have been greatly exaggerated.

The nation-state has a unique role in mediating globalization—directly or indirectly, supranational institutions still must deal with, or through, nation-states. Clearly, there are demonstrable differences in the wealth, strength, and prestige of actual nation-states, as well as in their receptiveness towards globalization. So far, only the authoritarian nations have been able to define the terms on which the global media corporations have entered their markets (Sinclair, 1998). The challenge for democratic nation-states is to find the political will to call the bluff of globalizing corporate interests, to shape relations with them for the benefit of the people the state ostensibly represents, and to selectively divert and filter the incoming flows of global culture.

Without denying the cosmopolitan freedoms that globalization can bring for many, the nation-state can and must do more than just watch while its citizens form themselves into consumers of all the kinds of global products and services now in circulation, from the blockbuster to the narrowcast. At its own level and below, the nation-state has to show itself willing to relinquish its claim as arbiter of an exclusive national culture and instead foster social and cultural pluralism within the population, as well as defend the public good within its mediasphere. These efforts should include the extension of citizenship, without making it conditional upon cultural background and affiliation, and the provision of active support for media industries at the national, micro-regional, and more local levels that depend on it. These steps will take the nation-state beyond the epoch that formed it and ensure that it fulfills its responsibilities in mediating globalization rather than throwing itself under the juggernaut's wheels.

◆ References

Abercrombie, N., Hill, S., & Turner, B. (1985). *The dominant ideology thesis*. London: Allen & Unwin.

Anderson, B. (1991). *Imagined communities: Reflections on the origin and spread of nationalism*. London: Verso.

Appadurai, A. (1990). Disjuncture and difference in the global cultural economy. In M. Featherstone (Ed.), *Global culture* (pp. 295–310). London: Sage.

Boyd-Barrett, O. (1977). Media imperialism: Towards an international framework for the analysis of media systems. In J. Curran, M. Gurevitch, & J. Woollacott (Eds.), *Mass communication and society* (pp. 116–135). London: Edward Arnold.

Boyd-Barrett, O. (1980). *The international news agencies*. London: Constable.

Boyd-Barrett, O. (1997). International communication and globalization: Contradictions and directions. In A. Mohammadi (Ed.), *International communication and globalization: A critical introduction* (pp. 11–26). London: Sage.

Castells, M. (1996). *The information age: Economy, society and culture: Vol. 1. The rise of the network society*. Oxford, UK: Blackwell.

Clifford, J. (1992). Traveling cultures. In L. Grossberg, C. Nelson, & P. Treichler (Eds.), *Cultural studies* (pp. 96–116). London: Routledge.

Collins, R. (1990). *Television: Policy and culture*. London: Unwin Hyman.

Crystal, D. (1997). *English as a global language*. Cambridge, UK: Cambridge University Press.

Cunningham, S., & Sinclair, J. (Eds.). (2001). *Floating lives: The media and Asian diasporas*. Boulder, CO: Rowman & Littlefield.

Featherstone, M. (1995). *Undoing culture: Globalization, postmodernism and identity*. London: Sage.

Ferguson, M. (1992). The mythology about globalization. *European Journal of Communication, 7*(1), 69–93.

Ferguson, M. (1993). Globalisation of cultural industries: Myths and realities. In M. Breen (Ed.), *Cultural industries: National policies and global markets* (pp. 3–12). Melbourne, Australia: Centre for International Research on Communication and Information Technologies.

García Canclini, N. (1995). *Hybrid cultures*. Minneapolis: University of Minnesota Press.

Giddens, A. (1990). *The consequences of modernity.* Cambridge, UK: Polity.

Golding, P. (1994). The communication paradox: Inequity at the national and international levels. *Media Development, 4,* 7–9.

Hall, S. (1992). The question of cultural identity. In S. Hall, D. Held, & T. McGrew (Eds.), *Modernity and its futures* (pp. 274–325). Cambridge, UK: Polity.

Hamelink, C. (1983). *Cultural autonomy in global communications.* New York: Longmans.

Harvey, D. (1989). *The condition of postmodernity: An enquiry into the origins of cultural change.* Oxford, UK: Blackwell.

Herman, E., & McChesney, R. (1997). *The global media: The new missionaries of corporate capitalism.* London: Cassell.

Hoskins, C., & McFadyen, S. (1991). The US competitive advantage in the global television market: Is it sustainable in the new broadcasting environment? *Canadian Journal of Communication, 16*(2), 207–214.

Hoskins, C., McFadyen, S., & Finn, A. (Eds.). (1998). *Global television and film: An introduction to the economics of the business.* Oxford, UK: Oxford University Press.

Hoskins, C., & Mirus, R. (1988). Reasons for the US dominance of international trade in television programmes. *Media, Culture and Society, 10*(4), 499–515.

Iwabuchi, K. (2000). To globalize, regionalize, or localize us, that is the question: Japan's response to media globalization. In G. Wang, J. Servaes, & A. Goonasekera (Eds.), *The new communications landscape: Demystifying media globalization* (pp. 142–159). London: Routledge.

Karim, K. (1998, July). *From ethnic media to global media: Transnational communication networks among diasporic communities.* Paper presented at the 21st Biennial Conference of the International Association for Media and Communication Research, Glasgow, Scotland.

Kotkin, J. (1992). *Tribes: How race, religion and identity determine success in the new global economy.* New York: Random House.

Lash, S., & Urry, J. (1994). *Economies of signs and space.* London: Sage.

Man Chan, J. (1996). Television in greater China: Structure, exports and market formation. In J. Sinclair, E. Jacka, & S. Cunningham (Eds.), *New patterns in global television: Peripheral vision* (pp. 126–160). Oxford, UK: Oxford University Press.

Massey, D. (1994). *Space, place and gender.* Cambridge, UK: Polity.

Mattelart, A. (1980). Cultural imperialism, mass media and class struggle: An interview with Armand Mattelart. *The Insurgent Sociologist, 9*(4), 69–79.

Mattelart, A., Delcourt, X., & Mattelart, M. (1984). *International image markets: In search of an alternative perspective.* London: Comedia.

McChesney, R. (2000). *Rich media, poor democracy: Communication politics in dubious times.* New York: The New Press.

Meyrowitz, J. (1985). *No sense of place.* New York: Oxford University Press.

Monsiváis, C. (1994). Globalisation means never having to say you're sorry. *Journal of International Communication, 1*(2), 120–124.

Morley, D. (2000). *Home territories: Media, mobility and identity.* London: Routledge.

Nederveen Pieterse, J. (1995). Globalization as hybridization. In M. Featherstone, S. Lash, & R. Robertson (Eds.), *Global modernities* (pp. 45–68). London: Sage.

Nordenstreng, K., & Varis, T. (1974). *Television traffic: A one-way street?* Paris: UNESCO.

Papastergiadis, N. (2000). *The turbulence of migration.* Cambridge, UK: Polity.

Richards, M., & French, D. (1996). From global development to global culture? In M. Richards & D. French (Eds.), *Contemporary television: Eastern perspectives* (pp. 22–48). New Delhi, India: Sage.

Roach, C. (1997). The Western world and the NWICO. In P. Golding & P. Harris (Eds.), *Beyond cultural imperialism: Globalization, communication and the new international order* (pp. 94–116). London: Sage.

Robertson, R. (1992). *Globalization.* London: Sage.

Robertson, R. (1995). Glocalization: Time-space and homogeneity-heterogeneity. In

M. Featherstone, S. Lash, & R. Robertson (Eds.), *Global modernities* (pp. 25–44). London: Sage.

Schiller, H. (1969). *Mass communications and American empire*. New York: Augustus M. Kelly.

Schiller, H. (1979). Transnational media and national development. In K. Nordenstreng & H. Schiller (Eds.), *National sovereignty and international communication* (pp. 21–32). Norwood, NJ: Ablex.

Schlesinger, P. (1999). Changing spaces of political communication: The case of the European Union. *Political Communication, 16,* 263–279.

Sinclair, J. (1998). Culture as a "market force": Corporate strategies in Asian skies. In S. Melkote, P. Shields, & B. Agrawal (Eds.), *International satellite broadcasting in Asia* (pp. 207–225). Lanham, MD: University Press of America.

Sinclair, J. (1999). *Latin American television: A global view*. Oxford, UK: Oxford University Press.

Sinclair, J., & Harrison, M. (2000). Globalisation and television in Asia: The cases of India and China. *UTS Review, 6*(2), 78–90.

Sinclair, J., Jacka, E., & Cunningham, S. (1996). Peripheral vision. In J. Sinclair, E. Jacka, & S. Cunningham (Eds.), *New patterns in global television: Peripheral vision* (pp. 1–32). Oxford, UK: Oxford University Press.

Sinclair, J., Yue, A., Hawkins, G., Kee Pookong, & Fox, J. (2001). Chinese cosmopolitanism and media use. In S. Cunningham & J. Sinclair (Eds.), *Floating lives: The media and Asian diasporas* (pp. 35–90). Boulder, CO: Rowman & Littlefield.

Sreberny-Mohammadi, A. (1991). The global and the local in international communications. In J. Curran & M. Gurevitch (Eds.), *Mass media and society* (pp. 118–138). London: Edward Arnold.

Straubhaar, J. (1997). Distinguishing the global, regional and national levels of world television. In A. Sreberny-Mohammadi, D. Winseck, J. McKenna, & O. Boyd-Barrett (Eds.), *Media in global context: A reader* (pp. 284–298). London: Edward Arnold.

Straubhaar, J. (2000). Culture, language and social class in the globalization of television. In G. Wang, J. Servaes, & A. Goonasekera (Eds.), *The new communications landscape: Demystifying media globalization* (pp. 199–224). London: Routledge.

Thussu, D. (2000). *International communication: Continuity and change*. London: Arnold.

Tomlinson, J. (1991). *Cultural imperialism: A critical introduction*. Baltimore: Johns Hopkins University Press.

Tomlinson, J. (1997). Cultural globalization and cultural imperialism. In A. Mohammadi (Ed.), *International communication and globalization* (pp. 170–190). London: Sage.

Tomlinson, J. (1999). *Globalization and culture*. Cambridge, UK: Polity.

Varis, T. (1984). The international flow of television programmes. *Journal of Communication, 34*(1), 143–152.

Wallerstein, I. (1990). Culture as the ideological battleground of the modern world system. In M. Featherstone (Ed.), *Global culture* (pp. 31–55). London: Sage.

Waters, M. (1995). *Globalization*. London: Routledge.

4

SOCIETY, CULTURE, AND MEDIA

Thinking Comparatively

◆ Annabelle Sreberny

◆ Introduction: Why a Comparative Frame?

Culture, Raymond Williams once wrote (1985, p. 87), is one of the most complex words in the English language. In addition, *society* and *media* are hardly simple terms. In the 21st century, it is clear not only that these are complex words but also, and more important, that the analysis of the relations between the three terms encounters some of the most contentious and complicated dynamics in the contemporary world.

I propose to take a comparative frame to explore these issues, using Britain, the United States, and Iran as the three national contexts of analysis. First of all, comparison allows us to see most readily that relationships between phenomena in one context are differently structured in another. Comparative method rapidly denaturalizes social relations and helps us understand that they are historically constructed, culturally inflected, and mutable. The choice of comparison here, as of 2002, of two of the most highly developed economies and media systems in the world with a non-Western, Middle Eastern system helps problematize some of our expectations. Beyond this commonly acknowledged duality,

Author's Note: I'd like to thank JD for his patience, support, and very helpful editing and Gholam Khiabany for help with Iranian materials.

though, there are multiple complexities. The United States and Britain are not just peas in a pod. There remain significant differences of ethos and orientation between them. Moreover, Iran has been producing a wide array of media products as well as a range of imported ones, giving Tehran a cosmopolitanism surprising to the uninformed outsider. Iran's population is very young and highly politicized, whereas the two democracies have aging populations and suffer from widespread political apathy.

Second, such a comparative approach is also based explicitly on the understanding that society, with its characteristic social divisions of class, gender, and ethnicity, is strongly intertwined with the nation-state. Indeed, it is very difficult to unravel the mutual development of modern societies, nations, and states (Mann, 1993, p. 737). Each society that is a sovereign social entity is also a nation-state that organizes the rights and duties of each societal member or citizen (Urry, 2000, p. 9). The social structure is not only material but also cultural, with members believing they share some common identity that is caught up with the territorial boundary of the state, much of this built up through an everyday "banal nationalism" (Billig, 1995) of repetitions: flag waving, anthem singing, a shared historical narrative, common literary and artistic fields, the rhythms of the annual calendar, and, increasingly, media usage.

A global system of national societies has developed, with each enjoying relatively clear boundaries and supported by its own pattern of "banal nationalism" in which one of the functions of the media is to articulate the different parts of society together in the creation and maintenance of a form of shared national culture. Here *culture* becomes identified with "national culture" and seems to demarcate the national territorial space, as per the well-known argument from Anderson (1991), which locates much of this development at the moment of the growth of print capitalism and the fixing of written languages in a national press and literature.

Yet, there are also preexisting, more local cultural groupings, such as regional cultural practices and urban cultural environments, that are not erased with the growth of a national mediascape and that media developments may help to revive, in the way that a good local newspaper can support urban affiliation and regeneration. Yet other "subnational" cultures that do not map straightforwardly onto national space may include class, gender, and ethnicity, whereas religious attachments clearly do not obey the territorial divisions of nations. Increasingly evident and widely shared are the flows of globalized cultural products, including television programs, pop music, feature films, and news imagery that serve to create global audiences, linking people in transnational taste cultures of various kinds. Although it is important to acknowledge the continuing differential access of poor and rural people to media, it is also important to recognize the real differences that mobile telephony, wireless/windup radio, satellite delivery, and affordable internet access have made in bringing ever more people into a mediated world.

Third, the complexity of, and constant changes within, the relationships between society, culture, and the media can be vividly demonstrated across these three very different social formations. In the West, the increasing ubiquity of several versions of mediated communication in our everyday lives has meant that the distinctions between our personal life, social networks, and "mediated" culture have long broken down. As Tolson (1996, p. x) puts it, "the "situated" and the "mediated" worlds gradually, but inexorably, interpenetrate. We live in highly mediatized societies. These processes are at work in Iran but are still somewhat less developed than in the United States and Britain, where the three elements are increasingly homologous, mapped onto each other in a process of mutual definition and redefinition. In Iran, there remains greater distance between the three levels of activity, meaning that there remain more areas of social life that are not mediated. To give two simple examples of this, in Iran, there are few sports bars, where media use begins to reshape social space previously focused on conversation. Iran also does not yet have reality TV, where media track ordinary people and their micro-interactions. The temporal caveats above in terms such as *remains* and *yet* are deliberate because the core process that international communication has shown is a world-historical tendency toward greater mediatization of society.

By reading the media environments of different societies against each other, we can see more clearly how the mediated environment is an essential part of wider yet still heavily nationally defined sociocultural and political milieux. Using these three national media systems as our cases, we will be able to explore the different ways in which the relationships between society, culture, and media have been defined within each system and the ways in which they have changed over time, as they deal with various pressures

- ◆ toward ever more commercially driven systems and oligopolistic tendencies;

- ◆ of convergence and digitization through new technologies to reconfigure older parts of the media system;

- ◆ from a range of internal underrepresented sectors, differently constellated in the three societies, for access and voice;

- ◆ from competing constituencies, some who wish to define and regulate the "national" cultural space and others who wish to protect or expand the space for free expression and communication;

- ◆ from external sources and global flows of media production that provide audiences with greater choice but alter the context in which internal production and meaning making occurs.

Let us begin with a rapid bird's-eye view of certain major distinguishing features of these three nations.

◆ *Comparative Societal Structures*

Both the United States and Iran are postrevolutionary societies, with their sociopolitical upheavals separated by some 200 years (1776/1978). Each is a republic with a written constitution; the United States makes a formal separation between church and state, whereas the Islamic Republic of Iran is a theocracy. Britain remains a constitutional monarchy without a written constitution, although the debates about the future of the royal family grow more frequent and intense, and entry into the European Union has meant that Britain has become signatory to European human rights law, amongst other constitutionally derived codes.

The United States and Britain are stable Western democracies with multiple political parties, although their first-past-the-post voting procedures have produced strong two-party formations that mean the political center generally dominates and constrains the growth of alternative political voices at all ends of the political spectrum. In both, corporate power constitutes the primary influence in public policymaking, even though it is often contested, especially at the present time regarding environmental issues, and even though frequently it is internally riven by clashing financial agendas. Neither country, however, has been invaded or experienced a revolution—or anything approaching it—over the past century. Both nations have experienced a steadily growing affluence at a level shared by rather few other nations worldwide.

Iran, in comparison, is an evolving political system that has experienced considerable changes throughout the 20th century. These have included a constitutional revolution in 1905–1907; the 1920s appointment by the British of a hereditary monarch, the shah; a democratic-nationalistic movement in the 1950s that nationalized its oil industry and removed a later shah, a process thwarted with his forcible reinstatement through U.S. and British support; another popular movement in the late 1970s that led to the final overthrow of the monarchical system, with its perceived dependency on the West, and the installation of an Islamic Republic; a bitter war with Iraq from 1980 to 1988, in which both governments were covertly supported by the United States and some other Western nations and in which a million died and many others were injured; floods of refugee immigrants from Afghanistan resulting from the wars there during the 1980s and 1990s; and, since the 1970s, the growth of a very substantial Iranian diaspora across the planet.

This political volatility has been matched by rapid social change that produced enormous disjuncture between a traditional, religious rural world and a modernizing middle-class urban life experience. The 1978 revolution was partly driven by a desire for greater political openness, the desire for which remains strong; from the late 1990s, this openness has fluctuated, taking a step forward and then retreating into new repression when the pace of change goes too fast for conservative forces in the establishment. Yet, with the franchise extended to women since 1963, Iran actually enjoys a greater degree of political freedom and mechanism of formal participation than many states in the Middle East. However, this is tempered by severe state interference in determining which political groups are authorized, in controlling the media, in closely monitoring university life, and through continuing to fill the jails with political prisoners.

Both the United States and Britain are exemplars of late capitalist economic development, with the service and financial sectors and global economic vectors playing an ever more significant role within their national economies. Iran's economy remains one of uneven development, a mix of traditional and mercantilist economic practices mixed with some highly industrialized sectors and a slowly growing information sector. But its core natural resource, upon which the national economy remains heavily reliant, is oil, and Iran remains a rentier state, as of 2000, earning 80%[1] of its foreign exchange from various forms of oil-based revenues (although it is only the world's 10th biggest exporter).

Demographically, Iran is heavily tilted toward youth, having approximately 59% of the population age 24 or younger,[2] with no memory of life under the shah or of the revolution but very attracted by new technologies and global popular youth culture (whose content, however, is severely frowned upon by the religious establishment). In contrast, the 2000 U.S. census and Britain's 2001 census revealed that, respectively, 42% and 36% of their populations are in the (slightly more extended) 1 to 29 age category, and their proportion of upper middle age and elderly is substantially higher than Iran's. Both Britain and the United States have highly differentiated family structures, including a high percentage of single people living alone. Iranian extended family ties, however, typically continue to be very strong. All these demographic patterns tend to influence lifestyle choices, social and cultural habits, media tastes, and even political priorities among the public.

The United States has a strong self-narrative of being an immigrant society, with different waves of European and other migrations and enjoying a highly mixed ethnic population base in its major cities; 13% of its population have a Spanish-speaking background. Minority-ethnic populations make up less than 7% of the British population. A more significant process of differentiation has occurred along the lines of "internal nations" with the establishment of a Scottish Parliament and a Welsh Assembly, which may carry long-term political, economic, linguistic, and cultural implications for weakening the unitary character of the British state. Iran's population is just over half Farsi

(Persian) speaking, but there are 26% whose mother tongue is a Turkic language, 9% who speak Kurdish, and other smaller minority-language groups,[3] as well as the 2 million or so Afghan refugees already mentioned.

In comparison with Britain, where only a tiny percentage regularly attends weekly worship, the United States remains a remarkably religious society, despite the formal separation of church and state. In certain of its states, a conservative religious morality rules even the privacy of the bedroom and affects school textbook content as well. Iran, a predominantly Shi'ite[4] Moslem culture with strong national cultural traditions, has historically been open to the absorption of other cultures. (This included a superficial Westernization under the second shah, but it lacked the formal guarantees of the rule of law that officially underpin most Western democracies.)

◆ *Comparative Media Structures*

These historical, political, and economic macro-structures help to define the nature of the media and communications environments in each country. Although some basic structural features will now be introduced, emphasis needs to be placed just as much on the ongoing movement within those structures and the constant negotiation of their limits.

Britain has one of the oldest press systems in the world, with *The Times* having been established in 1784. The press has historically been dominated by press barons, including Lords Northcliffe and Rothermere at the turn of the 20th century, Lord Beaverbrook from the 1930s through the 1970s, and the Lords Thomson (father and son) from the 1950s to the 1970s. The press is privately owned but nationally extensive, divided most clearly by the broadsheet-tabloid distinction. The physically larger and intellectually weightier broadsheets range from the conservative

The Daily Telegraph and *The Times* to the more liberal *The Independent* and *The Guardian*. The tabloids, physically smaller and more popular, include the *Sun* with its enduring daily bare-breasted "pin-up" on Page Three, an image as unlikely to appear in an American daily newspaper as an Iranian one. Through the 1990s, these stylistic and content divisions have begun to blur as "serious" newspapers such as *The Guardian* spawned multiple special sections in tabloid-sized format, underscoring the physical correlation with "soft" human interest and nonpolitical stories. Some press barons have turned into media moguls, most notably Rupert Murdoch, who already controlled the sensationalist *News of the World* and the *Sun* when he purchased *The Times* and *The Sunday Times* in 1980–1981 and who also owns Sky, providing multichannel TV packages through satellite and digi-box.

British broadcasting remains fundamentally divided into BBC channels supported solely by the government-approved annual license fee (although some parts of the BBC, such as BBC World, are now commercially driven) and three commercially financed channels, although all remain governed by the ethos of "public service"—a midway point between state-organized and commercially driven broadcasting. The British broadcasting model, based on its founder, Lord Reith's, principle of "bringing culture to the masses" (as though they had none of their own already), has acted as the paternalistic guardian of British culture and historically brought "high culture" to the general public. It even took on a strong role as public educator, not least in the relationship forged between the broadcast-based Open University and the BBC, with course programs broadcast early in the morning and late at night for all, not only its students, to watch. This system was, however, slow to grasp regional diversity, including Welsh and Scottish programming, and multicultural programming remains a contested arena of resource and programming output. The public service ethos of the system also works to strengthen civic society against the state, yet it is a contested democratic space continually squeezed "between the economics of the market place and the politics of propaganda and public relations" (Eldridge, Kissinger, & Williams, 1997, p. 59). The regulatory frameworks have also maintained reasonable editorial independence for the broadcasting networks.

The process of digitization and the pressures of convergence between media and telephony mean that powerful changes have been rippling through contemporary communication systems. In both the United States (from 1984) and Britain (from 2002), the ownership rules that have prevented oligopoly are being progressively relaxed (see Chapters 14 and 15, this volume). In Britain, a single agency for media and communications, OFCOM, has been setup, except that the BBC, originally founded in 1922 as a public corporation "at arm's length" from the government, will remain an aloof and self-regulating structure.

The United States exemplifies a privately owned, commercially driven media system. Its press has historically been city based and city bound, and even papers of repute such as *The New York Times* have never achieved a mass national readership. *USA Today*, which aimed to be the first to do so, never got beyond the tag of "McPaper." The U.S. broadcasting system of networks and affiliates better approximates a national system, although local differences of taste and interest help structure the content environment. For a long time, broadcasting was dominated by three major networks, but that system was blown open by the aggressive newcomer, Murdoch's Fox Television, in the 1980s. Public broadcasting—both television and radio—remain weak in reach and influence, supported by corporate donations and extended fundraising telethons from individual audience members.

Yet competition and concern about the bottom line of profitability can mean that new programming simply reworks highly formatted and successful genres (the sitcom, the talk show) with little creativity or innovation and with considerable amounts of time given over to advertising content. And despite the foundational significance of the First Amendment protecting free speech, there have always been some forms of regulation, most usually from within the media industries themselves to prevent government action (e.g., the Hays Code, the McCarthy-era shunning of supposed or actual Communists, the cinema and TV content ratings systems). The First Amendment has also come to be used by media corporations defining themselves in legal terms as speakers with free speech rights, thereby justifying their attempts to block low-power radio stations and cable public-access channels on the grounds that they are interfering with their corporate speech rights.

In terms of a putative "public sphere," the presence of different media voices in the U.S. system is only enabled by major capital investment in the development of a new broadcasting company or publishing title that vies with a multitude of others in a rather oligopolistic market. This model has fostered a demotic popular culture, with a generally superficial and skewed recognition of multiethnic diversity that entered the televisual mainstream already in the 1980s with *The Cosby Show* but also included some of the best examples of programming (*ER, Ally McBeal*) that put the idea of color-blind casting into practice. The ethnic mix of the U.S. population, coupled with the development of cable and satellite-based technologies, has helped to foster a broadcasting environment in which different communities, mainly differentiated on ethno-linguistic and religious grounds, enjoy their "own" small-scale broadcasting opportunities, whether a cable television network in Spanish (Univisión), an occasional metropolitan-city television program in Farsi, or a daily radio show in Mandarin or Hindi.

Iran's media system has always been dominated, either directly or at a short arm's length, by an elaborate state apparatus. Since the mid-19th century, the country has had a privately owned press that has operated under often harsh political control by the state. This has been particularly vigorous in recent years, such that in 2001 alone, more than 20 newspaper titles were closed down and a number of journalists and editors jailed, some even executed (Khiabany & Sreberny, 2001). Some of its best-known titles, such as *Keyhan,* have continued despite regime changes, whereas *Etela'at International,* a daily, has become a vehicle for Iranians dispersed globally since the revolution.

Iran has a state-run nationwide broadcasting system, which immediately changed its name after the revolution from National Iranian Radio and Television to Voice and Vision of the Islamic Republic, which was later renamed the Islamic Republic of Iran Broadcasting (IRIB). In 2002, there was talk of private television being allowed in the next few years, though possession of a satellite dish remained of dubious legality.

The Iranian media model, echoed in other parts of the Middle East and in the global South, has focused on national development and cultural protection in a global context where Western televisual products are readily available. There are two Farsi television channels, two in Arabic, and regular broadcasting in English. Domestic TV production has been building in recent years, including new soap operas.

Concerned about excessive Western influence, the Islamic Republic since 1979 has bought media programs from Eastern Europe, Latin America, and Japan. The IRIB Office of Communication and International Affairs coordinates an active program of television exchange with a number of countries, including Germany, Japan, China, Kuwait, Lebanon, Bosnia, Cuba, Brazil, Pakistan, India, Switzerland, Australia, and North and South Korea. Like the BBC World Service and VOA, IRIB broadcasts radio programs internationally in 21 languages, including Arabic, English, German, Hindi, French, Spanish, Turkish, Urdu, Hebrew, Russian, Chinese, Japanese, and Italian. A gradual recognition of the needs of the Iranian diaspora has precipitated greater international broadcasting in Farsi by the IRIB.

However, the political and cultural constraints are powerful. For example, women can only appear veiled—hence women's acting parts on television or in film are relatively few. Though a series of outstanding Iranian films were busily winning international awards, many of them are denied access to domestic screens. In 2002, a further chapter in the fight against Western cultural incursion was waged against the Barbie doll, with the Islamic Republic producing its own range of acceptable dolls wearing Islamic dress.

Because the state runs broadcasting and polices the press, any independent public sphere is severely curtailed, and "civil society" has little space within which to function (despite the phrase saturating political debate at the time of writing). The state even tried to close down internet cafés and thus control access to the Web, yet that remained a very hard task to achieve. At the beginning of the 2000s, a newspaper might be closed down one day, only to have its content publicized on the internet the next, potentially facilitating an even larger readership.

Such brief sketches cannot do justice to the complexity within each media system. But they already serve to signal the very different environments in which the media operate, as well as the different relations between media, the wider culture, and the political system in which each functions. Each exemplifies, up to a certain point, an ideal-typical form of media organization and power: The United States reveals the power of commercial forces, Iran shows the power of the state, and Britain still struggles to retain an ethos of "public service." Of the three, the United States also has the media system that most recognizes a full range of social and cultural difference, with Iran the most concerned about political coherence and ideological control. The

United States, despite its powerful and secure media industries, is paradoxically the most closed to mediated cultural products from abroad, but Iran, where the political rhetoric remains somewhat paranoid about external cultural influence, imports a considerable amount. Britain, the only monarchy, remains concerned about the continuity of tradition; Iran remains concerned about sustaining religious values; and the United States is the global leader in the production of popular culture, with its many shifts and fashion changes.

Thus, various forces external to the media—political, legal, economic, and cultural—are at work within each system, diluting the "purity" of the typicality of its structure, and it is vital to situate any analysis of cultural phenomena within these macro-structures. As Martín-Barbero (1993) has insisted is typically the case, in Iran, political and social issues are constantly played out on media channels and across social divisions. All three nations are, at the turn of the 21st century, highly mediated societies (at least in Iran's cities, which account for almost two thirds of its population[5]).

We will maintain this comparative analysis as we explore struggles over the definition and content of the media within these three nations in the context of three broad issues—namely, media communication and the power structure, media and the shifting boundaries of taste and decency, and social divisions, conflict, and their media representation.

◆ Media Communication and the Power Structure

In all societies, a complex web of law and regulation governs the ownership, operation, and content of the media. The comparison between these three systems is stimulating because it allows for a clearer exposition of the differences between processes of repression and processes of hegemony, which are probably best thought of as occupying a continuum of control from harsh and externally imposed to less harsh and more self-regulating, although in practice, repressive options are always in place if hegemony erodes.

In Britain, a variety of structures have framed and controlled permissible speech. The arcane office of the Lord Chamberlain, abolished only in 1968, was able to ban many of the staple plays of the contemporary and even classical theatrical repertoire—including Aristophanes, Shaw, Pirandello, Wedekind, Tennessee Williams, Arthur Miller, and Beckett—at one time or another, removing "the adult, the accurate and the outspoken from the British stage, as well as the lewd, the raucous and the plain dirty" (Hall, 2002, p. 14). Hints of homosexuality, suggestions of sex outside marriage, and questions about the existence of God were all enough to have plays banned from the stage for years.

Major laws that the courts could invoke included one pertaining to an "obscene publication" in which the test was whether the publication "tended . . . to deprave and corrupt those whose minds are open to such immoral influences." This law was invoked against works of recognized merit as well as against pornographic publications. Successful prosecutions were common, as were seizures of books by post office, customs, and police officials. Historical test cases included James Joyce's *Ulysses* and D. H. Lawrence's novel *Lady Chatterley's Lover,* books that could today be included on high school reading lists.

Probably the law that most limited and continues to limit journalistic activity has been the Official Secrets Act, first promulgated in 1911 at a period of growing spy scares in the countdown to World War I. By the 1980s, the enforcement of this act was looking frayed, with increasing and notorious breaches. One civil servant was jailed for leaking to the press details of the arrival in England of cruise missiles, and another was arrested but ultimately acquitted for leaking information that the government had misled parliament about the deliberate sinking, outside the official combat zone during the Malvinas/ Falklands War, of an Argentinian ship, the *General Belgrano,* with the loss of some 900 lives (Keeble, 1997). The new Official Secrets Act of 1989 concentrated on protecting official information, defining five areas where the publication of leaks was banned and journalists were denied a public interest defense. Yet it failed to address fears that it would help to suppress evidence of serious wrongdoing and ignored the natural other half of the argument, the need for more openness, so that as of 2002, a lobby still presses for a detailed Freedom of Information Act.

Another structure of control has been military governance of press access and information in times of conflict. The British Navy rigidly controlled coverage of the 1982 Falklands War (Morrison & Tumber, 1988), a policy that served as the model for the Pentagon's news "pools" during the Grenada invasion (1983), the Panama invasion (1989), the Gulf War of 1990–1991, and the Afghanistan invasion of 2001.

Unlike Britain or Iran, the legal framework of the U.S. media has as a major component the First Amendment, which forbids Congress from enacting laws that would regulate speech or press before publication or punish it after publication. Its simple existence is not magically or absolutely effective, however. Individual states have passed contradictory laws, for example, when abolitionist literature against slavery was outlawed in the South before and during the American Civil War. Only in the 1920s did the U.S. Supreme Court make the First Amendment applicable also to the states. Although prior restraint on publication is unconstitutional, exceptional circumstances such as war are held to justify it, for example, prohibiting the publication of the number or whereabouts of troops. Public officials and all official acts, including the government itself, may be openly criticized and denounced by speech or publication,

provided only that the words used are not of such a nature and are not used in such circumstances "as to create a clear and present danger." This is a hard argument even for the government to make, as in the 1971 *Pentagon Papers* case, when *The New York Times* and other papers began publishing classified material relating to U.S. policy in Vietnam. The government asked for an injunction to stop publication but the Supreme Court, by a majority vote, refused to bar the newspapers from reprinting the report. For the television and radio industries, the Federal Communications Commission (FCC) has promulgated rather vague rules about program content, containing an implied threat that a license can be revoked for repeated poor judgment involving program content.

In the United States, many different private groups attempt to influence government agencies, businesses, libraries, radio and television broadcasters, newspapers, and other communications media to censor material that they consider objectionable. Religious, ethnic, and racial groups have tried to prevent plays, movies, and television programs from being presented because of elements they deem offensive. In some states or local communities, textbook commissions or school boards have exerted pressure on authors and publishers to omit from or include in school texts certain materials relating to various sensitive areas such as evolution, the biblical account of creation, or discussions of religious or racial groups. Some groups have attempted to pressure public and school libraries to prevent circulation of books and periodicals they consider morally or otherwise offensive. On the other hand, the American Civil Liberties Union promotes the open flow of all types of information in the belief that individuals should have free access and opportunities for the exercise of their personal discretion and that no group should limit the availability of the resources from which such choices are made.

Another form of media control in the United States, as elsewhere, is self-censorship, often developed to prevent the state or the courts from breathing down an industry's neck. The Hays Production Code—promulgated by Will Hays's Motion Picture Producers and Distributors of America in 1922 and partly a response to the Catholic hierarchy's demands for strong controls—gave a movie a seal of approval if it complied with its rather conservative standards. Movies got the MPAA film classification system in 1967, which remains the basic guide to content and age-related suitability still today, and tussles about classification can make or break a film's circulation.

The broad moral code of Hays also governed television's depiction of family life and male-female relationships well into the 1960s. This meant that Lucy and Ricky on *I Love Lucy* had to sleep in separate twin beds and kept one foot on the floor at all times when kissing, despite being married in real life as well as on the show. The National Association of Broadcasters, the lobby organization for the biggest broadcasters, also promulgates a code that is voluntarily adhered to by station operators (www.nab.org). In addition, the major networks also have their own self-regulating system, especially the Standards and Practices departments that review scripts and watch everything that is aired, including commercials, and every contract with a producer provides that the project is subject to their approval.

Beyond the use of news pools in times of crisis and war, as a response to the terrible events of September 11, 2001, and the subsequent "war on terrorism," the passing of the 2001 Patriot Act widened the scope of the Foreign Intelligence Surveillance Act and weakened 15 privacy laws, whereas the Homeland Security legislation entailed serious repercussions on privacy as well as plowing a $1.5 billion technology budget into surveillance.[6]

Among the main technology-related provisions, the law created a huge database of information from government and the private sector to look for terrorist threats. It established longer sentences for hackers who cause bodily harm, invade personal privacy, hack government computers, or disrupt infrastructure. It widened the circumstances under which internet service providers, libraries, and other agencies can voluntarily turn over information about internet users without a warrant. It encouraged critical infrastructure providers such as power companies to share security information with the government and exempts this information from the Freedom of Information Act. It established an Office of Science and Technology within the Justice Department to provide law enforcement with recommendations and standards for high-tech tools. It created a technology clearinghouse to encourage technological innovation for fighting terrorism. It required federal agencies to self-assess and improve their information security measures for protecting all federal information and information systems, and it created "Net Guard," a high-tech National Guard to defend local internet infrastructure from attacks.

The legislation closed off large amounts of information previously open to the public. It had the effect of shielding from the public and from lawsuits any industry mistakes that threaten public health and would "data-mine hundreds of millions of records of Americans to figure out who may or may not be a terrorist threat" (Jerry Berman, executive director of the Center for Democracy and Technology, Washington, D.C., quoted in Kirby, 2002). An even more telling criticism might be that huge amounts of data were already available to U.S. agencies *before* September 11, so that the issue would center on the mechanisms of sifting and interpretation, rather than just the amassing of ever more raw information.

Beyond these and other explicit structures of law and regulation, the political economy of big business oligopolies in media ownership in the United States tends to produce an ideological conformity. An oligopoly of large players makes it hard to penetrate the market, which makes it very difficult for nonmainstream voices to be heard. It was only Murdoch's deep financial pockets that allowed him to launch Fox TV and gradually break into the former three-network oligopoly. For the press, all the evidence points toward competition for readers, which actually reduced the numbers of newspaper titles available to readers even in major cities. But it is not only vertical but also horizontal integration of media conglomerates that potentially make so worrying their disinterest in quality information and critical debate.

The convergence of broadcasting and communications technologies provided the backdrop for Reagan's media deregulation of the 1980s, when limits were eliminated for both radio and television on the amount of time that could be devoted to advertising, and guidelines were cancelled governing minimum hours for news, public affairs, local programming, and children's programming. The repeal of the Fairness Doctrine in 1987 ended the legal requirements for coverage of more than one side of controversial issues. And the way was paved for oligopoly through liberalizing rules governing the sale of broadcast channels (Demac, 1995). There remains little government policy for nationwide communications, and market forces are increasingly expected to self-regulate and construct policy by themselves (Demac, 1995, p. 281).

The FCC[7] deals with a business sector that accounts for about 15% of the American economy and important aspects of general daily life—telephone, television, radio, newspapers, and the internet. Yet many of the 2001–2002 "corporate scandals" concerned the economic crises or collapse of companies, many of which were regulated by the FCC (Qwest, WorldCom, Adelphi, Global Crossing, AOL Time-Warner); these companies lost trillions of dollars in stock market valuation and collectively pulled down the entire stock market. Part of the role of the FCC is one of industrial supervision—managing the competition among communications companies and supposedly looking out for the public's interest—though as Napoli (2002,

pp. 253–274) points out, it is one of the very weakest of the U.S. regulatory agencies, the most subject to corporate and/or congressional pressure. With deregulation and the increasing multimedia mix of communication platforms, the lines have blurred between telecommunications providers, broadcasters, and even publishers, and thus issues of "fairness" and market dominance are once again at the forefront of citizen debate about media ownership and concentration.

In Iran, at the time of this writing, the head of the IRIB was directly appointed by the "supreme religious leader" (Ayatollah Khamenei[8]), to whom he is ultimately accountable, despite the existence of a governing broadcasting council of six representatives of the three branches of the state. During the sixth *Majlis* (parliament), an attempt was made to bring the IRIB under the control of a new council, but this was rejected by the Council of Guardians, an institutional bastion of conservative policies, on the grounds that this was against the Constitution. By contrast, the minister of Islamic culture and guidance is directly appointed by the elected president. These appointments have often been the site of contention between competing forces. For example, in 1997, the reformist president Khatami appointed Ayatollah Mohajerani as minister, who promptly restored the licenses of many publications, angering the conservatives, who called for his impeachment.

The situation of the press is even more complex because it fell under often arbitrary rulings from various bodies. A publication needs to get a license from the Ministry of Islamic Culture and Guidance. If there are problems of content, the 1985 Press Law and the press courts should deal with them, but the revolutionary courts, set up as a temporary measure immediately after the 1979 revolution, have become a permanent part of the legal system of the Islamic Republic and are also empowered to deal with press offences. In addition, the Special Court for the Clergy, set up to deal with offences by the clergy, has also been used. For journalists, the biggest problems are the lack of separation between the executive and legislative branches and the general lack of clarity about what is permissible and what is not. We have already noted the paradox that internationally acclaimed Iranian films are often banned from domestic cinemas; in addition, there have been continual attempts to ban the possession of satellite TV dishes.

These brief examples from the three countries underscore the variety of external pressures under which media almost always operate. Although the particular mix of political, economic, legal, social, and cultural forces differs, no media system functions completely aloof from these, and different systems will absorb and handle them differently. In the field of media studies, these issues are often dealt with in singular fashion or not at all, with a fully developed theory of mediation still a long way off.

This chapter leans toward clarifying the significance of forces external to the media, but clearly, changes internal to the media can also alter the media environment in any country. These might include shifts in personnel—the appointment of a new chief editor or a top broadcasting executive, takeovers and mergers, the repositioning of channels, and the development of internal guidelines—but there is insufficient space to explore those important dimensions here.

◆ Media and the Shifting Boundaries of Taste and Decency

In this section, I try to highlight three arguments:

◆ that what is culturally "acceptable" changes over time within every social system;

◆ that media have been and remain a preferred target among political conservatives to account for socially distasteful behaviors, which often means conveniently avoiding the harder questions as to their real causation;

◆ that modern Western societies are as perplexed and divided about the limits of "free expression" as a more traditional and religious culture such as contemporary Iran's: The biggest difference is that the United States and Britain largely deal with materials produced within their culture, whereas Iran is mainly (although not solely) reacting to materials coming from outside and thus can use "cultural imperialism" as its rationale for controlling them.

The issue of media control also raises the thorny question of whether the media are agents of change or agents of stasis, as well as how media push or reflect changing sensibilities and tastes. In these debates, the old favorites of sex and violence reign supreme (see also Chapter 26, this volume), with much of the debate focused on the always arbitrary and socially imposed distinction between childhood (to be protected) and adulthood. Britain still offers one of the clearest demarcations, with its "watershed" of 9 p.m., after which "adult" programming content is allowed.[9]

Here, comparisons between Britain and the United States are particularly interesting because although the two systems share a great deal in common and, between them, have determined the nature of many media forms and genres over the past century, the nuances in the way the media systems and the cultures at large have dealt with issues of sexuality and violence have been rather different.

If the pure logic of the market were to rule, then, for example, we might expect the U.S. media environment to be more replete with explicit sexual material than Britain. But this is not the case. The very popular series *Sex and the City* was shown at 10 p.m. on a national British television channel, but the program was only shown in the United States on HBO, a subscription cable channel. The late-night talk show *So Graham Norton,* hosted by a very out gay man, or the explicit gay-theme drama *Queer as Folk* would also not have found their way onto broadcast network U.S. television. Thus, in the United States, the tension between free speech, commercial pressures, and puritanical sensibilities produces television that shows less sex but far more violence than in Britain. In turn, Britain, although it "enjoys" more nudity and swearing than the United States, has far less of both, as well as less hardcore pornography, than many continental European countries.

Yet any history of television reveals that what was disallowed at one point becomes quite banal at another, and each system will have its milestones of pivotal programming relaxations. Such a history would also show the important parallels between what was shown on the big screen of the cinema and the small screen of private television sets, as well as between what could be performed live on a theater stage and what was acceptable for presentation on the small screen. In Britain, the 1960s were the key decade for the representational challenge to accepted proprieties, with both film and television taking up hitherto unmentionable topics such as illegitimacy, adultery, homosexuality, and abortion. New movies such as *Room at the Top* (1959), *Saturday Night and Sunday Morning* (1960), and *A Taste of Honey* (1961)—all based on novels—challenged the conventions of British society, and television pushed the same sensitive buttons. *Up the Junction* (1965) was the first program to deal frankly with abortion. Dennis Potter's *Brimstone and Treacle* (1977) dealt with family sexual abuse, and *Bouquet of Barbed Wire* (1976) was the first program to tackle incest. For the United States and Britain, it would be possible to document the milestones of increased explicitness on television: the dates of the first bare breast, the first gay man, the first lesbian kiss, the first four-letter word, and a range of topics that now have come to be regularly discussed by ordinary people in talk show formats.[10]

Although some sections of the British-viewing public welcomed a greater explicitness and adult frankness, others did not. In the 1960s, Mary Whitehouse established a pro-censorship lobby, the National Viewers and Listeners Association (which changed its name to MediaWatch in 2002 after her death), and engendered many a moral panic about the declining moral environment in Britain, as with her 1984 campaign to outlaw "video nasties."[11] Her campaigners have long maintained a very media-obsessed conservative agenda about sex and violence, paying little attention to issues such as media coverage of unemployment, school dropout rates, or discrimination.

These concerns about sex and violence have an enduring resonance, now stretched across a wider range of communications technologies and modes of delivery. In 2002, Britain's Broadcasting Standards Commission, which investigates all complaints about television programming even if registered by only one person, still spends the bulk of its time focused on issues of profane or sexual language and "decency," the issues of most concern to the "active public" who complain. The internet has been blamed for the rise in child pornography and pedophilia, resulting in tougher legal measures, again blanketing the deeper and more disturbing question of why so much of contemporary male sexuality leads in that direction.

In a shift in relation to cinema, however, in 2001, the British Board of Film Classification's (BBFC's) annual report spoke of screen violence as an issue of particular concern to the British public, registering the BBFC as particularly concerned about the prominence of weapons and the portrayal of dangerous activities that could be copied by young and impressionable viewers. The report also paid particular attention to material in which the glamorization or "normalization" of drugs might be implicit and noted that the BBFC would continue to cut any material portraying sexual violence that might be harmful to individuals or to society, in line with the requirements of the Video Recordings Act. At the same time, portrayal of sexual activity within a loving relationship is increasingly accepted, and less attention is being given to explicitness of language (www. bbfc.co.uk). Indeed, as the first lesbian-theme drama hit British television screens (*Tipping the Velvet*, October 2002), critics were pointing out that with a changed media environment, including access to pornographic video and internet imagery, certain cinematic conventions (no erect penis, except in pornography) and television codes appeared outmoded and clichéd.

In the United States, the beginning of a more open legal approach was adopted by federal courts already in the 1930s, when they held that the Irish author James Joyce's *Ulysses* was not obscene and could be freely passed through customs. The courts ruled that the use of "dirty words" in "a sincere and honest book" did not make the book "dirty." Since the 1950s, many obscenity cases—involving books, magazines, and films—have been brought before the Supreme Court. In cases during the 1970s, the Court ruled that laws against obscenity must be limited "to works which, taken as a whole, appeal to the prurient interest in sex; which portray sexual conduct in a patently offensive way; and which, taken as a whole, do not have serious literary, artistic, political, or scientific value." There is a hierarchy of media in this regard, with the least permissiveness for broadcast television, radio, and basic cable subscriber packages; more permissiveness for supplementary cable and satellite subscriptions (especially some, such as the *Playboy* channel) and in the cinema; and effectively no constraints on novels, magazines, and comic books.

The Communications Decency Act, which was a discrete section of the 1996 Telecommunications Act, designed to control obscenity on the internet, was struck down in 1997 by the Supreme Court as being drafted in a way that contravened the First Amendment. The Court has further held that obscenity should be determined by applying "contemporary community standards" rather than national standards. This means that material acceptable in a cosmopolitan, urban environment may not be acceptable in a different community, but it also implies the silencing power of small groups. Thus, despite the powerful sway of the First Amendment, local outrage at art museum displays of Robert Mapplethorpe's homoerotic photographs or Andrés Serrano's "Piss Christ" photograph[12] aroused intense controversy in 1989 and the years following, all the way through to a Supreme Court decision in 1998 about the proper expenditure of public funding for the arts by the government-supported National Endowment for the Arts (NEA). The Court enjoined the NEA to fund only work that observed "general standards of decency."

It is interesting to observe how the denunciations of media permissiveness and their corruption of public moral standards by U.S. Christian fundamentalists echo, in many of their specifics, those launched by Moslem fundamentalists in Iran and elsewhere against the depravity of the Great Satan.

Nonetheless, in Iran, taste and decency operate within a very specific, but contradictory, political and cultural framing. Although there were women pop stars and actresses under the shah's regime, and women appeared unveiled in film and television, since 1978, the representation of women on big and small screens has been highly curtailed. All women have had to wear Islamic covering, and visual representations can include no sex, although political and revolutionary violence is allowed. As a consequence, fewer women appear in contemporary film, constraining narrative development.

Yet in Iran, there is a sense in which state repression both before and after the revolution actually promoted an underground and illegal circulation of cultural materials that often make Tehran seem far more cosmopolitan and trendy than many a European city. For example, even in the mid-1990s, it was possible to find many people who listened to both Iranian and Western classical music, contemporary Iranian pop illegally imported from Los Angeles, and current Western pop that had gone through many generations of copying. The recording formats included cassette tape, CD, and mini-CD (at a time when mini-CDs were hardly known in Britain). A new wave of women's magazines was being produced, with increasingly explicit articles about personal and sexual matters as well as political analysis. There were various pressures for different kinds of representation, especially of women, and key debates about Iranian politics were played out in the pages of the press.

Are the breasts and the gay sex yet to come (out in public) in Iran? That implies a West-centric model of communications development, permitting an increasing openness toward sexuality, and such changes do not appear imminent. However, even a kiss was not just a kiss in Iran in 2002: Ayatollah Khamenei ordered police to crack down on immoral behavior after a well-known actress, Gohar Kheirandish, kissed the film director Ali Zamani on the forehead when he collected a prize at a ceremony in the city of Yazd ("Not Just a Kiss," 2002). Yet one of the growth industries in Tehran is plastic surgery, and many a woman can be seen sporting nasal bandages under her enveloping scarf. Another, slightly more discreet, medical trend, popular in Iran as in other Muslim countries such as Egypt, is virginity restoration for brides-to-be, a powerful indication of the growing split between private practices and sociocultural norms. Many commentators on Iran focus on the considerable gap between public life and what happens behind closed doors, in private space. "Iranians delight in telling you that there is an indoor and an outdoor life, a mask for the street and a face for home, a uniform for the frump and a designer dress for the chador-less nymph, a public and a private morality" (Smith, 2002, p. 32). Thus, Iranian society operates

with a powerful front stage and back stage, to use Goffman's (1959) terms, and public representations seem to lag behind social practices.

Often, regime response lags behind public opinion, both in time and in values. In spring 2004, a film called *Marmoulak (The Lizard)* was released in cinemas across Iran. It told a humorous story of a thief who escapes from prison, takes on the garb of a mullah, and is welcomed by a village that has been looking for a new preacher. It was the fastest grossing film in Iranian cinema history, topping $1 million in a very short space of time, and played to packed houses until the head of the Guardian Council declared it un-Islamic (without having seen it), and it was pulled from all screens.

The huge emigration brought about by the revolution was unprecedented in Iranian history and has scattered Iranians all over the world. It is having a continuing impact on culture and everyday life inside Iran itself. Many families have contacts in more than one country and are thus receiving bits and pieces of other cultures—foodstuffs, mores, habits, news, language—through family networks. Diasporic cultural products also circulate back inside Iran. In many ways, Iranians have had cosmopolitanism thrust upon them. The dozen new Iranian television stations based in California have garnered significant audiences inside Iran, and two of them, ITN and Tapesh, attract advertising from Iran. It seemed likely that some of the style of these Irano-American cultural products would rub off on internal Iranian programming (not least in news, where the Los Angeles bulletins adopted a more detached form of coverage).

◆ Social Divisions, Conflict, and Their Media Representation

In the United States, as in Britain, many of the most important changes have been driven from within as various groups—minority-ethnic groups, women, gay men, and lesbians—have struggled and fought for both political representation and media recognition. All societies have internal divisions, and the media landscape is one site where these divisions may become visible. In the Iranian scenario, the principal focus of division remains the social standing of women, but the stereotype of an unchanging Islamic culture is blown apart by the increasing cultural and political ferment there. We will concentrate on issues of ethnicity and gender in this discussion, though obviously questions of social class also need to be put at center stage.

It is interesting to note that although the debates about propriety and decency noted in the previous section focused more on what was *included* in the media (and should not be), much of the debate about social division concentrated on what is *excluded*—namely, on groups who are not represented or poorly represented. As such, this latter debate has been spearheaded by social groups making demands about their own representation, rather than by a conservative concern about collective moral well-being.

A major problem in multicultural representation of difference would be created if it were solely to take the form of the growth of separate media channels, potentially leading to social fragmentation and socialization solely into one's "own" grouping. An alternate model is to develop an increasingly multicultural and diverse representation of people and themes within mainstream channels. Having said that, however, the contemporary plethora of broadcast, print, internet-based, and global channels itself challenges the idea of a cultural mainstream. We still think we know what it is, but it is no longer so clear whether any one group would actually fall into that category. As Richard Eyre (2001), the British theater director, said recently, "If there's one thing that is clear about our society, is that we are all members of minority groups of one sort or another" (p. 12). How to successfully address this reality through devising media policies with

pluralism, justice, and citizenship in mind remains a goal rather than an achievement.

In Britain, debate about cultural diversity in the media rages. The number of "minority" media channels in Britain has grown significantly, with around 200 Black and Asian print journals, including *Eastern Eye, Asian Times, The Voice,* and *Ebony.* Similarly for broadcasting, the number of radio and television channels for minority-ethnic populations and diasporic groups has grown, helped by the diffusion of satellite and cable.

Minority themes also have become more mainstream, and ethnic writers and creative artists have been producing novel forms that have crossed over into the mainstream. On television, this included the tremendously popular *Goodness Gracious Me,* the first program in which South Asian actors both laughed at quirks of South Asian daily culture in Britain and mocked common British prejudices, and *The Kumars at No. 42.* This second show deconstructed the talk show format by locating it within an Indian family's private house and upstaging the Indian host with his own parents and grandmother. Stronger Afro-Caribbean programming also emerged, including *Babyfather* and *Caribbean Summer.* British-made programming is explicitly addressing minority audiences, as with *Network East,* and there is also an increasing amount of imported programming, particularly from the Indian subcontinent, including *Bombay Blush.* Such crossover cultural productions can be seen in other forms, including Andrew Lloyd-Webber's musical *Bombay Dreams,* performed on the London stage with music written by one of India's best-known film score composers and staged by the top Bollywood choreographer. It also has been evident in film, with the popularity of *East Is East, Bend It Like Beckham,* and *Anita and Me,* written and played by British Asians. Radio is offering an Indian soap, *NAME,* that moves through English, Urdu, and Panjabi and is set to be the Asian equivalent of the long-running *Archers.*

Mainstream media slowly have been becoming more aware of the need to change their employment patterns. Although ethnic minorities comprise about 7% of the British population, that figure rises in some Midlands and Northern cities, as well as in London, where the minority-ethnic population is about 30%. The BBC has instigated a minimum 10% rule for guest actor appearances on long-running popular programs such as *East Enders* and *Casualty*. There are schemes to attract minority talent into both newspapers and broadcasting, but there are still very few executive positions within the media held by minority-ethnic individuals.

Also, minority-ethnic actors have increasingly become tired of "acting their skin," with the story line and characterization having them somehow represent an entire community. Many simply want to be cast in interesting roles (Sreberny, 1999). Slowly, program makers, especially on Channel Four, have shifted from making programs that are "monocultural," targeting specific ethnic groups, toward "multicultural" programming. The BBC has tried to maintain a twin-track approach, so that programs such as *Black Britain, Mega Mela,* and *Network East* have specific minority groups in mind, whereas *Heart of Harlesden* and *Babyfather* were designed to have broader appeal. An example of multiple cultural characteristics of contemporary Britain finding their way onto the TV screen was the 2002 television adaptation on Channel Four of Zadie Smith's award-winning novel *White Teeth,* a novel written by a young woman of Afro-Caribbean descent that included a mixed-race family, a Bangladeshi family, Moslems and Jehovah's Witnesses, and the power of science versus the loss of faith, all turned into a vivid and amusing televisual depiction.

After September 11, 2001, many media paid particular attention to increasing the representation and range of voices from within Islamic communities. *The Guardian* prepared a special insert on "Race in the Media" (2002) to discuss the political and

mediated representation of Muslims and to counter growing Islamophobia, and Channel Four's *Islam in Britain* season tried to depict the range of lifestyles and choices encompassed within British Islam (Poole, 2002).

In the United States, the dynamics of a commercial system in a very large country, the demographics of minorities (particularly African Americans and Hispanics), and perhaps also the popular rhetoric of an immigrant nation have all combined to produce a media environment that today includes specific channels, programs, and print media for minorities and localities. There is some visible integration of minorities into the heart of mainstream TV, at least at the level of household names such as Bill Cosby, Oprah Winfrey, Geraldo Rivera, and Connie Chung. Yet although African Americans are represented on the small screen in rough proportion to their percentage in the population, they are mostly to be found in sitcoms. Zook (1999) has shown how, in the mid-1990s, the brief explosion on the Fox TV network of Black-themed shows was only a phase in a strategy to contrast Fox's profile with the established networks. Smith-Shomade (2002) demonstrates how poorly Black women's roles have been scripted on TV and in music videos. Latinos are just visible, even though they are nearly 13% of the population, and Asian Americans and Native Americans hardly ever appear. People of color are rare indeed in the executive ranks of U.S. media industries, not least in the advertising industry, engine of the media system.

Progress appears patchy and inconsistent in other media. In 2002, Halle Berry was only the fifth Black woman to appear on the cover of *Cosmopolitan* since the magazine began using cover photographs in 1964 and the first since Naomi Campbell in 1990, and in many broad-circulation magazines, non-White cover subjects are still avoided for fear they will depress newsstand sales. A *New York Times* survey of magazine covers in November 2002 found that about one in five (or 20%) depicted minority faces, whereas 5 years previously, the figure had been only 12.7% (Carr, 2002). But with a non-White population of toward 30%, the incremental progress has not been impressive. The absence of cover model diversity has mirrored the industry's racial homogeneity, with only 6.1% of the magazine industry's professional staff non-White.

In Iran, debates about internal difference are differently constructed. The media do recognize the country's regional and language differences. All *ostan* (provinces) have their own regional television programs, which may include drama, comedy, and talk shows in their own regional languages and accents. Print media include publications in Arabic, Azeri, Kurdish, Armenian, English, German, and French (*Rasaneh* 9.1, Spring 1998, p. 63).

The most problematic issue still centers, as we have seen, on the visual representation of women. As noted already, there are now a number of publications designed for women, the best known of which is *Zan-e-Ruz,* that offer often quite frank discussions about health matters, sexuality, and the social situation of women (Khiabany & Sreberny, 2004).

◆ Conclusions

Julius (2002) argues that the modern period has seen three kinds of transgressive art: an art that breaks art's own rules, an art of taboo breaking, and a politically resistant art. The logic of this chapter has often focused on moments of media transgression and resistance. The challenge for all cultures is how to be adult, structurally speaking: how to facilitate freedom of expression but not hate speech, how to protect children from growing up too fast and too violently, and how to encourage individual and group access to all forms of expression without some voices becoming overly powerful and consistently drowning out others.

The public debates in these three nations about the power of the media focused on a similar set of issues—control over media, sexual explicitness and language, and social divisions—but they were addressed in very different ways. In the United States and Britain, commercial pressures and new national security laws construct the chief restrictions on a civil society that is pretty multivocal. The United States is one of the most multicultural nations yet also one of the countries that imports the least broadcast content, perhaps because—amongst a complex of reasons—it has an insular and introverted take on the world that became particularly salient in U.S. foreign policy after September 11. Some of the greatest homogeneity in national media form and feel comes from the single most powerful media producer. In Iran, Islamic theocracy attempts to stifle a vibrant opposition, whereas a pervasive traditional Islamic culture has produced profound splits between public conservatism and private permissiveness. Complexity rules.

Conflicts over media are ongoing. In 2002, Britain was in the throes of developing a totally new regulatory framework for media and communications that responded to technological convergence but left out the BBC and was thus the subject of considerable controversy. Increasingly beleaguered circles within the United States were debating the repercussions of post-9/11 security measures and the degree of political openness within the major media as a move toward war on Iraq gathered momentum. Iran was still locked in struggle about its form of political organization, and the divisions between conservatives and reformers remained far from resolved; hence, the contours of its media and communications landscape remained blurred, too.

Finally, our analysis needs to transcend a comparative frame, insofar as it tends to suggest that these three social and communicative systems exist in isolation from each other and other global forces (see Chapter 3, this volume). This is clearly not the case. Britain imports much of the best of U.S. television, as does the United States some of the best of British television (viewers in either country have little sense of how bad the other's bad stuff can be!). British television writers are challenged to make programs as novel as *24*, with its concept of a real-time narrative and its quartered screens, as taut as *The Shield* or as quirky as *Six Feet Under*. The Iranian revolution was partly mobilized through a fear of engulfment by Western cultural values and products, a sense that the society had become so "Westoxicated" that it had lost its own identity. Yet when it turned militantly Islamic, many people said that was not their identity either, and the private face of Iran is percolated with the most up-to-date videos, CDs, and other products of the abominated West. Some of the most popular programming originates outside Iran, from the diasporic communities of Los Angeles, organized by Iranian exiles, and from RTE Prague. Although this programming is popular because it offers entertainment and music, these channels also carry political interpretations unavailable inside Iran and thus become part of the propaganda struggle for the "hearts and minds" of the Iranian people.

Yet the comparative framework is also crucial. A major objective of this chapter has been to underscore how crucial it is to avoid media centrism in the analysis of media and to focus on social change. The media obsessiveness of some conservative groups mentioned is only an extreme version of a larger analytical error too common within media research itself. The very differences between these three nations' media systems, both structurally and in relation to the changes they are undergoing, demonstrate with one voice the necessity of centering media analysis in societal and cultural processes. Simultaneously, these differences make ludicrous any simple statement that attempts to encapsulate for all times and places what "the media" *are*.

◆ Notes

1. Accessed January 17, 2003, from www.rferl.org/nca/features/2000/04/F.RU.000406124546.html.

2. Accessed January 17, 2003, from unescap.org/pop/data_sheet/2000_tab3.htm.

3. Accessed January 17, 2003, from www.umsl.edu/services/govdocs/wofact2000/geos/ir.html#People.

4. Shi'ite Islam embraces some 10% to 15% of Moslems worldwide, including the great majority of southern Iraqis and many Lebanese. It traces its origins to the Prophet's younger cousin and son-in-law, Ali, and his son Husain, both of whom were martyred. This branch of Islam is distinguished (a) by the conviction that only these and certain other direct successors of the Prophet, in the earliest phase of the religion's development, possessed the authority to define its tenets; (b) by belief in the redemptive power of suffering; and (c) by the belief that eventually, the 12th of the original Imams will return and free the world from oppression and tyranny.

5. Accessed January 17, 2003, from unescap.org/pop/data_sheet/2000_tab3.htm.

6. See analyses by the Center for Democracy and Technology (www.cdt.org/security/usapatriot/analysis.shtml) and the Electronic Frontier Foundation (www.eff.org/Privacy/Surveillance/Terrorism_militias/20011031_eff_usa_patriot_analysis.html), both accessed January 17, 2003.

7. The following analysis borrows heavily from Lemann (2002).

8. Widely perceived as a firm supporter of existing controls, Khamenei's power appeared at least to balance the elected president's.

9. Once during the revolutionary period in Iran, when programs were running very behind schedule, a television commentator told the entire population to go to bed and that the long-awaited film would be shown on another night.

10. Ironically, it was Mrs. Thatcher's Conservative government that funded the biggest program of sex education in Britain and revolutionized representations of sexuality and sex talk on British television, all as part of AIDS education.

11. The term was coined to refer to a supposed wave of underground ultraviolent "reality" videos being made available to teens. A moral panic was whipped up, and new censorship legislation was passed to protect the innocent and impressionable (see Barker, 1984).

12. A photograph of a white plastic crucifix immersed in urine. Serrano's work consistently made use of bodily fluids, and he insisted that he did not intend to produce blasphemous art. For the controversies surrounding Serrano and Mapplethorpe, see Dubin (1992, pp. 96–101, 170–192).

◆ References

Anderson, B. (1991). *Imagined communities.* London: Verso.

Barker, M. (Ed.). (1984). *The video nasties: Freedom and censorship in the media.* London: Pluto.

Billig, M. (1995). *Banal nationalism.* London: Sage.

Carr, D. (2002, November 18). On covers of many magazines, a full racial palette is still rare. *New York Times,* pp. C1, C5.

Demac, D. (with Sung, L.) (1995). New communication technologies and deregulation. In J. Downing, A. Mohammadi, & A. Sreberny-Mohammadi (Eds.), *Questioning the media* (pp. 276–292). Thousand Oaks, CA: Sage.

Dubin, S. C. (1992). *Arresting images: Impolitic art and uncivil actions.* London: Routledge.

Eldridge, J., Kissinger, J., & Williams, K. (1997). *Mass media and power in modern Britain.* Oxford, UK: Oxford University Press.

Eyre, R. (2001). The art of television. In S. Higson (Ed.), *Culture and communications: Perspectives on broadcasting and the information society* (p. 12). London: Independent Television Commission.

Goffman, E. (1959). *The presentation of self in everyday life.* New York: Anchor.

Hall, P. (2002, February 10). Sleaze nation. *Guardian,* pp. 14–15.

Julius, A. (2002). *Transgressions: The offense of art.* London: Thames and Hudson.

Keeble, R. (1997). *Secret state, silent press: New militarism, the Gulf and the modern image of warfare.* Bedfordshire, UK: John Libbey Press.

Khiabany, G., & Sreberny, A. (2001). The Iranian press and the continuing struggle over civil society 1998–2000. *Gazette, 63*(2–3), 203–223.

Khiabany, G., & Sreberny, A. (2004). The women's press in contemporary Iran: Engendering the public sphere. In N. Sakr (Ed.), *Women in media in the Middle East.* London: I. B. Tauris.

Kirby, C. (2002, November 20). Trolling the Web for terror plots. *San Francisco Chronicle.* Accessed January 17, 2003, from www.sfgate.com/cgibin/article.cgi?file=/chronicle/archive/2002/11/20/MN55960.DTL

Lemann, N. (2002, October 7). The chairman. *The New Yorker.*

Mann, M. (1993). *The sources of social power* (Vol. 2). Cambridge, UK: Cambridge University Press.

Martín-Barbero, J. (1993). *Communication, culture and hegemony.* Newbury Park, CA: Sage.

Morrison, D., & Tumber, H. (1988). *Journalists at war: The dynamics of news reporting during the Falklands conflict.* London: Sage.

Napoli, P. (2001). *Foundations of communications policy: Principles and process in the regulation of electronic media.* Cresskill, NJ: Hampton.

Not just a kiss. (2002, July 10). *The Guardian,* p. 14.

Poole, E. (2002). *Reporting Islam: Media representations of British Muslims.* London: I. B. Tauris.

Race in the media [Special issue]. (2002, May 20). *The Guardian.*

Smith, H. (2002, July 1). The rebels with raging hormones. *New Statesman,* pp. 32–33.

Smith-Shomade, B. (2002). *Shaded lives: African-American women and television.* New Brunswick, NJ: Rutgers University Press.

Sreberny, A. (1999). *Include me in.* London: Broadcasting Standards Commission.

Urry, J. (2000). *Sociology beyond societies: Mobilities for the 21st century.* London: Routledge.

Williams, R. (1985). *Keywords: A vocabulary of culture and society* (Rev. ed.). Oxford, UK: Oxford University Press.

Zook, K.B. (1999). *Color by Fox: The Fox network and the revolution in Black television.* New York: Oxford University Press.

5

APPROACHES TO MEDIA TEXTS

◆ Ruth Wodak and Brigitta Busch

In our contribution, we focus on qualitative linguistic approaches to media texts—especially on the approaches developed within critical linguistics and critical discourse analysis. There are several important reasons for this choice: In recent decades, there has been a significant increase in international interest in applying qualitative research methods to the study of social and cultural processes. Although the traditional empirically oriented approach to media texts, mainly represented by quantitative content analysis, is still widespread in mass communication research (McQuail, 2000, p. 235), some observers (e.g., Jensen & Jankowski, 1991) speak of a "qualitative turn" in media studies. This shift of paradigm is not a question of preferences for particular methodologies but corresponds to conceptual and theoretical frameworks distinct from the traditional sender-receiver model.

We cannot, however, elaborate on all the important research in conversation analysis (CA) and sociolinguistics, which has been concerned with media analysis, due to the shift of paradigm mentioned above. CA emerged in the 1960s (see Titscher, Wodak, Meyer, & Vetter, 2000, for a summary). It is based on ethnomethodology (Garfinkel, 1967; Sacks, Schegloff, & Jefferson, 1974) as an interpretative approach to sociology, which focuses mainly on the organization of everyday life. Despite the specificity of its name, CA represents a generic approach to the study of social interaction. Much of the media text research in this field focuses on relevant aspects of broadcast news interviews (Greatbach, 1986; Heritage, 1985), talk radio (Hutchby, 1991), and talk shows

(Gruber, 1991; Kotthoff, 1997). CA describes the formal structure of conversations (openings, turn takings, closings, topic control, interruptions, etc.) and analyzes how they operate under the institutional constraints of media. The strength of CA is based in detailed linguistic description, focusing on the organization of interaction, without considering the context. Context is defined within the text, dependent on the explicit mentioning of relevant factors by the speakers (see Schegloff, 1998).

In recent approaches to media texts mentioned above, however, the "text" as such has been somewhat "decentralized," and the focus of interest has shifted to the (social, cultural, political) context and to the "localization" of meaning. A similar change of paradigm in approaches to texts has been occurring in linguistics. Media texts are also frequently being used as data corpora in linguistic analysis. Garrett and Bell (1998, p. 6) point out that more than 40% of the papers published in the leading journal *Discourse & Society* are based on media texts. In this chapter, we argue that the agendas in both disciplines are obviously converging and that interdisciplinary approaches to media texts can offer deeper insights.

◆ The Concept of the Text

The present trend in approaches to media texts can be characterized by turning away from "text-internal readings, where readers are theorized as decoders of fixed meanings, to more dynamic models, where meanings are negotiated by actively participating readers" (Meinhof, 1994, p. 212). It would be beyond the scope of this contribution to discuss the different strands that have led to a more dynamic view of the text. But we would like to emphasize that some of the works that have influenced the change of paradigms in media studies have been equally influential in critical linguistic approaches, such as aspects of the work of the Bakhtin Circle by the early 20th-century Russian semioticians, Halliday's (1978) work on social semiotics and pragmatics, the Foucauldian notion of discourse, and argumentation theories. Van Dijk's sociocognitive approach has also had a considerable impact (see below).

All these approaches endorse an interactive model of communication, which is far more complex than the traditional models in mass communication. Media texts are perceived as dialogic, and the readings depend on the receivers and on the settings. Researchers presume, therefore, that readers/listeners or viewers interact with media (not only by writing letters to the editor but also by interpreting and understanding them in specific subjective ways). Media texts also depend on intertextual relations with many other genres, diachronically or synchronically. Texts relate to other texts, represented by the media, through quotes or indirect references, thus already adding particular meanings or decontextualizing and recontextualizing meanings. Media thus produce and reproduce social meanings.

Barthes (1966/1994), in his essay "Introduction to the Structural Analysis of Narrative," differentiates between the work and the text. *Work* refers to the artifact, to the fixed pattern of signifiers on pages, whereas *text* refers to the process of meaning making, of reading. Fiske (1987/1989) takes up Barthes's differentiation to distinguish between a program (on television) and a text: "Programmes are produced, distributed, and defined by the industry: texts are the product of their readers. So a programme becomes a text at the moment of reading, that is, when its interaction with one of its many audiences activates some of the meanings/pleasures that it is capable of provoking" (p. 14).

LINGUISTIC AND NONLINGUISTIC METHODS OF TEXTUAL ANALYSIS

Titscher et al. (2000) provide an overview of current methods of text analysis that cover a broad and diverse range of methods such as grounded theory, ethnographic approaches, psychoanalytically oriented methods, qualitative heuristic text analysis, narrative semiotics, CA, and critical discourse analysis (CDA). On the basis of the definition of text provided by de Beaugrande and Dressler (1981), the authors suggest that the two dimensions of coherence (the semantic dimension, which is constitutive for the construction of meaning) and cohesion (the syntactic dimension) are constitutive of the text. The main difference between linguistic and nonlinguistic analysis is that nonlinguistic methods focus mainly on the semantic dimension of coherence, whereas linguistic methods are based on a systematic analysis of both dimensions. The aim is to make the interconnection between the cohesion and coherence dimensions apparent (Titscher et al., 2000, pp. 49ff).

Linguistic and sociolinguistic analysis pays attention to the linguistic detail, to the form and "texture" of the text (Fairclough, 1995, p. 21), aiming at illuminating sociocultural contexts. Garrett and Bell (1998) and Fairclough (1995) provide an overview of different text and discourse-analytical approaches and their application in media studies. Approaches situated within critical linguistics (CL) emphasize the importance of the context, the social and historical situativity of the text, and the intertextual/interdiscursive dimension. Thus, the claim is not to unveil "hidden meanings," as this

would imply a static, reified conception of the text, but to identify and analyze discursive strategies, argumentation schemes (*topoi*), and means of realization (in verbal as well as in other semiotic modes), as put forward by the discourse-historical approach (see below). Bell (1984), for example, while examining the microlinguistic level developed in audience design, considers consonant groups in word endings. Fowler (1991) applies some tools of functional linguistics (transitivity, use of passives, nominalizations, modality, etc.) in studying the language of news media. This means that media analysis is problem oriented and not dogmatically related to the one or other linguistic theory or methodology. What seems appropriate is a multimethod approach that combines different levels of analysis and thus different tools.

Linguistic methods are time-consuming in their detailed attention to the text, especially when it comes to audio or audiovisual texts, which necessitate accurate transcription. In approaches to media texts, mixed methods are very often employed. Examples of such mixed approaches are the work of the Glasgow Media Group (1976, 1980, 1985) on news programs or van Dijk's work (1998) comparing news reports in different countries. Both combine content analysis with text-linguistic and discourse-analytical approaches.

As far as media are concerned, linguistic approaches have so far been focusing mainly on the moment of the text, in the sense of Fiske's "program" or Barthes's "work" (see above). Although there has been increasing interest in audiences in the past years, studies that link media text and reception are still scarce (e.g., Lutz & Wodak, 1987; Meinhof, 1994; Morley, 1980; Richardson, 1998). Meinhof and Smith (2000) elaborate Kristeva's concept of intertextuality to frame the collection of papers concerned with this link.

The news genre has been the most prominent research focus so far in linguistic approaches to texts, especially in discourse analysis. The press has received comparatively more attention than television, and outside of conversation analysis, radio has been relatively neglected, except for some studies of news programs (e.g., Lutz & Wodak, 1987).

CDA

The terms *critical linguistics* (CL) and *critical discourse analysis* (CDA) are often used interchangeably. In fact, recently, the term *CDA* seems to have been preferred and is being used to denote the theory formerly identified as CL. The roots of CDA lie in classical rhetoric, text linguistics, and sociolinguistics, as well as in applied linguistics and pragmatics. The notions of ideology, power, hierarchy, and gender, together with sociological variables, were all seen as relevant for an interpretation or explanation of text. The subjects under investigation differ for the various departments and scholars who apply CDA. Gender issues, issues of racism, media discourses, political discourses, organizational discourses, or dimensions of identity research have become very prominent.[1] Bell and Garrett (1998) and Marris and Thornham (2000) provide excellent overviews on recent media studies and their relationships to CDA.

The methodologies differ greatly in all of these studies, on account of the aims of the research and also the methodologies applied: Small qualitative case studies are to be found, as well as large data corpora, drawn from fieldwork and ethnographic research. CDA takes a particular interest in the relationship between language and power. The term *CDA* is used nowadays to refer more specifically to the critical linguistic approach of scholars who find the larger discursive unit of text to be the basic unit of communication. This research specifically considers more or less overt relations of social struggle and conflict in all the domains mentioned above.

Deconstructing the label of this research program means that we have to define what CDA means when employing the terms *critical* and *discourse*. Most recently, Michael Billig (2002) has clearly shown that CDA has become an established academic discipline with the same rituals and institutional practices as all other academic disciplines. Ironically, he asks whether this might mean that CDA has become "uncritical" or whether the use of acronyms such as CDA might serve the same purposes as in other traditional, noncritical disciplines—namely, to exclude outsiders and to mystify the functions and intentions of the research. We cannot answer Billig's questions extensively in this chapter. But we do believe that he suggests some interesting and potentially very fruitful and necessary debates for CDA.

Researchers in CDA rely on a variety of grammatical approaches. The definitions of the terms *discourse, critical, ideology, power,* and so on are also manifold (see below; Garrett & Bell, 1998; van Dijk, 2002; Wodak, 1996a). Thus, any criticism of CDA should always specify which research or researcher they relate to because CDA as such cannot be viewed as a holistic or closed paradigm.

The Notions of Discourse, Critical, Power, *and* Ideology

CDA is concerned with "language as social practice" (Fairclough & Wodak, 1997) and considers the context of language use to be crucial (Benke, 2000; Wodak, 2000):

> CDA sees discourse—language use in speech and writing—as a form of "social practice." Describing discourse as social practice implies a dialectical relationship between a particular discursive event and the situation(s), institution(s) and social structure(s), which frame it: the discursive event is shaped by them, but it also shapes them. That is, discourse is socially constitutive as well as socially conditioned—it constitutes situations, objects of knowledge, and the social identities of and relationships between people and groups of people. It is constitutive both in the sense that it helps to

sustain and reproduce the social status quo and in the sense that it contributes to transforming it. Since discourse is so socially consequential, it gives rise to important issues of power. Discursive practices may have major ideological effects—that is, they can help produce and reproduce unequal power relations between (for instance) social classes, women and men, and ethnic/cultural majorities and minorities through the ways in which they represent things and position people. (Fairclough & Wodak, 1997, p. 258)

Of course, the term *discourse* is used very differently by different researchers and also in different academic cultures. In the German and Central European context, a distinction is made between *text* and *discourse,* relating to the tradition in text linguistics as well as to rhetoric (for summaries, see Brünner & Graefen, 1994; Wodak, 1996a). In the English-speaking world, *discourse* is often used both for written and oral texts (see Schiffrin, 1994). Other researchers distinguish between different levels of abstractness: Lemke (1995) defines *text* as the concrete realization of abstract forms of knowledge (*discourse*), thus adhering to a more Foucauldian approach (see also Jäger, 2001).

In the discourse-historical approach, we elaborate and relate to the sociocognitive theory of Teun van Dijk (1985, 1993, 1998) and view *discourse* as a form of knowledge and memory, whereas *text* illustrates concrete oral utterances or written documents (Reisigl & Wodak, 2001). Critical media studies view discourse as interactive, as negotiated between producers and audience, as a process in construction. Text is the (oral, visual, or written) manifestation of this (see Garrett & Bell, 1998).

The shared perspective and program of CDA relate to the term *critical*, which in the work of some "critical linguists" could be traced to the influence of the Frankfurt school or Jürgen Habermas (Anthonissen, 2001; Fay, 1987, p. 203; Thompson, 1988, pp. 71ff). Nowadays, this concept is conventionally used in a broader sense, denoting, as Krings argues, the practical linking of "social and political engagement" with "a sociologically informed construction of society" (Krings, Baumgartner, & Wildly, 1973, p. 808). At the same time, in Fairclough's (1995) words, "In human matters, interconnections and chains of cause-and-effect may be distorted out of vision. Hence 'critique' is essentially making visible the interconnectedness of things" (p. 747; see also Connerton, 1976/1996, pp. 11–39).

For CDA, language is not powerful on its own—it gains power by the use powerful people make of it, specifically in new public spaces or new genres provided by globalized media (Baudrillard, 2000; Fairclough, 2000a; Habermas, 2000; Hall, 2000a, 2000b). In agreement with its critical theory predecessors, CDA emphasizes the need for interdisciplinary work to gain a proper understanding of how language functions in constituting and transmitting knowledge, in organizing social institutions, or in exercising power.

Not only the notion of struggles for power and control but also the "intertextuality" and "recontextualization" of competing discourses in various public spaces and genres are closely attended to. Power is about relations of difference, particularly about the effects of differences in social structures. The constant unity of language and other social matters ensures that language is entwined in social power in a number of ways: Language indexes power, expresses power, and is involved where there is contention over and a challenge to power. Power does not derive from language, but language can be used to challenge power, to subvert it, to alter distributions of power in the short and the long term.

THEORETICAL AND METHODOLOGICAL APPROACHES

Kress (1990) concentrates on what he terms the "political economy" of representational media—that is, an attempt to understand how various societies value different modes of representation and how they use these different modes of representation. (This is a different sense of the term *political economy* from the one Wasko deploys in Chapter 15, this volume.) A central aspect of this work is the attempt to understand the formation of the individual human being as a social individual in response to available "representational resources." One by-product of this research interest has been Kress's increasing involvement in overtly political issues, including the politics of culture. Moreover, he has been concerned with multimodality and semiotics. Together with Theo van Leeuwen, Kress has developed a taxonomy that allows the precise description and interpretation of visual data (Kress & van Leeuwen, 1996). This work has influenced research on the new media (see Lemke, 2001; Scollon, 1999).

The work of Fowler, Kress, Hodge, and Trew (1979) has been cited to demonstrate the early foundations of CL. Later work of Fowler (1991, 1996) shows how tools provided by standard linguistic theories (a 1965 version of Chomskyan grammar and Halliday's [1985] theory of systemic functional grammar) could be used to uncover linguistic structures of power in texts. Not only in news discourses but also in literary criticism, Fowler illustrates that systematic grammatical devices function in establishing, manipulating, and naturalizing social hierarchies. Fowler concentrated on analyzing news discourses and in providing grammatical tools (transitivity and modality) for such an analysis.

Fairclough (1989) sets out the social theories underpinning CDA, and as in other early critical linguistic work, a variety of textual examples are analyzed to illustrate the field, its aims, and methods of analysis. Later, Chouliaraki and Fairclough (1999) explain and elaborate some advances in CDA, showing not only how the analytical framework for researching language in relation to power and ideology developed but also how CDA is useful in disclosing the discursive nature of much contemporary social and cultural change. Particularly the language of the mass media is scrutinized as a site of power and social struggle, as well as a site where language is often only apparently transparent. Media institutions often purport to be neutral, in that they provide space for public discourse, reflect states of affairs disinterestedly, and give the perceptions and arguments of the newsmakers. Fairclough shows the fallacy of such assumptions and illustrates the mediating and constructing role of the media with a variety of examples.

Van Dijk and Kintsch (1983) early on considered the relevance of discourse to the study of language processing. Their development of a cognitive model of discourse understanding in individuals gradually developed into cognitive models for explaining the construction of meaning at a societal level. Van Dijk turned specifically to media discourse, not only giving his own reflection on communication in the mass media (van Dijk, 1986) but also bringing together the theories and applications of a variety of scholars interested in the production, uses, and functions of media discourses (van Dijk, 1985). In critically analyzing various kinds of discourses that encode prejudice, van Dijk is interested in developing a theoretical model that will explain cognitive discourse processing mechanisms (Wodak & van Dijk, 2000). Most recently, van Dijk has focused on issues of racism and ideology (van Dijk, 1998) and on an elaboration of a theory of context (van Dijk, 2001). The sociocognitive model of van Dijk is based on the assumption that cognition mediates between "society" and "discourse." Long term and short-term memories and certain mental models shape our perception and comprehension of discursive practices and also imply stereotypes and prejudices, if such mental models become rigid and overgeneralized. The methodology used is eclectic, based primarily on argumentation theory and semantic theories.

In the Vienna school of CDA, the investigation of language use in institutional settings is central (Muntigl, Weiss, & Wodak, 2000; Wodak, 1996a). A new focus on the necessity for a historical perspective is also introduced (the discourse historical approach). A second important research focus of the Vienna school of CDA is the study of racism and anti-Semitism in the media and other public spaces (see Wodak, 1996b; Wodak et al., 1990; Wodak, de Cillia, Reisigl, & Liebhart, 1999; Wodak, Menz, Mitten, & Stern, 1994; Wodak & van Dijk, 2000; and below). Thirdly, and of course related to the latter two issues, is the study of identity constructions and changes of identities at national and transnational levels.

Recognition of the contribution of all aspects of the communicative context to text meaning, as well as a growing awareness in media studies generally of the importance of nonverbal aspects of texts, has turned attention to semiotic devices in discourse other than the linguistic ones. Pioneering work on the interaction between the verbal and visual in texts and discourse, as well as on the meaning of images, has been done by Theo van Leeuwen (Kress & van Leeuwen, 1996). Particularly the theory put forward by Kress and van Leeuwen (1996) should be mentioned here, as this provides a useful framework for considering the communicative potential of visual devices in the media (see Anthonissen, 2001; Scollon, 2001). Van Leeuwen studied film and television production as well as Hallidayan linguistics. His principal publications are concerned with topics such as the intonation of disc jockeys and newsreaders, the language of television interviews and newspaper reporting, and, more recently, the semiotics of visual communication and music. His approach has increasingly led him into the field of education. Van Leeuwen (1993) distinguishes two kinds of relations between discourses and social practices:

> discourse itself [as] social practice, discourse as a form of action, as something people do to or for or with each other. And there is discourse in the Foucauldian sense, discourse as a way of representing social practice(s), as a form of knowledge, as the things people say about social practice(s). (p. 193)

"Critical discourse analysis," according to van Leeuwen, is or should be concerned with both these aspects: "with discourse as the instrument of power and control as well as with discourse as the instrument of the social construction of reality" (van Leeuwen, 1993, p. 193). Van Leeuwen (1993) developed a most influential methodological tool: the actors analysis. This taxonomy allows for the analysis of both written and oral data, related to agency in a very differentiated and validated way. The taxonomy has since then been widely applied in data analysis.

The Duisburg school of CDA (Jäger, 1993, 2001) draws on Foucault's notion of discourse. According to Jäger (1999, p. 116), discourse is "materiality sui generis," and discourse theory is a "materialistic cultural theory." Jäger is also influenced by Alexej N. Leontjev's "speech activity theory" (*Sprechtätigkeitstheorie,* Leontjev, 1984) and Jürgen Link's (1988) "collective symbolism." As institutionalized and conventionalized speech modes, discourses express societal power relations, which in turn are affected by discourses. This "overall discourse" of society, which could be visualized as a "*diskursives Gewimmel*" (literally: "discursive swarming"), becomes comprehensible in different discourse strands (composed of discourse fragments from the same subject) at different discourse levels (science, politics, media, etc.). Every discourse is historically embedded and has repercussions on current and future discourse. The uniformity of the hegemonic discourse makes it possible that analysis requires only a "relatively small number of discourse fragments." Siegfried Jäger and Margret Jäger (1999) offer concrete model analyses dealing with everyday racism, the analysis of the "discourse strand of biopower" in a daily newspaper (S. Jäger), and an analysis of interwoven discourses relating to the "criticism of patriarchy in immigration discourse" (M. Jäger). The discourse of the so-called "new right" in Germany was also analyzed by M. Jäger and S. Jäger (1993), who based their research on different right-wing print media. They identified important common characteristics (e.g., specific symbols, "ethno-pluralism" [apartheid], aggressiveness, antidemocratic attitudes, etc.) as well as significant linguistic and stylistic differences dependent on the different target groups of the newspapers.

SOME RESEARCH AGENDAS

With the debate on globalization and on European integration, there is an increasing interest in media and multilingual audiences, cross-cultural and transnational perspectives, and the global-local articulation. Most of the research in these fields focuses on structural or political dimensions and/or on audience research, but there are only a few research projects concerned with media texts. Richardson and Meinhof (1999) contributed to filling the gap with a series of comparative case studies on satellite television programs proposed by news channels addressing a global audience (News Corp's Sky News and Germany's n.tv), local TV channels in Germany and Britain, and the European TV experience (ARTE, Euro-News), drawing on discourse analysis, applied linguistics, and social semiotics.

Equally interested in addressing multilingual audiences and in multilingual texts is a whole range of sociolinguistic and linguistic research covering a very diverse range of media and genres that vary from multilingual aspects in advertising (Grin, 1996), code switching in popular music (e.g., Bentahlia & Davies, 2002), and different aspects of subtitling and dubbing (Gambier, 1997) to the emergence of "Hinglish" and "Spanglish"—hybrid Hindi-English and Spanish-English spoken codes, respectively—in radio and TV. Nevertheless, researchers working in linguistics and media studies

point out that there is a serious lack of systematic research available on language and the media in multilingual settings (Boyd-Barrett, Nootens, & Pugh, 1996; Grin, 1996; Leitner, 1997; Robins, 1997). The new transnational configurations of media landscapes with their particular articulations between the local and the global would thus necessitate deeper insights. Concerning ethnic minorities, the media text-oriented research mainly investigates the representation of the "Other" in (mainstream) media (see below). In the field of minority media, a shift of paradigm has occurred (Busch, 1999b): In the past, questions of access to information and minority rights were a main focus, whereas present work concentrates more on constructions of (multiple) identities. Consequently, audience-centered approaches are now dominant. From the linguistic point of view, the role of media in supporting/reviving minority or less used languages has been a concern throughout. The scarce text-analytical studies of media in minority languages in Europe show that, particularly among smaller language communities, the spectrum of topics covered has considerably narrowed, leading to a focus on questions internal to the group (Busch, 1999a).

THE REPRESENTATION OF THE "OTHER"

The representation of the "Other," the representation of cultural diversity, and the reproduction of racism and xenophobia through media have been key research topics in the past few decades. Such studies have traditionally used a (critical) discourse analysis and cultural studies approach.[2] All these studies focus on the production and reproduction of stereotypes through print media and the internet, as well as through TV. Van Dijk's sociocognitive approach focuses on the schemata through which minorities are perceived and illustrated, as well as on headlines in the press. Headlines and their syntactic and semantic configuration typically represent "others" as perpetrators and agents, as anonymous and criminal, whereas the police and victims are passivized and presented as suffering.

The 1986 "Waldheim affair" in Austria, which exposed the former United Nations (UN) general secretary as having lied about his past in the German *Wehrmacht,* brought latent anti-Semitic prejudices to the fore. "Jews," "certain circles," "Jews full of revenge," "rich Jews," "Socialist Jews," and so on were accused of being part of a "world conspiracy" to attack Waldheim all around the world. The political party that launched Waldheim's candidacy for the Austrian presidency (the Austrian People's Party), functionalized old and new anti-Semitic stereotypes in this election campaign. Very characteristic of the Austrian variety of such discourses were subtle linguistic features, such as implications, insinuations, and facile categorizations because blatant anti-Semitic slander has been taboo in official contexts in postwar Austria. The election campaign for the right-winger Jörg Haider and the right-wing populist party (Freedom Party) in Vienna 2001 again made use of such stereotypes.[3] This illustrates how, whenever scapegoats are needed to channel anxieties, insecurities, aggressions, or failures, racist and anti-Semitic discourses appear and are reproduced through the media.

Stuart Hall (2000b) has also been able to demonstrate that the British media are biased when writing or talking about minorities and migrants. Specifically, in recent riots and conflicts (such as in Bradford in 2001), the unemployed young people who felt and were in reality excluded from access and participation in many social domains were depicted very negatively and associated with criminality and drug abuse. More and more in Europe, immigrants, especially African men, have come to be blamed for drug-related crimes.

Immigration laws throughout the European Union have become stricter, and hence discrimination and racism became stronger, legitimizing such restrictions. Fear of

unemployment was thus highlighted. These totally constructed fears and threats started immediately after the fall of the Iron Curtain in 1989–1990 (see Reisigl & Wodak, 2000, 2001). The media reporting went through three distinct phases: Firstly, a rather paternalistic, condescending tone was applied towards those countries and people "who had no democratic experience." Secondly, a discourse of "pity" took over, as soon as the living conditions of some population groups became known. And thirdly, as soon as migrants started crossing the borders to the West, racist beliefs and attitudes became loud. Thus, it was possible to study and exemplify the genesis of racism in media reporting (Matouschek, Januschek, & Wodak, 1995).

The terrorist attacks in the United States on September 11, 2001, reinforced anti-Islamic feelings and prejudices. The representations in the media of Muslims and the Islamic religion generalized the fear of terrorism to all people who "look different." Usama Suleiman (2001) has analyzed the reporting in the Israeli, Palestinian, and U.S. media about a number of important events since the founding of the state of Israel. He was able to show that the representation of Israelis in the Palestinian press, of Palestinians in the Israeli press, and of both conflicting parties in the American press was significantly biased because of the interests of leading political elites. One frequently had the impression that totally different events and people were being written about.

Arab reporting about Israel has become more and more laden with old anti-Semitic stereotypes since the new wars in the Middle East of 2001–2002 (see Wistrich, 2002). Conflicts in that period also led to more anti-Semitic clichés in the European press: analogies to Nazis and to concentration camps were drawn in the French and German media. European Jews—even all Jews—were made responsible for Israeli government policies.

Overall, strategies of generalization, blaming the victims, and victim-perpetrator reversal were increasingly prominent. Stories about one bad experience with "one Jew, Roma, Arab, Turk, and so on" were generalized onto the whole ethnic group. Such "prejudice stories" characterize media reporting as well as everyday racism (Essed, 1993). Disclaimers are another salient feature of such reporting: "Everybody has best Jewish, Turkish . . . friends, but . . . ." These clauses always introduce massive prejudices. The "denial of racism" (van Dijk, 1988a, 1988b) is another important characteristic. Denying racist, anti-Semitic, or xenophobic attitudes while latently functionalizing them in anti-immigrant reporting is necessary in pluralistic societies that claim to be "open" and "tolerant" (see Martín-Rojo & van Dijk, 1997; Wodak & van Dijk, 2000).

ter Wal (2002) has provided an overview of research in racism and cultural diversity in the mass media for the European Union, for the European Monitoring Center on Racism, Xenophobia and Anti-Semitism (www.eumc.at). She found that in the period researched (1995–2000), the predominant methodology used was quantitative content analysis, but in many studies, two or more approaches were incorporated. The most common combination was that of content and discourse analysis or of discourse analysis complemented by ethnographic fieldwork and semiotic analysis. Especially in the Scandinavian countries, Spain, Italy, Austria, and the Netherlands, qualitative discourse analysis was well established in the field. Another frequent approach to media texts was the cultural studies approach, which focuses on the mythical elements on which ideological significations have been built. The majority of the research was on the press, some on television, but virtually none on radio. The perspective gradually shifted from an analysis of news production and news content to a more contextualized analysis, taking into consideration the audience perspective and the possibility of negotiating identities. When the 15 member states of the European Union were compared, it could be shown that in all countries, a big difference existed between tabloids and more elite media,

which confirms the difference in modes of expression of prejudice between elites and ordinary people (see Wodak & van Dijk, 2000). On the other hand, all countries employed the linguistic features mentioned above in their reporting and news items. Access to the media was also very difficult for minority-ethnic professionals.

HATE SPEECH AND WAR

After the fall of the Berlin Wall and the outbreak of armed conflicts in Southeastern and Eastern Europe, media developments in the so-called countries of transition became a focus of interest. On the level of text analysis, the questions of hate speech, biased reporting, and representation of minorities have attracted research interest. Some of these works use quantitative content analysis; others combine quantitative aspects with qualitative text or discourse-analytical approaches. The scope ranges from case studies on particular media (e.g., Kuzmanic, 1999, on racism, sexism, and chauvinism in Slovenian print media; Valic, 1997, on war reporting on local radio in Serbia) to studies on the representation of particular groups (e.g., Erjavec, Hrvatin, & Kelbl, 2000, on Roma in Slovenia). Qualitative work mainly refers to the theoretical and methodological approaches developed by CDA (in particular, van Dijk, 1991; Wodak, 1996b).

During and after the war in former Yugoslavia, two major international text analysis projects were initiated and financed by nongovernmental organizations to investigate hate speech: The project "Media and War" (Skopljanac Brunner, Gredelj, Hodzic, & Kristofic, 2000) brought together a large interdisciplinary group of researchers from Croatia and Serbia, a difficult task in a period of complete communication blockade in the region. Its findings were based on a large body of data drawn from the print media—the two major dailies in the respective countries Vjesnik and Politika— and television news programs on the national (state) stations. Similar to van Dijk's (1991) comparative study of news discourses, the core of the "Media and War" study combined content analysis and discourse analysis methods complemented with a semantic field analysis (Skiljan, 2000) on the word *rat* (war), as well as background information on the political situation and the role of the media during the period of disintegration of former Yugoslavia and the outbreak of war in Croatia and Bosnia-Herzegovina. The publication (Skopljanac Brunner et al., 2000) that resulted from this study refrains from drawing general conclusions and does not extrapolate the findings to draw more general conclusions about hate speech. It is left to the reader to compare the conclusions drawn by different authors employing different methods of analysis (tacit triangulation). A main focus is the discursive strategies employed in constructing new national identities in which strategies of creating in-groups and out-groups by emphasizing differences between "us" and "them" play a key role, as well as strategies of internal homogenization, such as invoking "national unity and solidarity," and of victimizing one's own group while accusing the other of aggression. It was striking how frequently Croatian media dwelt on locating the newly founded state on a map of the imaginary: Croatia was depicted as an integral part of Europe, and Europe, in turn, was depicted as a centuries-old *Schicksalsgemeinschaft*—a community formed by historical destiny—based on Christian values.

Another recent major international text analysis project in Southeastern Europe was the "Balkan neighbors project," which involved researchers in Albania, Bulgaria, Greece, Macedonia, Romania, Turkey, and Yugoslavia (*Balkan Neighbours Newsletter*, 2000, Issue 10). It was also initiated and financed by nongovernmental organizations. Between 1994 and 2000, the project monitored mainstream print media. In each country, a range of several dailies and weekly political magazines with a different

global perspective were selected for the monitoring process. Each affiliated research center extracted from the press texts concerning the other countries involved in the project as well as texts concerning national, ethnic, linguistic, and religious minorities within the country. Within such texts, verbal realizations of stereotypes and prejudices were located and analyzed. As the project had a strong emphasis on dissemination, findings were published at 6 monthly intervals in a substantial news bulletin (*Balkan Neighbours Newsletter*, 1994–2000), which was circulated to opinion leaders in the different countries. The data were also available on the internet (www.access.online.bg/bn/newsletters). Each bulletin comprised a short description of the analyzed papers, an overview of the major political events, and a contextualized compilation of the extracted stereotypes. The long monitoring period made it possible to pin down moments of transformation of particular stereotypes in relation to certain events. Transformations occurred not only when armed conflict broke out but also, for example, after a major earthquake in Turkey, when Greece provided rapid help.

FEMINIST RESEARCH

Feminist readings of media texts have both an academic and a political focus (see Kuhn, 2000, 62ff). On one hand, many studies have compared representations of men and women in magazines as well as in newspapers or on TV talk shows (see Eggins & Iedema, 1997; Kotthoff, 1997; Lalouschek, 2002; Wetschanow, 2003; Winship, 1986). On the other hand, feminist criticism focuses on a different deconstruction of texts, on "women's genres" and the construction of femininity (see Kuhn, 1984). The aim of such studies is to question dichotomies and traditional distinctions, such as the public-private, the knowledge-pleasure, and the masculine-feminine splits (see also Marris & Thornham, 2000, pp. 330ff). The slogan that stems from the women's liberation movement—"the private is political"—has become very important for these analyses, which also include soap operas, infotainment, talk shows, crime stories, thrillers, and so on.

These first relevant studies were complemented recently by an attempt to include race, class, and ethnicity into such analyses (Squire, 2000). It was agreed that feminist analysis needs to be placed in context and that discourse analysis of media about gender roles needs to be context dependent (see Kotthoff & Wodak, 1997). Much work has also followed postmodern thinking (Brunsdon, 1991) by introducing new genres, the concept of "fragmentation," and an emphasis on deconstructing subjectivity and on the collapse of boundaries—including those of gender.

The study of Wetschanow (2003) analyzes media reporting on violence against women and on the reporting of rape cases in Austrian print media as well as TV. Although she concentrates on one central European country, the results could quite easily be generalized. By combining quantitative content analysis with qualitative critical discourse analysis of media texts, she illustrates convincingly how strategies of categorization are significantly different for the victims and perpetrators, as well as for men and women. The strategy of victim-perpetrator reversal is applied frequently, and the men who are accused of raping a woman are switched into the role of passive victims who were seduced and could not defend themselves against their sexual drives. Women are depicted as seductresses, as initiators, and thus possibly guilty of the harm done to them. The adjectives employed as attributes mark these differences and characteristics.

The same pattern holds true for violence. Patricia O'Connor (2002) has investigated and also worked with victims of violence (men and women), as well as with perpetrators in prisons. O'Connor (2002) and McElhinny (1997) were able to demonstrate empirically, through their discourse analysis of interactions and media texts, that

officials, police officers, and bureaucrats were always represented benevolently, whereas the victims, often enough women, were blamed for being weak, not remembering accurately, or being noncompliant. They are thus doubly harassed: first in the terrible situation and context of violence and, secondly, through the representation in the media and at court or through other bureaucracies that define them.

Eggins and Iedema (1997) studied not only the language of women's magazines in Australia but also the visual images of women by employing important features of Hallidayan functional systemic grammar and visual grammar, developed by Kress and van Leeuwen (1996) (see above). Eggins and Iedema compared two Australian magazines, *New Woman* and *She.* Although both magazines express similar topical dimensions (orientation to appearance, to heterosexuality, to women and men in isolation [without other variables], etc.), they address different audiences: *New Woman* calls for women's empowerment through individual change and thus neutralizes the possibility of real emancipation as a political process. *She,* in contrast, provides simple dichotomic answers to and evaluations of complex problems and constructs rigid boundaries between "women and men," between the "good and bad," the "beautiful and the ugly," and so on. The authors conclude that the magazines offer "difference without diversity" and thus—they claim—stabilize the status quo.

PERSPECTIVES

In our ever more globalizing world, media have gained more power. The impact of media on political developments and decision making still has to be fully explored. Moreover, the influence of media on the production and reproduction of beliefs, opinions, stereotypes, prejudices, and ideologies also has to be thoroughly investigated and compared throughout different countries worldwide. Qualitative in-depth studies on audiences, reception, and perceptions of readers, viewers, or listeners are also missing.

The cultural influence of the U.S. media on other media (e.g., in Europe) has slowly started to be perceived. This influence is apparent in the construction of new genres, new public spaces, new modes of advertisement, and so on. The impact of transnational media (such as CNN or ARTE) on identity construction has yet to be investigated.

Access to media is another relevant factor. Who are the decision makers; who are the journalists, producers, and investigators; and who is represented and how? And who watches, listens, and reads what? The problem of media literacy and of the comprehensibility of media poses big questions for participation in democratic societies.

Lastly, research is needed on new genres, which Lemke (2001) labels as "traversals," as encompassing time and space, such as the internet or channel surfing. Time-space distanciation and time-space compression (Giddens, 2000) have to be considered in their impact on our access to information.

We do not believe that we have enumerated all the relevant phenomena, which require more interdisciplinary and transdisciplinary research. We hope to have made clear that media research from a critical discourse-analytical point of view, in combination with many other theoretical approaches, might provide some answers to all these important questions.

◆ Notes

1. See Wodak, de Cillia, Reisigl, and Liebhart (1999); Blommaert and Verschueren (1998); Martín-Rojo and van Dijk (1997); Pedro (1997); many editorials in *Discourse & Society* over the years, specifically the debate between Michael Billig and Emanuel Schegloff (1999); Iedema and Wodak (1999); Wodak and Iedema (in press); Wodak and de Cillia (in press); and Wodak & van Dijk (2000).

2. See Hall (2000a, 2000b); Fairclough (2000a, 2000b); Wodak et al. (1990); Wodak (2001a, 2001b); Reisigl and Wodak (2001); Matouschek, Januschek, and Wodak (1995); ter Wal (2002); Suleiman (2001); van Leeuwen (2000); Wodak and van Dijk (2000); van Dijk (1997, 1998); Stern (2000); Mitten (1992); Gruber (1991); and Wodak and Reisigl (1999).

3. See Wodak and Pelinka (2002).

◆ References

Anthonissen, C. (2001). *On the effectivity of media censorship: An analysis of linguistic, paralinguistic and other communicative devices used to defy media restrictions.* Unpublished doctoral dissertation, University of Vienna.

Balkan Neighbours Newsletter. (1994–2000). Sofia, Bulgaria: ACCESS Association.

Barthes, R. (1994). Introduction a l'analyse structurale des récits [Introduction to the structural analysis of narrative]. In *Oeuvres complètes. Tome II. 1966–1973* [Complete works: Vol. 2. 1966–1973]. (Edition established and presented by Éric Marty). Paris: Éditions du Seuil. (Original work published 1966)

Baudrillard, J. (2000). The masses: The implosion of the social in the media. In P. Marris & S. Thornham (Eds.), *Media studies* (pp. 99–108). New York: New York University Press.

Bell, A. (1984). Language style as audience design. *Language in Society, 13*(2), 145–204.

Bell, A., & Garrett, P. (1998). *Approaches to media discourse.* Oxford, UK: Blackwell.

Benke, G. (2000). Diskursanalyse als sozialwissenschaftliche Untersuchungsmethode [Discourse analysis as social science methodology]. *SWS Rundschau, 40*(2), 140–162.

Bentahlia, A., & Davies, E. (2002). Language mixing in rai music: Localisation or globalisation? *Language & Communication, 22,* 187–207.

Billig, M. (2002). Critical discourse and analysis. In G. Weiss & R. Wodak (Eds.),

Critical discourse analysis: Theory and interdisciplinarity. London: Macmillan.

Billig, M., & Schegloff, E. A. (1999). Debate: Critical discourse analysis and conversation analysis. *Discourse & Society, 10*(4), 543–582.

Blommaert, J., & Verschueren, J. (1998). *The diversity debate*. London: Routledge.

Boyd-Barrett, O., Nootens, J., & Pugh, A. (1996). Multilingualism and the mass media. In P. Nelde, Z. Stary, & W. Wölk (Eds.), *Kontaktlinguistik. Ein internationales Handbuch zeitgenössischer Forschung* [Contact linguistics: An international manual of contemporary research] (Vol. 1, pp. 426–431). Berlin: de Gruyter.

Brünner, G., & Graefen, G. (Eds.). (1994). *Texte und Diskurse* [Texts and discourses]. Opladen, Germany: Westdeutscher Verlag.

Brunsdon, C. (1991). Pedagogies of the feminine: Feminist teaching and women's genres. *Screen, 32*(4), 360–383.

Busch, B. (1999a). *Der virtuelle Dorfplatz. Minderheitenmedien, Globalisierung und kulturelle Identität* [The virtual village square: Minority media, globalization, and cultural identity]. Klagenfurt, Austria: Drava.

Busch, B. (1999b). Von Minderheitenmedien zu Medien in multilingualen & multikulturellen Situationen. Versuch eines Überblicks über das Forschungsfeld [From minority media to media in multilingual and multicultural context: Overview of the field of research]. *Medienjournal, 23*(2), 3–12.

Chouliaraki, L., & Fairclough, N. (1999). *Discourse in late modernity: Rethinking critical discourse analysis*. Edinburgh, UK: Edinburgh University Press.

Connerton, P. (1996). *How societies remember*. Cambridge, UK: Cambridge University Press. (Original work published 1976)

de Beaugrande, R., & Dressler, W. U. (1981). *Einführung in die Textlinguistik* [Introduction to text linguistics]. Tübingen, Germany: Nie.

Eggins, S., & Iedema, R. (1997). Difference without diversity: Semantic orientation and ideology in competing women's magazines. In R. Wodak (Ed.), *Gender and discourse* (pp. 165–196). London: Sage.

Erjavec, C., Hrvatin, S., & Kelbl, B. (2000). *We about the Roma: Discriminatory discourse in the media in Slovenia*. Ljubljana, Slovenia: Open Society Institute.

Essed, P. (1993). *Everyday racism*. London: Sage.

Fairclough, N. (1989). *Language and power*. London: Longman.

Fairclough, N. (1995). *Critical discourse analysis: The critical study of language*. London: Longman.

Fairclough, N. (2000a). Critical analysis of media discourse. In P. Marris & S. Thornham (Eds.), *Media studies* (pp. 308–325). New York: New York University Press.

Fairclough, N. (2000b). The discourse of social exclusion. In M. Reisigl & R. Wodak (Eds.), *The semiotics of racism* (pp. 65–84). Vienna: Passagen Verlag.

Fairclough, N., & Wodak, R. (1997). Critical discourse analysis. In T. A. van Dijk (Ed.), *Introduction to discourse analysis* (pp. 258–284). London: Sage.

Fay, B. (1987). *Critical social science*. London: Polity.

Fiske, J. (1989). *Television culture*. London: Routledge. (Original work published 1987)

Fowler, R. (1991). Critical linguistics. In K. Halmkjaer (Ed.), *The linguistic encyclopedia* (pp. 89–93). London: Routledge.

Fowler, R. (1996). *Linguistic criticism*. Oxford, UK: Oxford University Press.

Fowler, R., Kress, G., Hodge, R., & Trew, T. (Eds.). (1979). *Language and control*. London: Routledge.

Gambier, Y. (Ed.). (1997). *Les transferts linguistiques dans les médias audiovisuels* [Linguistic transfers in the audiovisual media]. Villeneuve d'Ascq, France: Presses universitaires du Septentrion.

Garfinkel, H. (1967). *Studies in ethnomethodology*. Englewood Cliffs, NJ: Prentice Hall.

Garrett, P., & Bell, A. (1998). Media discourse: A critical overview. In A. Bell & P. Garrett (Eds.), *Approaches to media discourse* (pp. 1–21). Oxford, UK: Blackwell.

Giddens, A. (2000). *Sociology*. London: Polity.

Glasgow University Media Group. (1976). *Bad news*. London: Routledge.

Glasgow University Media Group. (1980). *More bad news*. London: Routledge.

Glasgow University Media Group. (1985). *War and peace news.* Buckingham, UK: Open University Press.

Greatbach, D. (1986). Aspects of topical organisation in news interviews: The use of agenda-shifting procedures by news interviewees. *Media, Culture and Society, 8*(4), 441–455.

Grin, F. (1996). Plurilinguisme en matière de publicité [Plurilinguism as regards advertising]. In P. Nelde, Z. Stary, & W. Wölk (Eds.), *Kontaktlinguistik. Ein internationales Handbuch zeitgenössischer Forschung* [Contact linguistics: An international manual of contemporary research] (Vol. 1, pp. 438–444). Berlin: de Gruyter.

Gruber, H. (1991). *Antisemitismus im Mediendiskurs. Die Affäre "Waldheim" in der Tagespresse* [Antisemitism into media discourse: The "Waldheim" affair in the daily press]. Wiesbaden: Deutscher Universitätsverlag/Westdeutscher Verlag.

Habermas, J. (2000). The public space. In P. Marris & S. Thornham (Eds.), *Media studies* (pp. 92–98). New York: New York University Press.

Hall, S. (2000a). Encoding/decoding. In P. Marris & S. Thornham (Eds.), *Media studies* (pp. 51–61). New York: New York University Press.

Hall, S. (2000b). Racist ideologies and the media. In P. Marris & S. Thornham (Eds.), *Media studies* (pp. 271–282). New York: New York University Press.

Halliday, M. A. K. (1978). *Language as social semiotic.* London: Edward Arnold.

Halliday, M. A. K. (1985). *Introduction to functional grammar.* London: Edward Arnold.

Heritage, J. (1985). Analyzing news interviews: Aspects of the production of talk for overhearing audiences. In T. A. van Dijk (Ed.), *Handbook of discourse analysis* (Vol. 3, pp. 95–119). London: Academic Press.

Hutchby, I. (1991). The organisation of talk on radio. In P. Scannell (Ed.), *Broadcast talk* (pp. 119–137). London: Sage.

Iedema, R., & Wodak, R. (1999). Introduction: Organizational discourses and practices. *Discourse & Society, 10*(1), 5–19.

Jäger, M., & Jäger, S. (1993). Verstrickungen—Der rassistische Diskurs und seine Bedeutung für den politischen Gesamtdiskurs in der Bundesrepublik Deutschland. [Entangled: racist discourse and its significance for overall political discourse in the Federal Republic of Germany]. In S. Jäger & J. Link (Eds.), *Die vierte Gewalt: Rassismus und die Medien* [The fourth force: Racism and the media] (pp. 49–79). Duisburg: DISS.

Jäger, S. (1993). *Kritische Diskursanalyse. Eine Einführung* [Critical discourse analysis: An introduction]. Duisburg, Germany: DISS.

Jäger, S. (2001). Discourse and knowledge: Theoretical and methodological aspects of critical discourse analysis. In R. Wodak & M. Meyer (Eds.), *Methods of critical discourse analysis* (pp. 32–62). London: Sage.

Jäger, S., & Jäger, M. (1999). *Kritische Diskursanalyse. Eine Einführung* [Critical discourse analysis: An introduction]. Duisburg, Germany: DISS.

Jensen, K. B., & Jankowski, N. W. (1991). *A handbook of qualitative methodologies for mass communication research.* London: Routledge.

Kotthoff, H. (1997). The interactional achievement of expert status: Creating asymmetries by "teaching conversational lectures" in TV discussions. In H. Kotthoff & R. Wodak (Eds.), *Communicating gender in context* (pp. 139–178). Amsterdam: Benjamins.

Kotthoff, H., & Wodak, R. (Eds.). (1997). *Communicating gender in context.* Amsterdam: Benjamins.

Kress, G. (1990). Critical discourse analysis. *Annual Review of Anthropology, 11,* 84–97.

Kress, G., & van Leeuwen, T. (1996). *Reading images.* London: Routledge.

Krings, H., Baumgartner, H. M., & Wildly, C. (1973). *Handbuch philosophischer Grundbegriffe* [Handbook of philosophical fundamental concepts]. Frankfurt: Kösel.

Kuhn, A. (1984). Women's genres. *Screen, 25*(1), 18–28.

Kuhn, A. (2000). The power of the image. In P. Marris & S. Thornham (Eds.), *Media studies* (pp. 62–67). New York: New York University Press.

Kuzmanic, T. (1999). *Hate speech in Slovenia: Slovenian racism, sexism and chauvinism.* Ljubljana, Slovenia: Open Society Institute.

Lalouschek, J. (2002). *Gesundheitkommunikation im Fernsehen* [Communication on health problems in TV]. Unpublished doctoral dissertation, University of Vienna.

Leitner, G. (1997). The sociolingistics of communication media. In F. Coulmas (Ed.), *Handbook of sociolingistics* (pp. 187–204). Oxford, UK: Blackwell.

Lemke, J. (1995). *Textual politics: Discourse and social dynamics.* London: Taylor & Francis.

Lemke, J. (2001). Discursive technologies and the social organization of meaning. *Folia Linguistica, 35*(1–2), 79–96.

Leontjev, A. N. (1984). Der allgemeine Tätigkeitsbegriff [The general activity term]. In A. A. Leontjev, A. N. Leontjev, & E. G. Judin (Eds.), *Grundfragen einer Theorie der sprachlichen Tätigkeit* [Basic questions of a theory of linguistic activity] (pp. 13–30). Stuttgart: Kohlhammer.

Link, J. (1988). Über Kollektivsymbolik im politischen Diskurs und ihren Anteil an totalitären Tendenzen [Collective symbols in political discourses and their impact on totalitarian tendencies]. *kultuRRevolution, 17–18,* 47–53.

Lutz, B., & Wodak, R. (1987). *Information für Informierte* [Information for the informed]. Vienna: Austrian Academy of Sciences.

Marris, P., & Thornham, S. (Eds.). (2000). *Media studies.* New York: New York University Press.

Martín-Rojo, L., & van Dijk, T. A. (1997). There was a problem and it was solved: Legitimation of the expulsion of illegal immigrants in Spanish parliamentary discourse. *Discourse & Society, 8*(4), 523–567.

Matouschek, B., Januschek, F., & Wodak, R. (1995). *Notwendige Massnahmen gegen Fremde?* [Necessary measures against foreigners?]. Vienna: Passagen Verlag.

McElhinny, B. (1997). Ideologies of public and private language in sociolinguistics. In R. Wodak (Ed.), *Gender and discourse* (pp. 106–139). London: Sage.

McQuail, D. (2000). *Mass communication theory* (4th ed.). London: Sage.

Meinhof, U. (1994). Double talk in news broadcasts. In D. Graddol & O. Boyd-Barrett (Eds.), *Media texts: Authors and readers* (pp. 212–223). Clevedon, UK: Multilingual Matters and The Open University.

Meinhof, U., & Smith, J. (2000). *Intertextuality and the media: From genre to everyday life.* Manchester, UK: Manchester University Press.

Mitten, R. (1992). *The politics of antisemitic prejudice: The Waldheim phenomenon in Austria.* Boulder, CO: Westview.

Morley, D. (1980). *The "Nationwide" audience.* London: British Film Institute.

Muntigl, P., Weiss, G., & Wodak, R. (2000). *European Union discourses on unemployment: An interdisciplinary approach to employment policy-making and organizational change.* Amsterdam: Benjamins.

O'Connor, P. (2002). Activist linguistics: Inside our method/inside our theory. In G. Weiss & R. Wodak (Eds.), *Critical discourse analysis: Theory and interdisciplinarity* (pp. 223–241). London: Macmillan.

Pedro, E. R. (1997). *Discourse analysis.* Lisbon: Ed. Colibri/Associação Portuguesa de Linguística.

Reisigl, M., & Wodak, R. (Eds.). (2000). *The semiotics of racism.* Vienna: Passagen Verlag.

Reisigl, M., & Wodak, R. (2001). *Discourse and discrimination.* London: Routledge.

Richardson, K. (1998). Signs and wonders: Interpreting the economy through television. In A. Bell & P. Garrett (Eds.), *New approaches to media discourse* (pp. 220–251). London: Blackwell.

Richardson, K., & Meinhof, U. (1999). *Worlds in common? Television discourse in a changing Europe.* London: Routledge.

Robins, K. (Ed.). (1997). *Programming for people: From cultural rights to cultural responsibilities* (Report for the United Nations Television Forum, New York, November 19–21, 1997). Rome: RAI.

Sacks, H., Schegloff, E., & Jefferson, G. (1974). A simplest systematics for the organisation of turn-taking in conversation. *Language, 50,* 696–735.

Schegloff, E. (1998). Text and context paper. *Discourse & Society, 3,* 4–37.

Schiffrin, D. (1994). *Approaches to discourse.* Oxford, UK: Blackwell.

Scollon, R. (1999). *Mediated discourse analysis.* London: Longman.

Scollon, R. (2001). *Mediated discourse: The nexus of practice.* London: Routledge.

Skiljan, D. (2000). Semantics of war. In N. Skopljanac Brunner, S. Gredelji, A. Hodzic, & B. Kristofic (Eds.), *Media and war.* Zagreb, Croatia: Centre for Transition and Civil Society Research.

Skopljanac Brunner, N., Gredelj, S., Hodzic, A., & Kristofic, B. (Eds.). (2000). *Media and war.* Zagreb, Croatia: Centre for Transition and Civil Society Research.

Squire, A. V. (2000). *Prinzessin Diana* [Princess Diana]. Working paper, University of Vienna.

Stern, F. (2000). The "Semitic" gaze from the screen: Cinematic discourse of the other. In M. Reisigl & R. Wodak (Eds.), *The semiotics of racism: Approaches in critical discourse analysis* (pp. 351–362). Vienna: Passagen Verlag.

Suleiman, U. (2001). *The other-territory-peace.* Working paper, University of Vienna.

ter Wal, J. (Ed.). (2002). *Racism and cultural diversity in the mass media: An overview of research and examples of good practice in the EU member states, 1995–2000.* Vienna: European Research Centre on Migration and Ethnic Relations.

Thompson, J. B. (1988). *Critical hermeneutics* (4th ed.). Cambridge, UK: Cambridge University Press.

Titscher, S., Wodak, R., Meyer, M., & Vetter, E. (2000). *Methods of text and discourse analysis.* London: Sage.

Valic, N. D. (1997). *Ricocheting words.* Belgrade: Argument.

van Dijk, T. A. (1985). *Prejudice in discourse.* Amsterdam: Benjamins.

van Dijk, T. A. (Ed.). (1986). *Discourse and communication: New approaches to the analysis of mass media discourse and communication.* Berlin: de Gruyter.

van Dijk, T. A. (1988a). *News analysis.* New York: Lawrence Erlbaum.

van Dijk, T. A. (1988b). *News as discourse.* New York: Lawrence Erlbaum.

van Dijk, T. A. (1991). *Racism and the press.* London: Routledge.

van Dijk, T. A. (1993). Principles of critical discourse analysis. *Discourse & Society,* 4(2), 249–283.

van Dijk, T. A. (1997). *Discourse as social interaction.* London: Sage.

van Dijk, T. A. (1998). *Ideology: A multidisciplinary study.* London: Sage.

van Dijk, T. A. (2001). Critical discourse analysis. In D. Tannen, D. Schiffrin, & H. Hamilton (Eds.), *Handbook of discourse analysis* (pp. 352–371). Oxford, UK: Oxford University Press.

van Dijk, T. A. (2002). The discourse-knowledge interface. In G. Weiss & R. Wodak (Eds.), *Critical discourse analysis: Theory and interdisciplinarity* (pp. 85–109). London: Macmillan.

van Dijk, T. A., & Kintsch, W. (1983). *Strategies of discourse comprehension.* New York: Academic Press.

van Leeuwen, T. (1993). *Language and representation: The recontextualisation of participants, activities and reactions.* Department of Linguistics thesis, University of Sydney, Sydney, Australia.

van Leeuwen, T. (2000). Visual racism. In M. Reisigl & R. Wodak (Eds.), *The semiotics of racism: Approaches in critical discourse analysis* (pp. 363–391). Vienna: Passagen Verlag.

Wetschanow, K. (2003). *Vergewaltigung. Eine diskursanalytische Studie zur medialen Repräsentationspolitik in Österreich* [Rape: A discourse-analytical study of the politics of representation in Austria]. Unpublished dissertation, University of Vienna.

Winship, E. C. (1986). *Reaching your teenager.* Munich, Germany: Reinhardt.

Wistrich, J. (2002, June). *Islam, Israel and the new anti-Semitism.* Paper presented at the Institut für Sprachwissenschaft, University of Vienna.

Wodak, R. (1996a). *Disorders in discourse.* London: Longman.

Wodak, R. (1996b). The genesis of racist discourse in Austria since 1989. In C. R. Caldas-Coulthard & M. Coulthard (Eds.), *Texts and practices: Readings in critical discourse analysis* (pp. 107–128). London: Routledge.

Wodak, R. (2000). Recontextualisation and the transformation of meaning: A critical discourse analysis of decision making in EU-meetings about employment policies. In S. Sarangi & M. Coulthard (Eds.), *Discourse and social life* (pp. 185–206). Harlow, UK: Pearson Education.

Wodak, R. (2001a). The discourse-historical approach. In R. Wodak & M. Meyer (Eds.), *Methods of critical discourse analysis* (pp. 63–94). London: Sage.

Wodak, R. (2001b). What CDA is about—a summary of its history, important concepts and its developments. In R. Wodak & M. Meyer (Eds.), *Methods of critical discourse analysis* (pp. 1–13). London: Sage.

Wodak, R., & de Cillia, R. (in press). Discourse and politics. In U. Ammon & K. Mattheier (Eds.), *Handbuch Soziolinguistik* [Handbook of sociolinguistics]. Berlin: de Gruyter.

Wodak, R., de Cillia, R., Reisigl, M., & Liebhart, K. (1999). *The discursive construction of national identity*. Edinburgh, UK: Edinburgh University Press.

Wodak, R., & Iedema, R. (in press). Communication in institutions. In U. Ammon & K. Mattheier (Eds.), *Handbuch Soziolinguistik* [Handbook of sociolinguistics]. Berlin: de Gruyter.

Wodak, R., Menz, F., Mitten, R., & Stern, F. (1994). *Die Sprachen der Vergangenheiten: öffentliches Gedenken in österreichischen und deutschen Medien* [The languages of past times. Public memory in Austrian and German media]. Frankfurt/Main: Suhrkamp.

Wodak, R., & Pelinka, A. (Eds.). (2002). *The Haider phenomenon*. New Brunswick, NJ: Transaction Press.

Wodak, R., Pelikan, J., Nowak, P., Gruber, H., de Cillia, R., & Mitten, R. (1990). *Wir sind alle unschuldige Täter! Diskurshistorische Studien zum Nachkriegsantisemitismus* ["We are all innocent perpetrators!" Discourse-historical studies of postwar antisemitism]. Frankfurt/Main: Suhrkamp.

Wodak, R., & Reisigl, M. (1999). Discourse and racism: European perspectives. *Annual Review of Anthropology, 28,* 175–199.

Wodak, R., & van Dijk, T. (Eds.). (2000). *Racism at the top*. Klagenfurt, Austria: Drava.

6

TECHNOLOGY

◆ Sandra Braman

The *media* in media studies are the technologies that mediate between those who make messages and those who receive them. Models of the communication process have long included the media, but for many years, research almost exclusively focused on message production and reception, with little attention to how messages got from here to there. The convergence of technologies that has resulted in the internet, however, has provoked a great deal of interest in just what makes one technology different from another. Today's global information infrastructure is a "pan-medium" (Theall, 1999) that combines all previous media, but differences among them still matter: Media developed earlier remain in use, many forms of communication use digital and analog media in combination, and although technologies may have multiple meanings and uses, they are not infinitely malleable; materialities still matter. The ways we use media and the policies we make for them are, in the end, always local and therefore technology specific.

This chapter opens by distinguishing among different classes of technologies and between stand-alone technologies and technological systems, looks at characteristics of technologies that make certain choices more or less appropriate in particular circumstances, examines how new technologies appear and come into use, reviews the technological features of the contemporary global information infrastructure that provides the context and conduit for the media, and concludes by looking at media themselves as technologies.

◆ From Tool to Meta-Technology

Across the long course of human history, the invention of new kinds of tools and technologies had such an impact on the nature of society that we distinguish between the premodern, modern, and postmodern periods by dominant type of technology. The ancient tools of premodernity, the industrial technologies of modernity, and the informational meta-technologies of postmodernity differ in the degree and kinds of social coordination they require, the materials they process, and the range of types of processes they enable. The specific features of meta-technologies go far toward explaining why the current period is also described as an information society (Braman, 1993).

The word *technology* has its roots in the Greek *techne* (making), referring to what both art and engineering have in common. This linguistic root has given rise to three different ways of *making:*

1. *Tools* can be made and used by individuals working alone and make it possible to process matter or energy in single steps. The use of tools characterized the premodern era. Although it is easy to think of examples of ancient tools for other things that people do, such as planting seeds or starting a fire, because communication is an inherently social act, it may only be when marks are made for the purposes of individual memory can it be said there are communication tools.

2. *Technologies* are social in their making and use; that is, they require a number of people to work together. They make it possible to link several processing steps together in the course of transforming matter or energy, but there is only one sequence in which those steps can be taken, only one or a few types of materials can be processed, and only one or a few types of outcomes can be produced. The shift from tools to technologies made industrialization

possible, and the use of technologies thus characterizes the modern period. The printing press and the radio are examples of communication technologies.

3. *Meta-technologies* vastly expand the degrees of freedom with which humans can act in the social and material worlds. Meta-technologies involve many processing steps, and there is great flexibility in the number of steps and the sequence with which they are undertaken. Meta-technologies can process an ever-expanding range of types of inputs and can produce an essentially infinite range of outputs. They are social but permit solo activity once one is operating within the socially produced network. Their use characterizes the postmodern world. Meta-technologies are always informational, and the internet is a premiere example of a meta-technology used for communication purposes.

There are four dimensions along which tools, technologies, and meta-technologies can usefully be distinguished: the degree to which they are social, the complexity of the processes they enable, their autonomy, and their scale. The movement from tool to technology to meta-technology is marked by an increase on each of these dimensions.

Buckminster Fuller (Fuller & Applewhite, 1975) introduced the notion of the social nature of technologies when he discussed writing as the first technology. The social coordination required for the use of technologies and meta-technologies explains why it is so important to agree on both technical standards and protocols for their use. It also explains why their use has such an impact on society, for each requires (or enables) the development of specific types of coordination and interaction.

Marshall McLuhan[1] drew attention to the second feature, complexity, when he noted that both tools and technologies change the field of possibilities and therefore of practice. French philosopher of technology Jacques Ellul (1964) offered a more detailed way of thinking about this when he defined *technique* as "a complex of standardized means for attaining a predetermined result." The complexity of each single step must also be taken into account, for the more complex, the more flexibility and creativity are possible (Novak, 1997; Scazzieri, 1993)—though an increase in complexity does not always mean a better technology. The only limits to the complexity of digital meta-technologies are those of mathematics and our imaginations.

Concern over the autonomy of technologies appeared first in the 11th century in the Golem stories that later inspired the novel *Frankenstein*. These tales of a creature made out of clay to serve human needs always concluded with the Golem becoming destructive because people were unable to be sufficiently detailed and accurate in their instructions. The notion of machinic autonomy as technological activity beyond the limits of human control thus appeared very early in the transition from tools to technologies. Economic historian Alfred Chandler Jr. (1977) pointed out in his seminal work, *The Visible Hand*, that beginning with the automation of production lines in the 19th century, society began turning its decision making over to machines, thus granting machines a second type of autonomy. In the digital world of meta-technologies, a third type of machinic autonomy has appeared in intelligent agents that roam the networks finding information, making decisions, and conducting transactions of their own on behalf of humans. It may go even further: There are now autonomously evolving nonhuman intelligences in the network that may well be making decisions and acting on their own behalf. George Dyson (1997) points out that machinic intelligence may now be operating autonomously in ways that humans cannot even perceive because the logics may be so different from what we know.

Other features of technologies also distinguish the modern from the postmodern era. Belief that technological development was always "progress" was a hallmark of modernity, but in the postmodern world,

there is growing concern about its risks. Technologies used to be viewed as standalone objects, but today, it is understood that each is inextricably part of a system. We used to apply the term *technology* only to material objects, but now use it to refer to ideas and ways of doing things as well. And despite the modern fancy that technology and culture have little to do with each other, by now it is clear that each deeply informs—indeed, creates—the other.

While keeping the distinction between tools, technologies, and meta-technologies in mind, for ease the remainder of this chapter will use the term *technology* to refer to all three.

◆ Technologies and Technological Systems

The difference between perceiving technologies as stand-alone and as embedded in systems is important for economic analysis, policymaking, and effects research. There are four types of technological systems.

1. *Mutually dependent systems.* There are systems that come into being because the use of one type of technology is dependent on the use of another, as use of the printing press required the technologies that make ink and paper. These relationships are significant because when there is a change in one of the technologies involved, it may require changes in others. When the printing press sped up as a result of electrification, for example, paper manufacturers started producing rolls of paper rather than sheets, and the quantities produced went up by orders of magnitude. An example of an indirect policy intervention possible with this type of technological system is the use of restrictions on access to paper as an effective way of preventing materials from coming into print without direct censorship.

2. *Linked systems.* In a linked technological system, individual technologies must

actually be linked with each other to be functional. Physical linkages, such as the couples between railroad cars, are one way of linking technologies in this way. Electronic networks are another. The telephone network is an example of a linked technological system in the field of communication. The internet is made up of many interlinked telecommunications networks, so we refer to it as a *network of networks*.

3. *Analytical systems.* A third type of technological system develops when social and technological forms are combined for the purposes of strategy and analysis. A good example of this from the perspective of information policy is the European use of the concept of the *filiere electronique* to refer not only to the telecommunications network but also to the organizations that exist only within and because of the network. The filiere electronique, rather than the telecommunications network by itself, has thus become the unit of analysis for economic and policy purposes.

4. *Personal systems.* A fourth sense of technological system is the information environment built and used by specific users as they choose particular technologies, networks, and interfaces for their own use. We refer to the entire world of communication and information technologies from which we choose those we will use as the *information environment*. Those we actually bring into our lives create a personal *information ecology*. Because the technological potential only becomes actual through such choices—and the effects of technologies can only be understood within this context—this type of technological system is of growing interest to researchers.

All of these types of technological systems lead to path dependency, the principle that each technical decision reduces the subsequent range of possibilities within its system by either making alternatives impossible or raising their cost so high that they are no longer economically feasible. An interesting consequence of path dependency is that it makes "leapfrogging" possible—societies that do not have certain technologies or find themselves blocked by those who control those technologies can circumvent existing power relations by taking up another. When Britain used its complete control over the global telegraph network to punish its political enemies during World War I, for example, other countries turned to the radio as a way of operating beyond British control (Headrick, 1990), and although it was long believed that every society had to repeat the stages of technological development seen in the United States and Western Europe, many countries have skipped the stage of ubiquitous wired telephony and moved directly into the wireless environment. Another implication of path dependency is that although the number of people who use a new technology early on will be relatively small, it is important to study their uses because they will play particularly influential roles in shaping the paths along which those technologies will develop (Winner, 1990).

◆ Characteristics of Technology

Within each class of tool or technology, additional critical distinctions are of fundamental concern to users and to policymakers. The features of any given technology are not inherent but depend instead on the context in which they are used. One of McLuhan's (McLuhan & McLuhan, 1992) "laws of media" is that information technologies can simultaneously yield contradictory effects. When the printing press came into use in Western Europe, for example, it both made it easier for an institution such as the Catholic Church to maintain control and, at the same time, made it easier for those who resisted that control, the Protestants, to develop their ideas and to organize (Eisenstein, 1979).

FUNCTIONAL VERSUS DYSFUNCTIONAL

Not every technology makes things easier, more efficient, more cost-effective, more pleasing, more aesthetic, or more healthful—or even does what it is intended to do. A technology may at times even be regressive. Capabilities can be lost, as when children who watch a lot of television fail to develop fine motor skills or organizations that take up new technologies find their productivity reduced. Dewdney (1998) uses the phrase "technological Maginot Line"[2] to describe those situations in which older technologies conquer newer ones, citing as an example the ability of Iranians to use ancient Persian rug-making techniques to piece together by hand pieces of paper shredded by the CIA at the time of the overthrow of the Shah. Osama bin Laden's reliance on transmission of information by word of mouth to avoid electronic surveillance after the terrorist attacks on September 11, 2001, is another example, as is the widespread practice known as *hawala* of using family ties rather than banks to manage and move money.

Some ideas just aren't very good at all. One example, from Lawless's (1977) wonderful book on communication policy proposals that were never implemented or that wildly failed: Before satellites came into use for communication purposes, the government seriously considered a proposal to put a belt of steel needles, each several inches long, in orbit around the Earth against which to bounce radio signals. The project was finally shelved only after numerous scientists and engineers pointed out that the needles would ultimately drop out of the sky, resulting in a rain of lethal projectiles moving at high speed as they hit the ground and anything or anyone in their way.

Sometimes ideas are good but the timing is wrong. The French minitel project provides a classic example. In the early 1980s, the then-new Socialist government in France took the dramatic decision to devote itself to development of a "dumb"[3] terminal so cheap to produce that the government could provide one free to every household in France, as a way of promoting the development of the service industry in that country while simultaneously increasing the media literacy of its citizenry and defining for itself a niche in the global information economy. Unfortunately, the plan didn't quite work out: It took much longer to get the terminals into distribution than originally projected, leading to a loss of political faith in the project. Tens of thousands of new services did appear that could be advertised and/or distributed through the minitel, but the majority involved the sex industry. And although it was a courageous guess that, with this product, France could both serve its own domestic market and offer a strong export product, by the time the minitel was fully available, personal computers had taken off, and there was little interest in dumb terminals (K. Dyson, 1988).

Because of the fundamental modern belief that more technology is better technology, it has been difficult for decision makers to acknowledge that it is possible for technologies to be dysfunctional or damaging. This, in turn, undercuts the possibilities of a rich public discourse about technological choice by leading to polarization—when those who question whether taking up a particular technology is in their own or society's best interests find that they have no way of bringing their concerns into decision-making processes, they are often left believing that resistance is their only alternative.

APPROPRIATE VERSUS INAPPROPRIATE

A technology may be ideal for one situation but disastrous in another. The experience of technology transfer—in which technologies are introduced into developing societies via aid or loans—has led to a great deal of discussion about the appropriateness of technologies. They may be too costly, as when cheap transistor radios go unused in the developing world because the batteries needed to run them are too expensive. They may be impossible to repair because they are in such poor condition upon arrival that they are irreparable, require maintenance knowledge or materials not available locally, or are so obsolete that the knowledge and/or materials needed aren't available anywhere. Technologies may not function at all within the material conditions of a particular environment, as when blowing sand and heat bring down telecommunications networks in desert areas. They may work on the wrong scale, as when wireless communication systems needed to extend service to unwired rural areas rely on technologies that have utility only in densely populated urban areas. Or they may be culturally inappropriate (Forsyth, 1990; Mansell & Wehn, 1998; Reddi, 1986); North American tribal groups, for example, are encouraged to move group decision making to an online environment when, traditionally, the most important decision makers are silent in group meetings.[4]

It is not that it is impossible for cutting-edge technologies to be valuable in the maintenance of traditional cultures. The telephone has enabled families to keep in touch even when employment disperses individuals geographically (Hudson, 1984). Australian Aboriginal peoples use contemporary technologies to enter the global art market as a way of generating the funds needed to sustain traditional ritual practices (Michaels, 1994). And tribal peoples in North America, like other historically marginalized groups, find that the Web provides the opportunity to reach a mass audience with their stories in their own voices.

Within the developed world, technologies may be inappropriate if they require too much energy (computers use a *lot* of energy) or if their use endangers the health of the user or others (as is the case with the sensitivity of fetuses to radiation emitted from the back of computers and, as many claim, with the increased incidence of brain tumors among heavy mobile telephone users).

Technologies may put in place information flows of a kind that conflict with personal or communal goals or values (Overman & Cahill, 1994; Overman & Loraine, 1994). When computer manufacturers, for example, move away from including disk drives that permit stand-alone use of databases and software in disk form in favor of forcing users to remain linked to a network for functionality, it may be "appropriate" for marketers but not at all so for those users who wish to protect their privacy, operate off the grid, or spend as little money on their computing operations as possible.

POTENTIAL VERSUS ACTUAL

Engineers, policymakers, and techno-enthusiasts often describe the most recent and sophisticated inventions as the "state of technology," but there are always great differences in access to technologies within and across societies. Many technologies are never available, except in the most specialized and well-resourced contexts. The result is that a gap always exists between the cutting edge of technology, as it may be available under ideal conditions with unlimited resources and before restrictive choices have been made (the potential state), and the level of technology actually available to most people with ordinary resources is enormous (the actual state). Many factors contribute to the latter, including level of knowledge, physical access, economics, and policy choices.

INCREMENTAL VERSUS DISRUPTIVE

Some innovations are incremental, involving minor changes in one technology that do not require changes in others within its technological system. The development of a new color of printing ink, for example, is not likely to require alterations to the printing press or to paper. Other innovations are "disruptive" or "radical" because their use demands transformations of other technologies with which they are involved and, often, of the organizations and societies that use them. The switch from the use of stand-alone manual typewriters by journalists and their editors to reliance on Web-based computers would be an example because it has completely changed the nature of journalistic practice. Disruptive innovations may come about as a result of the gradual accumulation of many small incremental changes over time, or they may appear as the result of the joint appearance of several radical innovations at once (Dosi, 1988). Some use the terminology of micro-inventions and macro-inventions to make this same distinction (Mokyr, 1992; Mowery & Rosenberg, 1989).

LOW- VERSUS HIGH-INFORMATION INTENSITY

Information intensity is the degree to which information itself has been used in the development of a particular technology. The information intensity of a technology is often invisible to the user. Very few are aware of the widespread embedding of artificial intelligence into objects of daily use, for example. An increase in information intensity does not always make a technology more difficult to use or require more training; indeed, it may make a technology easier to use. It does, however, affect the ways individuals experience their relationships with the environment (de Cauter, 1993; Wilson & Dissanayake, 1996) as well as with each other (Smith, 1990). Within organizations, technologies and organizational structure interact with each other to achieve the desired level of information intensity (de Landa, 1991; Demchak, 1991; Pondy, 1969).[5] The relative importance of information intensity for economic competition in today's environment is formalized in the concepts of "invisible assets" (Itami, 1991) or "intellectual capital" (Stewart, 1994), which refer to the edge that corporations must maintain between

their own information intensity and that of their clients. Governments are inherently information intense (Fletcher & Foy, 1994), and a vast increase in the information intensity of the nation-state is one of the demarkers of governance in the modern era (Giddens, 1984). In turn, governments increasingly recognize manipulation of information intensity as a policy tool in and of itself (Forecasting and Assessment in Science and Technology [FAST], 1983), as in support for the research and development (R&D) required for technological innovation (Kanter, 1992; Mokyr, 1992).

The relationship between information intensity and level of technological development, however, is not simple. The rate of innovation was slower than it might have been for much of the modern period because practice-oriented craft knowledge was kept away from knowledge-intense people in most societies for class reasons (Pearton, 1984). In addition, because the number of times information is processed is an indicator of information intensity, traditional bodies of knowledge as expressed in story cycles and cultural practices are very rich, whether or not they involve technologies. Recognition of the transformation to an information society, however, is an acknowledgment that the ever greater reliance on information technologies in turn increases the information intensity of society itself.

LOCAL VERSUS GLOBAL

One of the ways of distinguishing among technologies historically was by looking at how their users related to space, with the difference between local and global technologies appearing as a particularly important distinction. Local technologies produce specialized products to meet the needs of particular populations or places, usually rely on local materials as inputs, and operate on a small scale. Because they are usually labor intensive, many individuals in a particular locale are involved in their use. Global technologies, on the other hand, produce standardized products for world markets and are produced and used by large corporations. Because they replace labor intensity with information intensity, very few individuals in a particular locale in which the products are found may actually be involved with their production. Meta-technologies, however, make it possible to combine the two, producing small-batch or even one-off goods to meet very particular local needs when desired.

TRIVIAL VERSUS NONTRIVIAL

Those who try to develop new technologies are very interested in the difference between those they understand (trivial) and those they do not (nontrivial) (von Foerster, 1984). Indeed, the director of a major artificial intelligence project at Honeywell in the 1980s once commented that when they understood how a piece of computer programming got the results it did, they called it software, but when they couldn't figure how the results were achieved, they called it artificial intelligence.

CRITICAL VERSUS NONCRITICAL

There is a long history of government interest in encouraging the development of technologies that will serve military ends, but it is only since the mid-1970s that policymakers in the United States have begun to think in terms of technologies that are critical for society at large as they determine policy priorities. (Policymakers in Japan and Europe made this transition earlier.) The result is a shift from a focus on technologies that are mission specific to those that have utility in multiple environments. Technologies become defined as critical when they are expected to be beneficial to the public at large but do not provide enough immediate economic reward for the private sector to be able or willing

to develop without governmental support (Branscomb, 1993). Digital information technologies have been defined as critical since the category made its appearance (Wiegele, 1991).

Corporations that conduct R&D on critical technologies receive a number of policy advantages that include direct funding from the government, indirect financial support through tax breaks, and exemptions from antitrust law. Critics of the practice, however, note that often those technologies defined as critical fall in line with long-established R&D interests of the firms that benefit, the criteria for selection are arbitrary, and often definitions are so abstract that they are easily turned to corporate advantage. Restrictions on the international exchange of technical knowledge about such technologies work to everyone's disadvantage.

◆ Invention, Innovation, and Diffusion

Technologies do not appear all at once in their final form but rather go through long periods of development that often involve repeated iterations of experimentation, refinement of ideas, and responses to user feedback. Three stages of the process by which technologies come into being are distinguished. *Invention* is the operationalization of a new idea about how to do things, *innovation* takes place when an invention becomes logistically and economically feasible on a scale sufficient for the marketplace, and *diffusion* occurs when an innovation is taken up for use by the general population.

INVENTION

Of these three stages, the least is known about invention. It is ultimately a matter of individual creativity, but societies differ in the degree to which they encourage it—Czar Nicholas I actually banned the use of the word *progress* from Russia. It is generally believed that an abundance of resources is necessary to turn an invention into a successful innovation because there must be sufficient support both to continue doing things the way they have always been done and to simultaneously try doing the same things in a new way, but a lack of resources can inspire invention when materials or goods intended or habitually used for one purpose must be turned to another end. High labor costs or other barriers to the growth of capital present challenges that can tempt inventors (Mokyr, 1992). Societies in which the dominant religion asserts human dominance over nature have been more technologically inventive than those that stress the human as a part of or subordinate to nature.

Rewarding inventors economically through the mechanism of intellectual property rights is deemed to be so effective that such rights were included in the U.S. Constitution itself. Other factors that lead some individuals to be more inventive than others are a tolerance for risk and confidence that there is a safety net. Invention is often the result of sheer play (Stone, 1995) or of the desire to create something beautiful (van Creveld, 1991). There are cultures in which more time is spent decorating a tool than will be spent in its use. Personal frustration can also play a role—James Watt invented the steam engine after his workshop was closed down because he hadn't served an apprenticeship (Pearton, 1984).

There have been experiments in trying to design environments in which creativity will flourish, but it is difficult to determine all of the pertinent factors. The isolation of research parks is often not particularly successful, apparently because they lack the stimulation of urban environments (Massey, Quintas, & Wield, 1992). Invention is triggered when individuals with different types of knowledge come together to solve common problems, as happened notably with the printing press and is happening

again with the internet. There has been a lot of experimentation with "technology incubators" as a means of stimulating innovation by providing a technology-intensive working environment, but these are rarely successful, perhaps because this approach puts the working tools ahead of the problem to be solved or the idea to be implemented. One successful innovation can either enable—or require—further invention to cope with changes in the technological system (King & Cushman, 1995). Although the historical image of the lone inventor retains its rhetorical power, today invention is most often the product of teams (Dosi, 1988). When the same invention appears almost simultaneously in places that are far apart, as happened with television, it provides evidence of the fact that new ideas always rest on the ideas of others. The development of the scientific method stimulated technological creativity by providing a way of systematically breaking a problem down into its parts.

INNOVATION

Because economic thought developed before industrialization, technologies were not included among the factors of production considered to be of economic value (Blaug, 1978). This situation didn't change until the 1930s, when Schumpeter (1939) argued that innovation was responsible for launching long cycles of economic growth. There was an immediate response because his ideas were seen as offering a clue as to how to bring the worldwide Depression to an end (Dodgson, 1993). By the early 1980s, innovation had become an identifying characteristic of several information industries,[6] with some even arguing it should be its own subfield within economics (Hepworth, 1989).

Innovations affect the operations of the market because they present structural breaks (Kogut, 1993) through the alteration of technological systems. They offer the corporations that control them temporary monopolies that can be of enormous economic value (Dollar & Wolff, 1993; Hills, 1992). Because such monopolies are *only* temporary, however, corporations are encouraged to continually innovate. The sharing of knowledge that leads to innovation among networked firms is one of their important sources of value (Antonelli, 1992). A number of different inventions may appear in response to the same social or technical problem. It is a sign of movement to the innovation stage when there is rivalry between systems based on different inventions (Williams, 1975). "Standards wars,"[7] which pit different technical solutions to the same problem against each other, have been seen in media industries as diverse as television, mobile telephony, and computer operating systems.

Bringing people together is as important for innovation as it is for invention. Silicon Valley is a premiere example of the role of physical proximity in creating an "island of innovation" (Hilpert, 1992). It is for this reason that cities are increasingly described as information processing centers (Sassen, 1991), governments have sought to link geographically dispersed researchers via the network that became the internet (Abbate, 1999), and corporations form alliances to facilitate knowledge sharing and information flow (Antonelli, 1992). It used to be assumed that the invention-innovation-diffusion cluster was a linear process, but it is now acknowledged that invention and innovation can take place at any stage and that users can play important roles in product design (Greenstein, Lizardo, & Spiller, 1997).

DIFFUSION

The study of the diffusion of technologies has been an important stream of research in media studies since the 1950s. The findings of thousands of such studies have been synthesized by Everett Rogers (1983), who defines diffusion as "the process by which an innovation is communicated through certain channels over time among members of a social system" (p. 5). Diffusion may occur either through deliberate campaigns or through spontaneous "contagion" (Valente, 1995).

There are five steps in the diffusion process: (a) knowledge—learning about an innovation and how it functions, (b) persuasion—forming a positive attitude toward an innovation, (c) decision—making the choice to experiment with an innovation, (d) implementation—experimenting with the innovation, and (e) confirmation—making a commitment to either take up the innovation permanently or reject it. Features of an innovation that influence individual and collective decisions include relative advantage (Is it better than that it will replace?), compatibility (Will it work with other technologies already in use?), complexity (Is it difficult to use?), trialability (Is it possible to experiment with the innovation before committing to it?), and observability (Are the results of one person's experimentation with the technology visible to others?). Individuals may be free to make adoption decisions on their own, or they may be dependent on the decisions of their community or organization. One of the features of networked technologies is that they generate a binary condition in which one is either in or out of a circle of activity, which encourages adoption.

Thousands of studies in many different societies have shown that there are consistent differences in the rate at which individuals will take up innovations. Innovators (about 2.5% of the population) are those who take an invention and bring it into use; they may be marginal to society as a whole but have resources, a sense of adventure, tolerance of ambiguity, and a willingness to experiment. Early adopters (13.5%) tend to be well-educated and upwardly mobile individuals with some ambition and a capacity to cope with uncertainty and risk; they often play leadership roles in their communities as individuals whose actions are watched by others. The early majority (34%) are those who have observed the successes of early adopters but make their own decisions with some deliberation. The late majority (34%) start with skepticism but ultimately are convinced. Laggards (16%) are more traditional and may never take up an innovation, even if it is widely used in their communities.

Media tend to diffuse very quickly. It took only 50 years for the printing press to spread across Europe (Eisenstein, 1979), 20 years for the telegraph to develop into a global network (Headrick, 1990), and 10 years for television to appear in almost every home once it had been commercialized following World War II. A text-only internet became available to early adopters outside of the initial research community (though still confined to academia) in the 1980s, and it was with the inventions that led to the graphical and hypertextual features of the Web that the early majority began to develop in the mid-1990s. Because socioeconomic, political, or cultural factors often impede access to the Web—*adoption* in diffusion terms—the difference between those communities in which the late majority group has appeared and those in which it is still at an early adoption stage is often described as the "digital divide." Such differences are not new with digital information technologies, however. The same phenomenon in the print and broadcast environments was referred to as the "knowledge gap."[8]

◆ The Contemporary Global Information Infrastructure

The biggest single machine that has ever been created is today's global information infrastructure (GII), a medium that makes it possible to use one technological system for all the kinds of content and uses handled by multiple media in the past. The features of this infrastructure as a medium are so different from those of earlier media that it is worth examining them in some detail.

These differences begin with the shift from a technological to a meta-technological system. The global information infrastructure is best described as a "network of networks" (Noam, 1994), for what we experience as a single network is really made up of numerous networks that are owned and managed by different organizations and countries. Through the important regulatory mandate of interconnection—the rule that networks must connect with each other so that information can flow seamlessly through them—these networks pass messages along without user involvement, but the multiplicity of networks actually involved makes the legal and economic issues raised by the information infrastructure quite complex.

Although digitization of national infrastructures has proceeded at variable rates, it was in 1980 that it could be said that the system became global. In that year, the Consultative Committee for International Telephony and Telegraphy (CCITT), a specialized committee of the International Telecommunications Union (ITU) with responsibility for decisions regarding technical standards for telecommunications, decided that innovation had reached the stage at which it was possible to begin discussing global standards that would make it possible to transmit any kind of information anywhere via a single network that one could plug into as easily as one plugs in a telephone. The set of standards developed was called the ISDN, for the Integrated Services Digital Network. As an early participant in the development of those standards noted, the ISDN was a turning point that simultaneously served as an ideal type, a project goal, a specific set of standards, and a system put into place on the ground (Rutkowski, 1983).

THE CONVERGENCE OF TECHNOLOGIES

This network came into being as a result of what is known as the "convergence of technologies," meaning the convergence of computing and communication technologies. Technological convergence of this kind was made possible by the shift from analog to digital modes of transmitting information, discussed in more detail in Chapter 7 (this volume). Throughout the 20th century, these technologies were moving toward convergence as each underwent significant innovation, but World War II provided a great stimulus. The first legal problems arising from this convergence—which brought intelligence into the telecommunications network, thus vastly expanding its capabilities—arose in the 1950s (Pool, 1983). In the 1960s, it was widespread enough that its effects were beginning to be felt society-wide, and regulatory agencies such as the Federal Communications Commission (FCC) began to consider how the new technological systems should be regulated, undertaking a series of "computer inquiries" over a couple of decades to help the agency decide just what to do. By the early 21st century, the network of converged technologies is ubiquitous across the globe and used by millions on a daily basis.

This type of convergence appears within a long human history of finding ways to do more with media by bringing them together with other types of tools and technologies. The first medium of language converged with the material world when writing systems came into being about 6,000 years ago. Writing converged with industrial technologies with the printing press in the mid-15th century. Media converged with electricity in the mid-19th century, first producing the telegraph and then the electrified (and thus vastly more productive) printing press, the telephone, and finally the radio, marking the first stage in the history of the information society. And since the convergence of computing and communication technologies under discussion here, media are also converging with the human body.

The convergence of computing and communication technologies brought with it functional convergence, but it must be remembered that patterns of using particular technologies were themselves choices out of a wider array of potential uses with which there had been experimentation. The telephone, for example, provided a means of communal storytelling and singing in the rural Midwest—particularly valuable in the winter—as long as party lines[9] made that possible, and in the late 19th century in Hungary, the telephone was used as a news medium (Boettinger, 1976; Brooks, 1976; Casson, 1910; Pool, 1977; Pound, 1926). Social and cultural dimensions of convergence are referred to as globalization. Clearly, the type of information infrastructure that technological convergence brought about has made it easier for political convergence to take place in two senses: First, regional governance has grown in relative importance, as with the North American Free Trade Agreement (NAFTA) and the European Union (EU). And second, it has become easier for nation-states to harmonize their regulatory systems with each other and to enhance the transparency of the activities of each to each other (Florini, 2000).[10] Economically, the new technologies have also made it possible for corporations to grow larger in size and thus have contributed to convergence in the form of a reduction of competition in favor of oligopolies.

CHARACTERISTICS OF THE NET

A first global information infrastructure was built in mid-19th century with the telegraph system, but use of that infrastructure was limited because there were relatively few points of access, technical expertise was required, the length of messages was limited, only text messages could be sent, and it was expensive. Today's digital and broadband global information infrastructure exhibits very different characteristics.

Ubiquity. With the appearance of wireless means of accessing the internet, the system has become genuinely global, and the advent of the community wireless movement[11]—in which everyone within a community has free access to the internet if they have a wireless connection, itself rapidly dropping in cost—will go far toward enabling ubiquity within community as well as across it. Print had the potential of ubiquity, but transport of messages from one geographic region to another was slow, costly, and difficult. The ease of achieving global reach affects the scale at which Web-based operations may unfold in ways that are being seen in the nature of organizational form, the growing oligopolization of the mass media, and the social, political, and cultural aspects of globalization. Shifts in scale are one of the most important ways in which technologies differ from each other (Abu-Lughod, 1984). Of course, ubiquity is only a *potential*—actual use patterns depend on the many dimensions of access.

Accessibility. Although *access* is usually referred to as if it is a singular concept, in reality, a number of different factors are involved in determining whether there is *effective* access. Being within the technological reach of the network, now ubiquitous through wireless technologies but not nearly so with wired, is only one dimension of access. To actually use the network, one must also own or have the right to use a technology that interfaces with the network, the economic means to support an internet connection, training in how to use the interface, and knowledge of the benefits to be accrued through use. Language, culture, and literacy requirements can also be barriers to access.

Some of these dimensions of access are susceptible to policy interventions, such as the universal service mandate of the U.S. Telecommunications Act of 1996 that there must be internet access in schools, libraries, and medical facilities in an effort to ensure that everyone in the United States has a publicly available interface with the internet. Some barriers to access are

less amenable to policy but do respond to individual-, commercial-, and community-level efforts, as seen in the proliferation of language translation software, the posting of Web sites in multiple languages, and development of Web resources in languages that serve relatively small communities. Cultural and personal preference *not* to use the internet, however, will—and should—remain; studies show that even at the highest levels of income, 2% of the population consistently chooses not to have a telephone in the home.

Potentially Nonhierarchical. Broadcasting and telecommunications historically were always organized hierarchically, whether through the material design of a system (as with wired telephony) or through the organizational structure through which decisions regarding content and distribution were made (as with over-the-air broadcasting). It is popular to describe the internet, in contrast, as nonhierarchical, but it is important to remember that a *potentially* nonhierarchical environment can go either way and that it is possible for some areas within the internet to be organized hierarchically, while others are not.

There is no doubt that the internet was deliberately developed as a decentralized structure to serve the defense need for a communication system that could survive attack because there was no "center" and because there were myriad paths through which messages could get from here to there. Huber (1987) uses the term *geodesic* to refer to this characteristic of the internet, after Buckminster Fuller's development of geodesic architecture in which load and stress on a system are dispersed equally throughout rather than being focused on certain points. Although it has been discovered that certain patterns of information flow are repeated at every level of the structure—Huber describes this feature as "fractal," after the mathematics of self-repeating patterns—it is still possible for some of those patterns to be rigidly structured, but others are not, and for pockets of nonhierarchical uses to remain even within rigidly defined structures.

The degree to which the physical aspects of the infrastructure are hierarchically designed and the degree to which the organizational and communicative aspects are treated in this manner are two different things. Although the technological aspects of the infrastructure remain essentially nonhierarchical, the modes of control and use are becoming less so in response to several factors: With commercialization of the internet in the early 1990s, it was suggested that billing internet-based activities would require centralization (MacKie-Mason & Varian, 1994), although models have developed for doing this virtually without affecting the degree to which other internet-based activities might be bound by a hierarchical structure. The internet is often imaged as a diffuse cloud, but access to the internet is managed by internet service providers (ISPs) that themselves provide a structure and more regulation of speech than is permitted in the mass media in the United States under the First Amendment (Braman & Lynch, 2003). Many national governments would like to restrict the content to which their citizens have access and thus build firewalls that add structure to filter content. The most important factor reducing the nonhierarchical experience of using the internet, however, is the concern over national security that has spiked since September 11, 2001, which has provided a justification for centralized surveillance of personal, interpersonal, and public uses of the internet.

Interactive. However aggressively, the audience participates in determining for themselves the meaning of messages, television, and radio. Print can be two-way but is highly asynchronous when it is so. Telephony is interactive, but there are limits to the number of people who can be involved in any given conversation. One of the most important features of today's information infrastructure is that it enables group interactivity, making interactivity in effect a medium in itself.

Most games, hypertext narratives, and database interfaces claim to be interactive but actually offer only branching pathways, the content of each of which is predetermined. Stone (1995) identifies several characteristics of real interactivity: mutual and simultaneous activity on the part of both participants (usually working toward the same goal, but not necessarily), mutual interruptibility (each participant must be able to interrupt the other, mutually and simultaneously, so that the goal of a conversation may change as the conversation unfolds), graceful degradation (it must be possible to handle unanswerable questions in such a way that it doesn't halt the conversation), limited look-ahead (both parties must be interruptible, so that there is a limit to how much of the shape of the conversation can be anticipated by either party), no default (there must be no preplanned path for the conversation, which develops fully only in the course of interaction), and the impression of an infinite database (there is no limit to the information and types of responses each side may experience from the other).

◆ Media as Technologies

Analysis of the effects of use of media began to arise in the mid-19th century, once electrification began to change the scale, speed, and intensity with which they were experienced. It was not until the early 20th century, however, that the media began to be examined as technologies per se.

Over time, theories of the media have displayed increasing sensitivity to the difference the technologies make to media effects. A second trend has been a shift from seeing technology as unnatural to understanding it as a natural extension of the human body and environment.

TECHNOLOGY AS
BARRIER TO EXPERIENCE

The first discussion of media as technologies was offered by scholars associated with the German Frankfurt School. Theodor Adorno, Max Horkheimer, and Walter Benjamin were concerned about the industrialization of culture, made possible by technologies such as the electrified printing press, the radio, and the camera that could produce multiple copies of works that, in more traditional media, were created in single copies ("one-offs") or in limited numbers. With the production of multiples came the wide distribution and commoditization that, these authors argued, led to a loss of creativity and of the critical power of art. There was also a concern that the reproducibility of culture with these technologies meant that it was no longer the expression of authentic experience, exacerbating the alienation that was a consequence of all forms of industrialization and voiding the human capacity for making meaning through ritual (Negt, 1978; Ronell, 1989).

Frankfurt School analyses also saw technology as destructive of political experience, for without authenticity, it was believed to be no longer possible to have the kind of genuine public sphere envisioned by Habermas (1991) as the space in which public discourse about matters of public concern could take place separate from the state. The notion of the public sphere was predicated on the idea that an autonomous class politics could exist only with autonomous production of discourse—and such production was no longer possible because the media operate as a closed institution devoted only to commoditization.

Through contemporary eyes, it can be seen that these authors were educated in a "high" or elite art tradition and were reacting in large part to the development of popular culture forms that are now seen as creative and potentially critical in their own way. Their negative analyses of technology were also driven, however, by the experience of witnessing perhaps the most dangerous and destructive technologization of social life the world has seen, for Frankfurt School scholars had to flee the Nazis to save their jobs and, very soon, their lives.

Many of their insights were profound, and they have had an enduring impact on the development of critical theory (Held, 1980) both in North America and in Europe. The notion that commoditization vacates cultural forms of their fundamental human value has been further elaborated; Hyde (1983), for example, argues that once a gift is sold, it can no longer function as a gift. Whether the reproducibility of culture has led to standardization remains an open debate (Enzensberger, 1992; Forgacs, 1990). James Carey (1989), who was also influenced by the work of Innis and McLuhan (discussed below), characterized the kind of communication developed by the culture industries as transmission rather than ritual. Contemporary thought about the loss of authenticity includes identifying originality (Dewdney, 1998) and attention[12] as scarce resources.

TECHNOLOGY AS
SHAPER OF EXPERIENCE

The next stage of theorization about media as technologies took the position that they did not prevent but *shaped* experience. Lewis Mumford (1934) first presented the idea that civilizations are formed in ways determined by the medium that dominates. Harold Innis (1951) elaborated on this idea at some length in his investigations of the way in which media technologies shaped the Canadian experience of time and space. These ideas launched a stream of work that has become known as medium theory, devoted to analyzing the ways in which society is affected by changes in the technologies used to communicate. Medium theory is distinguished from other approaches to the study of media effects because it focuses on the technologies involved rather than message content. Examples of its application include both micro-level studies of individual relations with their immediate locales (e.g., Meyrowitz, 1986) and macro-level examinations of the impact of media technologies on international relations (e.g., Comor, 1996; Deibert, 1997).

TECHNOLOGY AS EXPERIENCE

Innis's work on entire technological systems and society writ large inspired his student, Marshall McLuhan, to turn to the impact on the individual human body. McLuhan's famous phrase "the medium is the message" summarized his insight that each communication technology extends a particular human sense—radio, for example, extends the capacity of the human ear; photography extends the eye; and the computer extends the central nervous system and the brain. It is for this reason, he argues, that human relationships are so deeply affected by the media technology through which communications take place.

McLuhan was writing during the period in which self-awareness of the transformation to an information society was taking place, and he was very much the theorist of the first "multimedia" experiences of the 1960s. Responding to the first experiences of global sharing of television content—with the President John F. Kennedy assassination and then with the Muhammad Ali boxing match—he suggested that electronic media were creating a "global village."[13] Both words in this phrase carried important meaning: The globalization he envisioned has undeniably become the dominant feature of social life at the beginning of the 21st century. The word *village,* with its premodern connotations, was important to McLuhan because he believed that the linear logics promoted by print would be disrupted by the aurally oriented electronic environment in ways that would encourage the development of social forms more akin to the premodern than the modern. Of course, we have not and cannot return to the world as it was experienced thousands of years ago; Ong (1982) describes the change McLuhan was talking about as "secondary" orality, necessarily different from the kind of orality experienced before there had been any exposure to print. However, McLuhan's work presaged much of postmodern thought as well as discoveries by cognitive psychologists about changes in the ways that people process information, depending on the dominant technologies in their environment.

McLuhan deeply influenced a generation of media scholars who were young during the 1960s, even though his work was ignored in academia for many years. The failure to immediately pick up McLuhan's ideas as a basis for research was probably due to the way in which he presented his thoughts. It was McLuhan who first broke up the rigidities of the printed page to produce books in which type ran in every direction, type and images were interspersed or overlay each other, and multiple texts were presented simultaneously so that their content interacted. The texts themselves had more in common with poetry than with scholarship. After his death, McLuhan's son made an attempt to systematize the work (McLuhan & McLuhan, 1992), but it may well have been the maturation as scholars of those who were influenced by his work in youth that has finally brought scholarly attention to McLuhan's work. Today, an entire stream of literature, referred to as work on media ecology,[14] has grown up around his oeuvre.

TECHNOLOGY AS REALITY

With postmodern theory, attention has turned away from the impact that media technologies have on our experience of reality to the argument that the world they create *is* reality. Baudrillard (1983) uses the concept of "hyperreality" as a way of talking about the use of media technologies to communicate about the symbolic rather than the material world. In the contemporary electronic environment, those symbols are agents that can actually make things happen. Hookway (1999) thus uses the term *demons* to describe the way in which many operations in our daily lives are triggered electronically, drawing on the medieval concept of agency that is neither human nor divine.

Although McLuhan talked about media technologies as extensions of human senses, today, increasingly, the biological and technological are literally merging in the "cyborg" (Haraway, 1991). The U.S. Department of Defense has issued calls for research on the codesign of humans and weapons, using biotechnology for the first and digital information technologies for the second. Meanwhile, artists are experimenting with use of their bodies as permanent roving cameras, computer chips have been implanted into animals for tracking purposes and into researchers who are experimenting with the consequences, and scientists are developing ways of linking silicon directly to the neural cells of our brains.

TECHNOLOGICAL DETERMINISM

The theories presented in the previous section all suggest that technologies shape the world in which we live. In its extreme form, this is the position of technological determinism, but this position is only one along a spectrum of positions in the direction and strength of causality between technologies and society. Differences in position matter because they suggest differences in attitude toward technology and, therefore, in its uses and in the analysis of risks, as well as opportunities taken into account during policymaking for technology (Kroker, 1984). None of the thinkers discussed here are extreme technological determinists. The opposite position is that society completely determines technology.

The position taken here lies midway along the spectrum. Theoretical pluralism is necessary to fully analyze any specific event or process, as each is always unique to its historical conjuncture and results from the intersection of multiple causal forces. Thus, although it is true that technologies can have structural effects on society as well as on individual cognition, it is also true that it is society that determines just how technologies will be used. And although it is true that technologies have changed human history at many points in the past, it is also the case that the continuity, speed, and ultimately radical nature of technological innovation over the past century and a half have made technological change of particular importance at this point in history.

Technomancy—projecting the future from technologies—is a variant on technological determinism that provided the basis of technological forecasting from the beginning of the 20th century (Schiffer, 1991). The phrase "neo-technological determinism" has been coined to refer to driving policy choices in service to the development and diffusion of technologies themselves rather than to social goals (Ferguson, 1986). Technological determinism in any form is damaging to policy processes because it makes critical work impossible (Rowland, 1986) and suggests that all problems can be solved. We can thus speak of "doing" infrastructure as a social process because of the mutually causative nature of the development of technological systems (Star & Ruhleder, 1996).

◆ Notes

1. Marshall McLuhan's prolific thinking about the effects of new information technologies stimulated numerous lines of theoretical exploration and research; among his books from the 1950s through the 1970s either still or back in print and thus easily available are *The Gutenberg Galaxy: The Making of Typographic*

Man (1962), *The Mechanical Bride: Folklore of Industrial Man* (2001), *The Medium Is the Massage* (with Quentin Fiore; 2001a), and *Understanding Media: The Extensions of Man* (1994).

2. The Maginot Line was the use of the ancient technique of building holes in the ground as a defense against new technologies such as airplanes during World War I.

3. A "dumb" terminal has no intelligence of its own but only provides an interface with another computer, enabling the user to access that computer's intelligence from afar.

4. Cultural tensions raised by moving communications to the internet are often the subject of discussion in meetings of the National Association of Media, Arts, and Culture (NAMAC) and the Association of American Cultures (TAAC).

5. When the level of information intensity within an organization is dependent on the extent to which it is networked, it is referred to as "network density" (see Hagedorn, 1993).

6. Fritz Machlup (1980) was the first to distinguish among specific industries in the information sector of the economy in the early 1980s; research and development (R&D) was one solely devoted to innovation, and others required innovation as an input.

7. "Standards wars" have taken place with almost every new information technology (see, e.g., Cerni & Gray, 1983; Crane, 1978; Kahin & Abbate, 1995).

8. Rural sociologists Donohue, Tichenor, and Olien (1975) developed the knowledge gap hypothesis and pursued it for decades. The powerful concept has provided the foundation for influential research programs by many others, including the following: Viswanath and Finnegan (1996), Ettema and Kline (1977), and Kwak (1999).

9. A party line was a telephone line shared by multiple households, each of which had a different ring so that a family could tell when a phone call was for its household. For most purposes, only a single party would respond to a telephone call, but communal purposes could be served by having everyone get on the party line at the same time.

10. The concept of "transparency" is a driving principle in international relations today; for a succinct synthesis of the literature on the subject, see Florini (2000).

11. The "community wireless movement" is the name given to the early 21st-century move by a rapidly growing number of cities in the United States that are in the process of providing free access to the internet through a community-wide wireless network provided by the municipality through a wireless hub.

12. The term *attention economy* was coined in the 1990s by Alan Froomkin, but the same concept is explored in treatments of social aspects of time in the work of authors such as Appadurai (1997) and Nowotny (1990).

13. The notion of the global village appeared in a number of Marshall McLuhan's writings of the 1960s and are newly accessible in republications of several of his books (e.g., McLuhan & Fiore, 2001b).

14. In addition to work by authors already discussed here such as McLuhan, Innis, Carey, Ong, Postman, Mumford, Eisenstein, Meyrowitz, Postman, and Ellul, other works that fall into the category of media ecology include Bolter (1984), Boorstin (1961/1992), Goody (1977), Havelock (1982), and Sontag (1977/2001).

◆ References

Abbate, J. (1999). *Inventing the internet.* Cambridge: MIT Press.

Abu-Lughod, J. L. (1984). Communication and the metropolis: Spatial drift and the reconstitution of control. *Asian Journal of Communication, 2*(3), 12–30.

Antonelli, C. (Ed.). (1992). *The economics of information networks.* Amsterdam: North-Holland.

Appadurai, A. (1997). Consumption, duration, and history. In D. Palumbo-Liu & H. Ulrich Gumbrecht (Eds.), *Streams of cultural capital: Transnational cultural studies* (pp. 1–21). Stanford, CA: Stanford University Press.

Baudrillard, J. (1983). *Simulations*. New York: Semiotext(es).

Blaug, M. (1978). *Economic theory in retrospect* (3rd ed.). Cambridge, UK: Cambridge University Press.

Boettinger, H. M. (1976). *The telephone book*. Croton-on-Hudson, NY: Riverwood.

Bolter, J. D. (1984). *Turing's man: Western culture in the computer age*. Durham: University of North Carolina Press.

Boorstin, D. J. (1992). *The image: A guide to pseudo-events in America*. New York: Vintage. (Original work published 1961)

Braman, S. (1993). Harmonization of systems: The third stage of the information society. *Journal of Communication, 43*(3), 141–148.

Braman, S., & Lynch, S. (2003). Advantage ISP: Terms of service as media law. In L. F. Cranor & S. S. Wildman (Eds.), *Rethinking rights and regulations: Institutional responses to new communications* (pp. 249–278). Cambridge: MIT Press.

Branscomb, L. M. (Ed.). (1993). *Empowering technology: Implementing a US strategy*. Cambridge: MIT Press.

Brooks, J. (1976). *Telephone: The first hundred years*. New York: Harper & Row.

Carey, J. W. (1989). *Communication as culture: Essays on media and society*. Boston: Unwin Hyman.

Casson, H. N. (1910). *The history of the telephone*. Chicago: A. C. McClurg & Co.

Cerni, D., & Gray, E. M. (1983). *International telecommunications standards: Issues and implications for the '80s*. Boulder, CO: National Telecommunication & Information Administration, Department of Commerce.

Chandler, A. D., Jr. (1977). *The visible hand: The managerial revolution in American business*. Cambridge, MA: Belknap.

Comor, E. A. (Ed.). (1996). *The global political economy of communication: Hegemony, telecommunication and the information economy*. New York: Macmillan/St. Martin's.

Crane, R. J. (1978). Communication standards and the politics of protectionism: The case of colour television systems. *Telecommunications Policy, 2*(4), 267–281.

de Cauter, L. (1993). The panoramic ecstasy: On world exhibitions and the disintegration of experience. *Theory, Culture & Society, 10*, 1–23.

de Landa, M. (1991). *War in the age of intelligent machines*. New York: Zone.

Deibert, R. J. (1997). *Parchment, printing, and hypermedia: Communication and world order transformation*. New York: Columbia University Press.

Demchak, C. C. (1991). *Military organizations, complex machines: Modernization in the US armed services*. Ithaca, NY: Cornell University Press.

Dewdney, C. (1988). *Last flesh: Life in the transhuman era*. San Francisco: Harper San Francisco.

Dodgson, M. (1993). *Technological collaboration in industry: Strategy, policy and internationalization in innovation*. New York: Routledge.

Dollar, D., & Wolff, E. N. (1993). *Competitiveness, convergence, and international specialization*. Cambridge: MIT Press.

Donohue, G. A., Tichenor, P. J., & Olien, C. N. (1975). Mass media and the knowledge gap: A hypothesis reconsidered. *Communication Research, 2*(1), 3–23.

Dosi, G. (1988). The nature of the innovative process. In G. Dosi, C. Freeman, R. R. Nelson, G. Silverberg, & L. Soete (Eds.), *Technical change and economic theory* (pp. 222–238). New York: Pinter.

Dyson, G. B. (1997). *Darwin among the machines: The evolution of global intelligence*. New York: The Perseus Group.

Dyson, K. (Ed.). (1988). *Local authorities and new technologies: The European dimension*. Kent, UK: Croom Helm Ltd.

Eisenstein, E. L. (1979). *The printing press as an agent of change: Communications and cultural transformations in early-modern Europe*. Cambridge, UK: Cambridge University Press.

Ellul, J. (1964). *The technological society* (J. Wilkinson, Trans.). New York: Vintage.

Enzensberger, H. M. (1992). *Mediocrity & delusion* (M. Chalmers, Trans.). New York: Verso.

Ettema, J. S., & Kline, F. G. (1977). Deficits, differences, and ceilings: Contingent conditions for understanding the knowledge gap. *Communication Research, 4*(2), 179–202.

Ferguson, M. (Ed.). (1986), *New communication technologies and the public interest: Comparative perspectives on policy and research.* Beverly Hills, CA: Sage.

Fletcher, P. D., & Foy, D. O. (1994). Managing information systems in state and local government. *Annual Review of Information Science and Technology, 29*, 1–25.

Florini, A. M. (2000, March). *The politics of transparency.* Paper presented to the International Studies Association, Los Angeles.

Forecasting and Assessment in Science and Technology (FAST). (1983). *Proceedings of a workshop on environmental biotechnology.* Brussels: European Commission.

Forgacs, D. (1990). *Italian culture in the industrial era, 1880–1980.* New York: Manchester University Press.

Forsyth, D. J. C. (1990). *Technology policy for small developing countries.* New York: St. Martin's Press.

Fuller, R. B., & Applewhite, E. J. (1975). *Synergetics.* New York: Macmillan.

Giddens, A. (1984). *The constitution of society.* Berkeley: University of California Press.

Goody, J. (1977). *The domestication of the savage mind.* Cambridge, UK: Cambridge University Press.

Greenstein, S. M., Lizardo, M. M., & Spiller, P. T. (1997). *The evolution of large-scale information infrastructure in the United States.* Cambridge, MA: National Bureau of Economic Research.

Habermas, J. (1991). *Structural transformations of the public sphere: An inquiry into a category of bourgeois society.* Cambridge: MIT Press.

Hagedoorn, J. (1993). Strategic technology alliances and modes of cooperation in high-technology industries. In G. Grabher (Ed.), *The embedded firm: On the socioeconomics of industrial networks* (pp. 116–138). New York: Routledge.

Haraway, D. J. (1991). *Simians, cyborgs, and women: The reinvention of nature.* New York: Routledge.

Havelock, E. (1982). *Preface to Plato.* Cambridge, MA: Harvard University Press.

Headrick, D. R. (1990). *The invisible weapon: Telecommunications and international relations, 1851-1945.* New York: Oxford University Press.

Held, D. (1980). *Introduction to critical theory: Horkheimer to Habermas.* Berkeley: University of California Press.

Hepworth, M. (1989). *Geography of the information economy.* New York: Guilford.

Hills, J. (with Papathanassopoulos, S.). (1992). *The democracy gap: The politics of information and communication technologies in the United States and Europe.* New York: Greenwood.

Hilpert, U. (1992). *Archipelago Europe: Islands of innovation.* Brussels, Belgium: Commission of the European Communities, FAST Programme.

Hookway, B. (1999). *Pandemonium.* Princeton, NJ: Princeton Architectural Press.

Huber, P. (1987). *The geodesic network: 1987 report on competition in the telephone industry.* Washington, DC: U.S. Department of Justice, Antitrust Division.

Hudson, H. E. (1984). *When telephones reach the village: The role of telecommunications in rural development.* Norwood, NJ: Ablex.

Hyde, L. (1983). *The gift: Imagination and the erotic life of property.* New York: Vintage.

Innis, H. A. (1951). *The bias of communication.* Toronto: University of Toronto Press.

Itami, H. (with Roehl, T.). (1991). *Mobilizing invisible assets.* Cambridge, MA: Harvard University Press.

Kahin, B., & Abbate, J. (Eds.). (1995). *Standards policy for information infrastructure.* Cambridge: MIT Press.

Kanter, R. M. (1992). The future of bureaucracy and hierarchy in organizational theory: A report from the field. In P. Bourdieu & J. S. Coleman (Eds.), *Social theory for a changing society* (pp. 63–86). Boulder, CO: Westview.

King, S. S., & Cushman, D. P. (Eds.). (1995). *High-speed management and organizational communication in the 1990s.* Albany: SUNY Press.

Kogut, B. (Ed.). (1993). *Country competitiveness: Technology and the organizing of work.* Oxford, UK: Oxford University Press.

Kroker, A. (1984). *Technology and the Canadian mind: Innis/McLuhan/Grant.* New York: St. Martin's.

Kwak, N. (1999). Revisiting the knowledge gap hypothesis: Education, motivation, and media use. *Communication Research, 26*(4), 385–413.

Lawless, E. W. (1977). *Technology and social shock.* New Brunswick, NJ: Rutgers University Press.

Machlup, F. (1980). *Knowledge: Its creation, distribution, and economic significance.* Princeton, NJ: Princeton University Press.

MacKie-Mason, J. K., & Varian, H. (1994). Economic FAQs about the internet. *Journal of Economic Perspectives, 8*(3), 75–102.

Mansell, R., & Wehn, U. (Eds.). (1998). *Knowledge societies: Information technology for sustainable development.* Oxford, UK: Oxford University Press, on behalf of the United Nations.

Massey, D., Quintas, P., & Wield, D. (1992). *High tech fantasies: Science parks in society, science and space.* New York: Routledge.

McLuhan, M. (1962). *The Gutenberg galaxy: The making of typographic man.* Toronto: University of Toronto Press.

McLuhan, M. (1994). *Understanding media: The extensions of man.* Cambridge: MIT Press.

McLuhan, M. (2001). *The mechanical bride: Folklore of industrial man.* New York: Gingko Press.

McLuhan, M., & Fiore, Q. (2001a). *The medium is the massage.* New York: Gingko Press.

McLuhan, M., & Fiore, Q. (2001b). *War and peace in the global village* (3rd ed.). New York: Gingko Press.

McLuhan, M., & McLuhan, E. (1992). *Laws of media: The new science.* Toronto: University of Toronto Press.

Meyrowitz, J. (1986). *No sense of place: The impact of electronic media on social behavior.* New York: Oxford University Press.

Michaels, E. (1994). *Bad aboriginal art: Tradition, media, and technological horizon.* Minneapolis: University of Minnesota Press.

Mokyr, J. (1992). *Lever of riches: Technological creativity and economic progress.* New York: Oxford University Press.

Mowery, D. C., & Rosenberg, N. (1989). *Technology and the pursuit of economic growth.* Cambridge, UK: Cambridge University Press.

Mumford, L. (1934). *Technics and civilization.* New York: Harcourt Brace.

Negt, O. (1978). Mass media: Tools of domination or instruments of liberation: Aspects of the Frankfurt school's communication analysis. *New German Critique, 14,* 61–80.

Noam, E. M. (1994). Beyond liberalization: From the network of networks to the system of systems. *Telecommunications Policy, 18*(4), 286–294.

Novak, M. (1997). Transmitting architecture: The transphysical city. In A. Kroker & M. Kroker (Eds.), *Digital delirium* (pp. 260–271). New York: St. Martin's.

Nowotny, H. (1990). *In search of usable knowledge: Utilization contexts and the application of knowledge.* Boulder, CO: Westview.

Ong, W. J. (1982). *Orality and literacy: The technologizing of the word.* New York: Methuen.

Overman, E. S., & Cahill, A. G. (1994). Information, market government, and health policy: A study of health data organizations in the states. *Journal of Policy Analysis and Management, 13*(1), 435–453.

Overman, E. S., & Loraine, D. T. (1994). Information for control: Another management proverb? *Public Administration Review, 54*(2), 193–196.

Pearton, M. (1984). *Diplomacy, war and technology since 1830.* Lawrence: University Press of Kansas.

Pool, I. de Sola. (Ed.). (1977). *Social impact of the telephone.* Cambridge: MIT Press.

Pool, I. de Sola. (1983). *Technologies of freedom.* Cambridge: MIT Press.

Pondy, L. R. (1969). Effects of size, complexity, and ownership on administrative intensity. *Administrative Science Quarterly, 14,* 47–60.

Pound, P. (1926). *The telephone idea: Fifty years after.* New York: Greenberg.

Reddi, U. V. (1986). Leapfrogging the industrial revolution. In M. Traber (Ed.), *The myth of the information revolution: Social and ethical implications of information technology* (pp. 85–98). Beverly Hills, CA: Sage.

Rogers, E. M. (1983). *Diffusion of innovations* (3rd ed.). New York: Free Press.

Ronell, A. (1989). *The telephone book: Technology, schizophrenia, electric speech.* Lincoln: University of Nebraska Press.

Rowland, W. D. (1986). American telecommunications policy research: Its contradictory origins and influences. *Media, Culture & Society, 8,* 159–182.

Rutkowski, A. M. (1983). The integrated services digital network: Issues and options for the future. *Jurimetrics Journal, 24*(1), 19–42.

Sassen, S. (1991). *The global city: New York, London, Tokyo.* Princeton, NJ: Princeton University Press.

Scazzieri, R. (1993). *A theory of production: Tasks, processes, and technical processes.* Oxford, UK: Clarendon.

Schiffer, M. B. (1991). *The portable radio in American life.* Tucson: University of Arizona Press.

Schumpeter, J. (1939). *Business cycles: A theoretical, historical, and statistical analysis of the capitalist process.* New York: McGraw-Hill.

Smith, A. (1990). Towards a global culture? *Theory, Culture & Society, 7,* 171–191.

Sontag, S. (2001). *On photography.* New York: Picador. (Original work published 1977)

Star, S. L., & Ruhleder, K. (1996). Steps toward an ecology of infrastructure: Design and access for large information spaces. *Information Systems Research, 7*(1), 111–134.

Stewart, T. A. (1994, October 3). Your company's most valuable asset: Intellectual capital. *Fortune,* pp. 68–74.

Stone, A. R. (1995). *War of desire and technology at the close of the mechanical age.* Cambridge: MIT Press.

Theall, D. F. (1999). The carnivalesque, the internet and control of content: Satirizing knowledge, power and control. *Continuum: Journal of Media & Cultural Studies, 13*(2), 153–164.

Valente, T. W. (1995). *Network models of the diffusion of innovations.* Cresskill, NJ: Hampton.

van Creveld, M. (1991). *Technology and war: From 2000 BC to the present* (Rev. ed.). New York: Free Press.

Viswanath, K., & Finnegan, J. R., Jr. (1996). The knowledge gap hypothesis: Twenty-five years later. *Communication Yearbook, 19,* 187–227.

von Foerster, H. (1984). Principles in self-organization—In a socio-managerial context. In H. Ulrich & G. J. B. Probst (Eds.), *Self-organization and management of social systems: Insights, promises, doubts, and questions* (pp. 2–24). Berlin: Springer-Verlag.

Wiegele, T. C. (1991). *Biotechnology and international relations: The political dimensions.* Gainesville: University of Florida Press.

Williams, R. (1975). *Television: Technology and cultural form.* New York: Schocken.

Wilson, R., & Dissanayake, W. (Eds.). (1996). *Global/local: Cultural production and the transnational imaginary.* Durham, NC: Duke University Press.

Winner, L. (1990). *Autonomous technology: Technics-out-of-control as a theme in political thought.* Cambridge: MIT Press.

7

DIGITAL MEDIA

◆ Jan van Dijk

I n the latter part of the 20th century, a number of media appeared that were called new. Every time this happens in history, it is wise to ask ourselves what exactly is "new" about these media. Hardly ever are so-called new media completely new. Most often, they combine characteristics of old media. Today, insecurity appears to be high as there is a whole range of expressions for contemporary new media—digital media, interactive media, multimedia, and information and communication technologies—or indications of particular new media, such as the personal computer and the internet.

In this chapter, the new media are called *digital media,* first of all. While defining their characteristics, we will come across the other indications, such as *interactive media* and *multimedia.* After these definitions, the capacities of digital media will be elaborated. What are the strong and weak capacities of these media as compared to other media? In the third section, we will deal with the most conspicuous process the digital media are engaged in: media convergence. Are the digital media integrating all known media in a single communication infrastructure? Or do they only mean another step in the process of media differentiation characterizing the 20th century? Subsequently, the main applications of the digital media are described: the internet, interactive broadcasting, mobile telephony, or computing and computer games. In the final section, four fundamental issues will be selected from the many social aspects accompanying digital media diffusion in society: information and communication freedom, intellectual property rights, the unification and fragmentation of society, and the so-called digital divide.

◆ *Characteristics*

DIGITAL CODE

The first defining characteristic of digital media has given them their name. Digital code is a *technical* media characteristic, with great substantial consequences for communication. Digital code means that in using computer technology, every item of information and communication can be transformed and transmitted in strings of 1s and 0s called bytes, with every single 1 or 0 being a bit. This artificial code replaces the natural codes of the analog creation and transmission of items of information and communication (e.g., by beams of light and vibrations of sound).

The first substantial effect of the transformation of all media contents in the same digital code is the uniformity and standardization of these contents. Form and substance cannot be separated as easily as many people think they can. Digital code is not a neutral form (van Dijk, 1999). It starts with initially cutting in pieces undivided analog items of information and communication (signs) and then recombining them in the digitized forms of images, sounds, texts, and numerical data. These forms are produced using not only the same basic code but also the same languages, such as HTML (hypertext mark-up language), the graphic code for all pages of the World Wide Web. The resulting forms are known for their great similarities in menu and navigation structures when they are programmed in computer software. The first perceivable cultural consequence is the growing practice of processing, reworking, and adapting sources other people have created, despite all diversity of original contents available in the digital media. This means more use of preprogrammed contexts and collages of contents after their initial fragmentation. Therefore, a related consequence is the fragmenting effect on information and communication processes, as it is observed in the cut-and-paste practice of word processing, for example (Heim, 1987).

Another effect of using uniform digital code is the increase in the quantity of items of information and communication. This code makes their production, recording, and distribution much easier. Supported by the exponentially rising storage capacity of computers and their disks, unlimited amounts of items are produced. This goes to such extremes that the selection of these items results in one of the greatest problems of using digital media: information overload.

A final and perhaps most important effect of using digital code is breaking up the traditional linear order of large units of information and communication, such as texts, images, sounds, and audiovisual programs, so that they can be transformed into hyperlinks of items liable to be perceived and processed in the order that the reader, viewer, or listener wants. This transformation from linear to hypertext media would have been impossible without digital code. The social and cultural consequences of this "revolution" in media production and use will be big. The reason why we do not yet realize the full potential of this transformation is that it has just started. Below it will be argued that digital media are still often used like the old linear analogous media, by simply converting existing printed forms into electronic ones and not using the capacities of the digital media to their fullest potential.

MULTIMEDIA FORM

Digital code enables a second defining characteristic of digital media, the *general* media characteristic of multimedia form. This means a combination of signs, symbol systems, communication kinds, and types of data in a single medium. Analogous media only possessed single media forms until the advent of television and motion pictures with sound. They were the media of the press (text), photography (images), and the telephone and radio (speech and sound).

The digital media give an extra impetus to multimedia forms beyond older multimedia such as film and television. All kinds of texts, figures, numerical data, windows, taskbars, and sound effects are added to the screens and speakers of traditional audiovisual media. In this way, the symbol systems (Goodman, 1968; Salomon, 1979) of linguistic, iconic, musical, logico-mathematical, and (partly) nonverbal signs are combined in a more or less artificial way.

Multimedia also can be called combinations of communication kinds (telecommunication, data communication, and mass communication) and data types (image, sound, text, and numerical data). Digital multimedia offer a potential stimuli richness and information density that are virtually unprecedented in media history. Multimedia forms may improve mental processing and learning (Salomon, 1979), provided that the plurality of signs, symbol systems, or types of data is combined in a reasonable way appropriate to the human mind and perception.

INTERACTIVITY

The third defining characteristic of the digital media is their interactivity. In a very general definition, *interactivity* is a sequence of action and reaction. It is remarkable how badly this crucial concept is (further) defined and made operational for research in media and communication studies. Jensen (1999) has produced an exhaustive account of the laborious search by social and communication scientists for a suitable definition. Jensen himself wishes to reserve the concept of interactivity for mediated communication. Van Dijk (1999) and van Dijk and de Vos (2001) offer an operational definition that is supposed to be valid for face-to-face communication as well. These authors define interactivity at four levels, acknowledging, like many other authors, that this concept is a multidimensional construct. The levels of interactivity are supposed to be appropriate to define how interactive a particular digital medium is.

The most elementary level of interactivity is the possibility of establishing two-sided or multilateral communication. This is the space dimension. All digital media offer this possibility to a certain extent. However, most often, the downloaded link or the supply side of Web sites, interactive television, and computer programs is much wider than the uplink or the retrieval made by their users.

The second level of interactivity is the degree of synchronicity. This is the time dimension. It is well known that an uninterrupted sequence of action and reaction usually improves the quality of interaction. However, some interactive media, such as electronic mail, are used for their lack of synchronicity. Producing and receiving messages can be done at self-chosen times and places, and one is allowed to think longer about a reply. Yet, this goes at the expense of immediate reactions and of the ability to send all kinds of verbal and nonverbal signs simultaneously.

The third level of interactivity is the extent of control exercised by the interacting parties. This behavioral dimension is defined as the ability of the sender and the receiver to switch roles at any moment. Furthermore, it is about the control over the events in the process of interaction. Interactivity in terms of control is the most important dimension in all interactivity definitions of media and communication studies (see Jensen, 1999). It means attention to the division of power in the interface of media and humans or between humans in both mediated and face-to-face communication. At this level, interactivity means, among other things, that the user is able to intervene into the program or representation itself, not simply to read it differently (Cameron, 1995). As digital media are more interactive than traditional media, they enable a shift in the balance of power to the user and the side of demand. However, this potential is not fully realized in present uses of digital media in which a supply-side view still dominates the design of the medium.

The fourth and highest level of interactivity is acting and reacting with an understanding of meanings and contexts by all interactors involved. This mental dimension is a necessary condition for full interactivity, for example, in physical conversation and computer-mediated communication. Currently, this level of interactivity should be reserved for the interaction between human beings and animals with a consciousness unless one has much confidence in interactions directed by artificial intelligence.

The digital media are defined by all three characteristics simultaneously. Traditional television possesses a multimedia form, but it is not interactive or based on digital code. Traditional telephony is interactive, but it has no multimedia form and does not work with digital code. In contrast, interactive television has all the characteristics of digital media, and advanced generations of mobile and fixed telephony incorporate both digital code and multimedia forms.

◆ Capacities

What are the strong and weak abilities of the digital media? In the past 25 years, much research has been done for the opportunities and limitations of mediated communication as compared with face-to-face communication. Since the 1980s, this has been extended to comparisons of the new media or computer-mediated communication and the old media. Items of comparison are the communication characteristics that these media possess and the communication needs they are able to fulfill. One tradition in this type of channel comparison research looks for the objective characteristics of media. Examples of this tradition are the social presence approach (Short, Williams, & Christie, 1976), the reduced social context cues approach (Kiesler, Siegel, & McQuire, 1984), and the information or media richness approach (Daft & Lengel, 1984).

The other tradition emphasizes the (inter)subjective characteristics. According to this tradition, media have no fixed, technologically determined properties but shifting qualities that are socially constructed and depend on their appropriation and use in particular social contexts. Examples are the social information-processing model (Fulk, Steinfield, Schmitz, & Power, 1987), the relational perspective (Walther, 1992, 1996), and social identity theory (Spears & Lea, 1992). Approaches classifying media according to the communication needs they are able to fulfill also form part of this tradition (Flanagin & Metzger, 2001; Rice, 1998).

Van Dijk (1993, 1999) has proposed an integrated objective and (inter)subjective approach identifying so-called communication capacities. These capacities are both defining and enabling the use of old and new media. They allow a systematic comparison of old media, new media, and face-to-face communication. The following capacities are briefly described now to assess what one is able to do with digital media.

Strong capacities of the digital media are their *speed* and *geographical reach* (place independence). In this respect, they look like the telephone and broadcasting. Using the internet, one can send a message to the other side of the world in a few seconds. Face-to-face communication and print media are only able to connect to proximate others instantly. However, the *social* reach of digital media lags behind as only a small minority of the world population has a computer and access to the internet. Even in the technologically advanced Western and Eastern Asian countries, less than half of the population, on average, had access to the internet in the year 2002.

Another strong capacity of digital media is their high *storage potential*. This potential is low in face-to-face communication, which depends on inadequate human memory. It used to be low in telephony before the invention of answering devices. In digital media, one can store much more than in printed media and analog broadcast media.

The *accuracy* or exactness of the information transmitted also is an advantage of digital media as compared with the telephone and face-to-face communication. In the latter, media signals often are ambiguous. Historically, accuracy also has been a strong asset of print media. Digital media add the exactness of numerical data and the informativeness of images. Both the storage capacity and the accuracy of the new media enable governments, politicians, and managers to control the rising complexity of organizations and society at large.

The *selectivity* of messaging and addressing is perhaps the most important capacity of digital media. Below, we will see that it has a strong impact on social relationships. Selectivity is rather low in the face-to-face communication of groups and other collectives. Here individuals have to make appointments and separate themselves from each other. Much of the communication using print media is not addressed, except for personal letters, of course. The same goes for broadcasting. The telephone was the first fully selective medium. Digital media advance this capacity, enabling systematic selections of (parts of) groups, individuals, and media content using electronic mailing lists, program guides, and the like.

One calls the digital media interactive, but actually their *interactivity* does not reach the high (fourth) level, which can be attained in face-to-face communication. Some digital media do not offer anything more than two-way traffic and a central store-and-forward agency serving as some kind of answering device. Clearly, this goes for electronic mail. In the other digital media, such as electronic journals, interactive broadcasting, and digital information services on the internet, the user has little control over content offered. The user does not intervene with this content; rather, she or he chooses from menus and reacts. Moreover, full-fledged conversation is lacking in digital media. One is not able to exchange all the signals (often) desired. This even goes for the high-quality videophone and videoconferencing.

In terms of *stimuli richness,* no other medium is able to beat face-to-face communication. The reason is clear: All current digital media are sensory poor. This is especially so for computer networks transmitting only lines of text and data. Broadband networks and offline multimedia offer a greater richness of stimuli, perhaps even an overload, in all kinds of combinations of images, sounds, data, and text. However, the combination of these stimuli is not natural but artificial. Some stimuli can be strengthened while others recede, but there is still a clear lack of the movement and body language provided by someone who is close.

As a consequence, of the last two capacities described, the *complexity* that one is able to achieve collectively by using them is not high. Research indicates that one is able to make contacts, ask questions, exchange information, and make appointments very well using computer networks, but it appears to be difficult to negotiate, decide, explain difficult issues, and really get to know someone (see Rice, 1998).

A drawback of the present design of digital media is the low capacity for *privacy protection* they offer. Face-to-face communication can be secluded to a large degree. Current broadcasting and the press can be received anonymously. This does not apply for the new interactive broadcasting and electronic press media. In fact, all usage and, often, the personal characteristics of users are registered in the digital media. This is certainly the case for computer networks. For stand-alone computers and multimedia, it is less so because they are under the control of the user, but these media have memories that can be accessed.

◆ Media Convergence

Digital media enable and stimulate the most important contemporary media development: the convergence of telecommunication, data communication, and mass communication (Baldwin, McVoy, &

Steinfield, 1996). What is the nature of this convergence? Does it mean that all media will flow together in a single medium—for instance, an all-embracing broadband internet with different kinds of media serving as terminals? Will the digital media completely replace the old analog media in the process of convergence?

It appears that both forms of integration and differentiation are marking convergence. First, we will describe the forms of integration. A clear picture is produced by the integration of media in the *combined infrastructures* of telecommunication, data communication, and mass communication. The process started with the integration of telecommunication and data communication using modems or fax machines and producing the most important digital media in the end: electronic mail and the information services of the internet. In the next phase, maturing in the first decade of the 21st century, mass communication has been integrated by means of broadband infrastructures. The digital mobile telephony of the so-called second and third generations—notably, the Global Packet Radio System (GPRS) and the Universal Mobile Telecommunications System (UMTS)—introduces the services of Web sites, e-mail, short-message service (SMS), the videophone, games, and other audiovisuals on the relatively small screens of cellular phones. Extending the capacities of these services by sizable data transmissions, the mass communications of the press, broadcasting, and audiovisual services are inserted into the digital media environment of the interactive press or broadcasting and mobile computing. The last-called medium consists of a whole range of palmtop and laptop computers with bigger screens and more weight than cellular phones and connected to computer networks or the desktop computers of offices and homes.

At the turn of the century, the infrastructures connecting all these media were traditional cable or satellite networks and a narrowband internet using telephone networks. In the first decades of the current century, a transition has been made to broadband networks increasingly using fiber-optic cable or very high frequencies in the air (by satellite and antenna). Sometimes, these connections are called electronic highways.

The integration of these media also means a *combination of sign systems and data types* that is enabled by digital code and multimedia form and that offers more potential interactivity (see above). This substantial instead of technical integration will produce the biggest social and cultural effects in the actual media practices of producing and consuming digital content, as argued in this chapter.

All types of integration are spurring the *concentration of media corporations*. Particularly in the 1990s, most media companies in the sectors of telecommunication, data communication, and mass communication were transforming themselves into general media companies. This was stimulated by the internet hype in that decade. At the turn of the century, many companies returned to their core businesses. However, this has not ended the financial and economic drives behind the process of media concentration. Large media corporations will certainly not only become telephone companies, broadcasting organizations, press institutions, or internet businesses again.

The integration of media, infrastructures, and contents enables a mixture of social and communication structures not known in any modern complex society before. The levels of interpersonal (micro), organizational (meso), and societal (macro) communication are directly linked to produce a *network society* (Castells, 1996, 2001; van Dijk, 1991, 1999, 2001, 2002). This is the combined effect of media convergence and social communication needs in the management of a complex society. Hitherto, media linked the societal and the individual levels (e.g., broadcasting) or the interpersonal and organizational levels (e.g., telephony) in separate ways. Currently, an integrated medium such as the internet offers interpersonal communication (e-mail), organizational

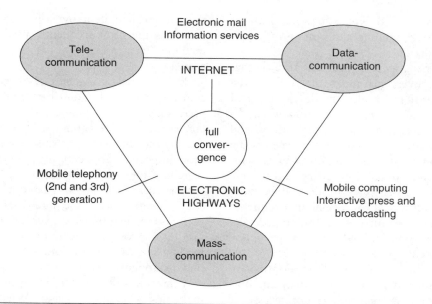

Figure 7.1   The Convergence of Telecommunication, Data Communication, and Mass Communication

communication (e-business), and societal communication (information services) all through the same channel. Even a single Web site of e-commerce, for instance, offers these opportunities all together.

These forms of integration inspire ideas of a complete mixture of digital media in a single medium (e.g., a broadband internet) and ideas of the disappearance of older analogous and digital media. These ideas are wrong. They are neglecting the tendencies of differentiation also appearing in the process of convergence.

The first form of differentiation is the present appearance of not less but *more media*. A prime lesson of media history in the former century was that most of the time, old media do not disappear with the advent of new ones, though this is predicted time and again. With the rise of the digital media, the printed press, the cinema, radio and television, the plain old telephone, the gramophone, and perhaps even the VCR will not disappear either. What happens instead is

that old media will acquire new uses and niches and be connected to the new digital media when this is deemed possible or desirable with the available technologies. When they cannot be linked, old and new media will refer to each other increasingly; for instance, this is presently being done in old media referring to www addresses.

A second form of differentiation involves all kinds of burgeoning *new communication groups, types, and applications*. The digital media do not produce less but more kinds of communication. Several more or less virtual groups and communities are being created between mass and interpersonal communication: mailing lists, newsgroups, target groups of interactive marketing, advertising and selling, (program) user groups, virtual teams and communities, and the producer or consumer groups of personal, Webcam, and interactive TV. New types of communication flourish, such as SMS telephony and chatting and playing in multiuser dungeons or domains (MUDs). Finally, new applications appear (e.g., reading and writing in hyperlink media).

Another aspect of differentiation is that media convergence means not only media concentration but also the development of many *small, formally independent media corporations*. This is an aspect of the period of innovation heading every new media development. It also is an effect of present-day organizational downsizing and the rise of network structures inside and between organizations. Their formal independence does not rule out their substantial dependence on financial holdings, venture capital, or large corporate media networks.

The final form of differentiation to be mentioned is the most important one. Technical convergence does not necessarily mean social or usage convergence in actual media practices. Contemporary society is in a process of *social and cultural differentiation* that does not fit into a unitary media environment. A single all-embracing medium that serves all applications and usage contexts is not a realistic prospect. It means that different social classes, age groups, and cultures might use different media or advanced and simple types of the same medium. It also means that, for example, the internet transmitted on TV or cellular phones might produce poorly matching media not fitting special needs in a particular context (e.g., the living room and the mobile environment).

◆ Main Applications

THE INTERNET AND THE WORLD WIDE WEB

The internet, the World Wide Web, and e-mail are the most important digital media today. The internet is a worldwide public network switching millions of local networks. The World Wide Web is a particular application of the internet. The Web does not link networks but (graphical) pages on them that are related in a hyperlink structure. E-mail is the most frequently used digital medium. It uses the internet as its main carrier.

The internet is a medium of information and communication, first of all. Other needs such as entertainment and e-commerce come second. All research worldwide shows that in the first years of this century, the most important applications are e-mailing; searching for specific information; looking for broader information related to work, study, leisure time, or the purchase of products; and reading the news. Surfing the Web just for fun or for orientation and downloading software, music, and videos are secondary applications. E-commerce, gaming, and chatting still were tertiary applications in the first years of this decade. As a medium of communication, the internet is used more to keep in touch with existing relatives, friends, and acquaintances than to contact new ones (Wellman, 2001).

Recent findings indicate that the use of the internet and computers does not displace print media or the use of broadcasting (Adoni & Nossek, 2001; Ferguson & Perse, 2000). Using the internet with its relatively active ways of information seeking and message exchange is not functionally equivalent to watching television or listening to the radio as a consumption of information and a relaxing pastime. Neither is it equivalent to reading printed material in a comfortable environment. In the second part of the 20th century, there had been a shift from reading to television viewing, but a shift from television viewing to computer and internet use has occurred only among young people (Ferguson & Perse, 2000; Social and Cultural Planning Authority of the Netherlands [SCP], 2001).

To many people, it may look like the internet is becoming the central medium connecting and even swallowing all others. It can be received on a television set, and television can be viewed on an internet computer screen. Increasingly, the internet is to be consulted everywhere—at home, at work, at school, and other public places.

Mobile telephony is making it available at all other places. Yet, the future of the internet as a giant crossroad of all kinds of public media is insecure. In the second half of the 1990s, the internet was "privatized," and it came under the influence of increased corporate and governmental control. It is being "coded" in all kinds of ways (Lessig, 1999, 2001). Governments are attempting to regulate the internet. Corporations are bringing forward all kinds of proprietary standards, access codes (user names and passwords), and obligations to pay for services that once were free. At the start of this century, a huge and decisive struggle for the internet is being waged between an open-source or open-standards movement—promoting the operation system Linux, freeware, shareware, and open-domain software—and the software and copyright industry. Microsoft is the head of the latter forces. It defends the present virtual monopolies of its operating system, browser, and office software at all costs and even tries to (partly) replace the open protocol of internet communication, transmission control protocol/internet protocol (TCP/IP), with its own present standards and infrastructures of network communication, enabling this corporation to collect toll and impose obligatory services on internet users.

The result of this struggle is insecure. The internet may persist as a predominant universal public medium, but it also may fall apart in all kinds of private (cyber) spaces, only connected by a public switching facility of addresses.

INTERACTIVE BROADCASTING

Interactive broadcasting is a collective name for digital audio broadcasting (DAB), internet radio and television, and interactive television delivered by cable, satellite, and set-top boxes. DAB is digital radio broadcasting in the atmosphere, offering the opportunity to select and record a large number of high-quality channels and items of music and information. Internet radio

and television are Web sites distributing audiovisual programs that are sometimes also transmitted on regular broadcasting. Interactive television is the use of cable, telephone, and satellite connections linked to television sets by set-top boxes for new applications of television viewing not known in traditional television. These applications are summarized in Table 7.1 and classified according to the levels of interactivity described above. Here it becomes evident that digital television is not (yet) interactive television. Better facilities to choose between channels and programs in digital television are not equivalent to making a difference to the supply and contents of programs by viewers. After all, interactivity means that communication partners influence each other.

The delayed arrival of interactive broadcasting proves that the internet is not swallowing all other media. Attempts to broadcast Web sites on TV, such as Web TV, have failed miserably. Apparently, watching television or listening to the radio and using the internet are different kinds of activities. This does not come as a surprise. Media usage patterns and the ritual daily use of media do not change so quickly. Looking at television viewing patterns, it is obvious that television is often used in the company of others; in the living room, kitchen, or bedroom with a small remote control at a particular distance from the screen; and in a relatively passive way or while doing other things at the same time. In contrast, the computer and the internet mainly are used individually, in a study or other special rooms, right in front of a screen and (inter)actively using a large terminal (van Dijk & de Vos, 2001).

Many services of interactive broadcasting have failed on the market (Jensen & Toscan, 1999). So, do television viewers and radio listeners have a need for interactivity in their relationship with this medium? Anyway, there is a definite demand for relatively passive viewing and listening behavior (see ARD Forschungsdienst, 1999; Lee & Lee, 1995). A need for more (inter)active

Table 7.1   Communication Capacities of Analogous and Digital New Media

Communication Capacity	Analogous Media Face-to-Face	Print	Broadcasting	Telephone	Digital Media Computer Networks	Offline Multimedia
Speed	Low	Low Medium	High	High	High	High
Reach (geographical)	Low	Medium	High[a]	High[a]	High[a]	Low
Reach (social)	Low	Medium	High[a]	High[a]	Low	Low
Storage	Low	Medium	Medium	Low	High	High
Accuracy	Low	High	Low Medium	Low	High	High
Selectivity	Low	Low	Low	High	High	High
Interactivity	High	Low	Low	Medium	Medium	Medium
Stimuli richness	High	Low	Medium	Low	Low	Medium
Complexity	High	High	Medium	Medium	Low	Medium
Privacy protection	High	Medium	High	Medium	Low	Medium

a. In developed countries only.

Table 7.2   The (Inter)activity of Applications in Digital and Interactive Television

Kind of Activity	Application	Level of Inter-Activity
Choice of channels and programs	◆ Conditional Access Systems ◆ Electronic Program Guides ◆ Decoder VCR	0 (Digital TV)
Choice from menus and transactions	◆ Video-on-demand ◆ Customization (choice of camera angle, replay, more item display, plots or story lines) ◆ Additional channels (for background information or advertisement) ◆ E-commerce (goods and services)	1-3 (ITV)
Producing information	◆ Participation in programs (directed) ◆ Reaction/commentary to programs ◆ Contribution to programs/channels (not directed) ◆ Production of own programs/channels	3 (ITV)
Exchange/ Communication	◆ Communication about/in parallel to TV programs (viewer/user communities)	4 (ITV)

(Source: Van Dijk & De Vos, 2001: 452).

behavior using broadcast media is likely to be found with heavy television viewers, young people, and experienced computer users (van Dijk & de Vos, 2001). Interactivity might be a latent need of some viewers and listeners to be developed, like the need for mobile telephony recently did, as an activity that has to be learned.

MOBILE TELEPHONY AND COMPUTING

The prospect of the electronic cottage in the 1980s showed that rarely ever before has futurism proven to be wrong so fast. Toffler (1980) popularized the idea that digital media would satisfy our presumed need to work, study, play, and live as much of our time as possible at home. In fact, telework and distance education have not become very popular in the first decades of digital media use. Instead, we have observed the tremendous rise of mobile telephony and computing. The rise is so impressive that the better opportunities for mobile communication must have been a latent need for many years. In the 1970s and 1980s, questionnaires appeared to show that users were satisfied with their plain old fixed telephones and considered cellular phones a luxury or status symbol. After their introduction on a mass scale, cellular phones were adopted within 10 to 15 years by a large majority of the population in developed countries and relatively even faster by the richer inhabitants of developing countries. What is this latent need?

Uses and gratifications research has given a preliminary answer to this question. Noble (1987) already classified the gratifications of the conventional telephone in a number of intrinsic or social and instrumental or task-oriented gratifications. His findings showed that social uses were more frequent than utilitarian ones. Leung and Wei (2000) conducted a telephone survey among cellular phone users in Hong Kong in 1998, producing a factor analysis of user needs. Seven factors were revealed. Intrinsic

and social gratifications were status, affection or sociability, and relaxation. Particularly in the early days of the mobile phone, its use was considered to be stylish and fashionable. A deeper and more lasting gratification might be the affection and sociability realized by permanently keeping in touch with family members, friends, and acquaintances. In addition, the cellular phone is used as a means of relaxation, that is, the pleasure of talking to people, to gossip or chat or simply to pass the time.

The instrumental or task-oriented gratifications analyzed by Leung and Wei (2000), which result from living in a fast-moving, mobile, and complex society, were mobility and immediate access. This means having the ability to phone everywhere without delay and to get immediate access to others. The mobile phone fulfills these needs by offering a large number of enhanced services such as call redirections, caller ID displays, and paging services such as voice mail. Finally, Leung and Wei found that the mobile phone provides the instrumental gratification of reassurance because it is a means for security in particular cases of emergency or when appointments have to be changed on short notice. A remarkable result of this investigation was that, contrary to the gratifications of fixed telephony use, Hong Kong cellular phone users valued the instrumental gratifications higher than the intrinsic or social gratifications (Leung & Wei, 2000, pp. 312–313).

The introduction of digital mobile phones enables the transmission of other kinds of data than speech and the storage of these data in the device. These features mark the transition from the first to the second and third generations of mobile telephony. In the first generation, text was already available; in the second generation came other sounds than speech, still images, Web pages, and numerical data. In the third generation, the moving images of videos and the videophone have been added.

In this way, the mobile telephone plays an important role in the process of media convergence. The boundary between the cellular phone as a medium of interpersonal communication and as a mass medium of the distribution of SMS, Web pages, videos, and games is dissolving. This is a fundamental transformation with unknown effects. In any case, mobile telephony will merge with mobile computing. All kinds of devices, from a very small cellular phone to a big laptop computer, will be offered, with all of them transmitting telecommunications, data communications, and mass communications that are only limited by the size of the screen and the weight and the processing capacity of the particular device.

COMPUTER GAMES

A digital media application that often is underestimated or downplayed is the use of computer games. This application attracts whole new generations of young people to the world of computing and networking. These generations keep playing when they get older. In 1997, games on PCs were played by 61.4% of 18- to 24-year-old Americans, 55.0% by people ages 25 to 49, and 44.7% by people age 50 and older in the United States (U.S. Census Bureau, 1997).

Modern computer games are a combination of microcomputer or home computer games, video games, and arcade games of the 1970s and 1980s. The following types of games are dominant. First, there are all kinds of driving or racing games simulating cars, airplanes, and spacecraft. Just like many other games, they simulate difficult movement through all kinds of environments. Then we have the loud and conspicuous set of war and shooting games. Another type consists of adventure games, which are explorations of artificial environments following all kinds of tasks. The most demanding games are simulation games—for example, building or managing a city under changing conditions, puzzle games, and games of physical skill during fast movement and the like. Finally, we

have a community type of games, most often played collectively, such as MUDs on the internet and based on role-playing.

The use of computer games has raised many concerns, especially among older generations having less or no experience with playing themselves and being suspicious about what is happening in these games. First, there is the fear of addiction as one observes the compulsive behavior engendered by electronic games. Playing computer games often means total immersion. Another fear is the presumed social isolation of adolescents playing with machines instead of building social skills in meeting peers. Game players who do meet sometimes hang around arcades all day, rousing the suspicion of early delinquency. The next concern is the violent nature of many computer games, which might provoke aggressive behavior or at least have a desensitizing effect on attitudes towards violence. A final worry is the overly masculine, if not sexist, nature of the stories in some computer games and the behavior expressed in playing them.

These fears should be tempered (see Haddon, 1999). Addiction to computer games is not widespread, and most often only temporary. People are using games mostly as a time filler between other activities or as a way of winding down after work. It is wrong to think that only young males play computer games. The social isolation of playing computer games is not bigger than the seclusion of heavy television viewing. Hanging around in arcades also is a particular way to develop social and cultural skills for (mainly) boys. Girls do not play computer games that much less than boys, but for them these games do not constitute a special culture or an important topic of conversation with peers (Haddon, 1999, p. 322). The violent and sexist nature of many computer games is the most serious problem, but it does seem to be a bigger problem, as compared to television programs, films, and comic books, only for one reason: the strong mental immersion produced by the interaction with the objectionable content of these games.

In contrast to these worries are the unnoticed potential advantages of playing computer games. According to Haddon (1999), they may be vehicles for learning. In computer games, the operating skills of working with a computer are learned in passing. In many games, the user learns to control animated computer graphics. Motor functions are practiced automatically. In adventure and simulation games, one learns to plan and get familiar with the structure of databases (Haddon, 1999, p. 321).

◆ *Fundamental Social Issues*

INFORMATION AND COMMUNICATION FREEDOM

Digital media have the capacities to advance and threaten information and communication freedom. Interactivity offers better chances for the freedom of all parties concerned than unilateral communication. The multimedia form enables the stimuli richness needed for information-rich expressions. Digital code boosts the opportunities to copy and exchange information ceaselessly. However, it also promotes storage and registration, enabling control both top-down and bottom-up.

Connecting digital media in networks with both central control and diffusion of power becomes a possibility. Presently, the internet, with its open and decentralized protocols, stimulates free speech. It is based on decentralized distribution and multiple points of access for people communicating relatively anonymously and crossing borders and jurisdictions without any notice. Furthermore, free speech is supported by a huge reservoir of public domain content or easy-to-copy intellectual property and tools of encryption to protect private communication. However, repressive regimes, terrorists, criminals, slanderers, racists, and (child) pornographers are also using these freedoms. Evidently, they threaten the freedom and safety of others and of society at large.

So, it depends on the particular social, political, and juridical state of affairs regarding what will result from using digital media for information and communication freedom. To start with, it is very important to know how governments and media regulators are classifying digital media in the context of media convergence. Should they be modeled on the press model, the common carrier (telephone) model, or the broadcasting model? The press has acquired most freedoms of information and communication in the past two centuries. However, common carriers and broadcasters were subjected to rather severe infrastructure regulation (telecommunications) or both infrastructure and content regulation (broadcasting). In the 1990s, most governments in the Western world and Eastern Asia tended to take the press model for economic freedom (on the market) and the common carrier or broadcasting model for social, cultural, and political freedoms in the digital media environment. With all their strength, these governments tried to stimulate global electronic commerce while trying to implement new restrictions or apply existing ones to the social and cultural uses of the internet. The Communications Decency Act, signed by President Clinton in 1996, was a case in point. It tried to subject the internet to more severe prohibitions than those existing in the media of broadcasting and the press.

There are three kinds of solutions in general to protect and stimulate information and communication freedom using digital media: legal changes, self-regulation, and technical solutions. They are only effective when used in combination (van Dijk, 1999, pp. 127–129). The adaptation of legislation and other general regulations is necessary to produce a legal framework for all more or less voluntary solutions of self-regulation and technical protection. This will take considerable time as the digital technology in question is still maturing and crossing borders, forcing international cooperation and agreements between national legislators.

Self-regulation is proposed for access and service providers. They are supposed to offer codes of conduct and hotlines (reporting offences) or to practice self-censorship in refusing unlawful sites, programs, and files. However, in the 1990s, other instruments of self-regulation became much more important: rating and filtering systems for internet content. Rating systems either mean a self-rating of content by providers themselves or by professional rating services. The quantity and quality of items, such as sex or violence, are put on a scale attached to a service or site and to be read by browsers. Then the software of filtering systems installed by the users themselves is able to offer the nature and level of protection required by parents, educators, and any other kind of authority. But a filtering system is a two-edged sword in defending information and communication freedom: It both protects against unsolicited contents or approaches and offers authorities new instruments of censorship.

Technical solutions are offered by "violence chips" and other hardware built into media and by all kinds of encryption protecting free and private communication. As they are able to protect both the good and the bad, they also are ambivalent solutions requiring a legal framework.

INTELLECTUAL PROPERTY RIGHTS

In offline digital media, it has become easier than ever before to copy any content. Computer networks simplify and expand the exchange and duplication of content even more. This also goes for material protected by intellectual property rights. To many people, the internet seems like a huge garden where valuable flowers can be picked for free. It looks as if the rights of publishers, authors, and producers are in grave danger. In fact, this may be the situation in the first "anarchic" phase of diffusion of the new digital media only. As soon as the legal adaptations to protect intellectual property rights

have become established and combined with instruments of technical and business protection (e.g., encryption and rights management systems), the situation might be reversed. The rights of information and communication freedom, like the so-called "fair use" of protected material (the use and reproduction of a single copy purchased; the rights of libraries, journalists, and scientists; etc.), may be threatened more. This is demonstrated convincingly by Lawrence Lessig (1999, 2001) and other observers of the American and European intellectual property right development (Boyle, 1997; Catinat, 1997; Halbert, 1999). They argue that more and more, the once completely open public domain of the internet is being closed by access codes for memberships, subscriptions or purchase, and the private appropriation of formerly public material. Circumventing the instruments of technical and business protection is forbidden by new legislation such as the Digital Millennium Copyright Act in the United States and the Directive on Certain Aspects of Copyright and Related Rights in the European Union.

These attempts at the private appropriation and protection of intellectual property, as well as their support by legislators, go against the basic trend of diffusion and socialization of intellectual material and knowledge in modern society boosted by the digital media, particularly networks. All existing laws of intellectual property rights only protect works that are *fixed*, enabling their originals to be copied and multiplied. However, in the dynamic environment of computer networks, these forms are continually changing, that is, re-created and reproduced. Other characteristics of networks are their so-called effects or externalities. The exchange and duplication of knowledge comes at the disposal of an increasing number of users, not losing but enlarging quality and intellectual value. Therefore, in practice, this value is passed on more and more in license agreements (e.g., of software) being a usage right instead of sale agreements (ownership right). In defending intellectual property rights, judges and lawyers increasingly speak about the protection of *labor* effort instead of creative effort. In this way, intellectual property rights—at least authors' rights, anyway—are moving from a cultural to an economic sphere.

Intellectual property rights have never been meant to increase the economic revenue for old contributions but, on the contrary, to reward new creative contributions (Perritt, 1996, p. 423). This means that the legitimate support of intellectual property rights to stimulate these contributions always has to be weighed against the fair use of these contributions by individuals and society at large for purposes of education, innovation, and citizenship (see Lessig, 2001).

The protection of this right and of fair use also is backed by a combination of legal protection, self-regulation, and technical solutions. As means of self-regulation, the markets of intellectual value are developing all kinds of new instruments of remuneration based not on the transfer of ownership but on a more or less free use (freeware, shareware, extra support by paid services, licensing) and backed by advertising or customer relationship management (Dyson, 1997). They mark the prime current business models of the internet. However, technical protection will become increasingly viable, too. This means all kinds of anti-copy codes inside the hardware being used, encryption of contents, and instruments of metering and billing use.

THE UNIFICATION AND FRAGMENTATION OF SOCIETY

The digital media are individualizing media, mainly because they are based on individual human-computer interaction. Simultaneously, they are media to be used collectively as these computers are connected in networks. This plurality of applications enables both divisions and commonalities among users and audiences.

Worries about a complete fragmentation of society by all kinds of subcultures and communities talking at cross-purposes in computer networks have been dominant from the start. Usually, social and media scholars had to argue in favor of the existence of homogeneity, integration, and unity in the media and society and against simplistic notions of a fragmenting society and media system. One example is Joshua Meyrowitz (1985, 1997; Meyrowitz & Maguire, 1993).

Against people expecting a breakup of American society into subcultural clusters of race, religion, ethnicity, and gender, a process supposedly reinforced by a fragmented media system of countless cable channels, pay-per-view programs, and internet sites, Meyrowitz and Maguire (1993) contend that "the current trend is towards integration of all groups into a relatively common experiential sphere—with a new recognition of the special needs and idiosyncrasies of individuals" (p. 43). Will the digital media primarily bring us together or tear us further apart? This is a question about the future of the public sphere. The most popular answer to this question emphasizes fragmentation as well. One refers to the uncoupling of public spheres and particular territories, the loss of the presumed unitary character of the public sphere of the past, and the blurring distinctions of the public and the private in contemporary society. However, will these changing conditions lead to the loss of all common ground for society at large and its media system?

For John Keane (1995), these conditions only mean that the conventional idea of a single, unified public sphere and its partner ideas of a marked public opinion, a common public good, and a particular public-private distinction are obsolete. Instead, we get a "complex mosaic of differently sized overlapping and interconnected public spheres" (Keane, 1995, p. 8). Keane may be right. The internet itself, with its hyperlink structure of connections and its numerous overlapping discussion forums, is a perfect model of this mosaic. It is complemented by the increasing number of cross-references and cross-fertilizations between new and old media, such as newspapers and television programs referring to Web sites or the other way round. These media are keeping common denominators in their coverage. The same themes and societal discussions are coming forward in a plurality of media, though they last shorter. So, it seems likely that public spheres will reappear in different shapes and reconstructed in ways that we cannot exactly anticipate yet.

THE DIGITAL DIVIDE

The diffusion curve of computers and the internet among the population at large in the United States has been steeper than that of the fixed telephone and cable but slower than that of television, radio, the VCR, and the cellular phone (Lievrouw, 2000). The diffusion of digital media is very uneven among different sections of the population and among different nations in the world. This refers to the problem of the so-called *digital divide,* a metaphor that became popular at the end of the 1990s after much older concepts such as information inequality and the knowledge gap.

Usually, the concept of the digital divide means unequal access to computers and the internet. One uses the term *access* freely in everyday discussions, not considering that there are many divergent meanings in play. Possessing a computer and a network connection is the most common meaning in the context of digital media. However, this only refers to the second of four successive kinds of access (van Dijk, 1999). I have distinguished four kinds of access:

1. *lack of elementary digital experience* caused by lack of interest, computer anxiety, and unattractiveness of the new technology (mental access);

2. *no possession of computers and network connections* (material access);

3. lack of *digital skills* caused by insufficient user-friendliness and inadequate

education or social support (skills access);

4. lack of significant *usage opportunities* (usage access).

Clearly, public opinion and public policy are strongly preoccupied with the second kind of access. Many people think the problem of information inequality regarding digital media is solved as soon as everyone has a computer and a connection to the internet. The first kind of access problem, the mental barrier, is neglected or viewed as a temporary phenomenon that only affects old people, some categories of homemakers, illiterates, and unemployed. The problem of inadequate digital skills is reduced to the skills of operation—managing hardware and software—and are called instrumental or operational skills. However, other digital skills are increasingly important in an information and network society: informational skills and strategic skills (van Dijk, in press). Informational skills involve the capacities to search, select, and process information from computer and network files. Having strategic skills means that users can take their initiatives in searching, selecting, integrating, valuing, and applying information from all kinds of digital sources to improve their position in society (see van Dijk, 2004, in press; van Dijk & Hacker, 2003).

Differential usage of computers and network connections is a neglected phenomenon as well. Usually, it is not seen as being of any importance to social and educational policies as differential usage is presumed to be the free choice of citizens and consumers in a differentiating postmodern society. However, when structural inequality in use of digital media appears among different categories of the population, this might become a problem for democracy and citizen participation in society. Previously, I have observed the growth of such a *usage gap:* People with high education and income are using the relatively advanced applications of digital media for work, business, and education (spreadsheets, databases, decision support systems, and searching for information on the internet), whereas people with low education and income are using relatively simple applications for entertainment and basic communication or transactions (gaming, surfing, e-mail, and looking for jobs) (see van Dijk, 1999, 2002, 2004).

The access problems of digital media gradually shift from the first two kinds of access to the last two kinds. Computer anxiety and motivational problems are decreasing as more people get used to the rapidly diffusing digital media and see the use of them. The divide in the material possession of computers and internet connections has widened among people with different income, education, and ethnicity in the high-tech countries of North America, Western Europe, and Eastern Asia between 1985 and 2000, but with the saturation of the diffusion of computers and networks among the highest social classes, the gap is beginning to close (van Dijk, 2002, 2004). It remains to be seen how large the remaining gap will be in the next decade and whether the lesser developed countries will be able to catch up. However, inequalities of informational and strategic digital skills and of usage opportunities will not disappear that easily. They are most likely to increase in a differentiating information and network society that is marked by growing socioeconomic inequality (Castells, 1996; Mansell & Wehn, 1998; van Dijk, 1999).

◆ **References**

Adoni, H., & Nossek, H. (2001). The new media consumers: Media convergence and the displacement effect. *European Journal of Communication Research, 26*(1), 59–83.

ARD-Forschungsdienst. (1999). Digitales und interaktives Fernsehen: Nutzererwartungen und Akzeptanzchancen [Digital interactive television: User expectations and acceptance chances]. *Media Perspektiven, 8,* 430–436.

Baldwin, T., McVoy, D., & Steinfield, C. (1996). *Convergence, integrating media, information & communication.* Thousand Oaks, CA: Sage.

Boyle, J. (1997). A politics of intellectual property: Environmentalism on the Net? *Duke Law Journal, 47,* 78–89.

Cameron, A. (1995). Dissimulations: The illusion of interactivity. *Millennium Film Journal, 28,* 33–47.

Castells, M. (1996). *The information age: Economy, society and culture: Vol. 1. The rise of the network society.* Cambridge, MA: Blackwell.

Castells, M. (2001). *The Internet galaxy: Reflections on the Internet, business and society.* Oxford, UK: Oxford University Press.

Catinat, M. (1997). *The "National Information Infrastructure Initiative" in the US: Policy or non-policy?* Cambridge, MA: Harvard University, Center for International Affairs.

Daft, R. L., & Lengel, R. H. (1984). Information richness: A new approach to managerial behavior and organization design. *Research in Organizational Behavior, 6,* 191–233.

Dyson, E. (1997). *Release 2.0: A design for living in the digital age.* New York: Broadway.

Ferguson, D. A., & Perse, E. M. (2000). The World Wide Web as a functional alternative to television. *Journal of Broadcasting & Electronic Media, 44*(2), 155–174.

Flanagin, A. J., & Metzger, M. (2001). Internet use in the contemporary media environment. *Human Communication Research, 27*(1), 153–177.

Fulk, J., Steinfield, C., Schmitz, J., & Power, J. G. (1987). A social information processing model of media use in organizations. *Communication Research, 14*(5), 529–552.

Goodman, N. (1968). *Languages of art.* Indianapolis, IN: Hacket.

Haddon, L. (1999). The development of interactive games. In H. Mackay & T. O'Sullivan (Eds.), *The media reader: Continuity and transformation* (pp. 305–328). London: Sage.

Halbert, D. (1999). *Intellectual property in the information age: The politics of expanding ownerships rights.* Westport, CT: Quorum.

Heim, M. (1987). *Electric language: A philosophical study of word processing.* New Haven, CT: Yale University Press.

Jensen, J. (1999). The concept of "interactivity." In J. Jensen & C. Toscan (Eds.), *Interactive television: TV of the future or the future of TV?* (pp. 25–66). Aalborg, Denmark: Aalborg University Press.

Jensen, J., & Toscan, C. (Eds.). (1999). *Interactive television: TV of the future or the future of TV?* Aalborg, Denmark: Aalborg University Press.

Keane, J. (1995). Structural transformations of the public sphere. *The Communication Review, 1*(1), 1–22.

Kiesler, S., Siegel, J., & McQuire, T. (1984). Social-psychological effects of computer-mediated information. *The American Psychologist, 39*(10), 1123–1143.

Lee, B., & Lee, R. S. (1995). How and why people watch TV: Implications for the future of interactive television. *Journal of Advertising Research, 35*(6), 9–18.

Lessig, L. (1999). *Code and other laws of cyberspace.* New York: Basic Books.

Lessig, L. (2001). *The future of ideas: The fate of the commons in a connected world.* New York: Vintage.

Leung, L., & Wei, R. (2000). More than just talk on the move: Uses and gratifications of the cellular phone. *Journalism & Mass Communication Quarterly, 77*(2), 308–320.

Lievrouw, L. (2000). Nonobvious things about new media: How fast is fast? *ICA Newsletter, 28*(2), 6–7.

Mansell, R., & Wehn, U. (Eds.). (1998). *Knowledge societies: Information technology for sustainable development.* Oxford, UK: Oxford University Press.

Meyrowitz, J. (1985). *No sense of place: The impact of electronic media on social behavior.* New York: Oxford University Press.

Meyrowitz, J. (1997). Shifting worlds of strangers: Medium theory and changes in "them" versus "us." *Sociological Inquiry, 67*(1), 59–71.

Meyrowitz, J., & Maguire, J. (1993). Media, place and multiculturalism. *Society, 30*(5), 41–48.

Noble, G. (1987). Discriminating between the intrinsic and instrumental domestic telephone user. *Australian Journal of Communication, 11,* 63–85.

Perritt, H. (1996). *Law and the information superhighway.* New York: John Wiley.

Rice, R. E. (1998). Computer-mediated communication and media preference. *Behaviour & Information Technology, 17*(3), 164–174.

Salomon, G. (1979). *Interaction of media, cognition and learning.* San Francisco: Jossey-Bass.

Short, J., Williams, E., & Christie, B. (1976). *The social psychology of telecommunications.* New York: John Wiley.

Social and Cultural Planning Authority of the Netherlands (SCP). (2001). *Trends in de Tijd.* Den Haag, the Netherlands: Sociaal en Cultureel Planbureau.

Spears, R., & Lea, M. (1992). Social influence and the influence of the "social" in computer-mediated communication. In M. Lea (Ed.), *Contexts of computer-mediated communication* (pp. 30–65). Hemel Hempstead, UK: Harvester Wheatsheaf.

Toffler, A. (1980). *The third wave.* London: Pan.

U.S. Census Bureau. (1997). *Current population surveys.* Washington, DC: Government Printing Office.

van Dijk, J. (1999). *The network society: Social aspects of new media.* London: Sage.

van Dijk, J. (2002, July). *Outline of a multilevel theory of the network society.* Paper presented at the 52nd annual conference of the International Communication Association, Seoul, South Korea.

van Dijk, J. (2004). Divides in succession: Possession, skills and use of the new media for participation. In E. Bucy & J. Newhagen (Eds.), *Media access: Social and psychological dimensions of new technology use* (pp. 233–254). Hillsdale, NJ: Lawrence Erlbaum.

van Dijk, J. (in press). *The deepening divide: Inequality in the information society.* London: Sage.

van Dijk, J. A. G. M. (1991). *De Netwerkmaatschappij, Sociale aspecten van nieuwe media* [The network society, social aspects of new media]. Houten, the Netherlands: Bohn Stafleu van Loghum.

van Dijk, J. A. G. M. (1993). The mental challenge of the new media. *Medien-psychologie, Zeitschrift für Individual- und Massenkommunikation, 5*(1), 20–45.

van Dijk, J. A. G. M. (2001). *De Netwerk-maatschappij, Sociale aspecten van nieuwe media* [The network society, social aspects of new media] (4th ed.). Alphen a.d. Rijn, the Netherlands: Samsom.

van Dijk, J., & de Vos, L. (2001). Searching for the Holy Grail: Images of interactive television. *New Media and Society, 3*(4), 443–465.

van Dijk, J., & Hacker, K. (2003). The "digital divide" as a complex and dynamic phenomenon. *The Information Society, 19*(4), 315–326.

Walther, J. (1992). Interpersonal effects in computer-mediated communication. *Communication Research, 19*(1), 52–90.

Walther, J. (1996). Computer-mediated communication: Impersonal, interpersonal and hyperpersonal interaction. *Communication Research, 23*(1), 1–43.

Wellman, B. (2001). Computer networks as social networks. *Science, 293*, 2031–2034.

PART II

AUDIENCES, USERS, AND EFFECTS

8

AUDIENCE AND READERSHIP RESEARCH

◆ Jenny Kitzinger

A ny theory about the media is incomplete if it does not take audiences (or "readers") into account. We may analyze texts and the processes through which they are produced, but without understanding *audiences,* such analyses can imply more than they deliver. To fully assess the media's role in society—its mediation, limitations, and sometimes unexpected implications—we need to study how people "read," use, and respond to the media. This is perhaps the most difficult task of all. The audience is an ephemeral and inherently relational concept. Audiences are defined, at least initially, in relation to texts (films, news bulletins, soap operas) or objects (such as books, radio, or TV sets). Quite *who* constitutes the audience, as well as when, where, and under what circumstances, is necessarily elastic. There is a corresponding wide variety in the techniques used to study audiences, the contexts within which they are placed, and the meanings made out of such research. Any one interested in audience research should also heed the warning offered by Nightingale (1996):

> Just as people as audiences cannot be separated from personal, social and cultural continuity, so texts cannot be isolated from their broader cultural significance, or from the history of that significance. The audience-text relation is a chimera, which can only ever be apprehended partially. We think we are seeing reality when what we

see is more like a holographic reflection, changing as our own point of reference changes and dependent on our ability to see—on the quality of our vision. Audience is a shifty concept. (p. 148)

When reviewing audience research, it is useful to reflect on who is interested in the audience, as well as how questions are framed and audiences envisaged. This chapter starts by outlining four different spheres of concern that prompt such research. It then focuses on debates between those investigating the media's role in relation to politics, culture, and identity. This sets the scene for outlining how researchers select the focus of enquiry and the diverse data collection methods they use. The following discussion thus covers the following:

◆ The impetus for audience research

◆ Framing the question—a review of diverse approaches and disputes

◆ Framing the audience—deciding *who* to study (when and where)

◆ Data collection techniques and approaches

This chapter is based on the premise that decisions about *where* to look and *how* to look are inextricably intertwined with ideas about what is important. Research is not an asocial, apolitical linear process based on selecting your question, choosing an appropriate method, and then simply analyzing and presenting findings. Research is embedded in a web of processes involving the socioeconomic conditions of production, disciplinary divisions, academic routines, historical context, knowledge paradigms, and interrelated decisions about questions, foci, and methods of enquiry (see Figure 8.1).

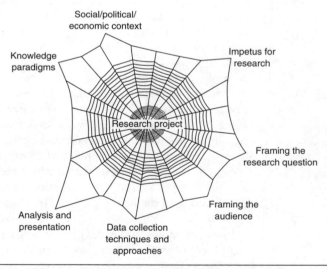

Figure 8.1   Conducting Research Involves a Network of Interrelated Decisions

NOTE: The spider's web is a more useful metaphor for research than the linear ladder.

◆ *The Impetus for Audience Research: Four Spheres of Concern*

The impetus for empirical research into audiences can be grouped under four broad spheres.

Market Imperatives. This research scrutinizes and seeks to manage audiences as consumers/commodities. People are approached as commercial units to be delivered to businesses, advertisers, or media organizations (Ang, 1991). Such research is concerned primarily with measuring audiences, identifying their sociodemographic distribution, and tracking issues such as attention flow and channel loyalty. This often involves audience panels, surveys, and monitoring via electronic means such as the "people meter" or continuous response measurements via handsets (Millard, 1992).

Concerns About Morality and Sex 'n' Violence. This research is concerned with the potential corrupting influence of the media. Much of this work is framed by psychological theories and relies on experimental laboratory-based studies. Such research is often conducted in response to long-running debates about copycat violence that have lasted from the first penny newspaper to the 1990s video nasties[1] controversies.

Responses to Technological Developments. This research asks questions about the implications of new media and communication devices. In the first part of the 20th century, research focused on cinema or the radio; today, it is more likely to focus on the Internet and interactive digital TV. Although this can involve a very narrow technological focus, such research is often conducted under the broader auspices of anthropology, history, or the sociology of science and technology. Such work thus shades into my fourth category as follows.

Questions About Culture, Politics, and Identity. The impetus for research inspired under this rubric is a concern with the media's role in the public and domestic realm. It examines how the media might frame public understandings and citizenship *and* how people use media texts and objects in negotiating interpersonal power relations or developing identities, pleasures, and fantasies. Such work includes much of the sociological enquiry into media effects and the cultural studies tradition, as well as questions about the role of media objects as items of domestic technology. This category embraces some uncomfortable bedfellows and cannot, of course, be completely segregated from the others outlined above. The division between approaching audiences as commercial units and as citizens is also not necessarily clear-cut and can itself be subject to analysis from within the "culture-politics-identity" perspective.

The above categories should thus not be seen as cast in stone. I offer them rather as basic navigational aids to help reflect on where specific audience research efforts are "coming from." In highlighting the different impetus *behind* research questions, the aim is to encourage reflective approaches to how research is framed and conducted. It would be a mistake to assume that certain areas of substantive enquiry are confined within one sphere.

Let me illustrate this with the example of enquiries into the media and interpersonal violence and abuse. This substantive area is often reviewed as if research were confined to the "morality and sex 'n' violence" tradition, addressing issues such as whether media representations of violence desensitize viewers or if such representations lead to copycat attacks. Examples of such research would include experiments by Bandura and colleagues with Bobo dolls (Bandura, Ross, & Ross, 1963) or the declarations made by psychologists about the dangers of certain videos (Barker & Petley, 2001). However, this substantive area can be explored from very diverse perspectives. Audiences can be approached as markets ("What type or level of violence makes viewers turn on or turn off; what is acceptable to viewers of this channel?"). Alternatively, a narrow interest in technological developments would prioritize questions such as the following: "Does the Internet create new channels for pedophiles?" Research under my fourth category (culture, politics, and identity) would take a very different approach, generating multiple enquiries concerning pleasure, identity, judgment, influence, and understanding. Researchers have studied how media representations of sexual violence influence public understandings, how viewers relate to victims and perpetrators on screen, and how responses are mediated by personal experience. They have also explored how the media resource survivor identities, the forms of pleasure found in violent movies, and how Black women negotiate with film representations that expose sexual violence but promote ideas of Black male brutality (Bobo, 1995; Hill, 2001; Kitzinger, 2000, 2001; Philo, 1999a; Schlesinger, Dobash, Dobash, & Weaver, 1992).

The range of questions that arise among those interested in culture, politics, and identity points to the broad nature of this fourth category and the need for further unpacking. It is this category that informs most academic work within media studies and has generated the most fruitful and diverse empirical approaches, as well as being the site of intense conflict. The next section therefore reviews the evolution of different research foci and theoretical approaches developed under this remit, both *reflecting* and *promoting* different research designs.

◆ *Diverse Questions on Audiences, Culture, Politics, and Identity: A Brief Review of Conflicting Theories and Approaches*

The origins of contemporary mass media studies are often located in 1930s Germany, where academics within the Frankfurt school responded to Germany's descent into fascism by developing theories about mass public responses to propaganda. Since then, the field has undergone many transmutations. The Frankfurt school's hypodermic model (of direct effects) was challenged by a two-step model of mediated influence (highlighting the importance of social networks and opinion leaders) and by "uses and gratifications," which argued that individuals use the media for their own purposes. Such approaches now compete alongside theories about the media's power to cultivate certain understandings of the world (cultivation theory; Gerbner, 1973) or priorities (agenda-setting theory; McCombs & Shaw, 1972). Each approach set up a new research question in opposition to others. Uses and gratifications theory, for example, demands that we ask "not what the media do to the public but what the public do with the media," whereas agenda-setting theory asserts that we should look at the media's role in telling us "not *what* to think but what to think *about.*"

A turning point in audience research was established in the late 1970s by Stuart Hall's model of encoding and decoding (Hall, 1980). Hall argued that texts are polysemic and that there is no necessary correspondence between the message encoded by the film or program maker and that decoded by audiences. To understand the role of the media, Hall argued that one must discover how different groups respond to any particular program. Hall promoted a *social* theory of subjectivity and meaning construction, arguing that audience research should be in the business of locating "significant clusters" of meaning and linking these to the social and discursive positioning of readers.

It was this understanding that laid the groundwork in the 1980s and 1990s for the burgeoning of a series of in-depth qualitative studies attentive to audience interpretation and activity. These studies focused on *groups* and sampled along diverse social variables because of the interest in "interpretative communities." The first and most famous of these is David Morley's (1980) study, "The Nationwide Audience." At first, class differences were the main focus of attention (at least within U.K. research), but debates about American cultural colonialism across Europe also helped encourage interest in ethnic diversity and cross-cultural interpretations (e.g., Ang, 1985; Katz & Liebes, 1985). At the same time, the rise of gay liberation and feminism influenced a growing interest in "queer" and "camp" readings, as well as prompting work into women's enjoyment of a despised cultural output, the soap opera. Distinct strands of research were developed that focused on exploring pleasure and identifying cultural competencies as well as claiming "fandom" as a crucial area of study (e.g., Hobson, 1982; Lewis, 1992).

During the 1980s and 1990s, researchers also increasingly focused on how the media were consumed as objects as well as texts. David Morley himself became dissatisfied with the artificial nature of showing videos to groups who might not have watched them otherwise and would certainly not have done so under the same circumstances (in the same groups, with the same degree of attention). He became interested in the home as a site of consumption and began to pursue more naturalistic research methods, leading to an increased interest in how people negotiated "living room politics" around media technologies (Morley, 1986). In a parallel development coming from a background in literary studies, Janice Radway (1984) highlighted the importance of the act of reading as much as the nature of the text. She argued that although the text might promote an anti-feminist message, the practice of reading could be women's way of creating space for themselves and resisting the demands of their families (Radway, 1984).

The 1980s and early 1990s, then, particularly within media/cultural studies in the United Kingdom, saw a turn to three dimensional qualitative work exploring many different dimensions of audiences: opening up new ways of researching media reception and new ways of theorizing power. These developments were not, however, viewed without some disquiet. Fierce disputes arose about the balance between attention to the "public" and "private" spheres and the extent to which audience activity was being exaggerated and "the message" ignored (see Corner, 1991; Eldridge, Kitzinger, & Williams, 1997; Gray, 1999; Miller & Philo, 2001). Many researchers insisted on the need to return to or retain a concern with how media texts might influence public understandings despite, or in light of, audience activity. Researchers at Glasgow, for example, built on previous text-based work carried out by the Glasgow University Media Group (1976, 1980) to explore how media representations might relate to public understanding. They used focus groups to research how people made sense of issues ranging from industrial disputes or "terrorism" to "mad cow" disease (bovine spongiform encephalopathy [BSE]) and AIDS. Much of this work sought to examine media "effects" while also taking into account how interpretation, pleasure, and social networks mediated audience-text relations. For examples of this work, see *Getting the Message* (Eldridge, 1993), *The Circuit of Mass Communication* (Miller, Kitzinger, Williams, & Beharrell, 1998), and *Message Received* (Philo, 1999b). Similar in-depth studies were being conducted elsewhere into issues such as the media's role in framing people's talk about Arab-Israeli conflict (Gamson, 1992), responses to nuclear energy (Corner, Richardson, & Fenton, 1990), and the influence of television programs such as *The Cosby Show* on racism (Jhally & Lewis, 1992). In combination, such work represents a body of "new effects research" (see Kitzinger, 1999, 2002).

It is against this backdrop that audience research needs to be understood. Studying audiences is never innocent. How audiences are investigated will always interact with the dimensions outlined above, although, at least in theory, this *should* be a two-way process. The next part of the chapter raises sampling issues—how to constitute audience research participants, as well as who, when, and where to study—before moving on to outline diverse data collection techniques.

◆ Framing the Sky: Defining the Audience and Deciding Who to Study

The elasticity and sheer scale of mass media audiences means that sampling for audience research is rather like trying to frame the sky. Researchers have to decide who constitute a meaningful group of research participants in the context of their particular research aims. The potential audience might include the whole population of a country (or even several countries) or everyone who owns a specific media technology. It might be people who watch a program genre (such as talk shows) or have watched a specific documentary or film. Researchers may opt for large-scale work that aims for a statistically representative sample (a scale of research often necessitating methods such as questionnaires), or they may opt to explore specific fan groups or communities (e.g., Radway's [1984] community of romance readers). Alternatively, the key research questions may mean that the best type of sample is one that maximizes possible diversity of interpretation or response (e.g., taking snapshots of different audience groups from very diverse backgrounds or across cultures).

Researchers also have to consider questions about the unit, place, time frame, and context of any audience study. Do people consume as individuals or families or communities? What constitutes "doing audiencehood," and is it separable from being a consumer, a citizen, or a member of the public? How do you study the reception of a particular text? How do you examine the experience of watching one news bulletin,

given all the other media messages and sources of information within which audience reception is embedded? Can reactions to a particular media episode be separated from the surrounding flow? Is it possible to look at the TV audience separate from the newspaper reader? What counts as watching television? What if the TV set is on and the individual is in the same room but not paying attention, or what if someone has not seen that episode of her favorite soaps but catches up on what happened through discussion during the lunch break at work?

Academics may try to tap into audiencehood through showing research participants a video of a program, but people consume the media in many different ways beyond the immediate process of watching, viewing, or listening and self-conscious postmortem discussions. People are arguably "doing audience work" when they exchange ideas on the bus or via the Internet. Fans may build up elaborate ways of relating to texts, which include how they decorate their rooms, what they wear, which catchphrases they integrate into their talk, and how they orientate their social lives. Arguably, the media may be implicated in this way even for people who do not consider themselves fans.

There is no perfect sample or single ideal time and place to research audiences. How researchers have addressed the above dilemmas varies with their research aims, resources, and disciplinary traditions. Questions about who, what, when, and where to study are inextricably intertwined with how audience research is conducted. The next section provides an overview of data collection techniques and approaches.

◆ Data Collection Techniques and Approaches

SURVEYS AND QUESTIONNAIRES

Large-scale questionnaire surveys are used within audience research to map audiences in broad brushstrokes (e.g., by sociodemographic variables and consumption patterns). Surveys are also used to access representative samples of audience views. In addition to providing basic profiles of the audience, surveys are employed to identify *correlations* between the mass media and the mass audience. Statistical analyses are used within cultivation theory to examine associations between amount of TV viewing and attitudes (Gerbner, 1973) and within agenda-setting research to compare the amount of media attention given to a particular issue and the priority assigned to it by the public (McCombs & Shaw, 1972). Surveys may also be used to compare the information presented in the media to what people know (e.g., Lewis et al., 1999, cited in Ruddock, 2001).

Questionnaires can also be used to complement qualitative work. Surveys help position qualitative findings in context and may highlight key factors unidentified in smaller scale qualitative enquiry (see Livingstone, Wober, & Lunt, 1994). They can also be offered to research participants as a means of private communication. For example, focus group participants can be explicitly invited to note down anything they felt unable to contribute to the group discussion. Discrepancies between what is revealed by questionnaires and what is discussed within the group can be used as a double check and might be interpreted as validation/invalidation. Alternatively, such discrepancies can be a source of insight into how media information is socially processed and the framing of popular discourse (see discussion of focus groups, presented later).

LETTERS, E-MAILS, ONLINE EXCHANGES, AND FAN WEB SITES

Another way of gaining access to audience data is to examine written correspondence (prompted or unprompted, on paper or online). The most famous letter-based research is Ien Ang's (1985) analysis of *Dallas,* in which she invited people to write to her describing what they liked or disliked about the program. Other studies have analyzed the letters or e-mails sent to news editors, program producers, or actors. These include, for example, analysis of Internet mail messages sent to *NBC Nightly News* (Newhagen, Cordes, & Levy, 1995), "parasocial interaction" in audience letters to a popular Indian television soap opera (Sood & Rogers, 2000), and meaning making and empowerment in letters to the South African media NGO Soul City (Tufte, 2002).

There are now also increasing opportunities to study audiences via online exchanges and Web sites. Indeed, this is not just an opportunity but also an imperative, as the World Wide Web becomes an extension of TV viewing and a new site of performing "audiencehood." Hine (2000), for example, examined online discussion of the Louise Woodward news story, and Baym (2000) studied online discussion of soap operas. Brooker (2001) looked at how teen audiences used dedicated Internet sites around the TV drama *Dawson's Creek,* and Pullen (2000) analyzed Web sites dedicated to the New Zealand–produced cult program *Xena: Warrior Princess.*

INTERVIEWS, GROUP DISCUSSIONS, AND FOCUS GROUPS

Actually talking to people (as individuals or as groups) offers the opportunity for researchers to pursue their particular questions (rather than focusing on the spontaneous interests of online correspondents) and to probe at length. *Individual* interviews have been employed to document the role of the media in relation to people's personal biographies, the influence of the media on their understandings of the world, and experiences and pleasures as readers, viewers, or listeners. *Group* interviews, however, are particularly popular and have a long history within mass communication research. They were used by sociologists during World War II, for example, to examine the impact of wartime propaganda (Merton, 1987). (For discussion of the history of this method within media studies, see Morrison, 1998.) Although focus groups became most closely associated with commercial research (as a quick way of generating new ideas), recently there has been a dramatic resurgence of academic interest in this method. It is now recognized as a potentially high-quality approach in its own right rather than a mere precursor to survey work. Indeed, group interviews are the cornerstone of much audience reception research (Lunt & Livingstone, 1996). Group discussions have been used extensively, for example, to examine the notion of "interpretive communities" and to explore diverse "readings" between groups from different classes, political perspectives, ethnic identities, or cultures, as well as in-depth studies of media influence. It is also used within research into media influence.

There is great variability, however, in the extent to which such studies fully exploit or take into account the key features of group work. It is here that the distinction between group interviews and *focus* groups becomes important. A group interview can only be defined as a *focus* group if the interaction between research participants is used both to generate data and as a focus of analysis (see Kitzinger, 1994). Group interviews are not focus groups if they are simply conducted as a convenient way to access several individuals simultaneously or if the group is used, in some quite static way, to represent certain sociodemographic characteristics (Jordin & Brunt, 1988). Unfortunately, the term *focus group* is often misappropriated in research reports in which there is a lack of attention, for example, to how the group operates as a group. At a very basic level, for example, researchers often fail to present even a single example of dialogue *between* participants. (For a full discussion of focus group methods, see Barbour & Kitzinger, 1999.)

Focus group research, which pays attention to interaction, can be very fruitful within studies of audiences. Such research can explore the negotiation of meaning, the sharing and building up of collective memories, the operation of dispute and consensus, and the performance of cultural repertoires. Groups' conveners sometimes aim to simulate naturally occurring conversation to identify the mediating processes via which mass media products enter culture (Liebes & Katz, 1990). They are used to explore how people discuss political or social issues, as well as how this relates to media frames, and to examine how particular programs or genres provide resources for thinking about issues ranging from racism to cancer (Gamson, 1992; Henderson & Kitzinger, 1999; Jhally & Lewis, 1992; Miller et al., 1998).

Interaction between research participants allows researchers to study how people respond to each other's perspectives and mobilize or resist media accounts in debate with one another. The unstable and dynamic processes within group discussions can propel researchers away from simplistic ideas about fixed attitudes and towards reflection on social processes. Focus group work can also generate very diverse types of talk—jokes, gossip, songs, anecdotes—all important forms of communication that help to illuminate how media messages are received, resisted, transmogrified, and incorporated into everyday exchanges. For example, focus groups on AIDS highlighted the importance of the "cultural currency" of media information (Kitzinger, 1993). This was illuminated by tracking how tales of "vengeful AIDS carriers" were used in group discussions and by exploring the circulation of "yuck" information about HIV risks from saliva ("you'd need to bathe in it, covered in open sores"). Another major research project using focus groups (this time discussing social work issues) highlighted the importance of high-profile "template" events in public debate. This research showed how journalists and their audiences used thumbnail sketches of previous scandals about social work intervention to inform how they respond to more recent events in the news (Kitzinger, 2000, 2004).

The relationship between media representations and collective or individual experience is a key question in debates about media influence. It is often argued, for example, that personal experience of a phenomenon decreases media power to shape perceptions. Focus group methods offer the opportunity to explore the relationship between private and public/media discourses. Researchers can use focus groups (especially if combined with interviews or questionnaires) to identify how individual experience and identity relate to the collective, exploring what is shared and withheld from the group. Where the dynamics of the discussion prompt new revelations, then researchers can identify how this influences the trajectory of debate. The focus groups I conducted on child sexual abuse allowed me to explore the impact of personal revelations within the group and identify how a media focus on stranger danger meshed with everyday exchanges (e.g., outside the school gate) about threatening outsiders (Kitzinger, 2004). Focus group work in this area has also highlighted how media messages can interact with and transform individual and collective understandings (Kitzinger & Farquhar, 1999).

OBSERVATION AND ETHNOGRAPHY

Direct observation of people as they go about their normal business—going to the cinema, listening to radio, watching television, using the Internet—is another very important research strategy for those wishing to understand audiences. Here the aim is to minimize intervention from the researcher, avoid problems of self-report data, and gain direct access to how people interact with and around the media texts and technologies. This technique does not isolate an issue or a program for discussion; rather, it examines everyday consumption in social context within the flow of actual practices. It is

particularly used by those interested in the domestic consumption of information and communication technologies (ICTs) in the home. However, observation can also be carried out at school or work, in a cyber-café, and at public events such as a religious rally conducted by American evangelist Billy Graham (Lang & Lang, 1991) or mourners at Princess Diana's funeral ("The Death of Diana," 1998). Observation is, however, often positioned within a broader ethnographic approach rather than being a data collection technique by itself.

Ethnography is a research approach that relies heavily on observation but can also incorporate a variety of (usually qualitative) methods. Drawing on perspectives developed by anthropologists such as Malinowski, audience ethnographies aim to produce deep, rich, and "thick" descriptions of how people relate to the media in their day-to-day lives. Ethnography is a way of understanding social life in holistic terms. Combining intensive observational fieldwork with interviews and group discussions, ethnographies present "audiencehood" through the eyes of the research participants, insofar as this is possible without reproducing a "colonial gaze" (Young, 1996). Linked to grounded theory, the ethnographer seeks to unravel the familiar and taken for granted and must be constantly open to being surprised by her or his data (an injunction that one hopes, however, would apply to any research). The aim is to locate patterns and the "informal logic of everyday life" (Geertz, 1973) but not to impose predetermined categories. Ethnographers are thus often more concerned about internal validity and situated representativeness than statistical significance. Where surveys segregate and decontextualize individual acts, the ethnographic approach insists that being an audience (or "doing audiencing" or "consuming technologies") should not be abstracted from its social context. Indeed, many of those interested in studying culture have been drawn to audience research (and vice versa) precisely because "the all-pervasive and symbiotic relationship between media and culture makes it impossible to analyse one in isolation from the other" (Johnson, 2001, p. 147). Research into audiences is certainly not confined to the moment of encounter with texts—it can include how people purchase and position technologies, interact around the television set, and talk about the media. As Gillespie (1995) argues,

> TV talk, though it may often seem esoteric and trivial, is an important form of self-narration and a major collective resource through which identities are negotiated. Ethnographic fieldwork makes it possible to document and analyse the forms, contents and implications of such talk as a ritualistic form of everyday interaction, whether in front of the TV set or elsewhere. (p. 205)

In practice, some so-called "audience ethnographies" fail to deliver either the intensity of involvement or the depth of analysis and reflexivity required to live up to the anthropological heritage of this term (for a critique, see Nightingale, 1989). However, ethnographic approaches have been fruitfully employed to explore communities of romance readers (Radway, 1984), how media technologies are integrated into the home (e.g., Lull, 1990; Morley & Silverstone, 1990), and how diasporic communities use television and video to re-create cultural traditions and create cultural change (Gillespie, 1995). It is also often the approach of choice among anthropologists interested in the impact of media technologies and texts as they penetrate different parts of the world. Such studies include a phenomenology of the media practices of Islamist women in Egypt (Werner, 2001); a study of radio, everyday life, and development in South India (Jayaprakash, 2000); and the modernizing influences of television in rural India (Johnson, 2001). New forms of ethnography are also now emerging as researchers develop techniques for studying Internet communities located in virtual, rather than geographical, space (Hine, 2000; Lindlof & Shatzer, 1998).

VIDEO VIEWING, SCRIPTWRITING EXERCISES, AND OTHER GAMES

Any of the above approaches can be combined with innovative ways of inviting people to think about, express, and reflect on their encounters with media texts and technologies. Morley and Silverstone's (1991) ethnography of domestic consumption included inviting research participants to complete time-use diaries, talk the researchers through their family photo albums, and draw mental maps of their household. Gray (1987) had her research participants color code their instruments of domestic technology (blue for masculine, pink for feminine). Showing videos to groups and inviting discussion have been used extensively to explore interpretation but have their limitations (see Morley, 1980, 1986). An alternative interesting array of games and exercises has been designed to explore people's specific engagement with media narratives, information, and messages. Much of the audience reception work by the Glasgow University Media Group involved scriptwriting exercises—in which research participants attempt to reproduce news bulletins or soap opera dialogue using still pictures taken from the TV screen (see Kitzinger, 1990; Philo, 1990). Other researchers have developed techniques such as having focus groups edit their own news bulletins or involving research participants in making their own videos (Gauntlett, 1997; MacGregor & Morrison, 1995). There is no space to outline such methods in detail here, but they have proved an invaluable complement to some of the data collection techniques discussed above.

EXPERIMENTAL RESEARCH

Experimental audience research involves studying controlled variables to test their effect. Such research is most closely associated with laboratory research into the impact of violence in the media (Bandura et al., 1963). However, experimental designs have been used to explore other theories, too. Iyengar and Kinder (1987) introduced an experimental approach to agenda-setting research in their study *News That Matters: Television and American Public Opinion*. They presented research participants with videotapes of television news broadcasts that had been altered by inserting extra news coverage of specific issues. Similar experimental approaches have been taken to examine the impact of "framing" (Price, Tewksbury, & Powers, 1997), test out cultivation theory (Rossler & Brosius, 2001), or explore how audiences view online news stories depending on the sources that they think have selected them (Sundar & Nass, 2001).

MULTILEVEL AND LONGITUDINAL RESEARCH

Any research is a snapshot in time and space, prioritizing an examination of some processes at the expense of others. However, understandings of the communication process can be increased by research that combines audience reception work (decoding) with studies of media content and production (encoding). (See, for example, the study of AIDS conducted by Miller et al., 1998.) Longitudinal work can also be invaluable. My own initial interviews with child sexual abuse survivors were conducted before the media "discovered" the issue. Comparing these early interviews with subsequent interviews with survivors a decade later provided insights into the media's role in constructing and transforming identities (Kitzinger, 2001, 2004). A longitudinal research design can be even more powerful when researchers go back to the *same* research participants. Reilly, for example, conducted focus groups in the early 1990s to explore how people in the United Kingdom made sense of mad cow disease. A few years later (1996), the mad cow crisis hit Britain with the admission that BSE could be linked with Creutzfeldt-Jakob disease (CJD).

Reilly was able to reconvene 13 of her initial 26 groups and explore their reassessment of the media coverage and their own views in light of such changes (Reilly, 1999).

HISTORICAL RESEARCH

Historical studies of audiences allow for even greater depth of insight into how meanings and practices have changed over time. Historians of "audiencehood" have been interested in issues such as the constitution of audiences for books, penny newspapers, or early cinema and the way in which reading, viewing, or listening was experienced. They have also explored how the media might interact with the creation of new forms of identity. Repeat focus groups or in-depth ethnographies, however, are rarely an option for those interested in such questions. Shifts within living memory can be accessed through interviewing people who were around at the time. Van Zoonen and Wieten (1994), for example, interviewed older people about the introduction of television into Dutch society in the 1950s. Beyond this, the historian is restricted to written and pictorial sources. This can include gleaning from editors' claims about their readers or from contemporary diaries or drawing on old mass-observation studies (e.g., Harper & Porter's [1996] study of crying in the cinema). Historians have documented family library holdings, newspaper subscriptions, and bookstore inventories and even examined how reading is illustrated in paintings (Darnton, cited in Schudson, 1991). Other data include archived letters to newspaper editors or radio broadcasters or fan letters to film producers (Nord, 1995; Ryfe, 2001; Stacey, 1994). Historians may need to be eclectic in their approach. Ehrenreich, Hess, and Jacobs (1992), in their work on "Beatlemania," for example, construct their argument using a variety of sources, including women's recollections of being Beatles fans, magazine articles, television viewing figures, a Gallup Poll, and quotes from DJs of the time. Other historians focus on specific types of viewers. Staiger, for example, analyzed comments by film critics (as a very specialized audience) in the 1920s and argued that they developed an aesthetic based as much on a film's expression of hyperpatriotic nationalist positions as on categories such as narrative or visual style (Staiger, cited in Smoodin, 1996).

◆ Reflections and Conclusion

The above discussion has offered a whistle-stop tour through audience research methods. This chapter is not intended to offer a "how-to" guide but, rather, introduces a range of approaches to this complex area of study. Readers wishing to learn more about specific research techniques will need to follow up specialist literature. I have also not touched on the broader debates about ethics, politics, and epistemology. Implicit in many of the approaches above are different models of what counts as meaningful knowledge and diverse ideas about how researchers can or should "represent" research participants. For each approach, there are also, of course, radically different ways of analyzing and presenting data (or, indeed, diverse degrees to which scholars place value on empirical data at all). Those debates are beyond the scope of the present chapter.

What I hope I have achieved is to introduce some of the strands running through the web of audience research. If nothing else, I hope to have highlighted the interconnection between theories about audiences, whom we study, how we study, and the questions we pursue. It is through conscious reflection on these interconnections, as well as awareness of alternative approaches, that understanding can be deepened and innovation developed.

◆ Note

1. A term used in Britain in the popular press to denote videos depicting extreme acts of violence supposedly perpetrated in real life.

◆ References

Ang, I. (1985). *Watching* Dallas. London: Methuen.

Ang, I. (1991). *Desperately seeking the audience*. London: Routledge.

Bandura, A., Ross, D., & Ross, S. (1963). Imitation of film-mediated aggressive models. *Journal of Personality and Social Psychology, 66*, 3–11.

Barbour, R., & Kitzinger, J. (Eds.). (1999). *Developing focus group research*. London: Sage.

Barker, M., & Petley, J. (Eds.). (2001). *Ill effects: The media/violence debate*. London: Routledge.

Baym, N. K. (2000). *Tune in, log on: Soaps, fandom and online community*. London: Sage.

Bobo, J. (1995). *Black women as cultural readers*. New York: Columbia University Press.

Brooker, W. (2001). Living on *Dawson's Creek*: Teen viewers, cultural convergence and television overflow. *International Journal of Cultural Studies, 4*(4), 456–472.

Corner, J. (1991). Meaning, genre and context: The problematics of "public knowledge" in the new audience studies. In J. Curran & M. Gurevitch (Eds.), *Mass media and society* (pp. 267–285). London: Edward Arnold.

Corner, J., Richardson, K., & Fenton, N. (1990). *Nuclear reactions: Format and response in public issue television*. London: J. Libbey.

The death of Diana [Special issue]. (1998). *Screen, 39*(1).

Ehrenreich, B., Hess, E., & Jacobs, G. (1992). Beatlemania: Girls just want to have fun. In L. Lewis (Ed.), *The adoring audience: Fan culture and popular media* (pp. 10–38). London: Routledge.

Eldridge, J. (Ed.). (1993). *Getting the message.* London: Routledge.

Eldridge, J., Kitzinger, J., & Williams, K. (1997). *The mass media and power in modern Britain.* Oxford, UK: Oxford University Press.

Gamson, W. (1992). *Talking politics.* Cambridge, UK: Cambridge University Press.

Gauntlett, D. (1997). *Video critical: Children, the environment and media power.* London: J. Libbey.

Geertz, C. (1973). *The interpretation of cultures.* New York: Basic Books.

Gerbner, G. (1973). Cultural indicators—The third voice. In G. Gerbner, L. Gross, & W. Milody (Eds.), *Communications technology and social policy* (pp. 553–575). New York: John Wiley.

Gillespie, M. (1995). *Television, ethnicity and cultural change.* London: Routledge.

Glasgow University Media Group. (1976). *Bad news.* London: Routledge.

Glasgow University Media Group. (1980). *More bad news.* London: Routledge.

Gray, A. (1987). Behind closed doors: Video recorders in the home. In H. Baehr & G. Dyer (Eds.), *Boxed in: Women and television* (pp. 38–54). London: Pandora.

Gray, A. (1999). Audience and reception research in retrospect: The trouble with audiences. In P. Alasuutari (Ed.), *Rethinking the media audience* (pp. 22–37). London: Sage.

Hall, S. (1980). Encoding/decoding. In S. Hall, D. Hobson, A. Lowe, & P. Willis (Eds.), *Culture, media, language: Working papers in cultural studies 1972–79* (pp. 128–138). London: Hutchinson.

Harper, S., & Porter, V. (1996). Moved to tears: Weeping in the cinema in postwar Britain. *Screen, 37*(2), 152–173.

Henderson, L., & Kitzinger, J. (1999). The human drama of genetics: "Hard" and "soft" media representations of inherited breast cancer. *Sociology of Health and Illness, 21*(5), 560–578.

Hill, A. (2001). Looks like it hurts: Women's responses to shocking entertainment. In M. Barker & J. Petley (Eds.), *Ill effects: The media/violence debate* (pp. 135–149). London: Routledge.

Hine, C. (2000). *Virtual ethnography.* London: Sage.

Hobson, D. (1982). *Crossroads: The drama of a soap.* London: Opera Methuen.

Iyengar, S., & Kinder, D. (1987). *News that matters: Television and American public opinion.* Chicago: University of Chicago Press.

Jayaprakash, T. (2000). Remote audiences beyond 2000: Radio, everyday life and development in South India. *International Journal of Cultural Studies, 3*(2), 227–239.

Jhally, S., & Lewis, J. (1992). *Enlightened racism: The Cosby Show, audiences and the myth of the American Dream.* Oxford, UK: Westview.

Johnson, K. (2001). Media and social change: The modernizing influences of television in rural India. *Media, Culture & Society, 23*(2), 147–169.

Jordin, M., & Brunt, R. (1988). Constituting the television audience: Problems of method. In P. Drummond & R. Paterson (Eds.), *Television and its audiences.* London: British Film Institute.

Katz, E., & Liebes, T. (1985). Mutual aid in decoding *Dallas:* Preliminary notes for a cross-culture study. In P. Drummond & R. Paterson (Eds.), *Television and its audiences* (pp. 187–198). London: British Film Institute.

Kitzinger, J. (1990). Audience understandings of AIDS media messages: A discussion. *Sociology of Health and Illness, 12*(3), 319–335.

Kitzinger, J. (1993). Understanding AIDS: Researching audience perceptions of acquired immune deficiency syndrome. In J. Eldridge (Ed.), *Getting the message* (pp. 271–304). London: Routledge.

Kitzinger, J. (1994). The methodology of focus groups: The importance of interactions between research participants. *Sociology of Health and Illness, 16*(1), 103–121.

Kitzinger, J. (1999). A sociology of media power: Key issues in audience reception research. In G. Philo (Ed.), *Message received* (pp. 3–20). Harlow, UK: Longman.

Kitzinger, J. (2000). Media templates: Patterns of association and the (re)construction of meaning over time. *Media, Culture & Society, 22*(1), 64–84.

Kitzinger, J. (2001). Transformations of public and private knowledge: Audience reception, feminism and the experience of childhood sexual abuse. *Feminist Media Studies, 1*(1), 91–104.

Kitzinger, J. (2002). Impacts and influences: Media influence revisited: An introduction to the new effects research. In P. Cobley & A. Briggs (Eds.), *The media: An introduction* (2nd ed., pp. 272–281). London: Longman.

Kitzinger, J. (2004). *Framing abuse: Media influence and public understandings of sexual violence against children*. London: Pluto Press.

Kitzinger, J., & Farquhar, C. (1999). The analytical potential of "sensitive moments" in focus group discussions. In R. Barbour & J. Kitzinger (Eds.), *Developing focus group research: Politics, theory and practice* (pp. 156–172). London: Sage.

Lang, K., & Lang, G. (1991). Studying events in their natural setting. In K. Jensen & N. Jankowski (Eds.), *A handbook of qualitative methodologies* (pp. 193–215). London: Routledge.

Lewis, L. (Ed.). (1992). *The adoring audience: Fan culture and popular media*. London: Routledge.

Liebes, T., & Katz, E. (1990). *The export of meaning*. Oxford, UK: Oxford University Press.

Lindlof, T., & Shatzer, M. (1998). Media ethnography in virtual space: Strategies, limits and possibilities. *Journal of Broadcasting and Electronic Media, 42*(2), 170–189.

Livingstone, S., Wober, M., & Lunt, P. (1994). Studio audience discussion programmes: An analysis of viewers' preferences and involvement. *European Journal of Communication, 9*(4), 355–387.

Lull, J. (1990). *Inside family viewing: Ethnographic research on television's audiences*. London: Routledge.

Lunt, P., & Livingstone, S. (1996). Rethinking the focus group in media and communications research. *Journal of Communication, 16*(2), 79–98.

MacGregor, B., & Morrison, D. (1995). From focus groups to editing groups: A new method of reception analysis. *Media, Culture & Society, 17*(1), 141–150.

McCombs, M., & Shaw, D. (1972). The agenda-setting function of the mass media. *Public Opinion Quarterly, 36*, 176–187.

Merton, R. K. (1987). The focussed interview and focus groups: Continuities and discontinuities. *Public Opinion Quarterly, 51*(4), 550–566.

Millard, W. (1992). A history of handsets for direct measurement of audience response. *International Journal of Public Opinion Research, 4*(1), 1–17.

Miller, D., Kitzinger, J., Williams, K., & Beharrell, P. (1998). *The circuit of mass communication: Media strategies, representation and audience reception in the AIDS crisis*. London: Sage.

Miller, D., & Philo, G. (2001). The active audience and wrong turns in media studies: Rescuing media power. *Soundscape, 4*. Retrieved from www.icce.rug.nl/~sound scapes/VOLUME04/Active_audience.html

Morley, D. (1980). *The "nationwide" audience: Structure and decoding*. London: British Film Institute.

Morley, D. (1986). *Family television: Cultural power and domestic leisure*. London: Comedia.

Morley, D., & Silverstone, R. (1990). Domestic communication. *Media, Culture & Society, 12*, 31–55.

Morley, D., & Silverstone, R. (1991). Communication and context: Ethnographic perspectives on the media audience. In K. Henson & N. Jankowski (Eds.), *A handbook for qualitative methodologies for mass communication research* (pp. 149–162). London: Routledge.

Morrison, D. (1998). *The search for a method: Focus groups and the development of mass communication research*. Luton, UK: University of Luton Press.

Newhagen, J., Cordes, J., & Levy, M. (1995). Nightly-at-NCB: Audience scope and the perception of interactivity in viewer mail on the internet. *Journal of Communication, 45*(3), 164–175.

Nightingale, V. (1989). What's ethnographic about ethnographic audience research? *Australian Journal of Communications, 16,* 50–63.

Nightingale, V. (1996). *Studying audiences: The shock of the real.* London: Routledge.

Nord, D. (1995). Reading the newspaper: Strategies and politics of reader response, Chicago 1912–1917. *Journal of Communication, 45*(3), 66–93.

Philo, G. (1990). *Seeing and believing.* London: Routledge.

Philo, G. (1999a). Children and film/video/TV violence. In G. Philo (Ed.), *Message received* (pp. 35–53). Harlow, UK: Longman.

Philo, G. (Ed.). (1999b). *Message received.* Harlow, UK: Longman.

Price, V., Tewksbury, D., & Powers, E. (1997). Switching trains of thought: The impact of news frames on readers' cognitive responses. *Communication Research, 24*(5), 481–506.

Pullen, K. (2000). I-love-Xena.com: Creating online fan communities. In D. Gauntlett (Ed.), *Web.studies: Rewriting media studies for the digital age* (pp. 52–61). London: Edward Arnold.

Radway, J. (1984). *Reading the romance: Feminism and the representation of women in popular culture.* Chapel Hill: University of North Carolina Press.

Reilly, J. (1999). "Just another food scare?" Public understanding and the BSE crisis. In G. Philo (Ed.), *Message received* (pp. 128–146). Harlow, UK: Longman.

Rossler, O., & Brosius, H. (2001). Do talk shows cultivate adolescents' views of the world? A prolonged-exposure experiment. *Journal of Communication, 51*(1), 143–163.

Ruddock, A. (2001). *Understanding audiences: Theory and method.* London: Sage.

Ryfe, D. (2001). From media audiences to media public: A study of letters written in reaction to FDR's fireside chats. *Media, Culture & Society, 23*(6), 767–783.

Schlesinger, P., Dobash, R. E., Dobash, R., & Weaver, C. K. (1992). *Women viewing violence against women.* London: British Film Institute.

Schudson, M. (1991). Historical approaches to communication studies. In K. Jensen & N. Jankowski (Eds.), *A handbook of qualitative methods for mass communication research* (pp. 175–191). London: Routledge.

Smoodin, E. (1996). The business of America: Fan mail, film reception and Meet John Doe. *Screen, 37*(2), 111–128.

Sood, S., & Rogers, E. (2000). Dimensions of parasocial interaction by letter-writers to a popular entertainment-education soap opera in India. *Journal of Broadcasting and Electronic Media, 44*(3), 386–414.

Stacey, J. (1994). *Star gazing: Hollywood cinema and female spectatorship.* London: Routledge.

Sundar, S., & Nass, C. (2001). Conceptualizing sources in online news. *Journal of Communication, 51*(1), 52–72.

Tufte, T. (2002). Communicating about domestic violence, rape and HIV/AIDS in South Africa: A reception analysis of viewers' letters. In C. Byerly & K. Ross (Eds.), *Mapping the field: Women and media.* London: Sage.

Van Zoonen, L., & Wieten, J. (1994). It wasn't exactly a miracle: The arrival of television in Dutch family life. *Media, Culture & Society, 16,* 641–659.

Werner, K. (2001). Coming close to God through the media: A phenomenology of the media practices of Islamist women in Egypt. In K. Hafez & D. Paletz (Eds.), *Mass media, politics and society in the Middle East.* Creskill, NJ: Hampton.

Young, L. (1996). Black women as cultural readers—Bobo, J. *Screen, 37*(4), 400–408.

TWENTIETH-CENTURY MEDIA EFFECTS RESEARCH

◆ Daniel G. McDonald

We don't know that what we're saying is particularly significant, but it is at least true.

—Robert K. Merton (1957,
describing mass communication research)

O ver the past 50 years, a number of authors have attempted to review the literature or offer conceptual schemes for classifying media effects (Hovland, 1954; McLeod & Reeves, 1980; Roberts & Maccoby, 1985; Weiss, 1969). Lazarsfeld (1948a) summarized the problem well:

> This dearth of substantial results is due to the difficulties of the field, which become apparent as one realizes what a complexity of problems the simple term effect produces. Mass media can affect knowledge, attitudes, opinions and behavior of individuals. These effects can be immediate or delayed, of short duration or long-lasting. Effects upon individuals might slowly become transformed into institutional changes. They can come about in simple reactions or complicated chains as when institutional changes produced by the media in turn affect individuals. (p. 249)

Along with variations in the conceptualization of the nature of what we mean by *effects,* studies of media effects may variously consider the mere existence of the media or a particular medium (Centerwall, 1989; McLuhan, 1964; Meyrowitz, 1985), the special characteristics of the media or a medium (McClure & Patterson, 1974; Munsterberg, 1916), the content of media or a medium (Gerbner & Gross, 1976), or a specific factor within certain forms of communication (McLeod, 1995). All of these conceptualizations, as well as many others, have been described as the causal agent in media effects studies. In addition, the notion of causality itself has undergone multiple changes in social scientific philosophy (Owens, 1992; Salmon, 1989). With these limitations in mind, this chapter will provide a brief historical overview of U.S. media effects research in the 20th century.

◆ *The Pioneer Phase*

Early in the 20th century, the field of social psychology was emerging at the crossroads between sociology and psychology. A small number of researchers and theorists began to explore such ideas as the psychology of being a member of a social group, group dynamics, and the impacts of the psychology of individuals on the organization. The era was also an important one in development of the mass media, for it saw the emergence of motion pictures, radio, and the telephone as mass communication devices. A few pioneering psychologists, sociologists, and social psychologists wrote about the impact that the new media were having on audiences and on society. Their writings and research set the groundwork for much of how we conceptualize media effects today.

Charles Horton Cooley, one of the first social psychologists, was one such theorist. In his extraordinary work, especially *Human Nature and the Social Order* (Cooley, 1902) and *Social Organization* (Cooley, 1909), Cooley set for himself the task of explaining the role of communication in society. First and foremost, Cooley saw the new communication media as providing an expansion of what has gone on before. For Cooley, the new media had certain defining characteristics, and those characteristics should indicate the types of effects we can expect.

Cooley suggests that the new media seem to be most clearly making gains over traditional communication in terms of speed of transmission and diffusion through the social classes. He noted two opposing strains as the result. On one hand, the media will encourage individuality by offering ideas that are congenial to a person's self-interest. On the other hand, the new media break down limits to the spread of ideas and customs, leading to a universal assimilation and sameness. Thus, Cooley sees the media as fostering individuality and conformity at the same time. The solution to this paradox, Cooley says, is that there are two types of individuality—one of isolation, the other of choice. The media should reduce the former but encourage the latter (Cooley, 1909, p. 93).

For Cooley, the new media have the same type of effects as interpersonal communication—and there is little to distinguish media from interpersonal communication. Starting from the premise that communication is that characteristic that makes us most human, Cooley deduces that what must happen, over time, is a gradual weakening of those things that separate us as individuals, communities, races, and nations as we come to understand that those who look, dress, or act differently are still very similar to us.

The negative media effects that Cooley foresees include the necessity of a public with a rather superficial understanding and concern for issues and other people. This superficiality is brought about by the fact that we learn so much about so many different things that we do not have time to think about, or understand, much of anything in detail. Because our time and attention are limited, he reasons, the addition of new issues to learn about or understand will decrease the amount of time and attention previously spent on fewer issues.

About the same time, Hugo Munsterberg, a psychologist at Harvard University, was thinking about effects that might be attributable to displacing real-world interaction by interaction with the symbolic world of motion pictures. Munsterberg wrote *The Photoplay: A Psychological Study* (Munsterberg, 1916), in which he combined the physiological aspects of perceiving depth and movement with the psychological characteristics of attention, memory, and imagination to examine what happens when someone views silent motion pictures.[1] This effect is based on the idea that the media provide an interaction with symbols or signs rather than with the objects or people those signs or symbols represent. Munsterberg makes the point that, for us to perceive continuous motion and depth[2] from the series of static images in a motion picture, our brain must integrate the information and produce a whole perception.

Munsterberg (1916) draws parallels between what motion pictures do and what our minds do as we make sense of reality. Just as our minds mold the objective world to our own interests through attention, imagination, and emotions, so too our minds bring together the details of the motion picture to form a coherent story. Motion picture techniques, such as flashbacks and cutaways serve to simulate memory, imagination, and attention processes.

For Munsterberg, then, mediated communication has its impact by presenting material that our mind must accept as real or true so that we can understand the communication.

The impacts arise from the manipulation of this symbolic reality and confusion of our perception of what is real with our knowledge that the presentation is completely symbolic. For Munsterberg, this confusion of reality and content is a necessary condition for understanding communication and a crucial part of how mediated communication works.

Other early researchers in this time period were similarly concerned about the effects of motion pictures but primarily concentrated on the effects on children (Bartholomew, 1913; Edwards, 1915; Phelan, 1919). A number of social workers and sociologists of the time were concerned about various aspects of the modern city, such as education, recreation, and leisure (Edwards, 1915; Gulick, 1909; Jones, 1922). Growing delinquency, increases in pregnancy rates, and other issues focused researchers' attention on potential causes and socialization influences, such as the motion picture and its theaters (Edwards, 1915; Gulick, 1909; Phelan, 1919).

Even in these early days of media effects study, direct media effects were typically conceived of as learning effects; other effects were a consequence of what was learned (Edwards, 1915; Phelan, 1919; Wilcox, 1900). Typically, that secondary effect was thought to be a negative effect (e.g., precocious involvement with the opposite sex, delinquency, learning about things that were "adult" in nature), although the idea that movie content could have a positive effect (morally uplifting or educational) was not lost on these researchers.

By assuming that content led to an effect, researchers were able to bypass the difficult process of relating content to effect and so spent much of their effort documenting the frequency of attendance, social aspects of attendance, and parental perceptions of motion picture effects. By the 1920s, there was a solid mass of evidence indicating that millions of children were attending motion pictures frequently—typically more than once per week—but, from a scientific standpoint, little could be concluded about the effects of motion pictures on those children beyond learning.

◆ The Payne Fund Studies

In 1928, to address the situation more completely, the Motion Picture Research Council set out to determine what effect motion pictures had on children. It did so by obtaining a grant from the Payne Fund, an organization with a history of interest in children and media. The grant was used to support the efforts of the Committee on Educational Research of the Payne Fund. Some of the best-known social scientists of the day were represented on the committee, and they devised a series of studies to investigate various aspects of potential effects of motion pictures on children. The results of that series of studies were completed by 1933 and reflected the state of knowledge regarding the effects of mass communication one third of the way through the 20th century.

Most of the Payne Fund researchers took a very practical stance, simply trying to document the effects of a medium that had, within about 30 years, become a major industry in the United States and around the world. The Payne Fund studies found that children and adults do learn from motion pictures. They could often remember what they learned for a long time afterward (weeks or months later) and that what they learned produced emotional responses. The Payne Fund studies documented many effects that would be restudied in research on radio or television decades later, including such phenomena as "sleeper effects," miscomprehension, imitation of positive and negative media role models, developmental differences in understanding and learning, and certain aspects of "perceived reality" research, such as the confusion of facts about motion picture reality for the real world.

After demonstrating that high levels of movie attendance were associated with declining morals, delinquent behavior, lower intelligence, and a number of other factors, the researchers faced a question: Does extreme movie attendance lead to conduct that harms reputation, or do children of low reputation go frequently to the movies (Charters, 1933)?

The authors of the studies were unable to answer the question after they raised it. Their conclusion is that there is no simple cause-and-effect relationship. They point toward the idea that all of their data support the notion of a reciprocal relationship—movies do have an effect on children, but those children who are most attracted to the worst movies tend to be those with the most problems to begin with. In phrasing that would echo throughout the later history of media effects research, two of the researchers noted that motion picture influence is specific for a given child and a given movie and that the same picture may influence different children in opposite directions (Shuttleworth & May, 1933).

The primary contribution of the Payne Fund studies was to document, as had not been done adequately earlier, that children and adults do learn from media and that what they learn has an impact on how they live their lives. Although the researchers were not able to specify exactly who would learn what or how learning affects behavior, it was clear that a simple process was not a viable explanation.

THE RADIO ERA

By the time the Payne Fund studies were published, a new medium was garnering research attention. Network radio had begun in 1927 and, by 1935, had millions of listeners each evening. Unlike the motion picture audience, for which attendance figures could be calculated directly from sales, the radio audience was invisible. Ratings services had been developed to estimate the size of the audience for particular programs to enable advertisers to get a sense of who was listening (Beville, 1985).

In 1933, President Hoover's commission on social trends compiled a two-volume set of studies devoted to understanding modern life. *Recent Social Trends* included one chapter devoted to the impact of radio, listing more than 100 effects of radio—as determined by the study's authors—on American society (President's Research Committee, 1933).

In 1935, Hadley Cantril and Gordon Allport published *The Psychology of Radio,* an attempt to clarify some of the descriptions of effects appearing in *Recent Social Trends* and take stock of what was known about radio, as well as what kinds of effects we might anticipate through radio. The authors noted that the medium's blending of interpersonal and impersonal characteristics should produce unique social effects. In their final chapter, Cantril and Allport describe the comparison of the degree of social participation afforded by radio and other forms of communication.

Given the thoughtful and careful nature of *The Psychology of Radio,* it is a bit ironic that Cantril is now better known for his study of an event that occurred in 1938, on the eve of World War II, when it became clear that the media were capable of achieving massive, dramatic effects.

Theater director Orson Welles was hosting a 1-hour weekly radio program in which works of literature were adopted for broadcast. For their Halloween broadcast, Welles and his writers had adapted H. G. Wells's *The War of the Worlds,* a science fiction story of an invasion by Martians. Because of a number of difficulties in working the original story (set in England) into a 1-hour U.S. radio broadcast, the setting was changed to New Jersey, and a somewhat unusual device was used to enable transitions between places and to speed up action: Much of the story, especially the opening, was told through radio news bulletins "interrupting" typical radio content.

Although the broadcast worked well for most of the audience, a small percentage of listeners that night had changed stations to the *War of the Worlds* from a more popular show a few minutes after the program started. As a result, they missed the opening announcements and thought they were listening to dance music—which was suddenly interrupted by news bulletins. In what was to become a dramatic demonstration of the power of radio to achieve effects, panic was induced among thousands of Americans. The actual extent of the panic will never be known, although some estimates run as high as 6 million who may have believed the Martians were invading the Earth. Cantril and a number of other researchers attempted to understand what had caused the panic (Cantril, Gaudet, & Herzog, 1940).

Cantril and his coauthors attempt to describe the individual characteristics that were associated with panicking or not panicking (Cantril et al., 1940). In other words, probably for the first time, researchers tried to sketch out the types of people and the types of conditions that might lead to such panic reactions. These conditions included such characteristics as suggestibility, critical ability, and fatalism. Such a conceptualization of media effects focused attention primarily on the psychological, rather than sociological, aspects. As the United States entered World War II, such psychological aspects dominated social science concerns as they worked to counteract the effects, or presumed effects, of enemy propaganda (Davison, 1983).

WORLD WAR II AND COMMUNICATION EFFECTS RESEARCH

The *War of the Worlds* phenomenon must have been in the minds of communication researchers as they assessed mass communication's role in the world war. In the case of propaganda, whether encouraging patriotism among one's own troops or hatred for the enemy, the effect was achieved primarily through emotional responses—fear, hatred, pride, love, and other affective responses to communication.

In some ways, those same feelings and emotions that had been roused by the "invasion from Mars" needed to be harnessed and used against an earthly enemy. It was clear that, under certain conditions, the media could achieve very powerful effects. The task of these researchers was to determine what those conditions were. Researchers were asked to determine how to construct the most effective propaganda material. Their attempts to determine the "magic bullets" of effectiveness are documented in *The American Soldier* (Stouffer, Lumsdaine, et al., 1949; Stouffer, Suchman, DeVinney, Star, & Williams, 1949) and *Experiments in Mass Communication* (Hovland, Lumsdaine, & Sheffield, 1949).

Although decidedly influenced by the *War of the Worlds,* Hovland and his colleagues clearly had a different research interest than did Cantril. Cantril was investigating the mechanisms associated with the multiple effects and different interpretations of one radio program, whereas Hovland et al. (1949) were attempting to uncover general principles related to the construction of messages (Lumsdaine, 1984).

For Hovland and his colleagues, the audience provided the measure of success of a persuasive argument. Hovland et al.'s (1949) use of controlled field experiments for gauging the effects of media programs on soldiers' knowledge, opinions, and attitudes set the parameters for investigations of mass and interpersonal persuasion for several decades. Hovland and his colleagues pursued such issues as differences in the channels of communication (e.g., lecture, documentary films, etc.) and were interested in being able to generalize effects across media—to motion pictures, radio, and newspapers (Lumsdaine, 1984).

Following World War II, it became apparent that there were not any easy answers or magic bullets that could be used in persuasive communication. After the war, Hovland directed the Yale University program on attitude change research, which brought the field study and experimental

work they produced to major prominence as methods of studying the social psychology of communication and attitude change (Himmelfarb & Eagly, 1974; Lumsdaine, 1984; McGuire, 1996; Rosnow & Robinson, 1967). The Hovland group (Hovland, 1954, 1957; Hovland, Janis, & Kelley, 1953; Hovland et al., 1949) advanced the study of one-sided versus two-sided arguments and source credibility, among other areas.

Paul Lazarsfeld and his colleagues at Columbia University had begun a program of research on the role of mass communication in modern society in the late 1930s (Katz, 1987; Katz & Lazarsfeld, 1955; Lazarsfeld, 1940, 1946; Lazarsfeld, Berelson, & Gaudet, 1944). After several publications related to the use and effects of radio, their interest broadened to the role of mass media in general and included newspapers, books, radio, and motion pictures. Several volumes of a journal, *Radio Research* (later *Communications Research*), were published, documenting their studies. In addition, Lazarsfeld focused heavily on the role of media in personal decision making. Their work dealing with the role of the media in political contexts is still heavily cited today.

Lazarsfeld's methods (primarily survey research) were very different from those of Hovland and his colleagues, and his conclusions were also very different. Hovland's research investigated the factors responsible for attitude or opinion change and so often pitted one version or one technique against another, whereas Lazarsfeld's work was set in the real world of elections, fashion and style, and one person's influence on another.

Lazarsfeld and his colleagues found that mass media were not often associated with simple directional change in attitude or opinion but were apparently often associated with a reinforcing effect (Katz, 1987). In a sense, the findings parallel those of the Payne Fund and other studies of media violence and behavior—that those predisposed toward violent behavior were most likely to consume violent motion picture content.

However, in the case of studies of violent content, the finding was generally considered an indicator of either a powerful media effect or evidence of reciprocal causation. In the case of political content, in which the search was for sources of attitude change, the same type of finding was interpreted as either no effect or reinforcement.

The difference in interpretation of the two similar findings might be explained through examining the connotations associated with the studies. On one hand, in studies of media violence, there is a strong negative sanction against the dependent variable, and any contributory increases in violent behavior are considered negative factors. On the other hand, political attitudes, whether based in typically Republican or Democratic Party ideals, are both equally acceptable and valid, so the only effect of consequence is a conversion from undecided to a decision or the very rare occurrence of a complete reversal from a Republican to Democratic affiliation.

A new form of communication effects research was begun in the 1950s as social psychologists interested in communication as an aspect of interpersonal interaction were developing theories of how communication works. Ted Newcomb's idea of co-orientation (Newcomb, 1953, 1961) focused on one person's orientation toward another person and how communication serves to increase the accuracy of our perceptions. Drawing on ideas from Charles H. Cooley (1902, 1909), Kurt Lewin (1951), George H. Mead (1982), Talcott Parsons (1953), and Fritz Heider (1958), Newcomb developed a model of co-orientation that was to have a major influence on the field of communication a decade later and that continued to exert an influence on the field throughout the rest of the 20th century and into the 21st century (Carter, 1965; Kenny & Acitelli, 2001; McLeod & Chaffee, 1973; Shin & Cameron, 2003).

Newcomb's idea of co-orientation was abstract and, although easily lending itself to most communication situations, the practical application of the principles and approach he developed were unclear. In addition,

Newcomb suggested that orientations, which were similar to attitudes, were inferred from behavior (Newcomb, 1961, p. 5), contradicting the then-current idea that behavior followed attitudes. Through the 1950s and 1960s, however, a number of mass communication researchers used Newcomb's notion of co-orientation and other similar models in which perceptions of others played a major role in explaining communication behavior and effects of communication (de Sola Pool & Shulman, 1959; Eisenberg, Monge, & Farace, 1984; Suzuki, 1997; White, 1950).

FRAGMENTATION, CONFUSION, AND DEEPER QUESTIONS

Reconciling the different ideas, approaches, methods, and findings became a major preoccupation of the late 1950s and early 1960s. The establishment of Ph.D.s in communication led to many more studies of media effects during the 1950s. Publication of Wilbur Schramm's *The Process and Effects of Mass Communication* in 1954 highlighted a number of these different approaches to media effects.

Schramm's (1954) reader provided communication students with research summaries and articles by sociologists, psychologists, anthropologists, historians, and a host of other researchers and theorists. That volume and later editions serve as exemplars of Schramm's idea that communication is "one of the great crossroads where many pass but few tarry" (Schramm, Riesman, & Bauer, 1959, p. 8), but the collections also highlight how different approaches yielded different answers, how little was known about the conditions under which media had effects, or even about the process of communication itself.

Amid these concerns, in 1959, Bernard Berelson pronounced the field of communication research as withering away, noting that "the innovators have left or are leaving the field, and no ideas of comparable scope and generating power are emerging" (p. 4).

Schramm et al. (1959) responded to Berelson's contention with a range of examples and explanations for what Berelson was observing, but it was clear, even in their comments, that the state of communication research was undergoing a transition period in which research would be different.

Other writers also noted the sea change in communication research. Joseph Klapper's (1960) book, *The Effects of Mass Communication,* described a shift from "hypodermic effect" models of media effects to what he termed "phenomenistic" models—those that saw the media as influences within a total situation. W. Philips Davison (1959) suggested that the audience was not a passive recipient of communication but an active, selective partner in the process. Raymond Bauer's "obstinate audience" (Bauer, 1964, 1965; Bauer & Bauer, 1960; Zimmerman & Bauer, 1956) suggested that a transactional model of give-and-take between audience and communicator is needed to understand communication effects.

◆ Growth in the Discipline, Fragmentation in Direction

By the mid-1960s, media effects research was firmly established within various departments and schools of journalism and communication. Partly because these schools were organized in accord with industry divisions (e.g., advertising, public relations, journalism, organizational communication, etc.), media effects research was similarly fragmented into contexts rather than process. Thus, by that time, effects associated with media were being studied as aspects of journalism, advertising, broadcasting, or whatever department or specialty area in which the researcher was teaching. Even as mainstream psychology and sociology took less interest in studying specific mass media effects, the new field of communication research continued to borrow broad theories and hypotheses from those fields as explanations for communication effects.

In the late 1960s, cognitive psychology began to provide raw material for advances in mass communication effects research. Armed with such concepts as salience and pertinence, media effects research began to abandon the question of whether media had effects to attempt to specify the mechanisms by which those effects were achieved. Across the field of communication research, it became clear, as Chaffee (1977) observed, that media effects often occurred within our minds and were not directly observable; more varied and inventive methods were needed to understand the processes by which media have effects.

RESEARCH ON VIOLENT CONTENT AND BEHAVIOR

Increasing crime rates, racial unrest, and generational tension of the 1960s led to a diversion of both researcher attention and grant money from the U.S. government to attempt to understand the causes of violent behavior. During the late 1960s and early 1970s, hundreds of studies investigated the link between media content and violent behavior. A group of studies by social psychologist Albert Bandura are among the best known of these.

Bandura's social learning theory formed the theoretical base for his (and many other) studies. Bandura (1977) advanced the discussion of media effects by specifying conditions under which he would expect people (especially children) to imitate antisocial and prosocial behaviors presented in the media. In social learning theory, those behaviors that are shown performed by attractive people or those behaviors that are shown to be rewarded are more likely to be imitated. Results of these studies were overwhelmingly consistent. Although some of these same principles were described in some of the Payne Fund studies of the 1930s (Charters, 1933) and even earlier (e.g., Phelan, 1919), Bandura's important contribution was to make these conditions explicit and test them in an experimental setting.

The success of social learning theory in explaining children's imitation of media role models led to additional investigations of how and when children imitate media characters. Long-term studies (e.g., Huesmann & Eron, 1986) found additional confirmation of an association of media violence with later aggressive and criminal behavior. The psychological notion of "priming" held importance for Berkowitz and his colleagues (Berkowitz & Geen, 1966; Berkowitz & Rawlings, 1963). They demonstrated that watching a film containing violent behavior, such as a fistfight, might arouse a set of responses that are associated in the viewer's mind with fighting. If the viewing is followed fairly quickly by a real event that is also associated with the same set of responses as those associated with fighting, the content can "prime" that second set of responses so that it may become more likely that the viewer will respond with a behavior associated with the fistfight.

The preponderance of the evidence pointed fairly quickly to the potential of television to contribute to violent behavior, yet not one of the studies could conclusively show that TV or movies caused violent behavior. Researchers could show that, within a laboratory setting, providing children or adults with violent content and the means to take violent action could result in violent behavior. In the general population, through survey and other studies, researchers could show that children and adults who were violent also tended to watch violent media content. Linking the two in a causal chain became a frustrating and difficult process.

The lack of clear demonstration of causal connections did not go unnoticed. Early on, Feschbach (1956) had advanced the catharsis hypothesis, which suggested that violent television viewing could be a means of reducing frustration and tension, similar to the effects the ancient Greeks believed to occur from attending dramatic theater. Although the catharsis hypothesis received somewhat mixed support and continues to live in some current approaches to mood management (e.g., Bryant & Zillmann, 1994), some

researchers, such as Sparks (2002), suggest that the evidence supporting the catharsis effect was primarily a result of problems in the method of investigation rather than evidence for the effect.

By the 1980s, television network executives were frustrated by a large number of studies (done with less than scientific accuracy) that blamed television for a range of violent behavior and attitudes. Centerwall (1989), for example, estimated that a large proportion of U.S. homicides were a direct result of television. A panel of academic researchers was commissioned by NBC to investigate the problem in detail, using an impressive data collection effort and advanced statistical procedures (Milavsky, Kessler, Stipp, & Ruben, 1982). The panel of researchers found little to connect television as a causal factor in later violent behavior. Most academic researchers, though, continued to believe that the evidence, although not completely clear, is strong enough to implicate media violence as a contributory condition. Such a conclusion was reached tentatively in the 1972 Surgeon General's Report (Comstock & Rubinstein, 1972), and more forcefully in the update sponsored by the National Institute for Mental Health (Pearl, Bouthilet, & Lazar, 1982). In addition, meta-analytic reviews of the media-violence connection during the late 1980s and 1990s provided additional clues to the nature of the relationships and the boundary conditions operating in the connection between content and behavior.

◆ Beyond Behavior: Construction of a Social Reality

Although the question of media as an antecedent or cause of violent behavior remained a popular one, the notion of cognitive effects and affective reactions to media were to dominate the last 25 years of media effects research in the 20th century. Among the highest profile and most researched areas was cultivation theory, developed by Gerbner and his colleagues (Gerbner & Gross, 1976; Gerbner, Gross, Signorelli, & Morgan, 1979) suggesting that television "cultivates" an outlook about social reality in the country. They hypothesize that the more one uses television, the more he or she will accept the "TV world" as reflective of reality.

Cultivation theory generated strong debate and numerous studies throughout the late 1970s and 1980s and remained an active area of research in the 1990s. Tests of the theory became complex and difficult, and modifications to the theory were developed as evidence became difficult to sort out (Gerbner, Gross, Morgan, & Signorelli, 1981). Results and conclusions have been criticized on both conceptual and methodological grounds (Doob & MacDonald, 1979; Hawkins & Pingree, 1982; Hirsch, 1981), and a recent meta-analysis by Morgan and Shanahan (1997) found no statistically significant cultivation effect.

◆ Media Effects and Social Issues

The early 1970s saw the emergence of several major strands of research associated with social issues and political knowledge. Although media effects had been an area of attraction for political science since the time of Lasswell (1948) and before (Wilcox, 1900), researchers in the field typically took ideas from political science and tested them as media effects. In the early 1970s, the field of communication began to develop a number of ideas about the way issues and knowledge about issues were communicated through the media that were to have a major impact on the field and allied areas such as political science.

One of these research areas, the knowledge gap hypothesis, developed by Tichenor, Donohue, and Olien (1970), suggested that,

as information diffuses into a social system, certain segments of the population learn the information faster than other segments. The result of the differential rate of learning is that gaps between social groups increase, rather than decrease, over time and with more information. The knowledge gap hypothesis became the focus of hundreds of studies from the 1970s through the close of the century. At first content with replication of the initial findings, later studies began to describe contingent conditions and antecedents of the basic effect (Gaziano, 1985). Although the knowledge gap remained an area of study throughout the century, research in the area peaked in the mid-1980s as more and more communication researchers tended toward psychological, rather than sociological, models for research.

Another area of study during the 1970s and 1980s was stimulated by changing news media. In the 1960s, for the first time, television news had overtaken newspapers in survey responses to the question ascertaining which medium people relied on most for news about current affairs and politics. The announcement generated a number of studies of "media reliance" or "media dependency" in which researchers attempted to unravel the consequences of this change in the social system. Although under experimental conditions, some researchers were able to show that television news was related to political cynicism and disaffection (McClure & Patterson, 1974; Patterson & McClure, 1976). The implications drawn for the social system were quite broad and alarming. A number of researchers demonstrated, through survey data, that those who relied primarily on TV news for their information were not as well informed or as trusting of politicians as those who relied on newspapers.

A flurry of research activity generated in the early and mid-1980s demonstrated similar results. However, because the bulk of the studies did not involve data that would enable causal inferences, some researchers questioned the validity of the conclusions drawn about the role of television and suggested that the findings might as easily be attributed to the type of person who seeks news from television rather than radio.

Studies by McLeod and McDonald (1985), Reese and Miller (1981), and a number of others found evidence that people did, indeed, learn from television news. By the late 1980s, the sweeping conclusions of the earlier research had had considerable doubt cast on it. In a situation that nearly mimics exactly Lazarsfeld's (1946) study of newspaper and radio reliance, the field essentially concluded that Lazarsfeld was correct in his assertion that those who reported relying on electronic media were less interested in the news in general than were those who reported relying on newspapers (Lazarsfeld, 1940, 1946, 1948b).

One area of study that was developed in the late 1960s and early 1970s illustrates in particular the general trend in media effects research during the past quarter century. Although the idea had been suggested earlier (Cohen, 1963; Lippmann, 1922), the agenda-setting hypothesis was most clearly enunciated by McCombs and Shaw (1972). The hypothesis suggested that the media set the agenda for public discussion of social issues by providing clues about which issues were important to think about.

Probably as a function of the heavy influence of cognitive psychology on media effects research in the late 1970s, agenda-setting research was recast from a social system effect; that is, the media "correlated" responses in social surveys (cf. Lasswell, 1948) to an individual psychological effect in which the media were seen as manipulating the salience of issues. Thus, although the theory originally focused on public discussion as being affected by media coverage, tests of the theory focused on media coverage being associated with issue salience or prioritization in people's minds. As cognitive psychology had greater impacts on media research in the 1980s and 1990s, a number of additional ideas were added to and complemented the agenda-setting framework (McCombs & Shaw, 1993).

Agenda setting was transformed from a hypothesis to a research area, incorporating earlier sociological concerns such as news diffusion (Breed, 1960) and gatekeeping (Becker, McCombs, & McLeod, 1975; White, 1950). Attempts were also made to link agenda setting to other theories, such as news framing, media priming, and the spiral of silence.

Research in news framing is concerned with how issues are presented in the news—which details are important, which are trivialized or peripheral. The area is based on early observations by Gitlin (1980) and studied by a number of researchers in communication and political science (Iyengar, 1991; Iyengar & Kinder, 1987). The research suggests that, by emphasizing certain aspects of issues, framing has implications for understanding the ebb and flow of public opinion.

Media priming effects take the notion of priming from cognitive psychology, which suggests that people can be "primed" to use certain stored sets of knowledge in making decisions or evaluations simply by exposing them to an associated stimulus (Higgins & King, 1981). Media priming is somewhat different from the psychological construct of priming in that it suggests that people are primed to make judgments on such things as presidential performance through repeated exposure to news reports on issues (Kinder, 1998a). The departure from the psychological area of priming is clear in that media priming refers to what might be seen as associative learning—people make connections between presidents and issues, for example, because they are taught those connections through news reports. Repeated presentations of the issues result in audience members' use of those learned links in evaluating the president. Whereas the psychological construct of priming refers to an activation of mental connections between the prime and the object of evaluation (Higgins & King, 1981), media priming refers to the dominance of certain learned connections in making an evaluation (Kinder, 1998a). Although the idea of media priming has generated a large amount of research, it is a relatively new idea. There are conceptual issues surrounding how it works and how it differs from other related media effects perspectives such as agenda setting or other phenomena such as salience, accessibility, activation, and the psychological concept of priming (Domke, Shah, & Wackman, 1998; Edelstein, 1993; Higgins & King, 1981; Kinder, 1998b).

◆ Media Effects and Public Opinion

A second major research area to emerge in the early 1970s and remain a fruitful avenue for research at the close of the century was in the area of public opinion research. Elisabeth Noelle-Neumann's (1974) idea of the spiral of silence appeared at first to attract little attention beyond that of members of her institute; however, by the early 1980s, it had emerged as one of the most researched theories in the field. The spiral of silence suggested that people tend to remain silent, rather than express opinions, if they perceive that their opinion is losing ground among the population. Mass media effects within the theory play a fairly minor but important role of providing information about the climate of opinion, and the perception of this climate is what is used in determining whether one's opinion is gaining or losing ground.

Most researchers studying the spiral of silence pick only certain components to study because the theory requires fairly substantial data to test completely. Although a number of early studies called some of the basic premises into question, empirical studies support various aspects of the theory (Glynn & McLeod, 1984). A meta-analysis conducted in the late 1990s (Glynn, Hayes, & Shanahan, 1997) found that the overall premise had small but statistically significant support. In addition, in one of the few studies testing the theory over time, McDonald, Glynn, Kim, and Ostman (2001) used the 1948 election data collected by Berelson, Lazarsfeld, and McPhee (1954) and found support consistent with the premises of the theory.

MEDIA USE AS EFFECT

As the first century of empirical mass media effects research in the United States was drawing to a close, research on the internet loomed large in journals and the popular press. A number of these studies are simply replicating older studies done with different media (see Wartella & Reeves, 1985). Some of these attempt to incorporate what has been established about our interactions with media. The best of these merge the interpersonal communication literature with mass media effects literature in a way that may not be too far off from what Cooley (1902, 1909) imagined at the beginning of the century and also incorporating more of the social element that had largely been missing from media effects research since the Payne Fund studies. The worst of them sink to what Chaffee (1979) described as the "synthetic competition"—a pitting of one medium against another to determine which is "best."

During the 1980s, physiological research methods began to be employed by a number of researchers working on media effects. Although some types of physiological measures were being used as early as the Payne Fund studies of the 1930s, these types of measures were seldom used between that time and the 1980s, when the need to look into the "black box" processes, or at least their outward manifestations, became increasingly important for communication theory. These researchers were most concerned with the areas where media had direct effects: attention, thought, memory, cognitions, arousal, skin conductance, and heart rate. Although the relevance or importance of the variables being studied in this type of research may not be immediately clear, what is clear is that the effect is a result of communication.

In concert with physiological studies that hark back to the early Payne Fund studies, the 1980s began to see affect and affective reaction return as a legitimate area of study in communication research (Dorr, 1981). Research proliferated on frightening mass media, led largely by the work of Joanne Cantor and her colleagues (Cantor, 1994; Cantor & Sparks, 1984; Cantor & Wilson, 1984). Offshoots of this research also examined the role of other people in modifying the mass media experience (Nathanson, 1999).

◆ New Directions

These studies, as well as others investigating how mass media fit into people's lives, suggest that Bauer's (1965) ideas of models of the transactional and interactive nature of communication might be on the horizon. As the second century in mass media effects research begins, there are a number of areas in which we may expect media effects research to be conducted over the next few years. Because of their generality, two broad areas may dominate media effects research in all of its contexts: issues of communication and reality and further exploration of the black box.

Issues of communication and reality, distinguishing reality from communication and other similar questions, follow from the earliest investigations of Munsterberg (1916) through the Payne Fund studies (Charters, 1933), Cantril and Allport (1935), Gerbner's cultivation studies (Gerbner & Gross, 1976; Gerbner et al., 1979), and contemporary issues of "presence" in virtual reality. It is one of the most basic questions in communication research: What is the difference between communication and reality? Although some studies frame the question as if blurring communication and reality is a particular problem, it is clear that blurring is the natural state of things, or else communication would have no relevance to reality. That is, communication is about reality, or it is worthless. The degree to which communication is isomorphic to reality is an extremely difficult question.

From one perspective, no communication is real—it is all communication. In some instances, however, we expect people to act on communication as if they were reacting to a reality—if someone yells "fire," for example. In other instances, we expect people not to treat the communication as reality—if someone yells "Godzilla," for example. As the new century of media research begins, we see that it is probably not an issue of deciding whether material depicted in the media is real; it is more likely an issue of deciding which dimensions of reality can be found in any particular communication. The idea of "real" may take on many visual, semantic, and meaning aspects—an affective reality (e.g., illustrating emotions that are consistent with the situation that is being dramatized), a reality of general social principles (e.g., suggesting that people who live fast lives die early), or a reality of visual appeal (e.g., that's real because it moves like a raptor should move). With computer-generated motion picture locations and characters, the field may find it profitable to study these and many other dimensions involved in how we use, rather than evaluate, communication and reality.

Further Exploration of the Black Box. Understanding how audience members understand reality is a subarea within the broader area of understanding what happens while communicating. Our first hundred years made a number of assumptions about communication; our models divided communication into various components, suggested stages in communication processes, described encoding and decoding of messages, and so forth, but all of these models and theories of communication were based on an assumption that either (a) we would never know the actual processes that occur or (b) the processes could be logically deduced. As we move into the second century of media effects research, we find that the assumptions of (b) are inadequate for a scientific study of media effects, and although (a) may be true in the strictest sense, psychological models and methods for studying information processing have gotten much more sophisticated and moved closer to modeling if not the process then at least the outcome, of thought.

◆ Notes

1. Commercial sound motion pictures were not available until 1927, 11 years after Munsterberg's book was published. Silent films were commonly exhibited in small towns even through the 1930s.

2. Depth is typically not thought of as being present in motion pictures; Munsterberg (1916) makes a case for the perception of depth by focusing on the difference between knowledge and perception. *Knowledge* refers to our awareness that the screen is flat; *perception* refers to our acceptance that the images on the screen move within a three-dimensional space. When someone walks behind a chair in film, for example, we do not think it odd when this person's legs "disappear" because we accept the image as having depth.

◆ References

Bandura, A. (1977). *Social learning theory.* Englewood Cliffs, NJ: Prentice Hall.

Bartholomew, R. O. (1913). *Report of censorship of motion pictures and of investigation of motion picture theatres of Cleveland.* Cleveland, OH: City of Cleveland.

Bauer, R. (1965). Communication as transaction. In D. E. Payne (Ed.), *The obstinate audience* (pp. 3–12). Ann Arbor, MI: Braun and Brumfield.

Bauer, R. A. (1964). The obstinate audience: The influence process from the point of view of social communication. *American Psychologist, 19,* 319–328.

Bauer, R. A., & Bauer, A. H. (1960). America, mass society and the mass media. *Journal of Social Issues, 16*(3), 3–66.

Becker, L. B., McCombs, M. E., & McLeod, J. M. (1975). The development of political cognitions. In S. Chaffee (Ed.), *Political communications: Issues and strategies for research* (Sage Annual Reviews of Communication Research No. 4, pp. 21–63). Beverly Hills, CA: Sage.

Berelson, B. (1959). The state of communication research. *Public Opinion Quarterly, 23,* 1–6.

Berelson, B. R., Lazarsfeld, P. F., & McPhee, W. N. (1954). *Voting.* Chicago: University of Chicago Press.

Berkowitz, L., & Geen, R. G. (1966). Film violence and the cue properties of available targets. *Journal of Personality and Social Psychology, 3,* 525–530.

Berkowitz, L., & Rawlings, E. (1963). Effects of filmed violence on inhibitions against subsequent aggression. *Journal of Abnormal Social Psychology, 66,* 405–412.

Beville, H. M. (1985). *Audience ratings: Radio, television and cable.* Hillsdale, NJ: Lawrence Erlbaum.

Breed, W. (1960). Social control in the news room. In W. Schramm (Ed.), *Mass communications* (pp. 178–194). Urbana: University of Illinois Press.

Bryant, J., & Zillmann, D. (Eds.). (1994). *Media effects: Advances in theory and research.* Hillsdale, NJ: Lawrence Erlbaum.

Cantor, J. (1994). Fright reactions to mass media. In J. Bryant & D. Zillmann (Eds.), *Media effects: Advances in theory and research* (pp. 213–245). Hillsdale, NJ: Lawrence Erlbaum.

Cantor, J., & Sparks, G. G. (1984). Children's fear responses to mass media: Testing some Piagetian predictions. *Journal of Communication, 34*(2), 90–113.

Cantor, J., & Wilson, B. J. (1984). Modifying fear responses to mass media in preschool and elementary school children. *Journal of Broadcasting, 28,* 431–443.

Cantril, H., & allport, G. W. (1935). *The psychology of radio.* New York: Harper & Brothers.

Cantril, H., Gaudet, H., & Herzog, H. (1940). *The invasion from Mars: A study in the psychology of panic.* Princeton, NJ: Princeton University Press.

Carter, R. F. (1965). Communication and affective relations. *Journalism Quarterly, 42,* 203–212.

Centerwall, B. S. (1989). Exposure to television as a cause for violence. In G. Comstock (Ed.), *Public communication and behavior* (Vol. 2, pp. 1–58). San Diego: Academic Press.

Chaffee, S. H. (1977). Mass media effects: New research perspectives. In D. Lerner & L. Nelson (Eds.), *Communications research: A half century appraisal* (pp. 210–241). Honolulu: University Press of Hawaii.

Chaffee, S. H. (1979, November). *Mass media vs. interpersonal channels: The synthetic competition.* Paper presented at the annual conference of the Speech Communication Association, San Antonio, TX.

Charters, W. W. (1933). *Motion pictures and youth: A summary.* New York: Macmillan.

Cohen, B. C. (1963). *The press, the public and foreign policy.* Princeton, NJ: Princeton University Press.

Comstock, G. A., & Rubinstein, E. A. (Eds.). (1972). *Television and social behavior.* Washington, DC: Government Printing Office.

Cooley, C. H. (1902). *Human nature and the social order.* New York: Scribner's.

Cooley, C. H. (1909). *Social organization.* New York: Scribner's.

Davison, W. P. (1959). On the effects of communication. *Public Opinion Quarterly, 23*(3), 343–360.

Davison, W. P. (1983). The third person effect in communication. *Public Opinion Quarterly, 47*(1), 1–15.

de Sola Pool, I., & Shulman, I. (1959). Newsmen's fantasies, audiences, and newswriting. *Public Opinion Quarterly, 23*(2), 145–158.

Domke, D., Shah, D. V., & Wackman, D. B. (1998). Media priming effects: Accessibility, association and activation. *International Journal of Public Opinion Research, 10*(1), 51–74.

Doob, A. N., & MacDonald, G. E. (1979). Television viewing and fear of victimization: Is the relationship causal? *Journal of Personality and Social Psychology, 37,* 170–179.

Dorr, A. (1981). Television and affective development and functioning: Maybe this decade. *Journal of Broadcasting, 25*(4), 335–345.

Edelstein, A. S. (1993). Thinking about the criterion variable in agenda-setting research. *Journal of Communication, 43*(2), 85–99.

Edwards, R. (1915). *Popular amusements.* New York: Association Press.

Eisenberg, E. M., Monge, P. R., & Farace, R. V. (1984). Coorientation on communication rules in managerial dyads. *Human Communication Research, 11*(2), 261–271.

Feschbach, S. (1956). The catharsis hypothesis and some consequences of the interaction with aggressive and neutral play objects. *Journal of Personality, 24,* 449–462.

Gaziano, C. (1985). The knowledge gap: An analytical review of media effects. In M. Gurevitch & M. Levy (Eds.), *Mass communication review yearbook* (Vol. 5, pp. 462–501). Beverly Hills, CA: Sage.

Gerbner, G., & Gross, L. (1976). Living with television: The violence profile. *Journal of Communication, 26,* 173–199.

Gerbner, G., Gross, L., Signorelli, N., & Morgan, M. (1979). Aging with television: Images on television drama and conceptions of social reality. *Journal of Communication, 30*(1), 37–47.

Gerbner, G., Gross, L., Morgan, M., & Signorelli, N. (1981). A curious journey into the scary world of Paul Hirsch. *Communication Research, 8,* 39–72.

Gitlin, T. (1980). *The whole world is watching: Mass media in the making and unmaking of the new left.* Berkeley: University of California Press.

Glynn, C. J., Hayes, A., & Shanahan, J. (1997). Perceived support for one's opinion and willingness to speak out: A meta-analysis of survey studies on the "spiral of silence." *Public Opinion Quarterly, 61,* 452–463.

Glynn, C. J., & McLeod, J. M. (1984). Public opinion du jour: An examination of the spiral of silence. *Public Opinion Quarterly, 48,* 731–740.

Gulick, L. (1909). Popular recreation and public morality. *Annals of the Academy of Political and Social Science, 34,* 33–42.

Hawkins, R. P., & Pingree, S. (1982). Television's influence on social reality and conceptions of the world. In D. Pearl, L. Bouthilet, & J. Lazar (Eds.), *Television and behavior: Ten years of scientific progress and implications for the eighties* (pp. 224–247). Washington, DC: Government Printing Office.

Heider, F. L. (1958). *The psychology of interpersonal relations.* New York: John Wiley.

Higgins, E. T., & King, G. A. (1981). Accessibility of social constructs: Information processing consequences of individual and contextual accessibility. In N. Cantor & J. F. Kihlstrom (Eds.), *Personality, cognition and social interaction* (pp. 69–121). Hillsdale, NJ: Lawrence Erlbaum.

Himmelfarb, S., & Eagly, A. H. (1974). *Readings in attitude change.* New York: John Wiley.

Hirsch, P. (1981). On not learning from one's own mistakes: A reanalysis of Gerbner, et al.'s findings on cultivation analysis: Part II. *Communication Research, 8,* 3–17.

Hovland, C. I. (1954). Effects of the mass media of communication. In G. Lindzey (Ed.), *Handbook of social psychology* (pp. 1062–1103). Reading, MA: Addison-Wesley.

Hovland, C. I. (Ed.). (1957). *The order of presentation in persuasion.* New Haven, CT: Yale University Press.

Hovland, C. I., Janis, I. L., & Kelley, H. H. (1953). *Communication and persuasion: Psychological studies of opinion change.* New Haven, CT: Yale University Press.

Hovland, C. I., Lumsdaine, A. A., & Sheffield, F. D. (1949). *Experiments on mass communication.* Princeton, NJ: Princeton University Press.

Huesmann, L. R., & Eron, L. D. (1986). The development of aggression in the American child as a consequence of television violence viewing. In L. R. Huesmann & L. D. Eron (Eds.), *Television and the aggressive child: A cross-national comparison* (pp. 45–80). Hillsdale, NJ: Lawrence Erlbaum.

Iyengar, S. (1991). *Is anyone responsible? How television frames political issues.* Chicago: University of Chicago Press.

Iyengar, S., & Kinder, D. R. (1987). *News that matters: Television and American public opinion.* Chicago: University of Chicago Press.

Jones, H. (1922). *Discussion—what do the people want? Proceedings of the National Conference of Social Work: 47th annual.* Chicago: University of Chicago Press.

Katz, E. (1987). Communications research since Lazarsfeld. *Public Opinion Quarterly, 51*(2), S25–S45.

Katz, E., & Lazarsfeld, P. F. (1955). *Personal influence.* Glencoe, IL: Free Press.

Kenny, D. A., & Acitelli, L. K. (2001). Accuracy and bias in the perception of the partner in a close relationship. *Journal of Personality and Social Psychology, 80*(3), 439–448.

Kinder, D. R. (1998a). Communication and opinion. *Annual Review of Political Science, 1,* 167–197.

Kinder, D. R. (1998b). Opinion and action in the realm of politics. In D. T. Gilbert, S. T. Fiske, & G. Lindzey (Eds.), *The handbook of social psychology* (4th ed., pp. 778–867). Boston: McGraw-Hill.

Klapper, J. T. (1960). *The effects of mass communication.* Glencoe, IL: Free Press.

Lasswell, H. D. (1948). The structure and function of communication in society. In L. Bryson (Ed.), *The communication of ideas* (pp. 37–51). New York: Harper.

Lazarsfeld, P. F. (1940). *Radio and the printed page.* New York: Duell, Sloan & Pearce.

Lazarsfeld, P. F. (1946). *The people look at radio.* Chapel Hill: University of North Carolina Press.

Lazarsfeld, P. F. (1948a). Communication research and the social psychologist. In W. Dennis (Ed.), *Current trends in social psychology* (pp. 218–273). Pittsburgh: University of Pittsburgh Press.

Lazarsfeld, P. F. (1948b). *Radio listening in America: The people look at radio—again.* New York: Prentice Hall.

Lazarsfeld, P. F., Berelson, B., & Gaudet, H. (1944). *The people's choice*. New York: Columbia University Press.

Lewin, K. (1951). *Field theory in social science* (D. Cartwright, Ed.). New York: Harper & Brothers.

Lippmann, W. (1922). *Public opinion*. New York: Macmillan.

Lumsdaine, A. A. (1984). Mass communication experiments in wartime and thereafter. *Social Psychology Quarterly, 47*(2), 198–206.

McClure, R. D., & Patterson, T. E. (1974). Television news and political advertising: The impact of exposure on voter beliefs. *Communication Research, 1*, 3–31.

McCombs, M. E., & Shaw, D. L. (1972). The agenda-setting function of mass media. *Public Opinion Quarterly, 36*, 176–185.

McCombs, M. E., & Shaw, D. L. (1993). The evolution of agenda-setting research: Twenty-five years in the marketplace of ideas. *Journal of Communication, 43*(2), 58–67.

McDonald, D. G., Glynn, C. J., Kim, S. H., & Ostman, R. E. (2001). The spiral of silence in the 1948 presidential election. *Communication Research, 28*(2), 139–155.

McGuire, W. J. (1996). The Yale communication and attitude change program in the 1950s. In E. E. Dennis & E. Wartella (Eds.), *American communication research: The remembered history* (pp. 39–60). Mahwah, NJ: Lawrence Erlbaum.

McLeod, D. M. (1995). Communicating deviance: The effects of television news coverage of social protest. *Journal of Broadcasting & Electronic Media, 39*, 4–19.

McLeod, J. M. & Chaffee, S. H. (1973). Interpersonal approaches to communication research. *American Behavioral Scientist, 16*, 469–500.

McLeod, J. M., & McDonald, D. G. (1985). Beyond simple exposure: Media orientations and their impact on political processes. *Communication Research, 12*(1), 3–33.

McLeod, J. M., & Reeves, B. (1980). On the nature of mass media effects. In S. Withey & R. Abels (Eds.), *Television and social behavior: Beyond violence and children*

(pp. 17–54). Hillsdale, NJ: Lawrence Erlbaum.

McLuhan, M. (1964). *Understanding media: The extensions of man*. New York: McGraw-Hill.

Mead, G. H. (1982). *The individual and the social self* (D. Miller, Ed.). Chicago: University of Chicago Press.

Merton, R. K. (1957). Social theory and social structure (Rev. ed.). Glencoe, IL: Free Press.

Meyrowitz, J. (1985). *No sense of place: The impact of electronic media on social behavior*. New York: Oxford University Press.

Milavsky, R., Kessler, R., Stipp, H., & Ruben, D. (1982). *Television and aggression: A panel study*. New York: Academic Press.

Morgan, M., & Shanahan, J. (1997). Two decades of cultivation research: An appraisal and meta-analysis. In B. R. Burleson (Ed.), *Communication yearbook 20* (pp. 1–45). Thousand Oaks, CA: Sage.

Munsterberg, H. (1916). *The photoplay: A psychological study*. New York: Appleton & Company.

Nathanson, A. I. (1999). Identifying and explaining the relationship between parental mediation and children's aggression. *Communication Research, 26*, 124–133.

Newcomb, T. M. (1953). An approach to the study of communicative acts. *Psychological Review, 60*(6), 393–404.

Newcomb, T. M. (1961). *The acquaintance process*. New York: Holt, Rinehart & Winston.

Noelle-Neumann, E. (1974). The spiral of silence: A theory of public opinion. *Journal of Communication, 24*(2), 43–51.

Owens, D. (1992). *Causes and coincidences*. Cambridge, UK: Cambridge University Press.

Parsons, T. (1953). *Working papers in the theory of action*. Glencoe, IL: Free Press.

Patterson, T. E., & McClure, R. D. (1976). *The unseeing eye: The myth of television power in national elections*. New York: Putnam.

Pearl, D., Bouthilet, L., & Lazar, J. (Eds.). (1982). *Television and behavior: Ten years* of scientific progress and implications for the eighties (DHHS Pub. No. ADM 82-1196). Washington, DC: Government Printing Office.

Phelan, J. J. (1919). *Motion pictures as a phase of commercialized amusement in Toledo, Ohio.* Toledo, OH: Little Book Press.

President's Research Committee. (1933). *American civilization today: A summary of recent social trends.* New York: McGraw-Hill.

Reese, S. D., & Miller, M. M. (1981). Political attitude holding and structure: The effects of newspaper and television news. *Communication Research, 8*(2), 167–188.

Roberts, D. F., & Maccoby, N. (1985). Effects of mass communication. In G. Lindzey & E. Aronson (Eds.), *Handbook of social psychology* (Vol. 2, 3rd ed., pp. 539–599). New York: Random House.

Rosnow, R. L., & Robinson, E. J. (1967). *Experiments in persuasion.* New York: Academic Press.

Salmon, W. C. (1989). *Four decades of scientific explanation.* Minneapolis: University of Minnesota Press.

Schramm, W. (Ed.). (1954). *The process and effects of mass communication.* Urbana: University of Illinois Press.

Schramm, W., Riesman, D., & Bauer, R. A. (1959). The state of communication research: Comment. *Public Opinion Quarterly, 23*(1), 6–17.

Shin, J. H., & Cameron, G. T. (2003). The potential of online media: A coorientational analysis of conflict between PR professionals and journalists in South Korea. *Journalism and Mass Communication Quarterly, 80*(3), 583–602.

Shuttleworth, F. K., & May, M. A. (1933). *The social conduct and attitude of movie fans.* New York: Macmillan.

Sparks, G. G. (2002). *Media effects research.* Belmont, CA: Wadsworth.

Stouffer, S. A., Lumsdaine, A. A., Lumsdaine, M. H., Williams, R. M., Jr., Smith, M. B., Janis, I. L., Star, S. A., & Cottrell, L. S., Jr. (1949). *The American soldier: Vol. 2. Combat and its aftermath.* Princeton, NJ: Princeton University Press.

Stouffer, S. A., Suchman, E. A., DeVinney, L. C., Star, S. A., & Williams, R. M., Jr. (1949). *The American soldier: Vol. 1. Adjustment during army life.* Princeton, NJ: Princeton University Press.

Suzuki, S. (1997). Cultural transmission in intercultural organizations: Impact of interpersonal communication patterns on intergroup contexts. *Human Communication Research, 24*(1), 147–180.

Tichenor, P. J., Donohue, G. A., & Olien, C. N. (1970). Mass media flow and differential growth in knowledge. *Public Opinion Quarterly, 34,* 159–170.

Wartella, E., & Reeves, B. (1985). Historical trends in research on children and the media: 1900–1960. *Journal of Communication, 35*(2), 118–133.

Weiss, W. (1969). Effects of the mass media of communication. In G. Lindzey & E. Aronson (Eds.), *Handbook of social psychology* (Vol. 5, 2nd ed., pp. 77–195). Reading, MA: Addison-Wesley.

White, D. M. (1950). The "gatekeeper": A case study in the selection of news. *Journalism Quarterly, 27*(4), 383–390.

Wilcox, D. F. (1900). *The American newspaper: A study in social psychology.* Philadelphia: American Academy of Political and Social Science.

Zimmerman, C., & Bauer, R. A. (1956). The effect of an audience on what is remembered. *Public Opinion Quarterly, 20*(1), 238–248.

10

PSYCHOLOGY OF MEDIA USE

◆ Tannis M. MacBeth

$\mathbf{I}$nterdisciplinarity is one of the hallmarks of research on media content, use, and effects. With regard to use, the preceding chapter focused on the sociology and anthropology of media use, that is, who uses which media, how much, where, when, and so forth. Scholars in communication studies often do such research. One of their theoretical perspectives on media use focuses on its functions and gratifications. Another communication studies perspective on media use and its effects, known as cultural studies, emphasizes the role of sociological factors—especially gender, class, and culture—in determining the different meanings, readings, and interpretations that people find in and take away from media communications. Like the preceding chapter, this one focuses on media use but from another social science perspective—that of psychology. The distinctions amongst sociological, communication studies, and psychological perspectives in media research are blurred rather than distinct, and all three types of scholars take an interdisciplinary approach. It is, nevertheless, useful to keep their varied theoretical and methodological approaches in mind when reading and evaluating media research.

From a psychological point of view, what processes are involved in media use? What is the research evidence regarding attention to, comprehension of, and memory for media products? What theories have been offered to explain these processes? These and related questions are the focus of this chapter. Rather than providing an exhaustive review of the relevant media research, examples are provided, most of which involve television, the most-studied medium. Let's begin by considering the theories.

◆ Psychological Theories and Processes Relevant to Media Use and Effects

SOCIAL LEARNING THEORY

The social psychologist Albert Bandura conducted his pioneering laboratory studies of the effects of watching filmed aggression on children's behavior (e.g., Bandura, Ross, & Ross, 1963) to illustrate his then-new theory that children could learn merely through observation, without reinforcement (reward or punishment), which had been the hallmark of earlier learning theories involving classical or operant conditioning. This process of vicarious learning through observation of models, in real life or the media, involves

1. noticing/attending to the modeled behavior (including, for example, verbal or facial expressions),

2. coding the behavior in memory visually or verbally,

3. enacting the behavior, and

4. motivation, that is, evaluating the consequences (Bandura, 1977, 1983, 1994).

In this process of social learning, Steps 1 and 2 comprise the acquisition phase and Steps 3 and 4 the performance phase. It is only when performance occurs, however, that learning can be demonstrated, even though behaviors may be acquired and not performed at all or not performed until much later. Whether an acquired behavior will be performed depends in part on observers' cognitions, including their perceptions of their own similarity to the model and their expectations that if they do imitate the behavior, they will be rewarded or punished. In short, the emphasis in social cognitive learning theory is on explaining the processes involved in the imitation of behavior observed in real life or through media use.

SCHEMA THEORY

Some cognitive psychologists (e.g., Abelson, 1981; Piaget, 1963; Schank & Abelson, 1977) emphasize that through their experience, humans construct and modify mental models, beliefs, and expectations, which govern their behavior. The term *schema*[1] (plural: schemas or schemata) is used to refer to a cognitive model or prototype, which could be relatively simple (e.g., a person's notion of the "average," or prototypical, dog) or complex (e.g., his or her gender schemas). The term *script* is used to refer to sequentially organized events, for example, going to a restaurant (Fiske & Taylor, 1984). The everyday notion closest to a schema is a stereotype. Schemas and scripts guide our information processing and social behavior. We try to fit incoming information into our existing models—that is, our schemas/scripts—and we notice, remember, and respond to information by making it consistent with those models. We tend not to notice information inconsistent with our stereotypes, and even if we do, we may forget it or distort it in memory, which is why schemas and scripts are so difficult to change and why stereotypes are so dangerous. For example, we make Fred, our hard-working friend, an exception to our belief that members of his group are lazy, when we should instead change our belief because the only person in that group whom we know doesn't fit the stereotype.

In the realm of gender, Cordua, McGraw, and Drabman (1979) found that 100% of a group of elementary school children who saw a film about a male physician and a female nurse correctly remembered their roles, but only 50% of those who saw a female physician and a male nurse did so. The other 50% presumably did not notice the role reversal when viewing or distorted the information in memory or at retrieval. That is, they either did not notice the mismatch between the film content and their gender-stereotyped schema(s) or changed the information to be schema (stereotype) consistent and recalled incorrectly that they had seen a male physician and a female nurse.

Children and adults construct schemas and scripts through their interactions and experiences, both in the real world and through media. North American infants show interest in television and begin watching regularly as early as 18 months, so it provides an "early window" (Liebert, Sprafkin, & Davidson, 1982) on the world. Media, including television, books, and videos, provide information about a variety of social interactions, types of people, and places before children have analogous real-life experiences. Thus, media likely play an important role not only in the maintenance but also in the initial construction of children's schemas. If so, these media-based schemas and stereotypes influence perceptions and behavior in the real world. For example, researchers who studied second and fifth graders' beliefs about occupations (nurse, police officer) concluded that children form separate schemata for social information acquired from TV and from real-world experience, but those who perceive fictional TV as socially realistic are more apt to incorporate TV messages into their schemata and their aspirations (Wright et al., 1995).

Story schemas/schemata are particularly useful for processing media content. They are organized clusters of knowledge about stories and how they are typically structured, and children with a good understanding of story schemas have better memory of central story content with reduced processing effort (Meadowcroft, 1985; Miron, Bryant, & Zillmann, 2001). Children in the preoperational stage of cognitive development—that is, up to about 5 or 6 years of age—can only use story schemas when the content is structured simply with clear causal links (Mandler & Johnson, 1977). With achievement of concrete operational thinking, around 5 to 7 years, children are more readily able to use them as frameworks for encoding, storage, and retrieval (Miron et al., 2001).

PSYCHOANALYTIC THEORY

Several aspects of psychoanalytic theory are potentially relevant for the psychology of media use. Media content (e.g., violence or sex) might trigger aggressive or sexual impulses. Or it might, through the concept of *catharsis,* predict a decrease rather than an increase in the probability that the viewer would behave aggressively or sexually because he or she would experience the violence or sex vicariously and, as a result, would cathartically release her or his own aggression or sexually related impulses. However, there is little, if any, empirical support for catharsis with regard to media use and effects.

Another psychoanalytic concept relevant to media use is Freud's distinction between *tendentious* and *nontendentious humor.* The current notion of being "politically correct or incorrect" is reminiscent of this concept. Zillmann (2000) discussed Freud's (1905/1958) psychoanalytic theory in this context of incongruity in humor. In tendentious humor, someone or something is victimized (ridiculed, debased, or humiliated), whereas nontendentious humor is victimless. Freud argued that, for reasons of social censure, people cannot enjoy blunt, demeaning hostility unless it is embellished with innocuous "jokework." The innocuous element camouflages the tendentious component of humor, so we can laugh and avoid social censure, but we also commonly misconstrue what we laugh about, making it possible to avoid self-censure.

Zillmann and Bryant (1980) formalized Freud's hypotheses in a *misattribution theory of humor* and tested it in an experiment involving comedy and misfortune. Their expectations were confirmed. "Amusement was exceedingly high when all the ingredients of good comedy were present: despised protagonists, their victimization, and humor cues that set the audience free to enjoy these characters' demise" (p. 149). The presence of an innocuous humor cue allowed the onlookers to be *"malicious with dignity"* (p. 149). Zillmann (2000) contended that comedy is the most popular genre of media entertainment for both the film and television industries in North America and cited research evidence in support of his *mood management theory* (Zillmann, 1988). Through trial and error, viewers acquire at least a tacit understanding of how to improve their affective state. They prefer comedy to drama when they are stressed or feel gloomy, frustrated, angry, and so forth (e.g., Anderson, Collins, Schmitt, & Jacobvitz, 1996; Zillmann, Hezel, & Medoff, 1980). There also is evidence, however, that they may avoid comedy when there is a reason to maintain negative emotions (O'Neal & Taylor, 1989) or when such emotions are very strong (Christ & Medoff, 1984). Other research addressing Zillmann's mood management theory in relation to empathy is discussed later in this chapter.

COGNITIVE SCIENCE

Behaviorism was, for many years, the preeminent psychological theory in North America. In part as a reaction to Freud's emphasis on the unconscious, the behaviorists argued that mental processes such as perception, memory, and emotion are not the concern of psychology, which must focus exclusively on predicting behavior. Indeed, they referred to all events between any sensory input and a behavioral response as a *black box*. Along with the development of computers and the field of artificial intelligence (AI) came the demise of behaviorism and the establishment of cognitive science, with its emphasis on the mind as an information-processing system. Cognitive scientists have subscribed to a *functionalist* doctrine that states that information processing and the functional organization of the mind can be studied and understood without reference to the underlying human hardware, that is, the brain (LeDoux, 1996). Moreover, they avoid the longstanding philosophical debate about the nature of consciousness and focus instead on the

mind's unconscious processes rather than on its conscious contents. These cognitive unconscious processes include perceptual analysis of the physical environment by our sensory systems, memory, speaking more or less grammatically, imagination, decision making, and so on, as distinct from Freud's darker conceptualization of the dynamic, emotionally charged unconscious. The cognitive unconscious processes "take care of the mind's routine business without consciousness having to be bothered" (LeDoux, 1996, p. 30). For most cognitive processes, mental operations, and computations, we are only aware of the outcome, not the operations themselves. "The inner workings of important aspects of the mind, including our own understanding of why we do what we do, are not necessarily knowable to the conscious self" (LeDoux, 1996, p. 32). Indeed, our conscious awareness consists primarily of the processes involved in our *working memory*, which consists of (a) a general-purpose temporary storage system used in all active thinking processes, (b) several specialized temporary storage systems (called *buffers*) used for specific kinds of information, and (c) *executive functions* that coordinate the working memory activities. Working memory creates and manipulates symbolic representations.

The cognitive science theoretical perspectives are particularly relevant for the media research on attention, comprehension, and memory, discussed later in this chapter.

EMOTION AND FEAR

LeDoux (1996) argues that subjective emotional states, like all other states of consciousness, are the end result of information processing occurring unconsciously. Cognitive scientists could have them fit into the cognitive framework, but instead, they made an artificial separation between cognition and the rest of the mind. LeDoux contends that the processes underlying emotion and cognition involve unconscious information processing and, sometimes, the generation of conscious content based on that processing. He would prefer to include both under the term *mind science*.

Cognitive scientists use the term *cognitive appraisal* to describe the processes we use to assess our situation. For example, when we encounter an animal while walking in the woods, we integrate our perception (visual, auditory, etc.) with our long-term memory to conclude, in our working memory, that it is a rabbit or a bear. According to LeDoux (1996), what is needed to turn our cognitive appraisal (rabbit vs. bear) into emotions (fear of the bear) is the activation of the physiological system built by evolution to deal with danger, and the *amygdala* plays a crucial role. He describes in some detail the connections between the amygdala and other parts of the brain, as well as other somatic responses that play a role in making an experience emotional. The essential components of his model are as follows. Working memory is the gateway to subjective experiences, emotional as well as nonemotional, and is indispensable for the creation of a conscious emotional feeling. The activation of the amygdala is crucial for a complete feeling of fear, and the activation of arousal is essential for a sustained feeling of fear. Bodily or somatic feedback, or long-term memories based on real-life feedback from the body, also is essential for a sustained emotional experience. You can, however, have an emotional feeling without direct projections from the amygdala to the cortex and without being conscious of the stimulus that elicited the feeling. "If emotions are triggered by stimuli that are processed unconsciously ([i.e.], if working memory is not involved) you will not be able to later reflect back on those experiences and explain why they occurred with any degree of accuracy" (LeDoux, 1996, p. 299).

So conscious emotional feelings and conscious thoughts both involve symbolic representation in working memory of subsymbolic processes carried out by systems that work unconsciously. The difference is that thoughts and emotions are generated by different subsymbolic systems and that emotions involve many more brain systems. In other words, the neurological and physiological processes involved in thoughts and emotions differ in important ways, though both involve unconscious processes and systems, and for both, our conscious awareness, if present at all, is through our working memory. Moreover, within the emotional realm, processing of negative material is quick and automatic, and this is primarily what LeDoux (1996) has described. Processing of positive material is elaborated, difficult, discretionary, and more likely to involve cognition (see Reeves, Newhagen, Maibach, Basil, & Kurz, 1991, for a discussion in relation to television messages).

According to LeDoux (1996), the amygdala has a greater influence on the cortex than the cortex has on the amygdala, so emotional arousal dominates and controls thinking, rather than vice versa. Our thoughts can easily trigger emotions (by activating the amygdala), but we are not effective at willing ourselves to turn off emotions (by deactivating the amygdala). I find this useful in trying to understand why people continue to watch scary movies even though they know they may have a long-lasting fright reaction that may interfere with their lives, as Cantor (e.g., 1996) has so well documented.

There is abundant evidence that most children and adults have been frightened by something they have seen or heard in the media and that these media-induced fears are often severe and long lasting (see Cantor, 2001, for a recent review). For example, in one study of undergraduates, all reported vivid memories of enduring media-induced fear (Hoekstra, Harris, & Helmick, 1999), and in another, 90% did so (Harrison & Cantor, 1999). It is common for children and adolescents who have been frightened by media to say they *like* scary films and TV but also to say that they have *regretted* watching them. What's the attraction? Why do people expose themselves to scary media? Zuckerman (1979) contends that sensation seeking helps people find their optimal arousal level. Apter (1992) argues that if danger is confronted in a "protective frame," the experience can be exciting rather than anxiety provoking. Cantor (2001) takes the position that a frightening depiction may alleviate anxiety on occasion but only under the limited circumstance that the story induces only mild fear and the outcome reveals that danger can be counteracted effectively (Bryant, Carveth, & Brown, 1981; Cantor & Nathanson, 1997). The psychoanalytic concept of catharsis, in which scary images might reduce rather than increase anxiety in a safe context, put forth by Bettelheim (1975) with regard to violent fairy tales presented orally, has not been substantiated (Cantor, 1998).

Zillmann (1980) proposed that *excitation transfer* might occur during media use; that is, media exposure may generate excitational states that intensify postexposure emotional responses. The physiological arousal experienced may be transferred or labeled by the viewer or reader in an effort to ascribe meaning to the experience. Zillmann has argued that what people like about being frightened by media is the suspense associated with threatened negative outcomes, which produces physiological arousal that, in turn, intensifies the enjoyment of a "happy ending" or resolution within the story as episodes induce and then reduce suspense (Zillmann, 1980; Zillmann, Hay, & Bryant, 1975). Different conceptualizations of arousal and some research relevant to each are discussed later in this chapter.

Johnson (1995) studied adolescents' motivations for viewing graphic horror and found that their reasons varied (gore watching, thrill watching, watching to deal with their own problems, watching to master fears), as did its impact. It is self-evident but worth mentioning that whereas some media-induced fears occur when an individual chooses to watch or read something known to be scary, others, some of which

may be very traumatic, are experienced unwittingly. This includes violent/frightening scenes in a film or story in which they were not expected, as well as events depicted in news that provide graphic images, whether in a print headline or story or on film.

BACKSTAGE BEHAVIOR, PARASOCIAL INTERACTIONS, MEDIA FRIENDS, AND SLIDING SIGNIFIERS

His experiences with television as a child led Meyrowitz (1985) to argue that his primary response to TV was neither to imitate behaviors seen on it nor to be persuaded that he needed to own products advertised. Instead, social interactions he saw on television, especially amongst adults, affected his willingness to accept other people's behaviors and claims at face value. He responded to television as a "secret revelation machine" that provided access to people's *backstage behavior*, that is, behavior not normally exhibited in public, including various aspects of adults' personal lives. Access to backstage behavior provides viewers with a sense of closeness/ intimacy with authority figures (i.e., familiarity) but often with a loss of respect (i.e., contempt). This occurs both for real-world people seen on TV (e.g., politicians) and for occupations and professional roles depicted by actors in fiction (e.g., lawyers, teachers, police).

According to Meyrowitz (1985), different media foster different patterns of information flow about social behavior. For example, television is likely to have a stronger impact than print on respect for authority figures because it provides more detailed images about behavior, including nonverbal behavior.

Media provide *parasocial interaction* (Horton & Wohl, 1956) to their users, that is, the illusion of knowing and interacting with characters depicted, whether real or fictional. These *media friends* (Meyrowitz, 1985) are especially important for people who are, in their own lives, socially isolated, socially inept, aged and/or invalid, or timid and rejected. Media convergence (e.g., Web sites and "chat" rooms for radio and television programs) undoubtedly intensifies the role of those media in our social world (Ward & Greenfield, 1998).

Just as Meyrowitz (1985) asked whether media, especially television, affect our understanding of the social word, Kinder (1991) asked whether growing up with television and other electronic media changes comprehension of the relationship between real-life things (e.g., elephants), that is, what is signified, and their signifiers (e.g., a photograph or video, or film). Meyrowitz finds Horton and Wohl's (1956) parasocial framework particularly useful for explaining why it is that when a "media friend" dies, millions of people may experience such a great sense of loss. He points out, as well, that the media provide the most ritualized channels of mourning, with the final irony that the parasocial performer does not die because the *only* means through which people came to know him or her (films, records, photographs, books, videotape) are still available. Does early experience with television encourage "the sliding of the signifier, so that by the time one first encounters, say, an elephant in the zoo, the living animal is merely another signifier of the image already seen on TV in documentaries and animated cartoons, that is, merely part of the paradigm of elephant signifiers?" (Kinder, 1991, p. 35). Ward and Greenfield (1998) asked what the impact of such media priority may be on our understanding of relations with real people, especially those for whom we have little real-world interaction, and how this influences our attitudes, beliefs, expectations, and stereotypes regarding age, gender, occupation, ethnicity, and nationality.

MOOD MANAGEMENT, EMPATHY, AND SOCIAL COMPARISON

With regard to emotional responses to media, Zillmann's mood management model (Zillmann, 1988; Zillmann & Bryant, 1985) predicts that people choose media that are likely to affect their mood positively. One of the ways that media can affect the viewer's mood is through empathy, which Zillmann (1991a) defines as an experience in response (a) to information about circumstances presumed to cause acute emotions in another, (b) to the facial and bodily expression of emotional experiences of another, and/or (c) to another's behaviors presumed to be caused by acute emotional experiences, and this experience (d) is associated with an appreciable increase in excitation that (e) someone interprets as feeling with or feeling for another. Mood management theory predicts that if empathy occurs, media users will prefer positive to negative portrayals and will feel better after exposure to positive material. It also specifies that when in a negative mood, people are drawn to media with a positive hedonic tone in the hope of improving their mood, whereas people in a good mood are less likely to select media content for its hedonic nature (Zillmann, 1988; Zillmann & Bryant, 1985). Results obtained by several researchers are consistent with these predictions. For example, people who report negative feelings early in the afternoon are more likely to report later that day that they watched a lot of TV, whereas those who report feeling better in the afternoon are more likely later to report a light evening of viewing (Kubey, 1984; Kubey & Csikszentmihalyi, 1990). These and other results (e.g., McIlwraith & Schallow, 1983) show that mood influences viewers' amount of TV viewing, but they do not speak directly to the impact of mood on type of content chosen.

Mares and Cantor (1992) studied elderly viewers' (mean age 75 years) responses to televised portrayals of old age. Participants in this study scored either in the top or bottom 20th percentile on a loneliness test but did not live in nursing homes. In an initial session, they were given descriptions of television programs. The lonely group showed greater interest in watching negative portrayals, and the nonlonely group showed greater interest in positive portrayals. In a second session, they were randomly assigned to watch a negative portrayal (an unhappy, isolated old man) or a positive one (a happy, socially integrated old man). The lonely elderly reported feeling better after watching the negative portrayal than they had felt before watching it, but there was no change in the mood of the lonely participants who saw the positive portrayal. The lonely also expressed less interest in the first session in watching a program about happy young people than in watching programs about unhappy elderly people. For the nonlonely, their mood became more negative after viewing the negative portrayal, but it did not change pre- to postviewing if they saw the positive portrayal of the integrated man. The only way in which these findings support the mood management theory is that the elderly participants did make choices in the first session that were found in the second session to have a beneficial effect on mood. But the choices they made contradicted mood management theory's predictions and, instead, were more consistent with social comparison theory.

In his social comparison theory, Festinger (1954) contended that people (a) compare themselves to others to evaluate themselves, (b) prefer to compare themselves to similar others, and (c) choose upward comparisons, probably because they want to feel similar to superior others or because this provides information about how to improve. More recently, it has been argued that comparison with a more successful person may produce negative affect because it highlights the individual's poorer situation or characteristics and that self-esteem may be enhanced in some situations through downward comparison with a less fortunate other (e.g., Brickman & Bulyer, 1977; Suls, 1977; Wills, 1981; Wood, Taylor, & Lichtman, 1985). The otherwise counterintuitive findings obtained by Mares and Cantor (1992) for elderly viewers fit this social comparison model better than the mood management one.

COGNITIVE NEOASSOCIATION THEORY

Leonard Berkowitz, (1984, 1986), another eminent social psychologist known for his research on the impact of media violence on aggressive behavior, has reframed his earlier version of social learning theory in terms of the cognitive neoassociationist theories of Anderson and Bower (1973) and Landman and Manis (1983). He contends that aggressive *thoughts, feelings, and actions* are linked within an associative network, with the pathways amongst these thought, feeling, and action nodes strengthened by similarity and semantic relatedness. Thus, media violence might *prime* other aggressive ideas, feelings, memories, and action tendencies, as might other cues (e.g., a gun) to one or more components of the *associative network*. Another psychologist, Rowell Huesmann (1986), also emphasizes cued imitation as important for understanding the role of media violence for viewers' behavior.

Josephson (1987) conducted a field quasi-experiment (MacBeth, 1998) in which she randomly assigned boys in Grades 2 and 3 to watch either a violent or a nonviolent, but equally exciting, television excerpt. In the violent excerpt, some snipers used walkie-talkies to communicate just before a SWAT team attacked them. After viewing their excerpt, the boys were taken to the school gymnasium, where a referee did a "pregame interview" using either a microphone and tape recorder or a walkie-talkie. Then they played floor hockey. Their teachers had previously rated them on trait aggression, that is, their characteristic level of aggression. During the floor hockey game, the boys who behaved most aggressively were those who had seen the violent excerpt, had been interviewed with a walkie-talkie, and were rated by their teachers as high in trait aggression. The walkie-talkie apparently served as a cue to activate their network of associations amongst aggressive thoughts, feelings, and actions.

Individuals who are characteristically more aggressive—that is, higher in trait aggression—are presumed to have more extensive associative networks of aggressive thoughts, feelings, and actions, so exposure to violence should have its strongest effect on such individuals. Experimental evidence from studies conducted with adults (e.g., Bushman, 1995; Bushman & Geen, 1990) and children (e.g., Josephson, 1987) using film/TV as well as video games (Anderson & Dill, 2000) supports this hypothesis. Immediately after exposure to media violence, people higher in trait aggression have more aggressive thoughts and ideas, feel angrier, and behave more aggressively than do those who are characteristically not aggressive.

Functional magnetic resonance imaging (fMRI) has been used in recent research to study 8- to 13-year-old boys' and girls' brain responses when viewing violent and nonviolent video images (Murray, 2001). TV violence viewing appears to activate brain areas involved in arousal and attention, detection of threat, episodic memory encoding and retrieval, and motor programming. These findings are consistent with the concept of associative networks involving aggressive thoughts, feelings, and actions, as well as LeDoux's (1996) cognitive models regarding emotion and fear (described earlier in this chapter).

COGNITIVE JUSTIFICATION

Research evidence indicates that the relationship between exposure to media violence and aggressive behavior, thoughts, and attitudes is *transactional* (Rosengren, Roe, & Sonesson, 1983). In a transactional model, one behavior (e.g., exposure to violence) increases the probability of another (e.g., aggression), which in turn increases the other, and so on.

Huesmann (1982) argues that people who are more aggressive watch violence in part because it allows them cognitively to justify their own beliefs and attitudes as normal. In their research on the effects of TV/film (Bushman, 1995) and video game (Anderson & Dill, 2000) violence, researchers have found that adults who are high in trait aggression report usually watching more violent fare and liking it more. As well, given a choice of what to view in a research setting, they are more likely than adults low in trait aggression to choose a violent movie or video game.

AROUSAL

A number of researchers working from a variety of perspectives have emphasized the importance of the viewer's arousal level for attention to, comprehension of, and memory for media products. Learning, which involves all three processes, is best when arousal is optimal, that is, in a middle range rather than too high or too low (Berlyne, 1960).

Some media researchers have focused on *physiological arousal*. For example, Krull and Watt (1973) talked about the independent contributions of the excitatory and violent components of television for viewers' aggressiveness. Both Berkowitz (1986) and Huesmann (1988) have emphasized the importance of viewers' preexisting emotional states, in terms of both their relatively stable physiological predisposition and their recently induced arousal just prior to viewing.

Vigilance is one aspect of selective attention; the viewer experiences it as alertness to expected stimuli (Miron et al., 2001). In terms of arousal, vigilance is performed by the cortical (reticular activating) system, as distinct from emotional (limbic or autonomic system) arousal. This distinction between cortical and autonomic arousal (Routtenberg, 1968, 1971) is useful because it separates arousal processes involved in attention, perception, and behavioral response preparation from those associated with affective/emotional reactions (Zillmann, 1991b). Zillmann (1991b) contends that for media research, the realm of cortical arousal is attention, alertness, and vigilance, on one hand, and information processing, acquisition, and retrieval, on the other. The realm of autonomic arousal, in contrast, is affective and emotional reactions that are induced, changed, or neutralized by media exposure or that occur shortly after exposure. Alpha wave blocking is most often used to measure cortical arousal, whereas heart rate, blood pressure, blood pulse volume, skin conductance, and skin temperature measure autonomic (limbic) arousal (Zillmann, 1982, 1991b). In television research, cortical arousal has been treated as a hypothetical construct (Zillmann, 1991b). Blood pressure is the least reliable of the measures of autonomic arousal (Zillmann, 1979). Miron et al. (2001) reviewed research evidence that contradicts the "zombie-viewer" line of research contending that TV viewing is associated with dominant alpha activity, that is, low cortical arousal.

As Zillmann (1991b) pointed out, for most North American viewers, television sometimes serves as an "unwinder." On such occasions, they choose content that will diminish their noxious states of hyperarousal. Kubey's (Kubey, 1984, 1986, 1996; Kubey & Csikszentmihalyi, 1990) research evidence documents the effectiveness of television for inducing relaxation. But viewers also, on other occasions, use television for excitement; exposure can be highly arousing. Zillmann discusses the circumstances under which television serves as an unwinder versus for excitement. The same is undoubtedly true of other media.

METACOGNITION

As Miron et al. (2001) point out, *metacognition* (Flavell, 1979; Flavell & Wellman, 1977) plays an important role in comprehension and memory. This term refers to an individual's knowledge about his or her own cognitive capabilities, including strategies to enhance performance (e.g., if I need to remember this phone number, it will help to repeat it in my head or, better still, write it down).

If we consider vigilance during television watching from a metacognitive perspective, a child's attentional self-regulation would involve awareness of his or her ability to sustain attention to television, assessment of how much attention is needed to understand a program (and eventually to learn from it), and the use of skills and strategies for maintaining attention. (Miron et al., 2001, p. 164)

Some media researchers have focused on conscious awareness of cognitive *arousal,* in a metacognitive sense. Salomon (1981, 1983), for example, emphasized the role of attentive involvement, which he called *amount of invested mental effort* (AIME), for learning from media. He found that in the United States, 12-year-olds believe both that it is easier for them to learn from TV than from print and that they are better at learning from TV (Salomon, 1984), which may lead them to invest less mental effort when watching TV than when reading. In a similar vein, Langer and Piper (1988) have distinguished between "mindful" and "mindless" viewing. References to using media as a "couch potato" or being "mesmerized" seem to reflect the distinctions made by these researchers. Unfortunately, if people habitually approach some media in a relatively mindless way and more often to relax/unwind than to learn, this will make it difficult for media designed to be educational to be effective. It is encouraging, therefore, that producers of TV programs such as *Sesame Street* have found ways to do so (Anderson, Huston, Smith, Linebarger, & Wright, 2001; Bickham, Wright, & Huston, 2001; Fisch & Truglio, 2001).

DESENSITIZATION OR HABITUATION

With repeated exposure to any particular type of media content, users may become *habituated* or *desensitized* to similar content, and this may have an impact on attention, comprehension, and memory. Thus, use of media with particular content such as violence or sex, or their combination, may influence subsequent media use as well as the impact of such content on the viewer's attitudes and behavior (see Zillmann, 1991b, for a review of relevant research).

DISINHIBITION

Through various socialization processes, we try to help children learn to inhibit antisocial and other negative behaviors. To the extent that such behaviors are portrayed in various media, especially if they are portrayed as justified, successful, and not penalized, previously acquired restraints against such behaviors may be *disinhibited*. This is likely to occur most readily for those with the fewest inhibitions—that is, those highest, for example, in trait aggression. Recall that in Josephson's (1987) field experiment, the boys who were most aggressive in the floor hockey game were those who were interviewed with a walkie-talkie, saw the violent excerpt, and were rated by their teachers as high in trait aggression. And in his laboratory experiment with adults, Bushman (1995) found that those high in trait aggression scored higher in anger/hostility and behaved more aggressively after watching a violent excerpt than did adults low in trait aggression, even after previewing anger/hostility was controlled.

Disinhibition probably occurred in the natural experiment my colleagues and I studied in Notel, Unitel, and Multitel (Joy, Kimball, & Zabrack, 1986; MacBeth, 1998, 2001). Aggressive behavior on the school playground was significantly higher 2 years after than before a town (Notel) acquired TV reception, and this was true for both physical and verbal aggression, girls and boys, and children initially low and high in aggressive behavior. In contrast, aggression in the comparison towns, Unitel

and Multitel, which had television reception in both phases of the study, did not change appreciably over the same period.

Note that if media are shown to have the negative effect that exposure leads to an increase in some antisocial behavior, the effect must be strong enough to overcome the child's or adult's inhibitions against behaving that way. For this reason, it may be easier to demonstrate a prosocial than an antisocial effect. Ethical constraints also play a role. Researchers cannot ethically expose participants in their studies to the levels of violence found in many films and other media.

GENDER AND MEDIA USE

As the popular phrases "chick flick" and "football widow" indicate, use of different media varies by gender, both in childhood and beyond (for reviews summarizing viewing patterns, see Huston & Wright, 1998; Comstock & Scharrer, 2001; see also Chapters 8 and 9, this volume). Oliver (2000) summarized this gender gap across genres—"The romantic yet heart-wrenching world of the melodramatic tear-jerker belongs to females, whereas the more action-packed and explicit world of sports, violence, and pornography belongs to males" (p. 222)—while making the important point that variations exist within same-gender groups. She went on to ask *why* females and males experience the world of entertainment in different ways, the question most pertinent to the focus of this chapter, the psychology of media use. She concluded that characteristics of both the media content and the viewer interact in complex ways.

Content characteristics that may contribute to gender differences in media use and exacerbate differences in reactions include the widely documented overrepresentation of male characters in most dramatic fiction (with soap operas the exception), as well as the greater coverage of male-oriented entertainment (e.g., in sports).

Oliver (2000) also reviewed evidence that more females than males enjoy dramatic content featuring issues about relationships, whereas more males prefer themes related to aggressive conflict. She distinguished between conflict and violence, pointing out that many females seem to have a strong distaste for the latter but not the former, which is featured prominently in soap operas. Females also enjoy the experience of suspense elicited by frightening films, but not if this is achieved through explicit, gruesome violence (Zillmann & Weaver, 1996).

What theories have been offered to explain the gender differences in preference for and response to media content (Oliver, 2000)? Sociobiologists and evolutionary psychologists say that males' lesser investment in rearing their offspring and greater concern for maximizing their genes in the next generation would predict a greater male interest in media content that provides many potential female "partners," even if only at a fantasy level (Malamuth, 1996). Evolutionary theorists use the same arguments to explain females' greater appreciation of pornography that more prominently features affectionate displays.

Cognitive-developmental, social learning, and schema theory perspectives emphasize the role of culture and socialization for gender differences in attitudes and behavior. Once children know the two gender categories and can label their own (there are girls and boys, and I am a _____), they seek self-relevant information, so attend selectively more to their own gender, which explains greater attention to same-sex models both in real life and in the media.

◆ *Attention, Comprehension, and Memory*

CHILDREN

Cognitive Development. Children's attention to the comprehension of and memory for events they encounter, in both the real world and through media, is constrained by their cognitive development. To the extent that their knowledge is faulty, their processing of information will be affected. For example, if their knowledge of time (e.g., tomorrow, today will be yesterday) is not yet fully developed, this will limit their ability to comprehend sequences of actions. They may not, for example, link the punishment at the end of a TV program or story to the crime committed at the beginning. Or, if their knowledge of money and related phenomena (payment for work, income, etc.) is not fully developed, they will be incapable of understanding their parent's response, "We can't afford it," to their request for something advertised. Instead of understanding that their parents haven't enough money for the purchase, such children may wonder why their parents don't just use their credit card and may think it's because their parents don't love them as much as do parents who buy such items for their children. Working from the perspective of Piaget's (1963) theory, Furth (1980) found that children's understanding of money, income, finances, and so on is surprisingly poor.

With regard to concepts of time, money, taking the perspective of another, hypothetico-deductive reasoning, reversibility of actions (concrete operational thinking in Piaget's [1963] theory) and ideas (formal operations), and many other important aspects of knowledge, children must construct that knowledge gradually through their interactions with people and objects. Unlike facts (e.g., "Ottawa is the capital of Canada"), such knowledge cannot be learned or memorized. And until such knowledge has developed to its mature form, children's attention, comprehension, and memory will be driven by their incomplete/inaccurate knowledge in any given domain. But, until their *schemes*[1] (the word Piaget used for the cognitive "building blocks" that others call *schemas, schemata,* or *scripts*) are able to process information in a mature way, the child will not (a) notice or attend to discrepant information, (b) comprehend their experiences fully, or (c) remember them accurately. Through the twin processes of assimilation (taking in relevant information) and accommodation (modifying the scheme, schema, or script in line with the new information), these cognitive structures gradually develop from their earliest to their most mature form.

Collins (1983a, 1983b) found that prior to middle childhood (Grade 4 or 5), most children watching adult programs (e.g., situation comedy, action adventure) could not make inferences or connect logically and causally related plot elements that were separated by subplot events, incidental content, or commercials. The separators commonly used in Saturday morning children's programs do not improve comprehension (Palmer & McDowell, 1979).

Attention. Most of the research on children's attention to media has focused on television, and in that research, attention has been most often defined as visual orientation to or looking at the screen. In their work in this area, Dan Anderson and his colleagues (e.g., Anderson & Burns, 1991) have found that the longer an individual either does or does not look at the TV screen when in the room with a set on, the greater the probability that the look (or nonlook) will continue. They call this resistance to change *attentional inertia,* in contrast to the more usual phenomenon in visual perception research in which an infant or child *habituates* to or tires of looking at something that was initially of interest and, with repeated presentations, looks for increasingly shorter periods. In the latter case, the same visual stimulus is presented repeatedly, whereas in the case of television, the visual material continually changes (Anderson & Burns, 1991). Some researchers have suggested that attentional inertia maintains looking during the less interesting moments or across content boundaries, for example, between different segments of *Sesame Street* during longer viewing periods (Anderson & Lorch, 1983; Anderson, Choi, & Lorch, 1987; Calvert, Brune, Eugia, & Marcato, 1991; Meadowcroft, 1996).

Rolandelli, Wright, Huston, and Eakins (1991) measured children's auditory attention to television by periodically degrading and distorting the soundtrack and observing how quickly children would manually respond to clear the soundtrack. Longer latencies imply listening less carefully. They found that auditory attention predicted auditory comprehension (recall of the verbal soundtrack) and that visual attention predicted recall of visual content, leading them to conclude that looking and listening contribute separately to understanding. They also found that for boys, there is less dissociation in attention to the audio and visual TV tracks, and that girls more often listen without looking but still retain as much information as boys.

In the preschool years, much of children's attention to television involves auditorily monitoring for sound signals associated with content they will likely find interesting or, more important, comprehensible, at which point they look at the screen and continue to do so until the content becomes incomprehensible (Lorch, Anderson, & Levin, 1979; also see summaries by Anderson & Burns, 1991; Huston & Wright, 1998). But attentional inertia serves to keep them attending longer and thus increases, up to a point, the probability that they will comprehend something. Children are likely to turn toward the screen at the sound of children's, nonhuman, and women's voices but to turn away from male adult voices, which tend to signal adult content (Anderson, Alwitt, Lorch, & Levin, 1979; Calvert, Huston, Watkins, & Wright, 1982).

These and similar findings form the basis of Huston and Wright's (1983, 1998) *feature-signal hypothesis* that the formal production features (e.g., animation, sound effects) are the recognizable constants of program genres and, like the superordinate story scripts underlying content, are its markers.

Children can, after a moment's glance at a new channel determine from form, rather than content, the genre of the program—whether it is for adults or children, whether it is funny or serious, whether it is informative or entertaining in intent, and whether it is worthy of their further investment of attention. (Huston & Wright, 1998, p. 1018)

The fact that young children use formal program production features as signals to attend to content that they are more likely to comprehend suggests that their TV viewing is an *active* rather than a *passive* process. But many television critics imply the opposite, describing the child as a passive, possibly addicted, victim. The either/or character of this debate is misleading. Sometimes, children monitor auditorily and selectively attend to content they comprehend. On these occasions, they often are time-sharing TV viewing with some other activity (e.g., playing with toys). Which one is the primary activity and which is secondary may shift. On other occasions, children may attend more constantly and be less physically actively involved with other objects or toys. For example, even Anderson (personal communication, April 1984), a leading proponent of the "child as active viewer" position, has found that young children's Saturday morning TV viewing is more likely to follow this latter model. That programming is typically cartoons intended for children, thus relatively easy for them to understand.

Anderson and Lorch (1983) differentiated between automatic viewing or processing, which probably is more characteristic of cartoon viewing, and strategic viewing, which involves active attention. The latter is usually schema dependent and schema driven—that is, by some prior knowledge, a story schema, or some other cognitive organizer that makes thoughtful processing possible (Meadowcroft & Reeves, 1989). An example given by Huston and Wright (1998) is the greater attention by boys to male characters in the media, once

they understand that gender is a constant and permanent attribute (Luecke-Aleksa, Anderson, Collins, & Schmitt, 1995). They proposed (Huston & Wright, 1983; Wright & Huston, 1983) that at very young ages or for very shallow, superficially humorous, or stereotyped material, the perceptual salience or "formal features" of the production techniques would determine selective attention and level of processing and that, with cognitive development, children's attention would become more internally governed and goal directed, based on their interest in the content.

In the context of this discussion of level of processing and the passive versus active child-viewer debate, it is important to remember that (a) there is considerable evidence that watching age-appropriate educational programming intended for children has a positive impact (e.g., Anderson et al., 2001; Bickham et al., 2001; Fisch & Truglio, 2001), (b) this is not the case for noneducational children's programming (indeed, there is evidence of negative effects; see MacBeth, 1996 for a review), and (c) most TV programs watched by children are intended for adults, so their comprehensibility will vary with the child's cognitive development.

A model describing the changes with development for children's attention to and comprehension of television, which in my opinion applies to other media as well, was proposed by Rice, Huston, and Wright (1982). This *traveling lens model* (see also Bickham et al., 2001) is based on Berlyne's (1960) notions of optimal levels of complexity, novelty, and so forth. In the traveling lens model, arousal, interest, and attention increase from low to high up the ordinate (*y*-axis) of a graph. Comprehensibility increases on the abscissa (*x*-axis) from low (boredom) up an inverted U-shaped curve to a maximum and then decreases again down the other side of the inverted U to incomprehensibility. An individual child's attentional lens travels with age and experience from left to right along the *x*-axis, with interest increasingly focused on previously incomprehensible media content.

Does attention to television vary by gender? Yes, and it does so fairly consistently. As was mentioned earlier, boys' visual attention to the set is greater than girls' (e.g., Alvarez, Huston, Wright, & Kerkman, 1988; see Miron, et al., 2001, for additional references). This gender difference in attention is not, however, associated with differences in comprehension or recall (Alvarez et al., 1988). Girls listen without looking more than do boys but remember equally well.

Comprehension. Just as comprehension does not guarantee recall, though it probably facilitates it, the link between visual attention and comprehension is not clear-cut. Anderson and his colleagues have argued that the correlation between the two occurs because comprehension increases subsequent attention (Anderson & Lorch, 1983), and they have shown that although children with toys available looked at the TV screen less than did children without toys, their comprehension was equivalent (e.g., Landau, Lorch, & Milich, 1992). In another study of children's programming, both visual attention to and comprehension of educational messages increased for 5- and 6-year-olds when humorous inserts were included, even though the inserts were not related to the educational messages (Zillmann, Williams, Bryant, Boynton, & Wolf, 1980).

In contrast, when adult-oriented rather than child-oriented formal production features were used (Campbell, Wright, & Huston, 1987) or narration was added (Rolandelli et al., 1991), comprehension varied, indicating that mental effort rather than just attention to the set was affected. Putting these and other findings together, Bickham et al. (2001) concluded that "looking and listening make separate and sometimes identifiable contributors to understanding, while perceptions of comprehensibility and interest strongly contribute to the decision to attend" (p. 103).

Some formal production features have more complex meanings that are acquired with experience with the medium in interaction with the viewer's level of cognitive development. For example, *montage* is used to indicate change in location, time passing, and other contextual information. Anderson and Field (1983) found that implied time changes were the most difficult and implied character actions the least difficult for children to draw inferences from, but both 4- and 7-year-olds could use and comprehend montage, although the older children were better at doing so. On the other hand, children younger than age 6 thought that an event had occurred twice if they were shown an instant replay (Rice, Huston, & Wright, 1986). As mentioned earlier, preschoolers have difficulty in distinguishing program from advertising content, even with separators (Palmer & McDowell, 1979). Younger children also have difficulty in distinguishing central from incidental information, but that difficulty is reduced if salient features are used to mark the central content (Calvert et al., 1982; Campbell et al., 1987; Kelly & Spear, 1991).

There is some evidence that playing interactive electronic games may facilitate the development of certain information-processing skills such as speed of mental rotation (spatial skill) and iconic representation (see Subrahmanyam, Kraut, Greenfield, & Gross, 2001).

Comprehension of various media, particularly for children but also on occasion for adults, is related to its perceived reality. Huston and Wright (1998) reviewed the evidence and proposed a three-dimensional structure for this issue with regard to television. The first, *factuality,* corresponds to what Hawkins (1977) called the "magic window" issue, which can be subdivided as follows:

Did the portrayed events actually happen in the real world pretty much as shown on TV? Did the TV show those events or part of them when they actually happened (as opposed to a reenactment of the factual event)? A yes answer to the main question establishes the content as factual. A yes answer to the second enhances the factuality, while a "no" answer diminishes it. (Huston & Wright, 1998, p. 1024)

Their second proposed dimension of perceived reality, *social realism,* refers to plausibility, that is, similarity to real life. It includes an actuarial judgment about the social realism of events/situations and a personal judgment based on identification by the viewer with one or more major characters portrayed. The third dimension, which Huston and Wright (1998) proposed more tentatively, is called *videotypy,* which refers to the degree to which the program's formal features, including editing and production techniques, dominate to remind viewers that "this is a television program" (e.g., sports and quiz shows, animated cartoons vs. most dramas and soap operas). Their three-dimensional model was proposed for television, but it also fits reasonably well to other media. The content of most other media, however, tends to be more homogeneous: Books are fiction or nonfiction with regard to factuality (but some, e.g., *Midnight in the Garden of Good and Evil,* fall in between); most movies are not factual, but some documentaries are; and most newspapers purport to be factual, but interactive games do not, and so on. The Internet, like TV, is mixed.

Memory. Children's memory for adult programs is better if it matches some of their prior knowledge, that is, their social schemas/scripts. For example, Newcomb and Collins (1979) showed a situation comedy about either a middle-class European American family or a working-class African American family to children from middle- and working-class families who were European or African American. Their recall was better if they saw the program that matched their family's social class, but ethnic group was not related to recall.

In studies conducted with elementary school children in the Netherlands, recall was better for television than for newspaper presentations, even after controlling for reading proficiency and whether the children expected to be tested (Walma van der Molen & van der Voort, 1997, 1998, 2000). The pattern of findings supported a dual-coding explanation in which the superior recall of television is due to the highly redundant audiovisual information in the children's television news stories used in these three studies. These results stand in contrast to those for recall by adults (described below) for adult news, which typically is much less redundant in its audio and visual characteristics. By comparison with North America, a much higher proportion of all TV programming, but especially children's TV, in the Netherlands is educational and informative, so viewers there may watch more attentively, mindfully, or with greater AIME. It also is true, however, that very few elementary school children in the Netherlands and North America regularly read newspapers.

ADULTS

With regard to adults' processing of media information, the work of Bryon Reeves and his colleagues is central to the intersection of psychology and mass communication (see Reeves & Thorson, 1986, for a review of their experiments on attention, mental effort, and memory for television content).

Attention. Whereas there has been considerable research on children's attention to television, in research with adults, attention has not often been studied directly. Instead, it has been inferred that if memory is enhanced, attention must have been high (Reeves et al., 1991). One example of research in which attention was measured assessed the impact of positive versus negative public service announcements (PSAs) (Reeves et al., 1991). While doing a secondary task, adults had to press a button on a game paddle when they heard a periodic tone while watching a videotape; the quicker the reaction time, the greater their attention. Negative PSAs were not attended to as closely as positive ones but were remembered better.

The PSA results are consistent with other evidence (Reeves, Lang, Thorson, & Rothschild, 1989) that positive and negative scenes in TV entertainment programs produce brain hemispheric differences in electroencephalograms (EEGs) (in the frontal region for the alpha frequency) identical to differences for nonmedia stimuli. Positive scenes evoke greater left hemisphere arousal and greater overall arousal (lower alpha values). Negative scenes evoke greater right hemisphere arousal.

Comprehension. In an attempt to explain the negative transactional relationship between television viewing and school achievement (see MacBeth, 1996, for a review), Armstrong and Greenberg (1990) studied first-year university students' performance on cognitive processing tests. They found that when TV was used as a secondary activity, significant performance decrements occurred for reading comprehension, spatial problem solving, and cognitive flexibility, suggesting that background television causes cognitive processing capacity limits to be exceeded on difficult and complex tasks.

Memory. Prior to widespread availability of news via the internet, about two thirds of adults in the United Kingdom and United States typically said that television is their main source of national and international news. As well, they said they trusted TV more than newspapers; if given conflicting TV and newspaper reports of the same story, they believed the TV one (Gunter, 1991). Given this preference for obtaining news via television, it is surprising how little of it people remember. For example, researchers who have conducted telephone interviews or experiments with adults who earlier that day watched a TV newscast

have found that spontaneous (unaided) recall was very poor, aided recall (e.g., providing the headline) was better but still poor, and the length of time between viewing and being interviewed (several minutes to 3 hours) made little difference (e.g., Faccoro & DeFleur, 1993; Findahl & Hoijer, 1985; Neuman, 1976). Moreover, distortion, misunderstanding, and confusions involving two or more stories (called *meltdown* by researchers) were common. Even when people subjectively believed that they had learned information, for example, about the weather, their recall, objectively speaking, was poor (Gunter, 1991).

Other researchers have compared recall rates from various forms of media. DeFleur, Davenport, Cronin, and DeFleur (1992) found that first-year university students in the United States remembered more from news stories when they were read in newspapers or off a computer screen than when seen on TV or heard on radio, and this was true for both unaided and aided recall. Faccoro and DeFleur (1993) conducted a cross-cultural version of that study in the United States and Spain. The results were identical to the previous study for students in the United States. Overall, across the four media and with aided and unaided scores combined, recall was similar for Spanish and U.S. students. But for Spanish students, computer recall was worst, newspaper was best, and television and radio were in the middle. The authors attributed this discrepancy to the more widespread use of computers at that time in the United States than in Spain.

Grimes (1991) conducted two laboratory experiments in an attempt to explain poor recall for news. He found that when the auditory and visual messages were highly redundant (which is not usually the case for TV news), adults perceived them as a single semantic unit, but when the two were mildly discrepant, they were perceived differently, which divided attention. In the latter case, typical of TV news, attentional capacity may often be exceeded, resulting in poor memory.

Two experiments with undergraduates provide some insight into the effect of prior experience schemas on mental encoding and retrieval of media events (Shapiro & Fox, 2002). The results suggest that

> the intrusion of schema-consistent information during memory reconstruction probably has as much to do with our judgments about memories as it has to do with our actual ability to retrieve the memory. Therefore, prior experience seems to strongly shape what we are willing to believe that we remember. (Shapiro & Fox, 2002, p. 131)

In these studies, memory was better for atypical than typical information even 1 week later, but the participants were less willing over time to believe that the atypical information was true if the topic was unfamiliar.

Graber (1990) found that for the adults in her study, recall of TV news stories was enhanced by visuals, especially those that were personalized through unusual sites and human figures. Her findings also indicated that schematic processing was a factor in faulty recall but less so for visual than verbal information.

◆ Conclusions

The main goals of this chapter have been (a) to provide a useful framework for understanding the psychological theories and processes relevant to media use and its effects and (b) to give examples of media research within that framework. Because of its preeminence to date, theories and research about television and, to a lesser extent, print and video games have been emphasized. Television is still the main leisure activity for children and adults in North America, but computers and other electronic media are increasingly heavily used as well (for reviews, see Montgomery, 2001; Subrahmanyam et al., 2001; Tarpley, 2001. Note that all three make the important point that use is strongly related to socioeconomic status, as is always the case

for new media). To date, most research on use of the internet and other new technologies has focused more on sociological than on psychological factors, but those media undoubtedly will be more prominent in future discussions of the psychology of media use and effects.

Where to from here? Looking back over the framework and examples of media research discussed in this chapter, what would be some interesting and potentially fruitful avenues to pursue in future research on the psychology of media use?

The availability of fMRI technology opens up a large and exciting set of possibilities for testing and validating or disconfirming many of our theoretical notions. Murray's (2001) work on children's brain responses when viewing violent and nonviolent video images provides a good starting point. For example, fMRI technology could potentially be used to explore the validity of the theoretical concepts of cognitive neoassociation theory, including linkages within associative networks of thoughts, feelings, and actions; priming of these networks by media violence or other aggression-related cues such as guns; and so forth. Bushman (1995) has shown that university students who score high on a measure of physical aggression—that is, high trait aggression individuals—are more likely than those low in trait aggression to choose to watch a violent videotape. Moreover, these students' moods (including anger) and behavior (aggression) were affected more by viewing violence than was the case for low trait aggression individuals. In a laboratory experiment that was analogous to Bushman's behavioral study but used video game rather than videotaped violence, Anderson and Dill (2000) found an increase in aggressive thoughts and behavior. What could fMRI or other technology tell us about the similarities and differences in the brain processes of high and low trait aggression children, adolescents, and adults in such situations?

Brain processing associated with preferences for different types of media content (e.g., comedy vs. drama) in relation to preexisting and subsequent moods and emotions would be interesting to explore. Other topics discussed in this chapter, including vigilance and its relation to cortical and emotional arousal, as well as children's media-related attention, comprehension, and memory also come to mind.

Cross-media comparisons—including internet and Web use as well as television, video games, books, radio, and so on—with regard to use, content, attention, comprehension, memory, and effects strike me as important to pursue.

Our role as adults in keeping children and youth safe has become much more difficult and complicated with the advent of some of the new technologies. We cannot regulate the internet. The cognitive development of children and preadolescents, for example, prior to the development of hypothetico-deductive reasoning, places limitations on their ability to perceive some of the possible consequences of their internet use, and this is exacerbated by their parents' lack of knowledge about their use, those with whom they are interacting and exchanging information, and so on. Pedophiles, who typically are very skilled at getting access to vulnerable children, are finding the internet ideal for this purpose. As researchers, we have a social responsibility to do what we can to understand how best to limit such negative consequences and to enhance the many positive consequences of the use of all types of media.

◆ Note

1. The cognitive structures for which cognitive psychologists use the terms *schema* (plural *schemas* or *schemata*) and *script* are based on Piaget's (1963) theory. Piaget used the term *schème* (plural *schèmes*) for this type of cognitive structure, which is of crucial importance in his explanation of cognitive development. In his theory, he also said that for some but not all schemes, there is an allied sensorimotor image, a figurative outline, and he used the term *schema* (plural *schemata*) for that concept. In this chapter, I have followed the cognitive psychology convention of using the terms *schema, schemas,* and *schemata,* as well as *scripts* for sequences, to refer to the concepts for which Piaget used the terms *schème* and *schèmes.*

◆ References

Abelson, R. P. (1981). Psychological status of the script. *American Psychologist, 36,* 715–729.

Alvarez, M. M., Huston, A. C., Wright, J. C., & Kerkman, D. D. (1988). Gender differences in visual attention to television form and content. *Journal of Applied Developmental Psychology, 9,* 459–475.

Anderson, C. A., & Dill, K. E. (2000). Video games and aggressive thoughts, feelings, and behavior in the laboratory and in life. *Journal of Personality and Social Psychology, 78,* 772–790.

Anderson, D. R., Alwitt, L. F., Lorch, E. P., & Levin, S. R. (1979). Watching children watch television. In G. A. Hale & M. Lewis (Eds.), *Attention and cognitive development* (pp. 331–361). New York: Plenum.

Anderson, D. R., & Burns, J. (1991). Paying attention to television. In J. Bryant & D. Zillmann (Eds.), *Responding to the screen: Reception and reaction processes* (pp. 3–25). Hillsdale, NJ: Lawrence Erlbaum.

Anderson, D. R., Choi, H. P., & Lorch, E. P. (1987). Attentional inertia reduces distractibility during young children's television viewing. *Child Development, 58,* 798–806.

Anderson, D. R., Collins, P. A., Schmitt, K. L., & Jacobvitz, R. S. (1996). Stressful life events and television viewing. *Communication Research, 23,* 243–260.

Anderson, D. R., & Field, D. E. (1983). Children's attention to television: Implications for production. In M. Meyer (Ed.), *Children and the formal features of television* (pp. 56–96). Munich, Germany: Saur.

Anderson, D. R., Huston, A. C., Smith, K. L., Linebarger, D. L., & Wright, J. C. (2001). Adolescent outcomes associated with early childhood television viewing: The Recontact Study. *Monographs of the Society for Research in Child Development, 66*(Serial No. 264).

Anderson, D. R., & Lorch, E. P. (1983). Looking at television: Action or reaction? In J. Bryant & D. R. Anderson (Eds.), *Children's understanding of television: Research on attention and comprehension* (pp. 1–33). New York: Academic Press.

Anderson, J., & Bower, G. (1973). *Human associative memory.* Washington, DC: V. H. Winston.

Apter, M. (1992). *The dangerous edge: The psychology of excitement.* New York: Free Press.

Armstrong, G. B., & Greenberg, B. G. (1990). Background television as an inhibition of cognitive processing. *Human Communication Research, 16*(3), 355–386.

Bandura, A. (1977). *Social learning theory.* Englewood Cliffs, NJ: Prentice Hall.

Bandura, A. (1983). Psychological mechanisms of aggression. In R. G. Geen & C. I. Donnerstein (Eds.), *Aggression: Theoretical and empirical reviews: Vol. 1. Theoretical and methodological issues* (pp. 1–40). New York: Academic Press.

Bandura, A. (1994). Social cognitive theory of mass communication. In J. Bryant & D. Zillmann (Eds.), *Media effects: Advances in theory and research* (pp. 61–90). Hillsdale, NJ: Lawrence Erlbaum.

Bandura, A., Ross, D., & Ross, S. A. (1963). Vicarious reinforcement and imitative learning. *Journal of Abnormal and Social Psychology, 67,* 601–607.

Berkowitz, L. (1984). Some effects of thoughts on anti- and prosocial influences of media events: A cognitive-neoassociation analysis. *Psychological Bulletin, 95,* 419–427.

Berkowitz, L. (1986). Situational influences on reactions to observed violence. *Journal of Social Issues, 42,* 93–103.

Berlyne, D. E. (1960). *Conflict, arousal, and curiosity.* New York: McGraw-Hill.

Bettelheim, B. (1975). *The uses of enhancement: The meaning and importance of fairy tales.* New York: Vintage.

Bickham, D. S., Wright, J. C., & Huston, A. C. (2001). Attention, comprehension, and the educational influences of television. In D. G. Singer & J. L. Singer (Eds.), *Handbook of children and the media* (pp. 101–119). Thousand Oaks, CA: Sage.

Brickman, P., & Bulyer, R. J. (1977). Pleasure and pain in social comparison. In J. M. Suls & R. L. Miller (Eds.), *Social comparison processes: Theoretical and empirical perspectives* (pp. 149–186). New York: John Wiley.

Bryant, J., Carveth, R. A., & Brown, D. (1981). Television viewing and anxiety: An experimental examination. *Journal of Communication, 31*(1), 106–119.

Bushman, B. J. (1995). Moderating role of trait aggressiveness in the effects of violent media on aggression. *Journal of Personality and Social Psychology, 69,* 950–960.

Bushman, B. J., & Geen, R. G. (1990). The role of cognitive-emotional mediators and individual differences in the effects of media violence on aggression. *Journal of Personality and Social Psychology, 58,* 156–163.

Calvert, S. L., Brune, C., Eugia, M., & Marcato, J. (1991, April). *Attentional inertia and distractibility during children's educational computer interactions.* Poster presented at the biennial meeting of the Society for Research in Child Development, Seattle, WA.

Calvert, S. L., Huston, A. C., Watkins, B. A., & Wright, J. C. (1982). The relation between selective attention to television forms and children's comprehension of content. *Child Development, 53,* 601–610.

Campbell, T. A., Wright, J. C., & Huston, A. C. (1987). Form cues and content difficulty as determinants of children's cognitive processing of televised educational messages. *Journal of Experimental Child Psychology, 43,* 311–327.

Cantor, J. (1996). Television and children's fear. In T. M. MacBeth (Ed.), *Tuning in to young viewers: Social science perspectives on television* (pp. 87–115). Thousand Oaks, CA: Sage.

Cantor, J. (1998). *"Mommy I'm scared": How TV and movies frighten children and what we can do to protect them.* San Diego: Harcourt Brace.

Cantor, J. (2001). The media and children's fears, anxieties, and perceptions of danger. In D. G. Singer & J. L. Singer (Eds.), *Handbook of children and the media* (pp. 207–221). Thousand Oaks, CA: Sage.

Cantor, J., & Nathanson, A. (1997). Predictors of children's interest in violent television programming. *Journal of Broadcasting & Electronic Media, 41*, 155–167.

Christ, W. G., & Medoff, N. J. (1984). Affective state and selective exposure to and use of television. *Journal of Broadcasting, 28*(1), 51–63.

Collins, W. A. (1983a). Interpretation and inference in children's television viewing. In J. Bryant & D. R. Anderson (Eds.), *Children's understanding of television: Research on attention and comprehension* (pp. 125– 150). New York: Academic Press.

Collins, W. A. (1983b). Social antecedents, cognitive processing, and comprehension of social portrayals on television. In E. T. Higgins, D. N. Ruble, & W. W. Hartup (Eds.), *Social cognition and social development* (pp. 110–133). Cambridge, England: Cambridge University Press.

Comstock, G., & Scharrer, E. (2001). The use of television and other film-related media. In D. G. Singer & J. L. Singer (Eds.), *Handbook of children and the media* (pp. 47–72). Thousand Oaks, CA: Sage.

Cordua, G., McGraw, K., & Drabman, R. (1979). Doctor or nurse: Children's perceptions of sex-typed occupations. *Child Development, 50*, 590–593.

DeFleur, M. L., Davenport, L., Cronin, M., & DeFleur, M. (1992). Audience recall of news stories presented by newspaper, computer, television, and radio. *Journalism Quarterly, 69*(4), 1010–1022.

Faccoro, L. B., & DeFleur, M. L. (1993). A cross-cultural experiment on how well audiences remember news stories from newspaper, computer, television, and radio sources. *Journalism Quarterly, 70*(3), 585–601.

Festinger, L. A. (1954). A theory of social comparison processes. *Human Relations, 7*, 117–140.

Findahl, O., & Hoijer, B. (1985). Some characteristics of news memory and comprehension. *Journal of Broadcasting and Electronic Media, 29*(4), 379–396.

Fisch, S. M., & Truglio, R. T. (2001). *"G" is for growing: Thirty years of research on children and* Sesame Street. Mahwah, NJ: Lawrence Erlbaum.

Fiske, S. T., & Taylor, S. E. (1984). *Social cognition*. Reading, MA: Addison-Wesley.

Flavell, J. H. (1979). Metacognition and cognitive monitoring: A new era of cognitive-development inquiry. *American Psychologist, 34*, 906–911.

Flavell, J. H., & Wellman, H. M. (1977). Metamemory. In R. V. Kailand & J. W. Hagen (Eds.), *Perspectives in the development of memory and cognition* (pp. 3–33). Hillsdale, NJ: Lawrence Erlbaum.

Freud, S. (1958). *Der Witz und seine Beziehung zum Unbewussten* [Wit and its relation to the unconscious]. Frankfurt, Germany: Fischer Bucherei. (Original work published 1905)

Furth, H. G. (1980). *The world of grown-ups: Children's conceptions of society*. New York: Elsevier.

Graber, D. A. (1990). Seeing is remembering: How visuals contribute to learning from television news. *Journal of Communication, 40*(3), 134–155.

Grimes, T. (1991). Mild auditory-visual dissonance in television news may exceed viewer attentional capacity. *Human Communication Research, 18*, 268–298.

Gunter, B. (1991). Responding to news and public affairs. In J. Bryant & D. Zillmann (Eds.), *Responding to the screen: Reception and reaction processes* (pp. 229–260). Hillsdale, NJ: Lawrence Erlbaum.

Harrison, K., & Cantor, J. (1999). Tales from the screen: Enduring fright reactions to scary media. *Media Psychology, 1*(2), 96–116.

Hawkins, R. P. (1977). The dimensional structure of children's perceptions of television reality. *Communications Research, 4*, 299–320.

Hoekstra, S. J., Harris, R. J., & Helmick, A. L. (1999). Autobiographical memories about the experience of seeing frightening movies in childhood. *Media Psychology, 1*(2), 117–140.

Horton, D., & Wohl, R. R. (1956). Mass communication and para-social interaction: Observations on intimacy at a distance. *Psychiatry, 19,* 215–229.

Huesmann, L. R. (1982). Information processing models of behavior. In N. Hirschberg & L. Humphreys (Eds.), *Multivariate applications in the social sciences* (pp. 261–288). Hillsdale, NJ: Lawrence Erlbaum.

Huesmann, L. R. (1986). Psychological processes promoting the relation between exposure to media violence and aggressive behavior by the viewer. *Journal of Social Issues, 42,* 125–139.

Huesmann, L. R. (1988). An information processing model for the development of aggression. *Aggressive Behavior, 14*(1), 13–24.

Huston, A. C., & Wright, J. C. (1983). Children's processing of television: The informative functions of formal features. In J. Bryant & D. R. Anderson (Eds.), *Children's understanding of television: Research on attention and comprehension* (pp. 35–68). New York: Academic Press.

Huston, A. C., & Wright, J. C. (1998). Mass media and child development. In W. Damon (Ed.), *Handbook of child psychology* (5th ed., pp. 999–1058). New York: John Wiley.

Johnson, D. D. (1995). Adolescents' motivations for viewing graphic horror. *Human Communication Research, 21*(4), 522–552.

Josephson, W. L. (1987). Television violence and children's aggression: Testing the priming, social script, and disinhibition predictions. *Journal of Personality and Social Psychology, 53,* 882–890.

Joy, L. A., Kimball, M. M., & Zabrack, M. L. (1986). Television and children's aggressive behavior. In T. M. Williams (Ed.), *The impact of television: A natural experiment in three communities* (pp. 303–360). Orlando, FL: Academic Press.

Kelly, A. E., & Spear, P. S. (1991). Intraprogram synopses for children's comprehension of television content. *Journal of Experimental Child Psychology, 52,* 87–98.

Kinder, M. (1991). *Playing with power in movies, television, and video games: From Muppet Babies to Teenage Mutant Ninja Turtles.* Berkeley: University of California Press.

Krull, R., & Watt, J. H., Jr. (1973, April). *Television viewing and aggression: An examination of three models.* Paper presented at the meeting of the International Communication Association, Montreal, Quebec.

Kubey, R. (1984). *Leisure, television, and subjective experience.* Unpublished doctoral dissertation, University of Chicago.

Kubey, R. (1986). Television use in everyday life: Coping with unstructured time. *Journal of Communication, 36*(3), 108–123.

Kubey, R. (1996). Television dependence, diagnosis, and prevention. In T. M. MacBeth (Ed.), *Tuning in to young viewers: Social science perspectives on television* (pp. 221–260). Thousand Oaks, CA: Sage.

Kubey, R., & Csikszentmihalyi, M. (1990). Television as escape: Subjective experience before an evening of heavy viewing. *Communication Reports, 3*(2), 92–100.

Landau, S., Lorch, E. P., & Milich, R. (1992). Visual attention to and comprehension of television in attention deficit hyperactivity disordered and normal boys. *Child Development, 63,* 928–937.

Landman, J., & Manis, M. (1983). Social cognition: Some historical and theoretical perspectives. In L. Berkowitz (Ed.), *Advances in experimental social psychology* (Vol. 16, pp. 49–123). San Francisco: Academic Press.

Langer, E. J., & Piper, A. (1988). Television from a mindful/mindless perspective. In S. Oskamp (Ed.), *Applied social psychology annual: Television as a social issue* (Vol. 8, pp. 247–260). Beverly Hills, CA: Sage.

LeDoux, J. (1996). *The emotional brain: The mysterious underpinnings of emotional life.* New York: Simon & Schuster.

Liebert, R. M., Sprafkin, J. N., & Davidson, E. S. (1982). *The early window: Effects of television on children and youth* (2nd ed.). New York: Pergamon.

Lorch, E. P., Anderson, D. R., & Levin, S. R. (1979). The relationship of visual attention to children's comprehension of television. *Child Development, 50,* 722–727.

Luecke-Aleksa, D., Anderson, D. R., Collins, P. A., & Schmitt, K. L. (1995). Gender constancy and television viewing. *Developmental Psychology, 31*, 773–780.

MacBeth, T. M. (1996). Indirect effects of television. In T. M. MacBeth (Ed.), *Tuning in to young viewers: Social science perspectives on television* (pp. 149–219). Thousand Oaks, CA: Sage.

MacBeth, T. M. (1998). Quasi-experimental research on television and behavior: Natural and field experiments. In J. K. Asamen & G. L. Berry (Eds.), *Research paradigms, television and social behavior* (pp. 109–151). Thousand Oaks, CA: Sage.

MacBeth, T. M. (2001). The impact of television: A Canadian natural experiment. In C. McKie & B. D. Singer (Eds.), *Communications in Canadian society* (pp. 196–213). Toronto: Thompson Educational Publishing.

Malamuth, N. M. (1996). Sexually explicit media, gender differences, and evolutionary theory. *Journal of Communication, 46*(3), 8–31.

Mandler, J., & Johnson, N. (1977). Remembrance of things parsed: Story structure and recall. *Cognitive Psychology, 9*, 111–151.

Mares, M., & Cantor, J. (1992). Elderly viewers' responses to televised portrayals of old age. *Communication Research, 19*(4), 459–478.

McIlwraith, R., & Schallow, J. (1983). Adult fantasy life and patterns of media use. *Journal of Communication, 33*(1), 78–91.

Meadowcroft, J. M. (1985). *Children's attention to television: The influence of story schema development on allocation of cognitive capacity and memory.* Unpublished doctoral dissertation, University of Wisconsin.

Meadowcroft, J. M. (1996). Attention span cycles. In J. H. Watt & C. A. Van Lear (Eds.), *Dynamic patterns in communication processes* (pp. 255–276). Thousand Oaks, CA: Sage.

Meadowcroft, J. M., & Reeves, B. (1989). Influence of story schema development on children's attention to television. *Communication Research, 16*, 352–374.

Meyrowitz, J. (1985). *No sense of place: The impact of electronic media on social behavior.* New York: Oxford University Press.

Miron, D., Bryant, J., & Zillmann, D. (2001). Creating vigilance for better learning from television. In D. G. Singer & J. L. Singer (Eds.), *Handbook of children and the media* (pp. 153–181). Thousand Oaks, CA: Sage.

Montgomery, K. C. (2001). Digital kids: The new on-line children's consumer culture. In D. G. Singer & J. L. Singer (Eds.), *Handbook of children and the media* (pp. 635–650). Thousand Oaks, CA: Sage.

Murray, J. P. (2001). TV violence and brain-mapping in children. *Psychiatric Times, 17*(10), 70–71.

Neuman, W. R. (1976). Patterns of recall among television news viewers. *Public Opinion Quarterly, 40*(1), 115–123.

Newcomb, A. F., & Collins, W. A. (1979). Children's comprehension of family role portrayals in televised dramas: Effects of socioeconomic status, ethnicity, and age. *Developmental Psychology, 15*, 417–423.

Oliver, M. B. (2000). The respondent gender gap. In D. Zillmann & P. Vorderer (Eds.), *Media entertainment: The psychology of its appeal* (pp. 215–234). Mahwah, NJ: Lawrence Erlbaum.

O'Neal, E. C., & Taylor, S. L. (1989). Status of the provoker, opportunity to retaliate, and interest in video violence. *Aggressive Behavior, 15*, 171–180.

Palmer, E. L., & McDowell, C. N. (1979). Program/commercial separators in children's television programming. *Journal of Communication, 29*, 197–201.

Piaget, J. (1963). *The origins of intelligence in children.* New York: Norton. (Original work published 1952)

Reeves, B., Lang, A., Thorson, E., & Rothschild, M. (1989). Emotional television scenes and hemispheric specialization. *Human Communication Research, 15*, 493–508.

Reeves, B., Newhagen, J., Maibach, E., Basil, M., & Kurz, K. (1991). Negative and positive television messages. *American Behavioral Scientist, 34*(6), 679–694.

Reeves, B., & Thorson, E. (1986). Watching television: Experiments on the viewing process. *Communication Research, 13*(3), 343–361.

Rice, M. L., Huston, A. C., & Wright, J. C. (1982). The forms and codes of television: Effects of children's attention, comprehension, and social behavior. In D. Pearl, J. Bouthilet, & J. Lazar (Eds.), *Television and behavior: Ten years of scientific progress and implications for the eighties* (pp. 24–38). Washington, DC: Government Printing Office.

Rice, M. L., Huston, A. C., & Wright, J. C. (1986). Replays as repetitions: Young children's interpretation of television forms. *Journal of Applied Developmental Psychology, 7,* 61–76.

Rolandelli, D. R., Wright, J. C., Huston, A. C., & Eakins, D. (1991). Children's auditory and visual processing of narrated and non-narrated television programming. *Journal of Experimental Child Psychology, 51,* 90–122.

Rosengren, K. E., Roe, K., & Sonesson, E. (1983). *Finality and causality in adolescents' mass media use* (Media Panel Report No. 24 [Mimeo]). Lund, Sweden: University of Lund, Department of Sociology.

Routtenberg, A. (1968). The two-arousal hypothesis: Reticular formation and limbic system. *Psychological Review, 75,* 51–80.

Routtenberg, A. (1971). Stimulus processing and response execution: A neurobehavioral theory. *Physiology and Behavior, 6,* 589–596.

Salomon, G. (1981). Introducing AIME: The assessment of children's mental involvement with television. In H. Kelley & H. Gardner (Eds.), *New directions for child development: Viewing children through television* (No. 13, pp. 89–112). San Francisco: Jossey-Bass.

Salomon, G. (1983). Television watching and mental effort: A social psychological view. In J. Bryant & D. R. Anderson (Eds.), *Children's understanding of television: Research on attention and comprehension* (pp. 181–198). New York: Academic Press.

Salomon, G. (1984). Television is "easy" and print is "tough": The differential investment of mental effort as a function of perceptions and attributions. *Journal of Educational Psychology, 76,* 647–658.

Schank, R. C., & Abelson, R. P. (1977). *Scripts, plans, goals, and understanding.* Hillsdale, NJ: Lawrence Erlbaum.

Shapiro, M. A., & Fox, J. R. (2002). The role of typical and atypical events in story memory. *Human Communication Research, 28*(1), 109–135.

Subrahmanyam, K., Kraut, R., Greenfield, P., & Gross, E. (2001). New forms of electronic media. In D. G. Singer & J. L. Singer (Eds.), *Handbook of children and the media* (pp. 73–99). Thousand Oaks, CA: Sage.

Suls, J. M. (1977). Social comparison theory and research: An overview from 1954. In J. M. Suls & R. L. Miller (Eds.), *Social comparison processes: Theoretical and empirical perspectives* (pp. 1–20). New York: John Wiley.

Tarpley, T. (2001). Children, the internet, and other new technologies. In D. G. Singer & J. L. Singer (Eds.), *Handbook of children and the media* (pp. 547–556). Thousand Oaks, CA: Sage.

Walma van der Molen, J. H. W., & van der Voort, T. H. A. (1997). Children's recall of television and print news: A media comparison study. *Journal of Educational Psychology, 89*(1), 82–91.

Walma van der Molen, J. H. W., & van der Voort, T. H. A. (1998). Children's recall of the news: TV news stories compared with three print versions. *Educational Technology Research and Development, 46*(1), 39–52.

Walma van der Molen, J. H. W., & van der Voort, T. H. A. (2000). The impact of television, print, and audio on children's recall of the news. *Human Communication Research, 26*(1), 3–26.

Ward, L. M., & Greenfield, P. M. (1998). Designing experiments on television and social behavior: Developmental perspectives. In J. K. Asamen & G. L. Berry (Eds.), *Research paradigms, television, and social behavior* (pp. 67–108). Thousand Oaks, CA: Sage.

Wills, T. A. (1981). Downward comparison principles in social psychology. *Psychological Bulletin, 90,* 245–271.

Wood, J. V., Taylor, S. E., & Lichtman, R. R. (1985). Social comparison in adjustment to breast cancer. *Journal of Personality and Social Psychology, 49,* 1169–1183.

Wright, J. C., & Huston, A. C. (1983). A matter of form: Potentials of television for young viewers. *American Psychologist, 38,* 835–843.

Wright, J. C., Huston, A. C., Truglio, R., Fitch, M., Smith, E., & Piemyat, S. (1995). Occupational portrayals on television: Children's role schemata, career aspirations, and perceptions of reality. *Child Development, 66,* 1706–1718.

Zillmann, D. (1979). *Hostility and aggression.* Hillsdale, NJ: Lawrence Erlbaum.

Zillmann, D. (1980). Anatomy of suspense. In P. H. Tannebaum (Ed.), *The entertainment functions of television* (pp. 133–163). Hillsdale, NJ: Lawrence Erlbaum.

Zillmann, D. (1982). Television viewing and arousal. In D. Pearl, L. Bouthilet, & J. Lazar (Eds.), *Television and behavior: Ten years of scientific progress and implications for the eighties* (Vol. 2, pp. 53–67). Washington, DC: Government Printing Office.

Zillmann, D. (1988). Mood management: Using entertainment to full advantage. In L. Donohew, H. E. Sypher, & E. T. Higgins (Eds.), *Communication, social cognition, and affect* (pp. 147–171). Hillsdale, NJ: Lawrence Erlbaum.

Zillmann, D. (1991a). Empathy: Affect from bearing witness to the emotions of others. In J. Bryant & D. Zillmann (Eds.), *Responding to the screen: Reception and reaction processes* (pp. 135–167). Hillsdale, NJ: Lawrence Erlbaum.

Zillmann, D. (1991b). Television viewing and physiological arousal. In J. Bryant & D. Zillmann (Eds.), *Responding to the screen: Reception and reaction processes*

(pp. 103–133). Hillsdale, NJ: Lawrence Erlbaum.

Zillmann, D. (2000). Humor and comedy. In D. Zillmann & P. Vorderer (Eds.), *Media entertainment: The psychology of its appeal* (pp. 37–57). Mahwah, NJ: Lawrence Erlbaum.

Zillmann, D., & Bryant, J. (1980). Misattribution theory of tendentious humor. *Journal of Experimental Social Psychology, 16,* 146–160.

Zillmann, D., & Bryant, J. (1985). Affect, mood, and emotion as determinants of selective exposure. In D. Zillmann & J. Bryant (Eds.), *Selective exposure to communication* (pp. 157–190). Hillsdale, NJ: Lawrence Erlbaum.

Zillmann, D., Hay, T. A., & Bryant, J. (1975). The effect of suspense and its resolution on the appreciation of dramatic presentations. *Journal of Research in Personality, 9,* 307–323.

Zillmann, D., Hezel, R. T., & Medoff, N. (1980). The effect of affective states on selective exposure to televised entertainment fare. *Journal of Applied Social Psychology, 10,* 323–339.

Zillmann, D., & Weaver, J. B., III. (1996). Gender-socialization theory of reactions to horror. In J. B. Weaver III & R. Tamborini (Eds.), *Horror films: Current research on audience preferences and reactions* (pp. 81–101). Mahwah, NJ: Lawrence Erlbaum.

Zillmann, D., Williams, B. R., Bryant, J., Boynton, K. R., & Wolf, M. A. (1980). Acquisition of information from educational television programs as a function of differently paced humorous inserts. *Journal of Educational Psychology, 72,* 170–180.

Zuckerman, M. (1979). *Sensation seeking: Beyond the optimal level of arousal.* New York: John Wiley.

11

CONTEMPORARY TELEVISION AUDIENCES

Publics, Markets, Communities, and Fans

◆ Virginia Nightingale

> *Remarkable as it may seem, Americans spend more of their lifetime being an audience than working or sleeping. This reflects the cornucopia of entertainment and communication that surrounds us in the latter part of the twentieth century. Its pervasiveness makes it central to understanding our culture and our society today.*
>
> —Richard Butsch (2000, p. 295)

There are several competing and sometimes overlapping ways of understanding audiences. *Publics, markets, communities,* and *fans* are the main terms used to describe people when they are "being an audience." This chapter will explore these audiences conceptually, using a variety of empirical examples.

◆ *The Changing Audience Experience*

As a mode of human *experience,* audience is a way of describing how humans come to know the world through systems of mediated representation. Nowadays, more and more of what we know is introduced to us via the media, and less and less of our access to received knowledge is moderated by teachers, other human intermediaries, or direct experience. As noted earlier, Butsch (2000, p. 295) has stated that Americans spend more time being audiences than working or sleeping. Audiences routinely expand the time they spend being audiences either by combining their audience time with other activities, such as working, traveling, and having fun, or by doubling up on audience activities, such as listening to the radio while reading the newspaper or watching TV while leafing through a magazine. Some people even monitor radio and TV while using the Internet, checking e-mail, or playing computer games. In this sense, the media multiply time and play havoc with our sense of duration (our sense of the passing of time). The more media surround us, the less attention we pay to any one medium or any one text, the harder it becomes to distinguish audience activities from other life skills, and the more widely the word is used to describe anyone doing anything with media.

Several media histories have documented the various and dramatic changes that have occurred in what it means to be an audience. Some writers have done so as part of tracing the history of particular media (Manguel, 1996; Small, 1998; Smulyan, 1994). Richard Butsch (2000) has traced the changing nature of audiences for theater and light entertainment in the United States over a period of 250 years. The U.S. conventions for being an audience were, of course, based in even older European, particularly British, theatrical traditions. Butsch describes Elizabethan audiences as an example of the great difference between past and present ways of being an audience, noting that

in Elizabethan theatres, courtiers and gallants treated theatre as their court where they could measure their importance by the attention they received. Fops sat on stage, interrupted performances, and even on occasion grabbed an actress. All of this annoyed the plebeian pit, who shouted, "Away with them." But pittites were hardly meek. They too ate, smoked, drank, socialised and engaged in repartee with the actors. (Butsch, 2000, p. 4)

Although some audiences today, particularly for rock music and major sporting events, continue aspects of past traditions of such audience "sovereignty," Butsch (2000) has noted that the experience of audience as an integrated component of *performance* has virtually disappeared. He explains that for 18th- and early 19th-century theater audiences, "The meanings from text (the play) and from social interaction (performers with audience) merged, since audiences interacted with actors as both text (the characters) and as social beings (actors)" (pp. 289–290). Such audiences were local but also microcosms of the community that the participants experienced daily, in the sense that the theater reproduced within its walls the discursive relations between participants as a replica of those that patterned the social world outside.

Butsch (2000) considers the difference between past and present experiences of being an audience to be so marked that he questions the appropriateness of using the term *audience* at all to describe the dispersed audience phenomena produced by broadcasting, with which we are most familiar today.

"The television audience" exists only with the text of a program. Beyond that, "the audience" does not exist; rather the individuals or households exist as entities unrelated to each other. In contrast to "the audience," these individuals are defined by environmental artefacts beyond the program, and TV is merely one of these artefacts. (Butsch, 2000, pp. 289–290)

This point is extremely important for understanding audiences and the nature of their power and agency in the contemporary world. It suggests that the "group" nature of audiences, inherent in the way we refer to audiences as just "people," needs to be reevaluated.[1] In particular, the tendency, following Raymond Williams (1980), to imagine the audience in terms of a polarity between "the masses," on one hand, and "community," on the other, has led in recent years to neglect of the *varieties* of mass audiences and of their social and political significance.[2] The focus on audience communities has created a better understanding of the nature of audience agency but deflected attention away from the evolving phenomenon of mass audience agency.

If, as Butsch (2000) suggests, audiences now derive their identity as audiences from other social groups or from their labeling by corporate entities (particularly those that control the media), then the parameters of what it means to be an audience in the contemporary world are derived from contexts outside the media. Extra-media groups, such as publics, market segments, families, cultures and subcultures, associations, and ethnicities, provide the contexts or social environments where being an audience is reworked as sociocultural meanings, actions, and ideas. These contexts of audience, in turn, leave their imprint on the nature of the audience experience. As a result, the activities associated with being an audience have multiplied and diversified in a manner to match the growth in new media, new media forms, the distribution systems arranged for them, and the new audience configurations they permit. This diversification suggests the value of

1. returning to the investigation of the mass audience,

2. introducing a more elaborate vocabulary for discussing and describing audiences in general and mass audiences in particular,

3. interrogating the sociocultural rights and privileges audience groups draw on to challenge the media, and

4. again addressing the diverse tactics that the institutions that finance the media industries adopt to minimize the impact of audience agency on the smooth operation of the media.

ENGAGING WITH MEDIA

Being an audience involves engaging with media. There are four dimensions to this engagement: a media time/space location is defined, people gather, media materials are presented, and a mediated event occurs. Elsewhere, I have discussed these components as four separate definitions of the word *audience* because in everyday talk, each may be used separately to refer to audiences. The definitions emphasize either the people involved—who the people in the audience are and how they have come together—or they emphasize aspects of the audience event that is occurring— who is holding audience with whom and what is happening (Nightingale, 1996, 2003). Audiences are complex mixtures of people and mediated events, but they are often defined primarily as "groups of people" or "events."

The "people" dimension of audience is dominant, for example, when we talk about audiences as the public, as markets, and sometimes even as communities. As audience publics and audience markets, people are thought of as aggregates of individuals. As audience communities, people are thought of as group members. By designating people as markets, publics, or communities, we are referring to their sociocultural status beyond the program or text and outside the mass communication process. The event component, by contrast, is dominant when the sociocultural significance of an audience event of actual media use is examined.

Although the terms *the public* or *the markets* have a metaphorical dimension when used to refer to audiences, these terms are not just ways of imagining the otherwise unknowable masses of people available as viewers or listeners. When applied to audiences, these terms are better understood as ways of identifying and addressing the specific rights and privileges that contemporary audiences exercise in the system of mass communication—and of assessing the limitations on those rights and privileges. Publics and markets are varieties of mass audiences—as well as ways of distinguishing among the variety of communication rights people command as human beings and as citizens—that contrast people's rights as audiences with the rights of the corporations, organizations, and institutions that own and control the mass media; the rights of advertisers and others who use the media to promote their products and corporate identities; and the rights of governments and other power elites who define the limits of media power (both political and commercial).

We often talk about "the public" without thinking of audiences, so audiences clearly are not the same thing as the public. We often talk about markets, and audiences never come to mind, so clearly audiences are not "the market." On the other hand, there is no dividing line between the audience market and the market or the audience public and the public. When we talk about audiences as the public, we are referring to the mediated nature of some aspects of being the public, as well as to the rights and privileges people bring to their engagements with the media, based on their political status. When we talk about audiences as markets, we are referring to the rights and privileges exercised by audiences as consumers. But when we talk about audiences as communities, we refer to the communal nature of cultural expression and to the rights that people possess as cultural beings to express their identity through texts. Part of being a

member of the general public involves using the mass media, part of being a consumer involves noticing (and acting on) advertising in the world around us, and part of being a member of our culture involves familiarity with the key texts of our times. It is possible to bring about change in the media by the choices we make about what to watch and what to turn off, what to buy and not buy, and what political information we ignore or accept. This action only has impact as mass action. Unless supported by a massive groundswell of like-mindedness, such action encourages little sense of agency and may instead make people feel powerless. Turning off particular program content makes a difference to the production of the program (and to the media) only if lots of other people, independently, act in the same way at the same time.

AUDIENCE POWER
AND AGENCY

The most important democratic reason for researching media audiences is to explore the scope for audience action. For this reason, I have chosen to focus this discussion of audiences on their power and agency.[3] In this context, I use the term *audience power* to refer to the social and political power of the social formation(s) from which an audience is drawn. In other words, questions of audience power arise in what Anthony Giddens (1984, p. 31) has described as the structures of domination and legitimation. This terminology has, however, tended to emphasize audience helplessness and to underestimate the value to audiences of the power they do have within these structures. National political structures are structures of domination, but they are also structures that underwrite human rights. National legal systems are systems of domination, but they are also the means by which ordinary people can seek redress for injury. From this perspective, audience composition, the basic information about audiences produced by audience measurement, for example, also provides a demographic profile of, or a rudimentary guide to, the sources of the social power of an audience. The basic demographics—age and gender—signal that these groups may have the scope to argue for special consideration in the development of media policy.

Audience agency, by contrast, is used here to refer to the situated and embodied practices that denote audience engagement with specific media products and that signal the cultural significance of audience activities for the participant and for the culture. Audience agency is awakened by the media, by texts, and by textual production. It is the process by which media materials are recycled in the cultural experiences of individuals, forming and transforming both the person and the social world. Again, we could think of audience agency as operating within an overarching and preexisting structure of meanings, but this would unnecessarily limit the range of creative action recognized as being linked to audience issues when power in discourse is linked with the capacity of audiences to undertake legal and social action to secure their media rights and interests.

From an audience perspective, audience is always a combination of people and event, power and agency. From a media management perspective, it is often considered useful, as we will see below, to minimize the importance of the "event" component of audience and to act as though audiences are in effect only people. Those working from within the structures of domination and legitimation often seek to maximize the focus on audiences as collections of individuals, as demographics or swinging voters, and to minimize the scope for meaningful audience action. As we will see, limiting media agency in an information-dominated world can result in unforeseen consequences.

THE PUBLIC, AUDIENCES, AND THE MEDIA

The position on audience power presented in this chapter differs somewhat from that advanced by mass society theorists who argued in the mid-20th century that audiences are alienated and marginalized by the structures of mass communication.[4] On the contrary, if, as Kellerman (2000) has suggested, contemporary society is an "information-dominated" one, then power, as Castells (1998) has asserted, "does not disappear" but is "inscribed, at a fundamental level, in the cultural codes through which people and institutions represent life and make decisions, including political decisions" (p. 347). There is no doubt that the introduction of mass broadcasting disrupted age-old patterns of expressing ideas and experiences through music, dance, and storytelling. Initially, it had the impact of silencing and depersonalizing some avenues for cultural expression, particularly among the working classes. As mentioned earlier, we know from the historical record that audience was once an experience that offered people both power and agency in relation to the performance of texts, the expression of cultural ideas, and the opportunity to affect social outcomes. But in the pre-broadcasting era, audience was also a less significant social activity overall. With the introduction of mass broadcasting, the balance of power in the control of the production and distribution of texts tipped in the favor of media organizations, corporations, companies, and government agencies. Audience power and agency split into discreet fields of influence: The exercise of social and political power shifted to the public or commercial domain, and the exercise of cultural agency, vested in remnants of communal commitment to (and control over) cultural forms, genres, products, and performances, began to be seen as private or personalized.

The separation of audience power and agency that characterizes audience publics and audience markets means that we engage with political debate as it is represented in the media but enact our judgments of those debates when we go to the polls. We view ads on TV but enact the social power inherent in that viewing, whether it is approving or disapproving of either the advertising or the product, in stores, supermarkets, and malls. Rather than destroying audience power, this reorganization relocated the site of enactment of audience power, shifting it from the media to the public sphere. In the public sphere, however, individuals count in the abstract as statistics rather than as "living bodies and as systems of consciousness" (Luhmann, 2000, p. 107).

We create our identities, by contrast, in the micro-contexts of both physical and mental engagement with texts and the flow of ideas and representations that fill the media spaces in our lives. The exercise of audience agency remains, in this sense, tied to the person and, as such, is politically insignificant until, in association with others, personal interests and needs are publicly represented in the form of communal or cultural intervention. Audience agency is realized only insofar as the "event" dimension of audience becomes recognized as politically and commercially significant by both audiences (as the basis for informed social action) and governments (as the basis for better informed policy development).

Today, the social and political power of audiences is based on the capacity of audience members to lobby governments, industry, and media organizations to make changes to what is broadcast or published. The targeted deployment of audience power requires the availability of, and access to, expert representation—legal teams, politicians, or activist organizations—to achieve its ends. Increasingly, those ends are achieved through media policy, media activism, and litigation—further evidence that the information revolution is changing the nature of power relations and facilitating new modes of audience affiliation, from which media action can be enacted. Manuel Castells (1998) has argued that, "in a sense, power, while it is real, becomes immaterial. It is real because wherever and whenever it consolidates, it provides, for a time, individuals and organizations with the capacity to enforce their decisions regardless of consensus" (p. 347). To achieve such outcomes, people engage in media activism

with political or social ends in sight, even though the existence of the group may be curtailed by the achievement of its sociocultural purposes.

PUBLIC ACTIVISM AND LITIGATION

From this perspective, litigation represents the hard edge of public advocacy and audience power. It is increasingly used to redress wrongs, imagined to be caused at least in part by media representation, particularly in advertising. Litigation is now part of the audience power repertoire. Examples of high-profile litigation include that directed against tobacco companies for misleading advertising and suppression of scientific evidence regarding the effects of smoking, as well as recent discussion of litigation against fast-food chains for advertising that encourages consumers to underestimate the health implications related to consumption of their products. Behind litigation, however, are public advocacy groups, working behind the scenes to further the interests of their constituencies and to right the wrongs they identify in the status quo. These groups act as intermediaries for audience associations, linked to common interests, and they make life uncomfortable for manufacturers, advertisers, and broadcasters.[5] The rank-and-file members of such groups often consider themselves victims of activities the group regards as oppressive and therefore seeks to change. The work of such groups depends, in turn, on their media activism, their representation of themselves in the media, and their capacity to convince others of the importance of their concerns and of the necessity to keep governments and the corporate sector in check.

Much of the research about the effects of the media—evident in moral panics over media violence, as well as in debates about the impact of the media on people's mental and physical health—is justified, ultimately, by reference to beliefs and values. In some cases, these values and beliefs are formalized in national, regional, or international legal systems, declarations, and charters that programmatically identify human rights, which include communication rights (von Feilitzen & Carlsson, 1999).[6] The formulation and explicit defense of human rights help to protect the interests of audiences by mandating the means by which "media harm" can be assessed and media power exercised. Such protection is particularly important for the media interests of groups such as children or indigenous minorities, who require specially designed and produced communication forms. In such cases, the costs of production often cannot be recouped by the sale of exhibition rights, so governments are called on to devise media policies to ensure the provision of suitable media materials.

A significant component of what we know about broadcast audiences has been the result of the demand for research to assist policy formation (Nightingale, Dickenson, & Griff, 2000) or to encourage industry and commercial interests to be proactive in the protection of audience rights, if only to avoid the regulation that would result from failing to defend those rights. Castells (1998) has suggested that, even though these power struggles are often enacted through the media, the media "are not the power-holders. . . . Power . . . lies in the networks of information exchange and symbol manipulation, which relate social actors, institutions, and cultural movements" (p. 349). And cultural movements are becoming ever more adept at using the broadcast media to mobilize their audience power.

ASSUMPTIONS ABOUT THE PUBLIC AS AUDIENCES

As members of the public, people act as informed citizens, as voters, as "everybody" in a particular jurisdiction. On behalf of the people, governments authorize ownership and control of the media. They retain responsibility for the regulation of the media, even when their regulatory responsibility is discharged through policies of media "self-regulation." Clearly, there are areas where governments and the media assist each other. Governments have a special interest in the media's management of public life, particularly in its representations of the actions and interests of the ruling elites. They therefore demand and are allocated a special place in media programming. Governments and opposition parties receive vast amounts of free publicity for their views and positions in the form of news and current affairs. News coverage provides ongoing representation of the public sphere, which is monitored regularly by public opinion polling and other political research. Political parties actively represent themselves in the media through political advertising and through their mandated access to the media during election campaigns. Campaign management requires access to the commercial audience data-gathering technology developed for measuring audience markets: ratings.[7] The media provide not only mandated election coverage but also an environment where political advertising and propaganda can be advantageously deployed.

Public opinion research often doubles as a form of audience research. Its findings inform electioneering and the expenditure on political advertising. The aim of public opinion research is primarily utilitarian—to produce research outcomes that will enhance the success of political campaigns. The aim is usually to develop an understanding of broad patterns of public opinion rather than to track the personal path individuals take in reaching political decisions. Like ratings research, public opinion polling is based on the misleading premise that the public is composed of rational individuals, who seek information relevant to the political decision making in which they are involved, when it is undertaken to facilitate often emotion-based persuasion and propaganda. Public opinion research, in a sense, focuses on finding ways to bring about shifts in community attitudes sufficient in scope and scale to alter voting intentions.

Some viewers and listeners clearly do not fit this assumption. Children, for example, cannot be assumed to have attained such a level of independent thought and action. Other special categories in the mass audience (e.g., victims of violence or those with hearing and sight impairments) fall outside the assumptions of political, moral, and ethical equality and individualism—if not permanently then at particular times or in particular circumstances. Recognition that materials freely available in the media may adversely affect some people often leads to public expression of concern about the effects of media materials on those groups. Russell Neuman (1991, p. 82) has described effects research as focusing on "the helpless audience." He suggests that public concern has been mobilized by the possibility that people suffer from information overload, that audience segmentation makes people vulnerable to persuasive messages, that the media use special effects to evoke emotion-laden responses from audiences, that communication flows attack the structures of communal knowledge, that people become addicted to the media and are more susceptible to media persuasion, and that the continuous exposure to media cultivates consent and discourages dissent.

Research about the public as audiences has intrinsic value to governments and broadcasting companies, at least to the extent that it is instrumental in the achievement of their aims. Unfortunately, research that pursues a critical and evaluative agenda and seeks to make the media reflect on its own practice is often of secondary interest to both governments and the media. Niklas Luhmann (2000) has argued that this happens because the media treat criticism of "the media" as though it is just another news story—not the media's concern but a problem for the public or the government to investigate. This strange inability to critically analyze their own performance or to take responsibility for their actions is, from Luhmann's perspective, a matter of the

media discriminating between information that is essential to their operation as media (such as having enough journalists to cover a particular event or getting the news to air on time) and information that, if they took it to heart, would slow down and complicate their performance because they would have to take account of the social and cultural implications of their practices. A systems theorist, Luhmann therefore distinguishes between information essential to the media's continuing operation and self-reflexive information that critically evaluates the quality of the media's performance. He has suggested that,

> by representing themselves as a system, [the mass media] generate boundaries with an inside and an outside that is inaccessible to them. They too reflect [or represent] their outside as public life, so long as specific external relationships, such as to politics or to the advertisers, are not in question. (p. 106)

The media contribute to the construction of reality by selecting and editing information for presentation to the public and by focusing attention on what is revealed rather than on the process by which information is selected and edited. "The effect if not the function of the mass media seems to lie, therefore, in the reproduction of non-transparency through transparency, in the reproduction of *non-transparency of effects* through *transparency of knowledge*" (Luhmann, 2000, p. 103).

Luhmann (2000) has hypothesized that, in general, audiences accept the media's representation of the world and forget to question how it was produced and in whose interests. Audiences are predisposed to accept the news agendas and criteria for inclusion of information because so much information is provided and because diverse viewpoints are included (even if the range of diversity given credence by the media is quite limited). This creates a sense of "transparency of knowledge" because audiences rationally evaluate the information provided and make decisions based on it, assuming that the range of information and opinion provided by the media includes all they need to take into account in reaching conclusions. Yet it is on precisely this point that the media are unable—and frequently unwilling—to reflect on their own performance and that audiences lack the time and the means to enquire further.

A number of structural factors contribute to this "nontransparency of effects." Audiences do not witness the production of news or other broadcast material. Though there is widespread understanding of the degree of human frailty at the core of journalistic practice, this seldom features as the content of news and so is represented as an issue of media workplace practice, not as one of legitimate audience concern. The media represent news about the world as "outside" the media system. News about audiences, in terms of coverage of moral panics and other concerns about media effects, is represented as existing outside the media system, as though the media system itself cannot be held responsible—though, of course, the media both generate the concern and represent it as though it were outside the system. The audience is positioned and addressed as though outside the media system, instead of being understood as an integral component of it. This permits a self-protective amnesia within media corporations, which protects their functionaries from recognition of their past contributions to present audience problems while simultaneously shielding their coverage of issues from being questioned as to its dependence on subsidization by advertising. Not least, there is amnesia concerning the dependence of the media on governmental good will. In the discourse on cigarette advertising (Chapman, 1986; Leiss, Kline, & Jhally, 1986; Schudson, 1984), for example, the subsidization of media operations by advertising budgets slips into the haze of the misremembered past, and biased coverage that serves to elect a government is seen to have been generated by the political parties rather than by the media.

AUDIENCE MARKETS

Although the media may displace their responsibility to the public onto the public or onto government regulation, they take their responsibilities to advertisers very seriously indeed. To this end, they sponsor a form of audience research (ratings analysis) that, in effect, parcels audience viewing into sellable commodities. The result is that people participate in the mediated commercial sphere in two ways: as consumers and as audiences. They are buyers in the marketplace (external to the media), and they are viewers or listeners (inside the media system). As audiences, people therefore possess a different meaning "inside" the media than they possess "outside" them. Inside the media, audiences are a resource (like forests, minerals, or agricultural products). They are considered to be the product of the media's work and, as such, a resource that can be offered for sale to recoup the costs of their production. Outside the media, viewers and listeners are clients or patrons. They are those whom the media, manufacturers, retailers, and others seek to serve.

The abstract representation of viewers by the media, for their own use as a commodity, means that they cultivate audiences as though they are a resource. They see audiences as a product of good programming, the result of their hard work, and therefore available to the media as goods for sale to outside bidders. As commodities, audiences are cultivated like crops—harvested, bundled, and sold in the media marketplace. Audiences, as people, are not actually sold, of course. In reality, the trade is in projected audience "exposures," and it is based on statistical estimates that certain numbers of people will tune their TV sets to particular channels at particular times in the future. In this, it resembles an often-risky futures market.

Audiences are consumers of both media services and advertised products. Their consumption of media services is reflected directly in the day-to-day operations of media companies. Their consumption of advertised products is, on the other hand, only indirectly related to broadcasting. It is registered and monitored as product sales, but in deciding where to situate their advertising and how to develop the best media mix to promote their products, manufacturers and advertisers draw on audience measurement services that are directly paid for by media industries. As a result of this close relationship, audience measurement services, such as ratings, combine measures of media patronage with indicators of the spending capacity and psychological profiles of segments of the mass audience.

Beville (1988) has explained this relationship in the following way: "Programs are the heart of broadcasting, while sales provide the muscle. Ratings with their feedback element are the nerve system that largely controls what is broadcast" (p. ix). Both Beville (1988) and Webster and Lichty (1991) have described how ratings, as well as other audience measurement services, are the most influential information available about audiences. Broadcasters, advertisers, governments, and activists all make use of them. Ratings inform media-buying negotiations between broadcasters and advertisers and are called on in decision making to license new products, plan programming, devise program schedules and formats, and structure public information campaigns. Most license renewal hearings and media policy development take audience measurement information into account. The reason for this importance is that ratings provide information about audiences that is integral to the operation of the media as an industry.

In most countries, mass broadcasting is dependent on advertising revenue. This dependence has a structural impact on audiences and the opportunities available to them. Audiences are the only resource at the disposal of the broadcasting companies. Broadcasters therefore use them to finance the broadcasting service and to generate funding for new program acquisition. This is the basic premise of advertising supported media. Broadcasters package audiences in forms that can be used to price advertising spots and to sell those spots to advertisers. The packaging involves the reduction of millions of complex life situations and events, occurring simultaneously around the world, into standardized, measurable, and comparable "packages" of information.

The first part of this packaging process involves separating audience program choices from the people making the choices. This is accomplished with the assistance of metering technologies, such as people meters, and with statistical analysis predicated on such abstraction. The activity of viewing or listening is reduced to the registration of a measurable action—the pressing of buttons on a meter or a remote control. Webster and Lichty (1991, p. 179) describe ratings as a "snapshot" of viewing, and they consolidate this analogy by referring to audience viewing as "exposure." Ratings involve taking numerical "snapshots" of audience button pushing and extrapolating general pictures of program and channel selection from that data. "Exposure" transforms the moment of meaningful engagement with the media into standardized and measurable time-based units (Webster & Lichty, 1991, p. 179). Viewing time is divided into day parts, quarter hours, 5-minute segments, and sometimes 1-minute segments to enable researchers to track movements in audience patterns of viewing. By these means, all evidence of audience interpretation or response to media content is extracted from the experience of being an audience for the purposes of statistical analysis. Being able to separate audience response from "exposure" enhances the reliability of ratings measures but also defines qualitative information about the *experience* of being an audience as irrelevant to the operation of media organizations.

Criticism of Ratings

There is evidence that the interests of audiences are not always the primary consideration for commercial media.

Making a profit, especially at the expense of an opponent, can prove to be, strategically, a higher priority. One manifestation of this is the practice of programming for the least objectionable program (LOP) rather than the best available programming, knowing that audiences will make this choice before switching off (Webster & Lichty, 1991, p. 153). Neuman (1991, pp. 153–159) provides an overview of the strategic thinking that encourages network executives to take advantage of the known propensity for viewers to continue viewing, even though they are not particularly interested in a particular program. Even the audience behavior known as *grazing*—"the tendency of viewers to frequently change channels" using a remote control device (RCD) (Webster & Lichty, 1991, p. 249), a clear indication of audience boredom—is rationalized as being caused by the RCD rather than being accepted as a response to poor programming. The behavior is dismissed as irrelevant to broadcasters because the technologies used to record audience exposures can be used for minute-by-minute tracking of audiences. As audiences, we experience the effects of these practices when we feel forced to choose from an unappealing range of programs or forced to choose one of two or more equally attractive programs. For the broadcaster, providing program options that are of similar value to the target audience, when compared with the program options offered by the opposition, is more likely to win the ratings chase. Offering diversity is seen as a sure way to lose the mainstream and is therefore regarded as the obligation of government-funded broadcasting. From an industry perspective, the strategically best programming option will always be to remain as close as possible to the main opposition but also slightly closer to the interests of most viewers. The competitive market structure of mass broadcasting, combined with viewer commitment to watching *television,* as opposed to watching particular *programs,* encourages broadcasters to engage in this practice, which brings about a regression to mainstream or middlebrow programming.

Segmentation

Joseph Turow (1997) has commented that

> when people read a magazine, watch a TV show, or use any other ad sponsored medium, then, they are entering a world that was constructed as a result of close cooperation between advertisers and media firms. Designed with marketing goals in mind, the formats and the commercials aim to signal to people whether and how they fit the proceedings. They also signal what people might buy or do to keep fitting in. (p. 16)

Such audience segmentation and targeting appear initially to work in the opposite manner to least objectionable programming. They address particular groups of consumers in the mass audience rather than the whole audience. Barban, Cristol, and Kopec (1987, p. 32) explain that three types of variables are taken into account when identifying target audiences: demographic, sociopsychological, and product usage variables. Of these, product usage variables are currently favored. Decisions to target audiences are made for commercial reasons, rather than to please audiences, yet they produce a comfortably complacent symbiosis between audiences and the "media vehicles" developed to attract them. As a result, Turow (1997) suggests, viewers who are targeted enjoy more satisfying media experiences but at the expense of the lack of enjoyment of people in the audience who fall outside the targeted segments. He is concerned that by always being in the comfort zone, the audiences targeted are encouraged to focus inwards on their own needs and aspirations. He is critical of this trend, arguing that it leads people to become less tolerant, to be more dismissive of the interests and viewpoints of others, and to ignore social responsibilities. The end result of this consumerist trend is that protection of the consumption function may eventually be taken to be the only justifiable public "good" (Turow, 1997, p. 127). Turow argues that rather than celebrating cultural diversity, this "hypersegmentation" encourages an "impulse to keep diversity hidden."

> Signalling, tailoring, and other targeting activities encourage people to join their own image tribes apart from other image tribes. As a result, marketers' concerns with diversity act to push groups away from one another rather than to encourage them to learn about the strengths of coming together to share experiences and discuss issues from different viewpoints. (Turow, 1997, pp. 199–200)

The Cultural Critique of Ratings

The research methods and practices developed for public opinion and ratings research treat "being an audience" as a form of industrial production, not by audiences but by industry. For media industries, mass communication is still understood as a component of "the hegemonic economic system and social contract that most powerfully propelled the post-war boom in the USA" (Soja, 2000, pp. 98, 169). The discourses of economic rationalism, emanating from the industrial power block, naturalize the ratings system. They also justify acceptance of the pictures of the audience it produces as accurate and as the only pictures worth having because of the economic value attached to the data produced. In the late 1980s and early 1990s, several academics challenged the ratings rhetoric by developing a cultural critique of ratings. John Hartley (1987), for example, pointed out that the reliance on ratings by media industries encourages media managers to infantilize the audience and avoid accountability for programming actions. Ien Ang (1991) criticized the inability of ratings to address the situated practices of actual audiences. Eileen Meehan (1990) took aim at the research methods used and attacked,

particularly, the inadequate representation of community viewpoints that is the end result of sampling practices and the length of life of TV ratings panels.

Lack of a Theory of Popular Culture

The central points of disagreement between ratings researchers and their cultural critics concerned the lack of a theory of popular culture. The same criticism was leveled at "uses and gratifications" researchers in the late 1970s (see Carey & Kreiling, 1974; Nightingale, 2003). If we really want to understand media audiences, we need to understand how culture works: the processes of both its production and reproduction. The absence of a theory of culture is most obvious, as previously mentioned, in the emphasis on "exposure" to media content rather than on responses to it or engagements with it. The ratings approach does not analyze media content but judges audience engagement as an irrelevant consideration in its pursuit of its limited but influential purposes. Although ratings speak directly to the interests of advertisers and broadcasters, they deflect discussion of the cultural significance of audience engagements with media onto the detail of ratings. The use of ratings as the ultimate guide to whether programs are scheduled encourages broadcasting companies to minimize their responsibility for program content, for the social and cultural implications of the discourses they produce and disseminate, and for their social and cultural responsibilities beyond the loose guidelines set by government regulation.

The suggestion that a theory of popular culture should inform audience research pointed to two aspects of "being an audience" that are systematically overlooked by the emphasis on publics and markets: the group nature of audiences and the sociocultural significance of the meanings produced when audiences engage with texts. The culture theorists (Carey & Kreiling, 1974; Morley, 1992) argued that the individualist approach to audience should be replaced by a cultural theory capable of explaining why some groups and audience communities enjoy better access to the media and find more to enjoy in the media than others. They argued that the sociocultural meaning of participation in media events should play a central role in defining our understanding of audiences. They have had some success with this project, particularly in documenting the ways indigenous and ethnic communities have been able to use their audience power to establish and maintain the capacity to express their histories and cultural heritage through indigenous production of media materials. In doing so, a clearer picture has developed of the crucial role mass media materials play in the formation and experience of identity.

AUDIENCE AGENCY

One achievement of the cultural approach in audience research has been to force a reconsideration of the individualist assumptions that are (nevertheless) still used to justify the abstract and impersonal understanding of audience publics and markets, focusing attention instead on audiences as groups and communities. The insistence on the importance of understanding audience agency as cultural action has allowed the fixation with audience composition and with economically exploitable audience data to be pushed aside, so that the spatial and experiential dimensions of being an audience can be added to the picture. Audiences can now be appreciated as places where things happen: Identity is developed, cultural meanings are shared, and new ideas are generated. In other words, *audience* describes the places where the most constructive and crucial reproduction of culture, meanings, and ideas occurs (Nightingale, 2003). This culturally rich world seldom figures in the "power" contexts of the public and the market, where the opportunities for audiences to exercise agency are deliberately minimized so that the media, advertisers, and policymakers

can operate as organizational entities with as little interference from the public as possible.

Emphasizing the communal and networked nature of audience shifts attention away from people as individuals and onto people in communal and associative contact with each other. People are audiences as cultures, subcultures, ethnicities, and diasporas; work teams in associations, clubs, and collectives; and families and other forms of domestic or cultural groups. The alienated individual of mass culture theory is as much a product of the structures of the mass production of audiences as an indication of the ways people operate in a media-dominated world. It is only when understood in the context of the complexity and diversity of associative contact that the nature of audience engagement with the practices of everyday media life can be appreciated. Associative contacts generate the real-world meaning systems where media information is debated, discussed, and enacted. Most people belong to, and participate simultaneously in, a range of both generalist- and interest-based sociocultural groups, so in seeking to understand how people enact media meanings, attention must be paid to the competition between ideas and affiliations originating from these groups, alongside the competition within media and texts.

Much of the cultural research about audiences has been motivated by two research aims: to demonstrate that audiences are active in their use of the media and to document instances of viewers who actively resist the hegemonic ideas produced by the mainstream media. It has been shown conclusively that audiences actively engage with media and also that they are sometimes systematically "resistant" in their information processing. Audience activity has been demonstrated to involve an impressive array of activity: "bricolage"[8] (Hebdige, 1979), "textual nomadism" (Radway, 1988), "textual poaching" (Jenkins, 1992), and improvisation, impersonation, and cultural transposition (Nightingale, 1996), in addition to information-processing activities of a receptive kind, such as cognition (Morley, 1992) and critical reflection and textual analysis (Buckingham, 1987), to name but a few examples. Yet it is the groupings within which such activity occurs that tell us most about the character of audience activity and that point to its cultural significance.

As mentioned earlier, I am using the concept of "audience agency" to talk about the meaningful actions people perform in engagement with media. Meaningfulness requires social convention—a sociocultural group or system of meanings that frame the particularity of personal experience. The use of the ethnographic method has underpinned the documentation of situated audience practices and expanded our knowledge of the many ways media are integrated in the development of identity. Audience groups make differential use of being an audience: Some focus on the representation of their group by the media, others focus on the access of their group to key media texts or to the media as a source of employment, and yet others focus on their modes of engagement with diverse media. Even if the meanings produced in audience engagement are personal in nature, they are interpretable only in terms of the conventions of meaning making used by the social groups in which the person was formed.

Audience agency therefore encompasses media engagements that affect identity and cultural participation. It involves cultural groups in the surveillance of, and commentary on, media representations. It attempts to acquire the resources to establish independent media controlled by specific communities rather than by commercial interests, and it engages media organizations in copyright skirmishes directed at textual poaching and other improvisatory activities based on existing media materials. For the most part, though, audience agency remains powerless to change the existing networks of mass communication. In the examples we consider next, audience groups seek power over media production, both as complements to and as alternatives for the mainstream media. Although they have established alternative broadcasting capacity, they nevertheless continue to exist in a complementary relationship with mainstream media. In this sense, audience agency is tactical rather than strategic in its focus.

ETHNIC COMMUNITIES AND AUDIENCE AGENCY

The structures and processes of mass broadcasting often fail to keep pace with changes occurring in the population. Once established, administrative structures and organizational hierarchies successfully reproduce themselves but fail to reflect the changing composition of the world around them. Charles Husband (1994) has pointed out that dominant ethnic groups in the developed world tend to co-opt the mainstream media. As a result, the diversity of represented culture underestimates the actuality (Husband, 1994, p. 2). In the shift from imagined monoculture to multiethnic state, this cultural lag[9] can have unintended outcomes. For some cultural minorities, lack of representation may reiterate a lack of sociocultural power linked to immigrant or indigenous status in ways that are disempowering for group members. Husband has noted that "ethnic minorities are marginalized not only through media images but through their exclusion from full and equitable participation in media industries" (p. 14).

Some of the most interesting audience research of the 1980s and 1990s has documented the diverse tactics that viewers of underrepresented backgrounds adopt to meet their needs for affirmation from the media. Early investigations into racist reporting in the British media documented the systematic nature of the much less-than-friendly representation of people of color in the British media (Hartmann & Husband, 1974). Such studies noted the absence of positive representation, the linking of ethnicity to reports of criminal activity in ways that create distrust and even fear of particular communities, and the patronizingly positive representation of particular "ethnic" individuals. Recently, Ross (2000, p. 138) has provided evidence that such practices do annoy Black British viewers, whom, she found, expressed concern about racial and ethnic stereotyping in the media, the marginality of Black minority characters, and the dominance of racism themes in programs featuring Black minority characters.

Many researchers in this field have drawn attention to the fact that media representations often imply that ethnic communities are homogeneous when, in fact, they are divided and differentiated. Sreberny (2000) has noted that the Iranian community in London is far from homogeneous. Its members see themselves as representing the diverse gender- and age-based differences from the "home culture" and are divided by whether members are political refugees waiting to return (looking back), immigrants preoccupied with starting a new life (looking forward), or members of either category just trying to get by in a strange environment (looking inwards). The different views community members hold on the relevance of their culture of origin for their current life circumstances suggest that their media needs will be diverse. No single type of media content will prove adequate.

In her ethnographic study of British South Asian youth, Marie Gillespie (2000) noted that coming to terms with their "limited" representation in mainstream media led many to experience disaffection with their British identity, fostering instead a "desire for new kinds of transnational and Diaspora identities." This disaffection precipitated more intense identification with transnational issues such as consumerism, feminism, environmentalism, and human rights, alongside "Diaspora identifications and connections." The Diaspora identifications and connections included viewing everything from Bollywood blockbusters to home videos that maintain family connections, exchange family information, and allow family members to engage in video tourism (Gillespie, 2000, p. 166). The distance between the personal meaningfulness of home video and the identification with global cultural issues leaves an unfortunate vacuum where national identity should be developed.

Naficy (1993) showed that independent video production could be a precursor to ethnic broadcasting capacity. In his ethnographic study of Iranian exiles in Los Angeles in the period from 1981 to 1992, Naficy documented the nature and extent of the media activities of this community. The Iranian exiles produced periodicals and radio broadcasts, sponsored newscasts and TV programs, and rented airtime and sold advertising space during its broadcasts. Access to broadcast materials were considered not an option but essential for the survival and mental health of the exiles. Naficy believes that "exile heightens the desire for constructing difference, for creating weight," and broadcast media offered opportunities to fulfill such desires. "Creating weight" for the exile culture is a significant concept. It refers to the ways that seeing one's culture on TV or encountering its language and stories on radio proves the importance of the culture because it sustains the shift from reminiscence to broadcast story. It bears testimony to the fact that media are one of the chief means for learning about the world. They give materiality to stories that would otherwise exist only as reminiscences and family folklore. Experiencing one's cultural heritage in the media gives an authority to the story that takes it beyond the personal and into the historico-social.

Naficy (1993) goes further, however, and notes that the popular culture produced in exile assisted the development of a grounded sense of self, from which engagement with mainstream American and other national identities could be negotiated. Paradoxically, the production of exilic popular culture also helped the exiles loosen their dependence on their "home" culture.

Exilic popular culture and television are instrumental in the survival of uprooted

Iranians. They constructed a cohesive semiotic and discursive space for exilic communitas and an exilic economy, but their commercially driven nature served ultimately to recuperate their resistive and counterhegemonic spin, turning them chiefly into social agencies of assimilation. (Naficy, 1993, p. 192)

Naficy's analysis signals ways groups within the mass audience may identify shared interests, define agendas for the production of particular media events, produce the required media materials, and identify exhibition strategies to counteract the problem of nonrecognition in mainstream media.

INDIGENOUS GROUPS AND AUDIENCE AGENCY

Desire for access to production, as well as control of both story content and cultural representation, appears to be routinely produced as a result of systematic underrepresentation or misrepresentation of ethnic and indigenous groups in the broadcast media. It is a trigger for audience activism not only among migrants, exiles, and refugees but also among indigenous peoples throughout the world. The situation for indigenous peoples is, however, rather different from that described above because the aim is to resist assimilation and the recuperative aftereffects sometimes produced by a media presence while "creating weight" for the group members. Jakubowicz (2001) has noted that

> the desire for a separate system over which Indigenous people can exert some influence and in which they can take pride of ownership reflects their exclusion from other mainstream media . . . there is an awareness in the Indigenous communities that the non-Indigenous media may speak about them, but speak neither to them nor for them. (p. 211)

Indigenous communities, then, use their agency as audiences to add their voices to the cultural mainstream, to make sure that they are speaking to each other and to the mainstream, but the maintenance of the indigenous community is their prime purpose.

Riggins (1992) has described indigenous groups as responding to the "media imperative of modern life" by seeking access to the means of media production while simultaneously (and usually unintentionally) encouraging "assimilation of their audiences to mainstream values" (p. 4). The "variability of interpretation"[10] in audiences virtually guarantees that outcomes other than those imagined will follow from the viewing experience. Riggins has suggested that, in some cases, politicians and mainstream media, to hasten assimilation, deliberately exploit the "dual role of ethnic media." Like minority-ethnic communities, indigenous groups have sought control of the means of media production (particularly of broadcast media) as a survival strategy. They see indigenous production of their own stories as a way to cure the cultural malaise created by the experience of systematic domination and exclusion and to restore their stolen cultural pride and integrity.

The policy initiatives pursued by indigenous communities are clearly demonstrated in the media project outlined by the Aboriginal and Torres Strait Islander Commission in Australia. They include the following:

1. "the right to full access to information and entertainment media";

2. access to the use of broadcasting for purposes associated with "cultural restoration, preservation and growth";

3. efficient access to the use of local radio and television for informational services of particular relevance to indigenous communities;

4. employment opportunities in indigenous media that open access to mainstream media employment; and

5. enhancement of self-image[11] (Jakubowicz, 2001, pp. 211–212).

Such policies demonstrate that indigenous communities are not content to sit back in reception mode and absorb visions of a world that systematically expunge the histories that explain their current sociocultural position, gloss over the richness and traditions of their cultural heritage, and "forget" their ongoing contributions and sacrifices to the status quo. They combine their independent media production capacity with their political activism to secure their achievements from recuperation by the mainstream media and, importantly, to educate the mass audience.

This institutionalization of the rights and opportunities for indigenous production contrasts starkly with the experience of fan groups, which operate solely within mainstream media culture. Although indigenous communities have had to prove the existence and importance of traditional culture, along with their communities' unique experiences of urban life, as worthy of independent media representation, this can be put into abeyance (at least for a time) once institutional recognition has been received. Fan communities seek, by contrast, to base their rights to engage in textual production on their pleasure in the text. For this reason, fan groups are more dependent on the media companies and increasingly insecure in their hold on an identity that is separable from mainstream media. Enforced independence from the media is a more threatening prospect for fan groups than assimilation into it.

FANS AND AUDIENCE AGENCY

In his definitive study of fans and fan culture, Henry Jenkins (1992) documented the richness of the cultural activities fans pursue: writing (producing stories and fan fiction), filking (composing fan music, songs, and lyrics), scripting new episodes, and constructing "reality" videos. The list of fan activities is potentially limitless. According to Jenkins, fan activity has demonstrated that media texts may inspire audience investment in complex interpretative play with texts,

joy in associating with others who share the fan's enthusiasm and detailed knowledge of the text, critical discussion of the textual "canon" and the relative worth of its component parts, and establishment and maintenance of Web sites, chat rooms, and other virtual spaces.

Jenkins (1992) chose the term *textual poachers*[12] to describe fan audience activities. The term captured the quality of rebelliousness in the appropriation of commercial texts and, in retrospect, prophetically anticipated the copyright and licensing disputes that now beleaguer some fan communities. Although fans enhance the cultural value of the originating texts, they are not the first writers of the stories. Their imaginative improvisation on the originating texts potentially sets them on a collision course with the registered owners or exploiters of copyright. Many fan activities are potentially lucrative, especially activities such as holding conventions and trading memorabilia. For this reason, fan activity has prompted awareness among copyright owners of the unexploited value that remains in the texts after broadcasting. Jenkins (in press) has noted that

in such a world, intellectual property, which has proven popular with mass audiences, has enormous economic value and companies seek to tightly regulate its flow in order to maximize profits and minimize the risk of diluting their trademark and copyright holdings.

The policing of intellectual property rights causes ongoing and widespread concern within fan communities about the types of materials that are and are not covered by copyright. Jenkins (in press) documents a veto by the Usenet hierarchy on the establishment of a filter site (a separate site devoted to the critique or discussion of another site) "where fans could post and critique original fiction set in the *Star Wars* universe." Usenet described the proposed activities as "illegal," and even though a compromise arrangement was finally agreed that provided free Web space and original content for fan sites, this was at the cost to fans of their rights to the intellectual property generated by the site. Jenkins has recalled that

> many believe that they made this decision based on a series of "cease and desist" letters issued by Lucasfilm attorneys aimed at shutting down Star Wars fan Web sites or blocking the circulation of fanzines.

This mirrors a similar incident in Australia, where the U.S. company Viacom issued "cease-and-desist" letters to *Star Trek* fan clubs in 1986 in an attempt to control the clubs.

Despite the ethos of sharing among fans, Jenkins (2001) has indicated a range of specialized roles pursued by fans. This specialization has centered on three activities: textual production; publication, distribution, and management of fan creative work; and criticism and cultural research.

1. Fans who specialize in creative production, particularly of scripts and stories based on the originating texts, are important to the fan group because they offer hope of tighter integration of the fan group with the production company. A similar effect is produced when media producers involve themselves in fan group activities and discussions.

2. Fan specialists who manage the production and distribution of fan materials: producing and distributing newsletters, organizing fan conventions, and taking on the management of clubs, meetings, fund-raising, and other activities. In the past, this group included fans who have been in the frontline of skirmishes and battles with copyright holders.

3. Fan specialists who are "academic fans," such as Jenkins himself. Though probably the least central to the ongoing existence of fan groups, academic fans have assisted the establishment of fan studies in university curricula and contributed to the critical analysis of the originating texts in academic publishing and conference contexts. They ensure that the sensibilities of fan communities are acknowledged and respected within the academy and generate better public appreciation of the value of fan "work" to the broader community (Jenkins, 2001).

However, it is possible to argue that the basis of fan specialization and creative improvisation was linked to the independence of fan communities, and the tightening of control over fan communities will curtail the opportunities for independent production and group maintenance. The intervention of the commercial sector in fan activities potentially threatens the creative freedom of fan communities. The increasing likelihood that fan groups are sponsored and monitored by copyright holders signals the imposition of limits on the future scope of fan activity. Although assimilation into the commercial mainstream is not necessarily a threatening prospect for fan communities in the ways it is for ethnic and indigenous communities, it suggests that some fans *work for* the copyright holders first and the membership second.

Fans actively pursue several of the media policy initiatives targeted by indigenous and ethnic communities—particularly those associated with employment opportunities in mainstream media, access to the use of broadcast materials for cultural and personal development, and enhancement of self-esteem (see Jenkins, 2001). Like indigenous and minority-ethnic communities, fans react vigorously to stereotyping or misleading characterizations in the mainstream media and by the public in general. Like indigenous and minority-ethnic groups, fans actively try to change these inaccurate perceptions. Correcting the misconceptions and enhancing the reputation of fans has been one of the tasks addressed by academic fans. Like indigenous and minority-ethnic communities, fans have taken to producing media materials that satisfy the particularity of their interests in the originating texts. Unlike the other audience communities we have considered here, their preservation and heritage activities have focused more on the originating texts rather than on their communities.

Fan communities are products of consumer society rather than victims of it; as a result, their relationship to the commercial producers of texts currently incorporates a degree of dependence. Jenkins (2002), Banks (2002), and others believe that the relationship between fans and media industries should be a collaborative one, capable of recognizing the contribution fans make to the broadcast or online text. This is not necessarily considered a bad thing by fans because commercial copyright holders increasingly include fan sites as part of their initial product designs and provide them with special privileges. Fan involvement in the production process can be a way of "adding value" to new media products, which now routinely include both merchandising and the establishment of an online fan base. The production companies benefit from the money fans are willing to spend to satisfy their interests and investments in texts, thus offsetting the company's initial financial risk. Fans are encouraged to discuss, share ideas, and, in doing so, publicize new products.

Jenkins (2001) has suggested that collaboration may prove to be a positive outcome for fans, especially if the types of engagement fans are seeking from media materials are taken into account in the production of the original texts. This "incorporation" of the mind of the fan into the media product is the equivalent for fans of indigenous and minority-ethnic participation in mainstream media. The other side of the equation involves the privileged access the fan is given to the commercial materials. Banks (2002) has documented requests by fans for rights to develop third-party commercial products that can be sold as add-ons for particular games. Such desires challenge the control of intellectual property by multinational corporations but may be more acceptable to independent games developers. Jenkins (in press) suggests that

> at the moment, we are on a collision course between a new economic and legal culture which encourages monopoly power over cultural mythologies and new technologies which empower consumers to archive, annotate, appropriate, and re-circulate media images. The recent legal disputes around Napster represent only skirmish in what is likely to be a decade long war over intellectual property, a war which will determine not simply the future direction of digital cinema but the nature of creative expression in the 21st century.

In the fan context, the preoccupation with the meaning of texts has given way to border disputes over the control of textual materials and the ownership of cultural materials that have been integrated into the foundations of cultural identity. Rather than protecting or promoting traditional cultural information, fans dispute the ownership of mainstream culture.

◆ Concluding Remarks

Emphasis on marginalized and sometimes spectacular audience groups has been a feature of the cultural approach in studies of audiences. Taken as a whole, this work has delivered a strong statement of the intensity of audience engagements with media texts and of the desire for greater involvement in, and control over, production among marginalized audience communities. It has demonstrated the importance to local communities of access to media materials that enhance rather than diminish identity development. Organized audience groups have established their own production and broadcasting companies and taken responsibility for ensuring that meanings often sidelined by mainstream media gain more attention, at least within their own communities. They have also fostered the production expertise of members and supported their efforts to gain employment in the mainstream media, so that group interests are better represented. Overall, they demonstrate the importance of the achievements that follow when audience groups are able to support their interests in ensuring that particular ideas and representations are available to group members first and also to the broader society. However, the cultural approach has also generated a deafening silence about the potential for the activation of mass audience agency.

Earlier in this chapter, I suggested that the introduction of mass broadcasting created a split between audience power and audience agency. This separation has proved of great value to both commercial organizations and government authorities involved in the administration of mass communication because it permitted them to minimize their responsibility for "signification" and allowed them to ignore the impacts of the audience events they produce. The separation of audience power and agency ensured that structures of signification were demoted, characterized as personal and private interest rather than as core components of the culture industries and the media system. Because audience agency was relegated to this personal space, the issues it raises were considered irrelevant to the ongoing work of the media. The personal and the private do not register in a world where representation through the abstraction of numbers is all that counts.

The cultural approach to audiences focused centrally on meaning making and the importance of the media for cultural survival. It identified and documented the ways minority-ethnic and indigenous communities have been able to combine their power as communities with their special interests, as audiences, in the preservation of key cultural ideas and values. By recognizing the achievements of indigenous and minority-ethnic communities in these respects, it is possible to notice the difficulties that confront groups such as fans, for

whom the basis of their affiliation (as groups) is textual—grounded in dependence on the mainstream media. Fans are as much products of the mass audience as they are of the originating texts, though researchers often fail to recognize this. In celebrating and reworking loved texts, fans have written themselves into a scriptural landscape that initially failed to register their agency as audiences—at least until a commercial value could be attached to it. Fans therefore point to the future of the mass audience and to new types of media engagement with increasingly interactive texts that demand more of the mass audience than television ever has.

◆ Notes

1. I am indebted to Richard Butsch (2000) for clarifying this matter in his book, *The Making of American Audiences*.

2. I have discussed this in my book, *Studying Audiences: The Shock of the Real* (Nightingale, 1996), where I advocated approaching audiences as communities. The argument presented here is a different one. The neglect and intellectual poverty of many studies of audience agency in the 1970s and 1980s demanded a textualized approach, the positioning of audience issues in a context of theories of popular culture. This situation was addressed, with a subsequent abandonment of the studies of mass audiences. In this chapter, I attempt to demonstrate why a framework that embraces both large-scale audiences and niche audience communities is needed.

3. By using this terminology, I am attempting to situate the power and agency of audiences, as audiences, in the operations of contemporary media. So *power* is understood in a Foucauldian sense as a property of the social community. *Agency* is also taken in the broad sense mentioned by Giddens (1984): "To be a human being is to be a purposive agent, who has both reasons for his or her activities and is able, if asked, to elaborate discursively upon those reasons (including lying about them)" (p. 3).

4. Russell Neuman (1991, p. 82) usefully summarizes the variety of positions taken over the years by mass society critics.

5. An interesting example was published while I was writing this chapter. A Sydney group called the Lebanese Muslim Association has written letters to the sponsors of an early morning program, drawing to their attention alleged racist statements by the program's presenter and accusing the broadcaster of failing to act on their comments. The broadcaster, in turn, is seeking police advice as to legality of the letters, alleging that they are defamatory. The escalation of the dispute between the broadcaster and the community group has achieved media attention for the group and its grievances (Brown, 2002).

6. The von Feilitzen and Carlsson (1999) reader includes an appendix, which documents the "International and Regional Declarations and Resolutions" that refer to children and the media.

7. I return to ratings later in this chapter.

8. Commenting on the use of the term *bricolage,* Ken Gelder (1997) notes that Dick Hebdige "borrowed John Clarke's (1975) borrowing of the anthropologist Claude Levi-Strauss's concept of *bricolage.* Bricolage is a mode of adaptation where things are put to uses in ways for which they were not intended, ways that dislocate them from their 'normal' context" (Gelder & Thornton, 1997).

9. The term *cultural lag* is borrowed from Williams (1980).

10. The reference here is to the term as used by Umberto Eco in his (1986) essay, "Towards a Semiological Guerrilla Warfare," in *Travels in Hyper-Reality.*

11. Jakubowicz (2001) notes that this list of the key elements of the ATSIC (Aboriginal and Torres Strait Islander Commission) media policy is taken from Meadows (1999).

12. The "poaching" metaphor was introduced by de Certeau (1988). The following statement is central: "Readers are travellers; they move across lands belonging to someone else, like nomads poaching their way across fields they did not write, despoiling the wealth of Egypt to enjoy it themselves. Writing accumulates, stocks up, resists time by the establishment of a place and multiplies its production through the expansionism of reproduction. Reading takes no measures against the erosion of time (one forgets oneself *and* also forgets), it does not keep what it acquires, or it does so poorly, and each of the places through which it passes is a repetition of the lost paradise" (p. 174).

◆ References

Ang, I. (1991). *Desperately seeking the audience.* London: Routledge.

Banks, J. (2002). Gamers as co-creators: Enlisting the virtual audience—A report from the net face. In M. Balnaves, T. O'Regan, & J. Sternberg (Eds.), *Mobilising the audience* (pp. 191–211). St. Lucia, Brisbane: University of Queensland Press.

Barban, A., Cristol, S., & Kopec, F. (1987). *Essentials of media planning: A marketing viewpoint* (2nd ed.). Lincolnwood, IL: NTC Business Books.

Beville, H. M., Jr. (1988). *Audience ratings: Radio, television, and cable.* Hillsdale, NJ: Lawrence Erlbaum.

Brown, M. (2002, July 26). Next stop police as 2GB and Muslims row over racism. *Sydney Morning Herald,* p. 2.

Buckingham, D. (1987). *Public secrets: "East Enders" and its audience.* London: British Film Institute.

Butsch, R. (2000). *The making of American audiences: From stage to television, 1750–1990.* Cambridge, UK: Cambridge University Press.

Carey, J., & Kreiling, A. (1974). Popular culture and uses and gratifications: Notes towards an accommodation. In J. Blumler & E. Katz (Eds.), *The uses of mass communications: Current perspectives on gratifications research* (pp. 225–248). London: Sage.

Castells, M. (1998). *End of millennium.* Maiden, MA: Blackwells.

Chapman, S. (1986). *Great expectoriations.* London: Comedia.

de Certeau, M. (1988). *The practice of everyday life.* Berkeley: University of California Press.

Eco, U. (1986). *Travels in hyper-reality* (W. Weaver, Trans.). London: Picador.

Gelder, K., & Thornton, S. (Eds.). (1997). *The subcultures reader*. London: Routledge.

Giddens, A. (1984). *The constitution of society*. Cambridge UK: Polity.

Gillespie, M. (2000). Transnational communications and diaspora communities. In S. Cottle (Ed.), *Ethnic minorities and the media*. Buckingham, UK: Open University Press.

Hartley, J. (1987). Invisible fictions: Television, audiences, paedocracy and pleasure. *Textual Practice, 1*(2), 121–138.

Hartmann, P., & Husband, C. (1974). *Racism and the mass media*. London: Davis Poynter.

Hebdige, D. (1979). *Subculture: The meaning of style*. London: Methuen.

Husband, C. (1994). General introduction: Ethnicity and media democratization with the nation-state. In C. Husband (Ed.), *A richer vision: The development of ethnic minority media in Western democracies* (pp. 199–214). Paris: UNESCO.

Jakubowicz, A. (2001). Australian dreamings: Cultural diversity and audience desire in a multinational and polyethnic state. In K. Ross (with P. Playdon) (Ed.), *Black marks: Minority ethnic audiences and media* (pp. 195–214). Aldershot, UK: Ashgate.

Jenkins, H. (1992). *Textual poachers: Television fans and participatory culture*. New York: Routledge.

Jenkins, H. (2001, Autumn/Winter). Matt Hills interviews Henry Jenkins. *Intensities* (2). Retrieved from www.cult-media.com/issue2/CMRjenk.html

Jenkins, H. (2002). Interactive audiences. In D. Harries (Ed.), *The new media book*. London: British Film Institute.

Jenkins, H. (in press). Quentin Tarantino's Star Wars? Digital cinema, media convergence, and participatory culture. In B. Cheever (Ed.), *d.film*. Cambridge: MIT Press.

Kellerman, A. (2000). Phases in the rise of the information society. *Info, 2*(6), 537–541.

Leiss, W., Kline, S., & Jhally, S. (1986). *Social communication in advertising*. New York: Methuen.

Luhmann, N. (2000). *The reality of the mass media* (K. Cross, Trans.). Cambridge, UK: Polity.

Manguel, A. (1996). *A history of reading*. Hammersmith, UK: Flamingo.

Meadows, M. (1999). *Indigenous media in Australia: A background paper*. Brisbane: Australian Key Centre for Cultural and Media Policy.

Meehan, E. (1990). Why we don't count: The commodity audience. In P. Mellencamp (Ed.), *Logics of television: Essays in cultural criticism* (pp. 117–137). Bloomington: University of Indiana Press.

Morley, D. (1992). *Television audiences and cultural studies*. London: Routledge.

Naficy, H. (1993). *The making of exile cultures: Iranian television in Los Angeles*. Minneapolis: University of Minnesota Press.

Neuman, W. R. (1991). *The future of the mass audience*. Cambridge, UK: Cambridge University Press.

Nightingale, V. (1996). *Studying audiences: The shock of the real*. London: Routledge.

Nightingale, V. (2003). The "cultural revolution" in audience research. In A. N. Valdivia (Ed.), *A companion to media studies* (pp. 360–381). London: Blackwell.

Nightingale, V., Dickenson, D., & Griff, C. (2000). *Children's views on media harm* (Monograph No. 10). Sydney: Australian Broadcasting Authority and University of Western Sydney.

Radway, J. (1988). Reception study: Ethnography and the problems of dispersed audiences and nomadic subjects. *Cultural Studies, 2*(3), 358–376.

Riggins, S. H. (1992). *Ethnic minority media: An international perspective*. Newbury Park, CA: Sage.

Ross, K. (2000). In whose image? TV criticism and Black minority viewers. In S. Cottle (Ed.), *Ethnic minorities and the media*. Buckingham, UK: Open University Press.

Schudson, M. (1984). *Advertising: The uneasy persuasion*. New York: Basic Books.

Small, C. (1998). *Musicking: The meanings of performing and listening*. London: Wesleyan University Press.

Smulyan, S. (1994). *Selling radio: The commercialization of American broadcasting*

1920–1934. Washington, DC: Smithsonian Institution Press.

Soja, E. W. (2000). *Postmetropolis: Critical studies of cities and regions.* Oxford, UK: Blackwell.

Sreberny, A. (2000). Media and diasporic consciousness: An exploration among Iranians in London. In S. Cottle (Ed.), *Ethnic minorities and the media* (pp. 179–196). Buckingham, UK: Open University Press.

Turow, J. (1997). *Breaking up America: Advertisers and the new media world.* Chicago: University of Chicago Press.

von Feilitzen, C., & Carlsson, U. (Eds.). (1999). *Children and media: Inage, education, participation.* Göteborg, Sweden: UNESCO and Nordicom.

Webster, J., & Lichty, W. (1991). *Ratings analysis: Theory and practice.* Hillsdale, NJ: Lawrence Erlbaum.

Williams, R. (1980). *Problems in materialism and culture.* London: Verso.

12

A CONCISE HISTORY OF MEDIA AND CULTURAL STUDIES IN THREE SCRIPTS

Advocacy, Autobiography, and the Chronicle

◆ Joke Hermes

Cultural studies has offered an unequalled number of stories and theories about popular media texts and audiences. Cultural studies has also produced work in other areas, such as fashion and style or the body and sexuality. In this short history of the tradition of cultural studies, I focus on the research that has engaged especially with media and popular culture, as well as on a small number of authors whose names have come to be associated with the recent fame and popularity of this area. I sort their work (rather than they themselves) into a limited number of "scripts." By using the logics of what I have called the advocacy, the autobiography, and the chronicler's scripts, the theoretical development of the field can be organized and periodized. My overarching aim is to explicitly understand cultural studies as a "web" of connections between authors or even texts, which has progressed in a certain direction. I would like to avoid implicitly understanding researchers as working in splendid isolation or bounded by the disciplinary boundaries of other fields. (Even if, in the case of Janice Radway's

[1984] *Reading the Romance,* this is actually true, as Radway explains in her introduction to the British edition of her book in 1987.) Also, although it is true that *grosso modo* cultural studies in the 1970s were mainly written in the advocacy script, whereas the 1980s saw the emergence of the autobiography and the mid-1990s the *chroniqueur,* my periodization is a means to an end. All the scripts can be found across the quarter century of cultural studies history I will discuss here.

This will be an ex-centric story of cultural studies, written from a vantage point outside of either Britain or the United States. As a nonnative speaker and writer of English, it is in my own interest to break up any complacent accepted view of media and cultural studies. This is a field dominated by those who master the English language best. This is a field in which studying certain media texts will push publishers' doors wide open, which would remain closed if it were, for example, Vietnamese, Swedish, Polish, Greek, or Chilean locally produced television drama that formed the backdrop for an investigation of the meaning-producing practices of audiences. The international success of Ien Ang (whose 1985 *Dallas* study was originally written in Dutch) or of Jostein Gripsrud (1995), a Norwegian media and cultural studies scholar, depended as much on their undisputed qualities as their choice to write about *Dallas* and, in Gripsrud's case, *Dynasty.* Despite their radical politics, media and cultural studies have been institutionalized directly in relation to Hollywood culture and Anglo-American concepts, to that globally recognizable world of audience pleasure and the biggest international language of academic scholarship. If political correctness can at all be called upon in one's favor, as an outsider, I will invoke the above reasons to politely disagree on such matters as where and when exactly cultural studies "originated" (and whether *origins* is a term a Foucauldian critic even wants to use) and whether it is a field that had founding fathers (Raymond Williams or Richard Hoggart) or should be read as poststructuralist feminism's most successful enterprise in academia ever. Below, I discuss the scripts more fully and illustrate them with references to concrete studies. It is not my intention to retain any author under a certain heading. Some authors can be found under two headings, though fewer than probably should be mentioned in various places. The script is no more but also no less than a position of enunciation.

◆ The Script as Speaking Position

Charlotte Brunsdon is a British film and television critic and a key cultural studies scholar. She has suggested that feminist intellectuals in television studies come in three varieties (Brunsdon, 1997). There are those feminist intellectuals who do not differentiate between themselves and "women"—there are no "others," the relationship is transparent, and "woman" is an unproblematic identity shared between the intellectual and those she talks about. Secondly, there are feminists who aim to recruit nonfeminist others: The relationship between feminists and women is a hegemonic one. The formerly undifferentiated group of women now comes in at least two categories: feminist women (including the academics) and nonfeminist women (the ones feminist women talk about). Lastly, there are postmodernist feminists, for whom "feminism" would appear to be the more stable identity and "woman" a profoundly unstable one. Biological gender ceases to be a reliable indicator of the discursive positions that the academic herself and those she studies may occupy (Brunsdon, 1997, p. 117). When seen as a developmental logic, feminist intellectuals moved from not questioning their own authority and superior, more powerful position (which included their automatic right to speak on behalf of other women) to a questioning of that position to—lastly—exploding the category on whose behalf, presumably, they had been politically active.

Like feminist television criticism, cultural studies is both an intellectual and a politically charged domain. Cultural studies is not practiced for the sole benefit of academics. Rather, these academics, myself included, understand themselves to also take issue with social questions that involve nonacademic others. In this chapter, I follow Brunsdon's logic to explore the success formula of media and cultural studies, as well as the direction in which the field is moving, by taking a closer look at how and on whose behalf its practitioners felt they were and are working. This is to question how cultural studies is an academic enterprise, in that it questions cultural processes of meaning production and is motivated by the need to make this questioning a socially and politically relevant practice to others inside and outside the academy. It is not that I hope to lay bare its ultimate appeal or to destroy its magic. As in the analysis of successful media texts, such as romances, magazines, or films, there is pleasure in the process of deconstructing the elements as well as the logic of the overall structure. Although I borrow the idea of a typology or

developmental logic from Brunsdon, I will recast it in terms of the "scripts" available in cultural studies to understand what cultural studies should be about and what the role and position of the researcher or intellectual should be. *Script* is a term I loosely borrow from the work of cultural historian Hayden White. It is similar to *plot*—the prescribed and mostly expected way in which the stories told by popular television or romance novels unfold. Positions for characters are a given, as are a number of elements in the overall story. All romance novels have feisty heroines who experience a struggle between head (this is an insufferable man) and heart (so why am I so attracted to him?). The heroes in romance novels should always be both manly and motherly. Likewise, a good cultural studies scholar has obligations to her head and her heart: to theory and methodology but also to the pleasures of the popular or the struggle on behalf of women's formula fiction. The scripts reconstructed below (*advocacy*, *autobiography*, and the *chronicle*) address the narrative inscription of cultural studies' academic audiences in cultural studies texts in relation to the researcher's or author's position, as well as how the relation between the author and the media public is structured.

The use of these labels allows me to write cultural studies' history and also trace back the current interest in and enthusiasm for the term *citizenship*, one of the areas cultural studies has come to be highly interested in. Arguably, cultural studies did not have much of an interest in the worthy and public causes that are part and parcel of being a citizen. This particular lack of interest has caused some of the fiercest criticism of cultural studies, especially from political economists and mainstream media scholars, who have acted as if stung by the success of this upstart interdisciplinary newcomer in the academy (cf. Ferguson & Golding, 1997; Morley, 1998). They charged cultural studies with having no method, no sustained ideological critique, and no backbone when it comes to being seduced by the naive pleasure audiences and academics themselves take in the products of global capitalism. To link such pleasures to democracy, as bravely suggested by John Fiske (1987) and John Hartley (1999), is to severely upset established notions of the relation between the public and the private and their relative importance. *Citizenship,* as used by Hartley (1999), Gripsrud (1999), or Miller (1998, 2001) but also by myself (Hermes, 2000), hardly had any connection to these criticisms. In light of the earlier scripts of the advocate and the autobiographer, however, to use the term *citizenship* makes absolute sense.

Citizenship or, to be more precise, *cultural citizenship* is a good term to use in the "chronicle" mode or script of cultural studies. It allows the researcher to take a certain distance and unfold the relation between larger social structures and practices and particular media texts and identity construction. The reader needs to take for granted the political engagement of the author. The agency of audience members (or members of subcultural groups) is a given, as is the importance of understanding how agency, identity, and politics are related to questions of pleasure and meaning production. Cultural studies has, from its earliest days, been post-Althusserian. This is to say that although a notion of how relations of power structure society has always been of the highest importance, cultural studies was never unreconstructedly Marxist and solely interested in class relations. There has always been a defining interest in how different social power structures (class, gender, race, and ethnicity) work together to produce located meanings and identities. Stuart Hall's directorship of the Birmingham Centre of Contemporary Cultural Studies (CCCS) in the 1970s is a useful if not undisputed starting point to tell this story, even if not everybody agrees (McNeil, 1998; Wright, 1998). Others have started similar tales of the history of cultural studies by referencing older British work, such as Hoggart (1958) or Williams (1963). There are also Australian (Morris, 1988a, 1988b), North American (Carey, 1989), and Latin American founding texts (García Canclini, 1995; Martín-Barbero, 1993) in addition to critiques of Anglo-American cultural studies as well as Asian ones (Chen, 1998).

I turn to Hall and the CCCS in more detail below. For now, it needs to be said that throughout these different traditions, there is a sense of the importance of recognizing how power relations shape meaning and identity. Althusser taught British cultural studies in the 1970s; in addition to this, he stressed that the meaning of power relations is not given but constructed historically and ritually. Although class difference shapes the local production of meaning and culture, these can only be understood through ideology or, more generally, through language and not directly in and of themselves. Another piece of Marxist heritage—namely, Gramsci's concept of hegemony—provided the other major building block. It states that power is all the more successfully imposed if the powers that be manage to seduce the underlings and have them participate in their own subordination. Both philosophers, though Marxists, understood that power is never total or all encompassing. They did not, however, take leave entirely of the modernist, avant-garde position inherent in classic Marxism. This is very clear in the "advocacy" script. It is defined by the speaking position of the advocate: one who speaks on behalf of others. Although the poststructuralist insights of Michel Foucault were referenced in this early cultural studies work (cf. Bennett, 1998b, pp. 62–63), they would become important a decade later, as part of the autobiography script.

Advocacy refers to cultural studies' concern for the working classes, women, and non-White people. Using Charlotte Brunsdon's (1997) typology, you could say that the political engagement that characterizes cultural studies in general in this particular script suggests a homology between the intellectual and his or her subjects. The intellectual does not understand those he or she writes about to be different from himself or herself. Rather, there is a shared identity. This identity can be grounded in class, gender, or ethnicity. Thus, as a woman, the intellectual can speak on behalf of as well as about other women. As working-class scholarship boys, Raymond Williams and Stuart Hall were in a position of knowledge and therefore authority to speak about culture and the working class in Britain. South American cultural studies scholars such as Nestor García Canclini (cf. Lull, 1998) have taken up this same rhetorical position that denies "otherness" and speaks from shared experience. The *advocacy* script also informs the enunciatory politics of many Black North American scholars such as bell hooks (1992, 2000) or Jacqueline Bobo (1995).

The *autobiography* script refers to the complications that arise when the Marxist project (whether in its class, feminist, or race and ethnicity variety) is felt to be a severely limiting theoretical framework, even if the political agenda it belongs to is still seen as valid. A famous cartoon depicted this problem as the endless stacking of dichotomous identities (man-woman, middle class–working class, White-Black, straight-gay). The more one found oneself on the "wrong" side, the more one was oppressed. As the authors (Littlewood & Pickering, 1998) of a chapter on television comedy put it ironically in the title of their chapter, "Heard the one about the White, heterosexual, middle-class father-in-law?" Overviews such as Davies, Dickey, and Stratford's (1987) *Out of Focus* absolutely seriously included every single classlike basis of oppression: race, religion, age, sexuality, handicaps, and so on. As with any kind of overstacking, the pile collapsed under its own weight. It could have done with more grounding. Categories such as class (or gender) introduced via the "advocacy" script in cultural studies are based on the idea that experience is a form of knowledge that does not need or, indeed, allow for mediation. Experience connects intellectuals and those they write about. In

Gramscian terms, experience is the founding entity of "the popular" (as opposed to the "populism" that serves the interest of the dominant classes). The autobiography script, Foucauldian rather than Marxist in orientation, suggested that things were slightly more complex. Identities are never singular and always contextual. Identities can be traced via different routes that do not necessarily include shared experience or hardship and oppression. Pleasure—especially in media texts—might be anything *but* naive. Given cultural studies' growing investment in self-reflexivity as a form of rebellion against mainstream scholarship, the critical autobiography was a natural form and starting point for understanding the power and meaning of popular media texts.

The *autobiography* script suggests a somewhat different relation of the author to the audience she or he studies (and the academic audience that she or he writes for) than the *advocacy* script. The unquestioned symbiotic relation between author and subculture, as in the early work of Paul Willis (1977/1980) but also in Grossberg's (1983–1984, 1986b) work on rock music, is questioned by authors such as Elspeth Probyn. There is no transparency to the system, and identity is complex and constructed locally and contextually. The author chooses to share theorized insights with her or his readers rather than offer a certified Truth to educate them. This means that there is a greater need for case study research than for the building of grand theory or the quantitative testing of hypotheses that covered attitudes or behaviors of entire populations. Grand theory was part of cultural studies via its "modern," strongly Marxist leanings in the advocacy script, even if ethnography and semiotic deconstruction of texts and practices were always the methods of choice. The two later scripts are decidedly "postmodern" and have little sympathy for classical Marxism, even though they do go on to work from a strongly felt political obligation to fight against multiple oppressions.

In the *autobiography* script, differences may be more important than the identities shared by researcher and researched. The researcher does not recruit; she or he offers media critique as a miniature. Her or his political engagement hardly takes the form of being the people's representative or advocate. "The people" have ceased to exist. Temporary, local alliances and coalitions are what remain. The personal experience of the writer encapsulates the kind of theoretical work she (or he) likes to do. An obvious example here could come from Ien Ang's work (Ang, 1985), ranging from her early 1980s *Dallas* study to her recent work on ethnic identity, or from Elspeth Probyn's (1993, 1996) work on gendered and sexual identity.

Read against this background, the *chronicle* script can be seen to have enormous theoretical baggage that it hardly explicates. The seeming emptiness of such terms as *citizenship* is strategic in that it allows the author to refocus on agency and subjectivity, to understand what used to be called "oppression" as a productive relationship of power that involves mediated pleasures as well as boredom versus excitement and social criticism versus unthinking acceptance of the status quo. In this script, the researcher can again speak about others. This researcher may posit that there is a difference between her or him and those she or he researches without immediately showing disrespect or breaking the political bond of advocacy. The researcher may suggest that cultural studies is itself embedded in governmental structures and trains students to take up positions within the system as cultural workers rather than to be anti-state rebels (cf. Bennett, 1998b; Hartley, 2003). Another intriguing effect of the *chronicle* script is to allow for the possibility that the researcher, as an intellectual and possibly as a fan of the genre she or he studies, is not more knowledgeable than the researched. The agency and respect that do form the core of the advocacy script have come into their own here. Occasionally, intellectuality may have all the earmarks of a rearguard action.

Audiences, fans, and informants are the ones "in the know." The researcher tags on to reconstruct responsibilities, hopes, and criticisms (Baym, 2000; Shein, 2002). She or he tries to chronicle, to reconstruct underlying logics. Such logics relate to a level of debate we do not always (or even often) engage with in everyday talk. When we do, it is usually in a piecemeal fashion. These reconstructions, or the substance of the chronicle, should not be read as "what was really meant or felt" by audience members. Rather, they are a reflective meta-discourse that may help understand how local practices are never fully autonomous microcosms but part of the fabric of culture and society, as well as, usually, of the global economy. The difference between intellectuals and "the people" in the *chronicle* script has become one of professionalism rather than (shared) experience.

◆ Advocacy and Early Cultural Studies

In the late 1970s, Stuart Hall was involved in several coedited collections. They dealt with youth culture (Hall & Jefferson, 1976); with constructions of deviancy, delinquency, and youth in the media under right-wing government (Hall, Critcher, Jefferson, Clarke, & Roberts, 1978); and, more generally, with theorizing meaning production and everyday culture (Hall, Hobson, Lowe, & Willis, 1980). These three collections of what were originally Working Papers in Cultural Studies (written at the Centre for Contemporary Cultural Studies at the University of Birmingham) together offer what would be hailed internationally as the program for a new type of interdisciplinary, politically engaged study of culture. The political engagement was Marxist (or its socialist-feminist counterpart), and Stuart Hall was its key intellectual force. The mode in which this work was written, or the script that can be discerned in it, is typically "advocatist."

In a 1986 special issue of the *Journal of Communication Inquiry* dedicated to Stuart Hall, Grossberg describes Hall's position as defined by his own social and intellectual history and situated within both Marxist and semiotic discourses (Grossberg, 1986a, p. 62). He goes on to say that

> there can be no radical separation between theory, at whatever level of abstraction, and the concrete historical context which provides both its object of study and its conditions of existence. This is not merely a political position (though it is that); it is also an epistemological one. (Grossberg, 1986a, p. 62)

Although some of Stuart Hall's work rightly belongs under the headings of the autobiography and chronicle scripts, his groundbreaking work in cultural studies can be typified as Marxist, structuralist, and typically "advocatist." There is little room within this framework for agency: We all live and experience reality in practices and histories that are not of our own making. This is as true of the intellectual as of the woman or man in the street.

In early cultural studies work, there is a strong tendency to use the language of the academy: theoretical, neutral, and distancing, whereas the positions taken and the subjects chosen bespeak anger and political outrage. With the benefit of hindsight, it seems obvious that early cultural studies had to "prove" itself in an academic context. Its combination of political engagement, social theory (Marxism) within a humanities framework (semiotics), and goal (to deconstruct practices of articulation and meaning production) was clearly felt to be challenging enough. There were counterexamples that did not bother with academic tradition: Best-selling academic feminists had written cynical but also personal defamations of traditional rules and roles for women and their cultural depictions that bespoke the same set of convictions and background, as well as epistemology, but were aimed at a general public and not at an academic audience.

Germaine Greer's (1971) *Female Eunuch* is an obvious example. It would take more time for cultural studies to radicalize also in the arena of writing style. It would also take stronger theoretical backup, in the form of the work of Foucault, which would initiate a poststructuralist and more self-reflexive turn. It is important to note, however, that a number of feminist authors were way ahead of the men.

Resistance Through Rituals (Hall & Jefferson, 1976), *Policing the Crisis* (Hall et al., 1978), and *Culture, Media, Language* (Hall et al., 1980) share a sense of vibrancy, of new ground tilled. They foretell one of the most strongly debated points of contention about cultural studies work on media and communication: the issue of pleasure. *Women Take Issue* (Women's Studies Group, 1978), a countercollection by women at the CCCS, and a later, non-CCCS-related collection, *Out of Focus* (Davies et al., 1987), fail to share this enthusiasm and bespeak a much grimmer socialist-feminist outlook on women's position. Perhaps the most telling example is Paul Willis's (1977/1980) *Learning to Labour*. In itself, this is a disturbing and confronting study of 12 young working-class boys and how their relation to school culture will predestine them to be locked into the harness of class relations in which their parents are also imprisoned. Willis's boys are a group who call themselves the "lads," to be distinguished from the "ear'oles." To be a lad is to occupy a position of considerable power and resistance against the school system. It also means that, as a lad, a boy will want to escape from the middle-class rules of school as quickly as he can. As a result, he will enter the workforce with nearly no education, to be a dispensable part of a system that hires and fires unschooled workers according to its own needs. The ear'oles, on the other hand, have a rough time at school. They take school seriously and are taken to task for this by the lads. They, however, have a much better chance of postsecondary education and a more satisfying work life.

Willis's (1977/1980) study is disturbing because of the iron, inescapable logic it describes. From a feminist point of view, it is also disturbing because Willis, without seeming to notice this, is so much taken with his lads that he, like them, appears to despise the ear'oles. The girls are a negligible factor altogether, objects of misogynist humor (if it can be called that) and attempted (or even successful) rape (Skeggs, 1992, p. 191). On the upside, Willis's enthusiasm and pleasure in his lads make him the epitome of the advocate. In terms of the script of the advocate, it is interesting to see how Willis moves effortlessly between imagining himself as "one of the boys" and his academic rendering of no less than the truth of their lives and being their spokesperson. There is a lack here of self-reflexivity that also pervades Hall's early work as well as early feminist work in cultural studies. The Marxist speaking position offers the author a magical solution for bridging the different worlds of the (oppressed) research subject and the more powerful academic. He or she may not be middle or upper class by birth but will have become so by virtue of education and acceptance into the academic world. This would be problematized by anthropologists in the early and mid-1980s as a result of ethnography's "linguistic turn." It was also famously analyzed by Angela McRobbie (1982) in one of the first pieces of self-reflexive feminist cultural studies, an article titled "Between Talk, Text and Action," in *Feminist Review*.

McRobbie's (1982) article and the fierce discussion in interpretive ethnography (provider of cultural studies' most favored research approach) signify a turn away from a structuralist Marxism to a poststructuralist cultural criticism (cf. Clifford, 1988; Clifford & Marcus, 1986; Marcus & Fischer, 1986). The studies cited were foreshadowed in turn by the work of Clifford Geertz (1973, 1983/1988). This body of work has been identified as initiating the so-called "linguistic turn" to self-reflexive academic authorship. It questions the position of the speaker. It wonders what her or his

right to speak is on behalf of others. How far is the speaker or author aware of the power difference between herself or himself and his or her research subjects, and how is it accounted for? For all its rhetoric and sometimes theoretical bombast on behalf of the oppressed, it now seems there was precious little room for the underdogs themselves in early cultural studies. After all, the kind of anthropology practiced in early cultural studies can, from the vantage point of its poststructuralist critics, be seen as yet another way of using the powerless for goals that have nothing to do with their own lives and everything with that of the researchers (academic prestige, jobs, publications, or idealistic high-flown politics). Marxism lent a theoretical and left-wing veneer to a criticism that did not require left-wing critics themselves to change all that much in their own lives, offer public space of sorts to others in their work, or be present in their own texts. Although ethnography is the method of choice, there is much description and interpretation by the observer/author, as well as fairly little interview transcript or comments by the observed.

A position of advocacy is more difficult to maintain in media criticism than in the kind of youth culture study undertaken by Willis (1977/1980). But in *Policing the Crisis,* Hall et al. (1978) manage to do so nonetheless. Their study focuses on demythologizing mugging, especially the myth of the dangerous young non-White man. Accounts of muggers themselves are eschewed on purpose. The authors claim that their aim "has been to examine 'mugging' from the perspective of the society in which it occurs" (p. 327). What does "mugging" (consistently put in quotation marks) mean? Or, how do we "trace out the terrain on which an answer to the question might be sought, and . . . identify the elements which such an explanation must include" (p. 327)? In a remarkable move, the book shows how an older myth (the dangerous Black male) is revived within a context of right-wing policy that chooses to ignore conditions of poverty or to attend to the economic crisis. Instead, it deflects attention by "policing" rather than helping the poor. Mrs. Thatcher (then party leader of the Conservatives) liked to speak of welfare scroungers, single mothers, and Black muggers as a collective of undesirables to indicate that the inner cities needed to be controlled (or policed). It was therefore both a matter of playing the media in the move towards policy decisions and, later, actual police deployments that could then be cast as appropriate measures against young Black men running amok: Together, these produced a right-wing consensus in Britain and a new "Black proletariat." The book traces this process both via the press (such as *The Sun* or *The Daily Telegraph*) and "letters to the editor." It is especially in the popular press that *mugging* became synonymous with *Black crime*. The book's project is also to reconstruct how news is constructed and profitably uses Cohen's (1973) notion of the "moral panic." Towards the end of the book, some quotations are given from ethnographic accounts collected by others to introduce the youth in question. These are grim, probably the more so for being offered in abstraction from a fieldwork account or of much other material. Here is one about school culture:

When you go to school, you realize the difference. You're made to realize it. They (the white kids) pick on you. First you try to bribe them—sweets, ices, the lot. But then, one day, you can't stand it any more. You get vicious, real vicious and you lick them. (quoted in Hall et al., 1978, p. 361)

All in all, it is an impressive and highly theoretical effort, drenched, from today's perspective, in what now feels like old-fashioned jargon. *Proletariat* is a term hardly used any more today, nor do I any longer see my colleagues and fellow academics quote *resistance* directly from Marx and Engels. I have never greatly liked this particular type of distancing jargon, although I do concur with its political

criticism. Gender held no prominent place in this work, as the women at the then Centre protested (cf. Tomlinson, 2001; Women's Studies Group, 1978). As a feminist, I have felt more comfortable with post-structuralist and postmodernist theory, which suggests that a more contextual theorizing can be stronger and more fruitful in capturing the moment of audiencehood, of how we construct our own identities while according meaning to the television programs we like or to the magazines or romances we love to read. This is to define the really important loci of meaning production as highly selective and fragmented and perhaps even to eschew the notion that overview is at all possible. The interesting question is whether cultural studies and media studies within cultural studies really needed the high Marxism of the late 1970s. Perhaps they did. Perhaps the feminist choice to start from the author's own experiences or, later, from highly local accounts would not have been strong enough to be effective within the wider context that academic studies also address. This would certainly explain why far more recent Latin American media and cultural studies have tended to hang onto the Marxist terminology (cf. Lull, 1998). In a situation in which academics are also political actors, who feel they are pitted directly against the institutions of the state or government, a personalized style is obviously not a highly attractive choice, even if ultimately it is more fitting within the type of political project that cultural studies enhances—which is to attend to local practices of articulation and meaning making to understand how relations of power will produce certain subjectivities and reproduce embedded societal structures.

It is worth looking at the work of Nestor García Canclini and Jesús Martín-Barbero to get a better sense of the effectivity of the advocacy mode, as well as of how media studies developed from a cultural studies perspective elsewhere. Both authors share a strong interest in mass media and popular culture from a customized mix of approaches.

Their work offers the only recent example of a classic Gramscian-Marxist outlook, though influenced by the work of Bourdieu and international relations theory. As in the earliest cultural studies, it combines analysis of the economic and the material with a semiotic decoding of media content. Whereas early cultural studies was mostly interested in television and fictional mass media texts from a somewhat distanced perspective, saving its enthusiasm for youth cultures, García Canclini (1995) and Martín-Barbero (1993, 1997) tend to spell out the relations of resistance and subordination that define the effectivity of such texts as the highly successful Latin American soap opera (cf. Martín-Barbero, 2000, p. 40). In contrast to later media and cultural studies, which based their notion of resistance on small audience studies (Brown, 1994; Fiske, 1987), Latin American cultural studies has taken a more general perspective. Martín-Barbero (1988) wishes to deconstruct what he calls the hegemonic paradigm in communication:

> The *hegemonic* paradigm is the one through which we "basically" think about the problems of communication today. This means that my critique is not one of a model from which I am detached, but rather of one inside which we critics to some extent live. This makes the task of outlining and deconstructing it so much more difficult. I believe that the first decisive step towards the construction of another way of thinking about the problem goes like this: we need to *re*-cognize that the hegemonic does not dominate us from without but rather penetrates us, and therefore it is not just against it but from within it that we are waging war. (pp. 447–448)

He then goes on to name two stages in the hegemonic construction of communication studies, which he calls "ideologistic" and "scientist." His goal is, recognizably, engaged criticism (cf. Hummel, 1995, p. 245) though couched in often uncomfortably strong politico-speak.

Intriguingly, the advocatist script in Latin American cultural studies appealed in the 1990s to academics who had voiced their criticism of the turn that cultural studies took from the mid-1980s onwards. This is a moment marked by the new audience studies (Corner, 1996), which consolidated a trend in media-oriented cultural studies to research small groups and devote energy to strong theorization of the material gathered, rather than engage in much methodological accounting. Those with a more sociological outlook tended to object. The earlier Marxism in cultural studies was, after all, firmly lodged in a social science perspective, which lost out against the interpretive "poetics" of the new postlinguistic turn that ethnography initiated by the work of, among others, Geertz, Clifford, and Marcus. Whereas before it had been legitimate to describe and interpret cultural phenomena and present this as objective results, after the linguistic turn, the constructedness of such accounts and the perspective from which they had been written were foregrounded. Objectivity had to make room for reflexivity and awareness of the power, authorship, and thus "authority" of cultural critics. The essence of cultural studies work relocated to writing and identifying forms of resistance rather than perceiving "the popular [as an emphasis of] the thick texture of hegemony/subalternity, [as] the interlacing of resistance and submission, and opposition and complicity," as Martín-Barbero (1988, p. 462) put it in a translated article that appeared in the journal *Media, Culture, and Society*. Philip Schlesinger, one of its editors, also provided an introduction to an English translation of Martín-Barbero's (1993) *Communication, Culture and Hegemony*. James Lull (1998), reluctant scholar of media and cultural studies and strong critic of its lack of rigorous methodology and over-the-top politics, offered an enthusiastic review of Mexican communication and cultural studies as a counterpoint to overly smug European and North American work. Quite rightly, he suggests that cultural studies today is a global phenomenon and that this is addressed by Latin American cultural studies.

Cultural studies is a global phenomenon these days. The reader, however, most certainly should not confuse British, North American, or Australian cultural studies with the cultural studies of Mexico and the rest of Latin America. Northern/Western cultural studies are luxuriant, often reflecting "problems" of abundance and boredom. Dominant discourses gravitate toward the navel-gazing, psychocultural stresses of repressed middle-class Western intellectuals, expressed in the most politically correct of arguments that are frequently supported with only the flimsiest empirical evidence (Lull, 1988, 1997), in self-congratulating competitions for "most exotic" status, or in endless claims and speculations about what cultural studies itself "really" is, where it originated, and who it represents (Lull, 1998, p. 404).

Clearly, then, advocacy is an effective script when combined with a strong and direct political agenda and an ambition to understand cultural studies as a sociology of mass communication. Without such a political agenda or its related constituency, the relation of the author to those she or he reports on, or whose media practices she or he interprets, becomes paternalist and emblematic of the conservative rather than the critical dimension of hegemony, part of the instruments of submission and subalternity. I happen to think that the advocacy script is inherently paternalist and too unaware of the academic's position of power and authority. But perhaps political enthusiasm and a good cause should be counted as redeeming factors.

◆ *Autobiography:*
   The Self-Reflexive
   Turn in Cultural Studies

Although much maligned as exercises in navel gazing (and not just by James Lull), the autobiographical script produced utterly fascinating studies. Whereas there had been an inclination in the advocacy script to break with the privileges of class and masculinity as they had been part of the academic establishment, by at least taking seriously the experiences and ideas of nonprivileged groups. The autobiographical script truly radicalized the revaluing of experience and knowledges of those not in positions of power as well as academic practice. By turning the distant and impersonal academic voice couched in the social science mode of doing research into one that had a body—that needed to be dressed, entertained, and fed and that was affected by what it saw and felt—while simultaneously turning to sophisticated theory to make sense of all that seemed so "natural" and "normal," a huge change was wrought in what could count as "science." The authors I will turn to here would probably not claim "science" as a label for their work, aware as they are that their project is cultural criticism rather than a renewed reification of cultural studies and its distancing beyond lay critique.

Ien Ang's (1985) *Watching Dallas* is a famous and much-quoted example. It is an account of her study of audience members' letters about the reactions they got from others in relation to viewing *Dallas*. Ang acquired these letters by inviting audience members to write to her in a personal ad in a (young) women's magazine. The ad states that Ang herself likes to watch *Dallas* but that she often gets strange reactions. Although *Watching Dallas* does not record Ang's personal experience beyond the text in the advertisement and goes on to theorize the "strange" reactions (which the letter writers immediately recognized) as part of two opposed ideologies, the study set a new landmark and, in a way, made Ang more vulnerable to predictable criticism and even derision. Her *Desperately Seeking the Audience* was certainly a more formal study of audience research practices (Ang, 1991). It is also highly critical of how research method and practice are used by networks and public broadcasting corporations alike as a regulatory technique to control the audience. Although Ang foregoes the classic Marxism of earlier cultural studies and casts her conclusion in terms of radical ethnography, her voice is political rather than personal.

Throughout her work, which she continued from Australia, Ang has stuck with an inspiring mixture of personal experience, observation, media research, and poststructuralist theorizing. As she puts it in her introduction to *On Not Speaking Chinese* (Ang, 2001),

> Imagining my Taiwanese audience [she has been invited to give a lecture] I felt I couldn't open my mouth in front of them without explaining why I, a person with stereotypically Chinese physical characteristics, could not speak to them in Chinese. (p. vii)

The title essay thus echoes Ang's theoretical and personal conviction that any identity, in a sense, is always mistaken (Ang, 2001, p. viii). Hybridity does not only make up Ang's personal history; it also informs her theoretical perspective, which she has also referenced to García Canclini's (1995) work. From the older advocacy perspective, Ang would seem to lose political persuasiveness here. If all identities are hybrids, there is no "natural" constituency for her work or group on whose behalf she may speak. Ang does have a political agenda, however, cast against elitist dismissal of popular entertainment and in favor of a feminist understanding of, for example, the soap opera. Rather than simply suggest that the soap opera is a crypto-feminist form that addresses an essential or unique feminine point of view, Ang suggests that viewers of soap opera may use this popular art form to come to (re)interpret their position in life and relationship to others. Politics in *Watching Dallas* are thus intimately bound up with a move towards self-reflexivity. This is both a more modest and a more ambitious form of politics than the politics of the advocacy script. It shifts discussion away from oppression, policy and economics, and a recognizable dominant class or group towards consideration of how identity is constructed. Who we (critics and other media users alike) are is understood to be

deeply and complexly implicated within the structure and practices of our societies. Power is diffuse and follows multiple logics. Its workings can only be understood contextually and as a practice in which all take part, even if relations of power are always unequal.

The radical quality of the autobiographical script is mostly theoretical. The theoretical framework favored is poststructuralist discourse analysis based on the work of Michel Foucault. In his *Discipline and Punish* (1979, English edition) and his *History of Sexuality, Part I* (1980, English edition), Foucault sketched a singularly persuasive account of how subjectivity can be accounted for both in terms of subjectivation and discipline, as well as in terms of seduction, of individuals as subjects of the discourses they speak and the practices they live. Contrary to the earlier structuralist framework, which held little room for human agency and subjectivity (all were determined by and in ideology), poststructuralism shows how we are seduced into feeling ourselves to be autonomous individuals. When we are invited to talk endlessly about ourselves, confessing to the deepest truth of our being, we are in a relationship in which power is with the listener, who determines whether truth has been spoken, and not with the confessor who speaks.

The media, then, can be understood to help us find or even speak deeper truths about ourselves. The melodramatic imagination that Ang understood to be crucial to enjoying *Dallas*, which functions as a counterpart to the tragic structure of feeling that the soap opera genre offers, is based on a sense of emotional realism. Those *Dallas* viewers who are not under the sway of the ideology of mass culture, which condemns mass-produced American television fare, hold that *Dallas* offers valuable insights into human relations and emotions from which they may learn. All the talk about themselves that the soap opera characters are engaged in consists, in a way, of exemplary confessions. A decade onwards, television was to take emotional realism that much further with the talk show, in which guests would confess to affairs they had not even told their partners about. I remember Oprah asking a Black businessman who was having an affair with his secretary, "So does your wife know about this?" Upon which he answered in deep shock, "I guess she must now." The harder a confession is to make, the truer it becomes, Foucault stated. Television took up this challenge with a vengeance.

Yet, the power of the Foucauldian framework perhaps does not lie in applying it literally to the media. It is in the work of Probyn, who offers a discourse analysis of cultural studies itself, that the political strength of the autobiography script is clearest. Like Ang, Probyn does not suggest she talks on anyone's behalf but her own. Like Ang, she does not generalize from a small set of data (cf. Emanuel, 1992, p. 22) or write from a position of superiority versus her audience or her respondents (Emanuel, 1992, p. 28). Her aim is to produce strong or stronger theory about popular media, the pleasures they offer, and the way such pleasures are also a means of disciplining oneself in terms of, for example, dominant definitions of gender or sexuality. In both *Sexing the Self* (1993) and *Outside Belongings* (1996), Probyn herself is very much present. Identity formation and subjectivity are the topics she wishes to explore via what she terms a "sociology of the skin" (Probyn, 1996, p. 5). Writing as a feminist and as a lesbian, Probyn offers perhaps the most thoroughly theorized autobiographical moment in cultural studies. This is not just "navel gazing": The subjects broached range from Québécois television production to childhood and nostalgia to interrogation of recent Western culture criticism and philosophy. They underwrite Probyn's interest in popular media, to which she is careful never to grant all-encompassing effectivity but understands, in their specific textuality, to be part of larger processes of disciplining, for instance, or seduction. Thus, she was one of the first to use the term *postfeminism* in a

careful way in relation to then recent American television series that appeared to celebrate newfound freedoms and enlightened traditionalism for women—comedies such as *Who's the Boss?* and *Roseanne*, as well as dramas such as *thirtysomething*. Here are women who apparently have a choice; indeed, they have chosen to have families, to be caregivers rather than have careers or to have families in combination with careers. This "choiceoisie" is of course, no choice (Probyn, 1988/1997, p. 133). Television appears to offer feminism, but it gives seductive traditionalism. Probyn's work stands out in that she grounds her reading in a combination of her own viewer experience as well as in precise, well-chosen philosophical quotations. In this case, from Louis Althusser: "I want to recall Althusser's description of the backwardness, forwardness, survivals and unevenness of development which co-exist in the structure of the real historical present" (Probyn, 1988/1997, pp. 128–129). This is a more subtle use of the Marxist philosopher than had become *usance* in earlier cultural studies work.

The autobiography script has especially been used to address issues of gender and ethnicity in relation to identity construction. The script has extended into newer forms of ethnographic research as well, in which the researcher is often present as a fan or as a gendered or colored person (non-White or White). This section opened with the example of Ien Ang's (1985) work as *Dallas* fan and as a woman of Chinese descent. Other examples would be Jacqueline Bobo's (1995) *Black Women as Cultural Readers*, Paul Gilroy's (1987) *There Ain't No Black in the Union Jack*, and Kobena Mercer's *Welcome to the Jungle* (1994). Stuart Hall's (1987) essays on multiculturalism, which relate his Caribbean descent, are perhaps the best known and, in the truest sense, autobiographical. It is also tempting to describe the composite cultural studies autobiographer "as a person of a certain sexual ambition and orientation." Probyn's (1988/1997) work is exceptional, however. Sexuality has mostly been slightly outside cultural and media studies and part of the neighboring interdiscipline of queer studies. Texts that move between the two, as it were, include Richard Dyer's work on film, sexuality, and ethnicity (in his collections *Only Entertainment* [[1992], *The Matter of Images* [1993], *White* [1997], and *Queers in Film* [2002]); they also can be found in collections such as *Inside/Out* (Fuss, 1991), which includes, amongst other interesting articles, an analysis of the star persona of Rock Hudson, who, until he was dying from AIDS, managed to hide his homosexual orientation from the public eye.

The fan ethnography, or audience research written within the autobiographical script, has—quite rightly, although often much too harshly—been criticized. Christine Geraghty's (1998) overview article of audience research in television studies is, by any standard, exceptionally good. Although there is audience research on other media as well, television-related work also offers a good example for other media and cultural studies work. Without disrespect, Geraghty manages to show how—in my terms—the autobiographer's script can be a severely limiting one. First of all, she points out that cultural studies should be criticized for using the term *ethnography* too lightly to describe a whole array of qualitative audience research. With the exception of Marie Gillespie's (1995) *Television, Ethnicity and Social Change*, there have been no truly long-duration projects in which the researcher has spent considerable time with her or his informants. Ang (1985) used 42 letters for her *Dallas* project; others have used time-use diaries or single long interviews, as I did in research on women's magazine reading (Hermes, 1995). In fairness, most of these researchers did not themselves call their projects "ethnographic," but a grey area was instituted between general qualitative audience research and ethnography. Any study that showed itself aware of the need to be self-reflexive as author/researcher—and that took into account the differential power

positions of interviewee and author—was more or less allowed to sport this label. After all, such collections as *Writing Culture: The Poetics and Politics of Ethnography* (Clifford & Marcus, 1986) had so thoroughly deconstructed the project of ethnography and, in effect, divorced it from its long anthropological tradition as based in fieldwork that the term was up for grabs. It came to stand, at least from the mid-1980s to the mid-1990s, for a particular type of writing practice.

Geraghty (1998) is also critical of the fact that the researcher's own fandom excluded critical television viewers or powerful respondents from all but a few audience studies. Gray (1992) mentions how much more difficult it was to keep control of her interviews with middle-class women than with her working-class respondents. Others have had the same experience. Given the strong feminist accent in the work on popular television, not many men were interviewed either. As will become clear below, this is changing. From the autobiography script, in which the researcher takes on a project that is firmly based within her or his own lifestyle and that will allow easier *rapport* with her or his informants or interviewees, the balance has recently been shifting to another script, which I have called the *chronicle*. Its main advantage is that it allows for a more distanced—if no less involved—position for the researcher. Although I can offer as proof only the body of feminist work produced and referenced in part above, I am convinced that the feminist efforts of over a decade and a half in media and cultural studies research have generated a lasting interest both in qualitative audience research as a method and in a self-reflexive mode of doing it—even if they have focused more on popular fiction rather than on news or nonfiction (as did early cultural studies in *Policing the Crisis* [Hall et al., 1978] or the work of the Glasgow Media Group). Although the small fan-meets-with-other-audience-members research started as a low-cost type of research conducted by newcomers to the academy who could not command large research budgets (Drotner, 1994, p. 342) and had to be based on the authority of personal experience to theoretically legitimate the break with the then current quantitative methods, it has become a method in good standing on its own.

◆ The Chronicle: The Late Theorization of Early Politics

The chronicle as a rule system or regime of writing has the obvious advantage that the author is allowed much more room to be critical of what she or he writes about. Rather than write as a fan or as one who is personally implicated in the research project, there is room for qualifying what interviewees have to say and for actually allowing the critical dialogue that anthropologists such as Clifford, Marcus, and Fischer so favored. Although power relations are taken into account, it is much less a codification of the media user or consumer as—implicitly—a victim. The victim was, after all, the natural counterpart of the advocate. Or rather, the advocate needed someone on whose behalf he or she could speak. In the autobiography script, this painful systematic positioning is undermined by suggesting that, in insofar as there are victims, the researcher also is one of them. As a fan amongst fans, moreover, the autobiographer can show a counterculture—forms of pleasure as forms of resistance against the system. John Fiske's (1987) work introduced this convention in his *Television Culture,* although his work in fact bridges all three moments. Starting from Marxist bearings, Fiske always allowed media texts, with considerable enthusiasm, to seduce him. This can been seen in his early work on television with John Hartley, in which they suggested that television is the bard of our times (Fiske & Hartley, 1978) but stuck with an overall Marxist frame of reference; in his autobiographical article on ethno-semiotics in *Cultural Studies* in 1990; and in his later work, which took a (slightly) more distanced view (Fiske, 1991).

The script of the chronicle can be found in the work of researchers whose interest is with culture, governmentality, and cultural policy (such as Tony Bennett) and in the current work on cultural citizenship that I mentioned earlier. Tony Bennett's work, like Brunsdon's, spans the entire (inter)discipline of cultural studies. Amongst his earlier work is a book on James Bond not only as a popular hero (Bennett & Woollacott, 1987), which is primarily a semiotic reading, but also as a complex phenomenon. It includes the novels, films, publicity, and critical commentaries. There is also a coedited volume, *Popular Culture: Past and Present* (Waites, Bennett, & Martin, 1982), on the history of popular culture for the British Open University. Bennett earned much of his international reputation subsequently while working in Australia on cultural policy and museology (Bennett, 1998c) and on cultural consumption. Quite extraordinarily, Bennett was one of three main researchers in an Australian government-funded research project on everyday consumption that was mainly based on quantitative data (Bennett, Emmison, & Frow, 1999), which in my definition places it almost entirely outside of cultural studies. All in all, Bennett, currently at the Open University as Stuart Hall's successor, has shown himself to be one of the most well-rounded cultural studies scholars. He is of interest here because of his style of writing, which has always been involved but distanced and never as overtly Marxist as the work of Hall. Bennett is in fact a true *chroniqueur* in cultural studies, and he was one long before most. He is also of interest because, in the course of his work on culture and policy, he addressed the issue of cultural citizenship. His primary interlocutor here, as Toby Miller (2001, p. 183) puts it, is government. Basically, governments should guarantee a set of cultural competences (i.e., cultural citizenship). Bennett's project, according to Miller, is to take cultural studies beyond "affect." Whereas the autobiography script allowed for the redefinition of politics or resistance as starting at a very low threshold—namely, the pleasure we take in popular forms—the chronicler wishes more dispassionately for stronger evidence of both cultural competence and (the possibilities for) cultural change. Bennett's aims for cultural policy studies, not surprisingly, include broadening the concept of culture used in the sphere of policy by introducing to cultural studies a wide anthropological definition. This should lead to a recontextualization of

> the somewhat narrow concerns of arts policy and administration as part of a much broader field in which a concern with culture as industry intersects with a concern with the ways in which cultural resources are deployed as parts of programmes of social management. (Bennett, 1998a, pp. 541–542)

Although Toby Miller sees Bennett's work as the first of three key sites of work on cultural citizenship, I personally favor a broader and less state-related understanding of cultural citizenship. I shall therefore bypass Renato Rosaldo and colleagues, whose work on cultural citizenship relates to Latina/Latino social movements and minority rights (Miller, 2001, p. 183; Torres et al., 1999), as well as Kymlicka and fellow liberal political philosophers who "seek rapprochement between collective minority cultures and individual majority culture" (Miller, 2001, p. 183). This is to argue (*pace* Miller) that there is the possibility of media and cultural criticism that includes political and social theory as part of the ongoing investigation and critique of processes and practices of meaning production. Because, indeed, there is more than "rat-chasing, undergraduate-invigilating psychology on the one hand, and armchair-therapizing, text-reading humanism on the other" (Miller, 2001, p. 185). I happen to like John Hartley's (1999) take on cultural citizenship and television in this regard, which he renamed do-it-yourself citizenship.

In his *Uses of Television*, Hartley (1999) interrogates how, via television, we may feel connected with others across the globe.

"If television is teaching, then it is a part of and 'witness to' the transmodern, transnational democratization of culture" (p. 47). But later on he states,

> Looking at the rest of the world through television, it is inevitable that differences can be both celebrated and erased, recognized and removed, insisted upon and ignored. So there's a curious "toggle" switching between television as a teacher of "identity" among its audiences, and as a teacher of "difference" among the same population. It seems to me that this "toggle" switch is itself historical—it was set to "identity" first, promoting what I've called "cultural citizenship" [i.e., as in citizens' rights] and identity politics (during the era of "golden-age" broadcast television) and to "difference" more recently, promoting "DIY" citizenship and semiotic self-determination. (p. 159)

One has to be a fan of Hartley's work to like his neologisms and sometimes quaint phrasing, but if you are, his work is not only a chronicle of how we have studied the processes of (everyday) culture and media and the articulation of meaning, identity, subjectivity, and power but also a commentary on how we have done that. Hartley, then, is a meta-chronicler. The only thing baffling about his work is why he has never engaged with audience studies at all. There is perhaps more of the early semiotic Marxism here then meets the eye. The point is that any media or cultural critique that wishes to present itself in public debate should be connected with both the everyday levels of media talk and its abstractions. From my perspective, small audience studies or "ethnographic intent" may keep us honest in our self-chosen profession of mediation and translation. It is the only direct way in which we may be held answerable for our views and interpretations. Apparently, in me too, there is more of the early political fighting spirit than I would normally realize.

◆ Conclusion

Cultural studies has many histories, and most of these include important work on media. These histories have developed in particular places and refer to particular, local circumstance. There is, however, also a strong sense of an ongoing process of dovetailing. The work of James Carey (1989), for instance, and his notion of a "ritual model" of communication (versus a "transmission model") provided many media and communication scholars with a useful point of departure. Carey argued against the dominant sender-message-receiver model of communication scientists. Like Stuart Hall's encoding-decoding model, this was as much an intellectual as a political intervention. Hall's model, developed originally in 1973, has, like Carey's notion, been overly used and is seldom seen for the critical observation it was. In a 1994 interview (quoted in Gray, 1999, p. 26), Hall explained that the original paper was a lecture for the Centre of Mass Communication Research at the University of Leicester, which was a thoroughly traditional communication science outfit. Hall wanted to present something they would both recognize and that could be offered as a critical comment. The model since then has had a life of its own. This is both positive—in that it pushed interest in both the production and the reception of media texts—and negative. The downside to the popularity of the model is that, as models tend to do, it has flattened understanding of how media texts have wholly separate lives among different audiences and during their production.

Dave Morley used the encoding-decoding model in a comprehensive study with Charlotte Brunsdon of the production, the text (or ideological meanings), and the reception of a BBC current affairs program called *Nationwide* (Brunsdon & Morley, 1978; Morley, 1980). If anything, this early audience study showed that the three reader positions Hall mentioned in the original paper (the dominant, the negotiated, and the oppositional reading positions) do not even come near to describing the complexity of readings invited by the televisual text. Morley himself has perhaps been the most incisive and important critic of the model in his postscript to The *"Nationwide" Audience* (Morley, 1981/1992). Morley suggests that the model misses a number of dimensions, such as whether audiences actually comprehend the text as encoded, which makes its usage problematical to say the least. Unfortunately, media and cultural studies find themselves in the bizarre position of being understood as collectively bound to a persistently popular model. Although critical of mainstream mass communication research, the encoding-decoding model echoes mainstream mass communication's central idea that communication and culture have to do with "getting the message across" (from a sender to a receiver). This hardly covers the wealth of insight that has been produced under the umbrella term of *cultural studies*, which is unique for its combination of qualitative empirical research and theorization of that material from engaged, politicized perspectives—whether these are in relation to media and media cultures or pertain to gender and feminism, postcolonialism, and issues of class, race, and ethnicity. Perhaps the chronicle script can give way to a new radicalization and a new set of terms if it turns out that *cultural citizenship* is not the magical term that will combine political engagement, sophisticated theory and cultural critique, and understanding, as we are now hoping it will be. Ultimately, the goal is simply to do a better job of our own global marketing and franchising. Or is that too much of an outdated postmodernist or, even worse, neoimperialist curse in terms of our equally outdated but nonetheless deeply lodged Marxist roots?

◆ References

Ang, I. (1985). *Watching* Dallas: *Soap opera and the melodramatic imagination*. London: Methuen.

Ang, I. (1991). *Desperately seeking the audience*. London: Routledge.

Ang, I. (2001). *On not speaking Chinese: Living between Asia and the West*. London: Routledge.

Baym, N. K. (2000). *Tune in, log on: Soaps, fandom and online community*. London: Sage.

Bennett, T. (1998a). Cultural studies: A reluctant discipline. *Cultural Studies, 12*(4), 528–545.

Bennett, T. (1998b). *Culture: A reformer's science*. London: Sage.

Bennett, T. (1998c). Pedagogic objects, clean eyes and popular instruction: On sensory regimes and museum didactics. *Configurations, 6*(3), 345–371.

Bennett, T., Emmison, M., & Frow, J. (1999). *Accounting for tastes: Australian everyday experience*. Cambridge, UK: Cambridge University Press.

Bennett, T., & Woollacott, J. (1987). Bond and beyond: The political career of a popular hero. Basingstoke, UK: Macmillan.

Bobo, J. (1995). *Black women as cultural readers*. New York: Columbia University Press.

Brunsdon, C. (1997). *Screen tastes*. London: Routledge. (Original work published 1995)

Brunsdon, C., & Morley, D. (1978). *Everyday television: "Nationwide."* London: British Film Institute.

Carey, J. (1989). *Communication as culture*. Boston: Unwin Hyman.

Chen, K.-H. (Ed.). (1998). *Trajectories: Inter-Asia cultural studies*. London: Routledge.

Clifford, J. (1988). *The predicament of culture: Twentieth century ethnography in literature and art*. Cambridge, MA: Harvard University Press.

Clifford, J., & Marcus, G. (Eds.). (1986). *Writing culture: The poetics and politics of ethnography*. Berkeley: University of California Press.

Cohen, S. (1973). *Folk devils and moral panics*. London: Paladin.

Corner, J. (1996). Reappraising reception: Aims, concepts and methods. In J. Curran & M. Gurevitch (Eds.), *Mass media and society* (2nd ed., pp. 280–304). London: Arnold.

Davies, K., Dickey, J., & Stratford, T. (Eds.). (1987). *Out of focus: Writings on women and the mass media*. London: The Women's Press.

Drotner, K. (1994). Ethnographic enigmas. *Cultural Studies, 8*(2), 341–357.

Dyer, R. (1992). *Only entertainment*. London: Routledge.

Dyer, R. (1993). *The matter of images: Essays on representation*. London: Routledge.

Dyer, R. (1997). *White*. London: Routledge.

Dyer, R. (2002). *Queers in film*. London: Routledge.

Emanuel, S. (1992). Ien Ang: Watching *Dallas*. In M. Barker & A. Beezer (Eds.), *Reading into cultural studies* (pp. 21–33). London: Routledge.

Ferguson, M., & Golding, P. (Eds.). (1997). *Cultural studies in question*. London: Sage.

Fiske, J. (1987). *Television culture*. London: Methuen.

Fiske, J. (1990). Ethnosemiotics: Some personal and theoretical reflections. *Cultural Studies, 4*(1), 85–99.

Fiske, J. (1991). For cultural interpretation: A study of the culture of homelessness. *Critical Studies in Mass Communication, 8*, 455–474.

Fiske, J., & Hartley, J. (1978). *Reading television*. London: Methuen.

Foucault, M. (1979). *Discipline and punish*. New York: Random House.

Foucault, M. (1980). *History of sexuality, Part I*. New York: Random House.

Fuss, D. (Ed.). (1991). *Inside/out: Lesbian theories, gay theories*. London: Routledge.

García Canclini, N. (1995). *Hybrid cultures*. Minneapolis: University of Minnesota Press. (Original work published 1990)

Geertz, C. (1973). *The interpretation of cultures*. New York: Basic Books.

Geertz, C. (1988). *Works and lives: The anthropologist as author*. Cambridge, UK: Polity. (Original work published 1983)

Geraghty, C. (1998). "Audiences" and "ethnography": Questions of practice. In C. Geraghty & D. Lusted (Eds.), *The television studies book* (pp. 141–157). London: Arnold.

Gillespie, M. (1995). *Television, ethnicity and social change*. London: Routledge.

Gilroy, P. (1987). *There ain't no black in the Union Jack*. London: Hutchinson.

Gray, A. (1992). *Video playtime: The gendering of a leisuer technology.* London: Routledge.

Gray, A. (1999). Audience and reception research in retrospect: The trouble with audiences. In P. Alasuutari (Ed.), *Rethinking the media audience* (pp. 22–37). London: Sage.

Greer, G. (1971). *The female eunuch.* London: Paladin.

Gripsrud, J. (1995). *The Dynasty years: Hollywood television and critical media studies.* London: Routledge.

Gripsrud, J. (Ed.). (1999). *Television and common knowledge.* London: Routledge.

Grossberg, L. (1992). *We gotta get out of this place: Popular conservatism and postmodern culture.* London: Routledge.

Grossberg, L. (1983–1984). The politics of youth culture: Some observations on rock and roll in American culture. *Social Text, 8,* 104–127.

Grossberg, L. (1986a). History, politics and postmodernism: Stuart Hall and cultural studies. *Journal of Communication Inquiry, 10*(2), 61–77.

Grossberg, L. (1986b). Is there rock after punk? *Critical Studies in Mass Communication, 3,* 50–74.

Hall, S. (1987). *"Minimal selves" in identity: The real me* (ICA Documents 6). London: ICA.

Hall, S., Critcher, C., Jefferson, T., Clarke, J., & Roberts, B. (Eds.). (1978). *Policing the crisis.* Basingstoke, UK: Macmillan.

Hall, S., Hobson, D., Lowe, R., & Willis, P. (Eds.). (1980). *Culture, media, language.* London: Hutchinson.

Hall, S., & Jefferson, T. (Eds.). (1976). *Resistance through rituals.* London: Hutchinson.

Hartley, J. (1999). *The uses of television.* London: Routledge.

Hartley, J. (2003) *A short history of cultural studies* London: Sage

Hermes, J. (1995). *Reading women's magazines: An analysis of everyday media use.* Cambridge, UK: Polity.

Hermes, J. (with Stello, C.). (2000). Cultural citizenship and crime fiction. *European Journal of Cultural Studies, 3*(2), 215–232.

Hoggart, R. (1958). *The uses of literacy.* Harmondsworth, UK: Penguin.

Hummel, R. (1995). Review of Jesus Martin-Barbero (1993) Communication, culture and hegemony: From the media to mediations. *Publizistik, 40*(2), 245.

Littlewood, J., & Pickering, M. (1998). Have you heard the one about the White middle-class, heterosexual father-in-law? Gender, ethnicity and political correctness in comedy. In S. Wagg (Ed.), *Because I tell a joke or two: Comedy, politics and social difference* (pp. 291–312). London: Routledge.

Lull, J. (1988). The audience as nuisance. *Critical Studies in Mass Communication, 5,* 239–243.

Lull, J. (1997). La "veracidad" política de Estudios Culturales [The political "truth" of cultural studies]. *Comunicación y Sociedad, 29,* 55–72.

Lull, J. (1998). Cultural studies in Mexico. *European Journal of Cultural Studies, 1*(3), 403–418.

Marcus, G. E., & Fischer, M. M. J. (Eds.). (1986). *Anthropology as cultural critique.* Chicago: University of Chicago Press.

Martín-Barbero, J. (1988). Communication from culture: The crisis of the national. *Media, Culture, and Society, 10*(4), 447–465.

Martín-Barbero, J. (1993). *Communication, culture and hegemony: From the media to mediations.* London: Sage.

Martín-Barbero, J. (1997). Cultural decentring and palimpsests of identity. *Media Development, 1,* 18–21.

Martín-Barbero, J. (2000). Transformations in the map: Identities and culture industries. *Latin American Perspectives, 27*(113), 27–48.

McNeil, M. (1998). De-centring or re-focusing cultural studies: A response to Handel K. Wright. *European Journal of Cultural Studies, 1*(1), 57–64.

McRobbie, A. (1982). Between talk, text and action. *Feminist Review, 12,* 46–57.

Mercer, K. (1994). *Welcome to the jungle: New positions in Black cultural studies.* London: Routledge.

Miller, T. (1998). *Technologies of truth: Cultural citizenship and the popular media*. Minneapolis: University of Minnesota Press.

Miller, T. (2001). Cultural citizenship. *Television and New Media, 2*(3), 183–186.

Morley, D. (1980). *The nationwide audience*. London: British Film Institute.

Morley, D. (1992). *Television, audiences and cultural studies*. London: Routledge. (Original work published 1981)

Morley, D. (1998). So-called cultural studies: Dead ends and reinvented wheels. *Cultural Studies, 12*(4), 476–497.

Morris, M. (1988a). Banality in cultural studies. *Block, 14,* 15–26.

Morris, M. (1988b). *The pirate's fiancee: Feminism, reading, postmodernism*. London: Verso.

Probyn, E. (1993). *Sexing the self: Gendered positions in cultural studies*. London: Routledge.

Probyn, E. (1996). *Outside belongings*. London: Routledge.

Probyn, E. (1997). New traditionalism and post-feminism: TV does the home. In C. Brunsdon, J. D'Acci, & L. Spigel (Eds.), *Feminist television criticism. A reader* (pp. 126-138). Oxford: Oxford University Press.

Radway, J. (1984). *Reading the romance: Women, patriarchy and popular literature*. Chapel Hill: University of North Carolina, Chapel Hill.

Radway, J. (1987). *Reading the romance: Women, patriarchy and popular literature* (2nd ed.). London: Verso.

Stein, L. (2002). Off topic: Oh my God, U.S. terrorism!: Roswell fans respond to 11 September. *European Journal of Cultural Studies, 5*(4), 471-491.

Skeggs, B. (1992). Paul Willis: Learning to labour. In M. Barker & A. Beezer (Eds.), *Reading into cultural studies* (pp. 181–196). London: Routledge.

Tomlinson, S. (2001). *Feminism and cultural studies*. London: Arnold.

Torres, R. D., Mirón, L. F., & Inda, J. X. (Eds.), *Race, identity, and citizenship: A reader*. Cambridge: Blackwell.

Waites, B., Bennett, T., & Martin, G. (Eds.). (1982). *Popular culture: Past and present*. London: Croom Helm.

Williams, R. (1963). *Culture and society: 1790–1950*. Harmondsworth, UK: Penguin.

Willis, P. (1980). *Learning to labour: How working class kids get working class jobs*. Farnborough, UK: Gower. (Original work published 1977)

Women's Studies Group. (Ed.). (1978). *Women take issue*. London: Hutchinson.

Wright, H. K. (1998). Dare we de-centre Birmingham? Troubling the "origin" and trajectories of cultural studies. *European Journal of Cultural Studies, 1*(1), 33–56.

13

EAST ASIAN MODERNITIES AND THE FORMATION OF MEDIA AND CULTURAL STUDIES

◆ Myungkoo Kang

In the past hundred years, East Asia, although being influenced by the West, achieved modernity in its own way and has a unique position and role in the world system. Japan has been in the center, South Korea and Taiwan have been in the semi-periphery, and China has been on the periphery struggling to capture a new position and role. Even on entering the 21st century, Japan has not been able to come out of its long-term depression. Due to the internally conservative and closed nature of Japanese nationalism, it has not been able to exercise political and cultural leadership commensurate with its economic size.

On the other hand, since it recently became a member of the World Trade Organization (WTO), China has been emerging as the single alternative force against U.S. hegemony; therefore, all countries have been paying attention to how China will change. The country is confronting a pivotal moment: Will it build a new empire that includes a Greater China economic bloc that, in turn, includes Southeast Asia, Taiwan, and the Philippines, as symbolized by the term *Greater China,* or will it play a role in constructing a peaceful global order while acting to limit U.S. hegemony?

If we take a close look at the map of the East Asian interior, it appears very difficult to group the countries into a single region other than for the reason of geographical proximity. When considering Confucian culture, East Asia must include Vietnam. North Korea and Mongolia do not figure easily on the map of East Asia because North Korea is half of the divided Korean peninsula that clings to its isolated socialist system and because Mongolia has a very underdeveloped economy. South Korea and North Korea are erstwhile cold war adversaries experiencing the pains of division. Taiwan, to China, is a part of China, but to those Taiwanese residents who argue for independence, it is not.

Despite such differences and geographical boundaries, within East Asia, the exchanges of finance, products, people, information, and culture have been rapidly increasing since the opening up of China and the collapse of the Soviet Union. Many East Asian people and the media have started to imagine East Asia as one regional community. In this regard, East Asia is a newly "imagined community."

Against this complex geopolitical background, this chapter will evaluate the accomplishments of critical media and cultural studies (MCS) in the past 20 some years in the region called "East Asia," in which, to reiterate, a new imagined community has been forming. However, just as research in other regions of the world cannot be tidily categorized as "North American MCS" and "European MCS," the phrase "East Asian media and cultural studies" is probably not an appropriate mapping. If the term *North American MCS* were used, many U.S. researchers would object, saying, "How can research in the United States be grouped into one category? It must be divided into subcategories." Canadian and Mexican researchers would certainly wish to talk about the special characteristics of their countries. If the term *European MCS* were used, there would be tumultuous criticism from European scholars, who would say how sharply different street culture is in Germany, France, and Britain. But to Western scholars, the categories "African," "Latin American," "Asian" and "European" do not sound abnormal. Keeping the politics of geopolitical mapping in mind, this review will take a look at the special characteristics of critical MCS in the past 20 some years, focusing on three localities:[1] Japan, Taiwan, and South Korea.

The next section looks back over the trajectories of the formative process of East Asian MCS. In it, I will examine how East Asian MCS identifies the formation of East Asian modernities in terms of the emergence of consumer society and consumer culture, as well as the formation of cultural identities mediated by communication industries in the era of globalization.

◆ Charting the Emergence of East Asian Media and Cultural Studies

This section raises two questions concerning the changes in East Asian MCS over the past 20 years:

1. Which research issues were prioritized?

2. Which particular features of MCS have Japan, South Korea, and Taiwan developed in response to their specific histories?

Research on media technologies—including newspapers, radio, television, and telecommunications—and on the media industries develops in response to their advances. It is axiomatic that media studies, always being an intellectual sphere connected to the media, are intimately related with the needs of the power structure and the communication industries.

Before World War II, Japanese newspaper studies mainly dealt with the social role of, and the propagandist use of, newspapers. After the war, due to the influence of the U.S. occupation, they changed to American-style social psychological public opinion studies (Yoshimi, 2001). Since the 1970s, in concert with changes in media industries, newspaper studies in Japan have begun to address journalism education and industry-oriented media studies—including theories of news production and audience surveys—and subsequently settled down as a mainstream trend in research. If we take a look at *The Fifty-Year History of the Japanese Society for Studies in Journalism and Mass Communication*, published by the society in commemoration of its 50th anniversary, topics such as media history, the content analysis of news, media responsibility, and ethics were the principal research tasks until the 1990s. From the 1980s, debate also got under way regarding the "information society."

Mori and Takaki (2000) have argued that Japanese researchers took British cultural studies as an alternative to microscopic media effects studies and to administrative research, but they did not see the local context out of which the agenda of British cultural studies emerged. Traditional mass communication studies and Japanese cultural studies, the other theoretical tendency, began in the mid-1980s. As an alternative to behaviorist and functionalist approaches to mass communication, which had previously dominated the scene, the approaches of Stuart Hall, David Morley, and John Fiske were introduced.

British cultural studies was not perceived as a theoretical attempt to supersede economic or class determinism in explaining the postwar British social order. As Hall's

study of Thatcherism demonstrated, British cultural studies tried to explain why workers supported Margaret Thatcher despite the fact that her economic and welfare policies worked against their class interests. Mori and Takaki (2000) point out that, due to its focus on theoretical discussion and its minimal concern with domestic cultural politics, Japanese cultural studies overwhelmingly focused on text-centered analyses, with an emphasis on ideological critique. When mapped as an interdisciplinary area, Japanese cultural studies was clearly distinct from deconstructionism, poststructuralism, and postmodernism, which were introduced into Japan as theories in literature and philosophy. Japan's researchers dealt with these European theories in the fields of art and philosophy, based on very promptly executed translations of such writers as Derrida and Baudrillard.

When British cultural studies was first brought into academic debates, literature and philosophy scholars expressed their doubt as to whether it made sense to have a separate cultural studies discourse about theories they had already introduced.[2] It was probably only after the main texts of European and American cultural studies of the 1990s were translated that Japanese cultural studies settled down institutionally.[3] After the phase of introducing foreign theories, Japanese cultural studies became interested in addressing the problems of the nation-state, memories of colonial history, and gender and sexuality—all of these in response to the changes taking place inside Japanese society, especially the long-term economic depression and the sudden increase in the power of conservative nationalism after the 1989 death of Emperor Hirohito.

A special feature of Japanese cultural studies is that it has fruitfully woven into its work the traditions of cultural critique that have developed since the very beginning of modern academic disciplines in Japan. By using the advances accumulated by cultural critique, Japanese cultural studies has deployed a methodological weapon called "historical analysis." For example, when working on the formation of urban consumption spaces, researchers use writings on urban culture done by Japanese cultural critics in the early 20th century. Good examples are Sangjung Kang's (1996) critique of Japanese Orientalism, Naoki Sakai's (1996) critique of Japanese nationalism, Chizuko Ueno's (1998) studies of the nation-state and Japanese patriarchy, Toshimaru Ogura's research on state violence, Shunya Yoshimi's (1992, 1999) analyses of consumer spaces and of the Japanese emperor system, and Yeonsuk Lee's (1996) perspectives on the national language. These are case studies that examine historically issues such as Japanese modernity and the nation-state, U.S. imperialism, and consumer culture.

At the same time, Japanese MCS is the response of critical intellectuals to a sense of crisis regarding the country's increasingly conservative culture, as well as to the historical revisionism that has been endeavoring to reformulate the history of modern Japan. The arenas for discussion among critical intellectuals were monthlies and quarterlies, rather than the purely academic realm. Such journals as *Thoughts, Impact, Modern Thoughts,* and *Situation* ran special issues on such topics as race, nationalism, and Japanese modernities. They addressed topics in a journalistic style, trying to communicate directly with the public instead of just with fellow academics.

After being liberated from Japanese colonial rule, South Korea and Taiwan achieved modernization through high economic growth, beginning in the 1960s. Until 1987, South Korea was under a military dictatorship, and until 1986, Taiwan was under permanent martial law. As a result of anticommunist policies, the media were subjected to stringent ideological control. Thus, within the realm of civil society, freedom of expression and freedom of the press were important rights that the public and journalists had to win through political struggle. Many journalists carried out protests to assert the freedom of the press, and this

became a tradition of the journalistic profession in both countries.[4] In the case of South Korea, however, in contrast to those reporters who struggled for the freedom of the press, there were also many others who, through cooperating with the power structure, succeeded in becoming government ministers, presidential chiefs of staff, and legislators.

In the latter half of the 1980s, the democratization processes in both South Korea and Taiwan at last sanctioned journalists' independent voice. Media studies, too, typically went through a number of changes as a result. Until the latter half of the 1980s, in Taiwan and South Korea, media studies had not been able to perform any significant research on journalism. From the beginning of the 1970s, researchers who came back to their own countries after receiving Ph.D. degrees in the United States taught the American liberal journalism model or devoted themselves to apolitical media effects studies (Xiu Qii Weng & Chong Gang Jing, 2000). Media researchers either kept silent or looked the other way in regards to the subjection of journalism to cold war ideologies.

Chen Bai Nian (2001) analyzed the topics of 295 media research proposals submitted to Taiwan's National Science Council from 1966 through 2000. He demonstrated that four issues had predominated in Taiwan's media studies for those 35 years. They were journalism and news media (14%), mass media effects and communication processes (14.2%), new media technologies (9.8%), and advertising, public relations, and marketing (8.1%). The subjects with the lowest frequencies were media ethics (0%), communication and gender (1.0%), international communication (1.4%), communication education (1.9%), and health communication (2.2%). The focus of research on journalism and news media was mainly media industry needs and production skills. Chen also showed that about 60% of the books on communication published over the previous 50 years had had an identical focus.[5]

Thus, in South Korea and Taiwan, due to the democratization movements that were strong from the mid-1980s, the dictatorial regimes could no longer control the public with cold war ideologies. In South Korea, a military dictatorship of more than 30 years' duration ended, and in Taiwan, the martial law system that had lasted for more than 40 years was dissolved. During this process, many new leftist theories from Europe and the United States were translated. Until the mid-1980s in South Korea and Taiwan, no leftist theory books, including even Marx and Engels's *Capital,* could be openly published or imported.[6] For both South Korea and Taiwan, the years 1986–1987 were a climactic moment in the move toward democratization. Coming in conjunction with the Soviet system's collapse, the ideological terrains became very complicated.

In the case of South Korea, many intellectuals and students concentrated on critical theories, and courses became available on both new and older leftist theories, including Marx's political economy. The social movements and intellectuals who, as their chief task against the military dictatorship, had struggled for democratization now sought alternative ideologies to fuel social reforms. As a result, the complicated ideological terrains of the early 1990s were generated. French poststructuralism, the Frankfurt school, British cultural studies, and postmodernist theories were all introduced at once. In South Korea, in 1986, Lee Sang-hee (1986) published a translated book under the title of *Critical Communication Theories,* which included theses introducing media political economy, cultural imperialism, semiotics, and other topics. Seizing on this opportunity, a great deal of MCS was translated through the first half of the 1990s. Theories of postmodernity became popular among intellectuals and students, so much so that Lyotard's (1984) *The Postmodern Condition* became a best-seller in 1992.

The U.S. communication debate between positivistic and critical researchers, signaled in 1983 by a special issue of the *Journal of Communication* titled "Ferment in the Field," surfaced in Korea in 1992 under the title "The South Korean Version of 'Ferment in the Field.'" The interesting thing here is that the South Korean version of the paradigm dispute did not focus on how South Korean media and cultural phenomena had been and should be researched. Rather, it concentrated on methodological and epistemological issues—including how the two paradigms are different and how the two research tendencies might be integrated—but imported the debate 100% as framed in the United States.

If we examine the panorama of South Korea's cultural studies, we see that MCS concentrated on introducing foreign theories and pursued its work separately from the grassroots popular culture movements that had formed a major feature of the democratization movement. From the 1970s on, these grassroots initiatives had intervened in social transformations in the cultural realm, centering on workers' and farmers' cultural movements. Even if these initiatives had failed through an excessive emphasis on class culture as a mechanical and deterministic formation, critical cultural studies did not attempt to generate a more adequate rendition of social reality and thereby wield any political impact. By choosing to operate separately from these initiatives, critical cultural studies made the mistake of introducing foreign theories or dealing with cultural formations on a strictly abstract level.

Cultural studies were busy just catching up with Western theories, as can be seen in the import of the postmodernism debate at the end of the 1980s and the importation of the modernity debate in the mid-1990s. It was not until the latter half of the 1990s that cultural studies research was carried out on such local and historical problematics as the Americanization of South Korean culture, the developmentalist mentality, and colonial modernity.

Cultural studies became actively institutionalized in Taiwan in 1993, when the

Asia Pacific Cultural Studies Center was established at the National Ching Hua University. This research institute has been engaged in such activities as the promotion of Asia-Pacific academic exchanges and expansion of the international cultural studies network. Good examples are the conferences organized under Kuan Hsing Chen's leadership, titled "Trajectories: Towards New Internationalist Cultural Studies" (1992 and 1995) and "Problematizing Asia: An International Forum" (1996). Taiwanese cultural studies can be largely divided into two activities—one that introduces cultural studies from Europe and America and one that investigates theoretically important issues in the Taiwanese context. The former is mainly composed of publications that introduce either the genealogy of Western cultural studies or postmodernism, gender and feminism, and postcolonialism. The latter comprises analyses of Taiwan's cultural phenomena and social structure. As can be seen in a special issue on cultural studies of the *Taiwan Journal of Social Studies* (Vol. 16, 2000), research on popular culture in Taiwanese and global contexts began from the end of the 1990s (Liao, 2000).

Viewed overall, South Korea's and Taiwan's critical MCS began at the end of the 1980s as a way to meet the hunger of the intellectual communities in these countries for critical theories, taking the democratization process as an opportunity to do so. It was only in the latter half of the 1990s that moves were made toward conducting research that analyzed and interpreted a variety of cultural phenomena in the local as well as global context. The *Inter-Asia Journal of Cultural Studies*, which started being published from 1999, has been playing the role of a forum, enabling networks of critical MCS researchers to form and explore common themes not only in East Asia but also in Southeast Asia.

From the above discussion, it becomes clear that East Asian MCS has formed its own special characteristics in the past 20 or so years while responding to the social situations that each society has had to face.

Japan has evinced a strong critical response to the sudden increase in power of postindustrial society and conservative democracy. Although in South Korea and Taiwan, critical MCS exhibited an excess of theories with few concerns about local historical realities, we must point out that many researchers had also been active in social movements.

By eagerly entering the journalists unions, media watch movements, and media reform movements, critical researchers have attempted to put their political visions into practice. The Solidarity for a Democratic Press movement and the Citizens' Alliance for Media Reform are the major engines of media reform activism in South Korea. In Taiwan, cultural studies provided the Taiwanese democratization movement with a theoretical foundation and carried out significant research on identity politics (with reference to Taiwan's independence), minority issues (including gender), and Japanese and American colonialism. These problematics came out of the historical realities faced by the Taiwanese, such as having been colonized by the Japanese, as well as the confrontations between and frustrations among native Taiwanese and the emigrants from Mainland China.

To look into how East Asian MCS responded to historical change within its own localities, the next two sections will examine the formation of consumer culture and the problematics of cultural identity, in relation to globalization in East Asia, mediated by the communication industries.

◆ The Coming of Modern Consumer Society and Consumer Culture

The question of when modern consumer society began in East Asia is an interesting and challenging one to ask. This is because, to answer it, one must first answer the questions of "What is consumption?" and

"What is the modern?" The answers to the question of what modern consumption refers to can be very different according to the theoretical positions adopted.

If we take a look at research on Western society, there have been two opposing assertions—one that modernity commenced in the 18th century and the other that it was in the 19th century. As regards consumption phenomena, which of their dimensions receives attention varies greatly with the century selected. U.S. researchers in the 1980s had a tendency to analyze the materials that they could straightforwardly access—including stores, exhibitions, and advertisements—whereas European researchers were interested in less visible forms of consumer behavior. Several researchers made no secret of their determination to critique consumerism rather than analyzing the phenomena themselves (Brewer & Porter, 1993; Campbell, 1989; Fox & Lears, 1983; McKendrick, Brewer, & Plumb, 1982).

Although there is no space here to argue in detail for the following assertions, there are some common characteristics of the beginning of consumer society. First, consumer society means that the majority of the citizens living in one society enjoy access, to a certain extent, to a diversity of consumer products. Also, the merchants introduce new marketing techniques to attract customers through exhibitions, advertisements, or other means. There are diverse retail networks connecting merchandisers and consumers. Second, in consumer society, not only does the market constantly change but also consumer behavior. It is when the consumers' behavior involved in purchasing goods gets intimately related to their own identities and is transformed into actions that give significant additional meaning to the products and their uses that a consumer society has begun. It is when the act of purchasing a product becomes an important part of the life of the consumer, rather than merely an aid to living, that simple consumption changes into a modern form of consumption.

Generating desire for products then becomes an important part of modern consumer culture, like the making of fads and fashions.

When seeking the origins of consumer society in East Asia, the general consumer culture tendencies in the West can be transposed with little problem. Although the cultural meanings of consumption—including the types of products, the formation of consumer groups, the relationships between the consumers and the products, and the signification of symbolic goods—will all appear different, we can assume that a few general features comprising modern consumer societies will be similar. However, while assimilating the West, East Asian consumer societies, in each country of East Asia, developed their own special characteristics. How East Asian modernities are different overall from Western modernity is beyond the scope of this chapter to consider. There is, however, no case of any non-Western society assimilating Western modernity 100%. When looking into the formation of East Asian consumer societies, each nation created a modern consumer society by hybridizing or adapting Western consumer culture according to its own socioeconomic conditions.

Research on the historical formation of Japanese consumer society finds it to have emerged after going through two world wars. Urban culture started to develop in Tokyo and Osaka in the 1880s. By the 1930s, a modern urban culture began to sediment. This urban culture was characterized by an elementary level of consumerism. Because a middle class was not fully formed in Japan, the younger generation and the elite class were leaders of the new urban popular cultural scenario. According to Maruyama Masao (1965), in the 1920s, a "privatized individualism," denoted by the everyday expressions "educated loafers" (*Kootoo Yumin*) and "tormented youths" (*Hammon-Seinen*), was common. Through popular music and sports—such as jazz and baseball—the youngsters of Tokyo and Osaka assimilated the nihilistic and hedonistic mass culture of the West as their own.

Japanese society went through the shock of losing the Asia-Pacific war, but in the 1950s and 1960s, the country experienced an unprecedentedly high degree of economic growth. During this period, the middle class got bigger, and thus a wide range of people entered into consumer society. In the latter half of the 1970s, Japan actually became an affluent society, luxury-item consumers emerged, and extravagant food, brand-name clothes, furniture, and home decor were on their shopping lists. In the West, consumer culture had expanded from the upper class to the middle class and then to the lower strata. In contrast, in Japan, it was young people who initiated consumer culture, and the older middle class followed their lead. Mita (1992) describes Japanese society from the mid-1970s until the beginning of 1990s as the "Age of Fiction." During this period, rapid economic growth ended and the economy became stable with zero percent growth.

Yoshimi (1992) identified the characteristics of Japanese consumer culture in late capitalist society in his studies of historical changes in Tokyo's urban spaces. According to him, Tokyo Disneyland, which opened its doors in 1983, was a typical expression of the fantasizing consumer reality that the Age of Fiction represented. It was an artificially constructed entity perfectly detached from external realities and a space in which hyperreality was materialized. Yoshimi established how Tokyo has historically developed a variety of symbolic spaces. Through tracing the transitions from the Asakusa district to the Ginza district, and then from Shinjuku to Shibuya districts, he has shown that the high-growth period was represented by Shinjuku and the Age of Fiction by Shibuya. In actuality, the whole Shibuya district is a space that embodies a hyperreal sensibility. Shibuya Street, in and of itself, is an enormous amusement park like Disneyland. It is, Yoshimi claimed, a space that excludes all that is unattractive and unclean and a space that is repelled by the activity of getting dirty and laboring to produce something.

According to Iwabuchi (2001), the leaders of Japan's consumer society at the beginning of the 1980s were called a "new human species." Although the term was not precisely defined, they were a counterpart of America's yuppies. As is well known, the term *yuppies* referred to a new city-dwelling affluent class in their 20s and 30s with a higher education and working in professional fields. Japan's "new human species" had several noticeable characteristics: (a) putting their individual interests and values first, (b) having extreme consumer preferences and expressing passionate likes and dislikes, and (c) having a powerful desire to assert one's individual identity.

Entering upon an affluent society with these particular traits, Japanese consumers began asking from the 1980s onwards, "What are we?" instead of just following Western consumer lifestyles. Pride in Japan as a country that makes the best electronics products now shifted to asking the meaning of Japaneseness. Notions of an "electronic nation" and "techno-nationalism" (Yoshimi, 1999) emerged in response, along with a postmodern consumer sensibility. From the beginning of the 1980s, the Mizukoshi Department Store started having product exhibitions, including an annual festival of Japanese traditional goods. Simultaneously, throughout Japanese society, the so-called *Matsuri bumu* (festival boom) blossomed.

Along with the formation of urban consumer cultural spaces with strong postmodern features, traditional culture festivals and Japanese products conveying traditional cultural tastes started getting popular among consumers. The special characteristics of this change in consumer culture in modern and postmodern Japan can be briefly outlined. Firstly, within the period of rapid economic growth of the 1960s and 1970s and the affluent society period beginning in the 1980s, new urban consumption spaces emerged: Shinjuku and Shibuya Streets were spaces that responded to rapid industrialization. The Shibuya district created a postmodern space that excludes any kind of ugliness and dirtiness, including labor and the act of manufacturing—a kind of space that is difficult to find, even in the West. Secondly, differently from the Western path by which the expansion of consumer culture took place—historically, from the upper to the lower class—the youth stratum, who wanted to express their identities through consumption, led Japanese consumer culture and, later, the middle class to adopt certain kinds of consumer behavior. Thirdly, postmodern consumer culture unfolded at the same time as the revival of Japan's traditional culture. The revival of traditional festivals and the revival of traditional costumes, furniture, interior decorations, everyday products, and food occurred at the same time. Instead of being a flawed imitation, a form of hybridized consumer culture appeared after accepting—but changing—the Western sensibility, confirming the cultural identity of Japaneseness.

If I were to add one more remark here, though, with regard to the diversity and quality of consumer products, the Japanese consumer market demonstrates a very high standard. At the same time, a large majority of the consumers display collective, uniform, consumption patterns.[7]

Whereas Japanese consumer society took shape at the beginning of the 20th century, South Korea and Taiwan experienced historical transformations distinct from that. As Japan's consumer culture was in its early formation, both were Japanese colonies. Under colonialism, consumer cultures were limited to a handful of urban upper-class groups.[8] After liberation in 1945, both South Korea and Taiwan were incorporated into the cold war order both politically and militarily. At the beginning of the 1960s, however, both societies entered the modernization on-ramp, based on export-centered, high-level economic growth. From 1961 to 1990, in contrast to the advanced capitalistic countries that achieved, on average, 2% to 3% annual growth during the same period, South Korea and Taiwan achieved nearly 10%. Indeed, in the 1970s, Taiwan

recorded exceptionally high-speed growth at an annual average of more than 20%. In tandem, people's consumption level continued to soar, too. Both societies became consumer societies in the 1980s, and from the end of this decade, they even became high-level consumer societies. Noticeably, instead of the products purchased, the very act of shopping itself became an important aspect of consumer culture. A postmodern consumer culture settled down, which appropriated symbols embedded in goods, through which people expressed themselves and formed their identities. In both localities, youth consumer culture became prominent. In Seoul and Taipei, just as in Japan a decade earlier, complex consumer culture spaces were constructed for young people to hang out.

According to *Taipei Review* (September 25, 2001), Taiwan's 15 to 25 age group, accounting for 25% of the total population, had reached 5 million. They were then spending a monthly average per head of about U.S.$29, totaling U.S.$1.74 billion, on consumption and entertainment. Their preferred locations included chain restaurants, internet cafés, karaoke parlors, and movie theaters. Thus, young people emerged in Taiwan as the category spearheading the consumer economy and consumer culture.

In the 1990s, thanks to the revival of the Asian economies (also including Singapore, Thailand, and Malaysia), consumer cultures in those countries also expanded and debates proliferated regarding young people's excessive consumerism (Chua, 2001). Describing the new generation as "Generations X and Z" and "new, new generation," its critics argued that, unlike the older generations who came from poverty, the present generation knew nothing of frugal ways, only about physical indulgence, and was immersed in materialism. Chua (1996), however, asserted that, even if these new generations were not frugal compared to their parents' generation, they were behaving rationally as regarded consumption and family budgets. This debate reflected a generation gap. The older generations had experienced quantum changes in terms of their living standards, from poverty to abundance. The young generation had no experience of poverty. At the same time, the debate showed that the relationship between the old and the young had been influenced by a Confucianist system of values. It further showed that the consumer culture realm, which is a site of the politics of self-expression and self-identity concerning how to live one's life, is a contested field in which different generational experiences and values clash and are negotiated.

With regard to how to view changes in consumer society from the perspective of cultural politics, cultural studies in South Korea and Taiwan did not produce locally contextualized research. In the case of South Korea, most research on consumer culture was content simply to introduce Western theories. Books by Baudrillard (1983), Featherstone (1995), Jameson (1991), and Haug (1986) were the most quoted. Whichever Western theory was used, many studies of consumer culture operated from the simple logic that monopoly capitalism creates the ideology called "desire" and generates consumer culture. Examples are the Lotte Department Store analysis (N. H. Kang, 1995), Seoul's city spaces (Kim, 1994), and youth consumer culture (Ju, 1994). These studies' basic framework imposed Western concepts on local phenomena. A typical argument, for example, was to say that that the representations of the female body shown in advertisements or television dramas have been dominated by capitalistic desires or that the everyday lifeworld has been colonized by monopoly capital. Local cultural studies researchers imported not only theoretical concepts but also even the research questions.

The theoretical framework for approaching postmodern consumer culture and its desires provided South Korean researchers with a set of concepts to analyze and critique consumer cultural phenomena. Yet the conditions of life of young South

Koreans are very different from those in America and Europe. The extremely competitive examinations for college entrance, the authoritarian family and school cultures, and the obsession with academic credentials are all diffused throughout the society, affecting the deepest personal identities of young people, even if they share superficially similar consumer cultures. In these studies, there were no considerations of such historical and everyday realities. They simply borrowed questions raised by Western studies of consumer culture.

Critiques of the desires created by urban consumer spaces followed the same logic. From the outside, the department stores and Apkujeongdong Street in Seoul appear havens of postmodern consumerism. However, the material foundation that produced such spaces and the lifeworlds of the consumers are very different. The regimes of desire created by the compressed modernization of the past 30 years could not but be different from the forms of consumption by Western consumers, which were shaped over two to three centuries. But these studies gave no consideration to the contrasts between such historically formative processes. I myself have characterized South Korea as a "postmodern consumer culture without postmodernity" (M. Kang, 1999).

In this chapter, the research accomplishments of MCS regarding consumer society and consumer culture have been evaluated as a form of East Asian intellectual modernity. Although the consumer culture of Japan, South Korea, and Taiwan followed the general pattern of capitalist modernity, the production and consumption processes exhibited different features. Japan was the first society to achieve its own non-Western modernity. With the shift from industrial capitalism to postcapitalist society, the form of consumer culture changed from the era of dreams to the era of hyperreal fiction. As it did so, simultaneously a demand for self-identity rose to the surface, a blending of both Japanese tradition and postmodernity.

In the cases of South Korea and Taiwan, although jointly experiencing compressed modernization, there has not been much empirical research about consumer society and consumer culture. As already argued, most studies were content either to introduce or mechanically apply consumer culture theories produced in the West. Recently, in both localities, the assertion has become more insistent that the global and local dialectics mediated in consumer cultures must be researched (Chua, 2001; Hsia, 1995).

As already pointed out by Appadurai (1990), Hall (1991), Dirlik (1996), and others, although the proposition is logical that research must examine the dialectics of the global and the local in forming and changing the cultures of regions, the actual task is not an easy one. The reason is that aspects of the multiple modernities manifest in consumer culture must first be analyzed, and then specific global and local details must be articulated with that analysis.

◆ East Asian Media Industries and Cultural Identities in the Era of Globalization

The objective of this section is to examine changes in the media industries and the problem of cultural identity in East Asia, within the problematics of globalization and postcolonialism. Changes in Asian media industries from the 1990s to the present can be placed in three categories. First, there is their expansion. Second, although American cultural products increased their presence, inside the Asian region, exchanges grew significantly of film and television programs, records, computer games, and comics. Third, there were not only exchanges of cultural products inside the region but also industrial exchanges in a variety of forms, including joint productions, joint ventures, and intraregional direct investment.

Generally, since 1980, the main topics of conversation within visual media industry circles have been synergy, convergence, and deregulation. Over the past two decades, the telecommunications, cable, satellite, television, and film industries have given birth to multimedia giants through many types of merger (Thussu, 2000). The massive investments required to become major players in the global market were what basically powered these industrial changes. These global market changes have equally extended to Asia, stimulated by the market potential of its media and cultural industries. In the early 2000s, dozens of regional international satellite systems covered Asia's sky. Cable and satellite television services were already operating in nearly all countries. With Star TV beginning its broadcasting from Hong Kong in the 1990s, American cable channels became available such as CNN1, ESPN, and HBO (Chan, 1994, 1996).

Secondly, together with these global market changes, trade between Asian media and cultural industries was greatly invigorated. As Sepstrup's (1989) analysis of Europe and Straubhaar's (1997) analysis of the global market both showed, in Asia too, instead of America's industry conquering the world, regional industries expanded simultaneously. Chan (1994), Barker (1999), and Hong (1999) showed that in the 1990s, the television programs of Asian countries interpenetrated. It is an undisputed fact that a new "geocultural market" (Straubhaar, 1997) emerged in which Japan's movies, music, and cartoons entered Asia; South Korean movies, music, and TV drama entered Taiwan and China; and Taiwan's and Hong Kong's movies and TV drama flowed into and out of China. A representative illustration is the Phoenix Satellite Service, which connects China, Taiwan, Hong Kong, and Southeast Asia. This was created through a joint venture between Star TV, two Hong Kong firms, and a mainland China firm (Chan, 1996). There were claims that Phoenix had captured second place among mainland Chinese viewers.

Regarding the kinds of cultural influences such changes in media and cultural industries might exert, Western scholars and many Asian scholars hold the view that globalization cannot be explained by the concept of cultural imperialism (Ito, 1990; Lee, Yoon, & Sohn, 2001). The critique of the cultural imperialism thesis is based on the following arguments. Firstly, there is the active audience theory, as put forward by Morley (1980), Fiske (1989), and Ang (1990), which insists that non-Western audiences do not passively consume the contents of programs but that they either appropriate them on their own terms or generate resistant interpretations. Secondly, scholars such as Featherstone (1995) and Tomlinson (1999) have embraced a post-colonialist or postmodernist perspective, proposing that cultural products imported into Asia get hybridized with local cultural elements, thereby generating new meanings. Thirdly, there is the thesis that globalization means not just the West expanding into the rest of the world but also Asian countries having active exchange with each other.

Indeed, we do often find that regional and local media markets have been growing. Another tenable claim is that national culture does not change easily and that cultural screens operate in the process of importing foreign programs. As the hybridization theory maintains, the thesis is feasible that every culture mingles and interacts with others to create a new one. These theories and data do not negate the fact, however, that colonialism was a powerful influence during the earlier formation of the modernities of East Asia.

On the other hand again, the contradictions of late capitalism are also growing, such as materialistic consumption, self-realization through acquisition, environmentally destructive economic growth, much more competition than cooperation, globally expanding inequality, and American-style business streamlining that focuses solely on the value of efficiency. These contradictions are what we describe as part of the tissue of the worldwide dominance of neoliberal capitalism, which regulates and influences the lives of most of us in this modern era when rapid globalization is continuing apace.

Even as regards news, documentary programs, and TV dramas, it has become a global cultural commonplace that people want to realize themselves through consumer commodities. The neoliberal corporate culture and work ethos that put productive efficiency before human welfare have become global. The most important thing is that Western modernity still serves as a reference point for almost every nation in Asia concerning the process of establishing and developing social institutions and operational rule making. This is what we call the "coloniality," which wields powerful influence over the formation of Asian modernity. This is a much larger issue than simply asserting that Hollywood movies are dominating Asian film markets or that McDonald's and Coca-Cola are standardizing Asian youngsters' tastes. It is more involved with fundamental questions such as the whole way of life that defines the conditions of human existence, how we live, and how we realize ourselves.

Japanese television programs and local tastes are strongly supported. The Mitzukoshi Department Store in Tokyo has innumerable kinds of foods, clothes, and furniture with the flavor of Japanese traditional culture. Many young people in Hong Kong continue to enjoy oolong tea, whereas many others drink Coca-Cola. Their lifestyles, however, such as their tendency to realize themselves through materialistic consumption—isn't that what we should mean by *culture*?—are all the same wherever you are. It is undeniable that materialistic and capitalistic lifestyles are the leading paradigm of our lives at the global level. More important, this paradigm is not being forced on us but is learned of our own free will. So it is not imperialist coercion. People do not refuse long working hours and are ready to sacrifice their own free time for material consumption. People work hard to consume more and to possess more. They are constantly worrying in case they get laid off from their companies, and when they lose their jobs, the whole family is thrown into crisis.[9] It is not just a matter of McDonaldization or how many hamburgers we have. It is more about the whole world accepting American-style culture, based as it is on consumption, a materialistic mode of self-realization, and the productivity-centered ethos of business and other organizations. The United States has been the frame of reference for the East Asian way of life as well as providing models for ways of operating social institutions.

Lastly, the hybridization thesis makes sense in part. There is no doubt that hybridity always occurs in the process of cultural exchange because we human beings are not stupid. One culture cannot simply dominate another. Each culture creates its own forms by appropriating aspects of other cultures. The hybridization thesis is tenable, including the proposition of "no cultural domination." However, an unequal relationship still exists in terms of social and cultural exchanges between the West and East Asia.

The historical opposition between the West and the rest still continues. What forms of modernity other than the Western model can we imagine? This is beyond the issue of how television viewers in non-Western societies appropriate or consume American television dramas. The crucial question is where alternative forms of modernity are to be found. East Asian critical MCS researchers always have a feeling of powerlessness vis-à-vis Western influence whenever they are pursuing alternative forms for their own societies. The West is not the "other" they can work together with on an equal footing but the model that non-Westerners always try to emulate.

◆ **Conclusion: Reconstructing East Asian Media and Cultural Studies**

For the past 20 years, MCS in the region has produced a number of texts on ideology and cultural representation through textual analysis and audience studies. Postmodernist theories and the Gramscian theory of hegemony have been introduced as the dominant theoretical frameworks. In addition, diverse, loosely connected intellectual constructs—such as the politics of the image, fantasy, and desire; the politics of representation; and the politics of space and location—were introduced simultaneously into the local intellectual arenas. Not only were concepts and theories imported but research questions, too. East Asian MCS has actively addressed new problematics and social realities—the formation of consumer society, the politics of the body and desire, and the identities of gender, ethnicity, and class—by employing sophisticated theories from metropolitan nations. Having said this, more often than not, East Asian MCS have dealt with the emerging politics of consumer culture and gender at abstract and generalized levels. In other words, by predominantly engaging in the theoretical construction of consumer and youth culture as well as gendered identity formation, East Asian cultural studies scholars have failed in large part to effectively contextualize local concerns and issues. Their work can be plugged into any industrialized modern or postmodern setting.

At the very end of this chapter, a number of important questions can be raised. Given that the state is still the dominant player and omnipresent disciplinary force in the arena of politics, culture, and the media in East Asia, any viable MCS should tackle its role and its mobilization of nationalisms, localisms, and cultural traditions. In which ways can MCS critique the deep-seated, "state-centered" cultures of East Asia? How can MCS diagnose the rampant "developmentalism" that has served as an essential part of state-driven economic development and state-centric ways of thinking, as well as their influence over the daily behavior of citizens? In which ways can MCS contribute to opening up new horizons regarding the democratic use of the media and more nuanced cultural politics? How can MCS critique the top-down mobilization of nationalism? I think that East Asian MCS has not effectively answered these vexing questions yet. After critically reviewing the lack of context-bound intellectual and political concerns in East Asian MCS, this study argues that MCS needs to embrace the historical dimension and be more self-reflexive. Such a historicized MCS comes out of concrete local contexts and not from borrowed theories or questions. Historical research requires that MCS look into the complex terrain of culture and everyday life, which is shaped by rapid historical shifts and particular sociopolitical struggles in the East Asian region.

◆ Notes

1. The reason why I am writing *three localities* instead of *three nations* here is as follows. First, South Korea is divided from North Korea. Regarding Taiwan, there is the position of the Chinese government that it is a province of China, but there are a significant number of Taiwanese residents who argue for the independence of Taiwan. After I told a Chinese professor, in order to obtain materials about the present condition of media studies in China, that I was planning to conduct a review of research in China, Taiwan, Japan, and South Korea, I received a letter back insisting that I could not deal with Taiwan separately as it is part of China. At a point in time when I was regretting being unable to review Chinese scholarship because getting materials from there was difficult, this letter made me even more uncertain how to proceed. Anyway, I make it clear here that the absence of China's media and cultural studies from this chapter is due to my lack of information sources.

2. According to a personal conversation with Professor Yoshimi, during a cultural studies conference in 1995 at Tokyo University at which Stuart Hall had made a keynote speech, these researchers in European philosophical theory and literature had presented an opposing view, arguing that the deconstructionism and poststructuralism that they had

been researching since the 1970s were now suddenly being reintroduced under the heading of "cultural studies."

3. If we take a look at the timing of the translation and introduction of a few important cultural studies books, in the 1980s, translations appeared of Richard Hoggart's *The Uses of Literacy* (1957 [1984]), Raymond Williams's *The Long Revolution* (1961 [1983]), Paul Willis's *Learning to Labor* (1977 [1985]), and Edward Said's *Orientalism* (1978 [1986]). In the 1990s, we can mention James Clifford and George Marcus's *Writing Culture* (1986 [1996]), Jeffrey Weeks's *Sexuality* (1986 [1996]), and Trinh T. Minh-ha's *When the Moon Waxes Red* (1991 [1996]). (The first date given is the original publication year, and the second date in brackets is the translation year.)

4. Western media studies have considered press freedom in terms of governments' control of the press. They have little interest in the fact that many journalists have struggled to assert their journalistic freedom in opposition to authoritarian regimes. As a result, in Third World journalism, as depicted by Western media studies, there are only oppressive political powers but no journalists who resist them and act independently.

5. These findings come from an analysis of the themes of books published on communication in Taiwan since the Newspaper Institute graduate program was established at the National University of Politics in 1954. According to the analysis, the studies were mostly on applied subjects, whereas studies related to human communication, the philosophy of communication, or oral communication were very rare.

6. When I was returning home to South Korea in 1987 after finishing my studies in the United States, a customs officer confiscated two books: Marx and Engels's *Capital* (Marx, 1886) and Althusser's *Reading Capital* (Althusser & Balibar, 1968).

7. This was pointed out not by a Japanese scholar but by a Western researcher, John Clammer. For example, although the fashion magazines introduce diverse styles and the latest popular fashions, nearly all Japanese men prefer black suits. As Clammer accurately pointed out, instead of purchasing a product to express

themselves, for the Japanese, clothes must not only be clean and tidy but also must express their gender, occupation, and position. At the same time, however, they must not be too different from those worn by others. When playing golf, golf gear must be worn; mountain-climbing clothes are worn while mountain climbing; and skiwear is worn on ski slopes (Clammer, 1997).

8. The assertion has been made that during the colonial period, modern mass culture became Americanized and significant consumer appetites became visible (Yoo, 2000). I believe that this was a phenomenon limited to a particular group. It is not tenable to assert that a consumer society and consumer culture formed under Japanese colonialism.

9. The suicide rate among Japanese in their 50s is the world's highest. About 6,000 people in their 50s kill themselves every year. Most of them do so in response to losing their jobs. In comparison, 6,000 people die each year in Japan from heart disease and 4,000 from strokes (*Yearbook of Social Indicators*, 2000).

◆ References

Althusser, L., & Balibar, E. (1968). *Reading Capital*. London: Gresham.

Ang, I. (1990). *Desperately seeking the audience*. London: Routledge.

Appadurai, A. (1990). Disjuncture and difference in the global cultural economy. *Theory, Culture and Society, 7*(2–3), 295–311.

Barker, C. (1999). *Television, globalization and cultural identities*. Milton Keynes, UK: Open University Press.

Baudrillard, J. (1983). *Simulations*. New York: Semiotext(e).

Brewer, J., & Porter, R. (Eds.). (1993). *Consumption and the world of goods*. London: Routledge.

Campbell, C. (1989). *The romantic ethic and the spirit of modern consumerism*. London: Routledge.

Chan, J. (1994). Media internationalization in China: Processes and tensions. *Journal of Communication, 44*(3), 70–88.

Chan, J. (1996). Television in Greater China: Structure, exports, and market formation. In J. Sinclair, E. Jacka, & S. Cunningham (Eds.), *New patterns in global television: Peripheral vision* (pp. 127–161). Oxford, UK: Oxford University Press.

Chen Bai Nian. (2001). The National Science Council research proposals in communication studies, 1966–2000: A preliminary analysis. *Journalism Studies, 67*, 1–24.

Chua, B. (1996). Culturalisation of economics and politics in Singapore. In R. Robinson (Ed.), *Pathways to Asia* (pp. 87–107). Sydney, Australia: Allen & Unwin.

Chua, B. (Ed.). (2001). *Consumption in Asia lifestyles and identities*. London: Routledge.

Clammer, J. R. (1997). *Contemporary urban Japan: A sociology of consumption*. New York: Blackwell.

Clifford, J., & Marcus, G. (1986). *Writing culture: The poetics and politics of ethnography*. Berkeley: University of California Press.

Dirlik, A. (1996). The global in the local. In R. Wilson & W. Dissayanake (Ed.), *Global/local* (pp. 21–45). Durham, NC: Duke University Press.

Featherstone, M. (1995). *Undoing culture: Globalization, postmodernism and identity*. London: Sage.

Ferment in the field [Special issue]. (1983). *Journal of Communication, 33*(3).

The fifty-year history of the Japanese Society for Studies in Journalism and Mass Communication. Tokyo: Japanese Society for Studies in Journalism and Mass Communication.

Fiske, J. (1989). *Understanding popular culture*. Boston: Unwin Hyman.

Fox, R., & Lears, T. J. (Eds.). (1983). *The culture of consumption: Critical essays on American History, 1880–1980*. New York: Cambridge University Press.

Hall, S. (1991). The local and the global: Globalization and ethnicity. In A. D. King (Ed.), *Culture, globalization and the world system: Contemporary conditions for the representation of identity* (pp. 19–40). London: Macmillan.

Haug, W. F. (1986). *Critique of commodity aesthetics: Appearance, sexuality and advertising*. Cambridge, UK: Polity.

Hoggart, R. (1957). *The uses of literacy.* London: Penguin.

Hong, J. (1999). Globalization and change in Taiwan's media: The interplay of political and economic forces. *Asian Journal of Communication, 9*(2), 39–58.

Hsia, C.-J. (1995). Taiwanese cities and society in the global economy. *Taiwan: A Radical Quarterly in Social Studies, 20,* 57–102.

Ito, Y. (1990). The trade winds change: Japan's shift from an information importer to an information exporter, 1965–1985. In J. A. Anderson (Ed.), *Communication yearbook 13* (pp. 430–465). Newbury Park, CA: Sage.

Jameson, F. (1991). *Postmodernism: On the logic of late capitalism.* Durham, NC: Duke University Press.

Ju, E. (1994). New generation and consumer culture in 1990s Korea. *Economy and Society (Seoul), 21,* 58–77.

Kang, M. (1999). Postmodern consumer culture without postmodernity: Copying the crisis of signification. *Cultural Studies, 13*(1), 18–33.

Kang, N. H. (1995). Space, body power: Everyday life in Apgujung Street. *Seoul: Cultural Science, 11,* 13–27.

Kang, S. (1996). *Beyond Orientalism.* Tokyo: Iyanami Publishing Co.

Kim, W. (1994). Consumption and everyday life within global capitalism. *Space and Society, 4,* 78–91.

Koichi, I. (2001). Uses of Japanese popular culture: Trans/nationalism and postcolonialLee, C., Yoon, T., & Sohn, S. (2001, September). *Reception of South Korean satellite television: In-depth interview with Korean-Chinese in Yanbian.* Paper presented at the "Transnational Program Flow and National Images, Identities in the Era of Globalization" conference, Seoul, South Korea.

Lee, S. (Ed. & Trans.). (1986). *Critical communication theories.* Seoul: Hangil.

Liao, P. (2000, October). *Theorizing the 90s: How not to talk about Taiwan in terms of the world system, global cultural economy, etc.* Paper presented at the 5th Annual Conference on the History and Culture of Taiwan, University of California, Los Angeles.

Lyotard, J.-F. (1984). *The postmodern condition: A report on knowledge.* Minneapolis: University of Minnesota Press.

Maruyama, M. (1965). Patterns of individualism and the case of Japan: A conceptual scheme. In M. Jansen (Ed.), *Changing Japanese attitudes toward modernization* (pp. 127–143). Princeton, NJ: Princeton University Press.

Marx, K. (1886). *Marx/Engels selected works* (Vol. 1). Moscow: Progress Publishers.

McKendrick, N., Brewer, C., & Plumb, J. H. (1982). *The birth of a consumer society: The commercialization of eighteen century England.* Bloomington: Indiana University Press.

Minh-ha, T. T. (1991). *When the moon waxes red: Representation, gender and cultural politics.* London: Routledge.

Mita, M. (1992). *Social psychology of modern Japan.* London: Kegan Paul International.

Mori, Y., & Takaki, O. (2000). Introducing cultural studies to Japan. In *Translators' introduction to British cultural studies: An introduction by Graeme Turner* (pp. 2–31). London: Routledge.

Morley, D. (1980). *The "Nationwide" audience: Structure and decoding.* London: British Film Institute.

National Institute of Population and Social Security Research. (2000). *Selected demographic indicators for Japan.* Tokyo: National Institute of Population and Social Security Research.

Said, E. (1978). *Orientalism.* New York: Pantheon.

Sakai, N. (1996). *Aborting Japanese language and Japanese.* Tokyo: New Light Publishing.

Sepstrup, P. (1989). Research into international television flows: A methodological contribution. *European Journal of Communication, 4,* 132–144.

Straubhaar, J. (1997). Distinguishing the global, regional and national levels of world television. In A. Sreberny-Mohammadi, D. Winseck, J. McKenna, & O. Boyd-Barrett (Eds.), *Media in a global context: A reader* (pp. 284–298). London: Arnold.

Thussu, D. K. (2000). *International communication: Continuity and change.* London: Arnold.

Tomlinson, J. (1999). *Globalization and culture.* Chicago: University of Chicago Press.

Ueno, C. (1998). *Nationalism and gender.* Tokyo: Paranto Co.

Weeks, J. (1986). *Sexuality.* Chichester, UK: Ellis Horwood.

Williams, R. (1961). *The long revolution.* Westport, CT: Greenwood.

Willis, P. (1977). *Learning to labor: How working class kids get working class jobs.* New York: Columbia University Press.

Xiu Qii Weng & Chong Gang Jing. (2000). Changes of epistemological models in communication studies. In *A case study of research proposals 84–99 for the National Social Council.* Taipei: National Cheng-Chi University.

Yoo, S. (2000). Americanization of Korean popular culture. *Media and Society, 17,* 28–39.

Yoshimi, S. (1992). Consuming "America": From symbol to system. In B.-H. Chua (Ed.), *Consumption in Asia: Lifestyles and identities* (pp. 202–224). London: Routledge.

Yoshimi, S. (1999). The cultural politics of the mass-mediated emperor system in Japan. In P. Gilroy, L. Grossberg, & A. McRobbie (Eds.), *Without guarantees: In honor of Stuart Hall* (pp. 395–415). London: Verso.

Yoshimi, S. (2001). The development of newspaper studies in the discursive space of 1930s Japan. Paper presented to the conference "New Dimensions of Cultural Studies," Chunchon, South Korea.

PART III

ECONOMY
AND POWER

14

MEDIA ECONOMICS

◆ Alan B. Albarran

M edia economics is a field of study that has experienced considerable growth and development over the past 40 years. Miller and Gandy (1991) identified 351 articles published between 1965 and 1988 in several key journals (the *Journal of Broadcasting and Electronic Media, Journalism and Mass Communication Quarterly,* and the *Journal of Communication*) that focused on "some economic aspect of communication" (p. 663).

Media economics involves the application of economic theories, concepts, and principles to study the macroeconomic and microeconomic aspects of mass media companies and industries. Concomitant with the increasing consolidation and concentration across the media industries, media economics emerged as an important area of study for academicians, policymakers, and industry analysts. Media economics literature encompasses a variety of methodological approaches involving both qualitative and quantitative methods and statistical analysis, as well as studies using financial, historical, and policy-driven data.

This chapter focuses on the topic of media economics by organizing itself around four separate sections. The first section examines the historical development of the field of media economics, tracing its roots to the founding of economics. The second section centers on theoretical and methodological dimensions of media economics. The third section addresses concepts important to the study of media economics. The fourth and final section reviews contemporary issues confronting media economics scholars. Illustrations will be drawn from the United States.

◆ Economics: Historical Development

To understand the historical development of the field of media economics, one must first begin with the study of economics itself. The initial literature on economic thinking began to evolve in the time period between 1500 and 1800, with much of the early work occurring in Western Europe (Landreth & Colander, 1989).

Mercantilism represents the earliest form of economic thought, originating in the 16th century. Mercantilists equated a nation's wealth with the accumulation of gold and silver. If nations lacked mines, they could acquire the precious metals via trade and commerce. This led to political intervention in the market via tariffs and subsidies, elevating commercial interests to national policy.

Physiocrats, a group of philosophers in 18th-century France, rejected mercantilism in favor of agriculture and called for a policy of laissez-faire, or minimal government intervention in the market. The physiocrats were among the first to view the economy as a constant flow of input and output.

Philosopher/scholar Adam Smith is credited with providing one of the first syntheses of economic thought with a collection of writings in 1776 commonly referred to as *The Wealth of Nations* (Smith, 1937). Smith defined land, labor, and capital as the three factors of production and the major contributors to a nation's wealth. Interestingly, Smith referred to the growing discipline as *political economy,* a term used much differently in contemporary economic thought (see Chapter 15, this volume, for a complete discussion of political economy).

Along with Smith, David Ricardo's (1953) theoretical contributions related to land, rent, and capital; Thomas Malthus's work on population theory; and the later writings of John Stuart Mill (recognized for noting the distinction between allocation of resources, distribution of income, and the theory of value) collectively formed the classical period of political economy. The work of these authors centered on the interplay of economic forces, the cost of production, and the operation of markets.

The classical school was eventually challenged by two new philosophies: marginalist economics and Marxism. Classical scholars believed price was determined by the costs of production, whereas marginalist economists equated prices with the level of demand, and in Marxism, price was controlled by the ruling class. The marginalists contributed the basic analytic tools of demand and supply, consumer utility, and the use of mathematics as analytical tools—all forerunners to the development of microeconomics. Marginalists also demonstrated that given a free market economy, the factors of production (land, labor, and capital) were important in understanding the economic system. The marginalists viewed value in a more rigorous manner than the classical school.

The Marxist school, built on the writings of Karl Marx (1926), identified labor as the source of all production. Marx rejected the market system that allowed the capitalists, the owners of the factories and necessary machinery, to exploit the working class and deny them a fair share of the goods produced. Marx predicted the fall of capitalism, as the disenfranchised labor class would ultimately rebel, overthrow the capitalists, and seize the means of production.

At the beginning of the 20th century, institutions of higher learning began to embrace the field, and the modern label of "economics" was used to represent courses of study in both America and Europe. At the same time, the focus of economic research was shifting from a classical approach to neoclassical economics. Neoclassical economics differed in its use of both analytical tools and mathematics (primarily differential calculus) to understand market behavior and price determination (Ekelund & Hérbert, 1990). Another important contribution of neoclassical economics was its refined interest in demand theory, as much of classical economics tended to focus only on production and supply. Many of the principles developed in neoclassical economics became the basis for the broader area of microeconomics.

The writings of William Stanley Jevons (1957), Carl Menger (1950), and Leon Walras (1954), along with the seminal contributions of Alfred Marshall (1961), helped fuel the growth of economics as a field during the neoclassical period. Marshall, perhaps one of the most prolific economic scholars, influenced numerous other graduate students during his tenure at Cambridge, forming the Marshallian approach to the study of economics. Marshall refined many aspects of economic theory and also made advances in the study of industry supply, consumer surplus, elasticity of demand, and resource allocation (Ekelund & Hérbert, 1990).

The 20th century also saw the field of economics move in other directions. Previously, market structure was theorized to represent monopoly, duopoly, or perfectly competitive markets. Edward H. Chamberlin (1950) theorized a new form of market structure, labeled as *monopolistic competition*. Monopolistic competition centered on the role of product differentiation, which offered application to a number of different markets. Both more traditional and general in its analysis as compared to Chamberlain's, Joan Robinson's (1969) theory of imperfect competition offered two important contributions: (a) analysis of monopoly and price discrimination and (b) the market for labor. The study of welfare economics (Pigou, 1932), or how economics can be used to promote better social policy, also came of age during the neoclassical period.

Significant changes in 20th-century economic thought were realized with the development of macroeconomics. Here the focus shifted to aggregate economics, which encompasses the gamut of monetary and market principles. Macroeconomics became a catalyst for fiscal policy decisions in both Western Europe and the United States during the 1950s and 1960s. John Maynard Keynes, a student of Alfred Marshall and the founder of Keynesian economics,

became the focal point for the development of macroeconomics.

Keynes's writings were numerous, but his most influential work was *The General Theory of Employment, Interest, and Money* (Keynes, 1936). Keynes's arguments would provide the pivotal rationale for the use of government spending and taxing to stabilize the economy. Keynes argued that government would spend and decrease taxes when private spending was insufficient and threatened a recession; conversely, government would reduce spending and increase taxes when private spending was too great and threatened inflation. Keynes's work, focusing on the factors that determine the total spending process, remains at the core of modern macroeconomic analysis.

Other scholars who helped refine macroeconomics as an area of study and economic thought (Ekelund & Hérbert, 1990) included Irving Fisher (money, prices, and statistical analysis), Knut Wicksell (public choice), A. C. Pigou (welfare economics), and Milton Friedman (economic policy and consumption). Today, macroeconomics is concerned with a number of topics, including economic growth, employment, aggregate production and consumption, inflation, and political economy (Albarran, 2002). Additional areas of study that coincided with this time period included the field of international economics, better methods of applied economics, and the adoption of more powerful analytical and statistical tools in econometrics.

Economic theories and economic thought are constantly changing and evolving. By the end of the 1960s, growing inflation and changes in productivity began to push economic thought in new directions. Monetarist theories reemphasized the importance of growth in the money supply as a determinant of inflation. Rationale expectations anticipate government intervention in the economy, arguing that the market's ability to anticipate government policy actions limits their effectiveness.

Finally, "supply-side" economics revisited a chief concern of the classical school regarding economic growth as a fundamental prerequisite for improving society's well-being. Supply-side economics emphasizes the need for incentives to save and invest if a nation's economy is to prosper, as well as the danger of canceling out those incentives through high taxation.

This review of major historical developments in economic thought illustrates the rich diversity of philosophies and theories found in the field of economics. As the study of economics became more refined, scholars began to investigate many different markets and industries, applying economic concepts and principles to different fields, including media.

◆ The Development of Media Economics

The rise of the mass media paved the way for the study of media economics. Research began to emerge during the 1950s. The media industries provided all of the elements required for studying the economic process. Content providers, offering information and entertainment, became the suppliers, whereas consumers and advertisers formed the demand side of the market. Various regulatory agencies (e.g., Federal Communications Commission [FCC], Federal Trade Commission, and other government entities) affected macroeconomic market conditions, and the relationship among suppliers in various industries created microeconomic market conditions.

Many of the early media economists addressed microeconomic concepts. Ray (1951, 1952) examined newspaper competition and concentration, whereas Reddaway (1963) reviewed economic characteristics of newspapers as firms. Steiner's (1952) classic work on competition in radio involves the application of microeconomic concepts to the radio industry. Early studies of the television industry examined market structure (Levin, 1958), competition with other media (Berlson, 1961), and the

impact on advertising revenues (Tijmstra, 1959–1960).

Concentration of ownership has been another topic studied across media industries. Representative studies of media concentration across industries include Albarran and Dimmick (1996), Bagdikian (2000), and Compaine (1985b), along with specific studies of industry concentration in newspapers (Lacy, 1984, 1985; McCombs, 1988; Picard, 1982, 1988a; Rosse, 1980), broadcast television (Bates, 1993; Litman, 1979), motion pictures (Gomery, 1993), and trade books (Greco, 1993).

Ownership structure has been examined in regard to management policy in the newspaper industry. Key works include Blankenburg's (1982, 1983) research on controlling circulation costs and pricing behavior and the impact on financial performance (Blankenburg & Ozanich, 1993). Further inquiry into press ownership and competition continues to develop, including the market for online newspapers (see Chyi & Sylvie, 2001; Lacy, Shaver, & St. Cyr, 1996; Lacy & Simon, 1997).

Other studies have examined variables such as media competition (Compaine, 1985a; Dimmick & Rothenbuhler, 1984), consumer expenditures and the principle of relative constancy (McCombs, 1972), barriers to entry (Wirth, 1986), demand (Busterna, 1987; Lacy, 1990), and utility (Albarran & Dimmick, 1993; Dimmick, 1993).

In 1988, the field of media economics gained further legitimacy by the debut of the *Journal of Media Economics* (*JME*), established by the first editor of the journal, Robert G. Picard. Initially published twice a year, *JME* moved to three issues a year by 1991 and quarterly distribution in 1994. The *Journal of Media Economics* has emerged as the premier journal for the latest research in the field. In addition to articles in scholarly journals, a number of books and edited volumes have contributed to the development of media economics.[1] Our focus now shifts to the theoretical and methodological dimensions of the field.

◆ *General Theoretical and Methodological Issues*

Media economics research combines a variety of theoretical and methodological approaches. The following paragraphs in this section detail some of the most widely used theoretical and methodological tools used in the field of media economics.

THEORETICAL FOUNDATIONS

In terms of theoretical development, three areas account for much of the knowledge regarding media economics. These areas involve microeconomic theories, macroeconomic theories, and studies related to political economy. Much of the literature base deals with microeconomics, which is particularly suited for media economics research because it centers on specific industry and market conditions.

Macroeconomic studies tend to take a much broader focus, examining such topics as labor and capital markets, as well as policy and regulatory concerns. The literature base involving macroeconomic theories is much smaller than that using microeconomic theories.

Political economy of the media also encompasses many areas, emerging as a response to positivist approaches in mainstream economics. The mass media became a natural area of study, drawing scholars from sociology and economics as well as communications (Golding & Murdock, 1997). For discussion of media political economy, consult the chapter by Janet Wasko (Chapter 15, this volume). Here we will focus on microeconomic and macroeconomic theories used in the study of media economics.

MICROECONOMIC THEORIES: INDUSTRIAL ORGANIZATIONAL MODEL

Among the most widely used frameworks for the study of media economics is the industrial organization model, developed by Scherer (1980), which in turn drew on the contributions of Bain (1968) and other neoclassical economists. The model offers a systematic means of analyzing many abstract concepts encountered in the study of a specific market. Scherer's explication of the market structure-conduct-performance (SCP) model as a tool for analysis has been widely used in the study of media markets and industries (Wirth & Bloch, 1995).

In its simplest form, the industrial organizational model posits that if the structure of the market is known, it allows explanation of the likely conduct and performance among firms. Each of the three areas (SCP) can be further defined by considering specific variables associated with each part of the model. For example, in terms of market structure, the variables used for analysis include the number of sellers/buyers in the market, product differentiation, barriers to entry, cost structures, and the degree of vertical integration (Albarran, 2002).

Gomery (1989) details the utility of the industrial organization model for media economics scholarship, echoed by Busterna (1988), Litman (1988), and Wirth and Bloch (1995). Several scholars have focused on just one part of the model, such as market structure (Wirth & Wollert, 1984), conduct (Picard, 1988b), or performance (Albarran & Porco, 1990; Litman & Bridges, 1986).

THE THEORY OF THE FIRM

Efforts to explicate a better understanding of market structure led to the development of the theory of the firm (Litman, 1988). The theory of the firm is an expansion of the industrial organization model, with the goal of gaining a better understanding of four common types of market structure: monopoly, oligopoly, monopolistic competition, and perfect competition.

The appeal of this approach lies in its simplicity and parsimonious nature. However, the defining of a market structure has become increasingly complicated due to increasing consolidation across the media industries and technological change. For example, the market for television could be thought of as simply the market for broadcast television or could encompass a much wider definition to include cable and satellite networks, premium and pay-per-view services, and VCR/DVD use. Bates (1993) and other scholars (Albarran & Dimmick, 1996) suggest that market structure cannot really be defined clearly using these broad and simplistic labels.

MEDIA CONCENTRATION

Another area of theoretical development relates to media concentration. In the United States, antitrust laws are designed to promote competition and limit concentration, making this an important area of inquiry for both public and social policy.

Media concentration is usually examined in one of two ways. Researchers gather existing data on firm/industry revenues to measure the degree of concentration by applying different methodological tools (e.g., concentration ratios, indices, or the Lorenz curve [see Albarran, 2002]), or researchers track concentration of ownership among the media industries (see Bagdikian, 2000; Compaine & Gomery, 2001; Howard, 1998). Regardless of the methods used, research documents increasing consolidation across all areas that make up the media industries, with many industries reaching "highly concentrated" status, indicating that the industry is dominated by a handful of firms (see Albarran, 2002; Albarran & Dimmick, 1996).

MACROECONOMIC THEORIES

There is a much more limited body of literature that involves macroeconomic analysis in the field of media economics. For example, some scholars have offered descriptive analysis of labor trends in particular media industries (Harwood, 1989).

Most macroeconomic research is related to policy and regulatory analysis, usually conducted at a national level of analysis. Policy studies typically attempt to analyze the impact of specific regulatory actions on existing markets and industries. Representative studies include Bates and Chambers (1999), Ford and Jackson (2000), and Lutzhöft and Machill (1999).

METHODOLOGIES USED IN MEDIA ECONOMICS RESEARCH

Media economics research is very eclectic in the sense that many different types of method are used to answer research questions and investigate hypotheses. However, much of the literature employs one of four methods: trend studies, financial analysis, econometrics, and case studies.

Trend studies compare and contrast data over a time series. In assessing media concentration, for example, scholars typically study concentration indices over time to gauge the impact of different policy decisions or other actions on media ownership. Most trend studies use annual data as the unit of analysis. Trend studies are useful due to their descriptive nature and ease of presentation, and they aid in analyzing the performance of media companies and industries. Representative trend studies include Dimmick and McDonald's (2001) look at network radio, Greco's (1999) examination of book publishing mergers, and Lewis's (1995) study of changes in newspaper pricing and subscription costs.

Financial analysis is another common methodological tool used in media economics research. Financial analysis can take many different forms and use different types of data. The most common data include information derived from financial statements and the use of various types of financial ratios.

For example, in the United States, all publicly traded companies operating must file various types of financial documents regularly with the Securities and Exchange Commission. Individual companies also distribute annual reports to their shareholders that contain a number of financial statements and other data. The Internet is an important source of financial data for researchers, easing the ability to collect and analyze data. Financial analysis is much harder to conduct on privately held companies, which are not required to disclose any financial information, and with companies domiciled outside the United States, where accounting practices and currency exchange rates vary.

Econometrics involves the use of statistical and mathematical models to verify and develop economic research questions, hypotheses, and theory. Econometrics has been more prevalent in the general economic literature because most media economics researchers coming from communication or journalism backgrounds lack the mathematical knowledge to pursue econometric modeling. Studies by Kennert and Uri (2001) and Miller (1997) represent research involving econometric analysis.

Case studies represent another useful method in media economics research. Case studies are popular because they allow a researcher to embrace different types of data as well as different methods. Case studies in media economics research tend to be very targeted and focused examinations. Representative case studies include McDowell and Sutherland's (2000) analysis of branding, Nye's (2000) review of litigation in music publishing, and Gershon and Egen's (1999) case study involving retransmission consent in the cable television industry.

Methods used in media economics research are not confined to these. Others can be found as noted above, such as policy analysis of regulatory policy and action on media markets and industries. Historical research is also found, although with less frequency (e.g., Dimmick & McDonald, 2001; Wolfe & Kapoor, 1996).

◆ Forces Driving Media Industry Change

The previous overview of the historical, theoretical, and methodological dimensions of the field of media economics provides a context for examining some of the key concepts important to media economics research. Prior to reviewing specific concepts, a review is warranted of the forces driving media industry change.

Four external forces continue to drive change across the media industries, leading to evolution of the study of media economics. These four forces consist of technology, regulation, globalization, and sociocultural developments. Each is briefly reviewed in the following paragraphs.

TECHNOLOGY

Because media industries are heavily dependent on technology for the creation, distribution, and exhibition of various forms of media content, changes in technology affect economic processes between and within the media industries. There are three critical areas where technology has done this. The first is the initial evolution of computers. Computing technology improved efficiency among workers in many areas and greatly minimized storage requirements for paperwork as well as increasing opportunities for communication (e-mail) and other software applications.

The second technological area, coupled with the rise of computing technology, has involved the transition from analog to digital content. As computers became more powerful and sophisticated, the ability to convert text and graphics digitally soon led to digital audio and video files. And once content is digitized, it can easily be distributed and shared with others. The media industries quickly moved to converting to a digital world, first in print and later in electronic media.

The third area of technological impact was and continues to be with the development of the Internet. First used primarily to exchange textual information, the advent of hypertext language led to the development of the World Wide Web, forever changing the user's experience with the Internet. Some media companies quickly recognized the power of the Internet, building Web sites to attract consumers and advertisers, whereas other companies floundered in their initial attempts to understand how best to use the new medium. The Internet offers media companies another way to connect audiences and advertisers, as well as a means to build and enhance brand development. By the late 1990s, the ability to stream audio and video files over the Internet was introduced, along with the rise of broadband services in the form of cable modems and digital subscriber lines. Early in the 21st century, wireless access was positioned to be the next major Internet innovation. The Internet also represents major challenges regarding intellectual property and copyrighted content.

REGULATION

Regulatory actions can always affect competitive market forces, and media industries are no exception. During the 1980s and 1990s, U.S. media industries benefited from a combination of deregulatory actions as well as liberalization of former policies. During the 8 years of the Reagan administration, the FCC took on a marketplace approach to regulation. Ownership limits were increased, and burdensome rules regarding program requirements and public interest standards were either removed or relaxed.

The 1996 Telecommunications Act, the most significant U.S. communications regulation passed since 1934, sought to eliminate competitive barriers in the broadcast, cable, and telecommunication industries. Ownership caps were relaxed yet again, and companies operating in one industry could now compete in others (e.g., cable companies could now offer telephone service, and telephone companies could offer cable-like services). Other rulings passed in 1998 and 1999 to stimulate competition in the emerging direct broadcast satellite (DBS) market allowed satellite operators to offer local television signals in addition to their regular lineup of traditional cable and pay networks.

These regulatory actions paved the way for increasing consolidation across U.S. media industries. For example, in the radio industry, some 75 different radio companies eventually were merged or acquired into one of two companies: Clear Channel Communications or Infinity (Viacom). In television, Viacom acquired the assets of CBS, King World, UPN, and Black Entertainment Television (BET). America Online merged with Time-Warner, creating the first company combining "old" and "new" media. The French utility company Vivendi, in a span of just 2 years, acquired the media assets of Seagram Universal and the USA Networks to become a global media giant, along with the likes of Disney, News Corporation, and Bertelsmann AG.

Court decisions, coupled with regulatory actions, also affect media markets. In early 2002, the U.S. Court of Appeals ruled in favor of separate cases brought forward by AT&T and Viacom regarding government-mandated ownership caps, declaring that the limits imposed by the FCC on cable and television station ownership were arbitrary and capricious. Trends strongly suggest that these decisions may lead to removal of all ownership caps at the national level for many media industries, leading to even more mergers and acquisitions. In a related matter, the FCC is expected to remove old restrictions barring newspapers from owning broadcast stations in the same markets in which they operate. If eliminated, the cross-ownership rules would give publishing companies the opportunity to acquire broadcast stations and cable systems within the markets they serve, leading to the development of multi-media-based companies offering content and advertising across multiple mediums.

GLOBALIZATION

With many American media markets heavily saturated, the global marketplace has become even more important in generating revenues for media firms and industries. Media products are often created with global audiences in mind, which is why so much content contains sex and violence—two topics that are easily understood across cultures.

Globalization of media content began with motion pictures and magazines but then expanded into other arenas, including television programming, VHS and DVD sales and rentals, and sound recordings. The United States has been the primary exporter of content, but the rise of international media conglomerates such as News Corporation, Vivendi Universal, Sony, and Bertelsmann demonstrated that a global oligopoly of media companies was increasingly dominating the marketplace for information and entertainment goods and services.

Globalization presents a challenge for media economics researchers, as accounting practices and regulatory structures differ from country to country. There are few reliable sources of global financial data related to media. Nevertheless, it is critical that scholars recognize that media companies compete and operate in a global as well as domestic marketplace for audience share and advertiser revenues.

SOCIOCULTURAL DEVELOPMENTS

Changes in demography and other aspects of society also affect the media industries and, ultimately, media economics. As noted, media content is often created with the desire to reach global audiences, so consumer tastes and preferences are critical in understanding audience needs and wants.

In addition, U.S. media users are changing. Census data clearly track the transition of the United States to a multicultural society. This has led to pressures from groups such as the National Advancement for the Association of Colored People (NAACP) to present network television programming that better reflects the actual makeup of society. In addition to becoming a nation of color, Americans are living longer and desire more content geared toward the needs of a mature audience. Aging baby boomers will demand more content devoted to issues related to retirement, health, travel, and leisure. Some cable networks were already beginning to address this market, but more will follow suit.

Audiences have an insatiable appetite for media-related content and services. As people live longer and obtain more discretionary income, spending on media will likely rise. These shifts in audience composition and makeup will present new pressures on media firms to develop content that will appeal to these unique and differing audiences.

Having reviewed these four macro-level forces, we now turn to some of the key concepts found in the study of media economics: media products, the dual-product marketplace, branding, competition, economics of scale and scope, mergers and acquisitions, and labor.

◆ Standard Concepts

MEDIA PRODUCTS

Media content, in the form of television programs, movies, sound and video recordings, and print (e.g., books, magazines, newspapers), represents some of the products supplied by media firms. Media products can be broadly classified into categories of information (news-related content) and entertainment (drama, comedy, action, music, games, etc.). Massive consolidation across the media industries has given rise to vertically integrated conglomerates (meaning they control many aspects of production, distribution, and exhibition) such as Viacom, AOL Time-Warner, Disney, and News Corporation. Media products such as television programming, feature films, and sound recordings can be repeatedly used and marketed to both audiences and advertisers, forming the "dual-product marketplace."

DUAL-PRODUCT MARKETPLACE

Many media industries function in a dual-product marketplace. That is, media firms produce or supply information and entertainment products that are consumed or demanded by audiences and, in most cases, advertisers. The dual-product marketplace is a unique characteristic of the media industries, allowing for separate transactions and potential revenue streams from both audiences and advertisers. Media firms try to strategically position their content so as to maximize potential revenues. The number one priority of media executives and managers is to generate positive cash flow (revenues less expenses, depreciation, taxes, and interest) to increase the value of their firm.

BRANDING

This is another key concept in media economics. Media companies use branding as a way to build awareness and identity connected with content products. Most audiences and advertisers recognize brands, and larger media companies have invested billions of dollars to develop and acquire different brands. Viacom is a multidivisional media company with a large cadre of recognizable brands, including MTV, Nickelodeon, Paramount, Blockbuster, CBS/UPN, Infinity, and King World. AOL

Time-Warner is another branded company, with well-known entities such as AOL, CNN, HBO, Warner Brothers, Netscape, Time, Sports Illustrated, and TBS/TNT. Branding provides not only instant recognition but also the opportunity to be recognized in a heavily competitive market environment.

COMPETITION

The dual-product marketplace operates at the distribution and exhibition levels once products are actually created. Prior to this, there are many competitive processes at work. For example, competition exists for ideas by writers that can be turned in to successful scripts for television programs and films. Securing experienced photographers, producers, directors, and editors for the production process involves competition, as well as the demand for the best available talent. An interesting aspect of studying media competition is the fact that, throughout the history of the media, no new media have completely displaced older forms of media (Dimmick & Rothenbuhler, 1984). Typically, some type of evolution or repositioning takes place, but traditional media learn to coexist and survive with newer media forms.

ECONOMIES OF SCALE AND SCOPE

Economies of scale and scope refer to the cost efficiencies realized by the operation of media firms in different venues. Economies of scale are realized when the average cost declines as multiple units of a product are produced. For example, the fixed and variable costs to produce a single newspaper would be very high, but the cost per newspaper drops dramatically as multiple papers are printed. Likewise, as radio stations have consolidated, there is no longer need for multiple offices and administrative and engineering staff.

Economies of scope allow multidivisional conglomerates to realize cost-efficiencies across horizontal media markets. Viacom has the ability to produce a motion picture via its Paramount Studios, air that movie on its pay channel Showtime, reap additional revenues from rentals via Blockbuster, and cross-promote the film through other owned programming and publishing outlets.

MERGERS AND ACQUISITIONS

The composition of the media industries has undergone considerable change due to mergers and acquisitions across many market sectors. Mergers and acquisition activity surged during the 1980s and 1990s due to a number of macroeconomic processes, including relaxation of ownership provisions, low interest rates available for financing, strong business performance, and technological convergence (see Ozanich & Wirth, 1998). As policymakers continued to relax ownership limits and more mergers took place, public interest watchdog groups became ever more concerned, fearing the growing consolidation of media would lead to constriction of news and information sources needed to nourish democracy.

LABOR

Media industries depend on talented technical, creative, and managerial personnel to function effectively. Personnel represent the greatest single expense for any organization. In the media industries, trade, craft, and technical workers are considered "below-the-line" employees, whereas producers, writers, directors, talent, and management are considered "above-the-line" employees (see Shanks, 1977).

Labor unions are common across many U.S. media industries. Various guilds and craft unions negotiate minimum pay grades for everything from scripts to directing. A common management responsibility is negotiating contract renewals, with unions representing media workers to avoid strikes and labor disruptions.

Technology continually changes the labor market for media firms, evidenced by the influx of computing systems used for many different applications. Media companies either invest in the development of personnel skilled in these new areas, or they may choose to outsource these responsibilities to firms specializing in specific applications. Labor markets are affected by consolidation, which typically creates a loss of some repetitive jobs, as well as general labor trends.

◆ Contemporary Issues in Media Economics

There are a number of issues scholars need to address in their efforts to further develop this important area of research. This final section considers three issues of particular relevance affecting media economics at the beginning of the 21st century: theory building, defining market structures more precisely, and better methods.

BROADER THEORETICAL DEVELOPMENT

Media economics research has primarily drawn on microeconomic concepts and principles, with a heavy reliance on the industrial organization model. Although this emphasis clarifies the relationship of various concepts in microeconomic analysis, it limits the development of the field. As a result, other economic theories, which have possible application to the mass media industries, have been ignored, especially those found in macroeconomics (Chambers, 1998; Lacy & Niebauer, 1995). For example, understanding the global consolidation of many media markets is an area that would be strengthened using macroeconomic approaches. The impact of global consolidation on general patterns of employment, economic development, and inflation are just three potential topics of interest.

In addition to drawing on the breadth of existing economic theories, scholars should consider new theoretical inquiries that could draw on multiple methods of investigation. The interplay of business structures, regulation, technology, and social policy implications across the media industries offers a unique playing field for scholars to generate new theories and hypotheses. To do so, researchers must be willing to move away from simply describing specific firms' structure and performance to more analytical and investigative analysis.

Theory building is never easy in any field, but given the rapid pace of change in the media industries, no area could benefit more from fresh ideas and news perspectives than media economics.

DELINEATING THE MARKET AND DEFINING MARKET STRUCTURE

A second issue involves better definition of what constitutes a market and expanding our understanding of market structure. Media economics research must grapple with the evolving definition of what constitutes a media market, a critical issue given the convergence under way across the media industries. Markets can no longer be defined cleanly. In reality, media companies tend to supply products in many different markets, in competition with other providers. Yet the tendency among policymakers and researchers is to still treat markets under traditional labels, such as television, newspapers, or motion pictures. This approach fails to recognize the realities of the media marketplace and can lead to inaccurate assumptions over which firms dominate a particular market.

One answer to this dilemma may be to consider the functions of a firm rather than focusing on the final product. If we begin to think of Viacom as a company with multiple brands engaged in content creation and distribution, it perhaps offers a clearer

interpretation of what the company was about and how it sought to be a leader in many different markets: network television, program syndication, cable networks, radio, and so on. Likewise, EchoStar was primarily a distribution company and the leader in direct-to-home satellite subscriptions, competing with the likes of AT&T/Comcast, Cox, and AOL Time-Warner in the market to capture multichannel households. Conceptually, this makes much more sense than to say AT&T/Comcast was the leading cable operator and EchoStar the leading satellite provider.

Coupled with the need for better understanding of the market is a need to expand or redefine the theory of the firm. For decades, media economists have tried to work within the three categories found in the mass media: monopoly, oligopoly, and monopolistic competition (Albarran, 2002). Yet other types of structures are evolving. Duopoly, a market with two primary firms, is becoming more common in media markets. U.S. examples at the beginning of the century included the market for new national digital satellite radio services, XM Radio and Sirius (Albarran & Pitts, 2001), and the market for Internet browsers, involving Microsoft Internet Explorer and Netscape.

But what was truly emerging in many media industries was a two-tiered market structure, with a limited oligopoly of firms (between three and five) controlling between 75% and 90% of the revenue/market share and a number of smaller firms on the other tier fighting for a small percentage of the remaining market share. Media industries representative of this type of evolving structure are the motion picture and recording industries, television networks, radio, consumer book publishing, and magazine publishing (Albarran & Dimmick, 1996).

BETTER METHODS OF ANALYSIS

Improvements in theory development and redefining of the media market and market structure must be realized in conjunction with enhancements in methods. In particular, one area deserves attention: measures used to assess competition and concentration.

Measures to assess competition and concentration have primarily relied on one of two available tools: concentration ratios and the Herfindahl-Hirschman Index (HHI) (Albarran, 2002). Concentration ratios provide a parsimonious way to measure concentration, using either the top four firms or the top eight firms in a market. Basically, if the top four firms control more than 50% of the market revenue, or if the top eight firms control more than 75% of the revenue, the market is considered highly concentrated. Although the measure is useful, it fails to address inequality of market shares. For example, using the four-firm ratio, one could encounter one firm dominating the market with 45% of the revenues, with the other three firms holding a combined 5%. In such a case, one might conclude the market was concentrated, but this would fail to offer a complete picture.

The HHI index seeks to be much more rigorous. The HHI squares the market share for each entity and then generates a total number for all the firms. Herein, however, lies a key problem. Researchers must have data on *every* firm in a market to calculate the index. Often, researchers lack access to data from all the firms, especially from privately held companies. Furthermore, calculating the index can be unwieldy.

More problematic for both measures is that they are designed only to measure concentration *within* a market segment. There are no generally accepted measures available to assess concentration *across* markets (see Albarran & Dimmick, 1996), yet this is an area of key concern. AOL Time-Warner, Disney, Viacom, and other media giants may have limited market share within individual market segments, but no tools exist to measure their combined influence across markets. With multiproduct firms engaged simultaneously in many media markets, developing measures to assess within-industry concentration and competition are badly needed.

◆ Conclusions

Media economics provides a means to understand the activities and functions of media companies as economic institutions. Only by understanding individual media companies as business entities can one fully appreciate their conduct within society. An understanding of media economics strengthens our understanding of the role and function of mass media in society. At a theoretical level, media economics complements existing mass communication theory by adding important dimensions regarding the structure, conduct, and performance of media firms and industries; the interplay of economics, policy, and regulation; and audience behaviors and preferences.

As a field of scholarship, media economics research offers important contributions to media studies. Media economics research faces many challenges as it attempts to analyze and evaluate the complex and changing world in which the mass media industries operate.

◆ Note

1. Research in media economics was spurred by a number of early volumes, including the following: *Economic Aspects of Television Regulation* (Noll, Peck, & McGowan, 1973); *Television Economics* (Owen, Beebe, & Manning, 1974); *Economics and Freedom of Expression: Media Structure and the First Amendment* (Owen, 1975); *Beyond Agenda-Setting: Information Subsidies and Public Policy* (Gandy, 1982); *Who Owns the Media? Concentration and Ownership in Mass Communications Industry* (Compaine, 1985b); and *Press Concentration and Monopoly: New Perspectives on Newspaper Ownership and Operation* (Picard, Winter, McCombs, & Lacy, 1988). Later volumes concentrated on broader coverage of the field, including *Media Economics: Concepts and Issues* (Picard, 1989); *Media Economics: Theory and Practice* (Alexander, Owers, & Carveth, 1993); *Media*

Economics: Understanding Markets, Industries and Concepts (Albarran, 2002); and *Global Media Economics: Commercialization, Concentration, and Integration of World Media Markets* (Albarran & Chan-Olmsted, 1998). Other volumes address specific industries such as newspapers (Demers, 1996; Lacy & Simon, 1993) and the evolving video entertainment industry (Owen & Wildman, 1992).

◆ References

Albarran, A. B. (2002). *Media economics: Understanding markets, industries and concepts* (2nd ed.). Ames: Iowa State University Press.

Albarran, A. B., & Chan-Olmsted, S. (Eds.). (1998). *Global media economics: Commercialization, concentration, and integration of world media markets.* Ames: Iowa State University Press.

Albarran, A. B., & Dimmick, J. (1993). Measuring utility in the video entertainment industries: An assessment of competitive superiority. *Journal of Media Economics, 6*(2), 45–51.

Albarran, A. B., & Dimmick, J. (1996). Concentration and economies of multiformity in the communication industries. *Journal of Media Economics, 9*(4), 48–49.

Albarran, A. B., & Pitts, G. G. (2001). *The radio broadcasting industry.* Needham Heights, MA: Allyn & Bacon.

Albarran, A. B., & Porco, J. (1990). Measuring and analyzing diversification of corporations involved in pay cable. *Journal of Media Economics, 3*(2), 3–14.

Alexander, A., Owers, J., & Carveth, R. (1993). *Media economics: Theory and practice.* New York: Lawrence Erlbaum.

Bagdikian, B. H. (2000). *The media monopoly* (6th ed.). Boston: Beacon.

Bain, J. S. (1968). *Industrial organization.* New York: John Wiley.

Bates, B. J. (1993). Concentration in local television markets. *Journal of Media Economics, 6*(1), 3–22.

Bates, B. J., & Chambers, T. (1999). The economic basis for radio deregulation. *Journal of Media Economics, 12*(1), 19–34.

Berlson, W. A. (1961). Effects of television on the reading and buying of newspapers and magazines. *Public Opinion Quarterly, 25,* 366–381.

Blankenburg, W. R. (1982). Newspaper ownership and control of circulation to increase profits. *Journalism Quarterly, 59,* 390–398.

Blankenburg, W. R. (1983). A newspaper chain's pricing behavior. *Journalism Quarterly, 60,* 275–280.

Blankenburg, W. R., & Ozanich, G. W. (1993, Spring). The effects of public ownership on the financial performance of newspaper corporations. *Journalism Quarterly, 70,* 68–75.

Busterna, J. C. (1987). The cross-elasticity of demand for national newspaper advertising. *Journalism Quarterly, 64,* 287–291.

Busterna, J. C. (1988). Concentration and the industrial organizational model. In R. G. Picard, J. P. Winter, M. McCombs, & S. Lacy (Eds.), *Press concentration and monopoly: New perspectives on newspaper ownership and operation* (pp. 35–53). Norwood, NJ: Ablex.

Chamberlin, E. H. (1950). *The theory of monopolistic competition* (6th ed.). Cambridge, MA: Harvard University Press.

Chambers, T. (1998). Who's on first? Studying the scholarly community of media economics. *Journal of Media Economics, 11*(1), 1–12.

Chyi, H. I., & Sylvie, G. (2001). The medium is global, the content is not: The role of geography in online newspaper markets. *Journal of Media Economics, 14*(4), 231–248.

Compaine, B. M. (1985a, Summer). The expanding base of media competition. *Journal of Communication, 35,* 81–96.

Compaine, B. M. (1985b). *Who owns the media? Concentration and ownership in the mass communications industry* (2nd ed.). White Plains, NY: Knowledge Industry Publications.

Compaine, B. M., & Gomery, D. (2001). *Who owns the media?* (3rd ed.). Mahwah, NJ: Lawrence Erlbaum.

Demers, D. P. (1996). *The menace of the corporate newspaper: Fact or fiction?* Ames: Iowa State University Press.

Dimmick, J. (1993). Ecology, economics, and gratification utilities. In A. Alexander, J. Owers, & R. Carveth (Eds.), *Media economics: Theory and practice* (pp. 135–156). New York: Lawrence Erlbaum.

Dimmick, J., & McDonald, D. G. (2001). Network radio oligopoly, 1926–1956: Rivalrous imitation and program diversity. *Journal of Media Economics, 14*(4), 197–212.

Dimmick, J., & Rothenbuhler, E. (1984, Winter). The theory of the niche: Quantifying competition among media industries. *Journal of Communication, 34,* 103–119.

Ekelund, R. B., & Hébert, R. F. (1990). *A history of economic theory and method* (3rd ed.). New York: McGraw-Hill.

Ford, G. S., & Jackson, J. D. (2000). Preserving free television? Some empirical evidence on the efficacy of must-carry. *Journal of Media Economics, 13*(1), 1–14.

Gandy, O. H. (1982). *Beyond agenda-setting: Information subsidies and public policy.* Norwood, NJ: Ablex.

Gershon, R. A., & Egen, B. M. (1999). Retransmission consent, cable franchising, and market failure: A case study analysis of WOOD-TV 8 versus Cablevision of Michigan. *Journal of Media Economics, 12*(3), 201–224.

Golding, P., & Murdock, G. (1997). *The political economy of the media* (Vols. 1–2). Cheltenham, UK: Edgar Elgar.

Gomery, D. (1989). Media economics: Terms of analysis. *Critical Studies in Mass Communication, 6*(2), 43–60.

Gomery, D. (1993). The contemporary American movie business. In A. Alexander, J. Owers, & R. Carveth (Eds.), *Media economics: Theory and practice* (pp. 267–281). New York: Lawrence Erlbaum.

Greco, A. N. (1993). Publishing economics: Mergers and acquisitions in the U.S. publishing industry: 1980–1989. In A. Alexander, J. Owers, & R. Carveth (Eds.), *Media economics: Theory and practice* (pp. 205–224). New York: Lawrence Erlbaum.

Greco, A. N. (1999). The impact of horizontal mergers and acquisitions on corporate concentration in the U.S. book publishing industry, 1989–1994. *Journal of Media Economics, 12*(3), 165–180.

Harwood, K. (1989). A surge in employment. *Feedback, 30*(1), 6–12.

Howard, H. H. (1998). The 1996 Telecommunications Act and TV station ownership: 1 year later. *Journal of Media Economics, 11*(3), 21–32.

Jevons, W. S. (1957). *The theory of political economy.* New York: Kelly and Millman.

Kennert, D. M., & Uri, N. D. (2001). Measuring productivity change for regulatory purposes. *Journal of Media Economics, 14*(2), 87–104.

Keynes, J. M. (1936). *The general theory of employment, interest, and money.* London: Macmillan.

Lacy, S. (1984). Competition among metropolitan daily, small daily, and weekly newspapers. *Journalism Quarterly, 61,* 640–644.

Lacy, S. (1985). Monopoly metropolitan dailies and inner-city competition. *Journalism Quarterly, 62,* 640–644.

Lacy, S. (1990). A model of demand for news: Impact of competition on newspaper content. *Journalism Quarterly, 67,* 40–48, 128.

Lacy, S., & Niebauer, W. E., Jr. (1995). Developing and using theory for media economics. *Journal of Media Economics, 8*(2), 3–13.

Lacy, S., Shaver, M. A., & St. Cyr, C. (1996). The effects of public ownership and newspaper competition on the financial performance of newspaper corporations: A replication and extension. *Journalism Quarterly, 73,* 332–341.

Lacy, S., & Simon, T. F. (1993). *The economics and regulation of United States newspapers.* Norwood, NJ: Ablex.

Lacy, S., & Simon, T. F. (1997). Intercounty group ownership of daily newspapers and the decline of competition for readers. *Journalism Quarterly, 74,* 814–825.

Landreth, H., & Colander, D. C. (1989). *History of economic thought* (2nd ed.). Boston: Houghton Mifflin.

Levin, H. J. (1958). Economic structure and the regulation of television. *Quarterly Journal of Economics, 72,* 445–446.

Lewis, R. (1995). Relation between newspaper subscription price and circulation, 1971–1992. *Journal of Media Economics, 8*(1), 25–41.

Litman, B. R. (1979). The television networks, competition and program diversity. *Journal of Broadcasting, 23,* 393–410.

Litman, B. R. (1988). Microeconomic foundations. In R. G. Picard, J. P. Winter, M. McCombs, & S. Lacy (Eds.), *Press concentration and monopoly: New perspectives on newspaper ownership and operation* (pp. 3–34). Norwood, NJ: Ablex.

Litman, B. R., & Bridges, J. (1986). An economic analysis of daily newspaper performance. *Newspaper Research Journal, 7,* 9–26.

Lutzhöft, N., & Machill, M. (1999). The economics of French cable systems as reflected in media policy. *Journal of Media Economics, 12*(3), 181–199.

Marshall, A. (1961). *Principles of economics* (9th ed.). London: Macmillan.

Marx, K. (1926). *Capital* (3 vol.). Chicago: Charles H. Kerr.

McCombs, M. E. (1972). Mass media in the marketplace. *Journalism Monographs, 24,* 1–104.

McCombs, M. E. (1988). Concentration, monopoly, and content. In R. G. Picard, J. P. Winter, M. McCombs, & S. Lacy (Eds.), *Press concentration and monopoly: New perspectives on newspaper ownership and operation* (pp. 129–137). Norwood, NJ: Ablex.

McDowell, W., & Sutherland, J. (2000). Choice versus chance: Using brand equity theory to explore TV audience lead-in effects, a case study. *Journal of Media Economics, 13*(4), 233–247.

Menger, C. (1950). *Principles of economics.* Glencoe, IL: Free Press.

Miller, K. M., & Gandy, O. H. (1991). Paradigmatic drift: A bibliographic review of the spread of economic analysis in the literature of communication. *Journalism Quarterly, 68,* 663–671.

Miller, I. R. (1997). Models for determining the economic value of cable television systems. *Journal of Media Economics, 10*(2), 21–33.

Noll, R. G., Peck, M. J., & McGowan, J. J. (1973). *Economic aspects of television regulation.* Washington, DC: Brookings Institute.

Nye, W. W. (2000). Some economic issues in licensing music performance rights: Controversies in recent ASCAP-BMI litigation. *Journal of Media Economics, 13*(1), 15–25.

Owen, B. M. (1975). *Economics and freedom of expression: Media structure and the First Amendment.* Cambridge, MA: Ballinger.

Owen, B. M., Beebe, J. H., & Manning, W. G. (1974). *Television economics.* Lexington, MA: D. C. Heath.

Owen, B. M., & Wildman, S. (1992). *Video economics.* Cambridge, MA: Harvard University Press.

Ozanich, G., & Wirth, M. O. (1998). Media mergers and acquisitions: A communications industry overview. In A. Alexander, J. Owers, & R. Carveth (Eds.), *Media economics: Theory and practice* (2nd ed., pp. 95–107). Mahwah, NJ: Lawrence Erlbaum.

Picard, R. G. (1982, April). Rate setting and competition in newspaper advertising. *Newspaper Research Journal, 3,* 3–13.

Picard, R. G. (1988a). Measures of concentration in the daily newspaper industry. *Journal of Media Economics, 1*(1), 61–74.

Picard, R. G. (1988b). Pricing behavior of newspapers. In R. G. Picard, J. P. Winter, M. McCombs, & S. Lacy (Eds.), *Press concentration and monopoly: New perspectives on newspaper ownership and operation* (pp. 55–69). Norwood, NJ: Ablex.

Picard, R. G. (1989). *Media economics: Concepts and issues.* Beverly Hills, CA: Sage.

Picard, R. G., Winter, J. P., McCombs, M., & Lacy, S. (Eds.). (1988). *Press concentration and monopoly: New perspectives on newspaper ownership and operation.* Norwood, NJ: Ablex.

Pigou, A. C. (1932). *Economics of welfare.* London: Macmillan.

Ray, R. H. (1951). Competition in the newspaper industry. *Journal of Marketing, 43*, 444–456.

Ray, R. H. (1952). Economic forces as factor in daily newspaper competition. *Journalism Quarterly, 29*, 31–42.

Reddaway, W. B. (1963). The economics of newspapers. *Economic Journal, 73*, 201–218.

Ricardo, D. (1953). On the principles of political economy and taxation. In P. Sraffa & M. Dobb (Eds.), *The works and correspondence of David Ricardo.* Cambridge, UK: Cambridge University Press.

Robinson, J. (1969). *The economics of imperfect competition.* New York: St. Martin's.

Rosse, J. N. (1980, Spring). The decline of direct newspaper competition. *Journal of Communication, 30*, 65–71.

Scherer, F. M. (1980). *Industrial market structure and economic performance* (2nd ed.). Chicago: Rand McNally.

Shanks, B. (1977). *The cool fire: How to make it in television.* New York: Vintage.

Smith, A. (1937). *An inquiry into the nature and causes of the wealth of nations* (E. Cannan, Ed.). New York: Modern Library.

Steiner, P. O. (1952, May). Program patterns and preferences, and the workability of competition in radio broadcasting. *Quarterly Journal of Economics, 66*, 194–223.

Tijmstra, L. F. (1959–1960, Winter). The challenges of TV to the press: The impact of television on advertising revenues and circulations of newspapers. *Journal of Broadcasting, 4*, 3–13.

Walras, L. (1954). *Elements of pure economics.* Homewood, IL: Irwin.

Wirth, M. O. (1986). Economic barriers to entering media industries in the United States. In M. McLaughlin (Ed.), *Communication yearbook 9* (pp. 423–442). Beverly Hills, CA: Sage.

Wirth, M. O., & Bloch, H. (1995). Industrial organizational theory and media industry analysis. *Journal of Media Economics, 8*(2), 15–26.

Wirth, M. O., & Wollert, J. A. (1984, Spring). The effects of market structure on television news pricing. *Journal of Broadcasting, 28*, 215–225.

Wolfe, A. S., & Kapoor, S. (1996). The Matsushita takeover of MCA: A critical, materialist, historical, and First Amendment view. *Journal of Media Economics, 9*(4), 1–21.

15

THE POLITICAL ECONOMY
OF COMMUNICATIONS

◆ Janet Wasko

◆ *The Historical/Theoretical*
Foundations of Political Economy

To fully understand a political economic approach to studying media
and communication, it is necessary to trace the foundations of political
economy itself. (Some of this background is similar to the discussion of
media economics by Alan Albarran in Chapter 14, this volume; the
differences in these approaches are discussed at the end of this chapter.)
The general study of political economy draws on 18th-century Scottish
Enlightenment thinking and its critique in the 19th century. For Adam
Smith, David Ricardo, and others, the study of economic issues was
called *political economy* and was grounded in social theory. Smith
defined political economy as the study of "wealth" (material goods) or
the allocation of resources and was concerned with "how mankind
arranges to allocate scarce resources with a view toward satisfying certain needs and not others" (Smith, 1776/1937, p. 14). Furthermore,
political economy focused on the production, distribution, exchange,
and consumption of wealth and the consequences for the welfare of individuals and society. More specifically, they studied one arrangement for
the allocation of resources—they studied *capitalism* as a system of social
production. Classical political economy evolved as capitalism evolved,

adding Karl Marx's and Frederick Engels's historical materialism and class analysis in the 19th century, emphasizing a radical critique of the evolving capitalist system through a moral stance in opposition to the unjust characteristics of that system.

During the last half of the 19th century, however, there was a fundamental shift in the study of economic issues, as the focus changed from macroanalysis to microanalysis. Emphasis was placed on individual rather than societal concerns, and methods were drawn from the social sciences rather than from moral philosophy. These basic changes were represented in a shift in the name of the discipline—from *political economy* to *economics*. The person often receiving credit for the name change, William Jevons, suggested that economics was the study of "the mechanics of utility and self-interest . . . to satisfy our wants to the utmost with the least effort . . . to maximize pleasure is the problem of economics" (Jevons, 1970, p. 24). As a more recent economist has explained, the "neo-classical economists made a sharper distinction than their predecessors had done between the explanation of What Is, in an economic system and the consideration of What Ought To Be" (R. D. Collison Black, quoted in Jevons, 1970, p. 10).

Although neoclassical economics prevails today, political economy has continued in different forms. Several conservative versions have emerged, including a corporatist approach and public choice theory (also known as the new or positive political economy). These approaches generally argue that individual freedom can be expanded by applying neoclassical principles to a wider range of issues than other economists.

Meanwhile, institutional political economy represents an approach that focuses on technological and institutional factors that influence markets. Although some work in communication studies draws on institutional analysis, a radical, critical, or Marxian political economy is likely the tradition that is represented when one refers to "the political economy of communication."

In *The Political Economy of Communication*, Vincent Mosco (1996) has defined this version of political economy as "the study of the social relations, particularly power relations, that mutually constitute the production, distribution and consumption of resources" (p. 25). He explains that political economy is about survival and control, or how societies are organized to produce what is necessary to survive and how order is maintained to meet societal goals. Mosco further delineates four central characteristics of critical political economy, which are helpful in understanding this approach:

1. *Social change and history.* Political economy continues the tradition of classic theorists, uncovering the dynamics of capitalism—its cyclical nature, the growth of monopoly capital, the state apparatus, and so on.

2. *Social totality.* Political economy is a holistic approach—or, in concrete terms, it explores the relationship among commodities, institutions, social relations, and hegemony and explores the determination among these elements, although some elements are stressed more than others.

3. *Moral philosophy.* Critical political economy also follows the classical theorists' emphasis on moral philosophy, including not only analysis of the economic system but also discussion of the policy problems and moral issues that arise from it. For some contemporary scholars, this is the distinguishing characteristic of political economy.

4. *Praxis.* Finally, political economists attempt to transcend the distinction between research and policy, orienting their work toward actual social change and practice, or as Marx

(1886/1969) argued, "Philosophers have only interpreted the world in various ways; the point is to change it" (p. 15).

Mosco's (1996) model is similar to the formulation developed by British political economists Graham Murdock and Peter Golding, who have distinguished critical political economy from mainstream economics: It is holistic, historical, and centrally concerned with the balance between capitalist enterprise and public intervention, and it "goes beyond technical issues of efficiency to engage with basic moral questions of justice, equity and the public good" (Golding & Murdock, 1991, p. 20).

In summary, a primary concern of political economists is with the allocation of resources (material concerns) within capitalist societies. Through studies of ownership and control, political economists document and analyze relations of power, a class system, and other structural inequalities. Critical political economists analyze contradictions and suggest strategies for resistance and intervention. The approach includes both economic *and* political analysis, with methods drawn from history, economics, sociology, and political science. These explanations set the stage or provide the groundwork for applying political economy to the study of communication.

◆ *Theoretical Discussions of Political Economy of Communications*

The academic study of communication has not always embraced economic analysis, much less a political economic approach. During the 1940s and 1950s, U.S. communication scholars focused primarily on individual effects and psychologically oriented research, with little concern for the economic context in which media are produced,

distributed, and consumed. Although there are examples of studies representing a radical critique or an institutional analysis of media structures and practices, explicit references to political economy were lacking.[1]

In the 1950s and early 1960s, former Federal Communications Commission (FCC) economist and University of Illinois professor Dallas Smythe urged scholars to consider communication as an important component of the economy and to understand it as an economic entity. In addition to offering a course at the University of Illinois as early as 1948, Smythe presented one of the first explications of a political economy of communications in 1960, defining the approach as the study of political policies and economic processes, their interrelations, and their mutual influence on social institutions (Smythe, 1960). He argued that the central purpose of applying political economy to communication was to evaluate the effects of communication agencies in terms of the policies by which they are organized and operated or, in other words, to study the structure and policies of communication institutions in their societal settings. Smythe further delineated research questions emanating from policies that related to production, allocation, capital, organization, and control, concluding that the studies that might evolve from these areas were practically endless. Although Smythe's discussion at this point did not employ radical or Marxist terminology, it was a major departure from the kind of research that dominated the study of mass communications at that time.

Smythe and a few other U.S. scholars—notably, Herbert Schiller and, later, Thomas Guback—continued to focus their research and teaching around the political economy of communication during the 1960s, influenced by institutional economics but inspired as well by the general political and economic developments of the period. Dan Schiller (1999) has pointed out that these scholars drew on the work of economist Robert Brady, who critiqued developments in the political and economic climate of the 1930s and 1940s from the vantage point of an emerging antifascist movement in the United States. Schiller concludes that

> the gestation of a political economic approach, in the United States at least, did not take the form of a direct carryover of analytical priorities from the established field of Marxian political economy—elements of which were indeed incorporated at a later stage. Nor, to be sure, was it a product of abstract academicism. Rather, the conceptual problematic that was elaborated by early political economic communications study was generally rooted in what Denning (1996) called "the cultural front" of the 1930s and 1940s and, specifically, in the antifascist intellectual synthesis that was the period's hallmark. (p. 90)

It was not until the 1970s that the political economy of media and communications (PE/C) was explicitly defined again but this time within a more explicitly Marxist framework. In 1973, Graham Murdock and Peter Golding offered their formulation of the political economy of communication, stating that "the mass media are first and foremost industrial and commercial organizations which produce and distribute commodities" (pp. 205–206). Thus, PE/C is fundamentally interested in studying communication and media as commodities produced by capitalist industries (Murdock & Golding, 1973). The article established a basic model for PE/C by focusing on the consolidation, concentration (including integration and diversification), and internationalization of media institutions and represented "a ground-breaking exercise . . . a conceptual map for a political economic analysis of the media where none existed in British literature" (Mosco, 1996, p. 102). A later piece by Murdock and Golding (1979) placed political economy within the broader framework of critical and Marxian theory, with links to the Frankfurt school as well as to other critical theorists.

Nicholas Garnham further outlined the approach in 1979, also drawing connections to the Frankfurt school and noting that the political economy of communication involves analyzing "the modes of cultural production and consumption developed within capitalist societies" (Garnham, 1979, p. 123). He further explained that media must be seen "first as economic entities with both a direct economic role as creators of surplus value through commodity production and exchange and an indirect role, through advertising, in the creation of surplus value within other sectors of commodity production" (p. 132). An important point emphasized by Murdock, Golding, and Garnham in the discussions cited above related to the contradictions inherent in this process. More specifically, as Garnham states, despite capital's control of the means of cultural production, "it does not follow that these cultural commodities will necessarily support . . . the dominant ideology" (p. 136).[2]

Meanwhile, also in 1979, Armand Mattelart, a Belgian scholar working in France, outlined a Marxist approach to the study of media and communication in "For a *Class* and *Group* Analysis of Popular Communication Practices" (Mattelart, 1979). He drew directly on Marx's *Capital* in outlining the mode of production of communication, including production instruments, working methods, and relations of production, adding special attention to issues relating to the global extension of media and communication or what he and others have termed *cultural imperialism* (see Chapter 3, this volume).

As PE/C has grown and developed over the years, a number of debates have emerged. One of the most interesting has been called "The Blindspot Debate," which was initiated by Dallas Smythe (1977). In an article intended to spark such a debate, Smythe pointed out that communication had been overlooked by Western Marxists, who were mostly interested in issues relating to ideology. He further argued that the main product of media was audiences that were sold by media to advertisers. In other words, Smythe argued that media programming was a "free lunch" and of little significance. Furthermore, he maintained that audiences' exposure to advertising should be considered labor that added value to the audience commodity.

Smythe's (1977) article prompted a series of replies, first from Graham Murdock (1978), who cautioned that the audience commodity was limited to advertising-dependent media and that dismissing program content was far too drastic. The debate raged on, with Smythe responding (1978), as well as Bill Livant (1979), Sut Jhally (1990), and Eileen Meehan (1993) entering into the fray. More recently, with the increasing spread of privatized, advertiser-supported media, the audience commodity concept has been accepted by many political economists, as well as other communication theorists.

During the 1990s, a few political economists directed special attention to "rethinking" political economy, especially in light of global political and economic restructuring (see Meehan, Mosco, & Wasko, 1994; Sussman, 1999). Mosco's (1996) book-length overview of PE/C is subtitled *Rethinking and Renewal* and presents a rethinking of political economy in the broad terms of commodification, spatialization, and structuration. In addition, he examines political economy's relation to cultural studies and policy studies. Mosco emphasizes that political economy is just one "entry point" to the study of communications, which must be studied within a wider social totality.

It is also important to note that there are different approaches to PE/C. In his 1996 overview, Mosco points out that British/ European political economists have generally attempted to "integrate communication research within various neo-Marxian theoretical traditions." On the other hand, North American political economy, drawing on both Marxian and institutional approaches, "has been driven more explicitly by a sense of injustice that the communication industry has become an integral part of a wider corporate order which is both exploitative and undemocratic" (p. 19).

Mosco also describes another variation that might be called Third World PE/C research, which relies on dependency and world systems theory, as well as other neo-Marxist traditions. This type of research has focused on challenging the modernization paradigm and analyzing various aspects of globalization processes (p. 20).

Recently, even more attention has been given to the distinctions between PE/C approaches. Hesmondhalgh (2002) discusses the differences between a "Schiller-McChesney tradition" and a "cultural industries approach." He is referring here to the criticism of U.S. media systems, especially media concentration, as developed by Herb Schiller and continued in the 1990s by McChesney and others, including Herman and Chomsky (1988). Hesmondhalgh argues that the tradition represented by Schiller and McChesney has provided invaluable documentation and analysis of the cultural industries. However, Hesmondhalgh feels that this version of PE/C has some shortcomings: It still "underestimates" contradiction in the system, fails to explain specific conditions of cultural industries, pays less attention to consumption than production, and mostly ignores "symbol creators" while focusing most often on information-based media than entertainment-oriented media. Hesmondhalgh finds solutions to these problems in a cultural industries approach—as outlined by Bernard Miège (1989)—but also draws on Raymond Williams (especially 1980) and thus is more sympathetic to a cultural studies tradition.

Early on in his book, Hesmondhalgh (2002) identifies the cultural industries approach as "European" and the Schiller McChesney approach as "a distinctive US tradition" (p. 8). Although a case can be made that the characteristics that Hesmondhalgh ascribes to the Schiller-McChesney tradition do indeed apply to some U.S. scholars, the wide range of PE/C work that has been done in North America has unfortunately been overlooked in this formulation, as may become clearer from the overview of PE/C research presented in the next section.

Ultimately, Mosco (1996, pp. 104–105) concludes that even though there are variations, all of these explications of PE/C at least attempt to decenter the media and emphasize capital, class, contradiction, conflict, and oppositional struggles. He further emphasizes that

> the political economy of communication covers a wide intellectual expanse including diverse standpoints, emphases, and interests which belie charges of essentialism that, in the extreme, dismiss the approach as economistic. The approach brings together an international collection of scholars who share not so much a singular theoretical perspective or even sense of community, but an approach to intellectual activity and a conception of the relationship between the scholarly imagination and social intervention. Moreover, it suggests that political economy faces numerous challenges that grow out of global social and cultural transformations as well as developments on its intellectual borders. (pp. 20–21)

◆ Exemplars of Political Economy of Communications

To further understand PE/C, it is useful to consider specific examples of the issues that political economists examine, as well as examples of research that has been influenced by this approach. (It is nearly impossible to completely trace the rich history and wide range of communication scholarship that draws on a political economic tradition because a wide range of themes pertaining to communication and media has been analyzed.) Although there are any number of ways to organize this discussion, the presentation that follows discusses some of the general themes that are fundamental to PE/C and provides some examples of research that exemplify these themes.[3]

HISTORICAL STUDIES

Most PE/C research incorporates historical analysis, for it is essential to document change as well as continuity. However, many notable historical studies have traced the development of specific media. The commercialization of the press has been documented in the United States by D. Schiller (1981) and Eisenstein (1979), and in Britain, emphasis on class relations and the press has characterized historical studies by Curran (1979) and Sparks (1985). Ewen's historical work (1976, 1998) presents the historical evolution of advertising and public relations, tracing the development of mass consumption and mind management.

Historical studies of broadcasting in the United States and Canada often have focused also on commercialization, as well as the relationship between corporate power and the state (e.g., Downing, 1990; Kellner, 1990; McChesney, 1993). Meanwhile, Attali (1985) has presented a historical overview of the music industry, and Flichy (1991) has discussed the history of media in Europe and North America.

The historical evolution of telecommunications has also received attention from political economists who have traced the growth and change of corporate power and state relations. Beyond Danielian's (1939) classic work on AT&T, more recent research includes Duboff's (1984) historical analysis of the telegraph and Becker's (1993) work on the telephone.

Historical work on the film industry also has been the focus of political economists, who have countered the typical emphasis by film scholars on texts and genres by focusing on the commercial and industrial aspects of film. Examples of work that includes a historical emphasis include Guback's (1969) research on the international film industry, Wasko's (1982) study of financial institutions and the film industry, and Pendakur's (1990) work on the historical dominance of the U.S. film industry in Canada.

THE MEDIA/ COMMUNICATIONS BUSINESS

A good deal of PE/C research has focused on the evolution of mass communications as commodities that are produced and distributed by profit-seeking organizations in capitalist industries. The trends that Murdock and Golding identified in 1973 have expanded and intensified not only within traditional media industries but across industrial divisions and into new technologically converged businesses as well. A market model now dominates much of the media landscape (Philo & Miller, 2000). Communication and information have become key components of this marketization process but have also developed as significant industries in their own right. In many countries, public media institutions have been privatized along with other public institutions, opening additional markets for growing transnational media and entertainment conglomerates. In addition, new communication and information systems, such as the Internet, are developing as commercialized space, contrary to earlier promises of public access and control. This commercialization process (including the growth of advertising and public relations) has been accompanied by an ever-expanding consumer culture, thus prompting the term *cultural capitalism* as a descriptor for the current period (see Murdock & Wasko, in press).

Analysis of media as a commodity and industry has involved various concepts and levels of analysis. First, we will discuss examples of these various tendencies, exemplified by the U.S. market and Time-Warner, followed by research examples of the different levels of analysis. (Internationalization, the global level of analysis, will be discussed in a separate section later.)

Commodification/Commercialization. Increasingly, media and communication resources have become commodities—products and services that are sold by profit-seeking companies to buyers or consumers. An example that seems obvious is the development of various forms of "pay" television since the 1980s (see Mosco, 1989). In addition, more and more of the media/communication landscape is filled with commercial messages. Numerous examples come to mind, but perhaps the evolution of product placement in Hollywood feature films is one of the most blatant (see Wasko, 1994).

Diversification. As media companies have expanded, new lines of business have been added in a process of diversification. Although most of the media industries in the United States began with a relatively large number of different companies, these industries today are dominated by huge media/entertainment conglomerates, such as TimeWarner, that are involved in a wide range of diversified activities. For instance, TimeWarner includes the following:

- ◆ publishing (Time Inc., Little Brown & Co., DC Comics),
- ◆ film (Warner Bros., New Line Cinema, Castle Rock Entertainment, Warner International Theatres),
- ◆ television production and distribution (Warner Television, WB Network, Turner Broadcasting),
- ◆ home video (Warner Home Video),
- ◆ music (Warner Music Group, including Atlantic, Elektra, Rhino, Warner Bros., Columbia House Co.),
- ◆ cable networks (HBO, Cinemax, CNN, Cartoon Network, Turner Classic Movies, etc.),
- ◆ cable systems (Time-Warner Cable, Time-Warner Telecom),
- ◆ computer services (America Online, CompuServe, Netscape, etc.),

◆ professional sports (Atlanta Braves, Atlanta Hawks).

Horizontal Integration. As media corporations have grown larger and more profitable, they often have added companies that are in the same line of business, thus integrating horizontally. TimeWarner, for instance, has added to its already sizable list of magazines that were owned by Time, Inc. and currently publishes more than 140 magazines.

Vertical Integration. Not only have companies such as TimeWarner expanded their range of businesses, but with new distribution technologies and deregulated markets, media companies have also integrated vertically by adding companies in the same supply chain or at different stages of production. For instance, at TimeWarner, Warner Bros. and New Line Cinema produce and distribute motion pictures that are shown on the company's cable networks (HBO, Cinemax) and television network (Warner Television network). As stated on TimeWarner's Web site at the end of 2002,

> Warner Bros. has evolved into a fully integrated global entertainment company, standing at the forefront of feature films, television, home video, animation, product and brand licensing, interactive media and international theaters.
>
> New Line's programming refreshes AOL Time Warner's libraries and provides valuable programming for its cable networks, in particular TNT, TBS and HBO.

Synergy. There is also the potential for the various businesses owned by these large diversified conglomerates to work together to more effectively market products, thus producing a synergy that maximizes profits. For instance, Warner films can be promoted via AOL as well as other company-owned media outlets, as well as serving as the basis for other media products (TV programs, books, etc.). Another example cited on TimeWarner's Web site in 2002 is the following:

> Time Inc. has taken advantage of extensive cross-promotion with America Online. Promotions of Time Inc. magazines on the AOL services generated 1.5 million subscriptions in 2001— about 100,000 a month. AOL discs poly-bagged with Time Inc. magazines and distributed at retail outlets led to some 800,000 AOL registrations.

It might be noted, however, that TimeWarner has been criticized for not taking full advantage of such strategies. In fact, some discussions in the popular and financial press during 2002 focused on whether TimeWarner (as well as a few other media conglomerates) had actually become too large to function efficiently at all. Indeed, some observers have even suggested that some mergers create corporations that are too large and unwieldy, thus arguing for more streamlined companies that can concentrate their efforts. However, other arguments have been made that synergies take time to develop and ultimately are advantageous for media and information companies such as TimeWarner.

Market Concentration. Of course, one of the major issues is the level of competition in various media markets. Although a competitive marketplace is the avowed goal of capitalism, there is an inevitable tendency for markets to become concentrated due to any number of factors (see Murdock & Golding, 1973). By documenting the actual level of competition (or lack of competition), PE/C challenges the myth of the competitive marketplace under late capitalism.

Indeed, TimeWarner holds a dominant share of the market in a number of different media industries. The company controlled more than 18% of U.S. cable systems in 2001 (which, together with AT&T

Comcast, represented 55% of the industry), whereas most of these cable systems represent a monopoly in their local cable service markets. In addition, with 31.5 million subscribers, AOL and its affiliated Internet service providers (ISPs) represent 21.1% of the online business in the United States, a considerable advantage over the next largest competitor (MSN) at 5.2%.

Essentially, most of the media industries or sectors in the United States are dominated by oligopolies. For instance, in 2001, Warner Bros. Pictures was the top film distributor in the United States, receiving $1.24 billion at the domestic box office. However, an oligopoly that includes Warner, Disney, Universal, Paramount, and Fox (all owned by giant media conglomerates) regularly receives between 80% and 90% of the total theatrical film box office, not only in the United States but many other countries around the world.

General Media Analysis. These various trends have been investigated by political economists in communications at various levels of analysis, including national media systems, specific media industries, and specific corporations. In addition, international level of analysis has been a special focal point of political economy and will be discussed in the next section.

Considering these developments across media/communication industries, it is not difficult to conclude that TimeWarner, together with a handful of other conglomerates, dominates the U.S. media landscape. Ben Bagdikian's (2000) ongoing countdown of the top media corporations is instructive here:

In 1983, fifty corporations dominated most of every mass medium and the biggest media merger in history was a $340 million deal. . . . [I]n 1987, the fifty companies had shrunk to twenty-nine. . . . [I]n 1990, the twenty-nine had shrunk to twenty three. . . . [I]n 1997, the biggest firms numbered ten and

involved the $19 billion Disney-ABC deal, at the time the biggest media merger ever. . . . [In 2000] AOL Time Warner's $350 billion merged corporation [was] more than 1,000 times larger [than the biggest deal of 1983]. (pp. xx–xxi)

Political economists are especially interested in the consequences of such media concentration. For instance, much attention has been focused on the influence of concentration on the availability and quality of news, as well as the tabloidization of news. In addition, researchers have documented the "blockbuster complex" and the homogenization of the content in cultural industries. More generally, political economists have analyzed these trends in relation to capitalism and power, confirming a class system with inherent structural inequalities and obstacles to meaningful democracy.

As noted previously, media concentration obviously has been a major focus of political economists in media studies for many years. However, the issues have become so blatant and intense over the past few decades that it not only is a theme for political economists but has also attracted the attention of other media researchers and activists, as well as some policymakers and journalists. Media economists also have paid special attention to this issue (see Chapter 14, this volume), though the type of analysis and the conclusions drawn are often quite different, as discussed below.

Examples of PE/C research in this area are abundant. Murdock (1990) has continued to provide keen analysis of these general trends, especially in Britain, and U.S. researchers have included (among many others) Barnouw and Gitlin (1998) and McChesney (1999).

Industry Studies. Political economists also have examined specific media and communications industries, describing industry

318 ◆ *Economy and Power*

structure and policies and looking more deeply into the trends described above, especially commercialization, commodification, and integration within these industries. Even though some of these industries are merging and converging, the analysis of industrial sectors is still often quite relevant.[4]

Meanwhile, other researchers within a political economic tradition have done research on the cultural industries, with Miège's (1998) work setting the foundations for work by other researchers, such as Sinclair (1999) and Hesmondhalgh (2002).

Telecommunication and information technologies have received extensive analysis in PE/C studies, with issues examined such as technological determinism and state support of technological development. Special attention has been directed at the unequal distribution of such resources, with analysis of issues such as access and equity, including discussions of "the information poor" or "the digital divide." Representative studies include H. I. Schiller (1981), Mosco (1989), Schiller (1986), Wilson (1988), Mosco and Wasko (1988), Hills (1991), Gandy (1993), Mansell (1993), and McChesney, Wood, and Foster (1998).

Corporate Studies. The examples thus far examine patterns of ownership within and across media sectors. Meanwhile, other work in PE/C has focused more specifically on issues relating to ownership and control of specific media organizations. Closer, more in-depth analysis of media and communication organizations is necessary to assess the precise mechanisms of corporate ownership and control but also to examine trends of commodification, integration, and diversification. This analysis often considers these developments in light of issues such as cultural creativity, diversity, equity, access, and democratic ideals.

The Walt Disney Company, for instance, provides a good example for such analysis (Wasko, 2001). Although the company has been known for producing children's or family-oriented entertainment—thus, gaining a somewhat sacred or pure image—it is important to analyze the company's business orientation and strategies. The Walt Disney Company was incorporated by Walt and Roy Disney in 1923, first as the Disney Brothers Cartoon Studio, then as the Walt Disney Studio. Based in Los Angeles, California, the company produced short animated films that were distributed by other film companies and appeared before feature-length films in movie theaters around the world.

Never one of the major studios, the company grew gradually, always with financial difficulties, and established itself as an independent production company in Hollywood. The Disney brothers built a reputation for quality animation, using cutting-edge technological developments such as sound and color and producing feature-length animated films. The popularity of Disney's products, which included merchandise based on its animated characters, was instantaneous and unmistakable not only in the United States but also in other countries.

Setting the foundations for the diversification that emerged in the ensuing decades, during the 1950s, Disney expanded to include television production and live-action feature films. In 1953, the company opened Disneyland, the first of many theme parks. During this period, the company also started distributing its own films. By the mid-1970s, however, the company appeared to be stagnating until a management and ownership shuffle rejuvenated its established businesses and developed new investments.

At the end of the 20th century, the Walt Disney Company was the second largest media conglomerate in the world (behind TimeWarner), with a wide array of domestic and international investments. The company's revenues for 2000 were more than $25 billion. Disney owns the American Broadcasting Company (ABC) television network, broadcast TV stations, and radio stations and networks and maintains partial ownership of several cable networks, including 80% of ESPN and 38% of A&E and Lifetime. Walt Disney Studios produces films under the Touchstone, Hollywood

Pictures, and Miramax labels. In addition, the company was also involved in home video, recorded music, theatrical productions, and consumer products, which are sold at more than 600 Disney Stores around the world.

Disney's theme parks and resorts division encompass six major theme parks in the United States, including Disneyland in Anaheim, California, and the Walt Disney World Resort in Florida (EPCOT, The Animal Kingdom, Disney–MGM Studios). Other theme park sites are Tokyo Disney, Disneyland Paris, and, by 2003, Hong Kong Disneyland. The company also owns extensive hotel and resort properties, a variety of regional entertainment centers, a cruise line, sports investments, and a planned community in Florida called Celebration. The Walt Disney Internet Group includes sites such as ABC.com, Disney Online, and ESPN.com.

The Disney Company represents an example of the diversified entertainment conglomerates that dominate the media industry, at least in the United States. The company's motivations are clearly stated in the following statements:

> Disney's overriding objective is to create shareholder value by continuing to be the world's premier entertainment company from a creative, strategic and financial standpoint. (www.disney.com/Investor Relations)

> Success tends to make you forget what made you successful. . . . We have no obligation to make art. We have no obligation to make a statement. To make money is our only objective. (Michael Eisner, 1981 staff memo, cited in Wasko, 2001)

A political economic analysis of the Disney Company would investigate the beneficiaries of these policies (shareholders and managers), as well as the mechanisms of control within the corporation that influence the production and distribution of its products and services. A complete study would look carefully at large stockholders, their relation to managers, and the composition of the board of directors. In addition, ties to other companies and financial institutions would be explored.

At this level of analysis, political economists are able to examine the consequences as well as the contradictions of capitalist ownership of media resources, not just as they relate to media concentration.

However, there are not as many academic studies that focus on specific corporations as one might hope. Examples would include Wasko (2001) and Banks (1996). However, books written by nonacademics are often useful in supplying relevant information for this type of analysis (e.g., Grover, 1996).

INTERNATIONALIZATION/ GLOBALIZATION

Political economy has concentrated especially on analyzing issues relating to international communication, even before the recent emphasis on globalization. This area includes not only the expansion of media corporations internationally but also the various political and economic issues related to a global communication system.

Of course, corporations such as TimeWarner and Disney have extensive global investments and activities. However, a particularly interesting example of the international expansion of media companies is Rupert Murdoch's News Corp. The corporation originated in Australia, where Murdoch owned several newspaper chains and numerous magazines. But over the next decades, the company expanded to include important media outlets on every continent except Africa, with particular strengths in satellite broadcasting systems. The company has holdings in film, television, home video, cable networks, magazines, newspapers, book publishing, and sports. The corporation's Web site boasted in 2002 of "producing and distributing the most compelling news, information and entertainment to the farthest reaches of the globe." Murdoch's global strategies have been varied but primarily have taken advantage of profitable opportunities, whatever and wherever they may exist, as well as focusing on popular, lowest common denominator media content.[5]

Although these issues were emphasized by Herman and McChesney (1997) and others, analysis of transnationalization of communication and media has been a theme for PE/C at least since the 1960s. For instance, Schiller's extensive work (beginning with H. I. Schiller, 1969/1992) was important in critiquing the U.S. communication system, its government and military ties, and its international extension.

Other PE/C work specifically embracing global issues includes Guback's (1969) studies of the international film industry, as well as his and others' work on international flows of media. Indeed, the discussion of a new world information order drew heavily on political economic analysis and became an important focus of research during the 1970s and 1980s (for overviews, see Nordenstreng & Schiller, 1993; Roach, 1993).

Meanwhile, in Latin America and Europe, numerous studies made important contributions to the discussion of international media development and cultural imperialism (see especially Dorfman & Mattelart, 1975). An overview of work done in Latin America is presented in Atwood and McAnany (1986), whereas Sussman and Lent (1991) gathered research focusing on the Pacific and Southeast Asia. In addition, as PE/C research expands, new and interesting approaches are emerging in various parts of the world. A few examples would include the work of Zhao (1998) and Morris-Suzuki (1998).

MEDIA-STATE RELATIONS

Even though studies of ownership patterns and the dynamics of corporate control are essential, political economic analysis is much more than merely identifying and then condemning those who control media and communication resources. To understand the media's role in society, it is essential to understand relationships between media power and state power, as well as the media's relationships with other economic sectors. Interrelationships between media and communication industries and sites of power in society are necessary for the complete analysis of communications and help to dispel some common myths about our economic and political system, especially the notions of pluralism, free enterprise, and competition. Thus, an important theme in political economic research has been tracking the relationships between political power and media power, especially those relationships that involve the state.

Although it is often assumed that corporations simply seek relief from government intrusion, it is crucial to understand the ways in which the state supports the economy and corporations. To cite only one example, the U.S. motion picture industry relies on the U.S. government for clearing barriers to foreign markets, as well as in tracking and punishing copyright offenders, both in the United States and elsewhere. This relationship involves the film industry's lobbying arm, the Motion Picture Association of America (MPAA), which regularly attempts to influence government policies affecting the industry and its members (for more details, see Guback, 1969; Pendakur, 1990).

Schiller's and Smythe's work paved the way for a range of issues and themes that focus on media-state relations. Smythe's (1957) early work on the electromagnetic spectrum pointed to the state's role in allocating communication resources and protecting corporate interests, whereas H. I. Schiller's (1969/1992) *Mass Communication and American Empire* provided an important analysis of the U.S. government's use of communication resources, especially for military purposes.

Meanwhile, other aspects of state policy have also been explored, particularly pertaining to support of the corporate interests in areas such as regulation, intellectual property, and so on. Bettig's (1997) work on intellectual property is an especially good example. Meanwhile, regulation and policy have been the focus of work by many of the previously mentioned researchers, as well as Hills (1986), Streeter (1996), and Calabrese and Burgelman (1999).

RESISTANCE/OPPOSITION

Despite the claims that political economy focuses only on the omnipotence of large corporations and a system that is impenetrable, political economists address issues relating to resistance and opposition in a wide range of research. Mattelart and Siegelaub (1983) presented many examples of these issues. Around the same time, studies of labor and the working class were gathered by Mosco and Wasko (1983) and later by Sussman and Lent (1998). Meanwhile, Douglas (1986) looked at trade unions in the media industry, Nielsen and Mailes (1996) studied labor in the film industry, and Winseck (1993) analyzed telecommunications unions in Canada.

Meanwhile, Miller, Govil, McMurria, and Maxwell (2001) have attempted to reframe the discussion of global Hollywood in terms of a new international division of cultural labor (NICL). The authors outline Hollywood's global dominance in political economic terms, analyzing the strategies that the U.S. film industry has used to "Americanize" the production, distribution, and exhibition of film. However, they frame their discussion in terms of the implications of this dominance for film workers as well as consumers, arguing that we need to "confront the NICL and imagine alternative, more salutary conditions and possibilities for our own cultural labour and for our brothers and sisters in the culture works everywhere" (p. 216).

Political economists also have discussed media developments specifically in relation to the public sphere, public citizenship, and democracy. Although acknowledging the powerful role that capital plays in media developments, researchers have argued that these issues have direct bearing on citizenship and public participation. These themes have characterized some of the work by Garnham, Murdock and McChesney, and many others.

♦ *Political Economy's Relationship to Other Approaches*

It also is instructive to consider PE/C's relationship to other approaches that focus on the study of communications and media. It has previously been noted that the application of political economy to communication or media most always indicates a critical approach, compared to what has been called an administrative or mainstream approach in communication research. Meehan (1999) has recently referred to the latter research paradigm as "celebratory" and concludes,

> If we begin with a shared valuation that "although some problems may exist, capitalism is fundamentally good," our research thereby takes a celebratory stance toward media products, audiences, and institutions. If our shared valuation suggests that "despite some progress, capitalism is fundamentally flawed," a critical stance is an integral part of our research. Attempts at dialogue across these mutually exclusive valuations seem bound to fail. (p. 150)

Several areas of mainstream research focus on issues similar to PE/C. Mosco (1996) has looked closely at policy studies that direct attention to important political influences on media and communications developments that are sometimes neglected by political economists. However, as Mosco observes, such analysis draws strongly on pluralist models, usually overemphasizes the state's roles (particularly in legal and regulatory policies), and tends to ignore relations of power and the fundamental dynamics of capitalism.

Here, we will focus on PE/C's relationship with another mainstream or celebratory approach, media economics, and the important relationship between PE/C and cultural studies.

POLITICAL ECONOMY AND MEDIA ECONOMICS

More deliberate attention to economics has been evident in the field of communication and media studies during the past decade or so, with scholars identifying *media economics* as a distinct focus of research activity. Examples include textbooks by Picard (1989), Albarran (1996), and Alexander, Owers, and Carveth (1993), as well as the *Journal of Media Economics,* which was launched in 1988. The goal of the journal, as stated in its Contributor Information section, is "to broaden understanding and discussion of the impact of economic and financial activities on media operations and managerial decisions." Generally, these media economics texts and the journal echo the concerns of mainstream (neoclassical) economics and seldom present serious critique of the capitalist media system. As the journal's first editor explains,

> Media economics is concerned with how media operators meet the informational and entertainment wants and needs of audiences, advertisers and society with available resources. It deals with the factors influencing production of media goods and services and the allocation of those products for consumption. (Picard, 1989, p. 7)

For the most part, the emphasis of media economics is on microeconomic issues rather

than macroanalysis and focuses primarily on producers and consumers in media markets. Typically, the concern is how media industries and companies can succeed, prosper, or move forward. In other words, this represents a celebratory position vis-à-vis capitalism. Although competition may be assessed, little emphasis is placed on issues posed by ownership of media resources or the implications of concentrated ownership and control. For instance, despite their title *Who Owns the Media?* the volumes prepared by Compaine (1982; Compaine & Gomery, 2000) represent a form of celebratory media economics and avoid discussion of the actual owners of media corporations or their overall connections to a capitalist system.[6] These approaches avoid the kind of moral grounding adopted by political economists, as most studies emphasize description (or "what is") rather than critique (or "what ought to be"). A common approach is the industrial organization model, as described by Gomery (1989):

> The industrial organization model of structure, conduct, and performance provides a powerful and useful analytical framework for economic analysis. Using it, the analyst seeks to define the size and scope of the structure of an industry and then goes on to examine its economic behavior. Both of these steps require analyzing the status and operations of the industry, not as the analyst wishes it were. Evaluation of its performance is the final step, a careful weighing of "what is" versus "what ought to be." (p. 58)

"What ought to be," however, is a competitive, democratically responsive, and multicultural media system. Even though it rarely makes this claim as such, the media economics tradition effectively reinforces and celebrates the status quo media system.

Along these lines, however, a few communication scholars also have contributed valuable organizational studies, which call attention to economic characteristics of media and communication industries, as well as emphasizing policy and regulatory developments, but not necessarily from a political economic perspective (see Tunstall & Palmer, 1991; Turow, 1984).

POLITICAL ECONOMY AND CULTURAL STUDIES

It is especially important to look more closely at the relationship between PE/C and cultural studies, as these two approaches are often identified (rightly or wrongly) as the primary and sometimes competing ways of critically examining media. Though PE/C and cultural studies focus on different areas of inquiry or objects of study, both approaches would seem to be needed for a complete critical analysis of culture and media.

Although cultural studies has expanded to the point where any definition is bound to be too limiting, a useful formulation is offered by O'Sullivan, Hartley, Saunders, Montgomery, and Fiske (1994): "Cultural studies has focussed on the relations between social relations and meanings—or more exactly on the way social divisions are made meaningful" (p. 71). It would seem, therefore, that PE/C and cultural studies would at least share a common critical analysis, even though the focus of study is directed at different elements of the media process.

However, PE/C is often considered by cultural studies scholars to be too narrow, deterministic, and economistic, despite the broad definitions and wide range of research outlined above. Many have charged that PE/C is primarily focused on the economic or the production side of the communication process, neglecting texts, discourse, audiences, and consumption. In addition, a simplistic notion of ideology is ascribed to political economists, with little room allowed for resistance or subversion by audience members.

Over the years, political economists have defended and expanded their theoretical positions in light of some of these critiques, clarifying extreme and inaccurate accusations but also responding to reasonable criticism (cf. Golding & Murdock, 1991; Murdock & Golding, 1973).

On the other hand, some political economists have found cultural studies to be lacking consistent and strong analysis of the institutional or structural context of cultural consumption, focusing too narrowly on issues relating to media texts, identity, and audience reception. Especially problematic are studies that argue that the audience's alternative interpretations of media texts represent a kind of subversive resistance to and undermining of dominant ideological definitions and thus are politically liberating (e.g., Fiske, 1988).

Over the years, numerous discussions and evaluations of this relationship have been offered by one side or the other in individual papers, articles, and books. However, the most focused debates have taken place in professional journals—for example, in the "Colloquy" in *Critical Studies in Mass Communication* in 1995. Here, Garnham (1995) and cultural studies specialist Larry Grossberg (1995) squared off, in what Meehan (1999) has called a "ritualized debate" based on stereotypes and unproductive posturing. In other words, the "debate" was not based on a constructive and well-mannered engagement but degenerated into spiteful and negative (sometimes false) characterizations of extreme positions within both approaches.

For many, however, there is still a need for an intellectual alliance (beginning with true dialogue, as Meehan, 1999, argues) between political economy and cultural studies. Such an integration of approaches is necessary not only to fully examine the complexities of mediated communication but also to challenge other celebratory approaches in communication research. As Murdock (1995) argues (in the debate cited above), we need to

work towards the construction of a more complete account of the central dynamics of contemporary culture and to mobilize those insights to defend the symbolic resources required to extend the rights and duties of citizenship in the service of revitalizing democracy. (p. 94)

◆ *The Future*

Even while the "debates" between PE/C and cultural studies have raged, a good deal of interesting work has integrated these approaches and may represent the most dynamic direction for future development. Many researchers who have identified primarily with PE/C have also integrated other approaches and disciplines with interesting and important results. More work has been done recently integrating feminism and political economy, represented especially in Meehan and Riordan (2002), as well as in work by Meehan and Byars (1995), Martin (1991), and Balka and Smith (2000).

On another front, Gandy (1998) offers an important look at race and ethnicity in the evolving systems of information media. As an indication of the integrated nature of such research, the book's description on the back cover is exemplary:

> It explores the concept of race through three streams of analysis: media systems and institutions, communication frames and symbolic representations; and social constructions. Borrowing insights from behavioral science, political economy, and the more interpretative strands of contemporary cultural studies, the book enters directly into the contemporary debate about structure and agency, and ends by proposing an agenda for the development of critical theory in the area of race and ethnicity.

In another recent collection (Hagen & Wasko, 1998), various researchers address the commonalities and tensions between political economy and audience or reception analysis. Although many of the authors in the volume see that the approaches share some theoretical perspectives, others point to issues relating to methodological and ideological differences.

In another development, several political economists represented in the previously mentioned volume present interesting analyses that integrate other disciplines. For instance, Murdock (1998) draws on anthropology to look more carefully at the historical roots of consumption. Elsewhere, Pendakur (1993) has integrated ethnography with political economy, delving more deeply into the impact of media technology in rural villages in India. And Mosco's (1999) recent work on New York draws heavily on geography to map the evolution of commercial space in the city. These researchers have maintained the theoretical foundations of political economy while expanding their analysis to embrace other relevant disciplines.

Increasingly, there are also studies that attempt to use political economy with other approaches to examine a particular media phenomenon holistically. An excellent example is Gripsrud's (1995) study of *Dynasty,* which traces the program's production context and discusses its textual elements, as well as examining its distribution and reception. In my own work on the Walt Disney Company, an attempt has been made to examine the history and political economy of the company, as well as explore various textual readings and the reception of and resistance to Disney products (Wasko, 2001).

It is important to note that these integrated approaches still at least attempt to maintain the essence of political economy—or, in other words, research that examines the relationships of power that are involved in the production, distribution, and consumption of media and communication resources within a wider social context. PE/C still privileges issues relating to class power, though not to the exclusion of other relationships, and emphasizes the complex and contradictory nature of such relationships. Most important, PE/C challenges media and communication trends that undermine the development of equitable and democratic societies.

◆ Notes

1. For instance, Danielian's (1939) classic study of AT&T and several critical analyses of the U.S. film industry, such as Huettig (1944) and Klingender and Legg (1937).

2. Recently, James Curran (2004) has labeled the work done by Garnham and those at the University of Westminster and associated with the journal *Media, Culture & Society* as the Westminster school or tradition. Curran explains that the Westminster school represents an approach to the media and a body of work analogous to the Birmingham school's contribution to cultural studies. Briefly, the Westminster school has produced empirical and historical studies of different media, as well as work on the evolution of the public sphere and public policy. Curran notes, however, that the tradition is not necessarily identified with PE/C, which has a broader scope than the Westminster school.

3. As noted, Mosco (1996) provides a more extensive and detailed overview. The work of researchers who do not refer directly to the PE/C tradition is also included in this discussion.

4. The television industry was dissected early on by Bunce (1976) and Collins, Garnham, and Locksley (1988) and later by Meehan (1984), Downing (1990), and Streeter (1996). Specific studies have analyzed the film industry, including Guback (1969), Garnham (1990), Pendakur (1990), Aksoy and Robins (1992), and Wasko (1994). Meanwhile, advertising has been examined by Janus (1984), Sinclair (1987), Jhally (1990), and Mattelart (1991) and public relations by Ewen (1998).

5. Murdoch's tabloids regularly feature heaps of sex and violence. An example of one of the more famous headlines from one of his tabloids, the *New York Post:* "Headless Body Found in Topless Bar."

6. For example, some of the differences between political economy and media economics; see the debate on media ownership between McChesney and Compaine (and others) that appears on opendemocracy.net at www.opendemocracy.net/forum/strand_home.asp?CatID=5.

◆ References

Aksoy, A., & Robins, K. (1992). Hollywood for the 21st century: Global competition for critical mass in image markets. *Cambridge Journal of Economics, 16*(1), 1–22.

Albarran, A. (1996). *Media economics: Understanding markets, industries, and concepts.* Ames: Iowa State University Press.

Alexander, A., Owers, J., & Carveth, R. (Eds.). (1993). *Media economics: Theory and practice.* Hillsdale, NJ: Lawrence Erlbaum.

Attali, J. (1985). *Noise: The political economy of music.* Minneapolis: University of Minnesota Press.

Atwood, R., & McAnany, E. G. (Eds.). (1986). *Communication and Latin American society.* Madison: University of Wisconsin Press.

Bagdikian, B. (2000). *The media monopoly* (6th ed.). Boston: Beacon.

Balka, E., & Smith, R. (Eds.). (2000). *Women, work and computerization: Charting a course to the future.* Dordrecht, the Netherlands: Kluwer.

Banks, J. (1996). *Monopoly television: MTV's quest to control the music.* Boulder, CO: Westview.

Barnouw, E., & Gitlin, T. (Eds.). (1998). *Conglomerates and the media.* New York: New Press.

Becker, J. (1993). The political economy of early telephony in Germany. In J. Wasko, V. Mosco, & M. Pendakur (Eds.), *Illuminating the blindspots: Essays honoring Dallas W. Smythe.* Norwood, NJ: Ablex.

Bettig, R. (1997). *Copyrighting culture: The political economy of intellectual property.* Boulder, CO: Westview.

Bunce, R. (1976). *Television in the corporate interest.* New York: Praeger.

Calabrese, A., & Burgelman, J.-C. (Eds.). (1999). *Communication, citizenship and social policy.* Boulder, CO: Rowman & Littlefield.

Collins, R., Garnham, N., & Locksley, G. (1988). *Economics of television: The UK case.* London: Sage.

Compaine, B. (Ed.). (1982). *Who owns the media? Concentration of ownership in the mass communications industry.* White Plains, NY: Knowledge Industry Publications.

Compaine, B., & Gomery, D. (2000). *Who owns the media? Competition and concentration in the mass media industry.* Mahwah, NJ: Lawrence Erlbaum.

Curran, J. (1979). Capitalism and control of the press, 1800–1975. In J. Curran, M. Gurevitch, & J. Woollacott (Eds.), *Mass communication and society* (pp. 7–11). Beverly Hills, CA: Sage.

Curran, J. (2004). The rise of the Westminster School. In A. Calabrese & C. Sparks (Eds.), *Toward a political economy of culture: Capitalism and communication in the twenty-first century* (pp. 13-40). Boulder, CO: Rowman & Littlefield.

Danielian, N. R. (1939). *The AT&T.* New York: Vanguard.

Dorfman, A., & Mattelart, A. (1975). *How to read Donald Duck.* London: International General.

Douglas, S. (1986). *Labor's new voice: Unions and the mass media.* Norwood, NJ: Ablex.

Downing, J. D. H. (1990). The political economy of U.S. television. *Monthly Review, 42*(1), 30–41.

Duboff, R. (1984). The rise of communications regulation: The telegraph industry, 1844–1880. *Journal of Communication, 34*(3), 52–66.

Eisenstein, E. (1979). *The printing press as an agent of change: Communications and cultural transformations in early Modern Europe.* New York: Cambridge University Press.

Ewen, S. (1976). *Captains of consciousness.* New York: McGraw-Hill.

Ewen, S. (1998). *PR! A social history of spin.* New York: Basic Books.

Fiske, J. (1988). *Television culture.* London: Methuen.

Flichy, P. (1991). *Une histoire de la communication moderne: Espace public et vie privée* [A history of modern communication: Public spaces and private life]. Paris: La Découverte.

Gandy, O. H., Jr. (1993). *The panoptic sort: The political economy of personal information.* Boulder, CO: Westview.

Gandy, O. H., Jr. (1998). *Communication and race: A structural perspective.* London: Edward Arnold.

Garnham, N. (1979). Contribution to a political economy of mass communication. *Media, Culture and Society, 1,* 123–146.

Garnham, N. (1990). *Capitalism and communication: Global culture and the economics of information.* London: Sage.

Garnham, N. (1995). Political economy and cultural studies: Reconciliation or divorce? *Critical Studies in Mass Communication, 12*(1), 62–71.

Golding, P., & Murdock, G. (1991). Culture, communication, and political economy. In J. Curran & M. Gurevitch (Eds.), *Mass media and society* (pp. 15–32). London: Edward Arnold.

Gomery, D. (1989). Media economics: Terms of analysis. *Critical Studies in Mass Communication, 6*(1), 43–60.

Gripsrud, J. (1995). *The* Dynasty *years: Hollywood television and critical media studies.* London: Routledge.

Grossberg, L. (1995). Cultural studies vs. political economy: Is anybody else bored with this debate? *Critical Studies in Mass Communication, 12*(1), 72–81.

Grover, R. (1996). *The Disney touch: Disney, ABC and the quest for the world's greatest media empire* (2nd ed.). New York: McGraw-Hill.

Guback, T. H. (1969). *The international film industry: Western Europe and America since 1945.* Bloomington: Indiana University Press.

Hagen, I., & Wasko, J. (Eds.). (1998). *Consuming audiences: Production and reception in media research.* Cresskill, NJ: Hampton.

Herman, E., & Chomsky, N. (1988). *Manufacturing consent: A political economy of the mass media.* New York: Pantheon.

Herman, E., & McChesney, R. (1997). *The global media.* London: Cassell.

Hesmondhalgh, D. (2002). *The cultural industries.* London: Sage.

Hills, J. (1986). *Deregulating telecoms: Competition and control in the United States, Japan and Britain*. London: Frances Pinter.

Hills, J. (with Papathanassopoulos, S.). (1991). *The democracy gap: The politics of information and communication technologies in the United States and Europe*. New York: Greenwood.

Huettig, M. D. (1944). *Economic control of the motion picture industry*. Philadelphia: University of Pennsylvania Press.

Janus, N. (1984). Advertising and the creation of global markets: The role of the new communication technologies. In V. Mosco & J. Wasko (Eds.), *Critical communications review: Vol. 2. Changing patterns of communication control* (pp. 57–70). Norwood, NJ: Ablex.

Jevons, W. S. (1970). *The theory of political economy*. Harmondsworth, UK: Penguin.

Jhally, S. (1990). *The codes of advertising: Fetishism and the political economy of meaning in the consumer society*. New York: Routledge.

Kellner, D. (1990). *Television and the crisis of democracy*. Boulder, CO: Westview.

Klingender, F. D., & Legg, S. (1937). *Money behind the screen*. London: Lawrence & Wishart.

Livant, W. (1979). The audience commodity: On the "blindspot debate." *Canadian Journal of Political and Social Theory, 3*(1), 91–106.

Mansell, R. (1993). *The new telecommunications: A political economy of network evolution*. London: Sage.

Martin, M. (1991). *"Hello, central?" Gender, technology, and culture in the formation of telephone systems*. Montréal: McGill-Queen's University Press.

Marx, K. (1969). *Marx/Engels selected works* (Vol. 1). Moscow: Progress Publishers. (Original work published 1886)

Mattelart, A. (1979). For a *class* and *group* analysis of popular communication practices. In A. Mattelart & S. Siegelaub (Eds.), *Communication and class struggle: Vol. 1. Capitalism, imperialism*. New York: International General.

Mattelart, A. (1991). *Advertising international: The privatisation of public space*. London: Comedia and Routledge.

Mattelart, A., & Siegelaub, S. (Eds.). (1983). *Communication and class struggle: Vol. 2. Liberation, socialism*. New York: International General.

McChesney, R. W. (1993). *Telecommunications, mass media and democracy: The battle for the control of U.S. broadcasting*. New York: Oxford University Press.

McChesney, R. W. (1999). *Rich media, poor democracy*. Urbana: University of Illinois Press.

McChesney, R. W., Wood, E. M., & Foster, J. B. (Eds.). (1998). *Capitalism and the information age*. New York: Monthly Review Press.

Meehan, E. R. (1984). Ratings and the institutional approach: A third answer to the commodity question. *Critical Studies in Mass Communication, 1*(2), 216–225.

Meehan, E. R. (1993). Commodity audience, actual audience: The blindspot debate. In J. Wasko, V. Mosco, & M. Pendakur (Eds.), *Illuminating the blindspots: Essays honoring Dallas W. Smythe* (pp. 378–410). Norwood, NJ: Ablex.

Meehan, E. R. (1999). Commodity, culture, common sense: Media research and paradigm dialogue. *Journal of Media Economics, 12*(2), 149–163.

Meehan, E. R., & Byars, J. (1995). Once in a lifetime: Cable narrowcasting for women. *Camera Obscura, 33–34*, 213–241.

Meehan, E. R., Mosco, V., & Wasko, J. (1994). Rethinking political economy: Change and continuity. In M. R. Levy & M. Gurevitch (Eds.), *Defining media studies: Reflections on the future of the field* (pp. 347–358). New York: Oxford University Press.

Meehan, E. R., & Riordan, E. (Eds.). (2002). *Sex and money: Feminism and political economy in the media*. Minneapolis: University of Minnesota Press.

Miège, B. (1989). *The capitalization of cultural production*. Paris: International General.

Miller, T., Govil, N., McMurria, J., & Maxwell, R. (2001). *Global Hollywood*. London: British Film Institute.

Morris-Suzuki, T. (1998). *Re-inventing Japan: Time, space, nation (Japan in the modern world)*. Armonk, NY: M. E. Sharpe.

Mosco, V. (1989). *The pay-per society: Computers and communication in the information age*. Toronto: Garamond.

Mosco, V. (1996). *The political economy of communication: Rethinking and renewal*. London: Sage.

Mosco, V. (1999). New York.Com: A political economy of the "informational city." *Journal of Media Economics, 12*(2), 103–116.

Mosco, V., & Wasko, J. (Eds.). (1983). *The critical communications review: Vol. 1. Labor, the working class and the media*. Norwood, NJ: Ablex.

Mosco, V., & Wasko, J. (Eds.). (1988). *The political economy of information*. Madison: University of Wisconsin Press.

Murdock, G. (1978). Blindspots about Western Marxism: A reply to Dallas Smythe. *Canadian Journal of Political and Social Theory, 2*(2), 109–119.

Murdock, G. (1990). Redrawing the map of the communication industries. In M. Ferguson (Ed.), *Public communication: The new imperatives* (pp. 1–15). Newbury Park, CA: Sage.

Murdock, G. (1995). Across the great divide: Cultural analysis and the condition of democracy. *Critical Studies in Mass Communication, 12*, 89–94.

Murdock, G. (1998). Peculiar commodities: Audiences at large in the world of goods. In I. Hagen & J. Wasko (Eds.), *Consuming audiences: Production and reception in media research* (pp. 47–70). Cresskill, NJ: Hampton.

Murdock, G., & Golding, P. (1973). For a political economy of mass communications. In R. Miliband & J. Saville (Eds.), *Socialist register 1973* (pp. 205–234). London: Merlin.

Murdock, G., & Golding, P. (1979). Capitalism, communication and class relations. In J. Curran, M. Gurevitch, & J. Woollacott (Eds.), *Mass communication and society* (pp. 12–43). Beverly Hills, CA: Sage.

Murdock, G., & Wasko, J. (in press). *Cultural capitalisms: Media in the age of marketization*. Cresskill, NJ: Hampton.

Nielsen, M., & Mailes, G. (1996). *Hollywood's other blacklist: Union struggles in the studio system*. London: British Film Institute.

Nordenstreng, K., & Schiller, H. I. (1993). *Beyond national sovereignity: International communication in the 1990s*. Norwood, NJ: Ablex.

O'Sullivan, T., Hartley, J., Saunders, D., Montgomery, M., & Fiske, J. (1994). *Key concepts in communication and cultural studies* (2nd ed.). London: Routledge.

Pendakur, M. (1990). *Canadian dreams and American control: The political economy of the Canadian film industry*. Detroit, MI: Wayne State University Press.

Pendakur, M. (1993). Political economy and ethnography: Transformations in an Indian village. In J. Wasko, V. Mosco, & M. Pendakur (Eds.), *Illuminating the blindspots: Essays honoring Dallas W. Smythe* (pp. 82–108). Norwood, NJ: Ablex.

Philo, G., & Miller, D. (2000). *Market killing*. London: Pearson.

Picard, R. (1989). *Media economics: Concepts and issues*. Newbury Park, CA: Sage.

Roach, C. (Ed.). (1993). *Communication and culture in war and peace*. Newbury Park, CA: Sage.

Schiller, D. (1981). *Objectivity and the news*. Philadelphia: University of Pennsylvania Press.

Schiller, D. (1986). *Telematics and government*. Norwood, NJ: Ablex.

Schiller, D. (1999). The legacy of Robert A. Brady: Antifascist origins of the political economy of communications. *Journal of Media Economics, 12*(2), 89–101.

Schiller, H. I. (1981). *Who knows: Information in the age of the Fortune 500*. Norwood, NJ: Ablex.

Schiller, H. I. (1992). *Mass communication and American empire*. Boston: Beacon. (Original work published 1969)

Sinclair, J. (1987). *Images incorporated: Advertising as industry and ideology*. London: Croom Helm.

Sinclair, J. (1999). *Latin American television: A global view.* Oxford, UK: Oxford University Press.

Smith, A. (1937). *An inquiry into the nature and causes of the wealth of nations.* New York: Modern Library. (Original work published 1776)

Smythe, D. W. (1957). *The structure and policy of electronic communications.* Urbana: University of Illinois Press.

Smythe, D. W. (1960, Autumn). On the political economy of communication. *Journalism Quarterly,* pp. 563–572.

Smythe, D. W. (1977). Communications: Blindspot of Western Marxism. *Canadian Journal of Political and Social Theory, 1*(3), 1–27.

Smythe, D. W. (1978). Rejoinder to Graham Murdock. *Canadian Journal of Political and Social Theory, 2*(2), 120–127.

Sparks, C. (Ed.). (1985). The working class press [Special issue]. *Media, Culture and Society, 7*(5).

Streeter, T. (1996). *Selling the air: A critique of the policy of commercial broadcasting in the United States.* Chicago: University of Chicago Press.

Sussman, G. (1999). Introduction: Special issue on the political economy of communications. *Journal of Media Economics, 12*(2), 85–87.

Sussman, G., & Lent, J. A. (1991). *Transnational communications: Wiring the Third World.* Newbury Park, CA: Sage.

Sussman, G., & Lent, J. (Eds.). (1998). *Global productions: Labor in the making of the "information society."* Cresskill, NJ: Hampton.

Tunstall, J., & Palmer, M. (1991). *Media moguls.* London: Routledge.

Turow, J. (1984). *Media industries: The production of news and entertainment.* New York: Longman.

Wasko, J. (1982). *Movies and money: Financing the American film industry.* Norwood, NJ: Ablex.

Wasko, J. (1994). *Hollywood in the information age: Beyond the silver screen.* Cambridge, UK: Polity.

Wasko, J. (2001). *Understanding Disney: The manufacture of fantasy.* Cambridge, UK: Polity.

Williams, R. (1980). *Problems in materialism and culture.* London: Verso.

Wilson, K. (1988). *Technologies of control: The new interactive media for the home.* Madison: University of Wisconsin Press.

Winseck, D. (1993). *A study in regulatory change and the deregulatory process in Canadian telecommunication with particular emphasis on telecommunications labor unions.* Unpublished doctoral dissertation, University of Oregon.

Zhao, Y. (1998). *Media, market and democracy in China: Between the party line and the bottom line.* Urbana: University of Illinois Press.

16

GOVERNMENT, THE STATE, AND MEDIA

◆ Erik Neveu

How can states influence media and news? For half a century, most textbooks have answered this question using the famous "four theories" developed by Siebert, Peterson, and Schramm (1956).

Two of these theories mirrored ideal types inherited from the 18th century. In the "authoritarian" theory, the one and only role of the press is to be the loudspeaker of the rulers. Censorship and a harsh system of penalties organize this subordination. Swift had no choice but to use the ruse of fiction in *Gulliver's Travels* to criticize the corruption of the English monarchy. Conversely, symbolized by the First Amendment in the U.S. Constitution, the "libertarian" pattern protects the freedom of the press and critical speech, as well as of newsgathering and its circulation. The 20th century would give birth to two other theories. In the "Soviet" model, the punishment of dissenting voices is no longer sufficient. All media belong to the state; all information and programming must serve the values and goals of a party-state and its totalitarian ideology. Lastly, the "social responsibility" pattern mirrors the contradictory demands of press freedom debated in 1947 by the Hutchins Commission in the United States. As pure market logic guarantees neither the quality of information and its access to all citizens nor the triumph of prosocial values and highbrow culture, state policies should combine incentives for both social responsibility and the preservation of freedom.

Naively normative and U.S. centered, this cold war typology—conveniently obliterating McCarthyism—transforms the United States into the only Holy Land of press freedom. It misunderstands the contradictory trends of European public service, both authoritarian and social responsibility influenced. The four theories neglect the important distinction theorized by Lijphart (1984) between majoritarian and consociational regimes. In the latter, the political management of media is based on a proportional system of influence and party control of media (German *Proporz,* Italian *lottizzazione*) that safeguard a minimal pluralism. The complete control of media by government thus concerns only majoritarian (France) or nondemocratic systems (Franco's Spain).

McQuail (1983) has pleaded for a richer typology. The debate that developed in the United Nations Educational, Scientific, and Cultural Organization (UNESCO, 1985) about the new world information and communication order made visible the rise in the Third World of a "development media theory." Media are considered here as the relays of strategies of development and cultural or linguistic autonomy. Journalists and media can then be enlisted to support these policies, with foreign influence limited. McQuail lastly suggests the appearance of a "democratic-participant" theory of media, pleading for the central influence of audiences and users over those of journalists or shareholders. Valuing active audiences and media as a forum, this pattern is illustrated by the U.S. civic journalism movement or Canadian community radio stations.

These theories appear today as outdated (Merrill & Nerone, 2002). Except for North Korea or Cuba, the "Soviet" model is now more a historical reference than an empirical case. A whole set of changes since the 1980s—privatizations, shrinking of the public sector, and development of huge media conglomerates—has emptied any meaning from the oppositions between "libertarian," "social responsibility," and even "authoritarian" theories. Long quoted as having "authoritarian" media systems, France and Italy have now a media market dominated by private channels. The strange situation in 2002 of Berlusconi, the Italian prime minister and media mogul, appointing some of his supporters to head the public broadcast network RAI questions the usefulness of the duo *libertarian/authoritarian.* Technological changes have disrupted state-media relationships. National borders have no sense for satellite TV or the Internet. International institutions (European Union [EU], World Trade Organization [WTO]) have gained enormous importance in managing communication networks or in regulating the circulation of cultural goods. The pertinence of the nation-state as the analytical unit of economic and legal media regulation appears more and more doubtful.

Relinquishing the illusion of a simple and clear classification of media systems into a few categories, we offer the following threefold exploration of contemporary relations between states, governments, and media.

The first part offers an inventory of the tools available to a state wishing to develop direct or indirect influence over media. Using this inventory, the second part questions some contemporary uses of this state repertoire of influence on media. What meaning can we assign to the spuriously clear distinction between state and civil society? Is it possible to speak—and, if yes, then how and to what extent—of a softening of state control over media? Does the market guarantee more freedom to media? Should one forget the old notion of "social responsibility"?

A third and final part deals more directly with the role of media and political communication in the functioning of modern democracies. It invites us to remain critical of the current offensive against "critical orthodoxy," led by the heralds of a naive celebration of the modern public sphere. Lastly, it poses other issues: Have media become cogs of a public representation service? How can the public sphere protect its dynamism?

◆ *The Repertoire of State Influence*

The ways and means of state influence on media are extremely complex. We could try to encapsulate them through the musical metaphor of the "repertoire" (Tilly, 1976). States can mobilize six repertoires of action on media, with each of them able to call upon a full family of instruments of action. The choice made by the state among repertoires and instruments might bring the press and media to offer the equivalent of military marches or the "Slaves' Song" in Verdi's *Nabucco,* or it could produce the freer tunes of "We Shall Overcome" or "I'm Free."

STATE OWNERSHIP AND DIRECT CONTROL REPERTOIRE

State ownership or direct control is the most visible tool or influence on media. This repertoire gathers extremely different levels of influence.

Orwell's novel *1984* with its Ministry of Truth offers the strongest picture of the process of production of a state-truth (*pravda* in Russian), the twin goal of the state's totalitarian control over media, and the enslavement of thinking through these media (Orwell, 1987). Such systems are today residual. This dark fantasy of a perfect policing of minds—paradoxically shared by the leaders of "socialist" countries and Western Kremlinologists—in fact never reached its goals, facing the denial of stubborn facts and the counterinformation of Western radio stations and underground *samizdat* media.

Public monopoly or a majoritarian influence over public media remained, until the 1980s, common in numerous European countries (Scandinavia, Italy, France). Blumler (1992) has highlighted the peculiarities of these European public services: universal service, quality programming for all audiences, noncommercialism, and political independence. On this last point, the range of situations covered by the repertoire of public service is very varied. But for the coverage of some controversial issues, such as Northern Ireland, the British political system has guaranteed a true autonomy to the British Broadcasting Corporation (BBC). The Netherlands invented as long ago as the 1920s a sophisticated system of *Verzuiling* (pillarization), parcelling out radio and TV channels among the major political forces (Protestant churches, the Catholic Church, Social Democrats, and Liberals). The French case mirrors conversely a situation of extreme media control by the ruling party. Alain Peyrefitte (1976),

De Gaulle's "minister of information," recalled his appointment in 1962:

> Christian de la Malène, whose position I inherit, shows me on the minister's desk a whole range of push-buttons. "This one is to call the usher, and those ones the director of television, the head of the news service, the director of TV programming, the director of radio programming. . . . Each day at five o'clock you will call them to decide on the headlines of the evening news bulletins on TV and radio. At any time you also can give them instructions by the internal phone network. Never leave your office before 1.30 and 8.30 PM! After the TV news, your ministerial colleagues will call you to object to anything of which they disapprove. (pp. 150–151)

STATE, MEDIA, AND NATIONAL SOVEREIGNTY

The state ownership and direct control repertoire can be difficult to distinguish from that pertaining to national sovereignty. As Silvio Waisbord shows in Chapter 18 (this volume), no state can ignore the importance of media for sovereignty or international influence. Three kinds of policies, used even by the most vocal champions of market forces, are to be found in this repertoire.

Even without public ownership, states play a central role in the funding, construction, and development of communication networks (telegraph, telephone, information highways) needed for the functioning and distribution of media. The communication needs of the army and colonial empires have given a decisive impulse to the extension of international telegraphic and radio systems (Mattelart, 1992). The takeoff of a popular press in the United Kingdom or in France is directly linked to the extension of a dense network of railway lines, in turn funded directly or indirectly by public money.

In the hidden or direct support that they provide to media, which are able to strengthen their international influence, the intervention of states is also visible. The genesis of German, British, and French press agencies during the 19th century is inseparable from the colonial and international strategies of their states. During the cold war, the United States (Voice of America, Radio Free Europe), United Kingdom (BBC), and France (Radio France International [RFI]) invested substantial amounts of money to broadcast news towards Soviet bloc countries (Mattelart, 1995; Semelin, 2000), which also developed their own broadcast propaganda to Third World nations. State support for national media and cultural industries has also been visible in international policies. On May 28, 1946, the Blum-Byrnes agreements were signed in Washington, D.C. Postwar financial aid from the United States for the reconstruction of France was made conditional upon a quota system offering 36 weeks a year of programming for foreign (de facto U.S.) movies in any French movie theater (Blum, 2001).

The sovereignty repertoire includes, finally, more reactive policies. Some limit the access of foreign participation and companies to national media. The trauma of Nazi occupation and "collaboration" gave birth to French laws that, in 1944, prohibited any foreign participation in French daily press. And if the Australian media mogul Rupert Murdoch chose in 1983 to become an American citizen, it was also to conform to the laws prohibiting the control of a U.S. TV network by foreigners (Tunstall & Palmer, 1991).

THE STATE AND GOVERNMENT AS INFORMATION SOURCES

Public authorities do not only influence news distribution. The modern state is the prime producer of data and information. Those in power dedicate more and more time to managing their relationships with media. Consultants and spin doctors help them to rationalize this activity, borrowing from the contributions of marketing and communication science. Symbolic gestures transform policies into images. One would see a French minister, in charge of humanitarian policies, unloading on his shoulders the heavy rice bags for the hungry Somali in Mogadishu's harbor. A British minister of agriculture would ask his own daughter to eat a huge British beef burger before the cameras—a mission that she would unfortunately relinquish, conspicuously nauseated after a few mouthfuls. Beyond the heights of the power elite, it is the whole system of state administrations and agencies that, since the 1930s, has organized a dense network of public relations officers and communication specialists in charge of promoting the image and policy of their institutions (Davis, 2002). This energetic supply activity is visible in the multiple press releases, journals, newsletters, and Web sites through which public authorities offer information that always includes the aim of justifying their actions.

Last but not least, the history of state construction is also the history of the construction of a huge machinery of production, centralization, and treatment of data (Neveu, 1994). From the census to the instant production of data on business and trade, via the growing number of statistical indicators of various kinds, the state is at the core of what French statistician Alain Desrosières (1993) termed "the politics of large numbers." When they comment on the unemployment figures, the budget deficit, or drug use, journalists work from state-produced news and data.

Crude lies are rare because they are risky. A French government office in charge of nuclear safety information claimed that the 1986 Chernobyl westbound nuclear cloud had sharply turned south over Switzerland and Italy, not daring to cross the French border. The credibility of its information collapsed to almost zero as a result. But the very conditions of production of official data and the variables used can hide, overstate, or understate certain kinds of facts (e.g., the underenumeration of female unemployment in the United Kingdom). Public authorities are also in good position to act as "primary definers." Hall, Clarke, Critcher, Jefferson, and Roberts (1978) use this notion to describe a power to define and frame events and issues. Through combining the authority of officialdom, a monopoly on certain kinds of information (for the police, crime statistics), and good public relations services, many administrations and ministries can operate as primary definers.

One might finally add that the budgets—often substantial—that public authorities can mobilize to promote and advertise their policies (struggle against AIDS, road safety) allow them to have their messages relayed by media but also to put gentle pressure on the press and the media by selecting those titles and channels to benefit from public service announcement budgets.

PRESS LAWS AND REGULATIONS

The core of the legal regulations concerning the influence of state on media is usually codified in specific press laws.

A first situation can be quickly mentioned if one does not forget that it still describes accurately the situation in numerous countries in Africa, the Near East, and Central Asia. In these authoritarian systems, media law can be put in a nutshell: Only the media that please the authorities are allowed to print and broadcast news pleasant for the authorities. A 1998 report from the watchdog organization Reporters Sans Frontières concerning Mauritania offers an illuminating case study. An "edict law" from July 25, 1991, creates de jure a system of preliminary declaration for creating a newspaper. This "declaration" works de facto as an arbitrary permit system. The home office can, without any need to explain why, censor or prohibit any media that "undermine the principles of Islam or State credibility, damage the general interest or disrupt public law and order." Such repressive regulations are strengthened by a direct political control of public media and numerous illegalities, such as the expulsion of journalists working for opposition media from government press conferences.

By contrast, and protected as early as 1766 in the Swedish constitution, freedom of the press is one of the bases of democratic systems. The First Amendment to the U.S. Constitution specifies the following: "Congress shall make no law respecting an establishment of religion, or prohibiting the free exercise thereof; or abridging the freedom of speech, or of the press; or the right of the people peaceably to assemble, and to petition the Government for a redress of grievances." True freedom of the press can be guaranteed by case law, as by the U.S. Supreme Court and other courts; by a "major" law, as in France (Derieux, 2000); or by a combination of the two, as in the United Kingdom.[1] However, it always presupposes at least four kinds of regulation, which inevitably open up other opportunities for state influence.

◆ The first one concerns the definition of press offenses. Although their definition and regulation can change from one country to another, libel exists in most legal systems (Barendt, Lustgarden, Norrie, & Stephenson, 1997). Basically, libel occurs when a false and defamatory statement about an identifiable person is published to a third party, damaging the subject's reputation. Invasion of privacy is another major case of press offense. Other offenses can be linked to practices betraying the principles of fair newsgathering: surreptitious recordings and use of hidden cameras. In continental Europe, some states punish the publication of racist statements and speeches, the justification of (war) crimes, and even (in France) any "revisionist" statement denying the reality of the genocide of European Jews by the Nazis.

◆ Press regulation also concerns the definition and the limits of the secrets that the authorities can set against journalists' investigations. Habermas (1989) has highlighted how the construction of the rule of law was also a process of extension of a "principle of publicity" by which the rulers must make their decisions with the fullest possible transparency, under the control of public opinion. One of the most basic dimensions of this publicity had been the right conquered by the press to cover, print, and comment on parliamentary debates. Freedom-of-information laws have enlarged the opportunities of access to government documents. In the United States, the "sunshine laws" allow free access for citizens and journalists to many meetings of public agencies. In France, a public agency (www.cada.fr) helps citizens confronted with the state's or any public institution's refusal to divulge public documents concerning their situation. The legitimacy conquered by the principle of publicity cannot, however, hide the importance of still other laws and regulations protecting various types of public secrets.[2] From the most justified to the most outrageous, they claim to protect national security, the secrecy of court proceedings or criminal investigations, and business imperatives. They can work during crisis as so many "darkness laws," as connective tissue between repression, intimidation, and illegalities.

◆ The rights of journalists are another basis of press freedom. These rights include freedom of access to and disclosure of public information, rights of access, and inquiry into public buildings and agencies. They require the protection and confidentiality of journalists' sources.[3] But states' contribution to the rights of journalists includes their protection from their own employers from threats emanating from private institutions. The "conscience clause" allows French journalists to resign without financial penalty if they disagree with a change in the editorial line of their media. The U.S. anti-SLAPP statutes[4] protect journalists from abusive lawsuits mounted for the simple purpose of threatening media to step back from launching public debate on topics considered embarrassing by powerful private interests.

◆ A last key element of media laws and regulations concerns the powers given (or not) to independent regulation authorities (the U.S. Federal Communication Commission, www.fcc.gov; the Australian Broadcasting Authority, www.aba.gov.au; the French Conseil Supérieur de l'Audiovisuel, www.csa.fr). Their roles can vary from allocating broadcast licenses, establishing the legal obligations of networks and the press, or functioning as watchdogs of journalistic ethics.

THE SPECIAL DISPENSATIONS SYSTEM

Press laws have always had their hidden partner. In most states, the specific laws on press and media are completed by a mosaic of texts whose principle is to free the press from the ordinary rules of law. Each of these dispensations can have liberating or, if there is a threat to remove them, chilling effects on the profits and/or critical freedom of media.[5]

These special dispensations have at least five aspects. Some are linked to tax regulations. The early 19th-century British system of "taxes on knowledge" was notorious. Its goal was, by high prices, to prevent the popular classes from reading the press, suspected of subversive influence. Conversely, today, most states grant the media sector preferential taxation rates. Until 2000, the income tax system exempted French journalists from any tax on 30% of their wages, a system often providing the equivalent of 1 or 2 bonus months' wages, funded by the state. Special dispensations are also visible in preferential postal rates for print media. They concern corporate merger law as well.

Many countries have voted in special rules to limit or prevent media monopolies or cross-ownership between media and press (Humphreys, 1996, pp. 97, 222). These dispensatory laws target advertising law, too. French law prohibits any advertising for alcohol, books, and supermarket chains on TV, so that these advertising revenues can be channeled to the press, considered as vital for its financial health. The bracketing of normal laws is visible again in many European countries in the public funding of the press, sometimes specifically organized to support a party and "opinion" press as agents of political pluralism (Finland, France, Sweden).

ILLEGALITIES

Aside from the fanciful dreams of naive lawyers, the state and political authorities rarely refrain from taking actions forbidden to them by laws and constitutions. Because of the power—both real and imaginary—usually attributed to them, media are one of the first targets in the use of illegalities. This notion, developed by Michel Foucault (1975), refers to organized strategies to infringe on the law, including what he terms the technique of "sanctioned illegalities," whose basic mechanism is to insert into laws and regulations the means to suspend their implementation by invoking crisis, threats, or secrets to safeguard. The repertoire of illegalities is difficult to describe, as it is precisely based on the fact that the authorities act against the law. It can, however, be summed up in two processes.

The first one is the misuse of laws—specifically, the use of legal regulations as alibis for prohibited actions. During the Algerian independence war, the French government "hijacked" many decrees concerning policing and public security to justify seizures in Algeria of issues of *Le Monde*, which criticized French colonialist policy. In 2002, the Turkish government used the broadcasting of Kurdish songs as a proof of a "separatist" plot to withdraw the licence of the network "Gun-TV" for 1 year. In all these cases, the courts would finally condemn the state—but months after the successful seizure of several of its issues for *Le Monde* or by permitting the chilling effect of military pressure on Turkish media. This family of illegalities is also visible when the political power uses a dominant or monopolistic public banking system to stifle the finances of a medium or when it makes an arbitrary use of tax controls or systematically sues a journalist or a magazine to silence it.

A second family of illegalities uses threats, surveillance, violence, or even murder, outside any legal framework. In 1973, the French counterespionage agency wiretapped the offices of the satirical weekly *Le Canard Enchaîné*. French President Mitterrand organized in complete contempt of law a sophisticated system of phone tapping targeting the journalists that he disliked. The watchdog organization Reporters Sans Frontières (2002) has reported that since the beginning of the second Intifada, more than 60 journalists have been wounded by bullets in occupied territories, mostly by the Israeli army. The report suggests that the ordinary risk of war coverage cannot explain such figures. The same organization highlights in each of its annual reports the situation of journalists arrested or tortured for their newspapers (Uzbekistan, Syria) or the suspicious role played by army and police units in the murders or "disappearances" of journalists (Algeria, Haiti).

These hard and brutal illegalities can be combined with soft ones that are allowed by the use of public sources to spread wrong information or hide facts unpleasant for authorities. One would thus agree with Keane (1991) to highlight that, over and above the traditional and crude style of repression by authoritarian states, great attention must be paid to the soft repertoire of the "democratic Leviathan." It mobilizes the smile of public relations officers and the art of constructing media events. It does not fear to turn to illegalities each time that the

authorities judge a situation critical or threatening for their power.

◆ Debating the Contemporary Uses of the Repertoire

Reflection on the uses of the state's influence through repertoires too often gives one the feeling of being framed by a new pattern of Whig history. Progress lies in having irresistible emancipation from civil society, conquering freedom of speech against the oppressive state, and using media and the press as checks and balances and a weapon of expression. The contemporary neoliberal mood suggests that the only regulations worth being produced by the state are those that "forbid it to forbid." Following a rhetoric studied by Hirschman (1991), the best of public interventions could only give birth to "perversity, futility, and jeopardy." Revisiting the history and contemporary uses of the repertoire in democracies, we would like to challenge these myths dressed up as science. It is not true that freedom of press had only been built against the state. The loosening of the state's direct control over media can sometimes hide other processes of influence. The reign of a "civil society" limited to mammoth companies and organized interests creates new threats for freedom of speech.

MEDIA FREEDOM AND STATE BUILDING

The excessively fashionable thought kit based on the state versus civil society duo always begins as the narrative of a fairy tale: "Once upon a time there was the state, almighty and oppressive." The casting of characters is clear: Kings and bureaucrats are seldom supporters of free speech and media. The story can mobilize a Foucauldian scenario celebrating micropowers and resistances, a Tocquevillean one emphasizing the role of the press among checks and balances, or a liberal one paying more attention to the strategic function of civil rights and of the rule of law. Basically, the plot remains the same: Free media and freedom of speech were born from the heroic struggles of "civil society" versus the statist Moloch.

This binary opposition takes for granted the existence of two clearly structured entities struggling one against another, but the real societal process is a cross-institutionalization. Two dimensions of this process deserve to be briefly highlighted here. One should first focus on the need to conceptualize together two contradictory dimensions of state history (Neveu, 1994). The state is both a machinery of control and repression and the instituting agent of "civil society." The monopolization of legitimate violence by the state is an absolute prerequisite for the central role conquered by speech and argumentation—and thus by media—to manage social conflicts as substitutes to force and violence. Nothing other than direct or indirect state action created the basis of the networks of physical communication (roads, railways) and news transmission needed by the press and public sphere. Only the generalization of literacy, most of the time boosted by public policies, creates the readership needed by the press. It is thus only in an imaginary history that one can depict a "civil society"—made of self-organized communities, companies, associations, or social movements—that militates for freedom of speech against the state, forgetting that such a civil society and its access to speech are simultaneously possible thanks to the process of state construction.

A second theme of reflection will come from a return on the repertoire of the state as a "source." The whole history of the state since the 16th century has been the construction-process of an institution centralizing and processing information. The soldier is certainly the first symbol of the state. But to recruit soldiers and equip them, one needs an informational machinery. Its first cogs were censuses, registry

offices, knowledge of the wealth and trade able to produce taxes, the production by civil or military authorities of reports on the spirit of the people, and the behavior of hostile powers. The state produces information, puts it in motion (roads, networks), and creates institutions to store and treat it (archives, libraries, research centers). By the sedimentation of statistics, court decisions, and administrators' reports, as well as through the typification of categories of citizens, the state produces information and knowledge that, in turn, institutionalize it as it simultaneously oversees, disciplines, and institutes a civil society.

Historian and French Prime Minister Guizot is one of the first liberal thinkers who, in the 1820s, theorized the role of the press in the cross-institutionalization and communication processes between state and society. For him, the freedom of press was a functional prerequisite of democracy. The press was much more than a check and balance: It was a tool of interpenetration between state and society, carrying towards the rulers the opinions and claims of the people. As it makes them visible to the whole society, so it catalyzes public opinion. The press is also the tool that, giving echo to parliamentary debates and governmental speeches, allows the rulers to explain their choices to the *demos*. Combining its own news production process and the freedom of press, "power becomes thus an information regulator; it is the pump which stimulates the circulation of social power, the purifying lung of opinions" (Rosanvallon, 1985, p. 71). Timothy Cook (1998) offers one of the most stimulating case studies illustrating the blind spots of a Manichean history of media, reduced to a struggle between civil society and the state. His approach to the history of the U.S. press highlights how its development was indebted to state grants, to policies based on dispensatory rules concerning business and industrial relation laws, and to the benevolence of legislators toward press and media companies. The press is a fourth estate. This is certainly one of its potentials.

But is it as an external and adversarial balance to the three other powers? Or is it much more by being integrated within the network of constitutional powers, which in turn adapt to its imperatives, offering it a flood of news, anticipating its formats and schedules?

THE HARD AND THE SOFT

The French poet Bernard Noel invented a distinction between *censure* (censorship) as the prohibition of speech and the term *sensure* (sense hollowing) he coined, signifying a freedom of speech emptied of any critical strength by the dulled consensus and asepsis of the speech produced. Such a notion can help one to understand the contemporary forms of state actions vis-à-vis media. It can make sense of the old Tocquevillean prophesy:

> The Sovereign . . . does not tyrannize. It bothers, it compresses, it enervates, it beguiles, it dazes, it condemns finally each nation to be nothing else than a flock of shy animals. This kind of organised, sweet and peaceful serfdom . . . may combine much better that one imagines with some of the external shapes of freedom. (de Tocqueville, 1981, p. 386)

The first tool of those soft weapons of influence on the press is to gain the status of primary definer. When the British Home Office wants to launch a policy of prison building (Schlesinger & Tumber, 1994), it multiplies the opportunities to visit jails— and firstly the most ramshackle ones— provided to journalists. Using the same techniques of agenda framing, the Bush administration has enrolled the press to build a moral panic on the impact of crack cocaine—with 1,500 articles on the topic in the *Washington Post* between October 1998 and 1999 (Reinarman & Levine, 1995)—even though no statistical data on the victims of the epidemic were initially available. The 1990–1991 Gulf War

offered another illustration of the smiling but efficient techniques of taming the press corps. The military provided media images in which war was nothing more than a real-life video game but where the thousands of corpses of Iraqi soldiers and civilians were invisible.

Symbolic action by the public authorities also consists of policing perceptions and analytical frameworks. State institutions and intellectuals can produce classificatory schemes that work as invisible spectacles or magnifying glasses. In 2000, the civil servants of the French ministry of finances went on strike against a reform of their administration. The press service of the ministry sent to all media a thick file justifying this reform with numerous arguments and explanations. A famous columnist from a left-oriented weekly soon wrote an article very critical of the strikers, an article that tasted like a cut-and-paste job that transformed the finance minister's speech into "journalism." Immediately, the central administration of the ministry had this article photocopied and faxed to all the locations still on strike, where it was distributed by the hierarchy as a handout.

The soft control of media is, lastly, composed by the production of media events. It may be the organization of press visits or travels, which has a secret goal of allowing the journalists to see, freely, what the authorities wish them to see. This event work is also based on the organization of rituals or events with high symbolic intensity. Prepared by an advertising executive, the 1989 parade commemorating the bicentenary of the French Revolution was completely structured by an interpretative frame à la Furet, the prominent historian, of that revolution as a universal symbol of the conquest of freedom, obviating any reference to the long dominant perception of 1789 as a social and egalitarian insurrection. To use Bourdieu's adjective, these weapons of influence are based on an *epistemocratic* power (Bourdieu & Wacquant, 1998). The stake is to impose schemes of perception of facts that, once transformed into something taken for granted, bring the media freely to limit themselves to a range of interpretations located in a space of consensus.

One must add that these soft strategies have flaws and can be superseded. Their success is never automatic. The criticism of the notion of "primary definer," developed by Schlesinger and Tumber (1994), is illuminating. It invites us to think relationally about the power of official sources. Despite their strong resources, they are also competing with other institutions, including other public bureaucracies. They are never fully shielded from the weakening of their messages by leaks, off-the-record statements, and blunders coming from their own members. An unpredictable event can sink the best media event to the bottom of the media agenda.

A supersession of these modern soft strategies is visible when, in situations of major crisis or war, they are often replaced by or mixed in with the old and harsh techniques of state lies and "propaganda." To justify the 1999 intervention in Kosovo, the North Atlantic Treaty Organization (NATO) and European governments amazingly exaggerated the crimes of the Serbian troops. With the zealous and uncritical reiteration on the part of most of the press and media, the massacres perpetrated by Yugoslav troops were multiplied through an imaginary body count, soon allowing a "genocide" to be announced (Halimi & Vidal, 2000). In his ethnography of the war correspondents in San Salvador, Pedelty (1995) shows how the American Embassy was both able to feed the journalists with daily press conferences and ready to contact the hierarchies of U.S. dailies to require the firing of stringers whose articles were considered "un-American."

The terrorist attacks of September 11, 2001, offered another illustration of the supercession of soft influence on media when certain journalists were denounced as unpatriotic, Web sites were closed, and repressive laws were voted in against the news media.[6]

THE HOLLOWING OUT OF THE STATE'S INFLUENCE: THE PROMISE OF FREEDOM?

The shift of the state's repertoire toward a symbolic management of media cannot thus be confused with a renunciation of attempting to influence them. The 1980s and 1990s saw substantial changes in media economics. Public service broadcasting was curtailed and privatized in many countries. Mergers gave birth to huge multimedia and "global" communication companies. In many cases, the real power of regulating the media system belongs to the headquarters of conglomerates or to independent authorities, escaping from governmental influence. As Janet Wasko reminds us in Chapter 15 (this volume), one must conceptualize these earthquakes in the media business according to the logic of a *political* economy. Changing media landscapes and policies are integrated into political narratives and strategies. Freed from the most visible forms of state control, brought back to the "state of nature" that the market is supposed to be, the media system seems to reach the harbor of a Fukuyamesque "end of history." Market and civil society—and no longer the state— rule media and communication.

Five arguments at least invite us to question this mythology. The first was suggested in the previous paragraph. The shift of the repertoire of state influence towards what can be labeled as "symbolic action" or strategic communication management cannot be confused with the state's withdrawal or powerlessness. The image and sound of an unreflexive patriotic choir presented by the U.S. press and media for a number of weeks after the Twin Towers slaughter is a strong illustration.

One should notice secondly that the very process of "rolling the state back" to put the media under the rule of the market has required and requires an enormous and hectic state interventionism. Scores of laws, rules, and court decisions—such as the end of the public network RAI monopoly, decided by the Italian Supreme Court in 1978—were needed to erase and destroy regulations that had been developed sometimes for more than a century. The results of these policies are rich in paradoxes. On one hand, U.S. court decisions have blurred the distinction between the rights of press and corporations to invoke the First Amendment (Allen, 2001). This change shakes the scaffolding on which were based the specific rights of press and media. On the other hand, struggles among mammoth media corporations reveal that the result of the natural functioning of the market threatens to be the birth of private monopolies, requiring more state intervention by antitrust laws and agencies. The theme of cross-institutionalization is illustrated here again: Even the most market-driven system of media needs permanent state action and regulation to exist and survive.

Thirdly, private media ownership has never been a perfect shield against state and government influence. The lasting connection between Murdoch's U.K. tabloids and the Thatcher government is a prime example. During the French presidential campaign of 1995, the most committed network was the private channel TF1, giving overfriendly coverage to the prime ministerial candidate Balladur. Were the executives of the channel conservatives? They were not socialists. And TF1 belonged to the Bouygues group, the leading French and world company for public works. Needing the public contracts, TF1 lost a reasonable bet whilst supporting a prime minister whom all opinion polls then anointed as the next president.

Fourthly, the result of less state intervention is not always automatically more freedom. French publishers have been complaining of a process of privatizing censorship. Flaubert and Baudelaire had to face legal actions requested by the empress and the minister of justice against their "immoral" novels. Freed from public censorship, writers and journalists face now costly and repeated suits triggered by extremist religious groups, powerful companies, and industrialists with their armies of attorneys.

Lastly, a market-driven press and media system creates no incentives to strengthen and reward the values and behaviors of citizenship. Most media and magazines target audiences as consumers interested in information concerning the stock exchange, soccer, fashion, and travel. The world of market-driven journalism (McManus, 1994) is populated by customers, not by citizens. It is dedicated to the satisfaction of human beings considered as market slots, not as responsible members from a polity. In the supply of cable television, the number of channels dedicated to information or documentaries, able to make sense of the social world, remains limited. Such media can offer pleasant entertainment and help people to identify useful goods and services. They also boost a very specific kind of freedom. The French liberal philosopher Benjamin Constant analyzed this "freedom of the modern" and its risks as early as 1819. Liberalism in its radical version opens the freedom to behave as though we were not living in society, as if the highest human goal were a selfish pursuit of happiness. But is it so reasonable to get "freed" from politics? To replace it by what, and whom, in the decision process?

◆ Conclusions: Reinventing "Social Responsibility"

It would seem strange to evoke with nostalgia the old classification of Siebert et al. (1956) after criticizing it. But at least the "social responsibility" pattern helped to highlight the strains between market logics and social needs (culture, information). A reasoned plea for an active public regulation of media threatens today to sound both outdated and more a matter of political commitment than being based on scientific grounds.

Such would be, however, our conclusion. It comes from the facts that suggest that market self-regulation creates new threats to media autonomy and quality. It also results from a syllogism. A polity is made up of citizens, not consumers. Citizens are requested to take part in debates and choices on the common good. To do so, they need information that is rich, pluralist, and clear. They need a press that acts as a mirror of all social worlds, not as the loud-speaker of institutions. If one agrees with this analytical frame, it is clear that the media cannot be reduced to a market or audiences reduced to consumers.

Rolling back the market and bringing back the state is a partial but compulsory answer (Cook, 1998; Neveu, 2001). Let us recall here that the first level of state inter-vention to guarantee an open and critical functioning of citizenship and the public sphere—and not only in the "underdevel-oped" world—is to provide the population with the prerequisites of citizenship: pro-viding a good and cheap education system, giving real access to jobs and social advance-ment, having an open and democratic politi-cal system that strengthens a feeling of civic self-esteem among citizens, and believing that citizens' opinions matter and influ-ence policies and politics. State interven-tion should also directly target media. Broadcasting rights and licenses, as well as access to public funding and subsidies, should all be conditional upon genuine respect for legal requirements. Such require-ments might be a minimum percentage of current affairs and debate programs, along with airtime and coverage given to voices from below. The challenge is to reinvent new regulations and new public funding systems able to prevent reducing audiences to a mere collection of consumers, as well as to channel the creativity of media profession-als toward making programs that are both attractive and trigger reflexivity, breaking the "dumbing-down spiral."

The risks of such policies are twofold. They may open new opportunities for party or governmental influence on media. They may be confused with the impossible return to life of the old Reithian pattern of public service, both paternalistic and rejected in a highly competitive mediascape. No one, neither the sociologist nor the political actor, is able today to draw up a perfect reform blueprint to address the threats we have identified. Facing these threats and challenges appears, however, as much more urgent and exciting than watching power-lessly the impact of market-driven media. And no doubt, there is much to be learned from the experience and actions of watch-dog organizations such as the Electronic Frontier Foundation or Reporters Sans Frontières. Undoubtedly, practical experi-ences and theoretical reflections suggest lines of action. In line with Sinclair's analy-ses (see Chapter 3, this volume), a new framework would need the interrelated action of supranational institutions and supranational regulations.[7] Internationali-zation also means comparing and borrow-ing laws, institutions, and successful experiences of public sphere engineering from foreign countries while simultaneously taming state intervention and market logic: The challenge is exciting for academics, media professionals, and citizens.

◆ Media, Government, and the Political Process

The analysis of media developed in the pre-vious sections focused on their relation to the state and their roles in the polity. It combined *longue durée* time frames and an institutional approach (Cook, 1998). Considered in shorter time frames, in an interpretative framework based on politics (parties, elections) and not only on the organization of the polity and its media policies, media must also be considered as central actors in political competitions. The research questions thus become the following: What is the impact of media on candidates, parties, and voters? How has broadcasting changed politics? What are the structures of interdependence between political journalists, spin doctors, politicians, and lobbyists? What is the impact of the media coverage of politics on public opinion and voting behavior?

POLITICAL COMMUNICATION

These questions are usually labeled in academia as *political communication,* a subspeciality of political science. This research field immediately suggests three challenges. The first comes from the flow, even the flood, of its productions. The amount of published material is enormous enough to justify its specific journals and handbooks (Nimmo, 1981) and is impossible to sum up in a few paragraphs. Another challenge comes from the almost obsessional focus of political communication studies on elections and campaigning. Of course, elections are the core of political struggle. Their results offer "actual-size" data to evaluate the impact of communication. The price of this overanalysis of campaign communication is that we know probably more about the possible electoral impact of the gimmicks or adulterous affairs of a candidate than about the daily coverage of politics and policies by the press and media. Last but not least, one may question the very notion of "political communication." It may invite us to think of communication as an autonomous process or to overrate the importance of communicative skills, whereas the forms and impacts of "communication" must also be considered as the results of a complex causal system, including the sociology of journalistic work, changes in the recruitment of politicians, and party functioning and funding. And this list should of course include evolutions in social morphology, collective identities, and beliefs in the power of politics to change the world.

Taking the risk of oversimplifying, it is possible to suggest four major changes identified by political communication studies. The first is the redefinition of the notion of public opinion. Formerly linked to the interpretations of *vox populi* expressed by intellectuals or elite journalists and politicians, since the 1960s, this notion has been identified with opinion polls, which have gained a central importance in politics (Champagne, 1990). A second change comes from the inflationary process of the professionalization of political communication by politicians and their spin doctors (Blumler & Kavanagh, 1999). This process triggers a third change that could be described as a symbolic arms race. Fearing to be put under control by politicians, journalists have become more adversarial. One of their skills becomes the decipherment, for their audience, of the media tricks and gimmicks of politicians, who in turn look for more sophisticated strategies to thwart the journalists' castrating know-how (Kuhn & Neveu, 2002). Fourthly, even if consensus weakens here, researchers quite widely agree on the growing role taken in campaigning by personalities, emotions, and pseudo-events to the detriment of programs and in-depth issue coverage. More than just detail these conclusions, the next paragraphs will try to highlight issues. How can we prevent political communication research from a bad remake of the old debate Umberto Eco (1965) once framed as between the "apocalyptic" jeremiahs declaiming against mass culture and its "integrated" celebrants? How do we make sense of the paradox of private media integrated within a "public representation service"? How can media support a renewal of the public sphere?

CRITICAL ORTHODOXY VERSUS DEMOCRATIC NEO-ORTHODOXY: THE WRONG DEBATE

Since the 1960s, most academics—and many journalists—have invited us to question the impact of media, especially TV, on the quality of democratic debate. Reports and comments have accused media of giving an excessive importance to polls, horse race politics, and power struggles to the detriment of in-depth coverage of politicians' programs and policies. The reduction of political speech into sound bites is claimed to weaken the quality of debate. During the 1968 U.S. presidential campaign, the average length of candidate sound bites during news bulletins was 40 seconds. The figure had collapsed to 7 in 1996. The criticisms have also targeted the growing importance given to artificial media events and the emphasis on the private, sometimes scandalous, dimensions of politicians' behaviors—such as the novel *Primary Colors* (Anonymous, 1996) that depicts, with realism, the story of a candidate specializing in bed hopping and saxophone playing.

In the United Kingdom, the target of criticism has firstly been the gutter press. But the use on both sides of the Atlantic of expressions such as "dumbing down," "tabloidization," "trivialization," and "Newzak" (Franklin, 1997) expresses clearly a shared "media malaise." The rising practice of inviting politicians on talk shows has triggered new debates. Could not the questions asked by hosts, lacking in serious knowledge of political issues, shield candidates from unpleasant discussions? Don't such interactions overemphasize the personal lives of interviewees and also reward the best actors, not leaders able to offer clear choices? The role given to boisterous audiences asking frivolous questions (about Clinton's underwear on MTV) has prompted fears of a TV "populism" (Blumler & Gurevitch, 1995; "La politique saisie par le divertissement," 2003). Especially in the United States, journalists have been targets of criticism. They have been accused of giving more time to adversarial comments than to politicians' speeches. Fallows (1996) even suggested that the upper crust of media pundits had become a privileged caste, no longer able to relay the worries and questions of laypeople. The final result of these processes would be a mistrust of politicians among citizens and civic apathy (Eliasoph, 1998).

This dominant analytical framework has recently been challenged. One of the first shots was fired by Kees Brants (1999), who asked, "Who's afraid of infotainment?" Mobilizing extensive data, especially from the Netherlands, Brants argued that infotainment, accounting for 22% of program content, has not yet become the main way that TV frames politics but also questioned whether its format might not spur the interest of those citizens least interested in political issues. But the books of McNair (2000) and Norris (2000) symbolize the declaration of war on "critical orthodoxy." Developing an in-depth case study of political news coverage in 1996, McNair argues that the public sphere works in a much more satisfactory manner than academia's laments suggest. Never has the supply of political information been so generous. And this information remains centered on issues and policies. McNair also argues that the interpretive turn in political journalism signifies a need for in-depth explanations, not a disease, and that beyond infotainment, talk shows offer ordinary citizens true opportunities for expression. In a very ambitious comparative study based on the Organization for Economic Cooperation and Development (OECD) and Eurobarometers data, Norris developed a similar analysis. If media can produce negative perceptions of some institutions (i.e., the EU Commission), such cases do not allow hasty generalizations. Conversely, Norris claimed that her data show that media do not primarily produce negative perception of politics. They do bring to citizens useful knowledge to make sense of the political stakes. The relationship between news consumption and political attitudes even inspires in Norris the image of a "virtuous circle" of better knowledge and greater attention to politics among major news consumers.

This discussion highlights important questions. Did the research on the political impact of media overrate their effects on the devaluation of politics? How, then, ought we to empirically evaluate their impact? But three reasons at least suggest questioning the new heralds of a "healthy public sphere."

The first one comes from the unfortunate oversimplification symbolized by the very notion of critical orthodoxy, which may suggest a shared and fierce radicalism among authors whose methods and conclusions differ and are usually based on serious empirical work. Another doubt comes from the fact that the new discourse on the democratic virtues of contemporary media seems no less simplistic than the outdated criticisms from the Frankfurt tradition. How can we avoid the task of developing an in-depth sociological analysis of the enormous differences in audiences' uses, interpretations, and receptions of information and news? Can one seriously argue from Eurobarometers that the fact that EU citizens know "their" 12-star flag is proof of the pedagogic virtues of media—without also commenting on the figure that reveals that less than 25% among them understood the countdown to the introduction of the Euro that would be in their wallets 1 year later?

A serious debate on the political role of media requires three levels of analysis:

1. a sociology of news production, combining the study of sources, journalistic work, and the impact of business imperatives;

2. a qualitative and quantitative data analysis of contents and formats, framings, and agendas;

3. a sociology of reception, including ethnographic case studies, such as those developed to analyze the soap opera *Dallas*.

One may agree that too much research has fallen into the shortcut trap of concluding, from the existence of framing or bias in content, the proof of its impact on audiences. Is this a good enough reason to remove the dusty functionalism of "uses and gratifications" from its mothballs? To forget its blindness to the production process of media messages, its reference to "uses" and "gratifications," whose social genesis remains a mystery? Such a method has, today as yesterday, the charm of simple and comforting answers, the alibi of a flood of data whose production process and actual meanings remain unchallenged.

MEDIA AS A COG IN THE PUBLIC REPRESENTATION SERVICE?

With the concept of "party cartel," Richard Katz and Peter Mair (1994) renewed the analysis of parties, suggesting a slow drift in the relation between parties and civil society. As often suggested by their very names (Greenbacks, Labour), parties had long defined themselves as expressing social groups inside political institutions. Katz and Mair suggest three dimensions of the weakening of such links. The exclusive relationship between parties and classes has loosened. The catchall party is no longer defined by a *classe gardée,* a particular social class constituency. Secondly, state intervention has become central in party functioning, straitjacketed by laws and statutes, funded by public money more than by activists. Finally, a kind of cartel solidarity has developed between established parties to keep control of the electoral market and prevent the arrival of newcomers. We can speak with Offerlé (1994) of parties as cogs in a public representation service organized by the state for voters more than as the expression of spontaneous citizens' voices challenging the state.

Can we compare the evolution of media to that of parties? Significant differences do exist. They come from the unprecedented weight of huge communication companies and market logic and sometimes from the state's withdrawal of financial support to the media. But if one considers the limited but strategic sector of the general information press and media, Katz and Mair's (1994) analytical framework still makes sense. Just as between voters and parties, the bottom-up linkage between the information press and its readership has loosened. Even in many countries where it was once powerful (France, Italy), the partisan party press now occupies a very limited space, like media linked to trade unions or social movements. Audiences and readerships have become markets to conquer more than a "base" with whom to reflect and to whom to give voice.

The information media have also become a full-fledged political institution. Cook (1998, pt. III) has clearly shown how the other constitutional institutions have adapted themselves to the imperatives of media, developing press services, rituals, and timetables to answer to the imperatives of newsworthiness, using the media for their own purposes. A newsroom is structured in an isomorphic relationship to public institutions. The political desk of a French newspaper has its specialists on the presidency, the parliament, and the prime minister. The structure and hierarchy of ministries are approximately mirrored by the hierarchy of the journalists who cover them. Because they are plugged into institutional sources, whose specializations and often ways of thinking and questioning they reproduce, journalists are trapped in mimetic "indexation" logics (Bennett, 1996). Their interpretative categories mirror those of the mighty. The simple question of what is political news is illuminating. This news section covers the cogs of representative democracy: institutions, parties, elections, and parliamentary debates. It pays conversely much less attention to realities whose political impact is nonetheless strong for ordinary citizens: lobbying, policy processes, social movements.

Let us finally note how the integration of news production and frames into the magnetic field of officialdom is also visible in the weak power of media to define an autonomous agenda. Following the agendas of the three main candidates and deriving their reporting priorities from them, journalists hammered the theme of law and order during the French presidential campaign of 2002—before expressing amazement when such framing and priming processes allowed the extreme-right politician Le Pen to get to the second round (Amalou, 2002). Because it restores the autonomy of the press, investigative journalism à la Watergate balances such trends. But it is strong in only a few countries. It can hardly develop without the partnership of actors or institutions having strategic interest in leaks. It also has to face the reaction of the powers that be to its challenges (Schudson, 1995, chap. 7).

Even if it does not suppress the existence of a space for debate, the location of news media in the shadow and interdependence network of public institutions and social power tends to make them share a common *episteme*. It threatens to transform them into loudspeakers of the official ways of framing news and events, rather than having them relay citizens' emotions, reactions, and ways of thinking.

REVITALIZING THE PUBLIC SPHERE

The historical analysis of the role of media in the public sphere looks often like a kind of horror story for intellectuals. Media are accused of transforming public debate into endlessly degenerating triviality. If they do mobilize factual data, their diagnoses often threaten to overinterpret them. The search for ratings pushes them to value the spectacular, the entertaining, and the emotive more than to enlighten debate or analysis of the issues. Epistemic closeness between questioners and questioned produces connivance. As "politics" appears ratings unfriendly, the media debates able to gather a significant audience have shifted toward talk show programs. And discussion focuses thus more on private matters (sex, family life, health), framed as manageable by individual therapy, rather than on social problems and people's stakes in the policies that address them (François & Neveu, 1999).

Despite these trends that threaten the very notion of public debate, we should conclude by considering new uses of media to revitalize political debate. The question of political debate in contemporary media need not be condemned to be framed in the nostalgia of an imaginary golden age.

Without developing a naive or populist celebration, one should first notice that many broadcast talk shows with active audiences contribute to modifying the agenda and style of debates. A clear example was offered by the public service French TV during the 1995 presidential campaign. Questions expressed from the studio by representatives of "civil society" or from cafés by "ordinary Frenchmen" were mainly about unemployment, the welfare state, AIDS, and political morality, whereas those from political journalists remained centered on the horse race and party bargaining (Neveu, 1999). The U.S. experiments in "civic journalism" can suggest similar comments. When they work to help local communities to identify their own agendas, define solutions, and organize debates, journalists give an opportunity to reconstruct local spaces for political discussion. One can question this approach. Is there a risk of seeing journalists replacing politicians? Does the quest of community consensus threaten minorities? Civic journalism, however, has often given a new energy to local politics.

One would finally note how the aim to regain young, female, popular readers has boosted new styles of reporting in the United Kingdom, the Netherlands, and France. Often written by women, these articles may use biographical material to make sense of issues, describe the practical impact of policies on laypeople, and give expression to their feelings and hopes. Such analyses can be expressed in portraits, in an "intimate reporting" (Harrington, 1997), or in reports linked to hard news and issues. They bring back into media and public debate a potential bottom-up approach to policies and their impact, as well as a sensitivity to collective stakes that may prevent stereotypical speech and revalidate social dialogue.

◆ Notes

1. Among the best Web sites concerning the U.S. First Amendment and the British libel law are the following: the Electronic Frontier Foundation (www.eff.org), the Reporters Committee for Freedom of the Press (www.rcfp.org), and the Libel Defense Resource Center (www.ldrc.com).

2. See, for instance, U.S. "Executive Order 12958: Classified Security Information" (1995), available at www.cmcnyls.edu/public/USLaws/ExOrder.htm.

3. See *Branzburg v. Hayes* (1972). Thirty U.S. states have adopted shield laws protecting journalists against subpoenas. Article 109-2 from the French "Code de procédure pénale" mentions "any journalist subpoenaed as witness about information gathered in the exercise of his job is free not to reveal their origin."

4. SLAPP stands for strategic lawsuit against public participation. See *Lafayette Morehouse, Inc. v. Chronicle Publishing Co.* (1995).

5. The Polish postcommunist government of Leszek Miller prepared in 2002 an antitrust law that had the central goal of weakening the private group Agora, publisher of the main opposition journal Gazeta Wyborcza.

6. See the 342-page USA Patriot Act bill (USAPA)—signed on October 26, 2001, by President Bush—and its analysis at www.eff.org.

7. The French authorities were unable to prevent the illegal sale—in France—of Nazi symbols offered on the Web from a site hosted by Yahoo in the United States.

◆ References

Allen, D. (2001). The First Amendment and the doctrine of corporate personhood. *Journalism, 2*(3), 255–278.

Amalou, F. (2002, May 28). La télévision a accru sa couverture de la violence durant la campagne [Television increased its coverage of violence during the presidential campaign]. *Le Monde*, p. 22.

Anonymous. (1996). *Primary colors*. New York: Random House.

Barendt, E., Lustgarden, L., Norrie, K., & Stephenson, H. (1997). *Libel and the media: The chilling effect*. Oxford, UK: Oxford University Press.

Bennett, L. (1996). An introduction to journalism norms and representations of politics. *Political Communication, 13,* 373–384.

Blum, R. (2001). *Parliamentary white paper on "Les faiblesses et les forces du cinéma français sur le marché international"* (Weaknesses and strengths of French cinema in the international market). Retrieved October 2, 2003, from www.assemblee-nat.fr/rap-info/i3197.asp

Blumler, J. (Ed.). (1992). *Television and the public interest: Vulnerable values in West European broadcasting*. London: Sage.

Blumler, J., & Gurevitch, M. (1995). *The crisis of public communication*. London: Routledge.

Blumler, J., & Kavanagh, D. (1999). The third age of political communication: Influences and features. *Political Communication, 16,* 209–230.

Bourdieu, P., & Wacquant, L. (1998). Sur les ruses de la raison impérialiste [On the cunning of imperialist reason]. *Actes de la Recherche en Sciences Sociales, 121–122,* 109–118.

Brants, K. (1999). Who's afraid of infotainment? *European Journal of Communication, 13*(3), 315–335.

Branzburg v. Hayes, 408 U.S. 665 (1972).

Champagne, P. (1990). *Faire l'opinion* [constructing public opinion]. Paris: Minuit.

Cook, T. (1998). *Governing with the news*. Chicago: University of Chicago Press.

Davis, A. (2002). *Public relation democracy: Public relations, politics and the mass media in Britain*. Manchester, UK: Manchester University Press.

de Tocqueville, A. (1981). *De La Démocratie en Amérique* [Democracy in America] (Vol. 2). Paris: Garnier Flammarion.

Derieux, E. (2000). *Droit de la communication* [Communication law]. Paris: LGDJ.

Desrosières, A. (1993). *La politique des grands nombres: Histoire de la raison statistique* [The politics of large numbers: History of statistical reasoning]. Paris: La Découverte.

Eco, U. (1965). *Apocalittici e integrati: communicazioni di massa e teorie della cultura di massa* [The Apocalyptists and the Assimilated: Mass communications and theories of mass culture] (2nd ed.). Milan: Bompiani.

Eliasoph, N. (1998). *Avoiding politics: How Americans produce apathy in everyday life*. Cambridge, UK: Cambridge University Press.

Fallows, J. (1996). *Breaking the news*. New York: Vintage.

Foucault, M. (1975). *Surveiller et punir* [Discipline and punish]. Paris: Gallimard.

François, B., & Neveu, E. (Eds.). (1999). *Espaces Publics Mosaïques* [Mosaic public spheres]. Rennes, France: PUR.

Franklin, B. (1997). *Newsak and news media*. London: Arnold.

Habermas, J. (1989). *The structural transformation of the public sphere*. Cambridge: MIT Press.

Halimi, S., & Vidal, D. (2000). *L'opinion ça se travaille: Les médias, l'OTAN et la guerre du Kosovo* [The Shaping of Public Opinion: Media, NATO, and the Kosovo war]. Marseille, France: Agone.

Hall, S., Clarke, J., Critcher, C., Jefferson, T., & Roberts, B. (1978). *Policing the crisis*. London: Macmillan.

Harrington, W. (Ed.). (1997). *Intimate reporting: The art and craft or reporting everyday life*. London: Sage.

Hirschman, A. (1991). *The rhetoric of reaction: Perversity, futility, jeopardy*. Cambridge, MA: Harvard University Press.

Humphreys, P. (1996). *Mass media and media policy in Western Europe*. Manchester, UK: Manchester University Press.

Katz, R., & Mair, P. (1994). *How parties organise: Change and adaptation in party organisations in Western democracies*. London: Sage.

Keane, J. (1991). *The media and democracy*. London: Polity.

Kuhn, R., & Neveu, E. (Eds.). (2002). *Political journalism: New challenges, new practices.* London: Routledge.

Lafayette Morehouse, Inc. v. Chronicle Publishing Co., 44 Cal.Rptr. 2d 46 (Cal. Ct. App. 1995).

Lijphart, A. (1984). *Democracies: Patterns of majoritarian and consensus government in twenty-one countries.* New Haven, CT: Yale University Press.

Mattelart, A. (1992). *La Communication-monde* [Communication-world]. Paris: La Découverte.

Mattelart, T. (1995). *Le cheval de Troie audio-visuel* [The media Trojan horse]. Grenoble, France: PUG.

McManus, J. (1994). *Market-driven journalism: Let the citizens beware?* London: Sage.

McNair, B. (2000). *Journalism and democracy: An evaluation of the political public sphere.* London: Routledge.

McQuail, D. (1983). *Mass communication theory: An introduction* (2nd ed.). Beverly Hills, CA: Sage.

Merrill, J. C., & Nerone, J. (2002). The four theories of the press four and a half decades after: A retrospective. *Journalism Studies, 3*(1), 123–136.

Neveu, E. (1994). *Une société de communication?* [A communication society?]. Paris: Montchrestien.

Neveu, E. (1999). Politics on French television. *European Journal of Communication, 14*(3), 379–410.

Neveu, E. (2001). *Sociologie du journalisme* [Sociology of journalism]. Paris: La Découverte.

Nimmo, D. (1981). *Handbook of political communication.* Beverly Hills, CA: Sage.

Norris, P. (2000). *A virtuous circle: Political communication in postindustrial societies.* Cambridge, UK: Cambridge University Press.

Offerlé, M. (1994). *Sociologie des Groupes d'Intérêt* [Sociology of interest groups]. Paris: Montchrestien.

Orwell, G. (1987). *1984* (Vol. 9 of Collected Works). London: Secker & Warburg.

Pedelty, M. (1995). *War stories.* London: Routledge.

Peyrefitte, A. (1976). *Le mal français* [The French disease]. Paris: Plon.

"La politique saisie par le divertissement" [Politics trapped by entertainment]. (2003). *Réseaux, 21*(118).

Reinarman, C., & Levine, H. (1995). The crack attack: America's latest drug scare, 1986–1992. In J. Best (Ed.), *Typifying social problems* (pp. 147–186). Berlin: Aldine de Gruyter.

Reporters Sans Frontières. (2002). *Annual report.* Available in English at http://www.rsf.fr/rubrique.php3?id_rubrique=144

Rosanvallon, P. (1985). *Le moment Guizot* [The Guizot moment]. Paris: Gallimard.

Schlesinger, P., & Tumber, H. (1994). *Reporting crime: The media politics of criminal justice.* Oxford, UK: Clarendon.

Schudson, M. (1995). *The power of news.* Cambridge: Harvard University Press.

Semelin, J. (2000). *La liberté au bout des ondes* [Freedom through airwaves]. Paris: Belfont.

Siebert, F., Peterson, T., & Schramm, W. (1956). *Four theories of the press.* Urbana: University of Illinois Press.

Tilly, C. (1976). *From revolution to mobilization.* Reading, MA: Addison-Wesley.

Tunstall, J., & Palmer, M. (1991). *Media moguls.* London: Routledge.

United Nations Educational, Scientific, and Cultural Organization (UNESCO). (1985). *Many voices, one world: The MacBride report.* New York: Author.

17

MEDIA, PUBLIC OPINION, AND POLITICAL ACTION

◆ Holli A. Semetko

R esearch on the subject of public opinion and political action from a media studies perspective has expanded considerably in recent years. Whereas in the mid-1980s, concern about media influence characterized a comparatively small portion of what Kinder and Sears (1986) described as research on public opinion and political action, nowadays it is hardly possible to think of the media as anything but central to research in this area. Many of the studies in this area can also be described as within the interdisciplinary subfield of political communication research, which has also expanded considerably over the past two decades.[1]

Some recent international examples illustrate the variety of reasons why the media are at the center of public debate in many societies around the world. Italy, for example, is classified as an established democracy in comparative research, but many have come to question this status given Prime Minister Berlusconi's controlling interest in commercial broadcasting in the country and his government's political influence over public broadcasting (see also Hallin & Papathanassopoulos, 2002). Central and Latin American countries, many of which are societies in transition from military regimes, provide numerous examples over the past two decades of how the news media contribute to the rise and fall of political power (see, e.g., Waisbord, 1995, 1997, 2000). In

Russia, Ukraine, and other post-Soviet societies in transition, the media are often at the center of debate not only because of their general pro-government bias (see, e.g., Mickiewicz, 1988, 1999; Semetko & Krasnoboka, 2003) but also because of the many human rights violations against journalists.[2] And in China, where the news media are heavily constrained and access is government controlled, concerns about press freedom to diverge from the party line take on special urgency in light of the sudden acute respiratory syndrome (SARS) epidemic in 2003.

Studies of public opinion and political action are at an interdisciplinary crossroads, and an array of quantitative and qualitative methods characterizes research in this area. The growing body of research on public opinion and political action can still be described as going the most deeply into the U.S. case. Although it may be appropriate to describe journalists as political actors and the news media as a political institution in any society (Cook, 1998; Patterson, 2002; Schudson, 2002), less is known about other parts of the world where different institutional conditions prevail. Growing scholarly interest in media, public opinion, and political action on a global scale is not only because of opportunities presented by the larger number of countries involved in democratization processes over the past two decades but also because of the global expansion of commercial media (McChesney, 1997).

Even in an established democracy such as the Netherlands, which is representative of European multiparty parliamentary systems, in which news organizations are largely independent from party influence and levels of party identification and electoral turnout are comparatively higher than the United States, there is evidence that one's viewing behavior has consequences that cannot always be thought of as "virtuous": Watching television news regularly on the public service channels, for example, has positive effects on political learning, feelings of political efficacy, and turning out to vote, whereas regularly opting for commercial television news has consistent and significant negative effects on these variables. This research thus supports a "dual-effects" hypothesis[3] (Aarts & Semetko, 2003). Especially given the wide range of commercial broadcasting options that citizens in most countries now have, the role of television in politics today is under conditions quite apart from, for example, Britain's first television elections in the late 1950s and early 1960s, when everyone had only a couple of channels to which they could turn for news and reporters were quite reverent and descriptive (as opposed to evaluative) in their coverage of candidates and leaders (Blumler & McQuail, 1969).

There is also special concern about the potential consequences of contemporary media environments for democracy building in societies in transition, in which party systems are still in their infancy, news organizations and journalists are often in precarious positions, and there are low levels of party identification and electoral experience among citizens. In these societies in transition as well as in established democracies, analysis of survey data can often show a positive relationship between media use and satisfaction with democracy, trust in institutions, and other measures of political attitudes (Dalton, 1996; Norris,

2000), but given the superficial and limited range of questions about media use in those surveys, such a general conclusion may mask the more complex set of relationships that may be operating.

In the limitations of one chapter, it is impossible to cover the historically important studies from communication, political science, psychology, and sociology that contribute to our present understanding of the media's role in public opinion formation, public political action, and the link between these two processes. I have therefore chosen to focus primarily on fruitful opportunities for interdisciplinary and multimethodological research in this area by reviewing some of the main findings from research that has been conducted from a media studies perspective over the past two decades. Such a perspective takes media as a key part of the focus of public opinion and political action research, with an emphasis on one or more of the following: use, contents, institutions, professionals, and media systems. I also do not include all of the research published in the past 10 to 20 years in this area but instead concentrate on some of the concepts, hypotheses, and perspectives that I believe are important for the future. In particular, I focus on the research about the formation of and changes in attitudes, the research on social movements, and studies of frames and framing effects.

◆ Studying Attitude Stability and Change

The question of consistency in political and policy attitudes was the focus of Philip Converse's seminal research on attitude stability. Converse (1962, 1964) argued that most Americans have no consistent pattern to their opinions or beliefs and that their opinions do not depend on ideological principles. An analysis of American National Election Study (ANES) panel data from 1956, 1958, and 1960 found that so many changed their opinions on policy issues that it appeared as if answers had been given at random. The general conclusion was that for most individuals, policy attitudes were for the most part *nonattitudes*. From this perspective, shifts in public opinion are largely explained by a lack of knowledge, interest, and ideology that results in randomness of opinion.[4]

There are many contrasting views on public opinion and what moves it. The work by Page and Shapiro (1992) stands

out because it describes a "rational public" whose opinions are moved by information in a way that reveals consistency between policy preferences and basic values. They focus on *aggregate public opinion* in the United States and show that it is largely stable over time on many aspects of public policy. This does not necessarily contradict Converse (1962, 1964), who described individual-level opinion change as largely random because these random changes at the individual level could appear stable at the aggregate level. Page and Shapiro (1992) argue, however, that public opinion moves in response to events or new information about an issue. They identified parallel publics (cohorts or demographic groups) who used similar standards to assess issues and whose opinions largely moved in the same direction, and they conclude that opinion is rational and that attitudes exhibit consistency.[5]

These two examples illustrate one of the central problems in public opinion research from a media effects perspective. It is the tension between the individual level and the aggregate level. Most studies tend to focus on one level or the other and often employ only a single methodological approach.

METHODS

Each method has its own advantages and disadvantages. Experiments allow for the maximum control on the part of the researcher of the environment within which the study takes place and therefore result in high internal validity, allowing us to specify cause-and-effect relationships. But media effects experiments also have special disadvantages, not the least of which is the laboratory (not a natural setting) and the stimulus material (which may distort what is actually in the news). Surveys, by contrast, may be nationally representative and are conducted in naturalistic settings. Cross-sectional surveys nevertheless rely on reported measures of communication exposure and correlations between these and reported attitudes. A panel survey, in which the same group of respondents is interviewed on separate occasions with the advantage of the naturalistic setting, permits causal analysis of effects. Panel studies are not without problems, however, the most common ones being attrition rates and contamination effects. In addition to these approaches, depth interviews, focus groups, and deliberative events are also common to research public opinion change and have been the basis for some pioneering studies on how people talk about and process political news (Gamson, 1992; Graber, 1988, 2001), frame it (Neuman, Just, & Crigler, 1992), and interpret, argue, and "deliberate" political issue information (Price, Cappella, & Nir, 2002). Content analysis has been often ignored by public opinion researchers, even though reliable and valid content indicators can be important for an understanding of the sources of media effects. Because each of the above methods of research has its own inherent strengths and weaknesses, a genuine understanding of the effects of communications

on attitudes ideally requires a design in which a number of methods are used in a complementary fashion.

MULTILEVEL ANALYSIS

Public opinion research that is survey based has also developed sophisticated tools for taking into account the contexts in which public opinion is measured. And data can be at different levels—for example, the individual level, the organizational level, and the system level. Multilevel analysis permits researchers to model the different layers in the structure of multilevel data and determine how layers interact and influence the dependent variable (Steenbergen & Jones, 2002). Multilevel analysis is an especially relevant form of modeling data for the study of media influence in a comparative research design in which contextual variables are also important (Shah, McLeod, & Yoon, 2001).

In the process of European political and economic integration, in which many countries are giving up some aspects of authority to another level of government and publics are forming opinions about national-level as well as European-level issues and institutions, multilevel analysis is especially useful for the study of opinion formation (Rohrschneider, 2002). It can also be useful to assess the impact of the news on political behavior—specifically, the decision to vote or, more appropriately, not to vote. In the 1999 European Parliament elections, for example, turnout was down from the previous election and reached the exceptionally low levels of 23% in the United Kingdom and 30% in the Netherlands and Finland, in comparison with highs elsewhere of 64% in Spain, 71% in Italy, and 70% in Greece.

Research on electoral turnout in European parliamentary elections has, for the most part, included some of these contextual variables alongside traditional demographic characteristics (education, age, gender) but, with few exceptions

(Blumler, 1984) and until recently, has largely ignored the contribution of the media or the campaign information environment to mobilizing or demobilizing electors (Niedermyer & Sinnott, 1998; Sinnott, 1995, 1998; van der Eijk & Franklin, 1996).[6] Theories about party competition and factors influencing electoral turnout, such as the day an election is held or the presence of more than one election in one country on the same day, can be tested using a multilevel analysis that permits the integration of quantity and tone of media reporting (about the 1999 European parliamentary election campaigns in each country) into the model predicting turnout or abstention. This model also includes potentially important national contextual influences such as, for example, concurrently held national or local elections, Sunday voting, and the presence of a viable anti–European Union (EU) party (Banducci & Semetko, 2002).

◆ The Media as a Facilitator of Opinion and Action: The Link Between the Individual Level and Societal Level

Media are often conceptualized as the primary connection between an individual and the society. One important line of research deals with the citizen as a consumer of news and media information, as well as a member of a community, and how mediated information and personal experience influence opinions and action. A central focus has been to identify the ways in which media uses and contents influence individual opinion, within the context of one's personal network of political discussants. This has emphasized the consequences of exposure to information in the media, in comparison with exposure to information via personal networks, for the development and perception of political attitudes.[7] Does the information in the media enhance or diminish the influence of personal experience and networks on the formation of political attitudes?

One study focused on individuals' personal experience with a problem or issue and how this can become politicized in the context of news and media information sources. By reporting people's experiences and linking them to the experiences of others, the media help people to interpret their own personal experience as part of a larger societal trend. According to Mutz (1994), for example, "Mothers who have lost their children to automobile fatalities have long been against drunk driving, but until the issue became highly publicized through the efforts of Mothers Against Drunk Driving, their personal experiences were not highly politicized" (p. 691). In this way, the media may help the victim of a crime or the unemployed worker to come to realize that she or he is one of many across the country or in the community. The media therefore may contribute to the politicization of one's personal experience because this can, in turn, affect political opinions and political preferences and can potentially induce people to take political action. The problem of unemployment is one that is often covered in the news and is one with which many individuals also have personal experience. According to Mutz (1994),

> Exposure to unemployment news appears to strengthen the impact of personal experiences [*with unemployment*] on presidential performance ratings. Heavy unemployment coverage also increases the extent to which perceptions of national unemployment conditions are generalized from personal experience. Overall, . . . mass media may . . . help legitimize the translation of private interests into political attitudes. (p. 689, emphasis added)

Another study addressed the extent to which individuals learn more about political views dissimilar to their own via the media in comparison with one's interpersonal network of political discussants.[8] This is an important question not least in the U.S. context, in which the media have been criticized for not offering a wide range of political viewpoints. Yet Mutz and Martin (2001) find that

> individuals are exposed to far more dissimilar political views via news media than through interpersonal political discussants. The media advantage is rooted in the relative difficulty of selectively exposing oneself to those sources of information, as well as the lesser desire to do so, given the impersonal nature of mass media. (p. 97)

The media are therefore described as "facilitating communication across lines of political difference." *Impersonal influence* refers to the important role played by media in shaping perceptions of societal-level trends and developments. According to Mutz (1998),

> Media play a particularly important role in shaping impersonal perceptions, and impersonal perceptions, in turn, play a particularly important role in shaping political judgments. Nonetheless, citizens are not necessarily doomed to excessive conformity or to puppet-like manipulation at the hands of those who control media content ... the normative social influence conveyed by interpersonal political discussion is obviously important, but the American public also demonstrate a great deal of independence, even in face-to-face settings. (p. 270)

The American penchant for demonstrating independence in political discussions is by no means a universal trait. The "spiral-of-silence theory," one of the most widely debated theories in public opinion research, is based on the idea that one's willingness to express one's own political opinions is constrained by how she or he perceives the climate of public opinion (Noelle-Neumann, 1974). Dozens of studies have

been conducted to address key hypotheses in the theory over the past two to three decades. A review of this body of research shows that inconsistencies in conceptualization, operationalization, and a lack of attention to macroscopic variables explain much of the variance in the spiral-of-silence effects. Scheufele and Moy (2000) conclude,

> Spiral of silence studies in different cultures have failed to take into account culture-specific variables that may mitigate the importance of opinion perceptions as predictors of individual behavior or attitudes. In other words, cross-cultural differences are key factors in predicting speaking out, the key dependent variable in spiral of silence research. As a result, we call for the return to a more macroscopic focus in spiral of silence research. (p. 3)

The perceptions of the climate of opinion, or the distribution of public opinion on an issue, can also influence an individual's willingness to participate in political activities such as expressing one's opinion and other forms of participation (Scheufele & Eveland, 2001). Another study has found an important interaction effect between reliance on hard news media and the frequency of political discussion. The effects of hard media use are different for people who often talk about politics with others in comparison with those who do not (Scheufele, 2002).

NEW MEDIA AND CIVIC ENGAGEMENT

How citizens connect and engage with civic life has been potentially enhanced with the arrival of the Internet. Amidst public concern about the lack of interest that young people have in reading newspapers or watching news, the Internet provides new opportunities for entertainment and information. A multilevel research design that takes into account individual-level media use and community-level variables explored the influence of both on civic engagement, measured as interpersonal trust and participation. Although, not surprisingly, the study found that reliance on the media for information purposes is positively related to the production of social capital,[9] whereas entertainment uses of the media are negatively related to civic participation,[10] there was also an important and surprising interaction effect (Shah, McLeod, et al., 2001):

> Informational uses of mass media were also found to interact with community context to influence civic engagement. Analyses within sub-samples find that among the youngest adult Americans, use of the Internet for information exchange more strongly influences trust in people and civic participation than do uses of traditional print and broadcast news. (p. 464)

A related study based on the same data set further explores the associations between Internet use as compared to other media among different age cohorts and reinforces the point that Internet influence on the production of social capital is primarily confined to the younger ("Generation X") cohort.[11] The authors conclude (Shah, Kwak, & Holbert, 2001),

> Although the size of associations is generally small, the data suggest that informational uses of the Internet are positively related to individual differences in the production of social capital, whereas social-recreational uses are negatively related to these civic indicators. Analyses within sub-samples defined by generational age-breaks further suggest that social capital production is related to Internet use among Generation X, while it is tied to television use among Baby Boomers and newspaper use among members of the Civic Generation. (p. 141)

Political Learning

Doris Graber's (2001) research demonstrates how vital visuals are for the retention and understanding of information, particularly political information. Television and, increasingly, the Internet, as it becomes more graphics than text driven, are therefore important sources of information for political learning. According to Graber (2001),

> Audiovisuals ease two major information-processing problems: failure to embed information in long-term memory and inability to retrieve it when needed. . . . All else being equal, when messages include visuals rich in relevant information, memory is enhanced . . . its accuracy improves as well. Good visuals make a situation more graphic and vivid . . . they are etched more deeply into memory initially than non-visual messages. In turn, because they are more easily recalled, they are frequently refreshed, which then prevents fading. (pp. 33–34)

Research shows that there is a difference between unsophisticated and sophisticated television viewers in coping "with messages that require complex processing at both the verbal and the audiovisual levels" (Graber, 2001, p. 35; see also Rahn & Cramer, 1996). One reason why audiovisuals do not consistently enhance learning or recall is because many TV news visuals are "totally uninformative" (Graber, 2001, p. 35). In comparison with television news, news on the Internet is received by a more interested, active (and interactive) audience.

◆ Media, Public Opinion, and Protest as Political Action

Much of the research on protest and collective action has taken a comparative historical approach with case studies from the

19th century or earlier. Political opportunity structure is an important theoretical concept in the arsenal of social movement theories that has provided a framework for much of the collective action research in which the 20th century is the focus (McAdam, Tarrow, & Tilly, 2001; Tarrow, 1998). Political opportunity structures refer to "consistent—but not necessarily formal or permanent—dimensions of the political environment that provide incentives for people to undertake collective action by affecting their expectations for success or failure" (Tarrow, 1998, p. 85).[12] Public opinion is one of those consistent dimensions of the environment. But the role of public opinion, particularly how the media reporting of events and of public opinion contributes to perceptions of "incentives" for undertaking collective action, has not been central to the research conducted from within this perspective. There has been attention to rhetorical framing of arguments from those working within a political opportunity structure approach (Koopmans & Duyvendak, 1995), but as a whole, the discussion of the media takes the form of references to other studies involving framing (Gamson & Modigliani, 1989) and some attention to the way various actors, including the media, frame political opportunity (Gamson & Meyer, 1996). There has been a call for an effort to "insert a dimension of public discourse within a political opportunity perspective"[13] (Koopmans & Statham, 2000, pp. 36–37), but although content analysis has been used, it has not been for the purpose of assessing the contribution of the media to collective action from a political opportunity structure perspective. A cross-national comparative study uses a content analysis of quality newspapers in Germany and Britain to provide a record of the "claims-making" activities of various groups, but the way this has been done fails to consider from a political opportunity perspective any questions about media power in shaping news agendas or media effects on collective action processes. There remains the problem of using the media as an indicator of claims-making activities in the public sphere, without acknowledging that the news organization or outlet can be an independent actor in the process.

Social protest, social movements, and collective action provide a fascinating setting for the study of the influence of media and communication process on public opinion, as studies of the student, antiwar, and environmentalist movements have shown (see, e.g., Gamson, 1988; Gitlin, 1980; Hallin, 1986). Public opinion and media coverage of events and opinions may help to facilitate or diminish opportunities for collective action. Research has shown that conceptions of public opinion are embedded in the news coverage of social protest (McLeod & Hertog, 1992). There are common approaches to framing protest in the news (Hertog & McLeod, 1995), and the term *protest paradigm* has been used to describe the formulaic approach that journalists take in reporting social protest (McLeod & Detenber, 1999). These common characteristics of protest reporting can have important consequences for the opinions of audiences. For example, when the news is framed in a way that supports the status quo in the coverage of one social protest, an experiment found that "viewers were more critical of and less likely to identify with the protesters, less critical of the police, and less likely to support the protesters' expressive rights" (McLeod & Detenber, 1999). Support for the status quo in the news coverage also led to lower estimations of the effectiveness of the protest, perceptions of its newsworthiness, and public support for the protest.

The framing of issues in the media also has effects on the mobilization of social movements. Media framing of issues has been described as an alternative or complementary explanation to the influence of public opinion, elite cues, and political opportunity structure on movement mobilization (Cooper, 2002). Cross-national comparative research on protest shows that "congruence" between the media's and the movement's framing of the issues, for example, can facilitate mobilization but that mobilization is hindered if there is "divergence" (Cooper, 2002).

The student peace movements during the intensification of the Vietnam War and the media coverage of the opposition to the war, along with the shifts in public support for the war over time, provide a basis for addressing questions about information, opinion change, and political action. The Vietnam War was the case used by John Zaller (1991, 1992) to explain both individual-level and aggregate-level changes in one model of U.S. public opinion. Whereas past research at the individual-level "modeled mass opinion change as a two-step process involving reception of political communication and acceptance or rejection of that communication," Zaller (1991, p. 1215) proposed "a two-message version of the reception-acceptance model, in which citizens are exposed to two opposing communication flows, either or both of which may affect their opinions." Different levels of attention to politics and different political values among citizens, along with variation over time in the intensity of oppositional messages in the media, interact in this model to explain both aggregate-level shifts and individual-level changes over time.

THE CONDITIONING EFFECTS OF POLITICAL INVOLVEMENT

The more politically involved are generally characterized by greater political knowledge, attentiveness, exposure to political information, and attachment to certain political values or beliefs. The literature does not provide a clear answer on what to expect concerning the relationship between attitude change and political involvement. Converse (1964) would predict that citizens with the lowest levels of exposure, interest, knowledge, and beliefs would change only randomly or not at all; those who were at the highest levels would remain stable or change systematically; and those in the

middle levels would be most open to influence from the information environment. Following Converse, Zaller (1992) also argues that a more detailed distinction in levels of awareness or attentiveness is necessary because the relationship between attitude change and political awareness may be nonlinear. Awareness or attentiveness is operationalized with the use of a scale or index of political knowledge by Zaller (1991, 1992), and the expectation is that citizens with intermediate knowledge levels would be most likely to be affected by information. His model of public opinion change has inspired a host of studies over the past decade.

There continues to be debate, however, about the validity of the measures used to establish political knowledge levels. The importance of political knowledge as a predictor of political involvement is acknowledged in the literature, but there remains disagreement over how it should best be measured (see, e.g., Delli Carpini & Keeter, 1993; Graber, 2001; Luskin, 1990; Mondak, 2001). Recent research likens the factual political knowledge questions used in most survey-based studies (including the ANES) to a high school civics exam and questions the ability of these questions to capture actual political understanding and awareness (Graber, 2001; Mondak, 2001).

◆ Agenda Setting, Priming, and Framing

Although some researchers have attached the word *theory* to each of the above terms, others refer to agenda setting, priming, and framing as key concepts or processes in public opinion research. There is also debate about whether and how these concepts, processes, or theories, in terms of effects on audiences, are actually related (McCombs, Lopez-Escobar, & Llamas, 2000; Scheufele, 2000). I do not wish to elaborate the debate over the status of these as concepts or theories or take sides in the discussion over their independence or interdependence. Below I discuss briefly the developments in agenda-setting research before turning to key questions in priming and framing research.

AGENDA SETTING

Much of the research testing the agenda-setting hypothesis has drawn on two sources of data. One is content analysis of the news. This is used to establish the most important issues in the news. The other measures public opinion. The latter has included cross-sectional designs, time series of comparable cross-sectional surveys, more elaborate panel studies, and experiments. Support for the hypothesis of media agenda-setting effects has been found in hundreds of studies over the past few decades (for reviews, see McCombs, 1981, 2004; McCombs, Einsiedel, & Weaver, 1991; McCombs & Shaw, 1993; Rogers & Dearing, 1988; Rogers, Dearing, & Bregman, 1993; Stempel, Weaver, & Wilhoit, 2003; Swanson, 1988; Weaver, McCombs, & Spellman, 1975; Weaver, Graber, McCombs, & Eyal, 1981). These studies provide substantial support for the hypothesis that the most prominent issues in the news are also the issues that become the most important in public opinion. The fact that support for the agenda-setting hypothesis has been found using all of these of methodological approaches further strengthens the argument for a powerful news media.

The term itself was first coined by McCombs and Shaw (1972), based on their community study of media agenda setting in a U.S. presidential campaign, which involved content analysis and cross-sectional survey data. The study was "pioneering" for providing evidence of a strong and significant correlation between the campaign agenda in the media and in public opinion, as well as setting forth the hypothesis that agenda setting is a process led by the news media (Rogers & Dearing, 1988).

A yearlong panel study of the 1976 U.S. presidential election, designed specifically to test the agenda-setting hypothesis, provided further evidence of the direction of the causal link from media agendas to public agendas (Weaver et al., 1981). The authors identified the relative strengths of television and the newspapers as influences on public opinion and established that agenda-setting effects varied over time, with the strongest during the spring and summer and the weakest during the final 12 weeks of the campaign, particularly with respect to unobtrusive issues such as foreign affairs, the environment, and government credibility. Patterson's (1980, p. 159) multiwave panel study of the same 1976 campaign also found that newspapers were more important vehicles than television news for voter learning about the issues and established that the more heavily the issue was reported in the press, the more readers with low or moderate interest in the election learned about the issue.

Iyengar and Kinder (1987, p. 12) tried to diminish the artificiality of the experimental setting and drew their sample from heterogeneous groups of people (not only college sophomores) and followed a strategy of conceptual replication in a series of experiments testing the agenda-setting power of television news. Findings combined from three sources—a series of sequential experiments each lasting 1 week (with pre- and postexperimental questionnaires), additional experiments that required only postquestionnaires, and an analysis of time-series data from national public opinion polls—provided further substantial support for the agenda-setting hypothesis. They thus concluded, "By attending to some problems and ignoring others, television news shapes the American public's political priorities. These effects appear to be neither momentary, as our experimental results indicate, nor permanent, as our time-series results reveal" (Iyengar & Kinder, 1987, p. 33). The study was innovative in its focus on television news as an agenda setter in normal (nonelection) periods.

Media power to influence public agendas may be conditioned by a number of factors. One is the extent to which real-world indicators reinforce or diminish the media message. Another is the type of issue—"unobtrusive" issues may be more susceptible to agenda setting. News about foreign affairs and foreign peoples, with whom viewers have little or no direct experience, is an example of an "unobtrusive" issue (see also Baum, 2002). Media influence may also vary with the type of public agenda. An individual's civic agenda (his or her perception of the most important issues or problems facing the community) may be quite different from an individual's personal agenda (his or her opinion about the most important problems he or she is facing). When an individual's personal agenda is the focus of research, then there is considerably less support for the agenda-setting hypothesis (McLeod, Becker, & Byrnes, 1974).

Election campaigns outside the United States have been the focus for a number of studies that have not found evidence in support of the agenda-setting hypothesis. British general elections in the 1980s and 1990s have provided more than one example in which media agendas and audience agendas failed to coincide (see, e.g., Miller, Clarke, Harrop, LeDuc, & Whiteley, 1990; Norris, Curtice, Sanders, Scammell, & Semetko, 1999), and in Germany too, agenda-setting effects failed to materialize in the historic 1990 election (Semetko & Schoenbach, 1994).

Priming

In a study of citizens' responses to Watergate, Weaver et al. (1975) argued

> that for persons with a high need for orientation about politics, mass communication does more than merely reinforce preexisting beliefs. In fact, the media may teach these members of the audience the issues and topics to use in evaluating certain candidates and parties, not just during political campaigns, but also in the longer periods between campaigns. (p. 471)

They refer to the process that came to be later described by the term *priming* in political communication research. Other early studies also provided evidence of the media's role in shaping the standards by which citizens evaluate political leaders and candidates (see, e.g., Patterson, 1980; Patterson & McClure, 1976; Protess & McCombs, 1991; Weaver et al., 1981). The term *priming* has been defined broadly by Fiske and Taylor (1984) as the effects of prior context on the interpretation and retrieval of information, as well as more specifically by Iyengar and Kinder (1987) and Krosnick and Kinder (1990) as changes in the standards used by the public to evaluate political leaders. Their experiments also provide support for the priming hypothesis.

Krosnick and Kinder (1990) used a simple knowledge test (a count of the number of political elites a respondent was able to identify correctly) to partition their respondents into two groups—political "novices" (with low knowledge) and "experts" (with high knowledge)—and argued that the novices are most susceptible to media influence. Krosnick and Brannon (1993) investigated the (separate and combined) roles of knowledge, interest, and exposure in the priming of evaluations of U.S. President George Bush over the period surrounding the 1990–1991 Gulf War when his approval ratings jumped more than 20 percentage points. They concluded that the relationship between knowledge and priming effects is more complex than previous research suggests and actually revised the conclusion of Krosnick and Kinder (1990) with respect to the effects of knowledge. Krosnick and Brannon point toward a social psychological model of information processing:

> Greater knowledge constitutes a greater ability to interpret, encode, store, and retrieve new information. And higher levels of exposure and interest are associated with a greater likelihood of forming on-line political evaluations and a

dilution of priming effects due to a wider range of knowledge being activated by media coverage. (p. 972)

Miller and Krosnick (2000) went further to elaborate the importance of trust when the moderating role of political expertise in information processing is considered. They argue,

> Media coverage of an issue does indeed increase the cognitive accessibility of related beliefs, but this does not produce priming. Instead, politically knowledge-able citizens who trust the media to be accurate and informative infer that news coverage of an issue means it is an important matter for the nation, leading these people to place greater emphasis on that issue when evaluating the President. Thus, news media priming does not occur because politically naive citizens are "victims" of the architecture of their minds, but instead appears to reflect inferences made from a credible institutional source of information by sophisticated citizens. (p. 301)

There are at least two recent overviews of the literature on priming. One brings together the 30-some studies from the fields of psychology, communication, and political science that deal explicitly with *media priming,* and its well-developed discussion of what constitutes media priming makes this a theoretically important study as well as a valuable critical assessment of the literature (Peter, 2002). Another is a meta-analysis of the priming literature that incorporates the research in the areas of violence as well as politics, based on 26 published articles representing 42 studies, and in conclusion raises questions about whether media priming actually shares common characteristics with the type of priming studied by cognitive and social psychologists (Roskos-Ewoldsen, Klinger, & Roskos-Ewoldsen, 2002). The study suggests that one of the important questions for future media priming research, which is a characteristic

of psychological priming research, is whether more intense media primes result in stronger priming effects.

These two overviews of the priming literature also emphasize the need to further distinguish, both theoretically and opera-tionally, priming effects from what has been described as that which is "chronically accessible" (see, e.g., Lau, 1989). Another relevant study of priming effects put it this way: "Future research should conceptualize priming more broadly to include considera-tions of both the accessibility of cognitions in short-term memory and the pathways among information in long-term memory" (Domke, Shah, & Wackman, 1998).

The priming literature as a whole sug-gests that effects are mediated by levels of political involvement, as measured by knowledge, exposure, and interest.[14] But the groups most likely to be primed and the sign or direction of the priming effect remain unclear. In fact, the complex inter-actions between knowledge, exposure, and interest led Krosnick and Brannon (1993) to revise the conclusion of Krosnick and Kinder (1990) on the knowledge and atten-tiveness (exposure and interest) groups most likely to be primed and the sign or direction of the priming effects of these variables. There is also some evidence to suggest that priming effects may occur across the board and may not always be mediated by levels of political involvement (see also Peter, 2002).

Framing

Framing research, like agenda-setting research, focuses on the relationship between issues in the news and the public perceptions of these issues. But it also goes further and "expands beyond agenda-setting research into *what* people talk or think about by examining *how* they think and talk about issues in the news" (Pan & Kosicki, 1993, p. 70; see also Pan & Kosicki, 2001). Another study actually concludes "that a model combining the theories of agenda setting and framing provides a better explanation for the shifts in aggregate opinion than either theory on its own" (Jasperson, Shah, Watts, Faber, & Fan, 1998, p. 205).

Our understanding of frames and framing effects has been the subject of much research over the past few decades (e.g., de Vreese, 2002; de Vreese, Peter, & Semetko, 2001; de Vreese & Semetko, 2004, in press; Edelman, 1993; Entman, 1991, 1993; Fiske & Taylor, 1984; Gamson, 1992; Goffman, 1974; Graber, 1988, 1993; Iyengar, 1991; Jasperson et al., 1998; Neuman et al., 1992; Price, Tewksbury, & Powers, 1997; Semetko & Valkenburg, 2000; Tuchman, 1978; Zaller, 1992). Frames set the parameters "in which citizens discuss public events" (Tuchman, 1978, p. iv). They are "persistent selection, emphasis, and exclusion" (Gitlin, 1980, p. 7). The process of framing refers to selecting "some aspects of a perceived reality" to enhance their salience "in such a way as to promote a particular problem definition, causal interpretation, moral evaluation, and/or treatment recommendation" (Entman, 1993, p. 53). Framing effects have been defined as "changes in judgment engendered by subtle alterations in the definition of judgment or choice of problems" (Iyengar, 1987, p. 816) or "one in which salient attributes of a message (its organization, selection of content, or thematic structure) render particular thoughts applicable, resulting in their activation and use in evaluations" (Price et al., 1997, p. 486).[15] A working definition of framing that brings together the study of frames and framing effects is proposed by Stephen Reese in the prologue to *Framing Public Life:* "Frames are organizing principles that are socially shared and persistent over time, that work symbolically to meaningfully structure the social world" (Reese, Gandy, & Grant, 2001, p. 11).

Two possible approaches to identifying frames in the news emerge from a review of the literature:

The inductive approach involves analyzing a news story with an open view to attempt to reveal the array of possible frames, beginning with very loosely defined preconceptions of these frames (see, for example, Gamson, 1992). This approach can detect the many possible ways in which an issue can be framed, but this method is labor intensive, often based on small samples, and can be difficult to replicate.

A deductive approach involves predefining certain frames as content analytic variables to verify the extent to which these frames occur in the news. This approach makes it necessary to have a clear idea of the kinds of frames that are likely to be in the news, because the frames that are not defined a priori may be overlooked. This approach has the advantage that it can easily be replicated, it can cope with large samples, and it can easily detect differences in framing between media (e.g., television vs. press) and within media (e.g., highbrow news programs or newspapers vs. tabloid style media). (Semetko & Valkenburg, 2000, pp. 94–95)

A number of news value-driven frames emerge from a review of the literature. The conflict frame, for instance, has been the subject of much discussion in the United States, where reporters have been criticized for being too negative in the coverage of politics (Capella & Jamieson, 1997; Patterson, 1993). Neuman et al. (1992) identified several different frames that were common in the U.S. news coverage of a range of issues, and these frames included conflict, economic consequences, human impact, and morality frames. Iyengar (1991) explicitly studied how audience members framed who was responsible for various social problems, after he exposed them to issues imbedded within what he described as frames: *episodic,* which refers to stories that report specific events, and *thematic,* which refers to stories that involve analytical, contextual, or historical coverage. One of the problems with much of the research on frames in the news is the lack of specification of measures and the lack of attention to the validity and reliability of measures.

Taking a deductive approach to analyzing frames in the news based on a review of the most common frames in the news—and in an effort to bring greater validity and reliability to the study of news frames—one study of national news coverage of politics in one European country developed reliable scales to measure "conflict," "human interest," "economic consequences," "morality" and "attribution of responsibility" frames in the news (Semetko & Valkenburg, 2000, p. 100). The authors found that although the use of frames varied significantly by news outlet (the more sensationalist outlets vs. the more sober ones), the most common frame in political news was attribution of responsibility, followed by conflict. They also measured the extent to which news was "episodic" or "thematic" in Iyengar's (1991) terms.

The attribution-of-responsibility frame was defined as that which presents an issue or problem in such a way as to lay blame or credit for its cause or solution either to the government or to an individual or group (Semetko & Valkenburg, 2000). This was an effort to further develop the work of Iyengar (1991), who studied how audiences framed responsibility but who never actually measured how the news framed responsibility for causing and solving social problems. Iyengar argued that the medium of television—specifically, television news, by covering an issue or problem in terms of an event, instance, or individual ("episodically") rather than in terms of the larger historical social context ("thematically")—encourages people to offer individual-level explanations for social problems. That explained why his framing experiments found that the poor woman on welfare is held responsible for her fate rather than the system or the U.S. government.

Television news in Europe, as in the United States, is also predominantly "episodic," but the content analysis of European political news revealed that at the same time, responsibility was often attributed to the government and not the individual. These findings suggest that although television news in many countries may be predominantly episodic because of news values and preferences for news formats, the way in which responsibility is framed in the news is influenced by the political cultures and social contexts in which the news is produced. In Western European democracies, unlike the United States, where the welfare state is comparatively strong, the government is expected to provide answers to social problems. Television news therefore can be episodic and at the same time frame the government (rather than the individual) as responsible for social problems such as poverty. Although much of the work on framing is conducted in one country and primarily the United States, it is nevertheless important to consider how other contexts may circumscribe the generalizations one may be tempted to draw from the data.

Media and Elections

Studies of elections and campaign-induced opinion change have incorporated some aspects of a media studies perspective. The sheer amount of U.S. literature now available on questions about opinion change and campaign influence, as well as media uses and impacts in elections at various levels, is so large that a thorough discussion of the findings cannot fit within the parameters of this chapter. A number of studies, for example, based on presidential campaigns in the past two decades emphasize the importance of presidential campaigns (Holbrook, 1996; Popkin, 1994), call into question the so-called "minimal effects" model of elections (Finkel, 1993), and identify the impacts of campaign events, media appearances, and advertising on voting (Shaw, 1999; Shaw & Roberts, 2000). The U.S. 2000 presidential campaign also saw major studies conducted by Thomas Patterson and others at Harvard University (see www.vanishingvoter.org), and there were a number of major research projects on the media and the campaign launched by researchers at the Annenberg School for Communication at the University of Pennsylvania. A special issue of *Political Communication* (Bimber, 2002) was devoted to the topic of political communication in this election, which ironically had more people paying attention to it after Election Day than before.

Media effects may be cognitive (effects on political knowledge), attitudinal (effects on political opinions), or behavioral (effects on turnout and vote choice). A number of election studies in the 1980s and 1990s identified significant media effects in national election campaigns in a number of countries outside the United States. These include Britain (Curtice & Semetko, 1994; Miller et al., 1990; Norris et al., 1999), France (Semetko & Bórquez, 1991), Germany (see, e.g., Finkel & Schrott, 1995; Pfetsch & Voltmer, 1994; Schmitt-Beck & Schrott, 1994; Semetko & Schoenbach, 1994), the Netherlands (Aarts & Semetko, 2003), Canada (Carty & Eagles, 2000; Jenkins, 1999; Mendelsohn, 1996), and New Zealand (Vowles et al., 2002).

The influence of media in referendum campaigns has only more recently received scholarly attention. Because a referendum is fought on one issue, and because that issue can often cut across party lines, the news media may be a more important source of information to voters who cannot fall back on their traditional party sympathies for guidance on how to vote or motivation on whether to vote. As the European Union member states increase from 15 to 25 in 2004, national referendums on issues about European integration will become increasingly common. Research on the influence of the media in European referendums to date has revealed that the campaign news matters not only for vote choice but also for citizens' perceptions about the campaign and the various aspects of the referendum issue, as well as for evaluations of political leaders during the campaign and in the period after the referendum result (de Vreese & Semetko, 2002a, 2002b, 2004, in press).

Negative Campaigning

The effects of negative political advertising in elections has been the topic of much U.S. research and was also the focus of a symposium in the *American Political Science Review* (Volume 93, December 1999). A meta-analysis of the large body of research into the effects of negative advertising, however, shows that there is no clear answer to the question of whether it is actually effective. Research by Kim Kahn and Patrick Kenney (1997, 1999) on the effects of information on intense and hard-fought campaigns in U.S. Senate races found that the uses and impact of information by those with high social capital were different from those with low social capital. The latter rely more on party identification, issues, presidential approval, and assessments of personal and economic circumstances, whereas those with higher social capital are less affected by changes in the campaign environment. And with respect to the likelihood of turning out to vote on Election Day, Kahn and Kenney (1999) found that negative campaigning also had an influence. But the tone of the campaign has a greater impact on those with low social capital, such as no party attachment, little or no interest in politics, and less political knowledge, particularly when the nature of the negative campaigns shifts from legitimate criticisms to unsubstantiated attacks.

◆ Conclusions

This discussion of public opinion and political action has summarized some of the developments in research from a media studies perspective, as well as some research that has not emphasized media and media effects as central in the processes of social change. Research from a media studies perspective considers the characteristics of media content and the factors that produce media content, the actions of journalists and news organizations, and how these together may influence public perceptions.

A media studies perspective provides a potentially fruitful avenue for theory building. In the study of collective action, for example, it would be worthwhile to devote more attention to the impressive sociological literature on political opportunity structures and how this might be elaborated from a media studies perspective. Such an approach would aim to integrate the media as a political actor into the larger arena of opportunity structure.

Another avenue for theory building that is becoming increasingly important to research conducted from a media studies perspective is a comparative angle. All research is comparative, in the sense that it is impossible to discuss change or absolutes without reference to something else. Comparisons over time are important, and assumptions about change over time are often looming in the background, if not already at the forefront, of statements about the media and society. More important for theory building are comparisons across groups. In highlighting some of the more recent research in public opinion and political action, this chapter has also mentioned a variety of different groups that have a special meaning for research from a media studies perspective. Age cohorts or generations are one example of such groups. As discussed above, Generation Xers, baby boomers, and the civic generation vary in their forms of civic engagement, and use of different media accentuated these differences. Apart from the issue of the digital divide, which exists between groups within countries as well as among countries, the Internet itself, even in a highly wired community, is found to be more meaningful for the civic engagement of young people than it is for older citizens. In societies in transition, cohort analysis might be important for understanding how journalists perceive and perform their jobs as well as for how citizens use the media and how they relate to different political actors and media institutions.

Another area that deserves closer attention concerns how to measure or describe those who are politically involved in comparison with those who are not, as this may have important consequences for understanding media effects. Political knowledge indicators have been commonly used to group individuals into "high" and "low" groups for purposes of distinguishing differences in media effects, but this needs to be seen within a larger perspective on what constitutes political knowledge and how knowledge may assist in the processing of political information. This is also part of a larger discussion on information processing, a topic that has generated considerable interest (Graber, 2001).

And given that party systems, media systems, and electoral systems are organized primarily at the national level, nation-states are also an important focus for cross-national comparison. These sorts of comparisons may be common to comparative political scientists (see, e.g., Gunther & Mughan, 2000), as well as those involved in comparative historical sociology and the study of cultural change, but the comparative perspective on media studies is (relatively speaking) rather underdeveloped (Blumler, McLeod, & Rosengren, 1992). A notable early study in the area of media theory shed light on the importance of considering post-Soviet and Eastern European examples for internationalizing media theory (Downing, 1996). Another study in political communications focused on innovations in party political campaigning in democracies and societies in transition (Swanson & Mancini, 1996). And another emphasized the importance of going beyond the typical "Western" case studies for building media theory (Curran & Park, 2000).

◆ Notes

1. *Political Communication* is the journal cosponsored by the divisions of the same name

in the International Communication Association and the American Political Science Association, and the journal's founding editor was Doris A. Graber. The *European Journal of Communication*, launched in the mid-1980s, is another source of much research on political communication in a broadly geographically defined Europe. In Italy, *Comunicazione Politica* was founded in 2000 by Gianpietro Mazzoleni and Paolo Mancini and now edited by Mazzoleni. The journal is owned by the CICOP (Centro Interuniversitario di Comunicazione Politica, in which four Italian universities are represented), and the publisher is Franco Angeli Editore of Milan. See www.com-pol.it for more about the journal and names of the members of the International Advisory Board. See Mutz (2001) for comments on the future of political communication research.

2. The Council of Europe has regular hearings that cover human rights abuses of journalists in Ukraine and Russia and other post-Soviet central European countries.

3. All of these relationships remain significant when controlled for political interest, age, level of education, and other types of media exposure. Aarts and Semetko (2003) also address a problem that is central to media effects research: the problem of endogeneity. Lacking panel data, they use two-stage least squares (2SLS) with a statistic to test for endogeneity to address these concerns. This strengthens their conclusions because it largely rules out self-selection. *Self-selection* refers to the process by which a politically interested or knowledgeable individual would select public news, whereas those who are not interested might choose to turn regularly to commercial news. This *Journal of Politics* article (Aarts & Semetko, 2003) was named the article of the year by the Political Communication Division of the International Communication Association in May 2004.

4. Converse's (1964) findings have been described as time bound in subsequent research by Pomper (1972) and Nie, Verba, and Petrocik (1976), and they suggested that ideological awareness, issue awareness, and attitude consistency had increased over the 1960s. A general discussion of this debate is found in Glynn, Herbst, O'Keefe, and Shapiro (1999, pp. 249–298).

5. Page, Shapiro, and Dempsey (1987) provided some of the strongest evidence of a direct link between the media issue agendas and aggregate public opinion, drawing on their analysis of 80 public policy issues over the 1970s and 1980s. Network television coverage accounted for nearly half the aggregate changes in public issue preferences. In a subsequent study of foreign issues in the news over 15 years, the same authors found that TV news was actually a significant predictor of the direction of public opinion on these issues (Page & Shapiro, 1992).

6. Grants from the Dutch National Science Foundation and the European Union (EU) Fifth Framework program funded a major 4-year research program involving all 15 EU countries to study news media impact on public opinion about European integration and political behavior in European elections. Two Ph.D. dissertations have been completed from the project (de Vreese, 2002; Peter, 2003). For more information about the project and various publications, e-mail Holli Semetko at holli.semetko@emory.edu.

7. This builds on the work of Katz and Lazarsfeld (1955) and also on the work of political scientists (see, e.g., Huckfeldt, Beck, Dalton, & Levine, 1995; Huckfeldt, Plutzer, & Sprague, 1993), who have focused on the parameters and forms of social networks as a facilitator of opinion and political action.

8. In recent election campaigns in the United States and other countries, James Fishkin, Robert Luskin, and Roger Jowell (2000) have conducted "deliberative polls." These involve intensive discussion among members of the public based on factual information about policy provided to them over the course of 2 to 3 days and that result in much debate, discussion, and more informed opinion.

9. The term *social capital* has been used by a variety of scholars to refer to a variety of specific qualities that an individual may have, such as general or specific knowledge on a subject, level of education, socioeconomic status, and so on.

10. The term *civic participation* has also been used by a variety of scholars and may refer to a number of forms of participation in civic life such as voting in elections, belonging to civic

and voluntary organizations, attending religious service, participating in demonstrations, signing petitions, writing to one's elected representative, writing a letter to an editor of a newspaper, and so forth.

11. The terms *Generation X, baby boomers,* and *civic generation* were used by the authors of this study to refer to the different generational groups. Generation X is the youngest of these three groups and refers to those born in the 1960s and 1970s and their offspring, and the civic generation refers to those in the oldest cohorts.

12. The concept of political opportunity structures developed out of the work of Charles Tilly and his colleagues, whose historical case studies revealed that revolution and popular uprising were more often a consequence of elite disagreement/dissent and political crises (such as after a defeat in war) than modernization processes such as urbanization or industrialization (Tilly, 1978). The concept of political opportunity structure has been used to study change over time (Tarrow, 1998) as well as cross-national variation in mobilization (Kriesi, Koopmans, Duyvendak, & Giugni, 1995), and these studies add different dimensions to the conceptualization of this approach.

13. Discourse analysis is a useful tool for identifying trends in elite opinions and issues in the public arena (van Dijk, 1988).

14. One of the earliest findings of agenda-setting research established variation in effects— not all of the people are influenced all of the time (McCombs & Shaw, 1972), and a number of studies have established that effects can be modified by the public's interest in information (see Weaver, Graber, McCombs, & Eyal, 1981).

15. Classic studies in psychology show, for example, that risk perceptions can be profoundly affected by slight changes in the way in which the problem is framed, with experiments using changes in question wording (Kahneman & Tversky, 1982). Frames have also been shown to shape public perceptions of political issues or institutions. The opinion of European publics about the European Union and various EU-related issues can easily be swayed in different directions, depending on how the issue is framed in the survey question, for example (Saris, 1997).

◆ References

Aarts, K., & Semetko, H. A. (2003). The divided electorate: Media use and political involvement. *Journal of Politics, 65*(3), 759–784.

Banducci, S. A., & Semetko, H. A. (2002, August). *Negative news, cognitive mobilization and European integration.* Paper presented at the meeting of the American Political Science Association, Boston.

Baum, M. (2002). Sex, lies and war: How soft news brings foreign policy to the inattentive public. *American Political Science Review, 96*(1), 91–109.

Bimber, B. (Ed.). (2002). Political communication in the 2000 election [Special issue]. *Political Communication, 19*(1).

Blumler, J. (1984). *Communicating to voters: Television in the 1979 European parliamentary elections.* London: Sage.

Blumler, J. G., McLeod, J., & Rosengren, K. E. (1992). *Comparatively speaking.* Newbury Park, CA: Sage.

Blumler, J. G., & McQuail, D. (1969). *Television in politics: Its uses and influences.* Chicago: University of Chicago Press.

Capella, J. N., & Jamieson, K. H. (1997). *Spiral of cynicism: The press and the public good.* New York: Oxford University Press.

Carty, R. K., & Eagles, D. M. (2000). Is there a local dimension to modern election campaigns? *Political Communication, 17*(3), 279–294.

Converse, P. E. (1962). Information flow and the stability of partisan attitudes. *Public Opinion Quarterly, 26*(4), 578–599.

Converse, P. E. (1964). The nature of belief systems in mass publics. In D. E. Apter (Ed.), *Ideology and discontent* (pp. 206–261). New York: Free Press.

Cook, T. E. (1998). *Governing with the news: The news media as a political institution.* Chicago: University of Chicago Press.

Cooper, A. H. (2002). Media framing and social movement mobilisation: German peace protest against INF missiles, the Gulf War, and NATO peace enforcement in Bosnia. *European Journal of Political Research, 41,* 37–80.

Curran, J., & Park, M. J. (Eds.). (2000). *De-Westernizing media studies*. London: Routledge.

Curtice, J., & Semetko, H. A. (1994). Does it matter what the papers say? In A. Heath, R. Jowell, & J. Curtice (Eds.), *Labour's last chance? The 1992 election and beyond* (pp. 43–64). Aldershot, UK: Dartmouth.

Dalton, R. J. (1996). *Citizen politics: Public opinion and political parties in advanced industrial democracies*. Chatham, UK: Chatham House.

Delli Carpini, M. X., & Ketter, S. (1993). Measuring political knowledge—putting 1st things 1st. *American Journal of Political Science, 37*(4), 1179–1206.

de Vreese, C. H. (2002). *Framing Europe: Television news and European integration*. Amsterdam: Aksant.

de Vreese, C. H., Peter, J., & Semetko, H. A. (2001). Framing politics at the launch of the euro: A cross-national comparative study of frames in the news. *Political Communication, 18*(2), 107–122.

de Vreese, C. H., & Semetko, H. A. (2002a). Cynical and engaged: Strategic campaign coverage, public opinion, and mobilization in a referendum. *Communication Research, 29*(6), 615–641.

de Vreese, C. H., & Semetko, H. A. (2002b). Public perception of polls and support for restrictions on the publication of polls: Denmark's 2000 euro referendum. *International Journal of Public Opinion Research, 14*(4), 367–390.

de Vreese, C. H., & Semetko, H. A. (2004). *Political campaigning in referendums: Framing the referendum issue*. London: Routledge.

de Vreese, C. H., & Semetko, H. A. (in press). News matters: Influences on the vote in a referendum campaign. *European Journal of Political Research*.

Domke, D., Shah, D. V., & Wackman, D. B. (1998). Media priming effects: Accessibility, association, and activation. *International Journal of Public Opinion Research, 10*(1), 51–74.

Downing, J. D. H. (1996). *Internationalizing media theory: Transition, power, culture: Reflections on media in Russia, Poland and Hungary 1980–95*. London: Sage.

Edelman, M. (1993). *Symbols and political quiescence*. New York: Irvington.

Entman, R. B. (1991). Framing US coverage of international news: Contrasts in narratives of the KAL and Iran air accidents. *Journal of Communication, 41*, 6–27.

Entman, R. B. (1993). Framing: Toward clarification of a fractured paradigm. *Journal of Communication, 43*, 51–58.

Finkel, S. (1993). Reexamining the minimal effects model in recent presidential campaigns. *Journal of Politics, 55*(1), 1–21.

Finkel, S., & Schrott, P. R. (1995). The effects of campaigns on voter choice in the German election of 1990. *British Journal of Political Science, 25*, 349–378.

Fishkin, J., Luskin, R., & Jowell, R. (2000). Deliberative polling and public consultation. *Parliamentary Affairs, 53*(4), 657–666.

Fiske, S. T., & Taylor, S. (1984). *Social cognition* (2nd ed.). New York: McGraw-Hill.

Gamson, W. A. (1988). Political discourse and collective action. *International Social Movement Research, 1*, 219–244.

Gamson, W. A. (1992). *Talking politics*. New York: Cambridge University Press.

Gamson, W. A., & Meyer, D. S. (1996). The framing of political opportunity. In D. McAdam, J. McCarthy, & M. Zald (Eds.), *Comparative perspectives on social movements* (pp. 275–290). Cambridge, UK: Cambridge University Press.

Gamson, W. A., & Modigliani, A. (1989). Media discourse and public opinion on nuclear power: A constructionist approach. *American Journal of Sociology, 95*, 1–37.

Gitlin, T. (1980). *The whole world is watching: Mass media in the making and unmaking of the new left*. Berkeley: University of California Press.

Glynn, C. J., Herbst, S., O'Keefe, G. J., & Shapiro, R. Y. (1999). *Public opinion*. Boulder, CO: Westview.

Goffman, E. (1974). *Frame analysis: An essay on the organization of experience*. Cambridge, MA: Harvard University Press.

Graber, D. A. (1988). *Processing the news: How people tame the information tide*. New York: Longman.

Graber, D. A. (1993). Making campaign news user-friendly: The lesson of 1992 and beyond. *American Behavioral Scientist, 37*(2), 328–336.

Graber, D. A. (2001). *Processing politics: Learning from television in the Internet age.* Chicago: University of Chicago Press.

Gunther, R., & Mughan, A. (Eds.). (2000). *Democracy and the media: A comparative perspective.* Cambridge, UK: Cambridge University Press.

Hallin, D. C. (1986). *The uncensored war: The media and Vietnam.* Los Angeles: University of California Press.

Hallin, D. C., & Papathanassopoulos, S. (2002). Political clientelism and the media: Southern Europe and Latin America in comparative perspective. *Media, Culture & Society, 24*(2), 175–195.

Hertog, J. K., & McLeod, D. M. (1995). Anarchists wreak havoc in downtown Minneapolis: A multilevel study of media coverage of radical protest. *Journalism Monographs, 151,* 1–48.

Holbrook, T. M. (1996). *Do campaigns matter?* Thousand Oaks, CA: Sage.

Huckfeldt, R., Beck, P., Dalton, R., & Levine, J. (1995). Political environments, cohesive social groups, and the communication of public opinion. *American Journal of Political Science, 39,* 1025–1054.

Huckfeldt, R., Plutzer, E., & Sprague, J. (1993). Alternative contexts of political behavior: Churches, neighborhoods, and individuals. *Journal of Politics, 55*(2), 365–381.

Iyengar, S. (1987). Television news and citizens' explanations of national affairs. *American Political Science Review, 81*(3), 815–832.

Iyengar, S. (1991). *Is anyone responsible? How television frames political issues.* Chicago: University of Chicago Press.

Iyengar, S., & Kinder, D. R. (1987). *News that matters: Television and American opinion.* Chicago: University of Chicago Press.

Jasperson, A. E., Shah, D. V., Watts, M., Faber, R. J., & Fan, D. P. (1998). Framing and the public agenda: Media effects on the importance of the federal budget deficit. *Political Communication, 15*(2), 205–224.

Jenkins, J. A. (1999). Examining the bonding effects of party: A comparative analysis of roll-call voting in the U.S. and Confederate houses. *American Journal of Political Science, 43*(4), 1144–1165.

Kahn, K. F., & Kenney, P. J. (1997). A model of candidate evaluations in Senate elections: The impact of campaign intensity. *Journal of Politics, 59*(4), 1173–1205.

Kahn, K. F., & Kenney, P. J. (1999). Do negative campaigns mobilize or suppress turnout? Clarifying the relationship between negativity and participation. *American Political Science Review, 93*(4), 877–889.

Kahneman, D., & Tversky, A. (1982). Choices, values and frames. *American Psychologist, 39,* 341–350.

Katz, E., & Lazarsfeld, P. F. (Eds.). (1955). *Personal influence: The part played by people in the flow of mass communications.* Glencoe, IL: Free Press.

Kinder, D. R., & Sears, D. O. (1986). Public opinion and political action. In D. T. Gilbert, S. T. Fiske, & G. Lindzey (Eds.), *The handbook of social psychology* (pp. 784–800). Oxford, UK: Oxford University Press.

Koopmans, R., & Duyvendak, J. W. (1995). The political construction of the nuclear-energy issue and its impact on the mobilization of anti-nuclear movements in Western Europe. *Social Problems, 42*(2), 235–251.

Koopmans, R., & Statham, P. (2000). *Challenging immigration and ethnic relations politics: Comparative European perspectives.* Oxford, UK: Oxford University Press.

Kriesi, H., Koopmans, R., Duyvendak, J. W., & Giugni, M. G. (1995). *New social movements in Western Europe: A comparative analysis.* London: UCL Press.

Krosnick, J. A., & Brannon, L. A. (1993). The impact of the Gulf War on the ingredients of presidential evaluations: Multidimensional effects of political involvement. *American Political Science Review, 87*(4), 963–978.

Krosnick, J. A., & Kinder, D. R. (1990). Altering the foundations for support for the president through priming. *American Political Science Review, 84*(2), 173–190.

Lau, R. R. (1989). Individual and contextual influences on group identification. *Social Psychology Quarterly, 52*(3), 220–231.

Luskin, R. C. (1990). Measuring political sophistication. *American Journal of Political Science, 31*(4), 856–872.

McAdam, D., Tarrow, S., & Tilly, C. (2001). *Dynamics of contention.* Cambridge, UK: Cambridge University Press.

McChesney, R. (1997). *Corporate media and the threat to democracy* (Open Media Series No. 1). New York: Seven Stories Press.

McCombs, M. (1981). The agenda-setting approach. In D. D. Nimmo & K. R. Sanders (Eds.), *Handbook of political communication* (pp. 121–140). Beverly Hills, CA: Sage.

McCombs, M. (2004). *Setting the agenda: The mass media and public opinion.* Cambridge, UK: Polity.

McCombs, M., Einsiedel, E., & Weaver, D. (1991). *Contemporary public opinion: Issues and the news.* Hillsdale, NJ: Lawrence Erlbaum.

McCombs, M., Lopez-Escobar, E., & Llamas, J. P. (2000). Setting the agenda of attributes in the 1996 Spanish general election. *Journal of Communication, 50*(2), 77–92.

McCombs, M. E., & Shaw, D. L. (1972). The agenda-setting function of mass media. *Public Opinion Quarterly, 36,* 176–187.

McCombs, M. E., & Shaw, D. L. (1993). The evolution of agenda-setting theory: 25 years in the marketplace of ideas. *Journal of Communication, 43*(2), 58–66.

McLeod, D. M., & Detenber, B. H. (1999). Framing effects of television news coverage of social protest. *Journal of Communication, 49*(3), 3–23.

McLeod, D. M., & Hertog, J. K. (1992). The manufacture of public opinion by reporters: Informal cues for public perceptions of protest groups. *Discourse and Society, 3*(3), 259–275.

McLeod, J. M., Becker, L. B., & Byrnes, J. E. (1974). Another look at the agenda-setting function of the press. *Communication Research, 1,* 3–33.

Mendelsohn, M. (1996). The media and interpersonal communications: The priming of issues, leaders, and party identification. *Journal of Politics, 58*(1), 112–125.

Mickiewicz, E. (1988). *Split signals: Television and politics in the Soviet Union.* New York: Oxford University Press.

Mickiewicz, E. (1999). *Changing channels: Television and the struggle for power in Russia.* New York: Oxford University Press.

Miller, J. M., & Krosnick, J. A. (2000). News media impact on the ingredients of presidential evaluations: Politically knowledgeable citizens are guided by a trusted source. *American Journal of Political Science, 44,* 301–315.

Miller, W. L., Clarke, H. D., Harrop, M., LeDuc, L., & Whiteley, P. F. (1990). *How voters change: The 1987 British election campaign in perspective.* Oxford, UK: Clarendon.

Mondak, J. J. (2001). Developing valid knowledge scales. *American Journal of Political Science, 45*(1), 224–238.

Mutz, D. C. (1994). Contextualizing personal experience: The role of mass media. *Journal of Politics, 56*(3), 689–714.

Mutz, D. C. (1998). *Impersonal influence: How perceptions of mass collectives affect political attitudes.* Cambridge, UK: Cambridge University Press.

Mutz, D. C. (2001). The future of political communication research: Reflections on the occasion of Steve Chaffee's retirement from Stanford University. *Political Communication, 18*(2), 231–236.

Mutz, D. C., & Martin, P. S. (2001). Facilitating communication across lines of political difference: The role of mass media. *American Political Science Review, 95*(1), 97–114.

Neuman, W. R., Just, M. R., & Crigler, A. N. (1992). *Common knowledge: News and the construction of political meaning.* Chicago: University of Chicago Press.

Nie, N., Verba, S., & Petrocik, J. R. (1976). *The changing American voter.* Cambridge, MA: Harvard University Press.

Niedermayer, O., & Sinnott, R. (1998). *Public opinion and internationalized governance.* Oxford, UK: Oxford University Press.

Noelle-Neumann, E. (1974). The spiral of silence: A theory of public opinion. *Journal of Communication, 24,* 24–51.

Norris, P. (2000). *A virtuous circle: Political communications in post-industrial societies.* Cambridge, UK: Cambridge University Press.

Norris, P., Curtice, J., Sanders, D., Scammell, M., & Semetko, H. A. (1999). *On message: Communicating the campaign.* London: Sage.

Page, B. I., & Shapiro, R. Y. (1992). *The rational public: Fifty years of trends in Americans' policy preferences.* Chicago: University of Chicago Press.

Page, B. I., Shapiro, R. Y., & Dempsey, G. R. (1987). What moves public opinion? *American Political Science Review, 81*(1), 23–44.

Pan, Z., & Kosicki, G. M. (1993). Framing analysis: An approach to news discourse. *Political Communication, 10,* 59–79.

Pan, Z., & Kosicki, G. M. (2001). Framing as a strategic action in public deliberation. In S. D. Reese, O. H. Gandy, & A. E. Grant (Eds.), *Framing public life* (pp. 35–66). Mahwah, NJ: Lawrence Erlbaum.

Patterson, T. (1980). *The mass media election.* New York: Praeger.

Patterson, T. (1993). *Out of order.* New York: Knopf.

Patterson, T. (2002). *The vanishing voter: Public involvement in an age of uncertainty.* New York: Knopf.

Patterson, T., & McClure, R. D. (1976). *The unseeing eye: The myth of television power in national elections.* New York: Putnam.

Peter, J. (2002). Medien Priming: Grundlagen, Befunde und Forschungstendenzen [Media priming: Foundations, findings, and research tendencies]. *Publizistik, 47,* 21–44.

Peter, J. (2003). *Why European TV news matters: A cross-nationally comparative analysis of TV news about the European Union and its effects.* Unpublished doctoral dissertation, Amsterdam School of Communications Research, University of Amsterdam.

Pfetsch, B., & Voltmer, K. (1994). *Geteilte Medienrealität? Zur Thematisierungsleistung der Massenmedien im Prozess der deutschen Vereinigung* [Divided media reality? How the mass media made issues the subject of discussion during the process of German reunification]. In H. Klingemann & M. Kaase (Eds.), *Wahlen und Waehler. Analysen aus Anlass der Bundestagswahl 1990* [Elections and voters: Analyses of the results of the 1990 federal election] (pp. 509–542). Opladen: Westdeutscher Verlag.

Pomper, G. M. (1972). From confusion to clarity: Issues and American voters, 1956–1968. *American Political Science Review, 66*(2), 415–428.

Popkin, S. (1994). *The reasoning voter.* Chicago: University of Chicago Press.

Price, V., Cappella, J. N., & Nir, L. (2002). Does disagreement contribute to more deliberative opinion? *Political Communication, 19*(1), 95–112.

Price, V., Tewksbury, D., & Powers, E. (1997). Switching trains of thought. The impact of news frames on readers' cognitive responses. *Communication Research, 24,* 481–506.

Protess, D., & McCombs, M. (Eds.). (1991). *Agenda setting: Readings on media, public opinion, and policymaking.* Hillsdale, NJ: Lawrence Erlbaum.

Rahn, W. M., & Cramer, K. J. (1996). Activation and application of political party stereotypes: The role of television. *Political Communication, 13*(2), 195–212.

Reese, S. D., Gandy, O. H., & Grant, A. E. (Eds.). (2001). *Framing public life: Perspectives on media and our understanding of the social world.* Mahwah, NJ: Lawrence Erlbaum.

Rogers, E. M., & Dearing, J. W. (1988). Agenda-setting research: Where has it been? Where is it going? In J. A. Anderson (Ed.), *Communication yearbook II* (pp. 555–594). Newbury Park, CA: Sage.

Rogers, E. M., Dearing, J. W., & Bregman, D. (1993). The anatomy of agenda-setting research. *Journal of Communication, 43*(2), 68–84.

Rohrschneider, R. (2002). The democracy deficit and mass support for an EU-wide government. *American Journal of Political Science, 46*(2), 463–475.

Roskos-Ewoldsen, D. R., Klinger, M. R., & Roskos-Ewoldsen, B. (2002). Media priming: A meta-analysis. In J. B. Bryant & A. R. Carveth (Eds.), *Meta-analysis of media effects*. Mahwah, NJ: Lawrence Erlbaum.

Saris, W. E. (1997). The public opinion about the EU can easily be swayed in different directions. *Acta Politica: International Journal of Political Science, 32,* 406–435.

Scheufele, D. (2000). Agenda-setting, priming, and framing revisited: Another look at cognitive effects of political communication. *Mass Communication and Society, 3,* 297–316.

Scheufele, D. A. (2002). Examining differential gains from mass media and their implications for participatory behavior. *Communication Research, 29*(1), 46–65.

Scheufele, D. A., & Eveland, W. P., Jr. (2001). Perceptions of "public opinion" and "public" opinion expression. *International Journal of Public Opinion Research, 13,* 25–44.

Scheufele, D. A., & Moy, P. (2000). Twenty-five years of the spiral of silence: A conceptual review and empirical outlook. *International Journal of Public Opinion Research, 12*(1), 3–28.

Schmitt-Beck, R., & Schrott, P. (1994). Dealignment durch Massenmedien? Zur These der Abschwächung von Parteibindungen als Folge der Medienexpansion [Dealignment through the mass media? Decreasing party attachment as a consequence of media expansion]. In H. D. Klingemann & M. Kaase (Eds.), *Wahlen und Wähler—Analysen aus Anlaß der Bundestagswahl 1990* [Elections and voters: Analysis of the results of the 1990 federal election] (pp. 543–572). Opladen: Westdeutscher Verlag.

Schudson, M. (2002). The news media as political institutions. *Annual Review of Political Science, 5,* 249–269.

Semetko, H. A., & Bórquez, J. (1991). Audiences for election communication in France and the United States: Media use and candidate evaluations. In L. L. Kaid, J. Gerstle, & K. R. Sanders (Eds.), *Mediated politics in two cultures: Presidential campaigns in the United States and France* (pp. 223–246). New York: Praeger.

Semetko, H. A., & Krasnoboka, N. (2003). The political role of the Internet in societies in transition—Russia and Ukraine compared. *Party Politics, 9*(1), 77–104.

Semetko, H. A., & Schoenbach, K. (1994). *Germany's unity election: Voters and the media.* Cresskill, NJ: Hampton.

Semetko, H. A., & Valkenburg, P. M. (2000). Framing European politics: A content analysis of press and television news. *Journal of Communication, 50*(2), 93–109.

Shah, D. V., Kwak, N., & Holbert, R. L. (2001). "Connecting" and "disconnecting" with civic life: Patterns of Internet use and the production of social capital. *Political Communication, 18*(2), 141–162.

Shah, D. V., McLeod, J. M., & Yoon, S. H. (2001). Communication, context, and community: An exploration of print, broadcast, and Internet influences. *Communication Research, 28*(4), 464–506.

Shaw, D. (1999). The effect of TV ads and candidate appearances on statewide presidential votes, 1988–96. *American Political Science Review, 93,* 345–361.

Shaw, D. R., & Roberts, B. E. (2000). Campaign events, the media and the prospects of victory: The 1992 and 1996 US presidential elections. *British Journal of Political Science, 30,* 259–289.

Sinnott, R. (1995). Ireland—Changing governments, parties and voters. *World Today, 51*(5), 89–92.

Sinnott, R. (1998). Party attachment in Europe: Methodological critique and substantive implications. *British Journal of Political Science, 28,* 627–650.

Steenbergen, M. R., & Jones, B. S. (2002). Modeling multilevel data structures. *American Journal of Political Science, 46*(1), 218–237.

Stempel, G., Weaver, D. H., & Wilhoit, G. C. (2003). *Mass communication research and theory.* Boston: Allyn & Bacon.

Swanson, D. L. (1988). Feeling the elephant: Some observations on agenda-setting research. In J. A. Anderson (Ed.), *Communication yearbook 11* (pp. 603–619). Newbury Park, CA: Sage.

Swanson, D. L., & Mancini, P. (1996). *Politics, media and modern democracy: An international study of innovations in electoral campaigning and their consequences.* Westport, CT: Praeger.

Tarrow, S. (1998). *Power in movement: Social movements and contentious politics* (2nd rev. ed.). New York: Cambridge University Press.

Tilly, C. (1978). *From mobilization to revolution.* New York: Random House.

Tuchman, G. (1978). *Making news: A study in the construction of reality.* New York: Free Press.

van der Eijk, C., & Franklin, M. N. (Eds.). (1996). *Choosing Europe? The European electorate and national politics in the face of the Union.* Ann Arbor: University of Michigan Press.

van Dijk, T. A. (1988). *News as discourse.* Hillsdale, NJ: Lawrence Erlbaum.

Vowles, J., Banducci, S. A., Karp, J., Miller, R., Sullivan, A., & Aimer, P. (2002). *Proportional representation on trial: New Zealand's second MMP election and after.* Auckland, New Zealand: Auckland University Press.

Waisbord, S. (1995). Farewell to public spaces? Electoral campaigns and street spectacle in Argentina. *Studies in Latin American Popular Culture, 15,* 279–300.

Waisbord, S. (1997). Can investigative journalism tell the truth? The modernity of journalism in Latin America. *Ecquid Novi, 18*(1), 115–131.

Waisbord, S. (2000). *Watchdog journalism in South America: News, accountability, and democracy.* New York: Columbia University Press.

Weaver, D. H., Graber, D. A., McCombs, M., & Eyal, C. H. (1981). *Media agenda-setting in a presidential election.* New York: Praeger.

Weaver, D. H., McCombs, M. E., & Spellman, C. (1975). Watergate and the media: A case study of agenda-setting. *American Politics Quarterly, 3,* 458–472.

Zaller, J. (1991). Information, values and opinion. *American Political Science Review, 85*(4), 1215–1238.

Zaller, J. (1992). *The nature and origins of mass opinion.* New York: Cambridge University Press.

18

MEDIA AND THE REINVENTION OF THE NATION

◆ Silvio Waisbord

This chapter discusses approaches to the study of media and nations by reviewing the place of the media in historical accounts of the rise of modern nations and nationalism, the past and present of the "national" media, and the impact of media globalization on nations. Notwithstanding developments that, to some authors, seemingly undermine the centrality of "the national" in political and cultural processes, it is argued that "the national" remains important as a basis for cultural identity in the contemporary world. Neither subnational (local) nor supranational (regional and cosmopolitan) formations and identities offer viable alternative identities to minimize, let alone eliminate, nationalistic feelings. Together with other factors, the media greatly contribute to the persistence of the national in a supposedly postnational era. Media studies can make a valuable contribution to nationalism studies by understanding how the media continue to articulate nationalistic sentiments. Rather than celebrating nationalism as a form of benign patriotism or condemning it for inflaming hatred, it is suggested that nationalism remains ambiguous. The complex and contradictory history of nations shows that nationalism can be equally associated with sentiments of human solidarity as well as with feelings of intolerance and exclusion. This remarkable and often frustrating ideological elasticity makes it difficult to predetermine the future of media patriotism on the basis of nationalism's past. Nationalism means different things to different people. One nation's intolerant chauvinism is the flip side of other nations' patriotic sense of difference and community. Media studies could offer explanations for why nations continue to grip people's imagination and identities, particularly given other potential choices in a globalized world, and understand what interpretations of the nation are made available for public debate.

◆ Media and the Origins of Nations

Benedict Anderson (1996) has remarked that neither nation nor nationalism occupied a central place in modern social thought. This gap is particularly significant considering that they roughly emerged at the same time and were similarly concerned with finding an answer to the problem of social order in the post–French Revolution era. Nationalists believed that culture, rather than economics or politics, keeps societies together. In response to the problems existing in a world turned upside down by political and socioeconomic revolutions, nationalism provided a cultural solution. It offered nations as the replacement to religion, a new cultural formation to give cohesion, and purpose to individuals and communities in an increasingly secular world. Nations provide a sense of unity and identity and establish differences among similarly culturally based groups. Nations simultaneously aggregate and separate people on the basis of cultural forms such as language, religion, history, and symbols.

How do people come to share the same national culture and identity? If nations are "culturally coordinated" communities, how does the process of cultural coordination happen?[1]

Two basic answers have been given to these questions. One answer states that political centralization was historically crucial in the development of modern nations. Nations resulted from a top-down political process that turned cultural diversity,

expressed in the existence of different languages, religions, and traditions, into cultural homogeneity. In this process, states played a key role in eliminating differences and imposing one culture. The second answer rejects the idea that centralization was a necessary precondition of nations and instead suggests that a variety of decentralized factors explains why nations emerged at a specific historical juncture. Nations and nationalism preceded, rather than followed, political centralization. In some cases, nations emerged even when states were absent (such as the cases of stateless nations); in other cases, states were unsuccessful in imposing a common culture to unify a myriad of nations living within its boundaries (see J. A. Hall, 1998).

Both positions assume that a network of social organizations is necessary for cultural coordination. Whether through state-sponsored institutions (schools, military service, national holidays) or private and civic associations, nations resulted from the dissemination of a set of practices, values, and rituals (Brubaker, 1996; Gillis, 1994; Liebes & Curran, 1998; Weber, 1976). The institutional necessity of nation making became more imperative as agricultural, rural societies gradually changed into industrial, large-scale societies during the 19th century. Traditional face-to-face communication was insufficient to coordinate the culture of large numbers of people. Nation building needed institutions to reach a vast population to foster feelings of common belonging. It was then when the mass media gained relevance as part of the institutional apparatus required to spread a common culture.

To understand their contribution to nation making, the media need to be understood as a set of institutions involved in the creation, maintenance, and transformation of cultural membership. National cultures are by-products of the process of social amalgamation and differentiation through which feelings of homogeneity and heterogeneity are developed and maintained. If nations are defined along a continuum of commonness and difference, how do the media contribute to create, solidify, perpetuate, and change feelings of belonging to a specific cultural community? If nation making implies establishing commonness and difference, how do the media establish cultural boundaries? To address these questions, it is useful to review arguments about the origins of nations.

Ernest Gellner's (1983) pioneering work has become the focal point of debates about the origins of nations. For Gellner, nations and nationalism were part of "the great transformation" (Polanyi, 1957) that Western societies experienced in the transition from agrarian societies to industrial capitalism. The relation between European modern nations and previous forms of collective identification varies in different cases (Gellner & Smith, 1996). Although in some cases, premodern ethnic groups were precursors to nations (Armstrong, 1982; Smith, 1986), some nations were basically invented during the modern era. For Gellner, an elaborate state system was responsible for the spread of a "national" culture to incorporate people into a new socioeconomic order characterized by markets, incipient industrialization, division of labor, and social mobility. Nations were functional to early capitalist development. Capitalism and the creation of domestic markets for labor and goods required the formation of nations.

Gellner's critics took issue with a number of points in his argument (see J. A. Hall, 1998). Some doubted that nationalism and industrialization shared the same time frame. Nationalism rose in societies that did not fit the classic model of capitalist transformations. Nor did nationalism

emerge in all societies that experienced industrialization. In many cases, nation building followed (rather than preceded) industrialism and modernity. If this argument is persuasive, then conditions other than capitalist development were necessary for nations to emerge (Calhoun, 1997).

What was the role of the media in this process? Even though the majority of standard texts on nation and nationalism only paid superficial attention to the media, the origins of modern nations and the mass media were separated by a few decades (see Thompson, 1995). The simultaneous emergence of nations and mass media was not mere coincidence. The rise of mass newspapers in the first decades of the 19th century, particularly with the advent of the penny press in the United States and other cheap dailies in many European countries, is commonly seen as the birth of the mass media. At the same time, different forms of printed literature gained a growing readership in bourgeois circles. The formation of an urban, middle-class public sphere that consumed a variety of printed materials (books, *feuilletons*, *literatura de cordel*, and magazines) was central to the formation of nations (Eley, 1996). During most of the 19th century, low literacy and technological factors limited the reach of the print media and, consequently, their nation-building potential.

Rising levels of literacy, coupled with technological developments, changed the conditions. The rise of consumer societies had important consequences for nation making. Advertising and the revolution in print, photography, and design became key instruments in the creation of national consumer markets (Leiss, Kline, & Jhally, 1997; Marchand, 1985). At the turn of the century, the coming of film and radio technologies expanded the media resources for shaping national cultures. Film and radio helped to overcome spatial and literacy obstacles. Literacy was no longer a requirement to become a member of a nation; sounds and images could convey representations of nationhood. Nor was distance an impediment to the formation of national consciousness. Together with advances in transportation, the massification of film and radio brought together an increasing number of people who, without mass communications, "were stuck in highly particularized segments, quite unable to share a sense of destiny with people they had no chance of meeting" (Hall, 1993, p. 3). If nation-building projects entailed the synchronization of politics and culture, as Gellner (1983) argued, the media played a crucial role by bringing together disparate populations under the same cultural roof.

The media as nation builder is one of the main interests of Benedict Anderson's (1983) influential work. He was not the first scholar interested in theorizing the role of the media in nation building. Karl Deutsch (1966) and Harold Innis (1972) also tried to understand the media-nation nexus, but neither one had the impact of Anderson's work in recent scholarship. The media are at the center of his much-discussed idea of nations as "imagined communities." For Anderson, print technologies had crucial importance in the formation of nations, specifically in the case of the formation of postcolonial nations in Latin America in the 1820s. He rejects primordialist arguments according to which "nations are natural, pre-given," as nationalist ideologues would put it, and functionalist positions à la Gellner that suggest that the rise of nations corresponds to specific stages of capitalist development. Anderson's position, however, differs from other constructivists for whom the *Bildungsprozess* primarily resulted from the interests of political and economic elites. Although some historians concluded that national consciousness served the advancement of capitalist interests (Hobsbawm & Ranger, 1983), Anderson was more interested in understanding the *ways* in which nations were "imagined" rather than attributing the timing of socioeconomic processes to specific class interests.

These differences are expressed in their argument about the role of the media in the origins of nations. Essays in Hobsbawm and Ranger's (1983) collection suggest that, together with official holidays and rituals, the media served bourgeois interests in bringing about cultural homogenization in the formation of national markets. Anderson (1983) did not question the presumed effectiveness of cultural institutions in creating new customs and identities, but he was more interested in showing that the consumption of print news introduced a novel opportunity for shared, "mediated" experiences among populations situated in distant locales. Print technologies were critical in the emergence of a common public culture, a fundamental condition in the shaping of modern nations. Newspapers were platforms for imagining nations by acting as meeting spaces for articulating national views and synchronizing time and space. Similar to the role of "national" novels (Bhabha, 1990; Carey-Webb, 1998; Larsen, 2001; Sommers, 1991), newspapers outlined the contours of the imagined nation and raised readers' awareness of common interests.

Despite growing interest in this point in recent years, the literature still lacks conclusive answers about the extent of media contributions to nation making. There have been successful and failed cases but no systematic explanation to understand under what conditions the media cultivated a sense of national membership.

Consider the role of public broadcasting systems in nation building. A number of studies, particularly on several Western European cases, have convincingly demonstrated that public broadcasting was specifically designed to provide a common culture to a diverse and fragmented audience (Curran, 2002; Scannell, 1996; Tracey, 1998). Founders were convinced that nation making was one of the central missions of public broadcasting. Weekly programs reflected the expectation that broadcasting would be an effort at cultural engineering. Personal memoirs and recollections are filled with anecdotes about how public broadcasting originally gave audiences their first taste of nationhood. The historical links between nations and public broadcasting seem beyond doubt.

Putting the media in the service of nation building did not always result in cultural unification. Centralized monopoly broadcasting systems were part of larger institutional networks to instill national sentiments, but such experiments were not always successful. The replication of various European models of public broadcasting in Africa and Asia hardly resulted in cultural unification (Reeves, 1993). Centralized media efforts to nurture national feelings were not effective in persuading local populations to abandon their cultures and embrace official national identity. Why did the media apparently contribute to the formation of nations in some cases and not in other cases? We still lack parsimonious arguments to account for the role of the media among other institutions and processes in the making (and unmaking) of national cultures. It would be safe to assume that the media and cultural institutions spread and renew sentiments of national belonging, but we still do not know why the media arguably gave support and sustenance to nation making in some cases but not in others. We have mostly detailed analyses of "successful" media nationalization but lack studies of failed media efforts in nation building.

◆ Media Globalization and the Crisis of "National Media"

The failure to consider the complex relations between media and national cultures is evident in current debates about nations and media globalization. The wave of post–cold war globalization has revitalized the sharp polemic about the consequences of international flows of information on cultural diversity in the world. The debate has been cast in familiar terms: Although critics have expressed anxiety about the cultural threats of globalization on nations,

advocates brush aside such fears. To globalophobes, globalization signals the cultural "Americanization" of the world and the disappearance of cultural diversity. Major shifts in media industries caused by privatization and liberalization of media markets, coupled with the spread of information technologies, have weakened political and cultural borders. The vast majority of the world's nations are virtually defenseless vis-à-vis the onslaught of Hollywood's content. Commercial media and consumerist interests promote a globally mass-produced, standardized media culture that paves over national differences. Nations are suffocated under the constant pressure of the corporate peddlers of global culture. Because national audiences are subjected to the same media culture, they have few opportunities for representing their own cultural specificity. Under these conditions, the chances for local cultural creation are bleak.

Globalophiles dismiss such concerns and consider that recent economic and technological changes contribute to cultural diversity. A superficial look at the current media order may suggest that U.S. media have the upper hand, but a closer analysis suggests that globalization brings positive consequences. The prospects for cultural expression are brighter. New technologies help to eliminate old barriers. The expansion of global trade opens new opportunities for cultural industries around the world. In fact, Hollywood's current status as all-powerful global cultural industry may be transitory. The maturation of media industries in several countries and audiences' preference for domestic content suggest that Hollywood's undisputed reign could be just a specific phase in the historical development of media industries (Hoskins, McFadyen, & Finn, 1997).

Despite their differences, neither critics nor defenders of media globalization offer a model that adequately captures the linkages between media and nation. Both positions offer a simple explanation to a complicated question: how cultures emerge, persist, and disappear (Elster, 2000). The relationship between media and national/cultural change is not adequately theorized. Globalophobes conclude that media dissemination and exposure lead to cultural change but fall short from offering an explanation for how culture works. There is no persuasive evidence that the media, regardless of other conditions, are able to induce and perpetuate long-term cultural transformations. If anything, available evidence seems to support the opposite: Exposure to global media actually intensifies sentiments of cultural difference. Audience studies have shown the limitations of inferring the impact of media globalization on national cultures from only examining media economics (Liebes & Katz, 1990). Rather than acting as "de-nationalizing" agents, global media offer opportunities for delineating boundaries, reaffirming identities, and combining cultures.

Globalophiles' explanation of the relationship between media and cultural change is not more convincing. It assumes that a combination of media technologies and market policies fosters national/cultural diversity (Berger & Huntington, 2002; Cowen, 2002). Too enthusiastic about the promises of new technologies and free markets, they ignore persistent power inequalities in cultural production and consumption. Certainly, technological innovations provide new opportunities for myriad nations to represent themselves. Among other examples, solar and windup radio, satellite communications, and cheaper video equipment provide, particularly to people with no access to electricity and traditional television, new chances for cultural production. These developments have limited reach and do not change political-economic structures responsible for inequalities in media production.

The debate on the impact of globalization on national cultures has reached an impasse largely because neither of the dominant positions seriously considers how nations are formed, maintained, and changed. Each position tends to cull examples that conveniently make its case, finding evidence that

"the global media substantially change nations" and that "the global media fail to eliminate national diversity." For every sign of cultural influence by Western media, there are also examples of national cultures resisting or being untouched by globalization. As long as it is framed as an issue of "effects" of global media on nations, the debate will continue a predictable course.

Therefore, a different set of questions needs to be asked to understand the linkages between media globalization and national cultures: How do the media intervene in the twin movements of inclusion and exclusion that underlie nation making? What is the role of the media among other institutions and processes responsible for shaping, maintaining, and undermining national cultures? What interpretations of "the nation" are disseminated? How should they be explained?

THE CRISIS OF THE "NATIONAL" MEDIA

To delve into these questions, one must examine the situation of the "national" media, an idea that articulated the mission of media industries worldwide during much of the 20th century.

The idea of "national media" needs to be revised (see Hjort & MacKenzie, 2000). Its ideological ambiguity has made it difficult to set apart whether *national* alludes to the right of cultural self-expression and democracy or the political ambitions of cultural commissars to impose a specific culture at the expense of pluralism. It has been used to achieve democratic and authoritarian goals. Its remarkable ideological flexibility is not surprising, considering that nationalism itself has been a maddeningly elastic concept, able to appropriate and be appropriated by a wide spectrum of political forces and ideologies. It is informed by essentialist and centralist conceptions of the nation that view "internal" cultural diversity as an obstacle to cultural unification and "external" cultures as a threat. The notion of "national media" belongs to a time when the principle of "cultural sovereignty" was upheld as a desirable and feasible goal of cultural policies, including the media, to impose cultural unification and cordon off an autonomous cultural space, free from foreign influences (Waisbord, 1995).

Beside its problematic ideological connotations, the idea of national media also needs to be reconsidered because the conditions of media industries have substantially changed since it was originally conceived. Three developments are responsible for severing the link between *national* and *media* and ultimately making *national media* projects unattainable.

First, the globalization of the media business—namely, the combination of technological innovations and the application of neoliberal policies—has shattered nationalistic hopes of establishing and monitoring cultural sovereignty (see Price, 2002). Although countries still have policies putting limits on foreign participation in domestic industries (investments, programming quotas), the intensification of cross-border capital flows and media trade has undermined traditional notions of "national ownership." It has become clear that the "national" origin of ownership and financing does not have a direct, predictable relationship with the "national" citizenship of cultural productions. Today, a Japanese corporation owns major Hollywood production studios, French banks cofinance Hollywood films, Hindi Americans bankroll Bollywood productions, and Mexican citizens control substantial media interests in Central America. But whose nationhood is represented by media output? Media products hardly represent anything that distinctively reflects the national origin of owners and funders.

Nor does it seem that a substantial amount of media product articulates the national sentiments of cultural workers. The presence of a globalized labor force in management and creative roles in media industries heightens the persistent difficulty of inferring the cultural/national affiliation of media productions from the citizen status of media personnel. There is no longer, if there ever was, a direct relationship between the citizenship of cultural workers and the national identity of media content. Defining the cultural citizenship of certain media content has become increasingly difficult when a multinational workforce produces, for example, a vast array of Hollywood movies and European coproductions, recordings of *rai* music in Paris studios or pan-American *salsa* in New York and Miami, and news in CNN and BBC newsrooms. The national identity of content is hard to pin down and cannot be predicted from the citizenship of cultural workers or the location of production.

Second, such forms of collaboration, coupled with a constant cross-pollination of ideas, have increased the blending of narrative styles, themes, and genres across borders. Two seemingly opposite forces, hybridization and standardization, are the norm in contemporary cultural production. This makes it difficult to attribute national citizenship to media content. Global television programming fits a limited number of genres and formulas. The business of television formats has substantially increased in the past decade, but whether formats are the ultimate example of standardization, actual productions reflect the preferences of national audiences and local contexts (Waisbord, 2001). The 3-minute pop song has been used and modified in thousands of recordings worldwide. Hong Kong, French, Indian, and Argentine filmmakers have added local color and twists to Hollywood's trademark action movies and thrillers. Some music is still indelibly associated with specific nations (Dominican *bachata*, Cuban *son*, Argentine tango), but a huge variety of sounds (Afro pop, Nordic jazz, Mexican rock, Swedish pop-rock, or Brazilian hip-hop) attest to the intensification of musical borrowing across nations (see Born & Hesmondhalgh, 2000).

Attaching national labels to media content is fraught with problems given the multileveled dynamics of contemporary media and cultural production. If the idea of national media is preserved, it better describes the media environment and resources of nations to articulate feelings of cultural belonging, rather than a certain media structure and companies whose products express something culturally unique to specific groups of population. It is a question of media capacity (institutions, technologies, policies, funding, and human resources) to nurture and perpetuate cultural identities and outline boundaries between in-groups and out-groups rather than their crystallization of cultural sovereignty.

NATIONS AND MEDIA INDUSTRIES

Media production capacity and access are unequally distributed across nations. Broad-brush, optimistic, or pessimistic conclusions about this situation fail to capture the nuances of the current state of global media industries and, consequently, the different opportunities for nation making. Neither the doom-and-gloom picture of Western/American cultural domination nor the upbeat techno-market vision accurately describes the situation (Sinclair offers a useful criticism of these positions in Chapter 3, this volume).

Most film industries around the world currently experience severe difficulties (Moran, 1996; Williams, 2002). The notion of "national" cinema that animated the establishment of film industries in many countries is questionable. It is rooted in a time when film and other media were primarily conceived as nation builders, mainly in opposition to Hollywood's early domination of world screens. The liberalization of film markets, Hollywood's uncontested box office power, and the dismantling of protectionist policies have weakened national industries. In past years, even nations that historically had a vibrant film industry have confronted a host of problems to produce a modest number of films

that compete with Hollywood for screens and audiences, nationally and internationally. Although many of the difficulties that film industries have experienced are not new, globalization has intensified perennial problems, particularly in distribution and marketing (Miller, Govil, McMurria, & Maxwell, 2002). Notwithstanding the sporadic success of a few non-Hollywood films in international markets, the situation is largely unfavorable for other industries. Moreover, considerations for coproduction and international distribution run contrary to the idea of "national" film, as producers tone down local/national themes and have an eye for content that "travels well" in international markets to attract sponsors, distributors, and audiences.

In contrast, the situation in the global television industry offers important differences. Lower fixed costs and different market conditions account for why many countries produce a substantial number of television hours but have weak (or simply lack) film industries. Television production in large- and medium-sized markets is considerable and generally commands local audience preferences (Sinclair, Jacka, & Cunnigham, 1996). With a few exceptions, domestic production is filled with low-cost productions such as game shows, talk shows, comedy, "reality" shows, and variety shows. In most countries, the production of drama, documentaries, and other more expensive programming is rare. Still, the intense traffic of television productions that originated in dozens of nations does not resemble Hollywood's undisputed supremacy of film screens and VHS and DVD rentals. Measured in number of hours and revenues, Hollywood continues to lead world production and exports, but given favorable market conditions, a substantial number of countries are still able to produce sufficient television hours to fill weekly schedules and attract domestic audiences.

Compared to film and television, the current state of the global music industry is different. Many sectors of the industry (production, distribution, retail, intellectual property rights) are more concentrated than in the past. The "Big 5" conglomerates currently capture nearly 90% of global sales. As in the film industry, globalization largely benefits big companies by expanding economies of scale, mainly in distribution and marketing (Frith, 2000; Negus, 1999). Business concentration, however, is not synonymous with the production of homogeneous content at the expense of national diversity. The global success of "American" music genres (pop, hip-hop, rock) is often mistakenly associated with the dearth of domestic music. Some analysts have noticed that product diversity has actually increased, rather than decreased, in recent years (Burnett, 1996). Faced with a substantial drop in global sales, coupled with short-lived profits from hits and genres, companies increased the number of releases to capture more fragmented and seemingly more fickle consumers. Produced and distributed by subsidiaries of global firms, local hits typically top charts and airwaves in most countries, particularly in wealthier, large markets.

The conditions in radio industries across the planet are quite different again from the situation in the industries described heretofore. With a few exceptions, radio remains essentially a local medium with a limited amount of foreign content (mostly music). The nation-building role that radio had in many countries (Hayes, 2000) has remained relatively unchanged. News and talk shows, two of radio's staple genres, are still important spaces for local/national voices. This is particularly evident in poor, rural areas where radio continues to be the primary source of news and information, given cost and lack of access to other technologies.

This brief summary suggests that opportunities for nation building largely vary because access to media production and consumption is different. Technology costs and the specific characteristics of each media industry provide different opportunities for media production. Low "barriers to entry" make access to radio easier than to any other medium or industry. Rapidly decreasing costs of technology have, in principle, facilitated access to print production. Likewise, cheaper equipment has eased access to music and film, video, and television production.

The economics of print and audiovisual industries, however, work against the prospects of significantly leveling the field. Media globalization has exacerbated the historical problems of small and poor nations in acquiring substantial media resources. New technologies have offered novel and still untapped opportunities but not to the point of correcting disparities in media access. Because the current hegemony of market policies favors business priorities, nations situated in markets that offer propitious conditions for capitalist interests (audience size, extensive advertising revenues, favorable media policies) have better chances to produce content. Nations in large and/or wealthier markets have more media resources at their disposal. Media consumption depends on literacy and technology costs. Literacy requirements make it harder for print media to be a primary site for nation building in nations with high illiteracy. No medium matches the accessibility and penetration of radio. Still, the massive increase in the number of television sets in the past decades around the world, coupled with the coming of several technologies for video distribution (cable, satellite, VHS), have consolidated the significance of television as a nation-building technology.

Differences in the availability of media resources do not imply that nations with poor access to media and/or weak media industries are condemned to cultural extinction. Cultural production entails much more than whether a nation has ample or limited media resources, as Gumucio-Dagron makes clear in Chapter 2 (this volume). Those differences are important to recognize, however, to understand the current prospects of media and national cultures in a globalized world. This is the subject of the next section.

THE PERSISTENCE
OF THE NATIONAL

Much of the recent discussion on nations and nationalism has dealt with the question of whether "the national" is waning or continues to be relevant. Although some observers argue that "the nation" is on its last legs, others consider it premature to discount its relevance. Several authors claim that nations and nationalism have entered an irreversible decline due to the passing of the conditions that originally made it possible (Greenfeld, 1992; Hobsbawm, 1990). If modernity was the cradle of nations, the end of modernity brings about the passing of the nation. The intensification of the movements of capital disrupts nations and the sense of home community (Harvey, 2000). For many, the death of the nation is not only an analytical conclusion but also a longing based on judging the past and present of the nation and nationalism, which are charged for having inspired some of the worst crimes against humanity of the past two centuries.

Against this position, other studies suggest that the nation maintains political and cultural relevance (Schlesinger, 1991). "The national" remains a primary form through which cultural identity and difference are maintained in the contemporary world. Nations have a future as long as human groups require a basis to establish unity and difference from others, and group identity is based on inclusion and exclusion (S. Hall, 1996). The consolidation of transnational cultures and identities, rather than eliminating individual and social identities, adds new layers to them. As John Hall (1993) writes, "All of us are composed of multiple social identities" (p. 152). There has been an increasing recognition that "concentric circles of belonging and identity" define cultural identities (Morley & Robins, 1995; Smith, 1990).

To have feelings of belonging to a national community does not exclude simultaneous feelings of belonging to local or supranational formations. Whether we call these feelings "patriotism" or "nationalism," it is doubtful that they are likely to vanish anytime soon or become less important as an identity-conferring basis. Patriotism, often associated with "good" love and pride for one's country, and nationalism, often associated with "bad" chauvinism rooted in prejudice, racism, and hate (see Calhoun, 1997), remain strong feelings that, for better or worse, ground social and cultural identities. Positive or pejorative connotations aside, patriotism and nationalism do not show signs of having receded as powerful identifiers of cultural belonging.

The persistence of nations and nationalism hinges on several factors. One factor is that globalization has not offered group identities that supersede national identities (Smith, 1990; Stevenson, 1997). It has not nurtured other cultural groupings that, like nations, are stirred by ideologies such as nationalism, a political project to attain self-determination (Hechter, 2000). Global communities of sport and music fans, fashion and art aficionados, academics, and religious believers are devoid of movements that appeal to historical and cultural bonds to achieve political recognition. They are integrated by people with similar cultural interests, but without a political movement claiming cultural distinctiveness and political rights, they are poor competitors to nations. They are "imagined" communities, but of a different nature compared to nations: They neither articulate political demands nor expect exclusive loyalty from their members.

Why would people abandon national identities and embrace other forms of identification? What alternatives exist to nations? What political and media discourses offer plausible substitutes to nations? Regional identities, sustained by media institutions, are unlikely candidates to replace national identities, as Philip Schlesinger (1991) has persuasively argued in the European case. As a form of transnational culture, religions have historically maintained a complex and tense relation of coexistence with nations (Hastings, 1997;

Piscatori, 1986). National identities have not been the secular replacement to religions as the basis for cultural identification in the modern world. Religious beliefs have typically articulated and been integrated into official conceptions of the nation.

Consider cosmopolitanism as a possible alternative to national identities. Much has been written recently on the tentative emergence of a "cosmopolitan civil society" (Beck, 2000; Hannerz, 1990; Rotblat, 1997). The affirmation of a global consciousness implies the expansion of sentiments of belonging to a community that appeals to individuals as "citizens of the world." Cosmopolitanism insists on the need to go beyond the lottery of birth that underlies national identities, so as to strengthen a universalist, humanitarian consciousness. It requires a simultaneous movement of transcending the cultural and political limits of nations and nurturing solidarity and commitment to universal values. Although national cultures divide, a cosmopolitan consciousness integrates by emphasizing commonality over difference.

Two developments have recently reinvigorated cosmopolitan hopes. First, genocide in the Balkans and Rwanda and crimes against ethnic groups in China, India, and Iraq, among other societies, have confirmed the conviction that nationalism unavoidably leads to massive violations of human rights and reinforces hatred and violence (Ignatieff, 2000; Nairn, 1997). Second, the consolidation of cross-national forms of participation around a host of global issues (human rights, environment, labor conditions, sexual and gender issues) has injected new energy into postnational and global solidarity movements (Held, 1995; Keck & Sikkink, 1998; Szerszynski & Toogood, 2000).

The challenge is the following: If nations have been invented (Chaney, 1994; Hobsbawm & Ranger, 1983), can cosmopolitanism also be invented? If national attachments are abstract but powerful identifiers, why can't cosmopolitan identity be possible too? If the media contributed to

cementing national cultures, why can't they be placed at the service of cosmopolitanism?

Recent media and technological developments have given more credence to such expectations. Together with developments in transportation, the media have emerged as a potential aid to cosmopolitanism by eliminating distance. The media offer a new global public sphere in which a cosmopolitan culture could be nurtured (J. Cohen, 1996; Hannerz, 1990; Nussbaum, 1996; Szerszynski, Urry, & Myers, 2000; Urry, 2002). In putting audiences in contact with other nations, global media are able to chip away at self-enclosed media cultures and open up new political possibilities.

Despite invigorated hopes, the case of cosmopolitan identity as a candidate to replace or supplement national identities seems dubious. Some authors have indicated that, in contrast to nationalism, cosmopolitanism lacks emotional grip (Calhoun, 1997). It is devoid of common symbols and a shared history on which cultural cohesion could be possible. As an example of global culture, it lacks, as Anthony Smith (1986) puts it, a "vital ingrained sense of historical experience, a sense of temporal continuity and shared memories" (p. 5). Others have observed that, in contrast to national citizenship, cosmopolitanism does not offer social and political entitlements. Citizenship rights continue to be rooted in specific states (Habermas, 1992). Rather than mutually exclusive, cosmopolitanism and national identities seem and need to be reconciled (McCarthy, 1999).

A cosmopolitan culture seems doubtful because the interaction between media and global publics does not seem to meet expectations about the activation of cross-border solidarity. World news organizations, for example, are hardly the catalysts of a cosmopolitan consciousness. The so-called "CNN effect"—television audiences familiar with world news who push for interventions in humanitarian crises—has yet to materialize. Despite expectations that they would contribute to broadening cultural horizons and fostering transnational communities, audiences are typically indifferent to the plight of others portrayed in world news (Tester, 2001), particularly when news reports suffering among populations believed to be geographically and culturally distant. Rather than bringing audiences together, the media increase a sense of distancing from (Boltanski, 1999) and denial of (S. Cohen, 2000) fellow world citizens.

The shortcomings of international news coverage probably offer a partial explanation for why the media fail to meet cosmopolitan expectations. News media tend to offer poor, sporadic, formulaic, and distorted visions of world news and humanitarian issues (Moeller, 1999). Media organizations typically resort to cultural narratives and stories that resonate with home audiences rather than seeking to understand developments and contexts better. However, it does not seem to be mainly a question of the limitations of news frames and journalistic practices: Unlike nations, cosmopolitanism lacks allied media organizations willing to become vehicles for transnational or postnational cultures. Perhaps expectations about the role of the global media in nurturing cosmopolitan sentiments are misplaced. With the exception of global media networks of activists, media institutions largely remain uninterested in aiding cosmopolitan causes and instead are better designed and willing to sustain national identities.

MEDIA AND THE PERSISTENT PULL OF THE NATIONAL

Although global media have yet to fulfill their potential in promoting cosmopolitan identities, media continue to make important contributions to supporting national cultures. The media-nation linkages need to be examined in the realm of everyday life rather than, as media studies have often done, on occasional moments when nations are ostensibly celebrated. The power of the media lies in making national feelings normal on an everyday basis. In providing the backdrop for daily life and fodder for routine conversation, the media help to perpetuate "banal nationalism" (Billig, 1995), that is, the defining context of everyday discourse and interaction. The contributions are threefold: making national cultures routinely available, offering opportunities for collective experiences, and institutionalizing national cultures.

First, the media nurture national sentiments by regularly making available cultural forms identified with the nation. National cultures require members to perceive that they share a "structure of feeling" (in Raymond Williams's [1977] sense). The media are one institution that provides an enabling environment to articulate a sense of proximity and coordination in national communities. Although the media are insufficient per se to generate cultural identities, the significance of media representations for nation making cannot be underestimated. The relevance of the media lies more in their having a great capacity to offer representations and interpretations of the nation on a daily basis. This is why the extent to which nations have media resources available is important.

Media languages remain one of the central elements that continue to articulate and reinforce a sense of cultural membership (Cormack, 2000). The media are largely responsible for the acceptance of specific languages, accents, and expressions as legitimate components of a national culture. The media also reinforce national belonging by constantly making reference to places, symbols, and memories that anchor national cultures and identities. If nationalism is a discursive formation (see Calhoun, 1997), then media discourses and representations of the nation need to be considered. In devoting attention to historical events, selecting news frames, or producing content to represent national sentiments, the media shape the cultural repertoire used to define nationhood. Although alternative discourses may contest media representations of the nation, the significance of the media in prioritizing and ignoring certain themes and interpretations cannot be minimized.

Journalism's choices of narrative frameworks and subjects to talk about the nation, for example, are worth considering to understand how nationhood is defined. Journalism regularly resorts to a stock of nationalistic discourses to report news (see Waisbord, 2002). It plays an important role in submitting different versions of the nation for public consideration, giving space to "ethnic" narratives that convey racist and hostile views, or stressing "civic" interpretations that emphasize tolerance, solidarity, and compassion as national values. The press and the media at large do make a great contribution to understanding patriotism as either the perpetrator of intolerance or as defined by a common commitment to democracy.

Second, the media continue to provide opportunities for shared media experiences that are central to nation making. If nations require collective experiences and shared memories, the media offer a suitable environment and resources to nurture national identities. "Media events" (Dayan & Katz, 1992) are examples of those experiences, moments when the daily lives of entire nations come to a full stop to watch or listen to the same event. In shaping a sense of time-space commonality, they coordinate the life of a nation. Millions watching presidential inaugurations, wars, the death of public figures, and other solemn occasions that put the nation on a center stage show cultural coordination at work.

The fragmentation of media audiences may be undermining the nation-building capacity that media events had in the past. They are still gripping collective acts of national communion, but the multiplication of channels makes it less likely that an "entire nation" will attend media events as in the past. When most audiences had a choice of one or two channels, and governments mandated all stations to broadcast simultaneously, media events could pull a nation together. Today, audiences are scattered across several media and channels.

Those media events are sporadic, however. If they become ingrained in national memories, it is not only because they convey powerful emotions and are attached to national rites of passage but also because they are rare. In contrast, there are other media events that sustain collective practices and stir national feelings on a regular basis. Media frenzy around national and international sports tournaments, as well as "national" celebrations (Carnival, saint's day festivities, military and civic parades on national holidays), are occasions for renewing nationalistic feelings. Likewise, nonstop news coverage of topics that absorb public attention also provides moments for pulling a nation to a common center. Media fragmentation and audience segmentation almost vanish when the media devote endless time and space to political scandals, celebrity murders, terrorist acts, and other news. The media may not be the central agora that they used to be when technological options were limited, but they still manage to reel in dispersed audiences and shape common collective experiences.

Third, the media contribute to the sustainability of nations by institutionalizing "national cultures." Institutional retention is fundamental for cultural continuity (Schudson, 1989). Nations appeal to a sense of stored memories passed from generation to generation. They are based on the idea of a historical continuity between past and present. To accomplish this, nations need institutions that permanently remind members of their commonality. Like educational systems, official calendars, and state rituals, the media store cultural elements that come to define nationhood. Certainly, institutional retention does not guarantee that a cultural element will remain intact or always be identified with the nation. Debates over the pantheon of heroes, historical events, symbols, and language show that national cultures are not "built" once and forever but are subject to change.

What postnational cultures and identities are missing is this institutional retention. Cosmopolitanism lacks institutionalization, as John Tomlinson (1999) argues, partially because global media do a poor job enforcing and maintaining cross-national identities. Global media allow audiences to retrieve common cultures and collectively experience common moments. They are not designed, however, to preserve common symbols and memories to sustain postnational sentiments. What symbols of cosmopolitan identities are constantly flagged by the media? How do global media regularly remind citizens of transnational belonging?

Having access to and participating in common experiences may be important in nurturing awareness of a supranational community. Allegiance requires more than retrievability and collective participation, however. It requires a set of institutions that routinely sustain and remind people about cultural allegiances. Undoubtedly, globalization penetrates and affects the daily lives of billions of people, but without institutions that constantly appeal to global identities, it is unlikely that the latter are permanently shaped. "National" media, in contrast, are still able to coordinate and articulate identities by drawing from a historical reservoir that has resulted from sedimented cultural labor.

In summary, because the media are an essential part of the infrastructure and resources required in the process of cultural formation in large-scale societies (Calhoun, 1997), the fact that media organizations are still attached to nations suggests that, despite the crisis of "national" media, the media still nurture the national.

THE FUTURES OF MEDIA PATRIOTISM

Developments "internal" and "external" to the nation have changed the environment that originally gave birth to ideas and policies about media and nation building. "From outside" the nation, globalization presents challenges to the traditional role of the media in nation building through dismantling barriers to cross-border flows of capital and information. The crisis of the "national" media, coupled with constant media spillovers and trade across political boundaries, has rendered it difficult, if not impossible, for nations to erect and patrol media borders to achieve cultural sovereignty. The sputtering emergence of a cosmopolitan consciousness and the burgeoning of nomadic identities (Joseph, 1999) add new dimensions to cultural belonging that are not captured by conventional definitions of national cultures and loyalties. "From inside" the nation, multiculturalism and hybridization have challenged nostalgic visions of nationalism (Poole, 1999; Rex, 1996). Intense migration movements have undermined national visions of "one race, one language, one culture" that shaped modern national identities. The global multiplication of "portable nationalities" (Anderson, 1996) and continuous flows of diasporic media (Sun, 2002) have undermined nation-states' projects that aimed to achieve a perfect alignment of politics and culture. In making cultural identities multilayered and contradictory, hybridization disputes reified conceptions of the nation.

Neither globalization nor multiculturalism has delivered a deadly blow to national cultures. The fact that the modern conception of the nation is questionable, both ideologically and practically, cannot lead us to infer the demise of actual nations. Several reasons account for why nations refuse to be left behind (McCrone, 1998; Miller, 1995). One of them is that nations are still equipped with a number of institutions that support and energize national sentiments. The media are one of those institutions that contribute to maintaining feelings of national membership.

Media patriotism adopts "chauvinistic" and "everyday" forms. Chauvinistic media patriotism propagates war-mongering, xenophobic discourses. The media fan the flames of nationalism in wars and other saber-rattling situations, debates over labor migration and economic issues, and the coverage of "moral panics" affecting the nation. The media contribute to heightening anxiety about "the foreign." Media alert us to "foreign" risks to the nation (from viruses and epidemics to the "Barbarians at the Gates" coverage of migrants and guest workers, from "blood-sucking" foreign investors to cultural invaders) and their demonization of "others" (Hallam & Street, 2000) considered ill-fitted to belong to the nation: All are examples of chauvinistic media patriotism.

More often, however, media patriotism has a quieter, "everyday" existence by bringing together members of the nation around language, symbols, and common experiences. The media still manage to nurture a sense of home, collectivity, and community linked to nationhood (Morley, 2000). The force of this kind of media patriotism lies in its apparent naturalness, in invisibly articulating feelings of national belonging. Although both forms of media patriotism delineate cultural boundaries, there is one important difference: Although chauvinistic patriotism at intervals noisily beats the national drum, everyday patriotism constantly and silently perpetuates national sentiments. Although much has been studied concerning the former, further research is needed to understand how everyday media representations of the nation are interwoven with the daily reproduction and transformation of national cultures and identities.

What remains unanswered is not whether "the nation" has a future but, rather, what kind of future (Beiner, 1999). Even critics of the nation accept that nations are likely to remain for quite some time (Poole, 1999). Media studies can provide valuable insights to elucidate whether nationhood is inevitably associated with horrible crimes and the politics of racial and ethnic marginalization, as cosmopolitans believe (Nussbaum, 1996; Robbins, 1999), or instead with a sense of place, pride, and community through which democratic life is possible, as progressive patriots insist (Barber, 1996; Rorty, 1998). Whether nationalism takes an ethnic or

civic expression is ultimately an empirical question that needs to be studied. In this sense, the media can equally act as a source of exclusion and murder in the name of the nation or as an ally of civic patriotism. Both possibilities are similarly viable, particularly in societies where patriotism is a contested, contradictory notion used to justify aggression and compassion, war and democracy.

There is nothing inherent in the functioning of media institutions to presuppose that, like patriotism, the media necessarily connect citizens through fostering sentiments of national superiority or nurturing a sense of home, solidarity, and moral obligation to compatriots and others. Like nations, the media still provide a cultural sense of "something to hold onto" in a world of shifting boundaries, growing uncertainty, and risk. The media can do much to define whether patriotic fears or a commitment to social justice articulate citizenship and a sense of cultural belonging.

◆ Note

1. I prefer to use *cultural coordination* instead of the commonly used *cultural integration*. Functionalist premises underlie the concept of *integration*, which is problematic for two reasons. First, integration needs to be a research question ("Does culture effectively integrate national communities?") rather than as a goal to be demonstrated. Framing nations in terms of cultural coordination helps us to avoid making ex post facto conclusions about whether integration effectively happens. Second, the idea of integration is still attached to functionalism's interest in culture as an element that contributes to the equilibrium of social systems. I am more interested in approaching the issue of media and national cultures as a question of collective behavior ("How do the media and culture contribute to coordinating actions among members of a nation?"), as opposed to seeing them as a quality of social systems.

◆ References

Anderson, B. (1983). *Imagined communities: Reflections on the origin and spread of nationalism.* London: Verso.

Anderson, B. (1996). Introduction. In G. Balakrishnan (Ed.), *Mapping the nation* (pp. 1–7). London: Verso.

Armstrong, J. A. (1982). *Nations before nationalism.* Chapel Hill: University of North Carolina Press.

Barber, B. (1996). Constitutional faith. In M. Nussbaum & J. Cohen (Eds.), *For love of country: Debating the limits of patriotism* (pp. 30–37). Boston: Beacon.

Beck, U. (2000). The cosmopolitan perspective: On the sociology of the second age of modernity. *British Journal of Sociology, 51,* 79–106.

Beiner, R. (1999). *Theorizing nationalism.* Albany: State University of New York Press.

Berger, P. L., & Huntington, S. P. (Eds.). (2002). *Many globalizations: Cultural diversity in the contemporary world.* New York: Oxford University Press.

Bhabha, H. (1990). *Nation and narration.* London: Routledge.

Billig, M. (1995). *Banal nationalism.* London: Sage.

Boltanski, L. (1999). *Distant suffering.* Cambridge, UK: Cambridge University Press.

Born, G., & Hesmondhalgh, D. (2000). *Western music and its others: Difference, representation, and appropriation in music.* Berkeley: University of California Press.

Brubaker, R. (1996). *Nationalism reframed: Nationhood and the national question in the new Europe.* Cambridge, UK: Cambridge University Press.

Burnett, R. (1996). *The global jukebox.* London: Routledge.

Calhoun, C. (1997). *Nationalism.* Minneapolis: University of Minnesota Press.

Carey-Webb, A. (1998). *Making subject(s): Literature and the emergence of national identity.* New York: Garland.

Chaney, D. (1994). *The cultural turn.* London: Routledge.

Cohen, J. (1996). The public sphere, the media and civil society. In A. Sajó & M. Price (Eds.), *Rights of access to the media* (pp. 42–58). The Hague, the Netherlands: Kluwer Law International.

Cohen, S. (2000). *States of denial: Knowing about atrocities and suffering.* Cambridge, UK: Polity.

Cormack, M. (2000). Minority languages, nationalism and broadcasting: The British and Irish examples. *Nations and Nationalism, 6*(3), 383–398.

Cowen, T. (2002). *Creative destruction: How globalization is changing the world's cultures.* Princeton, NJ: Princeton University Press.

Curran, J. (2002). *Media and power.* London: Routledge.

Dayan, D., & Katz, E. (1992). *Media events: The live broadcasting of history.* Cambridge, MA: Harvard University Press.

Deutsch, K. W. (1966). *Nationalism and social communication: An inquiry into the foundations of nationality* (2nd ed.). Cambridge: MIT Press.

Eley, G. (1996). Introduction. In G. Eley & R. Suny (Eds.), *Becoming national: A reader.* New York: Oxford University Press.

Elster, J. (2000). *Strong feelings: Emotion, addiction, and human behavior.* Cambridge: MIT Press.

Frith, S. (2000). Power and policy in the British music industry. In H. Tumber (Ed.), *Media power, professionals and policies* (pp. 60–83). London: Routledge.

Gellner, E. (1983). *Nations and nationalism.* Oxford, UK: Blackwell.

Gellner, E., & Smith, A. D. (1996). The nation: Real or imagined? The Warwick Debates on Nationalism. *Nations and Nationalism, 2*(3), 357–370.

Gillis, J. (Ed.). (1994). *Commemorations: The politics of national identity.* Princeton, NJ: Princeton University Press.

Greenfeld, L. (1992). *Nationalism: Five roads to modernity.* Cambridge, MA: Harvard University Press.

Habermas, J. (1992). Citizenship and national identity: Some reflections on the future of Europe. *Praxis International, 12*(1), 19.

Hall, J. A. (1993). Nationalisms: Classified and explained. *Daedalus, 122*(3), 1–28.

Hall, J. A. (Ed.). (1998). *The state of the nation: Ernest Gellner and the theory of nationalism.* New York: Cambridge University Press.

Hall, S. (1996). Who needs identity? In S. Hall & P. du Gay (Eds.), *Questions of cultural identity* (pp. 1–23). London: Sage.

Hallam, E., & Street, B. V. (Eds.). (2000). *Cultural encounters: Representing "otherness."* London: Routledge.

Hannerz, U. (1990). Cosmopolitans and locals in world culture. *Theory, Culture, and Society, 7,* 237–251.

Harvey, D. (2000). *Spaces of hope.* Edinburgh, UK: Edinburgh University Press.

Hastings, A. (1997). *The construction of nationhood: Ethnicity, religion and nationalism.* Cambridge, UK: Cambridge University Press.

Hayes, J. (2000). *Radio nation: Communication, popular culture, and nationalism in Mexico, 1920–1950.* Tucson: University of Arizona Press.

Hechter, M. (2000). *Containing nationalism.* Oxford, UK: Oxford University Press.

Held, D. (1995). *Democracy and the global order.* Cambridge, UK: Polity.

Hjort, M., & MacKenzie, S. (Eds.). (2000). *Cinema and nation.* London: Routledge.

Hobsbawm, E. (1990). *Nations and nationalism since 1780: Programme, myth, reality.* Cambridge, UK: Cambridge University Press.

Hobsbawm, E., & Ranger, T. (Eds.). (1983). *The invention of tradition.* Cambridge, UK: Cambridge University Press.

Hoskins, C., McFadyen, S., & Finn, A. (1997). *Global television and film: An introduction to the economics of the business.* New York: Oxford University Press.

Ignatieff, M. (2000). *Virtual war.* London: Chatto and Windus.

Innis, H. (1972). *Empire and communications.* Toronto: University of Toronto Press.

Joseph, M. (1999). *Nomadic identities.* Minneapolis: University of Minnesota Press.

Keck, M., & Sikkink, K. (1998). *Activists beyond borders.* Ithaca, NY: Cornell University Press.

Larsen, N. (2001). *Determinations: Essays on theory, narrative and nation in the Americas.* London: Verso.

Leiss, W., Kline, S., & Jhally, S. (1997). *Social communication in advertising: Persons, products & images of well-being.* London: Routledge.

Liebes, T., & Curran, J. (Eds.). (1998). *Media, ritual and identity.* London: Routledge.

Liebes, T., & Katz, E. (1990). *The export of meaning: Cross-cultural readings of Dallas.* New York: Oxford University Press.

Marchand, R. (1985). *Advertising the American dream: Making way for modernity, 1920–1940.* Berkeley: University of California Press.

McCarthy, T. (1999). On reconciling national diversity and cosmopolitan unity. *Public Culture, 11,* 175–208.

McCrone, D. (1998). *The sociology of nationalism.* London: Routledge.

Miller, D. (1995). *On nationality.* Oxford, UK: Clarendon.

Miller, T., Govil, N., McMurria, J., & Maxwell, R. (2002). *Global Hollywood.* London: British Film Institute.

Moeller, S. (1999). *Compassion fatigue: How the media sell disease, famine, war and death.* New York: Routledge.

Moran, A. (1996). *Film policy: International, national and regional perspectives.* New York: Routledge.

Morley, D. (2000). *Home territories: Media, mobility and identity.* London: Routledge.

Morley, D., & Robins, K. (1995). *Spaces of identity.* London: Routledge.

Nairn, T. (1997). *Faces of nationalism: Janus revisited.* London: Verso.

Negus, K. (1999). *Music genres and corporate cultures.* London: Routledge.

Nussbaum, M. (1996). Patriotism and cosmopolitanism. In M. Nussbaum & J. Cohen (Eds.), *For love of country: Debating the limits of patriotism* (pp. 2–20). Boston: Beacon.

Piscatori, J. P. (1986). *Islam in a world of nation-states.* Cambridge, UK: Cambridge University Press.

Polanyi, K. (1957). *The great transformation.* New York: Rinehart.

Poole, R. (1999). *Nation and identity*. London: Routledge.

Price, M. (2002). *Media and sovereignty: The global information revolution and its challenge to state power*. Cambridge: MIT Press.

Reeves, G. (1993). *Communications and the "Third World."* London: Routledge.

Rex, J. (1996). National identity in the democratic multi-cultural state. *Sociological Research Online, 1*(2). Retrieved from www.bsos.umd.edu/CSS97/papers/asencre.html

Robbins, B. (1999). *Feeling global*. New York: New York University Press.

Rorty, R. (1998). *Achieving our country: Leftist thought in twentieth-century America*. Cambridge, MA: Harvard University Press.

Rotblat, J. (Ed.). (1997). *World citizenship: Allegiance to humanity*. London: Macmillan.

Scannell, P. (1996). *Radio, television and modern life*. Oxford, UK: Blackwell.

Schlesinger, P. (1991). Media, the political order, and national identity. *Media, Culture, and Society, 13*, 297–308.

Schudson, M. (1989). How culture works: Perspectives from media studies on the efficacy of symbols. *Theory and Society, 18*, 153–180.

Sinclair, J., Jacka, E., & Cunnigham, S. (1996). *New patterns in global television: Peripheral vision*. New York: Oxford University Press.

Smith, A. (1986). *The ethnic origins of nations*. Oxford, UK: Blackwell.

Smith, A. (1990). Towards a global culture? In M. Featherstone (Ed.), *Global culture: Nationalism, globalization, and modernity* (pp. 58–174). London: Sage.

Sommers, D. (1991). *Foundational fictions: The national romances of Latin America*. Berkeley: University of California Press.

Stevenson, N. (1997). Globalization, national cultures and cultural citizenship. *The Sociological Quarterly, 38*, 41–66.

Sun, W. (2002). *Leaving China: Media, migration and transnational imagination*. Lanham, MD: Rowman & Litttlefield.

Szerszynski, B., & Toogood, M. (2000). Global citizenship, the environment and the mass media. In S. Allen, B. Adam, & C. Carter (Eds.), *The media politics of environmental risks* (pp. 218–228). London: Routledge.

Szerszynski, B., Urry, J., & Myers, G. (2000). Mediating global citizenship. In J. Smith (Ed.), *The daily globe* (pp. 97–114). London: Earthscan.

Tester, K. (2001). *Compassion, morality and the media*. Buckingham, UK: Open University Press.

Thompson, J. (1995). *The media and modernity*. Cambridge, UK: Polity.

Tomlinson, J. (1999). *Globalization and culture*. Cambridge, UK: Polity.

Tracey, M. (1998). *The decline and fall of public service broadcasting*. Oxford, UK: Oxford University Press.

Urry, J. (2002). *The global media and cosmopolitanism*. Unpublished manuscript, Department of Sociology, Lancaster University, Lancaster, United Kingdom. Available from www.comp.lancs.ac.uk/sociology/soc056ju.html

Waisbord, S. (1995). Leviathan dreams: State and broadcasting in South America. *The Communication Review, 1*, 201–226.

Waisbord, S. (2001, May). *McTV: The global popularity of television formats*. Paper presented at the meetings of the International Communication Association, Washington, DC.

Waisbord, S. (2002). Journalism, risk, and patriotism. In B. Zelizer & S. Allan (Eds.), *Journalism after September 11* (pp. 201–219). London: Routledge.

Weber, E. (1976). *Peasants into Frenchmen: The modernization of rural France, 1870–1914*. Stanford, CA: Stanford University Press.

Williams, A. (Ed.). (2002). *Film and nationalism: Depth of field*. New Brunswick, NJ: Rutgers University Press.

Williams, R. (1977). *Marxism and literature*. Oxford, UK: Oxford University Press.

19

NEWS MEDIA PRODUCTION

Individuals, Organizations, and Institutions

◆ D. Charles Whitney,
Randall S. Sumpter,
and Denis McQuail

T he mass media have been studied in reasonably formal and systematic ways for quite a long time, about as long as Western media systems have been composed of "true" mass media as we tend to define them today—as mechanisms for delivering content to large, heterogeneous, dispersed, anonymous audiences that have restricted opportunities to respond to the producers of that content (cf. McQuail, 2000). Because media organizations, industries, and institutions are sites of research—and at various levels of analysis, a variety of methods of studying them have been employed—we first briefly survey the history of systematically studying media, delineate the most frequently employed theoretical models used in the field, summarize an argument for organizing this study by levels of analysis, and then return to catalogue the methods with some research exemplars for each. We should note at the outset, however, that even though this is a chapter on research methods in studying media organizations and institutions, no methods that we know of are unique or peculiar to the study of them, and hence researchers seeking technical advice on methods should also consult more standard texts on research methodology.[1]

◆ The Advent of Media Sociology

The primary purpose of studying media is to understand why media organizations, a specific medium, or the mass media institution produces the kinds of content it does. The birth of "media sociology," however, around the turn of the past century, was *not* an academic enterprise but was in response to both practical and social problems engendered by the rise of mass commercial media.[2] On the business side, a nascent national advertising industry was eager to have credible circulation data on the rapidly expanding metropolitan press: The U.S. newspapers' Audit Bureau of Circulation dates from 1914, and "commercial research," such as magazine readership questionnaire studies, dates from 1911 (Beniger, 1986, p. 20). As early as 1880, N. W. Ayer & Son, the first national advertising firm in the United States, was publishing a national newspaper directory with independently gathered circulation data on the nation's newspapers and magazines.

Moreover, the rapid industrialization of newspaper production in Europe and the United States during the late 19th century triggered the systematic, if not yet scientific, study of media institutions as well. Sumpter (2001) notes that in response to public controversy over a "new journalism" that was commercial, sensational, and popular, the first content analyses were undertaken to document the actual content of the mass newspapers. In 1893, John Gilmer Speed, who had been managing editor of the *New York World* before its conversion to the "new journalism" formula, conducted the first recorded quantitative content analysis of a daily newspaper (Berelson, 1952/1971; Fenton, 1910; Krippendorff, 1980). Quantitative content analyses had been used before by Europeans to evaluate religious hymns and by Americans to analyze political documents and poetry (Kovring, 1954–1955;

Sherman, 1888, 1893. Speed, an amateur student of poetry and a relative of Keats, may have been aware of these earlier applications.

Speed's study, published in *Forum* magazine, compared four New York dailies—the *Times, Tribune, Sun,* and *World*—published on April 17, 1881, and April 16, 1893. Speed assigned the content of the newspapers to 13 categories, but he provided little explanation for how his classification system worked. Speed also used a unit of analysis, the newspaper column, which limited his ability to compare the newspapers. The *World,* for instance, employed a seven-column page format in 1881 but switched to eight by 1893. The *Tribune* used six columns; the *Times* and *Sun* used seven. Speed reported two major findings. First, the newspapers' size had nearly tripled since the 10-page average for the 1881 date. Second, "gossip," "scandal," and other sensational material dominated the additional columns. Crime news, which had not been used in 1881, according to Speed's coding system, now appeared in all but the *Sun.* Speed concluded that readers had not benefited from the newspaper expansion. Instead, he wrote, they had been harmed because news of "serious happenings" needed by readers to function in an urban society had been displaced by lesser stories that promoted "disjointed thinking" (Speed, 1893, p. 711).

A cluster of Progressive Era scholars adapted Speed's methodology to their studies of the "yellow" and "tabloid" press (Sumpter, 2001). Notable were civic reformer Delos Franklin Wilcox (1900), who undertook a massive content analysis of 240 English- and foreign-language dailies published during 1898 and 1899 in several major U.S. cities. Wilcox clearly explained how he derived his content categories. From the large study group, Wilcox selected 15 newspapers classified by "general appearance and reputation" (p. 77) as "yellow" dailies and 15 others classified in the same manner as "conservative" publications. He examined the newspapers within each group to determine what types of content they shared. "Yellow" newspapers, he found, commonly used crime and vice news, illustrations, and help-wanted, medical, and self-advertisements. "Conservative" dailies published political news, business news, letters and exchanges, and miscellaneous advertisements. Wilcox then used this eight-category system to code newspaper columns. In the process, he learned that increases in circulation accompany increases in sensational content. Mathews (1910) and Tenney (1912) could not exactly replicate Wilcox's findings, and both pointed to coding and definitional problems as possible explanations. Finally, Frances Fenton of the University of Chicago questioned the basic assumption that sensational content produced negative reader effects. Proof of this cause-and-effect linkage must be provided, and such a demonstration required more than a simple content analysis, she argued in a two-part study published in the *American Journal of Sociology* (Fenton, 1910, 1911). To test the linkage assumption, Fenton used several methods, including a content analysis of Chicago, New York, and Denver daily newspapers; questionnaires sent to prison and reformatory officials, juvenile court judges, and probation officers; reviews of court records; and interviews with criminal justice workers. The content analysis alone involved the coding of more than 10,000 individual copies of newspapers for what Fenton (1911) called "anti-social" material (p. 542). She concluded that newspapers contribute to antisocial activity because (a) publishers and editors distort or suppress facts when their publication would harm advertisers, and (b) readers who would not normally buy a newspaper do so when news treatments include "featuring, doctoring, and faking" (Fenton, 1911, p. 563).

However, early studies also had proceeded without a theoretically informed basis for predicting how the media might interact with other social institutions. Until those problems were addressed, the study of news remained stunted. Although Robert Ezra Park's ethnographic studies of the press are important, his greatest contributions perhaps are found in the scholarly essays that he devoted to the theoretical problems of media studies (Park, 1940). In them, Park worked out the framework for incorporating news into the sociology of knowledge and for studying the media as an institution. These contributions earned Park a reputation as the founder of media sociology (Frazier & Gaziano, 1979; Reese & Ballinger, 2001).

Park classified news as the oldest form of knowledge. The sociology of knowledge is concerned with the "conditions under which different kinds of knowledge arise and what the functions of each," Park wrote (1940, p. 682). News fell somewhere on a continuum stretching between formal, systematic knowledge, such as that derived from the natural sciences, and unsystematic knowledge, such as common sense. News's qualities, however, are so transient that its position on this continuum shifts. "News remains news only until it has reached the persons for whom it has 'news interest.' Once published and its significance recognized, what was news becomes history," Park concluded (p. 676). News, or at least the categories into which it fits, is routine, but the specific incidents reported in the newspapers are unexpected:

> The events that have made news in the past, as in the present, are actually the expected things. They are characteristically simple and commonplace matters, like births and deaths, weddings and funerals, the conditions of the crops and of business, war, politics, and the weather. These are the expected things, but they are at the same time the unpredictable things. They are the incidents and chances that turn up in the game of life. (Park, 1940, p. 680)

Sharing news or communicating it, Park believed, balances the competitive forces found in society. Sharing news not only integrates society by orienting public attention

(Park, 1940) but also transmits the "life history" and traditions of other social institutions and groups (Park, 1938). News per se is both a method of cultural diffusion and acculturation. As news spreads, the meaning of cultural artifacts, which can be different in different places, begins to converge and acculturation follows, Park wrote (1938), but many "selection" rules apparently govern this diffusion-acculturation dynamic because some news items travel farther than others. The more interesting and intelligible that news is, the farther it theoretically should travel, but this relationship is conditional. As social tensions increase, Park observed, public interest narrows, and the "range of events to which the public will respond is limited. The circulation of news is limited; discussion ceases, and the certainty of action of some sort increases" (Park, 1940, p. 684).

Park (1923, 1927) compared the institutional history of newspapers to the natural history of biological species. To survive the process of "natural selection," a newspaper needed to win the competition with other newspapers for readers, to interact successfully with other social institutions, and to provide social control for large population units in the same manner that gossip and public opinion do in villages or small towns. Park believed newspapers had very specific influences on other institutions. For instance, Sunday newspapers and their advertising columns made the creation of department stores possible (Park, 1923, 1927). By expanding the definition of news to attract more readers, newspapers also increased their political power because "news rather than the editorial" makes opinion in a democracy (Park, 1941, p. 4).

Park and academic "muckrakers" such as Fenton made important contributions to formalizing media studies, but they mainly viewed editors and reporters as passive conduits for the transmission of news (Frazier & Gaziano, 1979). They had little interest in how news workers shaped the news or in how news institutions, readers, and sources affected their decisions. By the late 1930s,

however, researchers were beginning to ask those questions, often with multiple tools such as those employed by Fenton. Their work, which often sought answers at several levels of analysis, deflected the institutional study of the media into the channel it followed for the rest of the 20th century. At the same time, too, research was broadening out: Although important contributions continued to come from sociology and social psychology, schools of journalism were for the first time contributing to media sociology research. Five of these post-1930 studies have particular significance. They are Harvard social psychologist Gordon Allport's (Allport & Faden, 1940) use of a content analysis of eight Boston newspapers[3] and of Gallup poll data to develop the rules of "newspaper psychology"; Leo C. Rosten's 1935–1936 survey study of Washington correspondents (Rosten, 1937/1974); Francis Prugger's (1941) extensive investigation of the backgrounds, attitudes, and opinions of reporters at a Midwest daily newspaper; Charles E. Swanson's (1949) "control" analysis of news workers and their readers in a one-newspaper town; and David Manning White's (1950) gatekeeper study of a small daily's wire editor.

Allport and his research associate, Janet M. Faden, hoped their study would discover the rules governing the psychological partnership between news workers and readers. Because their general research interest was public opinion formation, Allport and Faden (1940) selected for study the newspaper coverage of the 1939 congressional debate about the Neutrality Act. Their content analysis included all news stories, opinion columns, editorials, and letters to the editor published on the issue between September 1, 1939, and November 9, 1939. Items were coded for orientation (pro-, anti-, neutral, or ambivalent on repeal of the act) and news coloring (whether or not the coder detected the intrusion of the reporter's or editor's personal views).[4] In all, the study involved the analysis of 1,149 news items, 168 editorials, 483 letters to the editor, and an unspecified number of columns. The resulting data suggested to Allport and Faden the following "tentative" psychological principles: (a) News workers "skeletonize" public policy stories to simplify the issues and to highlight conflict, presumably because readers find fuller accounts "confusing and fatiguing" (p. 690). (b) The physical newspaper and its contents represent a highly structured and formalized "stimulus field." Editorial policy, the method of selecting letters to the editor, news coloration, and newspaper design are among the stimuli. (c) Based on a comparison of editorials with letters to the editors, the investigators concluded that editors demonstrate more emotional restraint than readers do. (d) Intensity of public interest in an issue, as measured by the space devoted to it in the newspaper, varies with time. Opinion polls confirmed this periodicity. (e) The more tension an issue causes in readers, the faster readers will seek relief.

Allport and Faden's (1940) study inferred news worker and audience behavior from content and poll data. Prugger, Swanson, and White—all working in midwestern U.S. journalism schools—wanted to describe news worker attitudes and opinions, their interactions with others, and the processes that produced content. Prugger hoped to learn more about the sources of news worker opinions and their beliefs about news work. To do that, Prugger (1941, p. 231) used questionnaires and interviews in what he claimed was the first study of the news personnel of a single newspaper, the 260,000 daily circulation *Milwaukee Journal*.[5] Prugger's reporters were often the oldest or the only child in a middle-class family. More than half held college degrees, often in journalism, but they did not believe a journalism degree should be a prerequisite for a news career. Most were 40-year-old social loners who preferred hobbies such as gardening or photography and who seldom joined clubs or political organizations other than the local press club. Unlike similar but later multisite or highly detailed studies (Breed, 1955a,

1955b; Stark, 1964), Prugger found no trace of social control in the newsroom, perhaps because the *Journal's* workers generally were content and believed their newspaper had a superior record for fair and unbiased reporting. At any rate, they were certain that policy considerations never influenced how the *Journal* reported the news.

Rosten's (1937/1974) book, based on research conducted when he was a University of Chicago graduate student, was the result of interviews with 127 Washington correspondents for U.S. newspapers, and it covered a wide range of demographic and attitudinal items; it is widely remembered today only because a majority of his respondents said both that they knew how their editors wanted stories slanted and that they "had had stories played down, cut, or killed for 'policy' reasons" (p. 352). This landmark work has been replicated at least twice in the United States, where less and less direct editorial interference was found (Hess, 1981; Rivers, 1962), and in Britain's Westminster lobby (Tunstall, 1970). Prugger's (1941) study produced a snapshot of the reporters, not a description of the news-making process. Swanson (1949) used a variety of methods, including newsroom observation, content analysis, interviews, and questionnaires to look for the "control" process in news work at an unidentified midwestern newspaper he called the *Midcity Daily*.[6] Swanson did the fieldwork for his newspaper ethnography between October 1946 and March 1948. To draw a complete picture, Swanson included editors in his analysis. Swanson found his news workers to be even more homogeneous than those studied by Prugger; however, the *Midcity Daily's* news workers believed a variety of forces controlled and shaped what was news. Swanson described them as being aware that they worked at "the crossroads among the pressure groups and powerholders" (p. 22) in Midcity. The editor ticked off the conflicting forces: liberals versus conservatives, labor unions versus management, a variety of civic organizations seeking publicity for their activities, religious denominations, political partisans, and unhappy advertisers. In the face of these conflicting demands, the editor and 30-member news staff told Swanson that they tried to function as a cooperative, integrative force for their community. When they were asked to rank traditional journalism values, the reporters ranked the 10th most important function as keeping "the people cooperating so they may discuss the issues" (p. 23). This function ranked right after reporting the day's events "without fear or favor to any individual or group" (p. 23). The news staff acknowledged they shared the power to decide what's news with city residents, the publisher, and business community. Later studies, particularly those that employed "thick" ethnographic descriptions, since have identified other participants in this news negotiation (Darnton, 1975; Gans, 1979; Tuchman, 1978). Although they were not asked to slant the news, the *Midcity* reporters admitted their stories were sometimes spiked for policy reasons. The reporters, however, felt free to criticize or praise the newspaper's performance.

If "media sociology" can be traced back to Robert Ezra Park, then the last of our "pioneering" research likewise deserves special attention—David Manning White's (1950) "gatekeeper" study of "Mr. Gates," the telegraph editor at a small daily newspaper.[7] White adopted a novel approach for mapping these news selection influences. In addition to observing the editor at work, interviewing him both daily and at the end of his fieldwork, and moreover performing a content analysis both of wire stories published and those that were rejected during a 1-week period by the newspaper, White also convinced "Mr. Gates" to annotate the rejected stories with the reasons why he spiked them. Many of the rejected stories were eliminated because of space, proximity, or redundancy issues; Mr. Gates eliminated a smaller group for subjective reasons (p. 387). White believed the latter finding indicated Mr. Gates's experiences and attitudes governed both the selection and

rejection of news stories. An aggressive multisite and multimethod extension of the Mr. Gates study by Walter Gieber (1956) proved that White had overgeneralized. Gieber used content analyses, ethnographic fieldwork, interviews, an experiment, and self-reports to study wire editors at 16 afternoon dailies in Wisconsin. His wire editors reported that they exercised minimal news judgment in their story selections because of deadline pressures. Gieber's series of content analyses revealed instead that the wire editors used "a statistically 'good sample' of wire traffic" (p. 430).

The White (1950) and Gieber (1956) studies are important ones for two reasons. First, the research allows the analyst simultaneously to make empirical statements at several levels of analysis[8]—the individual, the organizational, and, in the Gieber study, the industrial. Because "Mr. Gates" and his counterparts routinely determined, without consultation with others in the organization, what the national and international news content of their papers would be on a given day, *individual* and *organizational* behavior are one and the same. When Gieber observed a strong degree of uniformity of behavior across newspapers, he allowed generalization to the industrial level as well. The two studies, moreover, illustrated the strong desirability of using multiple methods to analyze news worker behavior, and they also stimulated examinations of the original Mr. Gates (Bleske, 1991/1997; Snider, 1967) and the gatekeeper roles of reporters and sources (Gieber, 1960–1961; Gieber & Johnson, 1961; Judd, 1961). Those case studies relied on ethnographic observation, focused interviews, and questionnaires, not quantitative content analysis.

In the United States, media sociology in the period of the 1950s and 1960s increasingly became the province of researchers in schools of journalism. As others (cf. Delia, 1987; Dennis & Wartella, 1996; McQuail, 2000) have noted, the disciplinary base of media studies, largely in professional schools, expanded as other disciplines' interests in media studies contracted, due in large part to widespread perceptions of limited or minimal effects of media messages. This was likewise true in media sociology, and in 1972, the sociologist Herbert Gans (1972) wrote of a "famine" in mass communication research, especially in what he called "institutional" studies—that is, research on the production of news and culture.[9] As noted elsewhere (Whitney & Ettema, 1992, 2003), by the end of the 1970s, a rebirth of media sociology in the United States had occurred, influenced by fresh theoretical influences from Europe and featuring research conducted generally at higher levels of analysis than in the pioneering studies. The relatively recent past has produced sufficiently large numbers of studies for two excellent collections of research spanning a variety of research methods and analytical levels to be published: Dan Berkowitz's (1997) *Social Meanings of News* and Howard Tumber's (2000) *News: A Reader*.

◆ Levels of Analysis and Theoretical Orientations in Media Sociology

The relatively recent past, too, has popularized the notion that it is practically and theoretically useful to subdivide media sociology—indeed, communication sciences more broadly (cf. Chaffee & Berger, 1987)—into "levels of analysis." At its most basic level of analysis, the production of mass-mediated symbol systems is the work of individuals or small groups. At a "higher" level, however, it is the product of complex organizations; at still another, higher level, it reflects the legal, economic, and other institutional arrangements of industry systems. Shoemaker and Reese (1996) speak of "hierarchies of influence" and identify five levels: individual, media routines, organizational, extra-media, and ideological. As they (see also Dimmick & Coit, 1982; Ettema & Whitney, 1987; McManus, 1994) note, the processes at

each level may be difficult to disentangle from the others, and thus the *research* conducted at each level poses distinctive questions about the production of media content; moreover, it is clear that in some "grand narrative" sense, *complete* explanations for why content looks as it does require attention to all levels in this hierarchy.[10] A full review of mass communicator studies at each level is beyond the scope of this chapter, but several reviews organized by level of analysis are available (see, e.g., Ettema & Whitney, 1987; Shoemaker & Reese, 1996; Whitney & Ettema, 2003).

Separate levels of analysis, too, generally involve differing theoretical orientations. In a literature review on the production of news, Schudson (1989) delineated three perspectives that inform research not only on news but other media content as well. Reflecting their disciplinary origins, he labeled them *sociological, political economic,* and *culturological*. Although not mutually exclusive, each perspective is grounded in a distinct tradition with its own assumptions about the social world and its methods for studying that world. The taxonomy usefully registers the increased theoretic diversity of communicator studies in the past few decades.

The *sociological* perspective in Schudson's (1989) taxonomy includes most of the studies cited above, as well as many of the "routines" and organizational behavior studies to be discussed below; in the recent past, too, it has come to embody a "social constructionist" (cf. McQuail, 2000; Scheufele, 1999) model that has given rise to a construct of *framing*. The majority of recent framing studies are studies of audience effects (i.e., that frames implicit in media content are learned by audiences) and of journalists' and other media creators' frames. Sometimes, these are taken as independent variables (cf. Gitlin, 1980, 1983; McLeod & Hertog, 1992), sometimes as dependent variables (Durham, 1998, 2001), or, frequently, as both, as communicators' frames are translated into content, which then frames future content that they and others produce.

We will pay scant attention to the political economic orientation here because it is the exclusive focus of Janet Wasko's chapter (see Chapter 15, this volume). It must be noted, however (see also Whitney & Ettema, 2003), that there is considerable conceptual overlap between the "ideological" level in Shoemaker and Reese's (1996) schema and the political economic work influenced by the British cultural studies tradition following, for example, Stuart Hall's (1980) classic "encoding-decoding" essay.

Schudson (1989), however, treats "culturological" theorization separately. Within media studies, of course, this realm of research is usually identified with various cultural studies traditions that privilege the text-audience nexus. However, even here there are two streams of research—that influenced by narrative theory and that flowing, again, from British cultural studies. From the latter perspective, Richard Hoggart, in his introduction to the Glasgow University Media Group's (1976) pathbreaking *Bad News,* pointed to four mass communicator filtering processes that shaped television news (and, we would argue by extension, most mass communicated content)—namely, those that related to the structural constraints of technology, time, resources, and geography; communicators' "news values"; medium-specific "television values"; and, finally and most important,

> the cultural air we breathe, the whole ideological atmosphere of our society, which tells us that some things can be said and others had best not be said. It is that whole and almost unconscious pressure towards implicitly affirming the status quo, towards confirming the "ordinary man" in his existing attitudes, towards discouraging refusals to conform, that atmosphere which comes off the morning radio news-and-chat programmes as much as from the whole pattern of reader-visual background-and-words which is the context of television news. (Glasgow University Media

Group, 1976, p. x, as cited in Eldridge, 1995, p. 8)

From such a perspective, then, cultural milieu serves as the overarching determinant of content. Below, we will offer several research exemplars from this tradition.

The narrative theory tradition has likewise recently animated communicator studies, and a narrative theory approach has been applied to nonfictional as well as to fictional content.[11] That news stories are just that—stories—was poignantly argued by Princeton historian Robert Darnton (1975), a former newspaper reporter from a noted family of journalists.[12] Recalling his summer job on the police beat, Darnton related an account of a dull day in which he found himself with no better item to write than a couple of paragraphs on a boy's stolen bicycle. A veteran competitor-colleague derisively, but apparently with some pity, typed out a different version. The young Darnton then phoned the boy's father with a few pertinent questions; for now he knew he had a *story* to tell. "Soon I had enough details to fit the new pattern of the story," he remembered. "I rewrote it in the new style, and it appeared the next day in a special box, above the fold, on the front page" (Darnton, 1975, p. 190). He got his first byline. Darnton concluded that facts and stories are mutually constituted: Although a story requires facts for its existence, the facts demand a story for theirs. In other words, a news story is, indeed, assembled from available and relevant facts, but those facts become available only if journalists know how to locate them, and those facts attain relevance only when the writer knows what to make of them. It is a story selected from a culturally given repertoire, Darnton argued. To this, Ettema and Glasser (1998) add, "The story lines that help to constitute the facts remain submerged in the unexamined common sense of the culture" (p. 152).

From this vantage, Schudson (1995) has famously noted,

The power of the media lies not only (and not even primarily) in its power to declare things to be true, but in its power to provide the forms in which the declarations appear. News in a newspaper or on television has a relationship to the "real world" not only in content but in form; that is, in the way the world is incorporated into unquestioned and unnoticed conventions of narration, and then transfigured, no longer a subject for discussion but a premise of any conversation at all. (p. 54)

An example of how journalists make sense of particular kinds of occurrences by invoking particular kinds of stories is Vincent, Crow, and Davis's (1989) analysis of the standardized story line in the network television news coverage of major airliner crashes. For journalists, such crashes are "the archetypal disaster of the technological age" and evoke stories with the theme of technology defeated by fate. There may be technical answers as to what happened, of course, but there will always be an eternal mystery (see also Frank Durham's 1998 treatment of the journalists' struggle to find a "cause" for the crash of TWA Flight 800). "The ever-present black box of airline stories is the perfect visual condensation of the fate versus technology conflict," Vincent et al. argued (p. 16). "But the whole concept of a 'black box' is invested with mystery and godlike omniscience, and the black box often refuses to tell what it knows." Whatever technical answers the authorities may eventually offer can never really resolve the eternal question: why? We can only listen in reverence and terror as the most ancient of stories must be told once again, as here in the form of an NBC report of an air crash in New Orleans:

Arthur Cunnings of Howell, Michigan, was in San Diego for the funeral of his son who was killed in a motorcycle accident there. His two daughters and three grandchildren were driving to that funeral from Florida when their car broke down Friday. So they got on an airplane in New Orleans: Pan Am Flight 759. In a week, Mr. Cunnings lost three children and three grandchildren. He was able to say today, "I cannot describe the sorrow." (Vincent et al., 1989, p. 16)

For other recent treatments of news myth, see Ettema and Glasser (1998), Bird and Dardenne (1988), Cornfield (1988), and Lule (1995, 2001). For parallel treatments of news as ritual, in addition to James Carey's celebrated 1989 statement of the idea, see Cazeneuve (1974) and Elliot (1972).

As James Ettema (2003) has noted,

Studies of news-as-narrative offer insight not only into the eternal question of life, they offer insight into the eternal question of journalism: what is news? The list of attributes or "news values" that journalists supposedly consider when judging newsworthiness typically includes the presence of conflictual or unexpected events, the prominence of those involved in the events, and the degree of impact on readers and viewers. In addition, the proximity of the events to the audience and the timeliness of the report are considerations in a story's newsworthiness. (quoted in Whitney & Ettema, 2003)

It is clear, however, that any textbook list of story attributes just cannot explain the diverse array of topics that constitute the news. What, then, does the press cover? Romano's (1986) tongue-in-cheek answer was "box scores, beauty pageants, press conferences, Richard Nixon and so on" (p. 42). Though Romano was teasing us, he went on to make a point that serves as a useful point of departure for any attempt to understand how journalists decide what is news. "The principles that govern those decisions, while rational, aren't scientific or logically compelling," he argued. "No one need accept them the way one must accept the rules of gravity" (p. 42). News stories, in other words, do not correspond to the reality of human affairs in the way that theories of physics, presumably, correspond to the reality of quarks and quasars. We should not expect elegant and timeless theories that can predict the sorts of occurrences that will become news. We should not even expect unambiguous criteria for recognizing news when we see it. Knowing what is news is partly just a matter of knowing what has always been news—politics, disasters, and so on—and, as Darnton (1975) wryly showed, it is partly a matter of knowing a good story when one hears it.

In brief, research at the individual level focuses on the characteristics (e.g., gender, ethnicity, attitudes, political or ideological biases, practices) of individual communicators or homogeneous small groups of communicators to predict or to explain continuities in content. For example, in concluding his study of "Mr. Gates," David Manning White (1950) observed (with real or feigned shock and regret, it might be added),

> Through studying his overt reasons for rejecting news stories from the press associations, we see how highly subjective, how based on the "gatekeeper's" own set of experiences, attitudes and expectations the communication of "news" really is. (p. 350)

Both subsequent reinterpretations of White's own data (Hirsch, 1977; McCombs & Shaw, 1977) and a considerable amount of later research have called this conclusion into question: As noted above, environmental constraints, routines, and the strong similarities between news coming into the editors' newsrooms and that which they process and then publish strongly suggest that other factors *at higher levels of analysis* exert stronger and more consistent influences on content (see also D'Alessio & Allen, 2000; Gans, 1979, 1985; Schudson, 1995; Shoemaker, Eichholz, Kim, & Wrigley, 2001).

At the next level of analysis up, the organizational, both different theories and different methods might be appropriate, and at still higher levels, still others might be. However, let us move now to examine a series of research studies that might be summarized under the heading of "manufacturing" news.

◆ The Manufacture of News: Key Themes

Research into news production in the sociological tradition, starting in the 1960s, has elaborated a number of tendencies that are encapsulated in the idea of news as a manufactured product (see Cohen & Young, 1973). Fishman (1980) titled his ethnographic study of news making *Manufacturing the News*. Bantz, McCorkle, and Baade (1980) reflected the same tradition of work by using the title "The News Factory" for their study of the television newsroom, arguing that a *"factory model* is a heuristic model for how work was accomplished." The shared notion guiding or emerging from research into news production (see also Berkowitz, 1997; Schlesinger, 1988) has been that news is largely made according to certain preestablished specifications as to not only form and composition but also content. News, as many have demonstrated, is a "construction of reality" rather than a picture of reality. This is not in itself surprising given the need to meet an inexhaustible and vast demand for such a staple media commodity, but it does sit oddly with conventional notions that contents are in some sense novel and unexpected and are also responses in the form of reports of unexpected events, claiming to be true reflections of reality. Lippmann (1922) had long before recognized the character of news as standardized, routinely produced, and made to order according to certain laid-down routines for finding and processing raw events from the public record. The main elements supporting the choice of a "factory model" of news production can be summarized under the following set of headings.

NEWS "DISCOVERY"

Following the assembly line image chosen by Bantz et al. (1980), the first stage of the manufacturing process is that of assembling the raw material for conversion into the typical contents of a newspaper or news bulletin. Several strategies have been described in research for organizing the search for material, although the underlying basis is typically laid down by a fixed allocation of resources to different topic areas and "news beats"—the places where "news events" typically become visible. There are *places* where this happens, and there are *people* around whom it happens, the people who are conventionally newsworthy. The places include law courts, police and military headquarters, parliaments, stock markets, and sport stadiums. The people include leading politicians, established celebrities of all kinds, prominent criminals or their victims, and so forth.

News discovery can also be accounted for according to the main sources of information about events that might be made into "news." These include news agency material (perhaps the most important single source of ready-made "news"); other news media that have appeared within the production cycle of the news organization in question; various databases, now including the Internet; incoming press releases from self-interested parties (a very large and productive body of material); routine material gleaned by the organizations' in-house reporters, following standard beats; and the results of intensive investigative activity by own correspondents and reporters (not rare but limited in overall yield). Many journalists also maintain their own networks of contacts or sources that can provide them with ready material, with some chance of originality in detail, but also likely to cover the same ground in the same stereotyped way as others (Elliott, 1972; Reese, 1991).

McManus (1994) classified the various discovery strategies along a continuum of "activity level." In his own study of a television news station, he classified three quarters of news used as "passively discovered"; 20% came from moderately active discovery and only 5% from highly active means. The key to this distribution is the fact that the more active the search, the more time or money it is likely to cost, and commercial news organizations typically seek to minimize costs in relation to audience attracted. He would call this the market model rather than factory model, but there is an overlap between the two.

LINKS TO SOURCES

One key to solving the problem of a constant supply of raw material for processing as news is to have dependable sources, but this can also mean having ties of interdependence with sources and opening the way to collaboration. An early study by Gieber and Johnson (1961) of relations between city journalists and local government officials reported a degree of assimilation between the interests of the two roles. They cooperated for mutual advantage rather than for the good of the readers and contrary to the theoretical independent informative and watchdog role of the press. Ericson, Baranek, and Chan (1989) refer to a special category of "source media" whose main activity is to supply journalists with what they are looking for on behalf of various source organizations that often have an interest in the news. The media concerned consist of press conferences, press releases, public relations, and so on. The organizations that supply news are not usually disinterested. Often, they consist of government officials, the police and other authorities or businesses, lobby groups, and special interests. The unwritten rules of journalistic objectivity seem to support such tendencies because "facts" often have to be validated as such by a reliable and authoritative source, partly to protect the news medium from charges of inaccuracy or bias (Tuchman, 1973).

Schlesinger and Tumber (1994) pursued this theme in their detailed study of the interactions with news media, and each other, among British criminal justice professionals, policymakers, and advocacy groups as sources of law-and-order news. Evidence from several countries has testified to the high proportion of material that is actually published as news that originates in self-interested sources or as public relations (PR). Herbert Gans, in his 1979 study of news content on national TV and news magazines, found three quarters to come from government sources. This is higher than most other findings suggest, but typically at least half of news originates in this way. The sources most successful at getting their "news" into the news are not representative of the community. According to Gans, again, these sources are likely to be powerful, well resourced, and well organized. They are likely to be "authoritative" as well as efficient, often with an official status or recognized community power. Gandy (1982) has charted the extent to which powerful interest groups provide the media in effect with "information subsidies" that also help their own causes. Regular access tends to be given on TV and in the press to the same relatively narrow circle of pundits and celebrities, leading to a relatively narrow consensus of information and perspectives on national media (Reese, Gandy, & Grant, 2001).

Molotch and Lester (1974) referred to those in a position to "make news" as having "habitual access." In their terms, they are also "event promoters" because they are sometimes in a position to cause events to happen in a way that will attract a predictable degree and type of coverage. This is in line with the notion of "pseudo-events," introduced originally in the context of political campaigning. Essentially, these are staged happenings, usually involving prominent and "newsworthy" figures. There are several implications of the tendencies and practices described. One, it confirms that much of the news flow is indeed planned and, to that extent, not really "news." Second, the sources are not at all balanced in terms of public interest.

Third, the established hierarchy or power and status are likely to be confirmed rather than challenged.

TIME AS A FACTOR IN NEWS MAKING

By definition, news is timely, and news media operate on fixed time schedules of production, with a cycle that may be one a week, a day, every few hours, or even more or less continuously. News production and news itself have to fit within the time available, with consequences for the kind of event that figures in the news and is most likely to have news value. According to Tuchman's (1978) study of news making, journalists and editors facilitate the allocation of their resources by typifying news events according to a certain time scale. They distinguish between events in terms of their degree of expectedness or prescheduling, ranging from those long predicted (such as an election) to the completely unexpected, that occur as the news is in its final moments of assembly. There is a third more or less "timeless" category consisting of "soft news" stories that are not tied to any particular schedule and can be saved up or used at will. Another dimension is news type, in which time is also a key component. A general category is of "hard news," which is always scheduled, with three subcategories: "spot news" (isolated and recently completed events), developing news (incomplete and ongoing news events), and continuing news (where stories are added to a sequence following a particular event or theme).

Preplanned events make up a large part of routine news coverage, but preplanning can have unexpected and undesirable consequences, from the point of view of accuracy and truth. Where news events are scheduled, they are also usually provided with a preexisting definition or frame of interpretation (see below) that the actual event may not confirm. The result can either be a distortion of events or disorganized reporting. A classic study by Lang and Lang (1953) described the news coverage of General MacArthur returning from the Korean War in 1951 as portraying a hero's welcome, when to direct observers it appeared low key and ambiguous in tone. Halloran, Murdock, and Elliott (1970) used the example as a basis for studying the reporting of an antiwar rally in 1968, showing that reported plans for violent conflict led to a failure to depict the relatively peaceful character of the event.

Time matters in other ways, especially in television news bulletins, where it is usually extremely limited and there is intense debate and competition over allocation amongst the journalists concerned and also amongst those affected by the news, especially political sources, which take relative time allocation as an indicator of favor of bias. Schlesinger (1988) refers to a "stopwatch culture" governing television news in the United Kingdom, with decisions about timing being seen as an essential aspect of professionalism. The general obsession with time in all media has a number of consequences. One is to reduce the meaningfulness of news when points have to be made in the form of "sound bites," which grow ever shorter. Another is the fact that items may lose a place in the news forever, if they do not find a time slot while they are immediately current. Third, it gives an extra advantage to well-placed sources who can time their own interventions and events to maximize the chance to gain access.

FRAMING

According to Entman (1993), framing is about selection and salience. It refers to the process by which journalists select topics, define the underlying issue, and interpret causes and effects. A frame is essentially a way of organizing otherwise fragmentary pieces of information in a thematic way that facilitates news gathering, news production, and, in principle at least, audience comprehension and learning. However, at this last stage, framing is more likely to be a source of bias and miscomprehension. A news frame has affinities with more familiar notions of news "peg" or "angle" or "theme," and it helps to connect apparently similar events into a connected whole. Tuchman (1978) likened a news frame to the "window" through which newspeople viewed and composed their picture of the world. Fishman (1978) used a similar idea of thematization in describing the "construction" of a crime wave in New York. Frames, according to Scheufele (1999), can be understood as either causes for the way issues are formulated or as consequences. Some writers would suggest that the professional rules of objective journalism themselves constitute frames; others, that media frames add to what can be observed and reported accurately and often introduce value judgments into reporting. It could also be argued that by establishing connections with values, they also establish the relevance of factual reporting and do help to make "news" more comprehensible and memorable. The problem remains, however, of reconciling framing with the pretence of objectivity.

Entman (1991) showed how two similar incidents, the shooting down of a Korean airliner by the Soviet forces and the downing of an Iranian airliner by the U.S. Navy, were framed in quite different ways, leading to quite different evaluative conclusions. The first incident was often framed as an unwarranted attack, an act of war, in the context of the ongoing cold war. The Iranian case was treated as an unfortunate accident and a tragedy, without any negative reflection on the motives or responsibility of the perpetrators. The example illustrates the fact that "frames" are rarely neutral or value free, not chosen by chance. They open the way to manipulation of news by interested parties and indeed are often used in this way, whenever a choice of frames is available. The research example cited above of reporting of political demonstrations in London against the Vietnam War (Halloran et al., 1970) showed media efforts, in line with the authorities, to frame the protest events as both violent and the work of foreign agitators. The struggle for power over media is often conducted initially as a struggle over definitions of events.

ECONOMIC INFLUENCES

The single largest influence on the production of news is probably that of money in one way or another (Bagdikian, 2000; Ettema & Whitney, 1994), especially where news organizations have a primary goal of making money. Even when that is not the case (there are nonprofit media and publicly owned news services), the high costs of modern news production and distribution introduce economic criteria at every stage, from selection to distribution. News that meets professional standards of originality and novelty value, as well as embodying production and presentation values, is bound to be expensive, not only because of the necessary costs but also because of market values under competitive conditions. This especially applies to investigative and other forms of depth reporting. There is no shortage of supply of low-cost content from agencies or free content from self-interested suppliers to fill space, but to be first and to be original with news almost always requires an organization to use its own well-qualified employees at all stages of the news process. It is the recovery of costs of expensive news that leads to strong influences on news content. If the main source of revenue is the paying reader, viewer, or listener, the audience has to be large or, if small, willing to pay over the odds for quality. The second case hardly applies to general-interest news services. To attract large audiences, news has to follow audience-maximizing strategies, with likely popularity guiding selection rather than judgments of significance.

Where advertising is the main source of revenue, much the same applies, with the additional factor of seeking to please and also not to offend key advertisers. Research into television news by McManus (1994)

makes it clear how the goal of maximizing audiences and minimizing costs has a clear impact on particular story choices, cutting across other journalistic criteria of value. Although well-established media companies, such as U.S. network news channels, could afford up until the late 1980s to cross-subsidize their news operations for reasons of prestige, news is increasingly required to make a profit for itself. The growing "free media" category, paid for by advertising, hardly makes a pretense of applying standards based on journalistic values and cannot claim independence of judgment in commenting on news. Although minority and alternative media can still offer news, and now more easily by way of the Internet, their chances of gaining a significant public reach are very limited.

To the general factors mentioned should be added the fact that established news media are likely to be owned or controlled by large media corporations or wealthy individuals. This both reflects a degree of monopoly and also opens the way for influence on news content that favors big business interests. Such influence is not unrestrained and is not often easy to demonstrate, but it does exist, with little effective counterweight.

◆ Conclusion

The study of news media production has broadened out and deepened considerably over the past century. The *themes* touched on here remain today much as they have been during that century, and, as we have noted, virtually from the beginning the methodological armamentarium of the news production researcher has included the tools of content analysis, survey research, and observation. We have demonstrated, too, an ebb and flow in theoretical orientation. We propose, too, that the recent past has firmly established the signal importance of production studies in the wider field of news media study.

◆ Notes

1. Suggested texts are in references.

2. Wartella and Reeves (1985) have noted that with the introduction of a new mass medium or media form, presumed social problems presented by that medium, rather than scholarly disciplines or theories, have uniformly been the initial stimulus to research. See also Delia (1987).

3. The eight newspapers were the *American, Globe, Herald, Post, Record, Transcript, Traveler,* and *Christian Science Monitor.*

4. To check the reliability of coding, Allport and Faden (1940) had two research assistants code the relevant items in the same mixed sample of 30 newspapers. For news coloring, the agreement was 95.9%. Coefficients for orientation of news stories, editorials, and columns were 86%, 90%, and 70%, respectively. An equivalent number was not reported for letters to the editor. These high coefficients, however, are problematic. The same coders scored poorly when deciding whether to include or exclude an item or when trying to determine an item's column inch length. For instance, the coders assigned only 66.7% of the same items to the news story category.

5. At the time of Prugger's (1941) investigation, at least one book-length study had been published of reporters from different newspapers but assigned to the same beat. See Leo C. Rosten's (1937/1974) *The Washington Correspondents.*

6. Swanson (1950) produced a three-part study of the *Midcity Daily,* but the final two installments dealt with audiences and their perceptions of the newspaper.

7. The term *telegraph editor* is now obsolete, as is its successor designation, the *wire editor.* Such editorial workers are now called news editors, and they select from news "wire" services the state, national, and international news and features now transmitted to the newspaper via the World Wide Web.

8. We discuss levels of analysis in the next section.

9. Paradoxically, his article was by way of introduction of research articles by young sociologists who would develop strong reputations for such media studies—Gaye Tuchman and Paul Hirsch—and it was at about this time that Gans himself was undertaking the research for his landmark *Deciding What's News* (1979).

10. The Shoemaker and Reese (1996, p. 64) "hierarchies" model shows its five levels as concentric circles, with the individual level as the smallest, inner circle and the ideological as the outermost one.

11. The following section is patterned after Whitney and Ettema (2003), in a passage written by James Ettema.

12. His father was a highly regarded foreign editor for The *New York Times,* where his brother won a Pulitzer Prize for international reporting.

◆ References

Allport, G. W., & Faden, J. M. (1940). The psychology of newspapers: Five tentative laws. *Public Opinion Quarterly, 4*(4), 687–703.

Bagdikian, B. (2000). *The media monopoly* (6th ed.). Boston: Beacon.

Bantz, C., McCorkle, S., & Baade, R. C. (1980). The news factory. *Communication Research, 7*(1), 45–68.

Beniger, J. (1986). *The control revolution.* Cambridge, MA: Harvard University Press.

Berelson, B. (1971). *Content analysis in communication research.* New York: Hafner. (Original work published 1952)

Berkowitz, D. (Ed.). (1997). *Social meanings of news.* Thousand Oaks, CA: Sage.

Bird, E., & Dardenne, R. (1988). Myth, chronicle and story: Exploring the narrative qualities of news. In J. W. Carey (Ed.), *Media, myths and narratives* (pp. 67–86). Newbury Park, CA: Sage.

Bleske, G. (1997). Ms. Gates takes over. In D. Berkowitz (Ed.), *Social meanings of news* (pp. 72–80). Thousand Oaks, CA: Sage. (Original work published 1991)

Breed, W. (1955a). Newspaper opinion leaders and processes of standardization. *Journalism Quarterly, 32*(3), 277–284, 328.

Breed, W. (1955b). Social control in the newsroom: A functional analysis. *Social Forces, 33*(4), 326–335.

Carey, J. W. (1989). *Communication as culture*. Boston: Unwin Hyman.

Cazeneuve, J. (1974). Television as a functional alternative to traditional sources of need satisfaction. In J. G. Blumler & E. Katz (Eds.), *The uses of mass communication* (pp. 223–231). Beverly Hills, CA: Sage.

Chaffee, S., & Berger, C. (1987). Levels of analysis: An introduction. In C. Berger & S. Chaffee (Eds.), *Handbook of communication science* (pp. 141–145). Newbury Park, CA: Sage.

Cohen, S., & Young, J. (Eds.). (1973). *The manufacture of news*. London: Constable.

Cornfield, M. (1988). The Watergate audience: Parsing the powers of the press. In J. Carey (Ed.), *Media, myths and narratives* (pp. 180–204). Newbury Park, CA: Sage.

D'Alessio, D., & Allen, M. (2000). Media bias in presidential elections: A meta-analysis. *Journal of Communication, 50*(4), 133–156.

Darnton, R. (1975). Writing news and telling stories. *Daedalus, 104*, 175–194.

Delia, J. (1987). Communication research: A history. In C. Berger & S. Chaffee (Eds.), *Handbook of communication science* (pp. 20–89). Newbury Park, CA: Sage.

Dennis, E., & Wartella, E. (1996). *American communication research: The remembered history*. Mahwah, NJ: Lawrence Erlbaum.

Dimmick, J., & Coit, P. (1982). Levels of analysis in mass media decision making. *Communication Research, 9*(1), 3–32.

Durham, F. (1998). News frames as social narratives: TWA Flight 800. *Journal of Communication, 48*(4), 100–117.

Durham, F. (2001). Breaching powerful boundaries: A postmodern critique of framing. In S. D. Reese, O. Gandy, & A. Grant (Eds.), *Framing public life* (pp. 123–136). Mahwah, NJ: Lawrence Erlbaum.

Eldridge, J. (Ed.). (1995). *Glasgow Media Group reader: Vol. 1. News content, language and visuals*. London: Routledge.

Elliott, P. (1972). *The making of a television series*. London: Constable.

Entman, R. M. (1991). Framing US coverage of international news. *Journal of Communication, 41*(4), 6–27.

Entman, R. M. (1993). Framing: Towards clarification of a fractured paradigm. *Journal of Communication, 43*(4), 51–68.

Ericson, R. V., Baranek, P. M., & Chan, J. B. (1989). *Negotiating control: A study of news sources*. Toronto: University of Toronto Press.

Ettema, J., & Glasser, T. (1998). *Custodians of conscience: Investigative journalism and public virtue*. New York: Columbia University Press.

Ettema, J., & Whitney, D. C. (1987). Professional mass communicators. In C. Berger & S. Chaffee (Eds.), *Handbook of communication science* (pp. 747–780). Newbury Park, CA: Sage.

Ettema, J., & Whitney, D. C. (1994). The money arrow. In J. Ettema & D. C. Whitney (Eds.), *Audience making: How the media create the audience* (pp. 1–18). Thousand Oaks, CA: Sage.

Fenton, F. (1910). The influence of newspaper presentations upon the growth of crime and other anti-social activity, Chapters 1–3. *American Journal of Sociology, 16*(3), 342–371.

Fenton, F. (1911). The influence of newspaper presentations upon the growth of crime and other anti-social activity, Chapters 4–7. *American Journal of Sociology, 16*(4), 538–564.

Fishman, M. (1978). Crime waves as ideology. *Social Problems, 25*, 531–543.

Fishman, M. (1980). *Manufacturing the news*. Austin: University of Texas Press.

Frazier, P. J., & Gaziano, C. (1979). Robert Ezra Park's theory of news, public opinion and social control. *Journalism Monographs, 64*, 1–47.

Gandy, O. (1982). *Beyond agenda-setting*. Norwood, NJ: Ablex.

Gans, H. J. (1972). The famine in American mass communications research. *American Journal of Sociology, 77*(4), 697–705.

Gans, H. (1979). *Deciding what's news*. New York: Pantheon.

Gans, H. (1985, November/December). Are U.S. journalists dangerously liberal? *Columbia Journalism Review*, pp. 29–33.

Gieber, W. (1956). Across the desk: A study of 16 telegraph editors. *Journalism Quarterly, 33*(4), 423–432.

Gieber, W. (1960–1961). Two communicators of the news: A study of the roles of sources and reporters. *Social Forces, 39*(1), 76–83.

Gieber, W., & Johnson, W. (1961). The city hall beat: A study of reporter and source roles. *Journalism Quarterly, 38,* 289–297.

Gitlin, T. (1980). *The whole world is watching: The role of the media in the making and unmaking of the New Left.* Berkeley: University of California Press.

Gitlin, T. (1983). *Inside prime time.* New York: Pantheon.

Glasgow University Media Group. (1976). *Bad news.* London: Routledge.

Hall, S. (1980). Encoding and decoding in television discourse. In S. Hall, D. Hobson, A. Lowe, & P. Willis (Eds.), *Culture, media, language* (pp. 128–138). London: Hutchinson.

Halloran, J., Murdock, G., & Elliott, P. (1970). *Demonstrations and communication.* Harmondsworth, UK: Penguin.

Hess, S. (1981). *The Washington reporters.* Washington, DC: Brookings.

Hirsch, P. (1977). Occupational, organizational and institutional models in mass media research: Toward an integrated framework. In P. M. Hirsch, P. V. Miller, & F. G. Kline (Eds.), *Strategies for communication research* (pp. 13–42). Beverly Hills, CA: Sage.

Judd, R. P. (1961). The newspaper reporter in a suburban city. *Journalism Quarterly, 38*(1), 35–42.

Kovring, K. (1954–1955). Quantitative semantics in 18th century Sweden. *Public Opinion Quarterly, 18*(4), 389–394.

Krippendorff, K. (1980). *Content analysis: An introduction to its methodology.* Beverly Hills, CA: Sage.

Lang, K., & Lang, G. E. (1953). The unique perspective of television. *American Sociological Review, 18,* 2–12.

Lippmann, W. (1922). *Public opinion.* New York: Macmillan.

Lule, J. (1995). The rape of Mike Tyson: Race, the press, and symbolic types. *Critical Studies in Mass Communication, 12,* 176–195.

Lule, J. (2001). *Daily news, eternal stories: The mythological role of journalism.* New York: Guilford.

Mathews, B. C. (1910, January 13). A study of a New York daily. *The Independent, 68,* 82–86.

McCombs, M. E., & Shaw, D. L. (1977). Structuring the "unseen environment." *Journal of Communication, 27,* 18–22.

McLeod, D. M., & Hertog, J. K. (1992). The manufacture of "public opinion" by reporters: Informal cues for public perceptions of protest groups. *Discourse & Society, 3*(3), 259–275.

McManus, J. (1994). *Market driven journalism: Let the citizen beware?* Thousand Oaks, CA: Sage.

McQuail, D. (2000). *McQuail's mass communication theory* (4th ed.). Thousand Oaks, CA: Sage.

Molotch, H., & Lester, M. (1974). News as purposive behavior. *American Sociological Review, 39,* 101–112.

Park, R. E. (1923). The natural history of the newspaper. *American Journal of Sociology, 29*(3), 273–289.

Park, R. E. (1927). The yellow press. *Sociology & Social Research, 12*(1), 3–11.

Park, R. E. (1938). Reflections on communication and culture. *American Journal of Sociology, 44*(2), 187–205.

Park, R. E. (1940). News as a form of knowledge: A chapter in the sociology of knowledge. *American Journal of Sociology, 45*(5), 669–686.

Park, R. E. (1941). News and the power of the press. *American Journal of Sociology, 47*(1), 1–11.

Prugger, F. V. (1941). Social composition and training of *Milwaukee Journal* news staff. *Journalism Quarterly, 18*(3), 231–244.

Reese, S. (1991). Setting the media's agenda: A power balance perspective. In J. Anderson (Ed.), *Communication yearbook 14* (pp. 309–340). Newbury Park, CA: Sage.

Reese, S., & Ballinger, J. (2001). The roots of a sociology of news: Remembering Mr. Gates and social control in the newsroom.

Journalism & Mass Communication Quarterly, 78(4), 641–658.

Reese, S., Gandy, O., & Grant, A. (Eds.). (2001). *Framing public life.* Mahwah, NJ: Lawrence Erlbaum.

Rivers, W. L. (1962, Spring). The correspondents after 25 years. *Columbia Journalism Review, 1–5.*

Romano, C. (1986). What? The grisly truth about bare facts. In R. Manoff & M. Schudson (Eds.), *Reading the news* (pp. 38–78). New York: Pantheon.

Rosten, L. (1974). *The Washington correspondents.* New York: Arno. (Original work published 1937)

Scheufele, D. A. (1999). Framing as a theory of media effects. *Journal of Communication, 49*(1), 102–122.

Schlesinger, P. (1988). *Putting 'reality' together: BBC News* (2nd ed.). London: Routledge.

Schlesinger, P., & Tumber, H. (1994). *Reporting crime: The media politics of criminal justice.* Oxford, UK: Clarendon.

Schudson, M. (1989). The sociology of news production. *Media, Culture & Society, 11,* 263–282.

Schudson, M. (1995). *The power of news.* Cambridge, MA: Harvard University Press.

Sherman, L. (1888). Some observations upon sentence-length in English prose. *University Studies of the University of Nebraska, 1*(2), 119–130.

Sherman, L. (1893). *Analytics of literature: A manual for the objective study of English poetry and prose.* Boston: Ginn & Co.

Shoemaker, P., Eichholz, M., Kim, E., & Wrigley, B. (2001). Individual and routine forces in gatekeeping. *Journalism Quarterly, 78*(2), 233–246.

Shoemaker, P., & Reese, S. (1996). *Mediating the message: Theories of influences on mass media content* (2nd ed.). White Plains, NY: Longman.

Snider, P. (1967). "Mr. Gates" revisited: A 1966 version of the 1949 case study. *Journalism Quarterly, 44*(3), 419–427.

Speed, J. G. (1893, August). Do newspapers now give the news? *Forum,* pp. 705–711.

Stark, R. W. (1964). Policy and the pros: An organizational analysis of a metropolitan newspaper. *Berkeley Journal of Sociology, 7*(1), 11–31.

Sumpter, R. S. (2001). News about news: John G. Speed and the first newspaper content analysis. *Journalism History, 27*(2), 64–72.

Swanson, C. E. (1949). *Midcity Daily:* The news staff and its relation to control. *Journalism Quarterly, 26*(1), 20–28.

Tenney, A. A. (1912, October 17). The scientific analysis of the press. *The Independent,* pp. 895–898.

Tuchman, G. (1973). Making news by doing work: Routinizing the unexpected. *American Journal of Sociology, 79,* 110–131.

Tuchman, G. (1978). *Making news: A study in the construction of reality.* New York: Free Press.

Tumber, H. (Ed.). (2000). *News: A reader.* New York: Oxford University Press.

Tunstall, J. (1970). *The Westminster lobby correspondents.* London: Routledge.

Vincent, R., Crow, B., & Davis, D. (1989). *When technology fails: The drama of airline crashes in network television news* (Journalism Monographs No. 117). Columbia, SC: Association for Education in Journalism and Mass Communication.

Wartella, E., & Reeves, B. (1985). Historical trends in research on children and the media: 1900–1960. *Journal of Communication, 35*(3), 118–133.

White, D. M. (1950). The "gate keeper": A case study in the selection of news. *Journalism Quarterly, 27*(4), 383–390.

Whitney, D. C., & Ettema, J. (1992). Current research on American mass communicators: Expanding the margins. *Mass Communication Review, 18*(3), 3–8.

Whitney, D. C., & Ettema, J. (2003). Media production: Individuals, organizations, institutions. In A. Valdivia (Ed.), *Blackwell companion to media studies* (pp. 157–186). London: Blackwell.

Wilcox, D. F. (1900). The American newspapers: A study in social psychology. *Annals of the American Academy of Political and Social Science, 16,* 56–92.

PART IV

SPECIFIC AREAS OF MEDIA RESEARCH

20

NARRATIVE AND GENRE

◆ Horace Newcomb

The significance of narrative and genre for the study of contemporary media can hardly be overestimated. Both are means by which the world of human experience can be reconstructed, rearranged, and reimagined. As ways of organizing, framing, and directing experience and knowledge and as industrial tools, these categories have been central to film and electronic media since the beginnings of these forms of communication.

Although both concepts can and should be applied to the structures of meaning in strictly "informative" or rhetorical works such as news reports, documentary film and television, and advertisements, this chapter focuses primarily on the functions of narrative and genre in fictional works of film and television. When appropriate, however, attention will be focused on other significant representational types. It is also important to note here that the focus of this chapter is on patterns generally associated with "Western" or "European" forms of narrative and genre, though it will be important at times to take note of this cultural specificity. Similarly, by way of introduction, it is equally significant to recognize that neither concept is founded in the creation, distribution, reception, or organized study of film and electronic media. Notions of narrative and genre are central to all forms of literature—and, in some instances, even of other arts such as painting, music, and dance—and to the study of those media as well. Indeed, drawing on this long history of the uses of narrative and genre is necessary to fully understand the significance of these concepts for media studies.

For example, there is perhaps no better illustration of the fundamental roles of narrative and genre than to notice their application in interpersonal communication grounded in human speech, in everyday exchanges with others. Ask of another any simple question, something such as, "What did you do last night?"

Answering such a question usually involves the making of a narrative. Certainly, no one would attempt to catalogue each action or every moment of the lived sequence time indicated as "last night." An appropriate answer would select certain events, highlight some of those selected, use others as linking devices, and move toward a conclusion. Even if that conclusion were no more "conclusive" than "Nothing. I stayed at home," a narrative would have been created, for "nothing" is an evaluative judgment and deletes all the things done there. It suggests other "something" alternatives that would have more significance for the questioner, and in these immediate, potential comparisons, a range of responses is implied and embedded.

If, of course, the events were much more involving than "nothing" suggests, if they were organized in such a manner as to invoke suspense, or laughter, or disbelief, specific types of organization might be used. In other words, the narrative might fall into a classification scheme—a genre. We might even suggest, for analytical purposes, that the question, "What did you do last night?" could itself constitute a specific genre that we might call the "stories about last night" genre, which would be distinct from "what did you do last summer" or "what did you do at school."

In most social interaction, a certain value is placed on narrative and on those who create good narrative—variously defined as entertaining, or enlightening, or informing. The person who embellishes, who makes good selections, who organizes, who draws us in, who allows us some sense of participation is important just for those skills. Our pleasure and our enlightenment is a part of life we appreciate.

Such simple examples suggest that the "work" done by narrative and genre can be understood as a process of rearranging the world for imaginative purposes. This imaginative activity occurs in at least two ways. First, the act of the one who answers the question, who selects events and orders them, is an imaginative action. Second, the one who listens, who anticipates, who believes or disbelieves, who laughs or fails to laugh, who places herself or himself into the circumstances by thinking something such as "I wouldn't have done it that way" is also engaged in an imaginative process. This "freedom" to participate in the constructed "worlds" of narrative and genre is perhaps one thing that contributes to definitions of being human. To "imagine" the future, or the past, or other worlds, or actions forbidden—or bidden—by our societies, enables a potentially rich consideration of and commentary on the actions we do perform.

This observation, however, requires central focus on yet another aspect of these two concepts that becomes significant for their study in contexts of contemporary media: The creation of narratives, as well as their classification into genres, is never a "neutral" act. The one who answers our question, the one who selects which features of "last night" to emphasize, pass over, or even delete, has the power to direct our attention, which also involves diverting our attention from other events. What if there are things the answerer, the narrator, wishes to hide from us? What if there are things the answerer selects as important but that for us overlook something far more significant? Indeed, what if the answerer is lying to us? Does it matter if the entire answer, the narrative account, is "made up"? Why and how is it that we value so highly the fictional worlds that "entertain" us?

From such questions, and out of such basic aspects of social activity, great and trivial art, huge industries, and, in the views of many who study such matters, powerful social and cultural influences arise. Understanding the roles of narrative and genre in media studies, therefore, requires rather precise study of those concepts and the wide range of approaches to them. Indeed, the study of these topics has produced an especially rich body of work related to expressive forms, a long history of engagement with narrative and genre. As should be expected, different theories (and theorists), different questions, and analytical strategies have focused on different aspects of the topics. Rather than seeing these as somehow more "right or wrong," these variations can be understood as an ongoing deliberation, a conversation of sorts, in which alternative perspectives enable a richer understanding, each offering reshaping the others as it forges its own argument.

Structuralist anthropologist Claude Lévi-Strauss's (1967) analysis of "binary oppositions," for example, offers formulas for recognizing relationships among features that have been used to examine both narrative and genre. Folklorist Vladimir Propp (1968) argued that "all" narratives share certain common features serving similar purposes. These "functions," he argued, might take varying shape in specific cultural contexts but could, on close analysis, be found to serve different narratives in the same manner. Tzvetan Todorov (1977) focuses the analysis of narrative on the shifting states of social formations, beginning in stability, moving through change, challenge, and instability, to arrive at an altered stable state "in the end." Seymour Chatman's (1978) study of the "branching" aspects of narrative, citing "nodal" points and movement away from and toward certain narrative events, offers yet another perspective.

Studies of genre are equally varied and suggestive of strategies for analysis. Much of the discussion surrounding genre relates to the ideological implications of shaping and organizing human experience in such specific ways, in forms that seem to have both an ongoing appeal to audiences and a sufficient resilience to be reshaped for social, cultural, or industrial change.

A key source in these explorations is Roland Barthes's (1972) *Mythologies,* a work that has generated its own body of commentary literature applying and exploring basic concepts. Many other studies focus on specific forms, such as the musical (Altman, 1981; Feuer, 1982), whereas others, such as Thomas Schatz's (1981) *Hollywood Genres: Formulas, Filmmaking, and the Studio System,* survey a range of film types. Similarly, Horace Newcomb's (1974) *TV: The Most Popular Art* examines a range of television genres.

In the apparently ever-expanding contexts of expressive culture, as new media wrestle with and modify traditional forms, even as "older" media such as film and television continue to churn out familiar examples, approaches to narrative and genre will require more precision. But the fundamental concerns—how, including the technological and industrial aspects, are stories told and experienced—keep us mindful of the significance of these topics.

◆ Narrative

A fundamental characteristic of narrative, as indicated above, is the arrangement of events in time. If we take as a central feature of this arrangement the Aristotelian dictum that all narratives have beginnings, middles, and ends, we must recognize or establish relations among these parts.

In *Film Art: An Introduction,* David Bordwell and Kristin Thompson (1986) offer a definition of narrative that suggests the significance of such an analytical approach: "A narrative is *a chain of events in cause-effect relationship occurring in time and space*" (p. 83).

A central question in the study of narrative, then, and one that is a good starting point for narrative analysis, is, "Why did it start here and end here?" A related question (or set of questions) asks, "Why are the events in the narrative arranged in this specific order?" What "causes" this narrative to occur and perhaps orders the causal relationship that follows? For analytical purposes, it is even helpful to ask, "What if?" What if the narrative had begun at another point, with another event contained within the narrative? What if the sequence had been rearranged so that the audience would have certain information at an earlier or later point in the narrative?

Such questions emphasize the fact that narratives are constructs, relatively arbitrary arrangements designed to appeal to certain desires or to shape certain responses. They also remind us that in certain circumstances, the audience has knowledge of "what might happen" in the narrative and that the creator(s) of the narrative can play upon expectation, defeating or confirming it, a point that becomes especially pertinent in the discussion of genre that follows.

To understand and make use of the constructed aspects of narrative, it is helpful to follow the work of scholars who make distinctions between *story* and *plot* (cf. Bordwell, 1985). In this distinction, the story involves events as they happened and includes all aspects of those events—as in everything that happened "last night." The plot, however, is the selection and arrangement of certain events, using "story" as the raw material, the body of resource events from which to draw—and construct—the narrative.

Clearly, one primary transformation of story into plot, of events into narrative, involves a reconstruction of time. In prose fiction, a writer might note the passage of time with a simple phrase: "As winter snows melted. . . ." Dramatic performances on stage might suggest time passage with lighting changes, fades down and up. In the quasi-literary form of the radio drama, we have a similar example with the classic line from narratives constructed for juvenile listeners tuned to western adventures: "Meanwhile, back at the ranch. . . ."

With cinematic narratives, the range of technical devices for indicating altered time, for changing story into plot, is quite large. As with printed narratives, dates and times can appear on the screen: "December 7, 1941." In sound, film characters can speak of specific dates and times of day. Passage of days and weeks can be signified by such clichéd techniques as the falling pages of a calendar or the churning wheels of a train. But more complicated alterations of time appear with the use of "fades" and "dissolves," as on the stage, to indicate passage of time. When the screen goes to "black," then fades into a new picture, we assume time has passed even if we are viewing the same people in the same location.

Flashbacks, also often indicated with a dissolve technique or other visual manipulation on the screen, take us into the "past" and beg the narrative question of what these past events will contribute to the plot emerging in this narrative. Parallel editing, however, implies that the events we see in a narrative sequence are occurring at the same time. We cut back and forth between events, having learned by experience that "real time" has not passed in the interval taken to enact the other scenes. The term *to cut*, of course, comes from the physical act of editing film. Pieces of film are cut apart and glued together again to construct narratives. (This practice is now generally accomplished electronically, with digital editing equipment that allows far more "efficient" selection processes from among a massive range of options for assembling filmed or taped content.) This physical capability to juxtapose visual content focuses attention on another aspect of the cinema, the ability to create narrative from filmed images alone. Some makers and theorists of silent film (Eisenstein, 1949) considered this the most significant aspect of the new medium and developed complex theories of narration based completely on relations among segments of filmed content.

Equally as significant as time in narrative is space. Again, literary narrative is quite capable of constructing spaces in which the events of a narrative occur. This is most often done with detailed description, though on occasion, a narrative may simply refer to a locale—"the desert," "the shore."

Obviously, narratives in film and television have advantages here. The photographic capabilities of these media are enhanced by the use of lighting techniques to give spaces more specific connotative meanings. Camera placement may limit or increase information available to the viewer. Design within space provides context for events that occur there, and the movement of performers to specific spaces may indicate a range of significance. Moreover, as we will see in the discussion of genre, space may carry significance for the meanings of the narrative in and of itself, as do the "wide open spaces" of a western or the tightly confined areas within a spaceship.

As with the sequence of events, the ability to edit film into specific spatial relationships is central to narrative. A cluster of conventional techniques blends events into visual sequences that contribute to meaning making. With the "eye-line match," the camera first photographs a performer looking in a certain direction, then focuses on what the performer sees. By filming "on axis," spaces are maintained in specific relation to one another, following the logic of conventional perspective. The familiar "shot-reverse-shot" or "over-the-shoulder" shot may maintain a conversation as if two people are speaking to one another in turn.

In point of fact, as this last example indicates, such uses of editing to construct the sense of a sequence are powerful devices. Films are almost always shot out of sequence. The last scene of a narrative could be the first to be filmed. Performers need not be in the same room at the same time to carry on a conversation. The "listener," who we see looking "at the speaker," is looking into a camera. The "speaker" may perform the same scene on a different day, looking into the camera now positioned from "the other side."

No matter the technological limitations or capabilities, however, no matter the construction or reconstruction of time or space, what happens within the most familiar cinematic narratives generally focuses on human experiences, some far more developed than others. These narratives often begin in a state variously described as "normal" or as in equilibrium. This state of affairs is then disrupted by an event or events, and the remainder of the narrative is given over to events leading to a changed state of affairs or to the reestablishment of equilibrium. In some cases, the disruption of the "normal" results in the presentation of an enigma that must be solved or, at least, explained. The sequence of events leading to this end state is often a series of complications that must be confronted or overcome. Questions surrounding the enigma are presented. Clues are hidden and discovered. The quest is completed.

In most media narratives common in the Western European American traditions, the attempts to complete the tasks set within and defining the plot—attempts to resolve the enigma, to reestablish equilibrium—become the responsibility of a central figure, often described as a "goal-oriented hero." This individual, usually male, must overcome difficulties and reassume a central position to satisfactorily conclude the narrative.

Within such commonly figured narratives, then, the sequences of events, scenes, and actions most often follow a logic of cause and effect. Each scene or sequence may in itself involve a beginning, middle, and end, and analysis of these scenes and sequences is central to an analysis of the narrative whole.

At this point, we come to a core issue for the study of narrative: Who is the creator of the narrative? Whose narrative is being constructed? A related question complicates this problem: Who is the narrator, and is the "narrator" the same as the "creator of the narrative?" Here I have purposely avoided the term *author* to describe the creator of the narrative. The notion of *authorship* is in itself a vexed topic and nowhere more problematic than in the study of mass media such as film and television. One school of thought suggests that the director of a film is, in some cases, its *auteur*. This term is variously used to suggest that the director has (a) created all elements of a film, from script

to final edit; (b) has final control over these elements; or (c) has established the "vision" of the film and stamped her or his concept on the elements involved. Challenges to this concept of authorship point out the highly industrialized nature of most filmmaking, involving multiple tasks and procedures that are impossible to control. Still other critiques argue that "authorship" is itself a sociocultural construct, that artifacts such as films or television programs are as much culturally created as they are individually or even collectively invented.

Neither side of this issue, however, quarrels with the notion of, the existence of, a "narrator" for narrative. The point is that the narrator is the voice or perspective within the narrative that guides the construction of the sequence of events, hence guiding the viewer's knowledge and perhaps reactions to these events. In some instances, the narrator is a performer, a character within the narrative. Indeed, one of the clearest indications of the complex nature of narrative and narration occurs in films such as *Rashomon* (directed by Akira Kurosawa, 1950), in which there are multiple narrators constructing the "same" narrative from different points of view—a technique that leads inevitably to the fact that the same narrative is, in fact, many different narratives and that this "external" philosophical observation is, in some sense, narrating the whole. More conventional narratives in which the narrator is clearly identified might be found in some instances of the hard-boiled detective film, or in *films noir,* where a central character "narrates" the film in the first person.

In a great many cases, however, the viewer's perspective on a given narrative is akin to an omniscient view in which "we" look "into" the world of the narrative. Even here, however, our perspective is limited, focused, forced, and guided by what the camera allows us to see and the sequence of events that constrains our knowledge. We may guess at what will happen—indeed, this is the source of much pleasure in narrative. We may do more than guess, relying on cues within the film that match lived experience or, as we shall see, more often match cues commonly found in other, similar films. In such cases, we may take pleasure from the confirmation of our guesses, or we may be more involved precisely because we do *not* know what will happen next or because our expectations have been defeated or channeled in new directions.

Among the most important features of narrative, then, and one of the factors that makes it useful and significant for human experience is its malleability. Narratives may, and often do, conform to patterns. But they may also suggest new patterns, new ways of considering the world, new perspectives on old topics.

◆ Implications of Preferred Narrative Structures

So familiar is narrative design that we often tend to overlook its highly constructed—one is tempted to say arbitrary—characteristics and, more significantly, overlook the implications of these specific features. But narratives also call for analysis of the factors underlying the specific formations described here. That is, the analysis must take into account the medium in which the narrative is created and the historical, social, and cultural circumstances surrounding that medium. Those circumstances would include, among other factors, the technological and economic resources available to the makers of narrative, the traditions of narrative construction associated with the "culture" in which it is produced, the expectations of audiences both within and outside of that specific cultural setting, and so on. But because of our focus here on fictional narratives, the circumstances would also include the intentions, capabilities, and resources of makers of narratives. For film and electronic media, these circumstances are, historically, directly related to industrial organization of a certain scale, and development of the "fiction film" or "fictional

television" offers a perspective on many aspects of narration.

As Bordwell, Thompson, and Staiger (1985) suggest in *The Classical Hollywood Cinema: Film Style and Mode of Production to 1960*, a key work on the history of cinematic narrative strategies (among other topics), nothing inherent in the invention of technologies of the cinema required "movies" to develop in specific ways, into certain familiar forms, or into specific narrative patterns. Nevertheless, they argue, by the mid-nineteen-teens, American film especially had narrowed into the structure viewers around the world recognized as the "Hollywood" film.

For media studies, the implications of this historical development are profound. One of the most telling implications is that films come to be associated primarily with entertainment. Once films are categorized in this manner, and once they are then distributed for profit, the entire process of filmmaking becomes highly industrialized. Industrialized filmmaking is expensive and potentially quite profitable. But to be profitable, films must attract large numbers of viewers. If certain narrative structures draw those numbers to theaters but others do not, the profitable narrative structures come to dominate the understanding of what constitutes "a movie," what it is to be entertained, what a cinematic narrative "is." No matter the specific content or, as we shall see, the specific genre, the conventional "Hollywood" film takes on those certain characteristics.

Thus, we can attend to the social, cultural, and ideological implications of reliance on the goal-oriented hero, the typical White male central character whose actions, choices, and values guide us through the fictional world he centers. We can attend to the prominence of heterosexual romance as a structuring feature in the Hollywood cinema, as well as the prevalence of coupling or marriage as a concluding moment in so many films. We can mark the subordinate roles of women in most of these films. We can observe the marginalization or demonization of members of other racialized groups or ethnic groups.

But such observations only begin to account for the implications of the dominance of specific narrative structures. Other factors include the fact that the necessary support systems are brought into alignment with the preferred narrative. Buildings and locations are constructed or designed to accommodate these kinds of films. Equipment is invented, modified, and improved to suit the form. Systems of distribution and exhibition must match the needs associated with particular film form.

Consider, for example, the expectation that fictional filmed narratives will be of a certain predictable length, roughly 90 to 120 minutes. We read of battles between studios and directors over films that are longer than this established criterion. But there is no factual reason for films to be of this length. Rather, it is the case that a film of 100 minutes can usually be shown more frequently in an evening, whereas films longer than 120 minutes would reduce the number of screenings in the social settings that have developed for the usual showing of films. Thus, even the notion of "going to the movies" is determined, in part, by the intersection of economic interests and narrative structures.

A similar implication can be attached to the ways in which creative personnel learn to "make" movies in particular ways. Handbooks and instruction manuals teach the Hollywood "three-act structure," and some go so far as to suggest page numbers in scripts as points at which certain types of actions should occur. Executives, agents, producers, and directors anticipate such structures and may reject works created on different patterns. If the "inciting incident" has not occurred at 25 to 30 minutes in the narrative, the movie is deemed "unconventional." When an unconventional narrative does become successful, it is often defined as an "art movie."

This points to the fact, of course, that describing the narrative structures of the "Hollywood cinema" barely scratches the surface of potential narrative strategies. Films are made around the world with different approaches to narrative. Popular Indian cinema regularly "disrupts" the central narrative with musical performances. In the classic Arabian narrative, *A Thousand and One Nights,* stories within stories connect in a variety of ways that do not fall easily into the conventions of "Western" narrative strategies. Multiple points of view, narratives within narratives, narratives that end ambiguously, in failure, without restoring equilibrium—all these are possible. A primary concern for culturally based analysis of narrative remains focused on the degree to which "Hollywood cinema" has forced such culturally specific narratives to the margins, even in their own societies. Still, it is worth noting that even the narrator of the tales in *A Thousand and One Nights* can be seen as a nearly classic example of the "goal-oriented hero(ine)," who exemplifies what might be the task of all narrative—to keep herself alive.

◆ Television Narrative

Though not immediately apparent, another alternative to classical Hollywood emerges in the structures of television narrative. In the earliest days of American television, a few plays written for television and performed live followed the more ambiguous structures found in dramatic productions for the stage. And a great many performative programs such as the variety show, stand-up comedy, the talk show, and children's programs were interspersed throughout the television schedule. Both types of programming—single play and performance—remain staple strategies in many national contexts that are, unlike the U.S. system, unable to provide financial support for extended fictional narratives.

One factor distinguishing television narrative from that of Hollywood film, however, resulted from the different economic structures underlying television.

Following the "broadcast model" developed for commercial radio, American television was planned as an advertising medium. Programs were designed not to "sell tickets" as were movies but to sell the attention of viewers to advertisers. The larger the audience, the higher the fees returned to producing and distribution/exhibition entities.

Much of the power of such a model lay in its domestic context. Although some alternatives such as "theater television" were considered, the medium quickly came to be designed for viewing in the home. A second fundamental characteristic of advertiser-supported television was quickly found in its regularity—the schedule. Popular programs maintained long-running places on the television schedule. New narratives had to be created for the same performers week after week. This fact was among the most significant in the shift from "live" to "filmed" television. Although it was nearly impossible to create an entirely new "play" on such a demanding schedule, it was quite possible to film new material for weekly presentation. Adopting familiar genres such as westerns, mysteries, medical and legal melodramas, and situation comedies, writers could regularly create "episodes" for familiar characters. The industrial structures of American television quickly made necessary alterations in the patterns of film production, and film studios, major and minor, became "factories" for the production of television. Most early fictional television programs did, in fact, follow the classic structure—beginning, middle, end; goal-oriented hero; and equilibrium disturbed but restored in the "conclusion." Thus, each week, the central recurring character of a western would defeat the violent intruder, or the police detective would solve the current crime.

The primary alternative to this narrative pattern was found in the fictions of "daytime television," the soap opera. Originally developed for radio, the soap opera was designed to attract female listeners/viewers, and, as the nomenclature suggests, many early programs were produced by the advertising agencies of their sponsoring domestically identified products such as soap powders. These narratives were programmed in short, usually 15-minute, episodes. But neither the story nor the plot was concluded in a single episode. Indeed, the longest running soap opera, *The Guiding Light*, began on radio in 1937 and continues on television at this time. It follows the lives of a group of families who are now in multiple generations and has appealed to multiple generations of viewers, often also members of the same families.

Although there were a few attempts to bring this continuing narrative structure to television, most significantly *Peyton Place* (1964–1969), it was not until the late-1970s that more significant programming trends adopted what is best referred to as *serial narrative*. Prior to this time, even with the limited success of *Peyton Place*, conventional wisdom throughout the television industry was that audiences would not return to "unfinished" stories during prime time. The prohibitions against the form often relied on condescending and patronizing attitudes toward the female viewers of daytime television, and the term *soap opera* was applied derisively to anything resembling serialization in the more "male-oriented" prime-time programming strategies.

With the astonishing success of miniseries such as *Roots* (1977), however, programmers began to consider the possibility of using the longer form as a means of attracting viewers. Indeed, longer running episodic comedy series, such as *The Andy Griffith Show* or the later *All in the Family* or *The Mary Tyler Moore Show*, already exhibited aspects of seriality in the development of their characters, in references to previous episodes, or in episodic plots that flashed back to previous narrative moments. By the end of the 1970s, with successful long-running programs such as *Dallas* and *Hill Street Blues*, television producers and programmers acknowledged the drawing power of stories and plots that could—at least in theory—go on without end.

This very complexity, however, can be seen as an economic liability in the television industry. Much of the profit potential for television lies in the repeat programming of content. This is known as *syndication*, the licensing, for a fee, of programs for use by other programmers. Particularly for American television, syndication provides the capital reserves for production of many highly expensive programs, most of which fail to attract viewers. A single successful series, however, can, when sold into syndication, fund many failures, and production organizations rely on secondary use of these successful programs by other television stations and networks and by programmers in other countries. But highly serialized series do not syndicate well. New viewers often see one episode and fail to watch others, thus losing the thread of the narrative.

As a result, modified forms of serial narrative have been developed. I have referred to one version as the "cumulative narrative" (Newcomb, 1985). In this pattern, each episode of a television series can "stand alone." That is, the plot is completed within the allotted time. Yet it relies on and frequently makes specific reference to aspects of character, motivation, and even story that have occurred in previous episodes. Regular viewers are rewarded with the pleasure of remembering these references, understanding complexities rising from new character developments, and recognizing the potential for future events and characterizations, whereas single-episode viewers take pleasure in the full completion of a specific plot. The "cumulative narrative" might be said to encompass something of a meta-plot that extends over the entire series, in a manner similar to, but distinct from, the fully serialized narrative.

Other series have come to rely on narrative *arcs,* plots completed within a few episodes, which allow the series to move on to another arc in subsequent episodes. These arc-driven narratives can be programmed as packages and stand between full serialization and cumulative narratives. Still other options emerge with new programming strategies developed for newer distribution systems such as cable television. Clusters of episodes are programmed serially but not in an ongoing manner. A number of episodes appear on a semiregular basis, allowing programmers and promoters to promote the next cluster by appealing to viewers to return months later to follow the exploits of characters. The fact that programs such as *The Sopranos* or *Sex and the City* are also distributed as video packages in rental outlets attests to the fact that they appeal to specific groups of viewers who may or may not follow the programs on television at the time of original programming.

Beyond the obvious economic advantage constructed by having audiences return week after week to follow an ongoing narrative, serialization offers potential advantage to the creators of such fictions and potential intensification of pleasure for viewers. Without the restriction of time imposed in most movies, serial narratives for television have the opportunity to explore events in a far more complicated fashion. The consequences of actions can be played out over weeks, even years in the case of daytime soap opera. Choices made by characters return to haunt or to relieve them in later sequences of events. Relationships are allowed to become more complicated and complex. "Good characters" can die, adding levels of emotional reaction for viewers.

In most serial narratives, the psychological and emotional aspects of characters' lives also become a layer of story and plot. If professions—policeman, doctor, lawyer—dominated earlier television, serialization allows for plots drawing on the personal "lives" behind the professional performance. Moreover, because serial narratives usually focus on groups, on ensembles of characters, the intertwining of relationships, both professional and personal, increases the potential for new story lines as well as for complications among plots and stories.

As a result of these and many other factors, the meaning and significance of events can be enlarged and made more uncertain, more ambiguous. They suggest that serial narrative in television is, in many ways, more like narration in novels, particularly the long, often serialized novels of the 19th century. If we return to the notion that all narratives potentially allow for imaginative capability, for the possibility of considering alternatives to our lived experience, these serializations can be seen to serve far more than escapist or economic ends. They allow viewers to engage the imaginative possibilities of choices in ways resembling those made in their own lives. And they suggest that television narrative can, though often it does not, become one of the most complex and complicated narrative forms in human experience.

◆ Genre

Genres are systems of classification or grouping. Traditional classifications of expressive culture originally grouped forms of presentation. Drama, poetry, and, later, the novel were listed as genres. Within drama, *tragic* and *comic* further distinguished among larger numbers of works, and within poetry, the epic, the lyric, and the dramatic forms contained specific examples. Clearly, in such large, general categories, only a small range of qualities sufficed to "place" a work.

In more recent periods, however, genre has taken on far more specific notions of classification, often focused on content. And even more significantly, genres are defined by their conventions or repeated, expected, to-a-degree-predictable qualities. Among these, in addition to conventions of character, setting, costume, and action, are conventions of narrative. Indeed, it is possible to see matters of character, setting, costume, and action as aspects or, at least, specified modifications of narrative. Put another way, certain narratives deal with similar topics and themes and employ similar character types (often resembling one another in physical features) to participate in similar types of actions and events (sometimes occurring in similar spaces). These narratives, then, can be classified as instances of specific genres.

As more and more specific characteristics have come to be noted, the concept of genre has been more widely and generally applied. Thus, across media—from literature to film to radio to television—patterned works such as the western, the mystery, the medical story, and the romance can all be considered genres. Even within these categories, further classification is possible. Thus, we have with the western the cavalry story, the trail drive/cattle empire story, the gunfighter story, and so on. Or within the detective story, we have the "English country house" story, the hard-boiled detective story, or the police procedural.

So common is this process of classification that it is possible to suggest that genres are completely arbitrary systems, created by critics who "invent" patterns as much as they discover them. This might be so in some instances of excessively fine-grained distinction. But the assertion is belied by the uses made both by creators who work within generic patterns and industries, from publishing to all forms of electronic media, which make use of them. Moreover, users of these patterned works—readers and viewers—display extraordinary knowledge dependent on familiarity with significant aspects of classified characteristics of bodies of work.

Despite any skill required, however, both the makers and users of expressive works defined as "generic" have faced forms of sociocultural denigration. Beginning in the late 18th century, genre works were often considered inferior to distinctive, highly individualized, "unique" works. Increasingly, especially with the rise of forms of mechanical reproduction such as film, the former were considered "industrialized" or "factory" works, whereas the latter were considered "works of art."

The counterview, that generically bound works of expressive culture are valuable in and of themselves, is eloquently expressed by Leo Braudy (1976) in *The World in a Frame: What We See in Films:*

> Critics have ignored genre films because of their prejudice for the unique. But why should art be restricted to works of self-contained intensity, while many other kinds of artistic experience are relegated to the closet of aesthetic pleasure, unfit for the daylight? Genre films, in fact, arouse and complicate feelings about the self and society that more serious films, because of their bias toward the unique, may rarely touch. Within film, the pleasures of originality and the pleasures of familiarity are at least equally important. (p. 105)

It is precisely this play, the oscillation between originality and familiarity, and the pleasures and knowledges attendant to both that make genre such a significant topic. But the relationship between originality and familiarity, between "product" and "art," does also acknowledge both the industrial/economic and the cultural aspects of genre. This relationship is fundamental to the utility of the concept of genre for media studies.

From the perspective of the film and television industries, genres provide substantial economic benefits. The stories/plots—the narratives—defining (and defined by) the genre are (to an ever more complicated degree) predictable. This enables producers who fund, distribute, and schedule the works to rely on an available pool of talent and technique. Writers who specialize in specific genres can provide material in line with the producers' expectations. Similarly specialized directors are skilled in managing the production process on tight schedules and precise budgets. Actors, despite their unwillingness to be typecast, are often identified with specific roles or role types and play to generic definitions. Locations can be used repeatedly or entire sets constructed for use in multiple productions. Props, such as costumes, weapons, vehicles, and decorations, can be purchased once with costs

amortized over many years and uses. In one way, then, genres are best understood as examples of industrial efficiency. It is this "assembly line" aspect that is often cited as evidence of qualitative inferiority. Adding to this evaluation is the factory-like use to which generic content is put in programming mass media—from the designation of the "B movie" as the film following a more distinctive feature on a double bill to the specific time slots associated with the situation comedy or the more "adult" action-adventure programs on television.

Related to this critique of generic works is their popularity, the fact that audiences rarely seem to tire of new versions of the same patterns. But it is precisely this sense of the popular, of the continuing appeal of certain narrative patterns, that complicates the critique. How are we to account for this response? What is the significance of highly patterned, familiar works for audiences/viewers and for the cultures and societies in which they are manufactured and experienced?

As the quote from Braudy (1976) suggests, genre films and television productions are powerful forms of expression. This argument depends on the assumption that popularity with large numbers of viewers rests, at least in part, in the fact that genres return to topics, issues, problems, and events that are historically, socially, and culturally significant. Moreover, as Thomas Schatz (1981) argues throughout his work on American film, *Hollywood Genres,* the social and cultural issues addressed by specific genres may be incapable of solution or resolution.

Thus, the western continually confronts a violent past, replete with divisions grounded in "race," class, and gender and played out in confrontations over territory, social control, and authority. The hard-boiled detective genre explores violent crime in an urban context, suggesting that contemporary divisions of class and gender, as well as issues of power and authority, remain as vexed as in the past. Science fiction allows for exploration of a range of topics and is perhaps less defined as a general category than in subgenres relating to technology, exploration, utopia, and dystopia. Social comedies in film and television explore interpersonal foibles and provide affirming laughter as evidence that all can be right within certain domestic or domestically inflected professional contexts. In all these and in other familiar genres, patterns of narrative construction work toward conventional conclusions.

And it is precisely these conventional endings that open genres to a far more complex critique. In this view, popular genres are inherently conservative, preserving the ideological status quo. In the western, certain racialized stereotypes contribute to the continuation of racism. In the police procedural, dominant authoritarian perspectives are solidified. In the situation comedy, traditional gender roles are confirmed.

This is a serious critique, often confirmed both by underlying story and narratively constructed plot. The key evidentiary factor in this analysis is the emphasis on repeated elements within the genre.

The counter to this argument focuses on differences within instances of a genre, finding them equally as significant as the similarities in the broad pattern. This view holds that genres offer a site for exploring alternatives to these views and sees the conventional endings as contrivances that cannot obliterate the conflict over social issues that constitutes the narrative itself. Recognizing genre as a site destabilizes the meanings conveyed. Instead of taking the familiar pattern at face value, emphasis is placed on a struggle over meaning, on the "work" required to reach the conventional ending.

In this view, genre and narrative come close together and suggest more complex explanations for the resilient "popularity" of generic productions. The industrial demand for "familiar novelty," for establishing a relationship between the conventional patterns and the "inventions" of material that "fits" those patterns, suggests that creators can place newer versions of

old issues within the expected formulas. Genres remain popular, in part, because they are flexible, resilient. The fundamental issues—authority, power, violence, relationships of gender, "race," age, sexuality, "family," and so on—remain present. Attitudes, behaviors, actions, choices—all available in alternative and imaginative form—can be explored in wild variations of narrative *within* genre.

And finally, these aspects of genre and narrative are again complicated by televisual practices. So dense and demanding is the television schedule, requiring "new" material in increasing amounts, that almost all conventional aspects of genre have become open to experimentation. This process is best defined as *genre blurring* and can be seen from the earliest days of television. A television western such as *Wagon Train* or *Bonanza* was as much a family melodrama as a more conventional example of the genre. Even a program such as *Have Gun, Will Travel,* much more closely aligned to the conventional western, usually focused on specific social issues. And programs such as *All in the Family,* from a later period, easily slid into noncomedic moments of great poignancy.

The trend has continued, particularly in line with the increased use of serialization and ensemble casts discussed above. Allowing police personnel, lawyers, or doctors to have richly personal lives explored in elaborately developed narratives shifts emphasis away from the underlying sociocultural "problem" that defined their "originating" genres. The result adds layers of significance by examining a far larger range of issues than those associated specifically with "establishing order," "administering justice," or "healing the sick." But the same "personal" problem continues to be inflected by those first associations.

Tony Soprano may face the same problems with his son as those faced earlier by Bill Cosby. The two may even offer similar advice for dealing with the problems, and there may even be a comic overtone to

Soprano's performance or something slightly fierce in Cosby's. But the generic support underlying each presentation and the elaborated narrative preceding the moment ultimately suggest differences within these moments. The result, as always with expressive culture taken at large and comparatively, suggests again that the significance of narrative and genre is the permission granted to consider alternatives to our own states of being.

◆ Genre and Narrative in the Postnetwork Era

Despite these general patterns of development and application, however, despite the resilience of particular narrative strategies and generic classification and discrimination, the economic and social contexts of television have in recent years shifted in such a way as to alter the application of these analytical categories. Here it is important first to recognize that within frames of the development of broadcasting as a means for presenting and experiencing forms of expressive culture, "programs"—the "content" of radio and television—were offered as segments in larger strategies of distribution. One of the most incisive descriptions of this form of experience was offered by Raymond Williams (1974), who described his experience of U.S. television as being caught up in the "flow" of broadcast offerings. Although there have been many applications of and arguments against the notion of television as a "flow" experience (notably, that viewers may watch specific programs or genres, not the entire schedule), the concept remained apt as an abstraction of the communicative model for most of the history of broadcasting. Put another way, it was an apt description of the model of broadcasting when limited to a small number of offerings, as in the case of U.S. television with its three over-the-air networks from the late 1940s through the mid-1980s.

If we describe this period and the experience of it as "the network era," however, we must recognize that the coming of many more channels of distribution via cable and satellite television, compounded by the use of devices such as remote control switchers, videocassette recorders, and digital video recorders has placed us in the "postnetwork era." Although television surely continues to "flow" all around viewers, indeed, in deeper and deeper eddies, the process of selection has become much more fragmented and segmented. In late 2002, for example, the portion of the audience viewing television networks broadcasting primarily over the air dropped below 50% for the first time. One result of this situation is the difficulty faced by programmers of attracting and holding viewers, of making them stop and watch their program rather than another program.

To accomplish this attraction, creators of programs, program buyers, and program schedulers have resorted to strategies of what John Thornton Caldwell (1995) refers to as "televisuality." The strategies so developed amount to a new set of genres, not distinguished so much by content, by cultural resonance or significance, but purely by the grasp for distinction, for differentiation among the mass of material available to viewers.

Caldwell (1995) offers five such categories. "Boutique" television is distinguished by its reliance on specific "designers," usually recognizable names from the world of film production who have moved to television. Notable directors such as David Lynch (*Twin Peaks*) or Barry Levinson (*Homicide: Life on the Street*) are strong examples. The "Franchiser" category is reliant on new video and digital technologies to emphasize visual surface and attach meaning to events. Here Caldwell cites events such as the Gulf War and the Los Angeles rebellion, events that were almost instantly repackaged into distinctive videographed images. More recently, we could cite the revisualizations of the attacks on the World Trade Center. His "Loss Leader" category focuses on such programs as the adaptations of well-known novels, usually as mini-series. These "major" television events can be heavily promoted, pushed as special events for which audiences are to make special arrangements for viewing. Although not programmed at the time of Caldwell's writing, we could include here the "event" programming of premium cable networks, such as HBO's *The Sopranos,* which, despite its relation to older genres, is programmed, packaged, and promoted as related to other HBO programs rather than in terms of specific content—"It's Not TV, It's HBO."

Caldwell's final two categories—two televisual "genres"—are the closely related "Trash TV" and "Tabloid TV." Trash TV is, in his words, made up of programs that "seek to overwhelm the viewer not with narrative or history, but with physical stuff and frenetic action" (Caldwell, 1995, p. 193). His primary example is *Pee-Wee's Playhouse.* Tabloid television, drawing on its print heritage, offers "heavy emphasis on pictorial stories and illustrative subject matter and an obsession with short, sensational topics" (p. 224). These programs "exploit the only viable presentational process left to them: the endless elaboration, dramatization, reiteration, and re-creation of some aberrant event or sensational hook" (p. 224). As should be clear from the preceding discussion, both these categories have also been "serialized" into extended "competitions" such as *Survivor* and *Big Brother,* and it is notable that "reality television" has become a highly successful genre, complete with its own plot patterns, narrative structures, conventions, and character types. As with other genres invented by individual creators, by "the industry," and by critics, "reality television" has already been divided into subgenres.

The developments Caldwell (1995) describes can be defined, as I have done here, as new "genres," or they can be seen as forms of modification, making use of newer technologies and techniques to emphasize certain qualities of older programming strategies. "Reality television,"

after all, relies heavily on familiar patterns of melodramas, often intensifying elements such as the "goal-oriented hero/heroine" and the significance of heterosexual romance. In either case, they indicate both the utility and the problems of generic classification, their potential for arbitrary application, and their use for comparative analytical purposes. It is doubtful that television creators and programmers, who commonly use more traditional generic systems of description to develop their ideas, will fall into comfortable use of categories such as Caldwell's. For analytical purposes, however, for the ability to think and write about the media without being drawn into "the industry's" own purposes, studies such as his should point the way for a more distanced and perhaps more distinctive application of theories of narrative and genre.

◆ References

Altman, R. (Ed.). (1981). *Genre: The musical.* London: Routledge.

Barthes, R. (1972). *Mythologies.* London: Cape.

Bordwell, D. (1985). *Narrative in the fiction film.* Madison: University of Wisconsin Press.

Bordwell, D., & Thompson, K. (1986). *Film art: An introduction.* Boston: McGraw-Hill.

Bordwell, D., Thompson, K., & Staiger, J. (1985). *The classical Hollywood cinema: Film style and mode of production to 1960.* New York: Columbia University Press.

Braudy, L. (1976). *The world in a frame: What we see in films.* Garden City, NY: Anchor Press/Doubleday.

Caldwell, J. T. (1995). *Televisuality: Style, crisis, and authority in American television.* New Brunswick, NJ: Rutgers University Press.

Chatman, S. (1978). *Story and discourse: Narrative structure in fiction and film.* Ithaca, NY: Cornell University Press.

Eisenstein, S. (1949). *Film form: Essays in film theory* (J. Leyda, Ed. & Trans.). New York: Harcourt, Brace.

Feuer, J. (1982). *The Hollywood musical.* Bloomington: Indiana University Press.

Lévi-Strauss, C. (1967). *Structural anthropology* (C. Jacobson & B. Grundfest Schoepf, Trans.). Garden City, NY: Anchor.

Newcomb, H. (1974). *TV: The most popular art.* Garden City, NY: Anchor.

Newcomb, H. (1985). *Magnum:* The champagne of TV? *Channels, 5*(1), 23–26.

Propp, V. (1968). *Morphology of the folktale.* Austin: University of Texas Press.

Schatz, T. (1981). *Hollywood genres: Formulas, filmmaking, and the studio system.* New York: Random House.

Todorov, T. (1977). *The poetics of prose.* Oxford, UK: Blackwell.

Williams, R. (1974). *Television: Technology and cultural form.* London: Fontana.

21

SOUND EXCHANGE
Media and Music Cultures

◆ Nabeel Zuberi

◆ **Disciplining Music**

Sounds have been recorded and played back through media technologies and music objectified in commodity form since the 19th century, yet remarkably, the study of mass-mediated music only became commonplace in colleges and universities during the 1980s and 1990s. Music teaching and research remain, however, scattered across such departments and programs as music, sociology, anthropology, ethnomusicology, cultural studies, media/communication studies, history, geography, education, and various ethnic and area studies. These academic formations have brought their own questions and analytical methods to bear on music as an object of serious study. The interdisciplinarity of music studies has been shaped by debates *within and between* disciplines about the relative importance of texts and contexts, social structures, and human agency. Arguably, we still do not share a clearly defined consensus about the direction of music studies.

MUSICOLOGY

The most obviously music-centered of the disciplines, musicology, has traditionally placed greater emphasis on musical form and style. But

◆ 429

critical musicologists have displaced the written or notated score foundational to a Western musicology tradition that privileges classical or art music. Against the notion of music as autonomous art, the so-called "new musicology" has produced semiotic readings that historicize musical texts. Musicologists have also turned to the performance preserved in the sound recording and applied close reading methods to folk and popular commercial styles such as jazz, blues, rock, soul, funk, and film music. Rhythm and timbre have joined melody and harmony. Many musicologists were instrumental in organizing initial interdisciplinary discussions that resulted in the formation of the International Association for the Study of Popular Music (IASPM) in 1981. Like sociologists and anthropologists, musicologists who study recorded music agree that musical sounds are linked to social structures, cultural processes, and the histories of particular groups of people (Brackett, 1995; Leppert & McClary, 1987; Middleton, 1990, 2000; Shepherd, 1991). Yet the relative importance placed on texts as opposed to people and contexts still fuels disagreements with music scholars in other disciplines.

SOCIOLOGY

Sociologists contend that formalism provides a limited understanding of music. They stress music as social activity and experience embedded in power relations (Longhurst, 1995; Martin, 1995). Sociology considers the political economy of music— its industrial production, distribution, and consumption—a particularly important critical intervention in the recent context of media industry consolidation. Through a series of mergers and acquisitions, the "big five" music corporations—AOL Time-Warner, Bertelsmann AG, Universal/Vivendi (UMG), Sony, and EMI—dominate the economy of musical commodities on an unprecedented global scale. Those sociologists influenced by Marxism have tended

to be suspicious of aesthetics as textually determinist and aesthetic values as markers of social distinctions and hierarchies. So sociologists have focused on how people make musical judgments. How can we understand, as Simon Frith (1998) puts it, "the gap between the sensual experience of music and the discursive means by which it becomes pressed into an experience" (p. 128)? This has returned sociologists of music to the unavoidable question of musical aesthetics (Frith, 1996). Yet musicologists continue to criticize them for their concentration on discourse about music and contextual factors at the expense of the music itself and its bodily pleasures.

ETHNOMUSICOLOGY

Ethnomusicology attempts to bridge the formal analysis of sounds à la musicology with the anthropological imperative to understand music "in the field," within the fabric of cultures—the customs, rituals, and institutions of particular people in communities located in specific places. The discipline has not isolated music as performance, text, or practice. Ethnomusicology's attention to culture as everyday life and its sensitivity to cultural difference have contributed to the development of music studies across the disciplines. By studying the music of "other cultures," regarded by the classical Eurocentric musicology tradition as relatively primitive or undeveloped, ethnomusicology advanced pluralism in music scholarship. Researchers sought to record and preserve local and national music traditions threatened by a hegemonic Western and globalizing music industry. However, this meant that the discipline tended to be suspicious of technologically mediated and industrially manufactured music as "inauthentic" and corrupting. Nonetheless, ethnomusicology has been forced to address the ubiquity of mass-mediated music in many cultures around the world and, ironically, has grown alongside the development of "world music" as a popular music market category since the late 1980s (Feld, 2000). Like its parent discipline anthropology, ethnomusicology has also become more self-conscious and reflexive about the way it produces knowledge of the "other." And with the impact of globalization discourse, the field has reassessed the notion of a stable, enclosed "local."

CULTURAL STUDIES AND POPULAR CULTURE

The interdisciplinary formation of cultural studies—fundamentally concerned with the relationship between culture and power—has cannibalized musicology, sociology, ethnomusicology, and anthropology and, in turn, has influenced these older disciplines. The widespread institutionalization of cultural studies in the late 1980s and early 1990s significantly shaped the emergence of *popular music studies* in the English-language academy. The term *popular music* remains a floating signifier that can mean any or all of the following: music liked by many people, music seen to represent particular populations, specific music genres usually derived from American and British rock and soul music, music that sells in large numbers or figures in polls and charts, or simply any music that is recorded and manufactured as a mass-reproduced commodity for the marketplace (Corbett, 1994, pp. 35–36). The latter open-ended definition tends to be favored by scholars in media studies.

In its neo-Gramscian mode, cultural studies engaged with popular culture as a site of ideological struggle within which popular music was one location for discussions of hegemony and resistance in civil society. In fact, much of U.S. media commentators' animosity to the new field focused on the teaching of apparently trivial and ephemeral popular music, which apparently threatened the canon of great works housed in the humanities of the Western university.

For cultural studies, the problem of the *popular* is central to a critical and political engagement with culture. Scholars continue to argue about the democratic impulse in the popular as well as its troubling mobilization in discourses of market populism and authoritarian populism. Many of these debates focus on whether studies of consumption, audiences, and fans simply validate or critique increasingly market-driven consumer cultures that perpetuate economic and social inequities. In recent years, the sociological and political economy wings of cultural studies have emphasized the need to return to analysis of cultural production to offset the drift toward consumption-based studies.

In the disciplines and "postdisciplines" that I have outlined above, the struggle for the academic legitimacy of popular music studies was waged primarily by Western academics who belonged to a generation shaped in significant measure by post–Elvis Presley rock, pop and soul, the civil rights movement, and 1960s counterculture (Grossberg, 1992). In the British context of postwar public education, studies of popular music were motivated by serious consideration of working-class cultures (e.g., Hall & Jefferson, 1993; Hebdige, 1979; Willis, 1978). As well as examining social class, popular music studies more concertedly considered gender, sexuality, race, and ethnicity in the 1990s when feminism, queer theory, multiculturalism, and postcolonial discourse ranked high as agenda items on and off campus. Courses on popular music integrating these political concerns sprang up as cultural studies gained a foothold in the curriculum. However, ethnic studies programs and departments such as African American studies and Latin American studies had also long studied music, though often without the same fanfare or support as new kid-on-the-block cultural studies.

POPULAR MUSIC STUDIES

Today, popular music studies remain marginal and dispersed in many colleges and universities, even though professional associations, several journals (e.g., *Popular Music, Popular Music and Society, Journal of Popular Music Studies, Perfect Beat*), publishers' series, Web pages, and a clutch of textbook readers are devoted to the field (e.g., Frith & Goodwin, 1990; Shuker, 1994). In one recent anthology, David Hesmondhalgh and Keith Negus (2002, p. 4) note that there has been no single synthesis of disciplines in an emergent popular music studies. A commitment to interdisciplinarity has not produced consensus about theory or methodology but led to the crystallization of the field around questions of musical meaning, value, power, industries, audiences, and place. Lawrence Grossberg (2002) contends that the inability of popular music studies to develop a specific theoretical framework around which to argue (unlike theory associated with the journal *Screen* in film studies) has been one of the failures of the field. Recent IASPM conferences attest to the continuing friction between musicologists and sociology/cultural studies academics. Each camp grapples with the other's technical vocabulary. Some IASPM members worry that the field's internationalism might lead to show-and-tell-and-listen about unfamiliar local music cultures with little sense of common theoretical urgency. Others complain that despite the wider spectrum of music represented and more cross-cultural exchange, the field is still dominated by the English language and by Anglo-American rock music (see Kärki, Leydon, & Terho, 2002).

If the struggle to have popular music taken seriously has (almost) been won, there is a growing sense that the emergent field might have made some major theoretical shortcuts along its path. In its efforts to institutionalize popular music in the academy, the field may have tried too hard to give its object a political use value as counterhegemonic. In celebrating the youthful, marginal, and spectacular, popular music studies might have been relatively deaf to the more ordinary, conflicted, and plural ways in which recorded music permeates the everyday lives of the vast majority of musicians and listeners.

◆ Media Studies and Mediation

Given the arguments and anxieties in the early institutionalization of popular music studies that I have sketched above, what do media studies contribute to popular music studies? Anahid Kassabian (1999) notes that "popular music is not an established field in the discipline of communication studies" (p. 116). Indeed, in most academic locations, it is still a relative newcomer alongside its siblings/rivals—film studies, television studies, and even "new media" studies of computer-mediated communication.

Media studies' emphasis on the apparatuses and techniques of particular technologies amplifies our understanding of music in films, videos, and the Internet; the material cultures of records, cassettes, compact disks, and radios; and the mediations of other hardware and software used in the recording and playback of music. The analysis of media technologies in situ might temper much of the present moment's techno-utopian hyperbole and force us to confront the continuities as well as discontinuities in the way different music technologies function in economic and cultural contexts. Jay David Bolter and Richard Grusin (1999) warn that in the current period of rapid transformations, "Our culture wants both to multiply its media and to erase all traces of mediation: ideally, it wants to erase its media in the very act of multiplying them" (p. 5). Music's multiple technological mediations offer ways of approaching the reality of "multimedia" that do not presume technological "convergence" as a unique phenomenon of the digital age. A return to the concept of mediation would thus appear timely.

Drawing on Raymond Williams's definition in *Keywords,* Keith Negus (1996, p. 70) argues that mediation should be considered in broad terms: firstly, as transmission (i.e., technologies used for the production, distribution, and consumption of the sounds, words, and images of popular music culture); secondly, as intermediary action by those cultural intermediaries involved in these processes; and thirdly, as the mediation of social relationships (i.e., differences in power relations that mediate the production and reception of music). Negus (1996) proposes "the concept of mediation as a way of starting to think about the range of processes, movements, relationships and power struggles that occur between and across the production and consumption of popular music" (p. 70). His approach has the virtue of not being technologically determinist, but it begs the question of how these different levels of mediation interact.

In an essay on mediation that indirectly returns to the textual/contextual tension between musicology and sociology/cultural studies, Johan Fornäs (2000) writes,

> *Mediation* as a key concept in cultural studies is basically contested from two sides. In a *reductionism of absence,* structuralist positions have reified textual autonomy in relation to both subjects and contexts, both of which are subordinated or reduced to it, and thus annihilated. . . . This has induced a sort of backlash in the form of a series of attempts to murder the text in order to regain space for either subjective experience or social reality. . . . A *reductionism of presence* strives to abolish mediation in favour of ideas of direct routes to external or internal reality. In such an anti-textualist cult of immediacy, a recourse to real subjective experience or hard social facts seems to escape any need for interpretive practice. (pp. 48–49)

Against both these reductive tendencies, Fornäs (2000) argues that we need to consider the material relations between texts, contexts, and subjects carefully, for "in mediated action, people use texts as cultural tools to create collective and individual identities" (p. 58). But how do these actors and forces interact? Negus (1996) draws on Stuart Hall's notion of "articulation" (Grossberg, 1986) to describe the links or connections made between different elements in an historical conjuncture, but Fornäs (2000) notes that the concept "unfortunately remains rather vague in its applications" (p. 53). John Downing (1996) has also pointed out that the term *articulation* is "either relatively banal, or bears such a gigantic weight that it cracks under the strain" (p. 214).

A modest critical step forward might first involve foregrounding the multiple technological mediations of music. Old and new academic formations have had to address the impact of sound-recording technologies and other media on music cultures. For scholars in media studies, these mediations usually offer the starting point for analysis. The strongest work in the field, however, is not media centric in its examination of the relations between music, media, culture, society, economics, and politics.

◆ The Social Life of Music Technologies

Technologies consist of techniques, discourses and representations, processes and practices in everyday life, and the materiality of machines, devices, objects, and artifacts. In line with developments in other areas of interdisciplinary media and cultural studies, work on music technologies increasingly examines the social life of these technologies. Timothy Taylor (2001) argues for a "practice theory" because

> any music technology . . . both acts on its users and is continually acted on by them; MP3s—or any software or hardware— have designed into them specific uses, which are followed by listeners, but at the same time, listeners through their practices undermine, add to, and modify those uses in a never-ending process. (p. 38)

Tia DeNora (2000) suggests that research into the ways that the specific properties of materials are appropriated in social and psychological processes illuminates "the social-technical *mélange* through which forms of agency and social order(s) are produced and held in place" (p. 36). Her *Music in Everyday Life* examines the uses of recorded music in hospital therapy, airplanes, aerobics, retail spaces, the romantic interludes of "intimate culture," and collective gatherings such as parties. Michael Bull's (2000) study of personal stereos in Britain combines a critical phenomenology of use with ethnographic methods, building on other studies of these mobile music devices (Du Gay, Hall, Janes, Mackay, & Negus, 1997). In her anthropology of Zambian radio culture, Debra Spitulnik (2002) points out that status, kinship networks, and economic factors make radio largely an outdoor device. Studies of karaoke singing illustrate the "liveness" of mediated performance in bars (Drew, 2001; Mitsui & Hosokawa, 1998). The emerging study of "piped" or background mood music as ways of ordering commercial and public spaces reveals new listening subjectivities in environments and activities filled with mediated music (Kassabian, 1999; Lanza, 1994). Such research influenced by theories of everyday life contributes to a critical theory of music technology as both commodity form *and* creative domain.

The meaning of music has been produced across the technological "sites" of print, photography, radio, film, television, video, records, cassettes, CDs, MP3 files, and so on, as well as amplified concert performances "mediated in the flesh." For most of its life as media, music has circulated in various commodity forms across related media industries. Music cultures develop as *assemblages* of old and new technologies. Many academic studies across the disciplines attest to the uneven distribution of music technologies as artifacts from context to context. For example, 7-inch vinyl record singles retain powerful currency in Jamaican sound system culture (Stolzoff, 2000) but are no longer produced in many countries. Twelve-inch vinyl singles pressed in Europe and the Americas revolve in transnational dance music scenes and networks associated with hip-hop, house, techno, and their various subgenres, accruing different types of value and cultural capital as they travel and are grounded in particular locations (Fikentscher, 2000). Yet 12-inch vinyl has all but disappeared in India, one of the fastest growing national markets for recorded music. The compact disk may be the dominant legal format in Australasia, Europe, and North America, but the humble cassette remains the most common and affordable music commodity in the Indian marketplace (Manuel, 1993). This mix of old and new media use reminds us of the difficulty in constructing an "evolutionist" narrative of music technologies.

TECHNOLOGICAL MEDIATION AND DISCOURSES OF MUSICAL AUTHENTICITY

Despite more than a century of industrialized recording that enabled music to become mobile matter in time and space, music technology studies have had to tackle resilient popular discourses that pit the "authentic" presence of the "live" unmediated music experience (whether produced or consumed) against the inauthentic fabrication of mediated music. Fans and critics have judged the value of musical forms and practices along a continuum of different mediations that include instruments and various audio and audiovisual media. Anxieties about music's commodification in devices and artifacts continue to haunt approaches to technology. Media studies keep returning (like a James Brown loop/sample) to the debates about art's mass reproducibility between Theodor Adorno and Walter Benjamin, even though only the former wrote much about music. The tension between the economic rationalization of media technologies and their democratic potential reverberates through music media studies. Fears lurk that electrical, electronic, and now digital technologies of production, reproduction, transmission, distribution, and consumption wither the power and immediacy of music in the collective and communal realm, sacrificing its life as communication between musicians and audiences in public spaces for canned music in the more privatized spaces of headphones, homes, and automobiles (Attali, 1985). But as Frith (2001) points out,

> The effect of twentieth-century media was less to privatise musical and other cultural experiences than to blur the distinction between the public and private spheres. . . . Rather than talking about the privatisation of music we should, perhaps, see music as the medium through which we negotiate the complex relations between our public and our private selves. . . . What has mattered for sheet music sellers and film star makers, for record companies and radio programmers, has not been the privatisation of music but its individualisation. (pp. 37–38)

◆ *Technologies and Musicianship*

A number of historical studies describe how technological mediations were integral to the changing sound of music in the 20th century (Chanan, 1995; Gronow & Saunio, 1998; Jones, 1992). In the composition/production of recorded music, the electric microphone facilitated more intimate vocal styles and made certain instruments audible for the first time in recordings. Magnetic tape and multi-track recording made recorded sounds more malleable after the fact of performance in the sound mixes of Glenn Gould, Karlheinz Stockhausen, and Miles Davis. The valve amplifier generated new sounds for instruments such as the electric guitar in live and studio performance. The studio console, with its many novel sound effects, became at

least another musical instrument in its own right in the work of producers and engineers such as Sam Phillips, Phil Spector, Joe Meek, Brian Wilson, George Martin, Lee Perry, and King Tubby.

The academic rise of popular music studies in the 1980s and 1990s coincided with the dissemination of digital technologies such as sequencers and samplers, which enabled the production of new music through the almost infinite recombination and treatment of previously recorded sounds. Academics tried to come to terms with digitization's effects on practices and discourses of musicianship. Andrew Goodwin (1992) argued that relatively inexpensive digital machinery facilitated greater access to the means of music production but that male-dominated cultures of music making still predominated. Paul Théberge (1997) contended that manufacturers of digital instruments such as Roland and Korg rationalize composition through their interfaces and programming options. Computer-made music may be indicative of broader developments in technical-creative labor, the "downsizing" and miniaturization of music production most sharply represented by the growing numbers of DJs, home studio producers and laptop musicians in commercial dance music, and experimental "electronica." Elie During (2002) suggests that these musical fields mark a significant shift to a craft regime of authorship:

> But contrary to the authorship of the author (composer or performer), the craftsman's authorship does not function like a principle of rarefaction (limiting the circulation of cultural goods, and the proliferation of meaning); on the contrary it seems to authorise and to beckon unbounded reproduction and transformation. It is above all characterised by a certain ethic of musical work, manifested by increased control over the whole production line. (p. 45)

The discourse of musicians, fans, and journalists familiar with this new technological terrain often, however, invokes quite traditional romantic ideas about art, authorship, and creativity. And producers such as Moby, Moodymann, and Fennesz have developed hybrid modes of recording and performance incorporating analog and digital media—the playing of "real" instruments with "pushing buttons live," as DJs Shadow, Cut Chemist, and Nu Mark put it in the title of one of their compositions.

Much of the academic writing and serious journalism about digital music has focused on the practice of sampling. Initial approaches enthused about the punk-meets-postmodernism aesthetics of détournement and the "plunderphonics" of artists such as John Oswald, Steinski, the Bomb Squad, Prince Paul, and M/A/R/R/S. But studies of sampling soon turned to the increasing economic and legislative regulation of sound bytes. Debates about the concepts and legal definitions of musical creativity and originality, intellectual property, and copyright dominated this second wave of sampling scholarship (Frith, 1993). As the practice has become ubiquitous across music genres, studies focus more on the ethical dimension—the moral responsibility of music producers in the exchange, appropriation, or "rip-off" of sounds. Musicians in the wealthy nations continue to disproportionately profit from sampling the recorded music of those with less power in transnational music economies (see Born & Hesmondhalgh, 2000).

The debates around sampling remind us that technologies of music production, distribution, and consumption have been intimately intertwined and are not neatly separated domains in the history of recorded music. Tricia Rose (1994) argues that sampling technology enables history-and-memory work as it holds and releases sound fragments from the recorded archive. The impact of digitization on listening, popular memory, and music historiography has yet to be gauged in any comprehensive scholarly study. With music transformed into bits and bytes in a digital culture of miniaturization, the storage capacity of musical machinery accommodates an expansive sonic archive. Compact disk technology enables music companies to profitably mine the past with rereleases from their back catalogues. These labels, as well as DJs and compilers of CDs, can reorder and reshape the history and meaning of music movements, genres, and local and national music traditions. Archivist labels such as Strut, Soul Jazz, and Rhino also serve a pedagogic function with their compilations of old recordings.

TECHNO-CULTURES, IDENTITIES, AND COMMUNITIES

Historical studies reveal that musical technologies and artifacts have played key roles in the formation of both subjective and collective identities. In her study of early women's blues recordings in the 1920s, Angela Davis (1998) describes how the blues as "the predominant postslavery African-American musical form . . . articulated a new valuation of individual emotional needs and desires" (p. 5). As the blues "came to displace sacred music in the everyday lives of black people, it both reflected and helped to construct a new black consciousness" (Davis, 1998, pp. 5–6). Billie Holiday learned to sing the blues in large part from the records of Bessie Smith that she listened to, rather than live performances. In his exemplary history of early American phonography, William Kenney (1999) argues that social listening in women's groups, gramophone clubs, and other social organizations acknowledged marginalized social formations whose expressive modes circulated *on wax,* contributing to the creation of collective memory and identity. These identities included emergent *cultures* as well as *markets* for hillbilly/country music and African American "race" records. The time-traveling capabilities of music media artifacts can change the course of music history. For example, Harry Smith's *Anthology of American Folk Music* (1952) comprised a six-record set of almost forgotten recordings from the 1920s and 1930s, idiosyncratically compiled and annotated by a maverick record collector. Following its 1997 reissue as a six-CD box set by Smithsonian Folkways, Greil Marcus (1997) wrote that the *Anthology* presented a sonic history of the "the old, weird America" and inspired the folk music movement during late McCarthyism and the cold war.

Scholars now take for granted that music recordings contribute to the contours of popular memory (Lipsitz, 1990). A film such as Woody Allen's *Radio Days* (1984) meditates on the relationship between private and public memory switched on by songs on the wireless. Radio imagined local, regional, and national communities of consumers and citizens who might never encounter each other in their local bars or musical venues. Thus, rhythm and blues crossed over to White America and was born again as rock 'n' roll in the 1950s. Radio solidified mass markets for advertisers and then helped to fragment them into niche demographics at home and behind the wheel. North American scholarship on the medium waned as television usurped radio's cultural and economic position in the 1950s. But Michele Hilmes (2002) notes a recent resurgence in interest because

> radio's demographically fragmented status made it a perfect arena in which to observe the operations of the many "subaltern counterpublics" . . . that had adopted the relatively low-cost and interactive medium as a place to mark out new forms of cultural identity and debate. (p. 11)

Free and pirate radio continue to provide models for participatory media communication taken up in the analysis of other technologies such as audiocassette tapes (James, 1992; Strauss, 1993). Bootleg tape trading by Grateful Dead fans, for example, constituted a networked community that became one template for the Internet file sharing of music.

Any utopianism about such technologically connected "virtual communities" needs to be tempered by analysis of the forces that structure and delimit their agency. In his account of hip-hop's transition from the primary arena of live performance to mediated narrative, Greg Dimitriadis (2001) describes how "rap moved from a local, party-oriented art form to one driven by closed-song structure, self-contained texts, and popular filmic images over the past 20 years" (p. 33). Rap is now primarily studio art, distributed by a global music industry that relies increasingly on visual media for the promotion of its audio products. Brian Cross (1993) has represented a lively but still fragile and besieged Los Angeles hip-hop culture composed of open microphone sessions in clubs, turntables, record collections, mixers, and samplers in homes, tapes circulated amongst friends, a few radio shows, and the poetics of DJs, MCs, break dancers, graffiti artists, and rappers. Such local cultures have to contend with heavily regulated and policed urban environments with few venues to play and limited opportunities (see Rose, 1994, for a New York City comparison).

THE VISUAL ECONOMY OF MUSIC

Debates about what John Mundy (1999) terms the "visual economy of popular music" highlight the issues and anxieties around the increasing "convergence" of media and media studies. Record sleeves, promotional posters, press photography, film, television, and video have substituted the image for the musical body. Grossberg (2002, p. 38) suggests that live performance is no longer the primary source of musical authenticity. Fans, journalists, and critics routinely state that the primacy of the visual results in the subservience of the sonic to an alien technological regime. Paul Gilroy (2000, pp. 272–274) laments that the call-and-response sociality of Black music in public performance has receded with the two-dimensional limitations of the screen and musical "de-skilling" due to digital technologies.

Despite the long-established visualization of music and the filmic presence of jazz singers and other popular music since the advent of the "talkies" in the late 1920s (Gabbard, 1996), film and television studies have been quite slow to listen to the music in their respective domains. Genre analysis of the classical Hollywood musical examined the function of pre–rock music as spectacular song-and-dance interruptions in the industry's narrative logic (Altman, 1981; Feuer, 1982). New musicology informed by feminism and psychoanalysis studied the musical semiotics of orchestral scores in response to the auteurist focus on composers (Flinn, 1992; Gorbman, 1987; Kalinak, 1992). The ascendancy of popular music in the Hollywood compilation score was signposted by *American Graffiti* (1972), *Saturday Night Fever* (1977), and *Top Gun* (1986). As music provides more marketing clout and potential revenues through the "synergy" of international films and soundtracks, a growing literature has emerged at the interface of film, television, and popular music studies (Robertson-Wojcik & Knight, 2001; Smith, 1998). This work is more open to the different identifications produced by the music of global Hollywood, as well as other cinema cultures such as Bollywood and Chinese and Egyptian film. Industries and texts address a broader range of listener competencies, taste cultures, and niche markets (Kassabian, 2001). With the digital convergence of musical and "nonmusical" sounds and images in bits and bytes, music is examined within the overall "sound design" of both film texts and sonic-viewing experiences in exhibition spaces (Brophy, 2000; Chion, 1994; Hayward, 1999).

Studies of television have primarily focused on music's place in the development of youth television (Frith, Goodwin, & Grossberg, 1993). In the 1980s, music television gave us the new genre of the music video, an advertisement for the sound commodity. Surprisingly, the study of music in television commercials remains an underresearched area. Initial debates about music television revolved around the apparently emblematic postmodernism of MTV (Kaplan, 1987). Goodwin's (1993) institutional analysis of MTV critiqued the visual bias of these studies and drew attention to sound and established discourses about popular music culture. Music video analysis is now a stalwart of the field. In recent years, anthologies and readers in popular music studies increasingly feature chapters on the globalization of music television. In what corporate-speak likes to call "glocalization," MTV and Channel [V] have shaped musical imaginaries; remodeled local, regional, and national styles; and opened up new markets for youth- and middle-class-targeted goods in Latin America and Asia. Music television networks with linguistic roots outside the European–North American axis of mainly English-language pop also compete for markets with "Western"-owned companies.

INTERNET MUSIC

As various permutations of network theory have spread across the disciplines, media and cultural studies have considered music's distribution and consumption in peer-to-peer networks that organize widely dispersed listeners. The reproduction of previously recorded sounds is key to arguments about "piracy" and the "free" circulation of music through downloadable MP3 files and burnt CDs. Through software design, the major music corporations seek to secure digital rights and more efficiently manage customer information while cutting storage and transportation costs with the Internet. Through litigation and legislation, they hope to more tightly control and regulate the distribution of music. Both the big corporations and the smaller independents seek to organize an increasingly mobile consumer who operates in many regards like a sampler. In fact,

Grossberg (2002) argues that the current popular music formation is dominated by a "neoeclectic mainstream," an apparatus that "operates with a logic of sampling, in both senses of the term (i.e., as a production technique and a habit of listening)" (p. 48). As a technological practice of music consumption and production, sampling seems to anticipate the networking culture of the Internet. Sampling as cultural logic dominates the radio show, DJ set and remix, the CD compilation, the file server, and the programming facilities of various playback technologies. But resisting a potential technological determinism, Steve Jones (2002a) reminds us that "music online exists side-by-side with music offline and side-by-side with cultural and industrial practices and processes offline" (p. 228).

MUSIC INDUSTRIES, WORK, AND THE POLITICAL ECONOMY OF MUSIC

Studies of the music industry have acknowledged yet seriously questioned the Frankfurt school's macro-theoretical and monolithic account of the "culture industry," which has had to come to terms with structural changes in capitalism. The consolidation of the music industry has involved the decentralization of production with management in networked systems. Production is dispersed within various divisions of corporations and across the many smaller companies that function like subcontractors (Roberts, 2002). Organizational sociologists, mainly in the United States, have focused on the actors and processes by which music is produced in specific institutions. These so-called "production-of-culture" approaches address the particularity of organizational structures and production processes in industries producing creative work (Peterson, 1976). They focus on the interplay of technologies, the law, the market, industry structure, economies of scale, and occupational careers (Burnett, 1996, pp. 65–66). For example,

Richard Peterson's (1997) major study of country music describes how its styles and sounds were institutionalized between 1923 and 1953 through the intersection of performers, songwriters, agents, record companies, radio broadcasters, and film studios.

However, the production-of-culture approach tends to cordon off production within economic and organizational processes. Ironically, cultural context recedes into the background. As Keith Negus (1992, 1999) points out, culture in the form of social relations, defined by such axes of power as race, class, gender and sexuality, and so on, necessarily affects the way musicians and other workers in the music industry make decisions. Recent work on the "cultural industries" (Hesmondhalgh, 2002; Negus, 1999) has been influenced by the French sociology of Pierre Bourdieu and Bernard Miège. A branch of this sociology of music work centers on the notion of music industry personnel as "cultural intermediaries," a category of worker deemed more significant in a global economy increasingly defined by "information," "knowledge," and the products of creative industries such as music, film, television, advertising, and design. Angela McRobbie (2002), for example, points out that the entrepreneurial economy of dance music and metropolitan club scenes in Britain has provided models for an emerging culture of individualized, mobile creative work marked by deregulation, longer hours, and a decline of politics. Studies of the degree of relative autonomy of small music organizations and changing notions of "independence" remain important for the construction of radical democratic modes of music work in generally hostile economic conditions.

Considerations of music policy have had to deal with issues of aesthetics and pleasure (Bennett, Frith, Grossberg, Shepherd, & Turner, 1993; Street, 2000). Therefore, cultural industries research has been generating sociological accounts of musical creativity and form that move beyond the romantic-genius discourses of authorship (Toynbee, 2000). One way to examine the relationship between industry and aesthetics has been to focus on genres. The social meanings of these relatively standardized music styles are negotiated between musicians, industrial forces, the media, and listener-consumers. Tracking the emergence of similar texts, their categorization and mutation as they travel can illustrate the various economic, cultural, and political forces that shape music forms in specific local and national contexts. Political economy approaches also register different points in the value chain of music commodities as they circulate in various media technologies and are grounded in listening experiences (Miklitsch, 1998).

IDENTITY POLITICS

Popular music studies have shown us that, rather than reflecting the authentic voice(s) of a community in a particular place, music mediates subjective and collective identities. One of the influential legacies of the "Birmingham school" was its concept of "homology" (Willis, 1978). Academics examined the "homological" relations or fit between social position, music, sartorial style, and the activities within (mostly working-class male) youth subcultures. Critics have since taken apart subculture theory for the discreteness and internal coherence it attributed to cultures. The theory posited too rigid a resistance versus incorporation model, too neat a formulation of the "underground" against the "mainstream" (Thornton, 1995). Nevertheless, claims about authenticity, place, and identity continue to hold a strong currency in popular discourse within and about many music cultures. Therefore, Jason Toynbee (2000) argues that there is room to retain a modified concept of homology "as just one kind of link between community and musical practice . . . as an 'authentic' expression of social being in musical style" (p. 114).

In staking their claims, political, social, and cultural movements based on the struggle for the rights of women, queers, and racial-ethnic minorities have met with skepticism from some left-liberal critics. But as Robin Kelley (1997) argues, this is the weakness of a "neo-Enlightenment position" that characterizes "race, gender and sexuality as narrow identity politics while class is regarded as some transcendent, universal category that rises above these identities" (p. 109). Ron Eyerman and Andrew Jamison (1998) argue for social movement theory and history that integrate music as central to the cognitive praxis of actors within political and social movements.

Feminist and gay/lesbian/queer scholars have, to an important extent, redressed the masculinist bias of rock-dominated music studies and popular music culture itself. Debates about gender in popular music have proliferated since the 1980s (Whiteley, 1997, 2000). Poststructuralist theories that emphasize "technologies of the self" and the "performance" of gendered and sexual practices and identities have influenced writing on many genres, including the rock canon, country, disco, rave music, and "tweenie" pop for girls (Bayton, 1998; Schwichtenberg, 1993). Feminist and queer academics were largely responsible for a greater critical engagement with audiences and fans, particularly questions of affect, structures of feeling, and emotion (Lewis, 1992).

African American sounds have been integral to the history of "Western" popular music, and some of the recent academic literature on Black music reveals current arguments about identity politics more broadly. Studies of rap and hip-hop culture assume that the music contributes to a mediated Black public sphere in the post–civil rights/post-soul era (Neal, 1999, 2002). The genre has become a focus for debates about Black modernism and postmodernism (Potter, 1995) and for working-class and sexual politics as they intersect with questions of race in America (Perkins, 1996). Paul Gilroy (2000) criticizes the nationalist paradigm in African *American* rap and its academic studies. He conceives of rap as part of a transnational Black Atlantic counterculture of modernity. Increasingly, studies of "Black music" stress the multicultural interactions and complex power relations involved in the affiliations and antagonisms, aesthetics, and commerce of musical forms and practices between Black and White, African Americans and Jewish Americans (Lott, 1993; Melnick, 1999). Tony Mitchell (2002) points out that the wider globalization of rap and hip-hop has produced distinct, unique, and hybrid cultures around the world that are ignored by the parochialism and imperialism of most American studies of the genre.

SPACES AND PLACES

Cultural geography and spatial theories of globalization have brought to the fore the question of place in music studies. Ideas of place have always been central to music cultures. The sound of music has been sold as representative or evocative of the local—for example, Mersey Beat, Philly Soul, and the Bristol Sound. A genre such as hip-hop also self-consciously projects locality as a crucial element in its sound and the discourse around the music (Forman, 2002). Ethnographic and other anthropological approaches have detailed the ecology of musical place identities in a literature on specific music forms and "scenes" in particular locations (Bennett, 2000; Cohen, 1991; Finnegan, 1989; Leyshon, Matless, & Revill, 1998; Mitchell, 1996; Shank, 1993; Stokes, 1994; Swiss, Sloop, & Herman, 1998). Dance music cultures have become sites for debates about the policing of youth, the struggle over public space, and the desiring "politics" of hedonism (Gilbert & Pearson, 1999; McKay, 1998). The geographical influence in youth culture studies has been more marked as music venues, events and festivals, urban leisure, and tourism become integrated in service economies from Glasgow to Goa (Skelton & Valentine, 1998).

Music studies increasingly mediate the local and the global through conceptions of music scenes and cultures as mobile networks and circuits rather than as geographically bounded structures and processes. These include diasporic and linguistically based networks such as those for salsa, Arabic, Cantonese, and Hindi film pop, as well as marginal electronic dance music genres that, enabled by Internet communication, circulate through distributors to specialist record shops in the higher ranking Organization for Economic Cooperation and Development (OECD) nations. In the emerging literature, places are represented as nodes in the network or "dangerous crossroads" that produce syncretic or hybridized forms and practices (Lipsitz, 1994). Though not completely disavowed, the concept of *national* music is turned inside out by much of this work (Perrone & Dunn, 2001; Zuberi, 2001).

The greater volume and rapid interconnectedness that marks today's music cultures often involve neocolonial encounters and transactions. *Cultural imperialism* may be insufficient a term to understand the complex trajectories of these mediations, but critical analysis continues to focus on power relations and the "exotic" desires that motivate the "placing" and trafficking of music in various networks (Hayward, 1999; Sharma, Hutnyk, & Sharma, 1996; Taylor, 1997). One challenge for an international popular music studies is to move beyond "the West and the rest" to consider the many alternative circuits and trade routes through which music travels between people and places—for example, Hindi film songs in the Maghreb and salsa in Japan.

◆ Conclusion

In a networked globe of scattered centers and peripheries—one in which music is on the move more rapidly than ever before—music studies are likely to pursue more interdisciplinary, cross-cultural, and relational analyses. This convergence will not be a smooth operation. Sociological approaches to music, including those of media studies, will have to be more sensitive to the specificity of musical forms and experiences. The more anthropological return to music production, distribution, and consumption in everyday life offers methods that historicize, localize, and situate musical cultures in a world characterized by "spaces of flows." Academic popular music studies will need to more actively engage with (largely anti-academic) music journalism and explore how talk and writing about music in various media institutions and public life might affect academic rhetoric and vice versa (Jones, 2002b). These debates might affect the discourse of multicultural music education in schools, colleges, and universities. Can we talk seriously about music without the specialized jargon that musicology and the other disciplines have handed down? Questions of power will remain central to critical popular music studies as they examine the social life of technologies in increasingly digital media economies. We will continue to listen to the musical noises in the foreground but need to be more attentive to the sounds in the background and to the silences in between.

◆ References

Altman, R. (Ed.). (1981). *Genre: The musical*. London: Routledge.

Attali, J. (1985). *Noise: The political economy of music*. Minneapolis: University of Minnesota.

Bayton, M. (1998). *Frock rock*. Oxford, UK: Oxford University Press.

Bennett, T., Frith, S., Grossberg, L., Shepherd, J., & Turner, G. (Eds.). (1993). *Rock and popular music: Politics, policies, institutions*. London: Routledge.

Bennett, T. (2000). *Popular music and youth culture: Music, identity and place*. Basingstoke, UK: Macmillan.

Bolter, J. D., & Grusin, R. (1999). *Remediation: Understanding new media*. Cambridge: MIT Press.

Born, G., & Hesmondhalgh, D. (Eds.). (2000). *Western music and its others: Difference, representation and appropriation in music*. Berkeley: University of California Press.

Brackett, D. (1995). *Interpreting popular music*. Berkeley: University of California Press.

Brophy, P. (Ed.). (2000). *Cinesonic: Cinema and the sound of music*. North Ryde, New South Wales: Australian Film Television and Radio School.

Bull, M. (2000). *Sounding out the city: Personal stereos and the management of everyday life*. Oxford, UK: Berg.

Burnett, R. (1996). *The global jukebox: The international music industry*. London: Routledge.

Chanan, M. (1995). *Repeated takes: A short history of recording and its effects on music*. London: Verso.

Chion, M. (1994). *Audio-vision: Sound on screen*. New York: Columbia University Press.

Cohen, S. (1991). *Rock culture in Liverpool: Popular music in the making*. Oxford, UK: Oxford University Press.

Corbett, J. (1994). *Extended play: Sounding off from John Cage to Dr. Funkenstein*. Durham, NC: Duke University Press.

Cross, B. (1993). *It's not about a salary . . . rap, race and resistance in Los Angeles*. London: Verso.

Davis, A. Y. (1998). *Blues legacies and Black feminism: Gertrude "Ma" Rainey, Bessie Smith, and Billie Holiday*. New York: Vintage.

DeNora, T. (2000). *Music in everyday life*. Cambridge, UK: Cambridge University Press.

Dimitriadis, G. (2001). *Performing identity/ performing culture: Hip hop as text, pedagogy and lived practice*. New York: Peter Lang.

Downing, J. (1996). *Internationalizing media theory: Transition, power, culture*. Thousand Oaks, CA: Sage.

Drew, R. (2001). *Karaoke nights: An ethnographic rhapsody*. Lanham, MD: AltaMira.

Du Gay, P., Hall, S., Janes, L., Mackay, H., & Negus, K. (1997). *Doing cultural studies: The story of the Sony Walkman*. London: Sage.

During, E. (2002). Appropriations: Deaths of the author in electronic music. In C. Van Assche (Ed.), *Sonic process* (pp. 39–57). Barcelona: Actar/Museu d'Art Contemporani de Barcelona.

Eyerman, R., & Jamison, A. (1998). *Music and social movements: Mobilizing traditions in the twentieth century*. Cambridge, UK: Cambridge University Press.

Feld, S. (2000). A sweet lullaby for world music. *Public Culture, 12*(1), 145–171.

Feuer, J. (1982). *The Hollywood musical*. London: Macmillan/British Film Institute.

Fikentscher, K. (2000). *"You better work": Underground dance music in New York City*. Hanover, CT: Wesleyan University Press.

Finnegan, R. (1989). *The hidden musicians: Music-making in an English town*. Cambridge, UK: Cambridge University Press.

Flinn, C. (1992). *Strains of utopia: Gender, nostalgia and Hollywood film music*. Princeton, NJ: Princeton University Press.

Forman, M. (2002). *The 'hood comes first: Race, space, and place in rap and hip-hop*. Middletown, CT: Wesleyan University Press.

Fornäs, J. (2000). The crucial in-between: The centrality of mediation in cultural studies. *European Journal of Cultural Studies, 3*(1), 45–65.

Frith, S. (Ed.). (1993). *Music and copyright*. Edinburgh, UK: Edinburgh University Press.

Frith, S. (1996). *Performing rites: On the value of popular music*. Cambridge, MA: Harvard University Press.

Frith, S. (1998). A note on "The value of value." *New Formations, 34*, 127–128.

Frith, S. (2001). The popular music industry. In S. Frith, W. Straw, & J. Street (Eds.), *The Cambridge companion to pop and rock* (pp. 26–52). Cambridge, UK: Cambridge University Press.

Frith, S., & Goodwin, A. (Eds.). (1990). *On record: Rock, pop and the written word*. New York: Pantheon.

Frith, S., Goodwin, A., & Grossberg, L. (Eds.). (1993). *Sound and vision: The music video reader*. London: Routledge.

Gabbard, K. (1996). *Jammin' at the margins: Jazz and the American cinema*. Chicago: University of Chicago Press.

Gilbert, J., & Pearson, E. (1999). *Discographies: Dance music, culture, and the politics of sound*. London: Routledge.

Gilroy, P. (2000). *Against race: Imagining political culture beyond the color line*. Cambridge, MA: Harvard University Press.

Goodwin, A. (1992). Rationalization and democratisation in the new technologies of popular music. In J. Lull (Ed.), *Popular music and communication* (pp. 75–100). Newbury Park, CA: Sage.

Goodwin, A. (1993). *Dancing in the distraction factory: Music television and popular culture*. Minneapolis: University of Minnesota Press.

Gorbman, C. (1987). *Unheard melodies: Narrative film music*. Bloomington: Indiana University Press.

Gronow, P., & Saunio, I. (1998). *An international history of the recording industry*. London: Cassell.

Grossberg, L. (Ed.). (1986). On postmodernism and articulation: An interview with Stuart Hall. *Journal of Communication Inquiry, 10*(2), 45–60.

Grossberg, L. (1992). *We gotta get out of this place: Popular conservatism and postmodern culture*. New York: Routledge.

Grossberg, L. (2002). Reflections of a disappointed popular music scholar. In R. Beebe, D. Fulbrook, & B. Saunders (Eds.), *Rock over the edge: Transformations in popular music culture* (pp. 25–59). Durham, NC: Duke University Press.

Hall, S., & Jefferson, T. (Eds.). (1993). *Resistance through rituals: Youth subcultures in postwar Britain*. London: Routledge.

Hayward, P. (Ed.). (1999). *Widening the horizon: Exoticism in post-war popular music*. Sydney, Australia: John Libbey/Perfect Beat Productions.

Hebdige, D. (1979). *Subculture: The meaning of style*. London: Methuen.

Hesmondhalgh, D. (2002). *The cultural industries.* London: Sage.

Hesmondhalgh, D., & Negus, K. (2002). Introduction: Popular music studies: Meaning, power and value. In D. Hesmondhalgh & K. Negus (Eds.), *Popular music studies* (pp. 1–15). London: Arnold.

Hilmes, M. (2002). Rethinking radio. In M. Hilmes & J. Loviglio (Eds.), *Radio reader: Essays in the cultural history of radio* (pp. 1–19). New York: Routledge.

James, R. (Ed.). (1992). *Cassette mythos.* Brooklyn: Autonomedia.

Jones, S. (1992). *Rock formation: Music, technology, and mass communication.* Newbury Park, CA: Sage.

Jones, S. (2002a). Music that moves: Popular music, distribution and network technologies. *Cultural Studies, 16*(2), 213–267.

Jones, S. (Ed.). (2002b). *Pop music and the press.* Philadelphia: Temple University Press.

Kalinak, K. (1992). *Settling the score: Music and the classical Hollywood film.* Madison: University of Wisconsin Press.

Kaplan, E. A. (1987). *Rocking around the clock: Music television, postmodernism and consumer culture.* London: Methuen.

Kärki, K., Leydon, R., & Terho, H. (Eds.). (2002). *Looking back, looking ahead: Popular music studies 20 years later.* Saarijärvi, Finland: IASPM-Norden/ Gummerus Printing.

Kassabian, A. (1999). Popular. In B. Horner & T. Swiss (Eds.), *Key terms in popular music and culture* (pp. 113–123). Malden, MA: Blackwell.

Kassabian, A. (2001). *Hearing film: Tracking identifications in contemporary Hollywood film music.* New York: Routledge.

Kelley, R. D. G. (1997). *Yo' mama's disfunktional! Fighting the culture wars in urban America.* Boston: Beacon.

Kenney, W. H. (1999). *Recorded music in American life: The phonograph and popular memory 1890–1945.* Oxford, UK: Oxford University Press.

Lanza, J. (1994). *Elevator music: A surreal history of Muzak, easy listening and other moodsong.* New York: Pantheon.

Leppert, R., & McClary, S. (Eds.). (1987). *Music and society: The politics of composition, performance and reception.* Cambridge, UK: Cambridge University Press.

Lewis, L. (Ed.). (1992). *The adoring audience: Fan culture and popular media.* London: Routledge.

Leyshon, A., Matless, D., & Revill, G. (Eds.). (1998). *The place of music.* New York: Guilford.

Lipsitz, G. (1990). *Time passages: Collective memory and American popular culture.* Minneapolis: University of Minnesota Press.

Lipsitz, G. (1994). *Dangerous crossroads: Popular music, postmodernism and the poetics of place.* London: Verso.

Longhurst, B. (1995). *Popular music and society.* Cambridge, UK: Polity.

Lott, E. (1993). *Love and theft: Blackface minstrelsy and the American working class.* New York: Oxford University Press.

Manuel, P. (1993). *Cassette culture: Popular music and technology in North India.* Chicago: University of Chicago Press.

Marcus, G. (1997). *Invisible republic: Bob Dylan's basement tapes.* New York: Holt & Co.

Martin, P. J. (1995). *Sounds and society: Themes in the sociology of music.* Manchester, UK: Manchester University Press.

McKay, G. (Ed.). (1998). *DiY culture: Party and protest in nineties Britain.* London: Verso.

McRobbie, A. (2002). Clubs to companies: Notes on the decline of political culture in speeded up creative worlds. *Cultural Studies, 16*(4), 516–531.

Melnick, J. (1999). *A right to sing the blues: African Americans, Jews, and American popular song.* Cambridge, MA: Harvard University Press.

Middleton, R. (1990). *Studying popular music.* Milton Keynes, UK: Open University Press.

Middleton, R. (Ed.). (2000). *Reading pop: Approaches to textual analysis in popular music.* Oxford, UK: Oxford University Press.

Miklitsch, R. (1998). *From Hegel to Madonna: Towards a general economy of "commodity fetishism."* Albany: State University of New York.

Mitchell, T. (1996). *Popular music and local identity: Rock, pop and rap in Europe and Oceania.* London: Leicester University Press.

Mitchell, T. (Ed.). (2002). *Global noise: Rap and hip-hop outside the USA.* Middletown, CT: Wesleyan University Press.

Mitsui, T., & Hosokawa, S. (Eds.). (1998). *Karaoke around the world: Global technology, local singing.* London: Routledge.

Mundy, J. (1999). *Popular music on screen: From Hollywood musical to music video.* Manchester, UK: Manchester University Press.

Neal, M. A. (1999). *What the music said: Black popular music and Black public culture.* London: Routledge.

Neal, M. A. (2002). *Soul babies: Black popular culture and the post-soul aesthetic.* London: Routledge.

Negus, K. (1992). *Producing pop.* London: Arnold.

Negus, K. (1996). *Popular music in theory: An introduction.* Cambridge, UK: Polity.

Negus, K. (1999). *Music genres and corporate cultures.* London: Routledge.

Perkins, W. E. (Ed.). (1996). *Droppin' science: Critical essays on rap music and hip hop culture.* Philadelphia: Temple University Press.

Perrone, C. A., & Dunn, C. (Eds.). (2001). *Brazilian popular music and globalization.* Gainesville: University Press of Florida.

Peterson, R. (Ed.). (1976). *The production of culture.* London: Sage.

Peterson, R. (1997). *Creating country music, fabricating authenticity.* Chicago: University of Chicago Press.

Potter, R. (1995). *Spectacular vernaculars: Hip-hop and the politics of postmodernism.* Albany: State University of New York Press.

Roberts, M. (2002). Papa's got a brand-new bag: Big music's post-Fordist regime and the role of independent music labels. In N. Kelley (Ed.), *Rhythm and business: The political economy of Black music* (pp. 24–43). New York: Akashic Books.

Robertson-Wojcik, P., & Knight, A. (Eds.). (2001). *Soundtrack available: Essays on film and popular music.* Durham, NC: Duke University Press.

Rose, T. (1994). *Black noise: Rap music and Black culture in contemporary America.* Hanover, CT: Wesleyan University Press.

Schwichtenberg, C. (Ed.). (1993). *The Madonna connection: Representational politics, subcultural identities, and cultural theory.* Boulder, CO: Westview.

Shank, B. (1993). *Dissonant identities: The rock 'n' roll scene in Austin, Texas.* Hanover, CT: Wesleyan University Press.

Sharma, S., Hutnyk, J., & Sharma, A. (Eds.). (1996). *Dis-orienting rhythms: The politics of the new Asian dance music.* London: Zed.

Shepherd, J. (1991). *Music as social text.* Cambridge, UK: Polity.

Shuker, R. (1994). *Understanding popular music.* New York: Routledge.

Skelton, T., & Valentine, G. (Eds.). (1998). *Cool places: Geographies of youth.* London: Routledge.

Smith, J. (1998). *The sounds of commerce: Marketing popular film music.* New York: Columbia University Press.

Spitulnik, D. (2002). Mobile machines and fluid audiences: Rethinking reception through Zambian radio culture. In F. Ginsburg, L. Abu-Lighod, & B. Larkin (Eds.), *Media worlds: Anthropology on new terrain* (pp. 337–354). Berkeley: University of California Press.

Stokes, M. (Ed.). (1994). *Ethnicity, identity and music: The musical construction of space.* Oxford, UK: Berg.

Stolzoff, N. C. (2000). *Wake the town and tell the people: Dancehall culture in Jamaica.* Durham, NC: Duke University Press.

Strauss, N. (Ed.). (1993). *Radiotext(e).* New York: Semiotext(e).

Street, J. (2000). Aesthetics, policy and the politics of popular culture. *European Journal of Cultural Studies, 3*(1), 27–43.

Swiss, T., Sloop, J., & Herman, A. (Eds.). (1998). *Mapping the beat: Popular music and contemporary theory.* Malden, MA: Blackwell.

Taylor, T. D. (1997). *Global pop: World music, world markets.* New York: Routledge.

Taylor, T. D. (2001). *Strange sounds: Music, technology and culture.* New York: Routledge.

Théberge, P. (1997). *Any sound you can imagine: Making music/consuming technology.* Hanover, CT: Wesleyan University Press.

Thornton, S. (1995). *Club cultures: Music, media and subcultural capital.* Cambridge, UK: Polity.

Toynbee, J. (2000). *Making popular music: Musicians, creativity and institutions.* London: Arnold.

Whiteley, S. (Ed.). (1997). *Sexing the groove: Popular music and gender.* London: Routledge.

Whiteley, S. (2000). *Women and popular music: Sexuality, identity and subjectivity.* New York: Routledge.

Willis, P. (1978). *Profane culture.* London: Routledge.

Zuberi, N. (2001). *Sounds English: Transnational popular music.* Urbana: University of Illinois Press.

22

ADVERTISING

A Synthetic Approach

◆ Todd Joseph Miles Holden

◆ Introduction: The Growing Centrality of Advertising

What was once a localized industry associated with a certain kind of economy in specific societies has now become a core societal institution in a wide range of contexts around the world. By 2000, advertising had grown from an American-centered industry in the 1950s[1] into a mega-billion-dollar global industry.[2] In the process, advertising has been transformed into a medium through which many of society's key entities and their publics communicate. O'Barr (1994) states that "advertising both reflects and constitutes social order" (p. 4), but I think we must go even further: Advertising has become a major force in ongoing societal re/production.

This re/productive role is rendered all the more weighty as society globalizes. To highlight but two examples: Today, we witness the increasing use of political spots as a major form of electoral communication in countries outside America and Europe (Holden, 1997b, 1999b; Sabato, 1981); so too are we experiencing the pell-mell insertion of symbols indigenous to one cultural context into product appeals in another (Holden, 2001b).

This burgeoning presence has meant that advertising has become a magnet for communication researchers, political scientists, psychologists, marketers, semioticians, sociologists, social philosophers, anthropologists, and cultural historians. At the same time, likely due to the great differences among these practitioners and the disciplinary, balkanized tendency of contemporary social science, a large amount of high-quality work in the field has gone mutually unrecognized. Bridges have remained unbuilt, channels of connection untraversed.

A certain core set of themes has emerged. These include gender,[3] cultural history,[4] organizational practice,[5] marketing,[6] branding,[7] audience,[8] and commodification.[9] Many studies of advertising reduce the subject to a specific topic, such as the language of advertising,[10] the art of advertising,[11] or its historical development.[12] Areas that have been identified, but in my view have yet to be adequately explored, include cultural and political nationalism, comparative political values, race, identity, the changing nature of the sign, advertising's agenda-setting function, and the presence and operation of the advertising institution on ad readers' perceptions and practices.

All of these are projects worthy of future attention. Yet in general, and unfortunately, advertising research has rarely proceeded in a comprehensive, synthetic way. For those seeking to clarify the wealth of disparate literature that has accrued over the years, the task is certainly formidable. It is just this project I believe media studies must take on. I wish, with this chapter, to offer a start.

◆ Toward a "Total Conception" of Advertising

From Marx, among others, sociology incorporated a holistic, totalizing vision—society as a complex composite of structural elements operating at numerous "levels" in simultaneous, cross-cutting, interlocking,

often contradictory ways, defying facile reduction. Among these levels are the political and economic, above all, but so, too, are the social, cultural, moral, and spatiotemporal. One element of the Marxist legacy is embodied in what Golding and Murdock (1991) call a "critical political economy of communication," a perspective that has come to exert an increasing presence in advertising scholarship.

What separates the totalizing conception argued for here from the kind of critical approach espoused by Golding, Murdock, and others is that a considerable amount of advertising research has illuminated aspects other than political economy or even cultural history. Although critical writers often argue that such studies miss the point, the fact is that a wealth of significant advertising information is generated outside the critical perspective. To accommodate such voices, a framework is required that is flexible enough to observe the many *sectoral* and *institutional* phenomena that may emerge within, but are not mere reflexes of, the larger system of capital reproduction. By *sectors,* I mean the dimensions of society as categorized by academic disciplines, such as sociology, political science, and the like. By *institutions,* I mean coherent sets of ideas, practices, roles, and norms that are regularized in social structure, such as "the institution of religion," "the institution of the family" or "the institution of advertising."

SECTORAL DIMENSIONS AND TOTALITY

Although totalities are very difficult to articulate in single analyses, a number of advertising studies excavate at least the footprints of other dimensions buried within society's complex architecture. In Baudrillard (1981/1994), for instance, one discerns the cultural and economic; in Mattelart (1991), the economic, spatial, and historical; in Williams (1980), the social, historical, and economic; in Habermas (1962/1995), the political and social; in

Kellner (1995), the social and economic; and in Schudson (1984), the cultural, economic, and moral. Advertising research has all too often contented itself with focusing on but one. What is needed is more of the kind of scholarship hinted at by Ewen and Ewen (1982/1992) in their social history of mass-mediated consumption in America: "Built on expanded production and the economic potential of consumer markets, advertising created the imagery, the aesthetic, of a social-democratic capitalism, one that understood and would claim to solve the most basic contradictions of modern life" (p. 20).

ADVERTISING AS A SOCIETAL INSTITUTION

Through its network-like connections not only to but also between the various sectors of society, advertising can be seen as linking various institutions, organizations, and publics; it serves as a re/productive mechanism through which various laws, rules, practices, conventions, beliefs, and ideologies flow. This mediation process is quite complex. It entails advertisers deriving the materials of their commercial communications from the social knowledge they gather about the audience, then translating this knowledge into information products in ways (formats, codes, signs) that can be understood by that audience. Leiss (1994) maps the dimensions of the advertising institution thus:

> [Advertising] incorporates a threefold process of mediation. One type occurs between producers and consumers, wherein advertising agencies assist producers in encoding products with symbolic meanings; another, between producers and the media, wherein agencies assist producers in choosing the right "media mix" (and the media content—advertising content relation) for attaining the strategic objectives of their marketing campaigns; and a third, between media

and their audiences, wherein agencies assist both producers and the media in understanding the decoding processes of audiences. (p. 131)

The complexity of the mediation equation provides further ground for a synthetic approach. For now, though, let us review some of the research literature's dominant perspectives on advertising, commencing with an ongoing, sometimes paradoxical dispute.

THE PARADOX OF ADVERTISING WITHIN MEDIA STUDIES

"Today," Baudrillard (1981/1994) has written, "we are experiencing the total absorption of all virtual modes of expression into that of advertising" (p. 87). A second French theorist, Mattelart (1991), opines, "Our society is immersed in advertising as the dominant mode of communication" (p. 214). Hyperbole? Perhaps. Yet these views are far from unique. There is, among those who contemplate advertising, a tendency to ascribe great power to it. This presents a paradox, of sorts, for in media studies—which includes advertising as its research object[13]—the trend over the past 40 years has mostly been away from attributing direct, powerful effects to media. And yet throughout that period, there has been steady public clamor about advertising's tremendous, malign influence. The litany is familiar to those in the field—generally seen as beginning with Packard (1957),[14] who gave voice to popular anxieties about "subliminal seduction"[15] and mass manipulation by characterizing advertisers as "hidden persuaders" capable of influencing unguarded consumers. In a few years, Raymond Williams (1961/1993, p. 334) would posit advertising to be a "magical system," without which capitalism would surely collapse.

Two decades later, having just entered the period of audience-mediated "negotiated" and "aberrant" readings of text (S. Hall 1980), Schudson (1984) produced a widely circulated book on advertising bearing the provocative subtitle *Its Dubious Impact on American Society.* Yet Schudson too saw fit to echo Williams's (1961/1993) line that advertising is "the official art of modern capitalist society." Even to Schudson, this "capitalist realist art" possesses "a special cultural power" for it "picks up some of the things that people hold dear and re-presents them to people as *all* of what they value" (p. 233). It has become commonplace to articulate this view of advertising as moral culture (e.g., Fox & Lears, 1983; Pope, 1983; Marchand, 1985): the notion that, under advertising's influence, society has become narrowly circumscribed by consumerist values.

Even at a point when some deemed the audience all-powerful (e.g., Fiske 1989), advertising was still perceived as potent. For instance, Habermas (1995/1962) advanced the view that advertising (rendered as *publicity* by his translators) possessed the power to transform public life by altering relations between political leaders and their public(s). He argued that the reduction of political messages to the form of ads meant that political and social affairs were no longer discussed collectively by rational citizens. Instead, public matters were aired in private spaces, if at all, by atomized consumers of mass culture.

No less sweeping have been claims by those who assert that "advertising is as concerned with selling lifestyles and socially desirable identities, which are associated with their products, as with selling the products themselves" (Kellner, 1995, p. 252). In the process, these critics allege, consistent images of gender and race, interpersonal relations, sexuality, health, body, age, and nation (to name only a few) are constantly reproduced. Crucially, it has been argued, rival images have been effectively barred from circulation. The result is a narrowing of discourse through the "agenda-setting function of advertising" (Holden, 1995).

PARADOX SQUARED: MINIMALIST VIEWS OF ADVERTISING POWER

To be fair, the notion of advertising as an omnipotent medium of communication is far from universally held. There are those who find advertising's effects tempered, contingent, negligible, if not entirely absent. Schudson's (1984) book produced sharp reactions because it argued, in part, that "[advertising's] power is not so determinative nor its influence so clear" (p. 11). Patterson and McClure (1976), in earlier path-breaking work, had studied voter reactions to political commercials and concluded that "the vast majority of Americans are immune to advertising's propaganda. They are not manipulated" (p. 130). Diamond and Bates (1984) observed an obvious but underrecognized reality: "Less than half of the advertising done in any specific election year will be for successful candidates and more than half for unsuccessful candidates" (p. 350). In light of such inefficacy, can one contend that advertising is influential?

For media researchers, witnessing a world ever more fashioned around the rhetoric of advertising, this dispute is a puzzle in need of unscrambling. Because advertising is a media institution, it has been subject to the currents that historically have coursed through media studies, including the long-running "paradigm wars" between competing camps of "process" (or "effects") and "meaning" (see Chapters 9 and 12, this volume). Neither model has been fully persuasive or completely shakable. Most often, now, the view of effects is that they are longer term or indirect,[16] whereas the notion of audience power has become more situational—tempered by medium, locale, social group, or specific issue (Dahlgren, 1998; Hay, Grossberg, & Wartella, 1997; Morley, 1988). Advertising research tends to adopt one of the two perspectives[17] but often does so with little recognition that it is contributing to or being shaped by particular long-running but contested paradigms. Let us now proceed to assess more specific traditions of research, beginning with two that pivot as much on a difference of objectives as of methods.

Research Traditions

Harms and Kellner (1990) contend that two broad traditions have characterized advertising research: (a) *administrative studies* and (b) *critical studies*.[18] The former focuses on the collection of data as a means of learning how to use advertising to influence audiences, sell products, and promote politicians. The latter centers on how advertising articulates with the institutional structures of contemporary capitalist societies, with an eye to grasping its negative effects.

The Administrative Tradition. Market research exemplifies the administrative tradition. In this approach, a range of methods (including focus groups, projective techniques, and association tests) are employed, all aimed at gaining feedback from potential consumers about themselves, products, or possible ad campaigns. Physiological responses, recognition testing, and attitude-tracking tests may also be employed. Much of these data are collected "in-house" at advertising agencies. Academic researchers also study a range of focused phenomena with applications to ad form and content: everything from whether subliminal perception alters consumer behavior—highly unlikely (Merikle, 2000)—to whether negative political advertising can change voting behavior (in specifiable cases, it does).[19]

The Critical Tradition. Critical media studies originated with the Frankfurt school. In more recent years, the label *critical political economy* has become more common, the avowed aim of which is to trace the interplay between the symbolic and economic in communications. This project can be found in Baudrillard,[20] but applied specifically to advertising, it is best embodied in the sophisticated work of Williamson (1978). This approach has also been pursued by

Jhally (1990) and Goldman (1992). Not all critical approaches, however, are Marxist or even centered on political economy. Goffman's (1976/1979) work—though critical of the gender system—centers on the socially reproductive function of ads (i.e., focusing on social definitions and roles) while de-emphasizing (or altogether ignoring) the economic dimensions.

Although the kinds of studies denoted by the *administrative* label are not "critical," it is unwise to insist on strict separation. A synthetic approach to advertising certainly would do well to keep all these traditions in mind without blindly favoring or derogating either. For this reason, other research traditions should also be considered. These are often not full-blown traditions as much as perspectives, as we will now summarize.

The Semiotic Tradition. Many media analysts have argued that underneath ad text (i.e., beneath the level of "primary discourse" or what the advertiser is trying to sell) lies a "secondary" discourse, consisting of social, cultural, or political meanings embedded in "sign-text." *Semiotics,* the method of analysis that explores this deeper discourse, saw its popularity steadily ascend during the 1980s and 1990s.

Barthes's (1957/1972, 1967) formulation has probably been the most influential version of this approach. He argues that individual signs can be excavated from social text and, if systematically demonstrated as recurrent, can be linked together in "chains of signification" that may reveal the deeper ideational structure of society, which he labels "myth." This formulation has proven quite fruitful in academic advertising research, even in cases where Barthes is not accorded explicit mention.

The full Barthesian lexicon of "signification," "orders of connotation," and "myth" has proven unnecessarily abstruse for many analysts. Consequently, they have favored a more straightforward coding of underlying cultural meaning. Two models in particular stand out, the studies already cited by Williamson (1978) and Goffman

(1976/1979). Each in its own way has served to establish systematic semiotic analysis as an important tool for advertising research. Williamson's study served to lay the foundation for much of the critical studies of advertising, whose political-economic bent has become popular in the past decade; Goffman's not only worked to spotlight gender as a major genre in advertising research but also served to inspire qualitative content analysis of other social groups (e.g., O'Barr, 1994).

The Cultural Studies Perspective: Insistence on the Negotiation of Meaning. The practitioners of cultural studies asserted that message production was an open process in which ad "readers" could (and did) negotiate multiple meanings encoded in the commercial message. The crux of this view is captured in the following statement by Tomlinson (1999):

> Advertising texts . . . though part of what Horkheimer and Adorno (1979) referred to disparagingly as the "culture industry" linked to the instrumental purposes of capitalism, remain significant cultural texts. The way people make use of advertising texts may often be similar to the way they use novels or films. This is because they [ads] offer narratives—however ideologically suspect—of how life may be lived, references to shared notions of identity, appeals to self-image, pictures of "ideal" human relations, versions of human fulfillment, happiness and so on. (pp. 18–19)

Such a view stands a significant distance from strong effects models of media, for it perceives that advertising has an indeterminate effect. Whatever impact ads might have are mediated, if not wholly determined, by the message recipients themselves. Postmodernist writers, as we will now see, occupy much of the same ground.

Postmodernist Perspectives. In the 1980s, with the popularity of postmodernism and

its application to reflexive ad products, the focus turned to tracing the unending routing and rerouting of signifiers and signifieds in ad text. As elements in the sign became detached from their referent systems, signifiers often become more important than the signifieds, it was argued, and in this way images come to rival—if not dominate—the intended message.

For analysts, this often meant tracing the implications of meaning exchange: the relative interpretations, use, or power, for instance, between message encoders and decoders. As an example, Fowles's (1996) widely cited study of the links between popular culture and advertising in America included the claim that ad consumers derive as much use from the images in advertising as the ad creators derive from consumers' attention to specific ad messages. In particular, the meanings contained in such communications (often unrelated to narrow product communication) can serve to prompt message recipients in negotiating the personal dilemmas of contemporary existence.

To postmodernist analysts, the polysemy of ad texts, coupled with greater sophistication of ad readers, means there is greater equality between encoder and decoder, an "opening up" in meaning transference and construction. We shall explore this line of argument later in the work of O'Donohoe (2001). To other writers, however, the "insights" of postmodernism have amounted to nothing more than irksome, even pointless, mental calisthenics. Goldman (1992), for instance, ends his critique of this interpretative "era" in advertising studies by writing,

> The culture of the image is, indeed, all surface; unfortunately, postmodernist critiques are as flat and one-sided as the world of simulations they refer to. In a world of free-floating signifiers that advertising celebrates and poststructuralism criticizes, the critiques become as free-floating as the celebration. (p. 231)

It would be fair to assert that this genre of advertising research has proven less definitive than suggestive. It may be true that ad "readers" have more latitude to construct meanings than advertisers might intend and that the ads currently crafted embody an array of practices (such as fragmentation, de-differentiation, hyperreality, pastiche, intertextuality, and pluralism) that would encourage *less* unity in meaning construction. However, advertising's agenda-setting function also helps determine the contextual frame within which ad messages circulate. For ad readers, cultural history, social values, economic organization, political institutions, and practices prove highly directive. Thus, provocative as postmodernist theorizing may be, the reality is that encoding and decoding do generally articulate with one another and in ways consistent with national cultural parameters. The process is far less random than postmodernism would predict.

The Question of Levels of Analysis. Part of any totalizing conception is integration between levels. For critical scholars, this often has meant contextualizing communications, embodied well in the "cultural studies" approach that has emphasized the manufacture, transmission, reception, and use of messages. This linkage of producer and consumer is a project that Moeran (1996) rightly notes advertising studies must take on. Unfortunately, his study offers no glimpse of the message consumer in context.

Other studies err on the opposite side, by focusing almost exclusively on the message recipient. A cottage industry of consumer-sensitive studies has arisen, showing that message recipients are becoming more favorably disposed to advertising (Meadows, 1983), although this appears to vary to some degree by geographic location (Bonnal, 1990). Moreover, ad recipients are apparently becoming more literate about ads (Goodyear, 1991)—to the point of understanding the motives of message producers and the aims of their messages (Mintel, 1998; Tynan & O'Donohoe,

1998)—although this level of sophistication evinces geographic patterning (Goodyear, 1994). Such focused, audience-centered research is often the province of the advertising agency, and thus either does not make it into the public domain or else fails to address linkage between levels.

In between these two ends of the "cultural circuit" (S. Hall, 1980) are the messages themselves. A staple research methodology on this front has been content analysis. Initially a strictly quantitative approach, more recently it has been wedded with semiotics. These approaches, which have become standard in advertising research, are not without flaws. As Harms and Kellner (1990) observe, the study of content often eschews discussion of the political-economic structure of mass media and neglects the audience. Overall, they assert, semiotics fails to

> adequately articulate . . . the linkage between the macro political economic structure of mass media and the micro mass communication forms and techniques so as to reveal both the socioeconomic functions of advertising and the ways that ads actually shape and influence perception and behavior which reproduce the existing social system.

Such criticisms are important to bear in mind in evaluating advertising research, the bulk of which—whether it is producer, consumer, or content based—generally neglects the synthesis of levels.

The Geography of Advertising Research. One way of working toward a synthetic portrait is to piece together research in a number of contexts. This is particularly imperative as advertising globalizes, intersecting national culture. Unfortunately, one of the most distinctive aspects of work on advertising in the English language is its Western skew. As the ship lists, it does so decidedly toward the shores of America, with few English-language accounts of advertising research in other regions. Some binational comparisons can be located, with the most common pairings being the United States and the United Kingdom (Katz & Lee, 1992; Nevett, 1992), France and the United States (Biswas, Olsen, & Carlet, 1992; Taylor & Hoy, 1995), and the United States and Japan (Holden, 1996, 1997a, 1999a; Lin, 1993; Mueller, 1987; Ramaprasad & Hasegawa, 1992; Sengupta, 1995; Tanaka, 1994). Overall, cultural differences continually emerge—differences that often are expressed via stylistic elements (such as soft-sell, rational, personalization, and lifestyle appeals) and communication tropes (such as natural imagery, the use of humor, or a focus on emotions).

One such study that bears mention is De Mooij's (1998). Although the bulk of her conclusions are inferential and/or analogical, she does manage to cull a large number of cross-cultural studies in service of her claim that, when it comes to advertising, national culture is central. Working in the main with other researchers' statistical studies on communication and cultural values, she then applies a number of parameters to a sample of print ads from 20 countries (from Asia, Europe, Africa, North America, and South America), as well as 5,000 television ads from 13 countries. Although she discerns eight basic forms of advertising (accompanied by numerous subcategories), she asserts that there is a geographic patterning to the forms. Importantly, though, format appears to be associated with the culture of origin of the advertiser or else the stage of development that the company is undergoing (either a "standardization" or else a "local adaptation" phase).[21]

In a conclusion, De Mooij (1998) underscores this thesis of cultural difference by highlighting the "advertising styles" of America, Britain, Germany, Italy, Spain, France, Belgium, Holland, Sweden, Poland, Japan, China, and South Korea. The author ends by asserting that failure to recognize cultural values will have demonstrable, deleterious consequences for marketers and advertisers. Above all, communication

models built for one context cannot be applied to (or imposed on) another. Advertising forms, as well as the specific symbols and ideas embedded in their content, will, of necessity, have to be crafted to the imperatives of each place.

Media Technologies and Advertising. A major goal of synthesis is to facilitate advertising studies' treatment of complex societal phenomena. This is achieved by providing a methodology that can simultaneously strike a variety of analytic postures. It is here that I wish to ask, "Does this flexibility extend, as well, to a focus on specific media technologies?" It is not uncommon to encounter advertising scholarship that rather indiscriminately fuses them. To offer a few examples, although Williamson (1978) employs magazine and newspaper advertisements to demonstrate how meaning is placed in service of ideology, Harms and Kellner (1990) invoke her work—along with other print-based analyses such as Leiss, Kline, and Jhally (1990)—to assist in arguing against the effects of *television* advertising as an institution of ideological reproduction and control. Similarly, Goldman (1992) rather indiscriminately draws on magazine and television advertisements in America—but inferentially generalized to *all* advertising contexts—in the course of arguing that advertising has generally precipitated an evolution toward a "privatized discourse of commodified desire." In her otherwise laudable effort to study advertising contextually, De Mooij (1998) mixes print and television ads to assist in comparing particular variables (such as "power distance" or "individualism/collectivism") across contexts.

The point here is *not* that media ought to be strictly segregated but that analysts should be sensitive to validity concerns that naturally arise as media are mixed. One has to ask whether it really is the case that all ad forms operate in the same way—either as a reflection of institutional linkages, in the transmission of cultural values via content, or else in terms of longer lasting societal effects. It must quickly be acknowledged that in working to model synthesis, this chapter has crept down the same path a tad. However, the aim here is to offer a panoramic snapshot of contemporary advertising research. In effecting *actual* synthesis, however, greater care would be called for.

So far, this chapter has focused on the varying perspectives that have been brought to bear on advertising, ultimately in service of my argument that careful synthesis is necessary to truly see advertising as a core societal institution. In the remainder of the chapter, I organize specific advertising research studies under three headings, any of which can help move us toward synthesis: (a) an inventory of 10 standard findings concerning advertising effects, (b) an assemblage of what I have termed *sectoral* studies, and (c) investigations that address advertising as a societal institution.

◆ An Inventory of Effects

One effect of the emphasis on meaning has been to cast doubt on the notion of advertising impact. Nonetheless, the view that it does have influence still persists. After so many decades, precisely what do we know, or think we know, about effects? First, they are not only measured in terms of a message recipient's perceptions, attitudes, or behavior; they are also reflected in the institution itself, its practices and behaviors. By this standard, the following 10 claims currently appear rather well settled among researchers:

1. *Advertising's impacts are longer term and indirect.* Ads do not generally make someone immediately buy a product; rather, the logic of consuming things, of defining people in relation to commodities, appears to have been built up from a steady diet of advertising over decades.

2. *Advertising operates at two levels of discourse:* the primary (or messages about product) and secondary (or messages about society).[22] Most academic researchers focus on the latter.

3. *Advertising possesses an educative function.* This is obviously true of primary discourse but runs as well to secondary discourse. In ad dicta, one finds social history, along with society's basic cultural patterns and deepest values—however truncated and discontinuous the presentation may be. In the repeated encoding of expected behaviors, cultural definitions, societal rules, and human possibilities, advertising socializes.

4. *Advertising focuses priorities.* In this role as socializer, advertising tells receivers less *what* to think than what to think *about.* Ads, like news media, work as agenda setters (see Chapter 19, this volume).

5. *Advertising is directive.* Primary and secondary ad discourses narrow viewers' focus to a consumer way of life. As a consequence, viewers are constantly operating within the parameters and with the vernacular of a conversation about goods. Other areas to which message recipients' attention is directed include body, sexuality, gender definitions and possibilities, and local cultural practices and values. Less explored by research but likely foci also include awareness of racial and national differences, as well as collective and personal identity.

6. *Advertising is selective.* Although ads direct recipients toward particular themes, they are also excluding others. This is especially true when, in secondary discourse, they privilege hallowed cultural values and social history.

7. *Advertising sets the agenda for much of what appears on television.* As

such, it has an invisible power that exerts influence over the types of shows and, by extension, the themes or specific content transmitted for viewer experience. Less clear is its effect on the content of other media, particularly newspapers, magazines, radio, and the Internet (although some impact would seem likely).

8. *The ad form has become a dominant mode of expression* in an increasingly mediated, consumption-oriented, spatiotemporally condensed world.

9. *Advertising has contributed to the proliferation of signs globally.* This is due to the pell-mell spread of capitalism as well as the dramatic proliferation of communication media, which in many cases has wrought increasing interconnectivity between once highly disparate societies. In turn, this has led to a greater dispersion of local sign/content from advanced economies that, when forged with indigenous signs in other local contexts, has become "reengineered" and then often retransmitted to still other contexts.

10. *Advertising affords greater audience agency.* Paradoxically, despite all the direction and narrowing of discourse, the symbolic explosion that modern advertising has assisted has meant that users not only have more communication content at their disposal but have also become conversant with an array of communicative forms, codes, and devices. This, in turn, has meant that they have been able to become much more savvy in their encounters with advertising text.

◆ Sectoral Approaches to Advertising

The listed effects lend themselves to synthetic studies of advertising, particularly when wedded to sectoral analysis. Below I indicate some areas in which sectoral analysis has been fruitfully pursued to date.

The Cultural. Culture is typically reduced to the shorthand "way of life." Remmling and Campbell (1976) specify eight universal elements,[23] all of which are evinced in advertising. Not only are ads "material culture." Their status as a shared form of communication and virtual presence across the globe certainly qualifies advertising for inclusion on the short list of "cultural universals."

Since the 1980s, a major tradition in advertising scholarship has been the historical/cultural approach. Reflecting the geography of scholarship already noted, these books have centered on America, Canada, and England (cf. Fox, 1984; Pope, 1983; Turner, 1952). In certain cases, such studies simply recount the evolution of an industry. Yet, more recently, efforts have been made to place that history in cultural context as a means of providing deeper cultural analysis (e.g., J. Lears, 1994; Leiss et al., 1990; Marchand, 1985; see also Chapter 13, this volume). Such work moves toward synthesis in that it links development of an industry (the economic) with societal values (the cultural) and consumer practices (the social). And although all accounts have almost singularly centered on the advertising industry within the burgeoning consumer society of late 19th-century America up into the 1980s, what they reveal are intimate sectoral connections. Specifically, they assert the emergence of what might be called a "public morality"— an ethic of consumer praxis.

A major contribution in this vein was Fox and Lears's (1983) collection, *The Culture of Consumption*. There, advertising took center stage—due to its status as "the central institution of consumer culture" (Fox & Lears, 1983, p. xiii). At the same time, advertising was part of "a network of institutional, religious, and psychological changes" (T. J. J. Lears, 1983, p. 4) assailing America prior to the 1920s. Not only did the consumer culture require a "national apparatus of marketing and distribution," Lears (1983) argued, but "it also needed a favorable moral climate" (p. 4). Above all, this meant a shift from Protestant salvation in the coming world to therapeutic self-realization in the present—a present in which "all overarching structures of meaning had collapsed," save for the well-being of the self. Advertising, in his view, served to accelerate that breakdown.

Quick on the heels of this work came Marchand's (1985) *Advertising the American Dream*. This is, without doubt, the most prominent book in the historico-cultural vein. Thoroughly researched and well supported, the book argues, in part, that advertising educated consumers to embrace modernity. Through repetition of moral parables and visual clichés, tradition became trivialized and the new enhanced. A consumerist way of life was sold to the viewing public. Marchand writes,

> Perhaps more than any other institution, American advertising adapted itself to the possibilities for exercising both a dynamic and stabilizing influence during such an age. Advertising served as the spokesman for modernism. It exalted technological advances and disseminated the good news of progress to the millions. It promoted urban lifestyles and sought to educate consumers to master the new complexities of social interaction. (p. 359)[24]

A further work with this focus is by Leiss et al. (1990), a richly detailed study consisting equally of empirical observation and social theorization. For instance, one fascinating dimension is a content analysis of more than 15,000 magazine advertisements from two Canadian popular general-interest mass-circulation magazines, published over the course of 70 years. The results reveal a historical sequence, from a *product-information* format in the late 19th and early 20th centuries to a *product-image* format from the 1920s to 1940s, then a *personalization* format in the 1950s and 1960s, and finally a *lifestyle* format in the 1970s and 1980s. Reflecting the claim by Lears (1983)—and underscoring a major theme of this chapter—it seems fair to conclude that the move to *personalization* was possible only in relation to a particular, changing conception of self. In the same way, the later emphasis on *lifestyle* is consistent only with a society that has "achieved" a certain measure of political freedom and economic growth, capable of enabling its citizen-consumers to pursue their own private desires.

Institutional developments also seem to have played a role in social transformation. As Leiss et al. (1990) suggest, the move away from rational appeals toward symbolic representations of products in consumers' lives appears to have been abetted by greater development of the visual dimension of ads. As a consequence, products became more tangible, more visible in the ad. Moreover, the development by which the product came to be presented as a totem within a consumer's life appears linked to advertising's increased demographic research and strategies of market segmentation. Such approaches suggested that agencies needed to address the questions of the social relationship associated with the product, questions such as the following: "What does this product mean in my life?" and "Who am I in relation to the others in my consumer tribe?" Obviously, the practice of social segmentation and the question of product meaning in everyday life have become even more pronounced since.

Applications Across Cultures. A comparison of cultural contexts is very suggestive. For instance, Holden (2000c) collected a sample of Japanese and Malaysian television ads and coded them in terms of format. He determined that although all four forms of ads were present in both countries, Malaysian ads were disproportionately of the "lower end" formats (product information and product image), whereas Japanese ads were overwhelmingly of the "higher end" variety (personalization and lifestyle). In addition, a fifth format was uncovered in

Japan—an approach that, for want of a better word, was labeled *postmodern*. This format consisted of seven characteristics and required an exceptionally high degree of "semiotic literacy" to decode the ad's primary discourse.

This contrast raises interesting questions about the capacity of ad readers in the respective information milieus. The issue of reception is consistent with a parallel line of research that has sought to document so-called "advertising literacy" (e.g., Ritson & Elliott, 1995; Tynan & O'Donohoe, 1998). For Goodyear (1991), the differential senses made by message consumers situated in differing locales correlate with (a) the amount of exposure to TV and film, (b) the amount of exposure to advertising, (c) the level of industrialization/consumerism, and (d) national cultural factors. Absent are the elements of state policy present in Holden's (2001a) study of Malaysia. Nonetheless, what is clear is that advertising's messages about what society is and the place of consumers and products within it appear strongly associated with socioeconomic development and, by association, consumer sophistication.

The Social. Leiss et al.'s (1990) work is about culture, but it carries the title "social communication." Marchand's (1985) book is about the creation and rooting within culture of a consumer ethic, yet he casts certain ads as "social tableaus"—ads that present relationships between those depicted and also their place in a larger social structure.

When advertising research consciously addresses the social structure, it often does so by focusing on representations of identifiable groups and the relationships within and between groups. Racial stereotyping is an area that has been identified, although it has gone surprisingly understudied by advertising researchers.[25] Reflective of current intellectual foci, of greater recent interest has been the question of cultural identity, which obviously has a close bearing on how advertisers define and seek to communicate to target groups.[26] In general,

such group-centered research has been effected via semiotically attuned content analysis, although the study of message consumers in context would seem equally important.

ADVERTISING'S GENDER OBSESSION

Of all the categories selected for attention in advertising research, men and women are first and foremost. Despite a wealth of work on this subject, it is Goffman's (1976/1979) that receives universal mention. Although his work fails to mention semiology or the French tradition of structural analysis, it is symbolically based, is systematic, and, through its aggregation of commonly repeated codes, delivers us to the stratum of deeply ensconced myth that Barthes (1957/1972) proposed for analysis. Goffman's study concentrated on magazine pictures depicting men and women in various activities, poses, and interrelationships. Following coding and sorting, Goffman was able to demonstrate distinctive patterns of what he called "genderisms." Among these invariant representations of men and women were "relative size," in which social rank, weight, and authority are expressed in social situations; "feminine touch," in which women were depicted in poses of ritualistic (as opposed to utilitarian) touching; "functional ranking," whereby men performed the executive role in face-to-face encounters with women; and "ritualized subordination," where women nearly always deferred to men.

Although Goffman's is the most detailed study, his was not the first research on gender in ads. A handful of studies conducted in the 1970s focused on sex role stereotyping in magazines (Belkaoui & Belkaoui, 1976; Courtney & Lockeretz, 1971) and TV commercials (Courtney & Whipple, 1974; Culley & Bennett, 1976; Dominick & Rausch, 1972; McArthur & Resko, 1975). Typical of the findings were those by Courtney and Whipple (1974), whose secondary analysis of four studies concluded that women were overrepresented in family and home settings and most often depicted performing domestic chores involving the product advertised. Men were inordinately presented as entertainers, businessmen, managers, and sellers and, unlike women, rarely demonstrated products. Moreover, they more often benefited from the tasks and activities performed by women. The other studies consistently found men depicted as authorities, more independent than women, less tied to the home, more scientific (or persuasive), and rewarded socially by career advancement.

Since the 1970s, many more studies have been conducted on gender. Typical of this focus are the following: (a) Archer, Iritani, Kimes, and Barrios (1983) measured the proportion of a picture in newspapers and magazines devoted to the model's face (65% for men, 45% for women). (b) C. Hall (1994) counted the number of bust shots in television beer ads (49% have at least one shot focused on a woman's chest, as opposed to 24% for men). (c) Coltrane (2000) determined that portrayals of male and female characters (as measured in terms of aggressiveness, passivity, instrumentality, and daily activity) systematically differed in about one third of the ads studied, depending on the target audience.

Such associations have been researched less often outside of the United States. The few studies that have been conducted suggest that gendered discourse is extant in ad text but differs depending on the cultural context. For instance, Wiles, Wiles, and Tjernlund (1995) showed that Swedish magazine advertisers appeared to display both men and women in a greater variety of nonworking roles than Dutch and U.S. advertisers. Cutler, Javalgi, and Lee (1995) found that although Korean women were portrayed in stereotypical ways in magazine ads, when compared to American ads, they were less likely to be shown as sex objects and just as likely to appear in ads for durable goods as men. Das (2000) assessed

more than 1,100 magazine ads from a wide range of Indian magazines in 1987, 1990, and 1994 and found that portrayals of women and men had changed over the period studied. In particular, men were portrayed in a greater variety of roles and also in more traditional ways than in the past, whereas women were depicted as housewives less often. At the same time, women were not cast in nontraditional or career-oriented modes. Most often, their appearance did not seem to be determinative; rather, it was neutral. Nonetheless, sex role stereotyping remained high. This differs considerably from findings in America or Japan.

In Japan, Holden (2000b) sought to replicate Goffman's (1976/1979) magazine-based findings in a sample of television ads from the 1990s. He established that every American genderism was present, in virtually identical codes of representation. Japanese ads, however, were found to partial female bodies more than male bodies, to emphasize women's sexual characteristics more, to transform women into objects more often, to depict women as sexually aggressive (with men as sexually passive), and (surprisingly) to treat men as objects for the woman's gaze.[27] In short, when it comes to gendered discourse in ads, wide zones of complementarity—even homogeneity—exist. Still, a certain measure of contextual variation suggests that researchers should pursue a carefully contextualized strategy of case-by-case comparison.

The Political. Of all the sectors touched by advertising research, the political has historically been treated the least synthetically, despite its linkage to other sectors and institutions. Undoubtedly, this stems from the field's strong American orientation, a society in which university disciplines have strongly emphasized the separation of societal sectors. In addition, segmentation may stem from the field's historical association with mainstream political communication research, again virtually an American creation. The most frequently explored format has been the *polispot,* and this has meant, in the main, a focus on technique and an emphasis on short-term effect.

Thus, the concern that has guided most research over the past three decades is the degree to which advertising influences voting behavior. The signal early work in this area was by Patterson and McClure (1976), which advanced the counterintuitive claim that political advertising manipulated very few voters. They found that ads (a) were rather effective at informing voters about issues—itself a surprising finding; (b) served to confirm what voters felt they already knew about candidates; and (c) activated their partisan sentiments. These were all significant effects, indeed, but by the standard of opinion change (still pervasive in political communication circles), ads ended up appearing to be rather *in*effective.

Today, however, the view of effect has shifted, if only slightly. Summarizing recent literature, Iyengar and Valentino (1999) reckon "there is an emerging consensus about the efficacy of (campaign) advertising" (p. 108). One reason for this is that there has been a move to reconceptualize effect in ways other than persuasion or behavioral change. Iyengar and Simon (2000), for instance, assert that advertising influence might be measured two other ways: (a) voter "learning," or the acquisition of information about the candidates and issues, and (b) "agenda control," or the use of campaign rhetoric to set the public's political agenda. Advertising effects might also be seen in terms of the voters' decision to disengage. In parallel work, Ansolabehere and Iyengar (1995) suggest that negative political spots have the ability to polarize an electorate along (extreme) partisan lines, turning off independent voters and thereby depressing voter turnout. Clearly, such effects have significant implications for political contexts in which advertising increasingly has become a central means of political communication. Such is the case in many of the postindustrial societies in the world today.

Although most research on political campaigning is focused on contemporary political processes, some is historical. Jamieson's work (1984/1992) presents a capsule account of the major media campaigns of American presidential candidates from 1952 to 1992. Diamond and Bates's (1984) book covers the same historical ground, but what recommends this effort is an extended analysis of the major "persuasive" techniques and visual styles employed in American political ads. In addition, attention is given to whether and how *polispots* actually work to influence viewers. Although they conclude that political advertising will remain a "problematic art," they also identify major social, cultural, economic, and political negatives ushered in by political advertising. These include (a) the escalating costs of campaigning, (b) the increasing weakening of the parties, (c) the rising prominence of political consultants, (d) the increasing estrangement of candidates from political affiliation, (e) reduced citizen participation in politics, (f) the debasing of political argument, and (g) the shift in political discourse toward entertainment and frivolity.

Spero (1980) also surveys the same historical terrain, with highly caustic conclusions: "Political advertising," he writes, "is without peer as the most deceptive, misleading, unfair and untruthful of all advertising" (p. 3). For this reason, he concludes, it should be legislated out of existence. His distaste is likely influenced by McGinniss's (1969) best-seller *The Selling of the President 1968,* whose steady undertow was concern about democratic political practice in the advertising age. McGinniss's work was significant because it ushered in a spate of books centered on the technocrats crafting the ads. Robinson's (1973), Sabato's (1981), and Blumenthal's (1980) studies stand out for depth, balance, and insight. What they revealed was not only the growing power of the consultants but also the relationship between their values, the messages they create, and impacts on the American political process. The consultancy phenomenon persists, and, if anything, ads increasingly dominate the electoral landscape. This is increasingly true globally, with political spots settling in as fixtures outside the United States. Fresh research is needed comparing *polispot* craft and impact across various national contexts.

Each of the works mentioned above moves in the direction of synthesis. Recent scholarship has sought a similar end via different means. The Annenberg Public Policy Center, for example, has developed an "online tracking study of issue advocacy advertising." The Web site contains profiles of advocacy organizations that broadcast issue advertisements in America, as well as a running estimate of the amount of money spent on issue advocacy advertising. In addition, the site contains a primer on issue ads, a glossary of key terms, and a list of issues and groups that have advertised on those topics.[28]

Despite the uncertainties surrounding the sustainability and accessibility of Web sites, the Annenberg site spotlights the advantage of the Internet in political advertising research—above all, its immediate, interactive, multitaskable, multimedia nature. As of 2002, a limited number of sites served as repositories for *polispots* and provided critical analysis (almost exclusively for American ads). Perhaps the most polished is PBS's site, based on its award-winning TV series *The 30 Second Candidate,*[29] with a history of polispots, key examples from the past 50 years, and expert analysis of select ads and famous cases. A more limited site, containing nearly a dozen of the more famous spots, has been assembled by CNN/*Time.*[30] In recent years, newspapers, such as *The Washington Post,* and research institutes, such as the Political Communication Lab at Stanford University, have developed sites during the course of campaigns. There, one can access an extensive number of ads by candidate or issue, though only for a particular election cycle.[31] The Internet, then, is an excellent tool for synthetic political advertising research.

The most fecund work in this sector to date may be Westbrook's (1983) effort to place the development of electoral politics within the larger panorama of American consumer culture. In his view, the consultants who shape the messages and place them into ad/products are themselves commodities for sale. Furthermore, the transformation of electioneering toward an institutionalized advertising model is considered part of the increasing rationalization of American society over the course of the 20th century, a rationalization incorporating surveillance, commodification, and information management (Westbrook, 1983, p. 146).

Although it is common to associate political advertising with commodification, one area that has been little explored is how commodity advertising is politicized. This would seem an essential area for research, given the consensus developing about advertising's long-term power to set the ad reader's agenda. Such research posits that product advertising selectively communicates a narrow range of political values for symbolic consumption. One study in this vein was by Holden (1995), who discovered that in a sample of more than 1,200 U.S. television commercials, about 12% contained clearly identifiable political values, such as equality, liberty, and community. In all, more than 700 distinct political codings were found, and, contrary to expectations, it was not liberty (84 instances, or 12%) or individualism (84 instances) that appeared most frequently. Instead, community appeared more often (206 codings, or 29%). Even more surprisingly, social control—in the form of laws, rules, displays of order, or other governmental organization—registered the highest number of appearances (247 instances, or 35%). The study requires replication, not only in American ads but also cross-nationally, as a means of comparing the form, content, and relative presence of specific political values in ads of various societies.

The Economic. Although we have explored numerous connections between advertising and various societal sectors, it is at root an economic entity. Although it has expanded into various forms and serves other purposes, it began as a simple industry aimed at promoting goods for sale. Not surprisingly, then, this economic function still commands a large part of scholarship. Textbooks, manuals, and consumer studies aim at transforming the persuasive arts into science. Specialized professional journals such as the *Journal of Advertising Research,* the *Journal of Advertising,* the *International Journal of Advertising,* the *Journal of Marketing Research,* the *European Journal of Marketing,* and even *Public Opinion Quarterly* (among numerous others) are valuable clearinghouses for results about ad form, content, and audiences. Trade journals such as *Advertising Age* and *AdAge Global* offer statistics, trends, and inside information about the industry. In addition, there is an enormous literature on advertising and marketing by practitioners: "How-to" books abound— ranging from writing better ad copy to tips on prospering in the trade.

Such professionally oriented approaches, however, tend to be more piecemeal and less synthetic than other lines of economics-focused scholarship, which generally fit into the critical studies tradition. Studies that focus on the structure and operation of the media institution are common, as are those centering on how audiences are conditioned by ad content. Within the latter, the semiotics approach has been particularly strong. Let us consider these threads in greater detail.

The Political Economy of Meaning. The origins of this approach lie distantly in Marxism but are traceable directly to statements on symbolic activity by Lefebvre (1971/1984) and Baudrillard (1981/1994). The true breakthrough, however, came with Williamson's (1978) work. This view has evolved to maintain that "advertising is an institutional process in a political economy of commodity-sign value" (Goldman, 1992, p. 224).

One of the assertions at the heart of Williamson's (1978, pp. 12–13) text was

that advertising translates factual use value of products into their humanly symbolic exchange value. She also spoke of a kind of sleight of hand in which commercials substitute false categories for real ones: Social class, for instance, gets replaced by consumer preferences. Consequently, what people consume is how they come to identify themselves, rather than what they produce or their role in the larger system of production. Through this process, advertising gives "things" an additional (and alternative) social meaning.

Williamson (1978) explored technical issues in semiotics: how ads work by using symbols, referent systems, magic, and history. However, the most important contribution—at least to the political economic genre—was the idea that the signs in the ad have a currency that is transferred. The transfer occurs both within the ad (between an element of a referent system and the product), as well as outside it (in terms of buying and consuming). This transference is a process conducted by the audience: They derive meaning rather than having that meaning imposed on them externally. In this respect, Williamson observed, the audience "works" to produce meaning.

It is here that Williamson's (1978) writing resonates with later developments. For the idea that sign readers are workers who make value underlay the thinking of Smythe (1980), who saw audiences as laboring for advertisers. This, in turn, inspired Jhally (1990) to argue that "commercial time is labour watching time ... subject to the same process of valorization as labour time in the economy in general" (pp. 111, 120). To Jhally, this means that the study of advertising messages can and should be approached from a "proper materialist perspective" (p. 121); just as is true in the economic realm, the constitution of meaning in advertising involves the subjugation of use value by exchange value (p. 121).

This Marxist/semiological treatment of signs is also present in the work of Haug (1971/1986). Looking at the development of the advertising industry in Germany, he identifies what he calls "commodity aesthetics"—"one of the most powerful forces in capitalist society" (p. 10). Commodity aesthetics is "the sensual appearance and the conception of (a product's) use-value" (p. 17). Appearance becomes attached to the product and becomes just as important—if not more so—than the object itself. Thus, the role of advertising is to enhance or elevate the consumer's perception of the commodity's aesthetic. To achieve this, Haug reckons, the consumer is offered the promise of use value. As he explains,

> [Use value's] opposite (i.e. exchange-value) interest elicits from the standpoint of exchange-value an exaggeration of the apparent use-value of the commodity, the more so because use-value is of secondary importance from the standpoint of exchange-value. Sensuality[32] in this context becomes the vehicle of the economic function. . . . Whoever controls the product's appearance can control the fascinated public by appealing to them sensually. (p. 17)

This line of analysis has achieved some synthesis. As Goldman (1992) argues, ads not only embody commodity culture but also structure social relations. In the quest to locate and attach meanings that will add value to their product or service, advertisers succeed in colonizing the sphere of cultural life. The symbols produced and exchanged are the province of those who control the means of cultural production. But who is in charge? Possibly the information producers and distributors (i.e., the television networks or publishers), but possibly also the advertisers. In the case of television, we know that advertisers are searching for specific audiences, and because networks seek advertisers to garner profits, this places pressure on them to develop programming that will deliver audiences the advertisers will invest in. If this is true, it would mean, in essence, that advertisers dictate the overall types of content transmitted.

Whether or not this is so, there is growing support for the view enunciated at the outset of the chapter that "precisely because . . . the circulation of symbolic values becomes integral to the circulation of commodities, advertising is growing in importance" (Garnham, 1990, p. 13).

Global Political Economy. Two factors, in particular, appear to be fueling this growth. The first is the proliferation of media technologies as outlets for advertising's messages, with the Internet and satellites being but the two most recent developments and thus the greater frequency with which the symbols and images of advertising are circulated and experienced.

The second factor stoking change, as noted, has been the increasing globalization of the advertising industry. A key dimension has been the transnational presence of a number of ad agencies. This has resulted in standardized advertising techniques often applied to singularly shared products and delivered to once-unique local contexts, with a concomitant explosion in the universe of symbols present in any one culture. However, early research on ad-induced globalization suggests that cultural/psychological filters exist capable of offering ad consumers some defenses against exogenously framed ad messages. This occurs for at least two possible reasons: Either ad readers are too sophisticated to fall prey to many appeals, or else the framing features of their context insulate them from "alien" communications.

Nonetheless, the internationalization of advertising has remained an underexplored phenomenon. One study on this theme is Mattelart (1991), which moves toward deeper questions of democracy in the age of a communications-based "network society." In the main, though, it traces the multiple strategies approached by advertising agencies in globalizing their products and brands. Deregulation—the pressures exerted on governments to liberalize their markets—is seen as playing a major factor. So, too, are the twin developments of advanced techniques in audience measurement and the steady ascendancy of public surveillance. The effects, Mattelart concludes, are profound: above all, "the absorption of the market in collective and individual life ceaselessly push[ing] back the limits of the intolerable" (p. 159).

Mattelart (1991), however, also posits advertising as now commanding "greater social legitimacy" (p. 206). If so, this carries some potentially troublesome implications, not the least of which is that the advertising form has given rise to information condensation (e.g., McLuhan & Fiore, 1967; Ranney, 1983), preeminence of the image (e.g., Baudrillard, 1975; Boorstin, 1961), ascendancy of "schizophrenic" narrative (e.g., Jameson, 1983) or "pastiche" (Goldman, 1992), and the swelling of private symbols—whether in the guise of the commodity itself or the design, logo, symbol, or packaging (Mattelart, 1991). Not only has this worked to elicit from message recipients a general desire for products and a motivation to engage in consumption (Haug, 1971/1986), but it has served to blur the bounds between the economic and cultural sectors—a "profound modification in the public sphere [that] needs to be theorized" (Jameson, 1990, p. 109).

This reminds us of Habermas's (1962/1995) claim that the logic of advertising (which his translators render as *publicity*) has led to significant transformation in the public sphere. In his words, "the public sphere has to be 'made,' it is not 'there' anymore" (p. 201). It is made through political discourse that has become "staged display" (p. 206); political "transactions are stylized into a show" (p. 206). Under these conditions, the rhetorical form of advertising has come to predominate. Such rhetoric has wrought change in terms of the stakes, expectations, and goals enumerated through political discourse. These represent effects of the greatest magnitude. The fact that these claims are being advanced globally suggests that they are unlikely to be evanescent. This only increases the imperative to accord them greater consideration in the years to come.

We turn finally to advertising as a societal institution and studies that have treated it in such a way.

◆ Analyses of Advertising as Societal Institution

Role in Sociocultural Development. Advertising's position between societal institutions and their various publics means that it is often ripe for use as an instrument to reproduce key values or power relations. In many instances, such reproductive work transpires independently of (or at least invisible to the tracing of) direct influence by the dominant political and economic institutions of society.[33] As such, the institution—embodied in the acts of its members (agencies and their personnel)—possesses "productive capacity." This dual feature—advertising as product and producer, influenced and influential—is a hallmark of advertising as institution.

Leiss et al. (1990) have analyzed this compound character in their exploration of advertising as social communication in North America. An express aim of the authors is to show that "economic and socio-cultural changes were institutionally mediated by the emergence and development of two key symbiotically related industries: the commercial mass media and the advertising agencies" (p. 7). In an historical moment when working hours were decreasing and more time was available for leisure and the pursuit of personal goals, the satisfaction of alternative ends was both spotlighted and enabled by media. Advertising, in particular, served as the delivery system for discourse about goods, consumption, ways of life, and social values. This discourse was formulated by the ad agencies on behalf of their manufacturing clients via continuous, ever-shifting "marketing strategies."

The research of Leiss et al. (1990) persuasively demonstrates how shifts in the content of communication emanating from the ad agencies matched changes in the larger society. This integrated process of economic organization, capitalist ideology, promotional practices, and changes in lifestyle and social ideas clearly played a central role in the development of American and Canadian society.

Advertising Organizations. The ad agency is a significant site of this process. And because one can find people to interview, tasks to observe, decisions to record, and productions to analyze, these organizations have historically served as highly attractive sites for scholarly attention. Nonetheless, short of confessional accounts, such as Reeves's (1960/1986) or Ogilvy's (1963), gaining access to agencies can be difficult.[34]

One exception was McGinniss's (1969) landmark *The Selling of the President 1968*—a book that, in hundreds of telling details, exposed how image consultants (and their advertising products) were employed to transform American politics. In the words of one practitioner, "What we're really seeing here is a genesis. We're moving into a period where a man is going to be merchandised on television more and more" (McGinniss, 1969, p. 117). In the words of another, "This is the beginning of a whole new concept. This is it. This is the way they'll be electing forevermore. The next guys up will have to be performers" (McGinniss, 1969, p. 160). Aside from its prescience, what marks this book's value is the deep schism it revealed between rival organizational cultures: those of the politicians and their media professionals. It is a tension that has endured to the present but, as we shall see below, has tended to be resolved in favor of the image crafters.

The "danger" of exposing unseemly inner dynamics is likely the reason why agencies are leery of outsiders. One of the few books based on access is Moeran's (1996). His year of participant observation inside one of Japan's largest ad agencies provided a valuable snapshot, albeit that of a single agency in a particular country at a specific moment in time (prior to the so-called "bursting of the economic bubble" and, therefore, reflecting a different production milieu). Through the author's eyes, the reader sees the inner culture of the agency concretized.

At the fore is how intra- and interdivisional relations bore on the process of ad production. Most peculiarly (from a Western perspective), we witness the common Japanese practice of agencies simultaneously holding rival accounts in the same product category. This serves to spin a complex web of social relations, one that ensnares economic competitors, links institutions, and also sets up a climate of competition among factions within the same organizational entity. Outwardly, one can also trace the wide reach of this web: how the agency's media partnerships and cross-ownership of other media can play a role in social communication. Such intercorporate/ intra-institutional ties are distinctive to the Japanese context,[35] and it is out of such arrangements that a particular power formation has resulted. A few agencies have the ability to influence a range of advertising-related phenomena, from the "branding" of corporate identity to the alteration of product design to the shaping of commercial message.

Lacking, though, in Moeran's (1996) study is systematic treatment of how agency thought and action concretely articulated with the external worlds of popular culture, social trends, and consumer practice. This is a key issue (not only in Japan) and begs scholarly consideration. And although one of the author's avowed goals was to work toward a theory of consumption, little effort was made to capture the re/actions of the target groups to whom the organization was advertising. This was impossible by merely observing the organization because, by Moeran's own admission, most agency interactions with the consumer were "slapdash . . . brief survey(s)—usually presented to clients as 'focus interviews'" (p. 124). Not only does this unwittingly underscore the limitations of localized organizational anthropologies in tracing macro-linkage, but it also serves to remind us that the extent of societal excavation required to demonstrate actual institutional "effect" may outstrip most advertising researchers' resources.

Moeran's (1996) conclusions take the form of (a) generalizations regarding advertising as institution and (b) the assertion of consumerism as pervasive and dominant. Based on a single case, these claims (even if true) are difficult to make stick. Moreover, they completely ignore recognition of the pervasive cultural and/or political influences operating on the agency, as studies have shown from contexts as diverse as North America (e.g., J. Lears, 1994; Leiss et al., 1990; Marchand, 1985) and Malaysia (e.g., Frith, 1984; Holden, 2001a; Ngu, 1996).

Placing the Institution in Context. What is needed, then, if one is to focus on the agency as a unit of analysis is to explore how it articulates with the larger matrix of *institutions* connecting to it, as per the studies of Ewen (1976), Fox and Lears (1983), Marchand (1985), and Leiss et al. (1990). In particular, these scholars apprehend agencies *as a category,* whose activities and products stimulate sociocultural development.

Other studies have sought to cast the institution in comparative context. In this way, the relative position, activity, and impact of advertising in various national settings can be assessed. This is a tack Frith (1996) adopted in her study of Asian advertising. One problem with such a gambit, however, is the volatility of political regimes and the specificity of economic systems in countries outside the traditional geographical purview of advertising research (i.e., the West). As one indication of this limitation, consider that since 1996 restrictions were imposed on the media in Myanmar, Malaysia, and Indonesia, political upheaval has been experienced in the Philippines, reintegration came to Hong Kong, and independence was gained by East Timor. The implications of such volatility? Within 5 years of publication, Frith's book was retired from print. Though a laudable and

important project, no comparable work has yet been penned to take its place.

The foregoing all serves to underscore the following point: Despite the ease with which one can locate the organizations producing ads, the vectors governing their work are often external to them. This is so whether we are talking about information formation, transmission, reception, consumption, or social use. Holden and Husin's (2002) exploration of Malaysian advertising manifested a clear pattern of "top-sensitive" ad content: text that reflected government-sanctioned communication rules, informal cultural codes, and publicly announced policy shifts. Despite episodic swings between liberalization and crackdown, Malaysian advertising has served for more than 30 years as an intentional governmental tool for nation building. The secondary discourse that Malaysian ad text delivers reflects a narrow, repetitive set of prosocial values, focusing on family, education, nationalism, secularism, racial segregation (yet, paradoxically, ethnic harmony), urban development, and a common political-geographic center.

Searching for Synthesis. Among seminal studies in advertising, overwhelmingly the focus is top-down: producers' intentions and actions, gatekeepers' rules and ideologies, a mapped "system" of meaning, and an exposition of a culture of values. Few, if any, studies on the list gaze bottom-up: providing sustained treatment of what the consumers of advertising make of the messages.[36] Virtually no study on the list would draw the deep lines of connectivity between the two levels.

To do so, one has to demonstrate how the perceptions, attitudes, preferences, and practices of ad viewers—as well as the media these viewers interact with—are part and parcel of the larger social contexts in which they live. To date, the best work in this regard has been merely inferential. Consider Husin's (1999) grounded study, aimed at determining whether and how

Japanese viewers construct and use ad text. Her panel design revealed that viewers were not only quite attentive to advertising but that they decoded and employed ad messages in highly personalized, unanticipated, even idiosyncratic ways. Such findings are consistent with the cultural studies and postmodernist perspectives discussed above. Husin also argued that ad viewers' attention, actions, and frame of reference were highly concentrated on consumerism and popular culture. In a word, their reception was consistent with the predominant values of advertising. Moreover, the values they primarily embraced did not acknowledge competing or antithetical values— ideas and practices that may once have been central to them but now more often lurked at the periphery. As she concluded, "The audience, though active and free to apply his/her meanings to a commercial text, is bounded by the meaning structures of the media."

A study with different conclusions is O'Donohoe's (2001). After sifting through considerable literature on consumer attitudes, she suggests that there is decided "ambivalence" in response to ads. She codifies her findings into three sets of tensions, or what she labels "postmodern paradoxes":

> [First] consumers experience advertising as a distinct yet intertextual entity: they see advertising as having its own historical and cultural identity, yet they draw on their understanding of genres and conventions from other cultural texts to make sense of it. Second, consumers appear to treat advertising as something to be enjoyed as well as endured: as a form of popular culture it offers various hedonic, aesthetic and intellectual rewards, but at the same time its repetition of form and content can jade sophisticated palates. Finally, it seems that consumers' advertising literacy skills encourage them to feel immune yet vulnerable to the persuasive and ideological powers of ads. (pp. 103–104)

The discrepancies excavated by studies of ad audience in context, therefore, demand more extensive investigation.

◆ Conclusion

At the dawn of a new century, there is no simple way to summarize all that has been written and thought about advertising in a single chapter. What can be stated is that advertising has grown to occupy a greater space in the consciousness of academicians and that this development is certainly due to the widened orbit advertising has carved out. This growth, in turn, can be traced to changes wrought by the increasing liberalization and specialization of markets, the pell-mell expansion and interrelation of economic organizations, the proliferation of variegated media technologies with which humans communicate, the increasing heterogeneity of cultures, and the hybridization of value systems.

In the years to come, advertising is certain to increase its societal position. The reasons for this have to do with its inextricable relationship to capitalism but also the increasingly mediated nature of society. Not only in terms of human organization and interaction but also humans' relationship to knowledge: More and more such encounters are expressed through and experienced in terms of media. Moreover, it is, in its insinuation in these multiple media channels, that advertising may come to command an ever-increasing position in media studies.[37]

As an instrument of communication and a social force, advertising will be more and more central to our experience and understanding of the social world. In turn, this necessitates better approaches, capable of deciphering advertising's expanding place in society. What I have sought in this chapter is to present a set of schemes as a means of making better sense of our field. Achieving a total conception of advertising has been and may continue to be beyond the ken of most research on advertising; it is, however, in that direction that the best scholarship in the field has pointed.

◆ Notes

1. Coen (n.d.) estimates that in the 1950s, advertising expenditures in the United States were $5.7 billion, compared to $1.7 billion for the rest of the world. Steadily, this distribution has drawn toward parity. In 1955, the figures were $9.2 billion to $3.9 billion, respectively; in 1960, $12.0 to $6.1 billion; and in 1965, $15.3 to $10.1 billion. In 1975, the figures became roughly equal: $27.9 to $26.8 billion. Finally, in 1980, America lost its lead for the first time since such records had been kept. Nevertheless, it was not until 1989 that the rest of the world posted consecutive years of expenditure advantage. In 2000—due in part to a strong dollar—the United States reclaimed the lead.

2. Following the terrorist attacks of September 11, 2001, worldwide advertising experienced its first decline since World War II. Nonetheless, global expenditures in 2002 were projected to reach $466 billion. This figure splits roughly equally between the U.S. market ($239.3 billion) and the worldwide market ($226.8 billion), as has been the case since 1998 (see Coen, 2002). At the time of this writing, the most recent statistics were for the year 2000. In the top nine markets worldwide, total ad spending for the six major types of media (i.e., TV, radio, magazines, newspapers, cinema, and outdoor) exceeded $240 billion. More than half of this amount ($134 billion) was spent in the United States. When combined with the next largest market, Japan ($33.2 billion), two national markets accounted for more than 69% of worldwide ad expenditures. The top four European markets comprise an additional 23%. Following the United States and Japan, then, the largest markets (with expenditures listed in billions of dollars), include the following: Germany ($21.6), the United Kingdom ($15.8), France ($11.1), Italy ($8.3), Brazil ($6.9), Spain ($5.4), and Canada ($5.3) (see www.adageglobal.com).

3. Goffman (1976/1979) is the first that generally springs to mind. Others, whose work has strayed beyond the North American continent, include the following: Wiles, Wiles, and Tjernlund (1995) in Sweden; Cutler, Javalgi, and Lee (1995) in South Korea and America; Das (2000) in India; and Holden (2000b) in Japan.

4. Marchand (1985); Ewen and Ewen (1982/1992); Lears (1994).

5. Reeves (1960/1986); Ogilvy (1963); Clark (1988); Perrin (1992); Rothenberg (1994).

6. Practitioners occasionally offer public commentary on selected cases in marketing strategy (and mindful of PR, on their successful ones). Visit, for instance, Young & Rubicam Inc.'s "case studies" corner of its Web site www.yr.com/knowledge/case.php (last accessed August 20, 2002).

7. Aaker (1995); Ries and Ries (1998); Klein (1999); Bedbury and Fenichell (2002). A number of research papers on branding can be found at the "brandchannel" Web site: www.brandchannel.com/papers.asp (last accessed August 20, 2002).

8. Meadows (1983); Goodyear (1991); Tynan and O'Donohoe (1998); Mintel (1998); Ritson and Elliott (1999). An excellent resource for locating studies on audience is the World Advertising Research Center (WARC): www.warc.com (last accessed August 20, 2002).

9. Haug (1971/1986); Jhally (1990); Goldman (1992).

10. Vestergaard and Shroeder (1985); Tanaka (1994).

11. Rutherford (1994).

12. Fox (1984).

13. Implicit in the inclusion of advertising in a *Handbook of Media Studies* is the following question: "What is advertising's relationship to the medium?" If it is merely a *type of communication* that is channeled through a variety of media (e.g., newspapers, magazines, handbills, posters, billboards, digital displays, radio, television, Internet), then its treatment should be in terms of how it operates in relation to specific media. Viewed thus, advertising is merely a communication form, within which numerous subtypes of message packaging and transmission can be located, assessed, and compared. Traditionally, such technical studies of advertising

form have been conducted; the forms they have enumerated include factual messages, demonstrations, comparisons, problem solution, slice of life, endorsements, and testimonials. However, advertising has often been viewed in broader terms: as an institution or medium in its own right. In this version, ads comprise a self-contained system of communication that transmits societal content. That content may appear in a variety of tropes, symbols, representations, and settings. Whatever form it takes, though, it provides information about societal structure, social relationships, cultural practices, values, and ideas. It is this latter conception of advertising that is adopted here.

14. Packard (1957) was responding to a view of media, persuasion, and the mass that had existed for well over 50 years. From the 1890s onward, European intellectuals such as LeBon and Singhele, as well as American writers such as Lippmann, Dewey, Mencken, and Lewis, were sold on what later was termed the *bullet* (or *hypodermic needle*) theory of media effect (see Chapter 9, this volume). This vision of media manipulation did not die with Packard's long-dismissed rant. The 1970s saw movies such as *The Candidate* and *Network* ratifying the power of what Michael Ignatieff called in a BBC documentary "the 3-minute culture" of ad-based, mass-mediated, stimulus-response, manipulative communication. In the 1990s, eminent thinkers such as John Kenneth Galbraith (1992) were reductively complaining that "[it is due to advertising that] consumer wants are shaped to the purposes and notably to the financial interests of the firm" (p. 134).

15. The term was popularized in another polemic (Key, 1973). Research on subliminal advertising has been extensive and unconvincing. The original claims—about dramatically increased sales of Coca-Cola and popcorn in movie theaters after exposure to subliminal imagery—were always suspect. The author never made his data available for scrutiny, the study was never independently verified, and, in fact, he actually admitted to *Advertising Age* that the results were fabricated. Some proponents argue that it is "semi-subliminal" messages that are of concern as, by definition, anything subliminal cannot be perceived. For a spirited

defense of the power of semi-subliminal advertising, see Hagart's Web site: www.subliminalworld.com/FULL.HTM (consulted March 2002). The preponderant position, however, is that rather than subliminal *messages*, it is subliminal *perception* that is being measured, and although perception may be demonstrable, influence cannot.

16. For instance, Noelle Neumann (1973) and her "spiral-of-silence" theory that media's effects can work over a long period of time to diminish—even entirely quell—opposing public sentiment. As for advertising, Schudson (1984) and Iyengar and Simon (2000) offer similar conclusions concerning long-term effects (though they provide differing grounds for believing so).

17. A third stream is suggested by Jhally (1990). He follows up on Livant's (1981) observation that communication studies has heretofore been fixated on the analysis of messages, and he also takes up Garnham (1990) and Smythe (1980), who both sought to move away from the cultural studies–induced propensity only to assess systems of meaning. This third stream turns from the content of messages to the form that constrains the content. It looks at the place of communication in the wider system of social reproduction and the reproduction of capital.

18. We should note, however, that others view this as both a "weary" and "false" dichotomy—at least as applied to the larger field of communication research. See Golding and Murdock (1991).

19. See, for instance, Ansolabehere and Iyengar (1995) whose laboratory and real-world evidence suggests that negative advertising (a) drives away independent voters, thereby diminishing the pool of voters and reducing elections to contests between the partisan extremes; (b) works better for Republicans than for Democrats; (c) appeals to men more than women; and (d) overall, exerts a stronger effect than positive ads.

20. See Baudrillard's (1981/1994) *For a Critique of the Political Economy of the Sign.* Little is said here about advertising, and according to Harms and Kellner (1990), Baudrillard "increasingly erases political economy from his theory and provides a vision of society, especially in his later writings, in which signs

proliferate and come to determine the course of social development" (www.uta.edu/huma/illuminations/kell6.htm, last accessed June 4, 2004).

21. This emphasis contrasts with a focus on the stage of political-economic development of the society in question, as well as the decoding competency (the so-called "semiotic literacy") of message recipients—a claim that, in varying forms, Goodyear (1991) and Holden (2000c) have advanced.

22. This is what Barthes (1957/1972) termed *first-order* and *second-order* connotation, respectively.

23. These include language, age and sex differentiation, knowledge and beliefs, social control, social institutions, technology, art, and recreation.

24. In many ways, this is strikingly similar to the themes that flow out of Malaysian ads 60 years later (Holden & Husin, 2002). This suggests implications for advertising research that move in a number of directions—above all, advertising's relationship to socioeconomic development, its ability to help measure globalization, and its use as a tool for conducting cross-cultural research.

25. O'Barr (1994) looks at representations of the "other" in magazine advertisements. He generally focuses on African Americans, although he also treats images of Americans and the West in Japanese print ads. Other interesting work on television advertising in the 1990s is by Coltrane (2000), who looked at depictions of Caucasians and African Americans. This is an area of research crying out for further research attention.

26. For how identity is treated in Japanese television ads, see Holden (2000a).

27. Work soon to be published has revealed the following strong associations: women in harmony with nature, generally, and water, specifically; men in competition with nature, generally, and water, specifically; women disproportionately clothed in red and men disproportionately clothed in black; women more often than men depicted as free of organizational ties; and women more often than men depicted indoors and in nurturing roles. For a further look at these relationships, visit Todd Holden's "Sold on Gender" page at www.intcul.tohoku.ac.

jp/~holden/Presentations/IAMCR-genderPres/Gender-index3.html (last accessed June 4, 2004).

28. www.annenbergpublicpolicycenter.org/ISSUEADS/ (last accessed June 4, 2004).

29. www.pbs.org/30secondcandidate/index.html (last accessed June 4, 2004).

30. www.cnn.com/ALLPOLITICS/1996/candidates/ad.archive/ (last accessed June 4, 2004).

31. *The Washington Post* site devoted to the 2000 campaign has been retired. However, the Stanford 2000 campaign site can be found at http://pcl.stanford.edu/campaigns/campaign2000/index.html (last accessed June 4, 2004).

32. The terms *sensuality* and *sensual* are the translator's attempt to render the German words *Sinnlichkeit* and *sinnlich*. The single German word is much more comprehensive than *sensual,* meaning also *sensuous* and *sensory. Sensual* strongly implies human sexuality; *sensuous* strongly implies the tactile, olfactory, or both; and *sensory* strongly implies a purely scientific definition of the five senses. It is clear from Haug's (1971/1986) argument that sensuality is sometimes, though not necessarily, included. Rather, the essence of his argument is that advertising and the commodity aesthetic, even since feudalism, appeal to the physical senses, to the range of material human desires beyond simple practical use value. This is to be distinguished from the *sensory,* which has no sense of appeal or attraction in it.

33. Much of the signal work in this vein has been done on news routines and organizational values. See, for instance, Tuchman (1978), Gans (1979), and Gitlin (1980, 1983). For general reviews, see Berkowitz (1997).

34. A recent exception is Aitchison and French (1999), who coupled their own analysis of more than 300 famous print ads with the ex post facto assessment of the ads' creators. Thus, this insider account details the decisions that led to the ads and explains why many of the precepts and techniques of the 1950s and 1960s are no longer valid. Important to note, however, is that this was not a particularly "scientific" study. Its criterion for inclusion in the sample ("successful") did not specify how "successful" was measured, and it was

restricted to English-language-based campaign examples.

35. Despite numerous mergers between media groups (worldwide) over the past two decades, only the rare case involves film, television, music, or print publishers attempting to purchase an interest in advertising agencies—and then never for strategic (i.e., self-promotional) purposes. Not only does this phenomenon occur in Japan, but the reverse case—of ad agencies purchasing media outlets—is not unheard of.

36. The study by Patterson and McClure (1976) is an exception. They collected responses to national political spots over time from a panel of TV viewers. They coupled this with content analysis of both ads and national television news programs, thereby affording some comparison across media forms while also seeking to draw linkages between institution and public.

37. There are a few outstanding Web sites that assist advertising research. They include everything from academic scholarship to marketing and popular criticism to fan appreciation and parody. Perhaps the best all-purpose site yet constructed is that hosted by the University of Texas (http://advertising.utexas.edu/world/). A site housed at the University of Iowa (www.uiowa.edu/~commstud/resources/advertising.html) is not as well organized but still rather extensive. Among privately maintained sites, KnowThis.com has assembled a fine (but limited) collection of advertising resources, under the title "Marketing Virtual Library" (www.knowthis.com). (All URLs last accessed on June 5, 2004.)

◆ References

Aaker, D. A. (1995). *Building strong brands.* New York: The Free Press.

Aitchison, J., & French, N. (1999). *Cutting edge advertising: How to create the world's best for brands in the 21st century.* Upper Saddle River, NJ: Prentice Hall.

Ansolabehere, S., & Iyengar, S. (1995). *Going negative: How attack ads shrink and polarize the electorate.* New York: Free Press.

Archer, D., Iritani, B., Kimes, D., & Barrios, M. (1983). Face-ism: 5 studies of sex-differences in facial prominence. *Journal of Personality and Social Psychology, 45*(4), 725–735.

Barthes, R. (1967). *Elements of semiology.* London: Jonathan Cape Ltd.

Barthes, R. (1972). *Mythologies.* London: Jonathan Cape Ltd. (Original work published 1957)

Baudrillard, J. (1975). *For a critique of the political economy of the sign.* St. Louis, MO: Telos.

Baudrillard, J. (1994). *Simulacra and simulation.* Ann Arbor: University of Michigan Press. (Original work published 1981)

Bedbury, S., & Fenichell, S. (2002). *A new brand world: Ten principles for achieving brand leadership in the twenty-first century.* New York: Viking Penguin.

Belkaoui, A., & Belkaoui, J. J. (1976). A comparative analysis of the roles portrayed by women in print advertisements, 1968, 1970, 1972. *Journal of Marketing Research, 13,* 168–172.

Berkowitz, D. (Ed.). (1997). *Social meanings of news: A text-reader.* London: Sage.

Biswas, A., Olsen, J. E., & Carlet, V. (1992). A comparison of print advertisements from the United States and France. *Journal of Advertising, 21*(4), 73–81.

Blumenthal, S. (1980). *The permanent campaign.* New York: Touchstone.

Bonnal, F. (1990). Attitudes to advertising in six European countries: National feelings about advertising are positive, improving . . . and fairly consistent. *Admap, 26*(11), 19–23.

Boorstin, D. (1961). *The image: A guide to pseudo-events in America.* New York: Athenium.

Clark, E. (1988). *The want makers: Inside the world of advertising.* New York: Penguin.

Coen, R. J. (2002). Bob Coen's insider report (December 9). Retrieved June 5, 2004, from www.universalmccann.com/Bob_Coen_Report_July_2002.doc

Coen, R. J. (n.d.). Bob Coen's historical advertising data. Retrieved June 6, 2004, from www.universalmccann.com/coen_report_files/sheet008.htm

Coltrane, S. (2000). The perpetuation of subtle prejudice: Race and gender imagery in 1990s television advertising. *Sex Roles: A Journal of Research,* March. Retrieved June 5, 2004, from http://articles.findarticles.com/p/articles/mi_m2294/is_2000_March/ai_63993940

Courtney, A. E., & Lockeretz, S. W. (1971). A women's place: An analysis of the roles portrayed by women in magazine advertisements. *Journal of Marketing Research, 8,* 92–95.

Courtney, A. E., & Whipple, T. W. (1974). Women in TV commercials. *Journal of Communication, 24,* 110–118.

Culley, J., & Bennett, R. (1976). Selling women, selling Blacks. *Journal of Communication, 26,* 160–174.

Cutler, B. D., Javalgi, R. G., & Lee, D. (1995). The portrayal of people in magazine advertisements: The United States and Korea. *Journal of International Consumer Marketing, 8*(2), 45–55.

Dahlgren, P. (1998). Critique: Elusive audiences. In R. Dickinson, R. Harindranath, & O. Linné (Eds.), *Approaches to audiences: A reader* (pp. 298–310). London: Arnold.

Das, M. (2000). Men and women in Indian magazine advertisements: A preliminary report. *Sex Roles: A Journal of Research,* November. Retrieved June 5, 2004, from http://articles.findarticles.com/p/articles/mi_m2294/is_2000_Nov/ai_75959822

De Mooij, M. (1998). *Global marketing and advertising: Understanding cultural paradoxes.* Thousand Oaks, CA: Sage.

Diamond, E., & Bates, S. (1984). *The spot: The rise of political advertising on television.* Cambridge: MIT Press.

Dominick, J. R., & Rausch, G. E. (1972). The image of women in network TV commercials. *Journal of Broadcasting, 16,* 259–265.

Ewen, S. (1976). *The captains of consciousness.* New York: McGraw-Hill.

Ewen, S., & Ewen, E. (1992). *Channels of desire: Mass images and the shaping of American consciousness.* Minneapolis: University of Minnesota Press. (Original work published 1982)

Fiske, J. (1989). *Understanding popular culture.* London: Routledge.

Fowles, J. (1996). *Advertising and popular culture.* Thousand Oaks, CA: Sage.

Fox, R. W., & Lears, T. J. J. (1983). *The culture of consumption: Critical essays in American history, 1880–1980.* New York: Pantheon.

Fox, S. (1984). *The mirror makers: A history of American advertising and its creators.* New York: Vintage.

Frith, K. T. (1984). The social and legal constraints on advertising in Asia. *Media Asia, 14*(2), 100–104.

Frith, K. T. (1996). *Advertising in Asia: Communication, culture and consumption.* Ames: Iowa State University Press.

Galbraith, J. K. (1992). *The culture of contentment.* London: Penguin.

Gans, H. (1979). *Deciding what's news.* New York: Pantheon.

Garnham, N. (1990). Contribution to a political economy of mass-communication. In F. Inglis (Ed.), *Capitalism and communication: Global culture and the economics of information* (pp. 20–55). London: Sage.

Gitlin, T. (1980). *The whole world is watching.* Berkeley: University of California Press.

Gitlin, T. (1983). *Inside prime time.* New York: Pantheon.

Goffman, E. (1979). *Gender advertisements.* New York: Harper & Row. (Original work published 1976)

Golding, P., & Murdock, G. (1991). Culture, communications and political economy. In J. Curran & M. Gurevitch (Eds.), *Mass media and society* (pp. 15–32). London: Edward Arnold.

Goldman, R. (1992). *Reading ads socially.* New York: Routledge.

Goodyear, M. (1991). The five stages of advertising literacy: why different countries respond to different levels of ad sophistication. *Admap, 26*(3), 19–21.

Goodyear, M. (1994, September). Keeping up with the Joneses: The evolution of the superconsumer. *Admap.* Retrieved March 26, 2002, from www.warc.com

Habermas, J. (1995). *The structural transformation of the public sphere: An inquiry into a category of bourgeois society* (T. Burger with F. Lawrence, Trans.). Cambridge: MIT Press. (Original work published 1962)

Hall, C. (1994). Women and "bodyism" in television beer commercials. *Sex Roles, 31.*

Hall, S. (1980). Culture studies and the center: Some problematics and problems. In S. Hall, D. Hobson, A. Love, & P. Willis (Eds.), *Culture, media, language: Working papers in cultural studies* (pp. 15–47). London: Hutchinson.

Harms, J., & Kellner, D. (1990). Toward a critical theory of advertising. Retrieved June 4, 2004, from www.uta.edu/huma/illuminations/kell6. htm

Haug, W. F. (1986). *Critique of commodity aesthetics: Appearance, sexuality and advertising in capitalist society.* Minneapolis: University of Minnesota Press. (Original work published 1971)

Hay, J., Grossberg, L., & Wartella, E. (Eds.). (1997). *The audience and its landscape.* Boulder, CO: Westview.

Holden, T. J. M. (1995). Common threads in the tapestry: Mythical values in American commercials. *Journal of American and Canadian Studies, 13,* 1–33.

Holden, T. J. M. (1996). The commercialized body: A comparative study of culture and values. *Interdisciplinary Information Sciences, 2*(2), 199–215.

Holden, T. J. M. (1997a). The color of meaning: The significance of Black and White in television commercials. *Interdisciplinary Information Sciences, 3*(2), 125–146.

Holden, T. J. M. (1997b). "How can we say it in 15 seconds?" Assessing Japan's first mass media election. *Japanese Society, 2,* 77–97.

Holden, T. J. M. (1999a). The color of difference: Critiquing cultural convergence via television advertising. *Interdisciplinary Information Sciences, 5*(1), 15–36.

Holden, T. J. M. (1999b). Commercialized politics: Japan's new mass mediated reality. *Japanese Studies, 19*(1), 33–47.

Holden, T. J. M. (2000a). Adentity: Images of self in Japanese television advertising. *The International Scope Review, 2*(4). Retrieved June 4, 2004, from www.internationalscope.com/journal/volume%202000/issue4/holden.htm

Holden, T. J. M. (2000b, February). "I'm your Venus"/ "You're a rake": Gender and the grand narrative in Japanese television advertising. *Intersections: Gender, History and Culture in the Asian Context.* Retrieved June 4, 2004, from http://www sshe.murdoch.edu.au/intersections/issue3/holden_paper1.html

Holden, T. J. M. (2000c, March). Reading Malaysian and Japanese television commercials: Postmodernism, semiotic literacy and political-economic development. *Proceedings of the 6th International Conference on Japanese Studies: Japan–Southeast Asia Relations, National University of Singapore,* pp. 200–213.

Holden, T. J. M. (2001a). The Malaysian dilemma: Advertising's catalytic and cataclysmic role in social development. *Media, Culture and Society, 23*(3), 275–297.

Holden, T. J. M. (2001b, April 2). Marilyn Monroe hawked a red car, while a cranky sarariman debated Bill Clinton, to the tune of "All You Need is Love": Resignification and cultural re/production in Japanese television commercials. *M/C: A Journal of Media and Culture.* Retrieved June 4, 2004, from www.media-culture.org.au/0104/japtele.html

Holden, T. J. M., & Husin, A. (2002). Moral advertising: Messages of development and control in Malaysian television commercials. In T. Craig & R. King (Eds.), *Global goes local: Popular culture in Asia* (pp. 138–159). Vancouver: University of British Columbia Press.

Husin, A. (1999). *Living with television commercials: Media cultural literacy and symbolic consumption in meaning construction.* Unpublished doctoral dissertation, Tohoku University.

Iyengar, S., & Simon, A. F. (2000). New perspectives and evidence on political communication and campaign effects. *Annual Review of Psychology, 51,* 149–169.

Iyengar, S., & Valentino, N. A. (2000). Who says what? Source credibility as a mediator of campaign advertising. In A. Lupia, M. D. McCubbins, & S. L. Popkin (Eds.), *Elements of reason: Cognition, choice and the bounds of rationality* (pp. 108–129). New York: Cambridge University Press.

Jameson, F. (1983). Postmodernism and consumer society. In H. Foster (Ed.), *The anti-aesthetic essays on postmodern culture* (pp. 111–125). Port Townsend, WA: Bay Press.

Jameson, F. (1990). Postmodernism and the market. In R. Miliband, L. Panitch, & J. Saville (Eds.), *1990: The retreat of the intellectuals* (pp. 95–110). London: Merlin.

Jamieson, K. H. (1992). *Packaging the presidency: A history and criticism of presidential campaign advertising.* Oxford, UK: Oxford University Press. (Original work published 1984)

Jhally, S. (1990). *The codes of advertising: Fetishism and the political economy of meaning in the consumer society.* New York: Routledge.

Katz, H., & Lee, W.-N. (1992). Oceans apart: An initial exploration of social communication differences in US and UK prime-time television advertising. *International Journal of Advertising, 11,* 69–82.

Kellner, D. (1995). *Media culture: Cultural studies, identity and politics between the modern and the postmodern.* London: Routledge.

Key, B. W. (1973). *Subliminal Seduction: Ad media's manipulation of a not so innocent America.* New York: Signet.

Klein, N. (1999). *No logo: Taking aim at the brand bullies.* New York: Picador.

Lears, J. (1994). *Fables of abundance: A cultural history of advertising in America.* New York: Basic Books.

Lears, T. J. J. (1983). From salvation to self-realization: Advertising and the therapeutic roots of the consumer culture, 1880–1930. In R. W. Fox & T. J. J. Lears (Eds.), *The culture of consumption: Critical essays in American history, 1880–1980* (pp. 1–38). New York: Pantheon.

Lefebvre, H. (1984). *Everyday life in the modern world* (S. Rabinovitch, Trans.). New Brunswick, NJ: Transaction. (Original work published 1971)

Leiss, W. (1994). Risk communication and public knowledge. In D. Crowley & D. Mitchell (Eds.), *Communication theory today* (pp. 127–139). Oxford, UK: Blackwell.

Leiss, W., Kline, S., & Jhally, S. (1990). *Social communication in advertising: Persons, products and images of well-being.* London: Routledge.

Lin, C. A. (1993, July/August). Cultural differences in message strategies: A comparison between American and Japanese TV commercials. *Journal of Advertising Research,* pp. 40–47.

Livant, B. (1981). On a historical turning point in making audiences as commodities. Unpublished Xerox. New York: Brooklyn College.

Marchand, R. (1985). *Advertising the American Dream: Making way for modernity, 1920–1940.* Berkeley: University of California Press.

Mattelart, A. (1991). *Advertising international: The privatisation of public space.* London: Routledge.

McArthur, L. Z., & Resko, B. G. (1975). The portrayal of men and women in American television commercials. *Journal of Social Psychology, 97,* 209–220.

McGinniss, J. (1969). *The selling of the president 1968.* New York: Washington Square Press.

McLuhan, M., & Fiore, Q. (1967). *The medium is the massage: An inventory of effects.* New York: Bantam.

Meadows, R. (1983, July/August). They consume advertising too. *Admap, 18,* 408–413.

Merikle, P. M. (2000). Subliminal perception. In A. E. Kazdin (Ed.), *Encyclopedia of psychology* (Vol. 7, pp. 497–499). New York: Oxford University Press.

Mintel. (1998). *The sophisticated consumer.* London: Author.

Moeran, B. (1996). *A Japanese advertising agency: An anthropology of media and markets.* Honolulu, HI: Curzon.

Morley, D. (1988). Domestic relations: The framework of family viewing in Great Britain. In J. Lull (Ed.), *World families watch television* (pp. 22–48). Newbury Park, CA: Sage.

Mueller, B. (1987, June/July). Reflections of culture: An analysis of Japanese and American advertising appeals. *Journal of Advertising Research, 27,* 51–59.

Nevett, T. (1992). Differences between American and British television advertising: Explanations and implications. *Journal of Advertising, 21*(4), 73–81.

Ngu, T. H. (1996). Malaysia: Advertising in a multiracial society. In K. T. Frith (Ed.), *Advertising in Asia: Communication, culture and consumption* (pp. 241–257). Ames: Iowa State University Press.

Noelle-Neumann, E. (1973). Return to the concept of powerful mass media. In H. Eguchi & K. Sata (Eds.), *Studies of broadcasting: An international annual of broadcasting science* (pp. 67–112). Tokyo: Nippon Hoso Kyokai.

O'Barr, W. M. (1994). *Culture and the ad: Exploring otherness in the world of advertising.* Boulder, CO: Westview.

O'Donohoe, S. (2001). Living with ambivalence: Attitudes toward advertising in postmodern times. *Marketing Theory, 1*(1), 91–108.

Ogilvy, D. (1963). *Confessions of an advertising man.* New York: Dell.

Packard, V. (1957). *The hidden persuaders.* London: Longmans, Green.

Patterson, T. E., & McClure, R. D. (1976). *The unseeing eye: The myth of television power in national politics.* New York: Putnam.

Perrin, W. (1992). *Advertising realities.* Mountain View, CA: Mayfield.

Pope, D. (1983). *The making of modern advertising.* New York: Basic Books.

Ramaprasad, J., & Hasegawa, K. (1992, January/February). Creative strategies in American and Japanese TV commercials: A comparison. *Journal of Advertising Research,* pp. 59-67.

Ranney, A. (1983). *Channels of power: The impact of television on American politics.* New York: Basic Books.

Reeves, R. (1986). *Reality in advertising.* New York: Knopf. (Original work published 1960)

Remmling, G. W., & Campbell, R. B. (1976). *Basic sociology: An introduction to study of society.* Totowa, NJ: Littlefield, Adams.

Ries, A., & Ries, L. (1998). *The 22 immutable laws of branding: How to build a product or service into a world-class brand.* New York: HarperInformation.

Ritson, M., & Elliott, R. (1995). A model of advertising literacy: The praxiology and co-creation of advertising meaning. In M. Bergaada (Ed.), *Proceedings of the 24th Conference of the European Marketing Academy* (pp. 1035–1054). Paris: ESSEC.

Ritson, M., & Elliott, R. (1999). The social uses of advertising: An ethnographic study of adolescent advertising audiences. *Journal of Consumer Research, 26,* 260–277.

Robinson, D. L. (1973). *The election men: Professional campaign managers and American democracy.* New York: Quadrangle.

Rothenberg, R. (1994). *Where the suckers moon: The life and death of an advertising campaign.* New York: Knopf.

Rutherford, P. (1994). *The new icons? The art of television advertising.* Toronto: University of Toronto Press.

Sabato, L. J. (1981). *The rise of political consultants: New ways of winning elections.* New York: Basic Books.

Schudson, M. (1984). *Advertising, the uneasy persuasion: Its dubious impact on American society.* New York: Basic Books.

Sengupta, S. (1995). The influence of culture on portrayals of women in television commercials: A comparison between the United States and Japan. *International Journal of Advertising, 14,* 314–333.

Smythe, D. (1980). *Dependency road.* Norwood, NJ: Ablex.

Spero, R. (1980). *The duping of the American voter: Dishonesty and deception in presidential television advertising.* New York: Lippincott & Crowell.

Tanaka, K. (1994). *Advertising language: A pragmatic approach to advertisements in Britain and Japan.* London: Routledge.

Taylor, R. E., & Hoy, M. G. (1995). The presence of la seduction, le spectacle, l'amour and l'humour in French commercials. In S. Madden (Ed.), *Proceedings of the 1995 Conference of the Academy of Advertising* (pp. 36-42). Waco, TX: Baylor University.

Tomlinson, J. (1999). *Globalization and culture.* Cambridge, UK: Polity.

Tuchman, G. (1978). *Making news: A study in the construction of reality.* New York: Free Press.

Turner, E. S. (1952). *The shocking history of advertising.* Harmondsworth, UK: Penguin.

Tynan, C., & O'Donohoe, S. (1998). Beyond sophistication: Dimensions of advertising literacy. *International Journal of Advertising, 17*(4), 467–482.

Vestergaard, T., & Shroeder, K. (1985). *The language of advertising.* Oxford, UK: Blackwell.

Westbrook, R. (1983). Politics as consumption: Managing the modern American election. In R. W. Fox & T. J. J. Lears (Eds.), *The culture of consumption: Critical essays in American history, 1880–1980* (pp. 143-173). New York: Pantheon.

Wiles, J. A., Wiles, C. R., & Tjernlund, A. (1995). A comparison of gender role portrayals in magazine advertising: The Netherlands, Sweden and the USA. *European Journal of Marketing, 29*(11), 35–49.

Williams, R. (1993). Advertising: The magic system. In R. Williams (Ed.), *Problems in materialism and culture* (pp. 170–195). London: Verso. (Original work published 1961).

Williamson, J. (1978). *Decoding advertisements: Ideology and meaning in advertising.* London: Marion Boyars.

23

BROADCASTING, CABLE, AND SATELLITES

◆ Michele Hilmes

I t is impossible to understand the function and impact of the media of broadcasting, cable, and satellites without attention to the historical processes and tensions that have produced them. More than any other previous or subsequent medium, broadcasting and its adjuncts have been structured within the needs of *nation*. Born during the period of heightened nationalism following the struggles of World War I, radio and later television became deeply nationalized forms of communication, largely confined within the borders of individual nations, either completely run by or at least heavily regulated by government, shaped to serve the needs of national identity formation during a century marked by bitter national struggles, increased displacement and immigration, and national debates over "who we are, who we are not" (Hilmes, 2002).

These debates also essentially included negotiations over *internal* hierarchies and power. Radio, and later television, functioned as a public medium in private space, and its voices and representations became the sites of struggles over participation, inclusion, and control during decades in which nations struggled with massive immigration and the challenges of assimilation, the enfranchisement of women destabilized gendered social structures across the globe, racial struggles led to a period of decolonization and civil rights, and the first stirrings of a global popular culture disrupted national cultures and prerogatives. Broadcasting often served the needs of political elites, keeping cultural power out of the threatening hands of those deemed second-class citizens, even as subordinate groups made use of media on the margins to organize, define themselves, and share their messages with the greater public (Collins, 1990; Hayes, 2000; Scannell & Cardiff, 1991). Broadcasting institutions and industries became enormously powerful and increasingly central not only to national but also to individual life.

Cable, arriving at the height of television's power as a medium, promised at first greater localization of culture within the national address of television (Streeter, 1987) but, combined with the globalizing power of satellites in the late 1980s, began the process that today challenges national sovereignty over media even as it hands ever greater power and global reach to the media productions of certain nations such as the United States, France, Great Britain, India, and China. Broadcasting also developed a significant propaganda presence in the latter half of the 20th century, as nations sent out their political messages to other nations during times of war, tension, and peace. Thus, the social and political significance of broadcasting, cable, and satellites cannot be understood as merely technological, something simply applied to a culture and held in place by laws, structures, and practices (Williams, 1975; Winston, 1990). Rather, just as broadcasting has shaped culture over the past century, cultural processes have shaped the development and uses of broadcast technologies. This chapter traces that process.

◆ Radio Nations

The late teens and early 1920s were a period of immense social and political upheaval in the United States and in much of the world. Immigration, population flows, and the struggles over national identity and assimilation; the nation-defining paroxysms of the "War to end all wars"; the expansion of democracy to include women and other long-subordinated groups; the growth and problems of urban life; and an emerging, increasingly powerful sphere of popular culture challenged preexisting notions of social order and control. In countries around the world but especially in the United States, a new world of popular entertainments—in publishing, advertising, sports, movies, and vaudeville—rose up to amuse, inform, cajole, and educate the polyglot breed of Americans. A different kind of culture developed at the grassroots level that many, especially the established elites, feared and resisted. "Mass communication" began to be recognized as a powerful new social phenomenon in an atmosphere of expanding democracy and social instability.

The advent of radio drew on and affected all these trends. Far from arriving as a finished, uncontroversial technology that could be easily fitted into existing structures and hierarchies, radio stirred up conflicts, offered competing uses, provoked struggles over whose interests would win out over others, and raised fears about the dangerous cultural forces that might be unleashed by this invisible medium of connection and communication (Douglas, 1999; Goodman & Gring, 2000). Out of these many forces, radio broadcasting arose as a vital and necessary participant in the national experience, both in the United States and in other countries developing this promising new technology.

◆ *Founding Concepts*

Drawing on key technological innovations by Marconi, Fessenden, Armstrong, and DeForest, the idea of "wireless" radio broadcasting emerged from its previous domain in the garages and attics of the amateurs and became a nationally defining social practice. Joining the social upheavals and disturbances of the "Jazz Age," a time of rising affluence, increasing social tensions, technological advancement, and cultural experimentation, radio added its own unique voice to the mix. New institutions arose to address and control the growing business of radio. The Radio Corporation of America was formed in an atmosphere of nation building following World War I. Though many of its structures were similar to those being built in other nations, significantly, the United States, alone among the major nations of the world, chose to entrust its rapidly growing broadcasting system to the hands of major private corporations rather than to the state, producing its unique commercial network system.

The British Broadcasting Corporation chose another route, one that would be emulated by most of the nations of Europe and put in place in colonial locations around the globe. Based on the idea that a central contradiction existed between the needs of commercial owners and the needs of the state, public service broadcasting provided an alternative model to the American one (Hendy, 2000). Run by state-owned or state-chartered organizations, usually financed by a license fee paid by all and restricted to one or two national channels, public service broadcasting radio sought to educate, uplift, and preserve central cultural values. All association with vulgar commercial influences was to be avoided, and up until the post–World War II period, most nations regarded radio broadcasting primarily as a medium of information, education, and social control and much less as a popular entertainment form.

Many counties adopted some variation on the British model in the 1920s, with its combination of state ownership of broadcasting stations, a centralized programming service, public funding via license fee, and a public service mandate. Sweden, Norway, Denmark, and Finland all modeled their basic government-chartered broadcasting institutions after the BBC from the 1920s until the late 1960s or 1970s, with central control in a licensed corporation providing a mix of national and local service. France and Belgium, although allowing commercial radio to exist in the first decade or two, adopted public service systems after World War II. Other countries such as Germany and Italy, whose central governments exercised tight control and state ownership of radio before and during World War II, adopted a more British system after the war. Germany founded the Allgemeinschaft Rundfunk Deutschland (ARD) to provide a national programming service but placed ownership of radio stations in the hands of regional governments, which supplied the programming distributed by ARD as well as local offerings. Funding was provided by a combination of license revenues and sale of advertising. Italy formed the Radio Audizioni Italia (RAI), which operated several national television and radio channels again with a combination of public and commercial funds. France formed Radiodiffusion/Télévision Française (RTF) after World War II, with four national radio channels and one television channel after 1959. The Netherlands, virtually from the beginning, adopted a unique approach, with stations financed by subscription and public subsidy operated by "pillar" groups: organizations that represented large social formations in Dutch society. These were the conservative Protestant channel, the liberal Protestant channel, the Catholic channel, and two operated by radio amateur societies. Some shared facilities, and programming services were provided by a central broadcasting organization, the Nederlanse Radio Unie (NRU) (Emery, 1969).

In Asia, Japan formed the forerunner of its Nippon Hoso Kyokai (NHK) broadcasting authority in 1925 on a publicly funded basis but expanded to include commercial channels after World War II. India, under British rule, established the Indian Broadcasting Company in 1926 as a private enterprise, but it was replaced by the All India Radio service (AIR) in 1936 under government operation. In the early 1960s, television developed under the auspices of Doordarshan, the state-sponsored national network, which expanded to include regional stations and satellite-delivered services in the 1970s and 1980s and began to allow commercial sponsorship of programming.

Other countries made radio broadcasting a direct function of the state. In the Soviet Union, broadcasting was centralized in Moscow and directed by the state under the Ministry of Culture. The Moscow central station sent out programs by shortwave links to other cities across the Soviet Union's great expanse. In China, though the early 1920s saw a certain number of foreign-owned, private radio stations originate along the east coast and in some major cities, all were closed down in the late 1920s as the civil war raged between the Nationalist Party and the Communists under Mao Ze Dong.

A few nations combined private and public ownership in partnership since the earliest years. Canada actually started out with an American-style privately owned, advertising-supported system, which also imported a steady diet of American programs. Fearing the loss of its national culture in broadcasting altogether, in 1932, the Canadian government made the decision to completely redesign its broadcasting system and fashion a less American-influenced alternative. It created the Canadian Radio Broadcasting Company, which in 1936 became the Canadian Broadcasting Corporation (CBC). The CBC's mission was to build a network of both public-owned and privately owned stations, using a combination of public and commercial funding to provide the entire Canadian public with programs built on Canadian identity and culture. It dedicated itself to seeing that all of its widely scattered and often very sparse population, sprinkled across the immense expanse of Canada, could receive the kind of broadcasting service that a private system would not find profitable and one that focused on Canadian concerns and talent. With a mix of privately owned and public stations as affiliates, financed by a combination of public funding from license fees and the sale of advertising time, the CBC produced national programs and funded local productions (Collins, 1990).

BROADCAST CULTURES

In the United States, after a brief period of amateur experimentation and relatively uncontrolled local entrepreneurship, the National Broadcasting Company (NBC) and its smaller but more adaptable rival, the Columbia Broadcasting Service (CBS), quickly became the two major players, exerting a strong oligopolistic control over radio broadcasting in the United States. Regulators, though expressing the occasional doubt over their highly commercialized operations and the networks' monopolizing tendencies, in fact built a licensing system that privileged the control of large corporations over radio, to ward off the populist dangers the ineffable medium posed. By the time of the passage of the Communications Act of 1934, the majority of nonprofit stations had been driven off the air, and by 1940, the two major networks controlled most of the nation's more powerful stations (McChesney, 1993). However, control over programming had been largely turned over to the major advertising agencies and their sponsors, who designed and produced the programs, merely buying blocks of time on the networks. Between them, radio networks, advertising agencies, and the taken-for-granted American public created what some have called the "golden age" of U.S.

radio broadcasting. In other countries, such as France, Great Britain, and Germany, the radio units of the state owned the stations and provided the broadcasting service, making radio an increasingly effective means of political propaganda by the late 1930s (Hayes, 2000; Lacey, 1996).

From a collection of individual stations offering an eccentric mix of local entertainments, radio by the 1940s grew into an enormously profitable industry and a central focus of American life. Advertising agencies, networks, and stations, with a heavy dose of influence from Hollywood, created unique new forms of entertainment, information, and expression. Though primarily intended to sell consumer goods, the avenues of creative innovation opened up by this amazingly successful medium allowed a variety of programs, genres, stars, and audiences to emerge that spoke to the hopes, fears, and desires of the American public. Jack Benny became "America's fall guy" on the most popular type of radio show, the comedy/variety format, providing sophisticated and humorous satire of social pretensions and hierarchies to a new "middlebrow" audience. As the networks divided their schedules into distinct daytime and nighttime realms, daytime became the territory of women. Innovators such as Irna Phillips invented a new form, the daytime serial or "soap opera," that addressed the interests of women in highly melodramatic, continuing narratives, and Mary Margaret McBride set out on the path that would lead to *David Letterman* and *Oprah* (Douglas, 1999; Hilmes, 1997; Smulyan, 1994).

Yet despite radio's popular success, the medium came under increasingly heavy criticism as the war years drew near. Both conservative and left-wing critics objected to radio's cultivation of lowbrow tastes and interests and its heavy permeation by advertising. Radio's very success became a mark of its limitations, and as war rumbled in the distance, it seemed change might be on the horizon. Nowhere was this tension more marked than in Great Britain, where efforts to popularize the BBC service became

increasingly difficult because of their association with "Americanization." It would take the war years to turn public service broadcasting, in Great Britain and in other nations, in a more popular, entertainment-based direction.

◆ National Conflicts

Radio broadcasting played an extremely central role in nations around the globe during the war-torn years of the 1940s. Wartime tensions would change the medium forever and eventually usher in its greatest rival, television, whose structure and practices would reflect the deep changes wrought by war and peace. Because of the importance of recruiting national publics for war, radio would expand its mission and address, reaching out to groups disdained and overlooked before the war to draw them into the national fold. At the same time, radio would allow nations to turn their politics and culture outwards, creating international services such as the Voice of America and the BBC World Service as adjuncts to the war machine, which would become even more important during the different kind of conflict brought about by the cold war. Radio would become a crucial news medium, overturning pressures that had kept news coverage minimal in most nations in the 1920s and 1930s. Television would enter into this cauldron of political and cultural tensions promising education, international understanding, and the "end of ideology" but would end up embroiled in bitter cultural battles of its own.

Much of the concern over radio involved ideas about the audience, the "national public," that broadcasting, more than any other medium, addressed: Did radio create a susceptible, easily manipulated "mass public" that needed to be firmly directed by "experts" disseminating the "right kind" of information? Or did radio reach a rational, reasonable group of responsible individuals who could make informed decisions based on a range of information and opinion? In Europe, Hitler's Nazi state used radio as a central means of propaganda. Mussolini brought Italian radio under his control. In the United States, demagogues such as Father Coughlin inflamed the debate even as the Roosevelt administration approached radio as an adjunct of state. Roosevelt sought to tighten the regulatory framework under which broadcasting operated, commissioning a series of investigations that led to industry reforms. As a result of one of these, NBC was forced to divest itself of one of its two national networks—the Blue, which became the American Broadcasting Company (ABC) in 1943.

At the same time, as the war heightened the need to define "who we are and why we fight," radio offered up increased opportunities for marginalized and oppressed groups to demand the ability to speak for themselves, to address the inequities and antidemocratic aspects of American life. For the first time, programs that explicitly addressed the history of racism and prejudice in the United States reached a broad public on the airwaves (Savage, 1999). Though these first efforts were cautious and hampered by oppositional views, they provided a vital forum for the momentum that would lead to civil rights reforms after the war. Other programs recruited American women into a newly defined sphere of paid work and public service (Horten, 2002). Advertisers, stations, networks, and government agencies worked hand in hand, though not without friction, to build public morale and spread important wartime information and encouragement. Programs produced for American troops abroad boosted morale overseas but also reflected the racial divide in U.S. culture (Meckiffe & Murray, 1998).

Beginning in the World War II years and intensifying during the cold war, the U.S. government began to take an active interest in aggressively promoting its capitalist, democratic ideology abroad via the strategic use of media. International shortwave

radio, in particular, was able to break into the closed nationalistic broadcasting systems with a rival, outsider's voice. The international radio service, Voice of America (VOA), was initiated in 1944 to spread American values and propaganda messages worldwide and to counterbalance the radio propagandists of the Axis powers. Originally operated by the Office of War Information, in 1948, Congress passed the Smith-Mundt Act to create the U.S. Information Agency, which took over the VOA as well as a host of other activities designed to "tell America's story to the world," as its motto states. Interestingly, the law authorizing the agency to distribute information about the United States to other countries forbade it to disseminate this information at home, to offset any fears about domestic propaganda. In 1951, another outreach service, Radio Free Europe (RFE), was created by the Central Intelligence Agency (CIA) with broadcasts aimed specifically at Eastern Europe under the Soviet bloc; in 1953, it formed Radio Liberty (RL), transmitting directly into the Soviet Union (Nelson, 1997).

These stations did not just spread information about the United States and U.S. culture; they provided an oppositional source of news about the recipient nations themselves. The VOA showcased the United States to other nations; RFE and RL showed other nations to themselves from an American perspective, countering Soviet-centered news and information with anti-Communist propaganda. The United States was not the only country transmitting outward. The BBC's World Service became the single most-listened-to radio program around the world, with an estimated regular audience of 120 million. France created Radio France International to bolster French culture worldwide. Both the USSR's Radio Moscow and China's Radio Beijing maintained extensive shortwave broadcasting services to spread political messages throughout their areas of influence.

During the war, U.S. radio networks proved themselves the best and most trusted avenues of news from the fighting fronts for the majority of the American public. NBC and CBS had been slow to take on news programming as part of their in-house duties, preferring instead to allow sponsors to provide commentators and analysts in commercial programs. But in the late 1930s, with the resolution of the press-radio war, networks began to establish news bureaus across the nation and in hotspots overseas. The journalists who made their reputation on radio during the war would become not only household names but also television's first news anchors in the postwar period. CBS in particular served as the home of distinguished journalism, with Edward R. Murrow, Lowell Thomas, Erik Sevareid, William L. Shirer, Chet Huntley, Elmer Davis (head of the Office of War Information from 1942–1945), Charles Collingwood, and Howard K. Smith as primary figures. Murrow served as CBS's European news director. His live reports from London during the blitz, in the air over Berlin in 1943, and as American troops entered German concentration camps in 1944 still mark a high point in journalistic immediacy and impact. NBC had H. V. Kaltenborn and George Hicks. As NBC Blue became ABC after 1943, it too established a lineup of news commentators, including H. R. Baukage, Martin Agronsky, and Raymond Gram Swing.

The sheer popularity and centrality of news during the war years made sponsorship of news programs irresistible. This meant that sponsors, who in effect owned and produced the programs, could if they wished intervene in editorial content. Under pressure from sponsors, a change took place in the rhetoric of news delivery. From frankly personalized accounts—in which reporters spoke in first person and delivered the news through the lens of their own opinions—an openly expressed, less personalized, more generalized, and neutral style came into use. In 1939, CBS announced a new policy encouraging this change: It would no longer have news *commentators*; it would have news *analysts*.

Erik Barnouw gives an example of how that affected one of H. V. Kaltenborn's newscasts from 1940, covering a speech by presidential candidate Wendell Wilkie. Kaltenborn's first version read, "I listened to Wendell Wilkie's speech last night. It was wholly admirable." But Kaltenborn crossed this out and substituted a new introduction: "Millions of Americans of both parties listened to Wendell Wilkie's speech last night. Most of them agreed that it was a wholly admirable speech" (Barnouw, 1968, p. 136). This was both less honest (because Kaltenborn had no information about how most Americans felt) and less controversial (masking editorializing behind a tone of objective reporting). It was the shape of things to come.

But despite the networks' growing commitment to news provision and despite the high level of confidence expressed in radio news by the American public, broadcast news as an objective presentation of fact, untainted by product pitches or by overt editorializing, had yet to appear as an industry standard. This state of affairs would continue into television—only breaking free after the "quiz show scandals" helped to reduce the power of sponsors and news coverage developed enormously—but still struggled with the conflicts between commercial and informative agendas, between self-interest and objectivity. The line between entertainment and news, always a slippery one, had begun to formalize in a way that network television would negotiate anew.

THE SHINING CENTER OF THE HOME

Television rolled off the war-greased assembly lines and into America's living rooms with astonishing ease and rapidity after the disruptions of the war years were over. From the beginning, dominated by the forces of big industry, there was never any doubt that television would develop along the lines laid out by radio into a commercial network system, controlled by the former radio networks and funded by advertising. Cold war tensions only heightened the close relationship between government and industry, and despite considerable social unrest brewing among America's minorities and redomesticated former wartime workers, television promised a "normalizing" nation the good life. Decisions made in the regulatory sphere consolidated the big networks' hold over the developing medium and put them in a strong position once the Federal Communications Commission (FCC) "freeze" on TV station licenses had ended.

Television programs resembled their radio counterparts more than a little. The networks encouraged the transition to TV by siphoning off radio profits to support the new medium and encouraging sponsors, agencies, and stars to jump onto the TV bandwagon. Overseas, commercial television had made its debut in Britain in 1955, amid much debate that had echoed across the Atlantic. The careful separation of advertising from production, mandated by the new British Independent Television Authority, set a model that many U.S. critics thought American TV should follow. In the British system, commercial station operators produced their own programs and bought others from the United States and elsewhere, although in 1982, Channel 4 (the then-new second commercial channel) initiated a new system of buying programs from domestic independent producers as well. Advertisers were allowed to buy time in a totally separate process without even knowing what program their ads would appear next to. Selection and scheduling of programs stayed in the hands of licensed station operators exclusively, with no input from advertisers. In addition, advertising was restricted to set points at the beginning and end of programs only, cutting out the intervention of commercials mid-program that so many found so intrusive—and advertisers found so effective.

In the United States, meanwhile, a corrupt and lazy FCC seemed to have abandoned its regulatory responsibilities. In 1946, the New Deal–influenced FCC, under Clifford Durr, had published the most critical and proscriptive report in its history, the so-called "Blue Book," more than a little influenced by the BBC-derived perceptions of its primary author, former BBC executive Charles Siepmann (Hilmes, 2003). Yet its reforms had been largely ignored and barely considered in the light of television hoopla. U.S. critics and reformers looked for a way to reverse this downward spiral, especially in light of the British example, and seized on a few reports in the press about unfair quiz show practices as a way to intervene. In September 1958, a New York grand jury launched an investigation of quiz show fraud (most of the popular game shows were produced in New York), and in 1959, the FCC began its own investigative efforts. What made the scandal influential, though, was the second set of tensions operating during this time: the desire of the networks to break free of the domination of sponsors and advertising agencies that they had tolerated for the past 30 years.

The networks, led by NBC, had already begun to advocate a new kind of relationship of sponsors to TV: the magazine concept, developed by NBC chief Pat Weaver after the style of women's daytime talk shows, which substituted multiple sponsorship for single sponsors and made spot advertising the new order of the day. This system prevented a single sponsor from exercising the power over programming and scheduling that it previously had, and it let the networks regain the control over programming and scheduling decisions that they had lost in the 1930s. Seizing on the opportunity presented by the quiz show scandal and investigations, the networks promised that from now on they would take on a new, activist role in programming. Gone would be the dependence on corrupt, ratings-driven advertisers; here to stay would be a new era of centralized network responsibility and control. It was the blueprint for the classic network system, the era of network dominance that would reign supreme from the 1960s until cable and new regulations broke it up in the late 1970s. Unfortunately, instead of ushering in reforms, the profitable oligopoly of commercial television simply consolidated its power. The U.S. television industry would experience the most tightly centralized, vertically integrated, standardized, and profitable period in its history. The rest of us would experience *Mr. Ed, My Favorite Martian,* and *Happy Days,* our now-classic television heritage.

Radio, though diminished, did not die but morphed into a new form. The all-music DJ format emerged from Black radio practices, and a new kind of sound filled the airwaves. Rock and roll debuted as a new musical form out of the collision of Black and White audiences, crossover DJs, and the newly opened sphere of radio (Barlow, 1999). On television, meanwhile, a brief period of live drama, influenced by the New York theatrical scene, brought bold new fare to the small screen and launched dozens of new careers. Many consider this TV's "Golden Age." But variety shows, westerns, and situation comedies also thrived and prospered. The situation comedy, in particular, developed in large part by radio's female stars during the war years, would bring a new, feminine voice to prime time and soon came to dominate television schedules. News experimented and adapted to the visual demands of television, as did sports. The daytime remained a relatively undeveloped part of the schedule until the late 1950s.

Yet barely had the quiz show scandal faded away when the period of tight network control began to totter under a new dystopian rhetoric that blamed the vertically integrated commercial network oligopoly for a host of problems. The emergence of PBS in 1968 pointed exactly to all those things that the commercial networks failed or refused to do: educational programs for kids, serious public affairs and documentary series, coverage of art and culture, inclusion of racial minorities,

and a host of other long-awaited program initiatives. The commercial networks responded by creating "youth-oriented" shows that either stifled political comment, as with the *Smothers Brothers,* or created double-edged, compromised messages (Bodroghkozy, 2001). Network news covered the struggle for civil rights and for women's equal rights but reproduced the repressive racial and gender system in its own organization and basic orientation.

Pressures from reformist, political, and competing industry groups created a groundswell for regulatory measures that would undermine the tight network cartel. The financial interest and syndication (fin/syn) and prime-time access rules (PTAR) were passed to reduce the power of the "big three" networks over their increasingly vertically integrated business. Simultaneously, newly deregulated cable television pointed to a new, diverse, multichannel television universe still unavailable, yet beckoning.

ENTER CABLE

Community antenna television started out as a way for communities inaccessible to over-the-air television signals to bring TV into homes via a wire. A monthly fee could be levied for such a service, and the local cable TV operator could also set aside a channel for televising local events and send those out too, as a freebie. As station building spread in the late 1950s, local affiliates began to serve these communities, but many customers found that they enjoyed having a few distant signals from nearby cities beamed in as well. This was especially true when the nearly metropolis had a high-power independent television station that aired programming different from the networks, even more so if it included local sports or lots of old movies. By 1975, almost one sixth of the nation's homes were wired for cable. There were more than 3,500 local cable companies serving these homes, and most of them had the capacity to send 10 or more channels over the wires to their customers. A few companies began to buy and consolidate local systems, becoming the first cable multiple-system operators (MSOs). The National Cable Television Association (NCTA) was formed to lobby against its usual foe, the National Association of Broadcasters (NAB), and to push for cable expansion. As early as 1970, the FCC, worried about concentration of ownership, passed rules forbidding local telephone companies or existing broadcasters to operate cable television systems.

It had been unclear exactly how much power the FCC had to regulate cable because cable did not use the public airwaves that the FCC had been formed to supervise. In 1968, a Supreme Court ruling upheld the FCC's authority over cable, as long as it had a direct relationship to over-the-air broadcasting, as it clearly seemed to. In 1972, the FCC finally issued some clear rules that both inhibited cable development in some ways and yet also signaled its legitimacy and viability as a medium. Cable was free to expand in the top 100 TV markets. Cable operators had to offer at least one public/educational/government access channel, and the "must-carry" rules required that "all significantly viewed local stations" had to be retransmitted over the cable wires. This change had been sparked by a coalition of interest groups, which, despite competing agendas, had all seen in cable a solution to some of the problems that were beginning to be identified with commercial broadcast television (Streeter, 1987). Cable was seen as providing a useful alternative to the big-three bottleneck of the airwaves (largely produced by the VHF frequency allocation decisions of the 1940s) and as a way to bring more diversity and innovation onto the tube. Pay TV over cable, now permitted, promised a new market for movies and sports. Hollywood, which had been thwarted in its earlier pay TV plans, began to take notice (Balio, 1990).

But a potentially greater market began to open up as cable systems put the must-carry rules into effect, and small, low-power UHF

independent stations found themselves rubbing shoulders on cable TV dials with their formerly dominant VHF rivals. This provided an enormous boost for independent and educational stations, raising viewership levels and program ratings and lifting the price that they could charge for advertising. Formerly shoestring stations began to buy more expensive programming, often network reruns, but also movie packages, older syndicated series that had reverted from network ownership, and a few so-called *first-run syndication* productions. These were shows produced especially to be sold to stations, not to nets. In the 1960s and 1970s, they usually consisted of "specialty" formats, such as game shows, talk shows, and specials. More independent production companies began to specialize in these types of programs, sold directly to independent stations.

In addition, the syndicated market for off-network programs—reruns—also boomed in the 1960s. Not only independent stations but also affiliates—using the extra hour of prime time that they gained—and even networks themselves, especially in the summer months, began to rerun their own shows. In many ways, syndicated programs were the ideal broadcast fare: Already successful, a known quantity that took little promotion, a series successful in prime time could be recirculated for years to eager audiences (Kompare, 1999). Though network deals meant that often the producers of these series received only limited compensation for their afterlives in syndication, studios and independents became increasingly unwilling to sign away their rights as the 1970s progressed. The promise of the cable-enhanced syndication market swelled the agitation for regulatory and structural change.

In other countries, where television began as a state-sponsored public service monopoly, great effort was expended to ensure that broadcast reception was available nationwide from the beginning. Competition with state broadcasters was not allowed. In areas where reception difficulties abounded—within large apartment buildings in major cities or in mountainous areas—cable was used much as in the United States, as a retransmission device, from the early 1950s on. But until satellite transmission promised an outside source of programming, cable was limited in more public service–based systems to the two or three state services available. Few incentives for expansion existed. In some countries, however, particularly Belgium, Luxembourg, Switzerland, and the Netherlands, cable was used more extensively to relay multiple public service stations into areas outside their reach (Humphries, 1996). In Canada, with its mix of public and commercial broadcasting, cable expanded much more rapidly, mostly as a vehicle for bringing American programming into Canadian homes via microwave. Thus, cable's ability to serve local communities, fulfilling the principle of localization so predominant in U.S. thinking about broadcasting, swiftly became secondary to its national and even global capabilities, thanks to its conjuncture with satellites.

◆ *Global Footprints*

Opposed by broadcasters and regulators, limited to 12 or fewer channels, and faced by high system construction costs, cable might have remained forever a secondary medium were it not for two technological developments of the late 1970s: satellite broadcasting and fiber optics. Yet even before these technologies expanded cable's abilities, the early 1970s in the United States, as well as in Canada, Europe, and other leading television nations, began to witness a rise in perceptions of cable's social potential. Pressure was building to break free of broadcast television's limitations, whether commercial or public, and expand the number and types of service available.

In the United States, commercial network television was increasingly perceived as a "vast wasteland" dominated by greedy sponsors and a "lowest common denominator" programming mentality. Cable promised the "narrowcasting" of more specialized minority programming, local access channels that could pick up the community television function that local commercial stations had long since dropped, and commercial-free film channels: a television of abundance rather than scarcity. (The fact that the UHF band remained largely empty and might have provided many of these same services went unexamined in the rush to embrace the "new" technology.)

In Europe, where some countries had begun to privatize broadcasting and expand the number of public channels, the promise of cable's interactivity proved compelling, evoking visions of public participation in civic decision making. Cable was seen as the potential backbone of the burgeoning deployment of information technology. It also allowed the growing pressure toward expansion of media systems to bypass the difficult battles over terrestrial broadcasting and move into a new, promising arena uncolonized by established interests. In Canada, regulators' attempts to limit cable to communities that already had two or more Canadian stations available, as well as allow only one commercial and one public U.S. channel on those that met that standard, sparked general outrage, and the proposal was dropped (Rutherford, 1990). In Great Britain, cable began to be studied for its potential, and in 1983, a few companies would begin to offer regional services. Yet cable was expensive to install and still depended largely on broadcast programs for its material. In 1975, cable subscription rates stood at only 12% of homes in the United States. Struggling local franchisees began to sell out to larger companies, creating the first MSOs (Parsons & Frieden, 1998).

However, in 1975, Time Inc.'s subsidiary, HBO (Home Box Office), launched the first service to take advantage of satellite distribution of unique, film-based programming to local cable franchises nationwide. Leasing a commercial satellite transponder and using it to beam its signal across the satellite footprint, HBO was only the first of cable's rapidly expanding specialized services that began to find a niche. Simultaneously, fiber-optic technology—sending data through bundled glass fibers in place of the old copper wire—allowed cable systems to expand their channel capacity exponentially in the 1980s. Atlanta station owner Ted Turner beamed his WTBS, with its exclusive franchise over the Atlanta Braves (also owned by Turner), up onto a satellite transponder, founding the first cable "superstation."

These developments depended on the vital technology of the geostationary satellite. The first satellites used for communication purposes were launched in the early 1960s by U.S. telecommunications companies such as AT&T, Hughes, and RCA. COMSAT (the Communications Satellite Corporation) was formed in the United States in 1962 with the encouragement and participation of the U.S. government, much as RCA had been formed earlier at the outset of radio, to coordinate American satellite development, investment, and use. In 1964, INTELSAT (the International Telecommunications Satellite Organization) brought together a consortium of countries to serve a similar purpose for international satellite operation; at first managed by COMSAT, it became an independent corporation in 1973, with shares owned by its more than 100 member nations (the United States, through COMSAT, owns 25%) (Parsons & Frieden, 1998).

At first, satellites orbited around the Earth at speeds faster than the Earth's own rotation; this meant that they had to be tracked as they moved across the sky by large arrays of receiving dishes. But the development of the geostationary, or synchronous, satellites in the early 1970s meant that now satellites could be launched into orbit in the exact spot—22,300 miles above the equator—that allowed them to remain stationary in relation to the rotation of the Earth. A dish could be set to receive the continuous signal of one satellite in one particular place in the sky and never be moved. This made distribution and reception of satellite signals much more regular and reliable. Early satellites transmitted back to Earth on the C-band, between 4 and 6 gigahertz (GHz), and required enormous, bulky dishes for reception; more recent ones operate on the higher frequency Ku-band, between 11 and 14 GHz, and enable the use of tiny, pizza-size receiving dishes. Most satellites contain 24 transponders, or individual channel transmitters, though today's technology allows each transponder to be split to handle two or more separate signals.

New satellite-distributed cable channels began to proliferate in the 1980s, from Turner's second effort, the Cable News Network (CNN), to music video–dominated MTV, all sports all the time on ESPN, and other more varied offerings such as CSPAN (televising Congress and other governmental activities), USA (a varied-format channel owned mostly by movie studios), the Christian Broadcasting Network (CBN), Black Entertainment Television (BET), various home shopping channels, and pay TV services such as Showtime and The Movie Channel. Must-carry rules imposed by the FCC meant that cable operators were obliged to carry all "significantly viewed" local stations in each franchise area, giving a boost to independent stations that would eventually lead to the inception of new, movie studio networks Fox, UPN (United Paramount Network), and the WB (Warner Bros.).

The demand for programming created by this upsurge in venues sparked the growth of independent production in Hollywood and elsewhere and created new television outlets for such marginalized forms as independent films, documentaries, children's programs, and ethnic/foreign language film and television. Eventually, the film and television industries would become so tightly intertwined through cross-investment and production that they could hardly be separated any longer. Original production for cable would, in the 1990s, begin to rival both network television and film for audience and critical acclaim, as with HBO's series *The Sopranos*. In 1999, the networks' combined audience share dropped to a new low of 58%, with cable making up the difference. By 2001, the number of television channels available in the average U.S. home had reached 55, up from 39 only 8 years before (Rutenberg, 2001).

Cable expanded across the globe. Canada's subscription rates had exceeded 80% by the early 1990s. In Europe (Kelly, Mazzoleni, & McQuail, 2003; McQuail & Siune, 1998), as a wave of privatization and commercialization transformed the public service environment, cable was envisioned as playing a key role in the new telecommunications infrastructure. It could be used to open up limited national systems to the new, combined public and commercial multichannel service now prevalent in most countries. By 1992, cable had become very popular in the smaller European nations, reaching as many as 92% of homes in Belgium and 87% in the Netherlands, but remained much less in demand in the larger nations such as Britain, France, and Italy. The availability of satellite TV was a significant factor in this scenario (Humphries, 1996).

By the mid-1980s, satellite broadcasting and cable had become deeply intertwined. Cable as we know it could not exist without the national and international distribution that satellites make possible. On the other hand, as direct broadcast satellite (DBS) became a medium in its own right, it promised the first real competition to cable television services. With the success of HBO and other cable channels, the demand for commercial transponder space, usually leased from the satellite operator, soon rose to such an extent that the aerospace industry could hardly keep up. Not only cable but also network and syndicated programming are distributed via satellite, as are radio, data, and voice communications, all vying for transponder space. Live coverage of events across the globe depends on it. Add to this most nations' use of satellite communications for defense and

information-gathering operations—not to mention the burgeoning cellular phone industry and, increasingly, wireless Internet transmission—and the demand for satellite capacity seems infinite. The geostationary band is becoming full.

GLOBAL IMPACT

The half-hemisphere-sized footprint of the typical satellite signal began to change the rules of the national media game radically. Because in the early stages of satellite television, transmission dishes were so large and expensive to install, most satellite reception was done through cable channels: Cable systems provided the middleman between service providers and the home audience. This fact alone helped to slow the development of cable in some European countries, such as France and Great Britain, because so much of the early television material available via satellite consisted of U.S.-based entertainment and news programming. State broadcasters and agencies (particularly those that already produced the bulk of programs viewed in their home countries) saw no need to invest public dollars to bring American programming to their national audiences, and would-be commercial providers needed government permission to operate, usually meeting with opposition from state broadcasting interests. However, in more heavily cabled countries, the importation of American and other European programming on the satellite channels was widespread.

In the United States, DBS—sending satellite signals directly to receivers in people's homes—became a small but thriving industry in the 1980s, subscribed to mostly by residents of rural areas with no access to cable and by some city dwellers through SMATV (satellite master antenna TV) systems that wired apartment buildings, dormitories, and hotels with a dish on the roof and wires running to the units within. It did not yet present much of a challenge to the expanding cable industry. However, by the mid-1990s, with the deregulation of cable television and with most local franchises remaining monopolies in their areas, dissatisfaction with rising subscription rates, limitations on channels carried, and the kind of less-than-perfect service that monopolies tend to provide began to encourage DBS ownership. Yet in the United States, satellite broadcasting's role up until now has been primarily linked to the cable television revolution. In an already commercial and fairly diverse environment, DBS presented simply one more option for delivery of the same kinds of entertainment, news, and specialty channels that American audiences have regarded as normal since the 1980s. And the United States' large landmass (nearly the size of a satellite footprint) meant that importation of other countries' signals was not an immediate challenge, though Canadian and Mexican channels should certainly be receiving more widespread distribution in the United States than they currently are.

In Europe and across the globe, however, the impact of satellite broadcasting has been profound. Coming at a time in the late 1980s, when deregulation and commercialization of broadcasting systems was taking place in most countries, as one author puts it, "The rapid expansion of satellite channels had a tremendous impact. It removed, effectively, all practical constraints on the prompt development of private commercial channels" (Humphries, 1996, p. 169). For many countries, one of the primary cultural effects of satellite broadcasting was an influx of American films and series, as well as entire channels of American programming, offered via satellites services that crossed the borders of many nations. It is also significant that the late 1980s saw the collapse of the Soviet Union and renewed movements toward political reorganization and liberalization across the globe. Satellite broadcasting played a significant role in the liberalizing and globalizing of media systems that went along with this process.

The first commercial satellite to debut in Europe was the Astra satellite operated out

of Luxembourg, launched in 1988 with 16 channels. In Great Britain, the Independent Broadcasting Authority in 1986 had authorized British Sky Broadcasting (BSB), a consortium composed mostly of U.K. commercial TV providers, to introduce satellite television to Britain in a regulated, public service context. However, due both to technical and administrative problems, its launch was delayed until 1990; in 1989, Rupert Murdoch's Sky Channel beat it to the punch, broadcasting into Britain from the Astra satellite, outside of British regulatory control. By 1991, Murdoch had bought out the struggling BSB operation and renamed it BSkyB (Crisell, 1997). Despite offering a mix of music videos, news, popular films and television series (many of them American), and sports, BSkyB's success has mainly been limited to Britain and Ireland.

The European Community Directive on Television attempted to impose some order on satellite channels, including a vague ruling that "a majority proportion of their transmission time, excluding the time appointed to news, sports events, games, advertising and teletext services" be reserved for European-produced programs, yet it simultaneously confirmed the fact, now raised to a principle, that if a satellite service launched from one member country passed its own local regulations, it could not be screened out by any other member nation (Negrine, 1994). By 1991, a host of pan-European satellite services were on offer: 21 English-language services, 10 German, 11 French, and 29 others. Some of the most popular channels were Sky1, Eurosport, MTV, CNN, Euronews, Canal Plus, and the TNT Cartoon Network. In Québec, satellite channels became an important source of French-language programming.

The rise of satellite television was not confined to the United States, Canada, and Europe. Satellites were a much-commented on feature of the globalization process in the 1990s. CNN, MTV, and HBO, along with competitors from other nations such as the BBC World News, the European ARTE, India's Zee-TV, and Mexico's Televisa, were amongst those broadcasters who took the lead in this area. In India, the first major competitors to state broadcasters emerged, often based around regional cultures and languages (Kumar, 1999). In Taiwan, pirate cable systems began to spring up, bringing in foreign television channels via satellite but also providing one of the few spaces for oppositional political programs (Lin, 2000). In mainland China, illegal home dishes picked up Murdoch's STAR TV signals from Hong Kong, breaking the communications isolation that had for so long prevailed in that country.

Satellite transmission also opened up whole new vistas for state-sponsored propaganda services. The CIA ceded its broadcasting operations to the United States Information Agency (USIA) in 1971. In 1985, President Reagan authorized a service to Cuba, called Radio/TV Martí, committed to an anti-Castro mission. In 1996, the USIA began its Radio Free Asia (RFA) service into China and Southeast Asia. All are operated under the auspices of the U.S. State Department/USIA's International Broadcasting Bureau as of 1994. Though television did not work as well as radio in terms of global reach and ease of reception, most countries set up satellite-distributed international television services in the 1980s and 1990s. The USIA initiated its World Net channel "to present a balanced picture of American society" in 1983, broadcast from Washington, D.C. to stations and cable channels, as well as U.S. embassies and cultural centers, around the world. The BBC initiated its World Television News service, and France set up Canal France International and TV5, a joint venture with other francophone state broadcasting organizations. In 1991, the BBC launched a more extensive World Service Television but as a commercial cable subscription venture because the British government declined to provide funding, broadcasting to Europe, Asia, and Africa.

In the globally connected world of the 1990s, World Net and the USIA radio services compete as well with the Cable News Network and other commercial cable nets to provide U.S.-oriented news and information to the world. In more developed countries, the Internet provides additional global information that threatens to make more traditional forms of radio and television obsolete. However, it must be remembered that 80% of the world's population still cannot rely on regular electric service, placing television and computers out of reach. Radio is the medium, still, that speaks to most of the world. In Africa, a continent whose continuing struggles with poverty, political instability, and war have kept broadcasting from developing consistently, digital satellite radio promises to reach populations long isolated. WorldSpace, a commercial enterprise owned by Noah Samara of Ethiopia, extends its broadcasts to 80% of the world's population with three satellites positioned over Africa, Asia, and Latin America and the Caribbean. A wide variety of radio services in languages including English, French, Spanish, Arabic, Turkish, Wolof, Swahili, Portuguese, and Afrikaans, with a diversity of styles and content, is available for those who can get access to digital receivers—still a minority, but growing (Whelan, 1998).

◆ *Conclusion*

As the new millennium begins, we are witnessing a very rich period in U.S. and global media, with a plethora of channels, media, products, and voices to choose from. Despite some disturbing tendencies for power to concentrate at the top in global industrial mergers and consolidations, here on the ground we seem to be experiencing an exponential breakthrough in the quantity, diversity, inclusiveness, and even quality of the media that surround us. However, we should remain mindful of the disparities and inequities that such abundance can conceal. New technologies do not "automatically" take care of social problems; indeed, they tend to become the heart of the next social problem unless we keep our historical perspective firmly in mind.

Culture, rather than nation, promises to define the media of the 21st century and to present the battleground on which most of its struggles will be waged. Yet the means of culture still fall under the sway of nationalized organizations, as of now, or of commercial concerns that threaten to replace the flawed power distribution of national governments with the often even less scrutable mechanisms of marketplace and profits. Although technology—inseparably allied with culture, the market, and the state—does occasionally hand us ways to redistribute communicative power in a more equitable manner, the forces of containment and control just as rapidly move in. As concentration, economic power, and political containment seek to find their own self-interested path through the maze of new opportunities, it is more crucial than ever to work to ensure that access, choice, diversity, and freedom continue to characterize the media environment in which we live and breathe.

◆ References

Balio, T. (Ed.). (1990). *Hollywood in the age of television*. Boston: Unwin Hyman.

Barlow, W. (1999). *Voice over: The making of Black radio*. Philadelphia: Temple University Press.

Barnouw, E. (1968). *A history of broadcasting in the United States: Vol. 2. 1933–1953*. New York: Oxford University Press.

Bodroghkozy, A. (2001). *Groove tube: Sixties television and the youth rebellion*. Durham, NC: Duke University Press.

Collins, R. (1990). *Culture, communication, and national identity: The case of Canadian television*. Toronto: University of Toronto Press.

Crisell, A. (1997). *An introductory history of British broadcasting*. London: Routledge.

Douglas, S. (1999). *Listening in: Radio and the American imagination*. New York: Times Books.

Emery, W. B. (1969). *International systems of broadcasting: Their history, operation, and control*. East Lansing: Michigan State University Press.

Goodman, M., & Gring, M. (2000). The Radio Act of 1927: Progressive ideology, epistemology, and praxis. *Rhetoric and Public Affairs*, 3(3), 397–418.

Hayes, J. E. (2000). *Radio nation: Communication, popular culture, and nationalism in Mexico, 1920 to 1950*. Tucson: University of Arizona Press.

Hendy, D. (2000). *Radio in the global age*. Cambridge, UK: Polity.

Hilmes, M. (1997). *Radio voices: American broadcasting 1922–1952*. Minneapolis: University of Minnesota Press.

Hilmes, M. (2002). Who we are, who we are not: Battle of the global paradigms. In L. Parks & S. Kumar (Eds.), *Planet television* (pp. 53–73). New York: New York University Press.

Hilmes, M. (2003). British quality, American chaos: Historical dualisms and what they leave out. *The Radio Journal: International Studies in Broadcast and Audio Media*, 1(1), 13–27.

Horten, G. (2002). *Radio goes to war: The cultural politics of propaganda during World War II*. Berkeley: University of California Press.

Humphries, P. J. (1996). *Mass media and media policy in Western Europe*. Manchester, UK: Manchester University Press.

Kelly, M., Mazzoleni, G., & McQuail, D. (Eds.). (2003). *The media in Europe*. London: Sage.

Kompare, D. (1999). *Rerun nation: The regime of repetition on American television*. Unpublished doctoral dissertation, University of Wisconsin–Madison.

Kumar, S. (1999). An Indian personality for television? *Jump Cut*, 43(2), 92–101.

Lacey, K. (1996). *Feminine frequencies: Gender, German radio, and the public sphere 1923–1945*. Ann Arbor: University of Michigan Press.

Lin, S.-P. (2000). *Prime time television drama and Taiwanese women.* Unpublished doctoral dissertation, University of Wisconsin–Madison.

McChesney, R. W. (1993). *Telecommunications, mass media, and democracy: The battle for the control of US broadcasting 1928–1935.* New York: Oxford University Press.

McQuail, D., & Siune, K. (Eds.). (1998). *Media policy: Convergence, concentration and commerce.* London: Sage.

Meckiffe, D., & Murray, M. (1998). Radio and the Black soldier during World War II. *Critical Studies in Mass Communication, 15*(4), 337–357.

Negrine, R. (1994). *Politics and the mass media in Britain* (2nd ed.). London: Routledge.

Nelson, M. (1997). *War of the black heavens: The battles of Western broadcasting in the cold war.* Syracuse, NY: Syracuse University Press.

Parsons, P. R., & Frieden, R. M. (1998). *The cable and satellite television industries.* Boston: Allyn & Bacon.

Rutenberg, J. (2001, July 15). Much in a name. *New York Times,* p. B4.

Rutherford, P. (1990). *When television was young: Primetime Canada, 1952–1967.* Toronto: University of Toronto Press.

Savage, B. (1999). *Broadcasting freedom: Radio, war, and the politics of race 1938–1948.* Chapel Hill: University of North Carolina Press.

Scannell, P., & Cardiff, D. (1991). *A social history of British broadcasting.* Oxford, UK: Blackwell.

Smulyan, S. (1994). *Selling radio: The commercialization of US broadcasting, 1920–1934.* Washington, DC: Smithsonian Institution Press.

Streeter, T. (1987). The cable fable revisited: Discourse, policy, and the making of cable television. *Critical Studies in Mass Communication, 4*(2), 174–200.

Whelan, C. (1998, June 8). WorldSpace aims to reach 200M Third World homes. *Electronic News,* p. 48.

Williams, R. (1975). *Television: Technology and cultural form.* New York: Schocken.

Winston, B. (1990). How are media born? In J. Downing & A. Sreberny-Mohammadi (Eds.), *Questioning the media* (pp. 55–68). Newbury Park, CA: Sage.

24

HOLLYWOOD

◆ Thomas Schatz and Alisa Perren

Any effort to assess, analyze, or even describe "Hollywood" inevitably begins with a definitional dilemma. The term *Hollywood* refers to an actual place, of course—a community north of Los Angeles that emerged, nearly a century ago, as a primary base of operations for the burgeoning American film industry. But the industry involved far more than the Hollywood environs even then, and as it continued to develop, the meanings associated with the term *Hollywood* became increasingly complex and multivalent.

Most fundamentally, the term *Hollywood* refers to three interrelated aspects of American cinema: the industrial, the institutional, and the formal-aesthetic. As an industry, Hollywood is a vast, integrated commercial enterprise with specific business practices and standard operating procedures geared primarily to producing and distributing feature-length films ("Hollywood movies"). The film industry, like most capital-intensive entertainment and media enterprises, has always tended toward an oligopoly structure—that is, a system whereby a few companies control a particular industry. This invokes the institutional aspect, in that the film industry has been dominated from the outset by a handful of movie studios—Paramount, Fox, Warner Bros.—many of which still operate and still rule the industry. During the "classical" era of the 1920s through the 1940s, the most powerful studios controlled all phases of the industry (production, distribution, and exhibition) through a vertically integrated system that mass-produced movies for a receptive mass audience. The studios lost their collective control of the industry during the postwar era due to a combination of factors, including antitrust litigation, the rise of independent film production, and the juggernaut of commercial television. The studios adapted and survived, and since the 1970s, they have enjoyed a remarkable resurgence and have reasserted their collective control of the so-called New Hollywood. Now the studios' film divisions produce far more than simply feature films, however, and the studios themselves are all subsidiaries of massive, transnational multimedia conglomerates such as Sony, Viacom, News Corp, and TimeWarner. But even as subsidiaries, the studios represent the "core assets" of these media conglomerates due to the enormous popularity of Hollywood movies in the global entertainment marketplace.

The widespread appeal of Hollywood movies is due not only to the studios' economic power and marketing prowess but also to the formal-aesthetic qualities of the films themselves. This third aspect of the term *Hollywood* has changed somewhat less than the industrial and institutional aspects, in that the cinematic style and narrative structure of Hollywood movies have persisted over the decades, despite the obvious need for novelty and innovation. In other words, what we call a "Hollywood movie" is much the same artifact today as it was in the late teens and early 1920s. Recent changes in Hollywood's industrial and institutional operations threaten this formal-aesthetic stability, however, due to demands of the global entertainment marketplace and the conglomerates' quest for "synergy" between their hit movie and other media-related divisions (TV, music, publishing, theme parks, etc.). But another crucial aspect of the New Hollywood, and one that may help maintain the formal-aesthetic integrity of its movies, is the parallel development of independent films and filmmaking. Throughout the 1980s and 1990s, the studios' blockbuster mentality has been offset by an unprecedented "indie boom." Consequently, the film industry has been increasingly split between big-budget, franchise-spawning, global-marketed blockbusters and low-budget "specialty films" designed for carefully targeted niche markets. Although these so-called independent films generally are produced outside the direct control of the Hollywood studios, the studios often provide financing and distribution. Thus, most indie films are scarcely independent of the Hollywood system. And in terms of style and content, independent films tend to be every bit as conservative and classical as their blockbuster counterparts.

As the entertainment industry has become an increasingly global enterprise in recent years, Hollywood continues to occupy the central role in the production and commercialization of culture. Just as classical Hollywood's domination of the movie industry a half-century ago induced critic Gilbert Seldes (1978) to say that "the movies come from America," so might one argue today that "entertainment comes from America"—and, more specifically, from Hollywood. And when one considers the widespread appeal of Hollywood movies and thus the colonization of cultural consciousness on a global scale, it is worth noting that the term *Hollywood* becomes increasingly conflated with the notion of "Americanization" (Seldes, 1978). This further complicates our definitional dilemma, particularly in the era of the New Hollywood with its blockbuster films, new delivery technologies, and expanding entertainment marketplace dominated by a cadre of global media conglomerates.

As even these preliminary comments should indicate, Hollywood has experienced a rich and dynamic history. The aim of this chapter is to chart that history in more detail and also to trace the efforts of film critics and scholars to make sense of it. Journalistic film criticism dates back to Hollywood's earliest years, and the film industry always has been subject to heavy coverage in both the trade and popular press. But the systematic scholarly study of Hollywood did not really take hold, interestingly enough, until after Hollywood's postwar collapse. Not until the studio system and classical era were pronounced dead, in other words, were scholars and academics ready to conduct an autopsy. And not until the emergence of the New Hollywood several decades later did "film studies" approach the status of a mature academic discipline. Much of that scholarship has looked back at Hollywood's classical era, of course, whose reputation has undergone rehabilitation over the past few decades. This is due not only to enduring appeal of Hollywood's "classic" films but also the increasingly sophisticated understanding of its interdependent industrial, institutional, and formal-aesthetic aspects—an understanding we hope to share in the pages that follow.

◆ *A Brief History of Hollywood*

The colonization of Hollywood in the 1910s actually occurred as an "independent" initiative in defiance of the industry's earliest oligopoly: the so-called Motion Picture Patents Trust, a cartel of film companies (Edison, Biograph, et al.) that controlled the patents for cameras and projectors. The Trust was broken via aggressive commercial competition and relentless legal challenges by men such as Carl Laemmle, William Fox, and Adolph Zukor—the studio pioneers and oligopolists of the Hollywood era. Meanwhile, the cinema rapidly matured into a modern business enterprise due to the combined effects of the standardization of the feature-length narrative film as the key movie commodity, the regulation and centralization of feature filmmaking in a factory-based mode of production, the development of a nationwide distribution system, and the brisk evolution from nickelodeon and storefront theaters to lavish movie palaces and downtown theaters catering to a middle-class clientele (e.g., see Balio, 1985; Finler, 1988; Jowett, 1976).

These developments fueled the emerging Hollywood film industry, although the signal factor in the formation of the Hollywood studio system, per se, was the integration of factory-based production, nationwide distribution, and first-class exhibition within individual motion picture corporations. The first of the Hollywood studios to pursue vertical integration was Adolph Zukor's Paramount Pictures, which utterly dominated the industry in the late teens. Others followed suit, and during the 1920s, a cadre of integrated companies—Paramount, MGM, Warner Bros., Fox, and RKO—became the ruling studio powers in Hollywood. A second tier of studios was occupied by Universal, Columbia, and United Artists, which were deemed "major minors"—major because they produced A-class features and had their own nationwide distribution arms and minor because they did not have their own theater chains.

The movie industry at the time was essentially bicoastal, with the direction of capital and the control of distribution and exhibition handled out of New York, while feature films and various other commodities (shorts, newsreels, etc.) rolled off the assembly line of the West Coast studio. The cost of converting to sound film ("talkies") in the late 1920s and the subsequent economic devastation of the Depression brought Wall Street into the picture, enabling the studios to consolidate their collective—and increasingly collusive—control. The "Big Five" integrated major studios owned only about one sixth of America's theaters, but this included most of the crucial urban and downtown theaters where Hollywood did the bulk of its business. And together with the three major minors, these companies completely controlled all feature film distribution in the United States. Other studios, such as Monogram and Republic, did emerge in the 1930s but were relegated to "Poverty Row" status as producers of B-movies for secondary markets. "Major independent producers" such as Samuel Goldwyn, David Selznick, and Walt Disney also emerged, who produced A-class pictures through financing-and-distribution deals with one of the studios.

Control of the marketplace ensured the studios sufficient income to maintain production operations geared to a blend of A-class star vehicles, B-grade program fodder, and occasional "prestige pictures." Their cash flow also enabled the big studios to maintain thousands of contract employees, including "stables" of top talent— producers, directors, composers, and, most important, stars—under long-term contract. Each studio developed a distinctive personality and "house style" during the 1930s and 1940s, keyed to specific star-genre formulations that often were produced and maintained by specialized "units" of top contract talent. Warner's gangster films with Edward G. Robinson and James Cagney, for instance, or RKO's dance musicals with Fred Astaire and Ginger Rogers were essential to the company's success. They brought stability

and efficiency to production operations while differentiating the studio's output; they also carried the studio's entire program of pictures (through a trade practice known as block booking) with the nation's independent theaters. Moreover, given the importance of stars (and the "star system"), these star-genre formulations were money in the bank for the studios, veritable insurance policies against box-office failure.

Collectively, the Hollywood studios developed a repertoire of genres and house styles that were variations on what has been termed *Hollywood's classical narrative paradigm* (Bordwell, 1986; Bordwell, Thompson, & Staiger, 1985). The key attributes of this paradigm are a three-act (fundamentally Aristotelian) story design of exposition, complication, and resolution; a goal-oriented protagonist whose objectives and obstacles (invariably accompanied by a secondary "love interest") define the plot line and narrative trajectory of the film; and patterns of psychological editing and "invisible narration" in which the camera work, cutting, and production design are geared to the psyche of both the central character(s) and the viewer. A combination of commercial, regulatory, and ideological imperatives induced the studios to develop narrative variations that not only generated and resolved conflict but did so in a fundamentally prosocial fashion—that is, through a "Hollywood ending" that conveyed both a moral and ideological resolution to the conflicts raised in the course of the film and one that invariably reinforced the status quo. This is not to say that all Hollywood movies blindly or naively reinforced the dominant ideology. On the contrary, many top filmmakers—writer-directors such as Billy Wilder, John Huston, and Preston Sturges, for instance, or producer-director teams David Selznick and Alfred Hitchcock—created films that were highly complex in their treatment of American ideology and whose "happy endings" were patently ironic or ambiguous. Moreover, various genres and period styles such as the women's film, the gangster and horror genres, and film noir did as much to flesh out and critique certain aspects of the American experience as they did to systematically reinforce the status quo.

By the late 1930s, as French film critic André Bazin (1968/1999) aptly noted, Hollywood cinema had reached a certain "equilibrium" whereby its social, economic, industrial, and stylistic aspects were in balance. Hollywood feature film output from 1939 to 1941 (generally regarded as the height of the classical era) certainly supports this view, as evidenced by such productions as *The Wizard of Oz, Gone With the Wind, Stagecoach, Mr. Smith Goes to Washington,* and *Dark Victory* in 1939; *The Grapes of Wrath, The Great Dictator, Philadelphia Story,* and *Rebecca* in 1940; and *Citizen Kane, How Green Was My Valley, The Lady Eve, The Little Foxes, Sergeant York,* and *The Maltese Falcon* in 1941.

The 1940s brought monumental changes to Hollywood, from the unprecedented wartime boom to the industry's rapid postwar decline. World War II was, in many ways, Hollywood's finest hour as a social institution, considering its contribution to the "war effort," and the studios enjoyed enormous profits due to war-related economic conditions. A key factor here was the suspension "for the duration" of the government's antitrust campaign against the Hollywood studios that had been initiated by the Justice Department in 1938. That campaign resumed after the war, however, culminating in a 1948 Supreme Court decision—the legendary *Paramount* decree, so named for the first company cited in the suit—which forced the integrated studios to sell their theater chains and also put an end to the marketing practices (block booking, blind bidding, etc.) that had enabled the eight studio-distributors to control the movie business. The *Paramount* decree effectively disintegrated the industry, forcing the studios to produce and market movies on an individual basis. This ruling, along with two other major postwar developments— namely, suburban migration (with its attendant baby/family/housing "boom") and

the introduction of commercial television— brought an end to the studio system and to Hollywood's classical era. The impact of these factors on American moviegoing was swift and devastating. After peaking in 1946 at 80 to 100 million theater admissions per week (when the U.S. population was only about 130 million), attendance fell to barely half that by 1950. Although the population surged during the 1950s, theater admissions continued to fall, and "watching TV" replaced "going to the movies" as America's preferred ritual of narrative entertainment. And the studios, without the cash flow from their theaters and a tightly controlled marketplace, were forced to abandon their factory-based mass-production system, with its regular output of A-class features and its legions of contract personnel.

The studios survived the 1950s, due mainly to three distinct and eminently successful strategies. The first was their collective decision to maintain control of distribution and to cut back significantly on active production, which they left to the growing ranks of independent producers. The studios still produced films of their own, but they dramatically cut production and began to focus primarily on financing-and-distribution operations—an effective strategy that persists today. The second successful survival strategy, and another trend that continues today, was the studios' shift to "big" pictures. The 1950s saw a massive increase in the number of big-budget "blockbusters" augmented by Technicolor and new widescreen formats, from costume spectacles such as *The Robe* (1953) and *The Ten Commandments* (1956) to epic westerns such as *Shane* (1952) and *The Searchers* (1956). This burgeoning blockbuster mentality was countered, significantly enough, by independent outfits such as American International Pictures (AIP) that turned out low-budget "exploitation films" for specific target markets, particularly for the teenage crowd that flocked to rock 'n' roll films such as *Rock Around the Clock* (1956) and horror teenpics such as *I Was a Teenage Werewolf* (1957). Many of these films were geared specifically for the drive-in market, whose explosive growth (from virtually nil after the war to some 6,000 screens by 1960) provided yet another indication of suburban migration and the emerging teen culture, as well as of postwar America's obsession with the automobile.

A third factor facilitating Hollywood's postwar survival was the major studios' eventual coming-to-terms with television. This involved opening their "vaults" of old pictures for TV syndication and also their move into "telefilm" series production. Following the lead of Disney, which allied with ABC and produced the hit *Disneyland* series in 1954, several of the majors began TV series production in 1955, the same year that the majors began syndicating their pre-1948 films—and, in effect, began thinking of their vaults as "libraries." The most aggressive studio in terms of telefilm production was Warner Bros., which, by the late 1950s, was producing one third of ABC's primetime schedule. All the majors took the plunge by 1960, and by then, Hollywood was producing far more hours of TV programming than feature films.

Although the studios adapted both to independent film production and to the burgeoning television age, other industrial and institutional developments during the 1950s significantly altered the Hollywood landscape. The most obvious was the relocation of network production from New York to the West Coast, as well as the related shift from live video for film as the preferred primetime program format. Another was the enhanced status and authority of top talent in both the film and TV industries, particularly stars who formed their own production companies. These companies generally were created by talent agencies such as William Morris and the Music Corporation of America (MCA), whose status also changed dramatically during the postwar era. The key player here was MCA, which grew from a band-booking operation in the 1920s and 1930s to become the most powerful entertainment company in

Hollywood. Indeed, the development of MCA during the 1950s and 1960s provided a template for the media conglomerates that would rule the New Hollywood, with MCA itself as the dominant industry force for the next half century.

The seeds of MCA's postwar rise were planted just before the war, when founder Jules Stein moved the agency headquarters to the West Coast and began signing movie talent. Stein's second-in-command, Lew Wasserman, oversaw MCA's Hollywood operations and became company president in 1946 at the age of 33. Wasserman was the chief architect of MCA's subsequent success, which came in three distinct areas of endeavor. The first involved top film stars, whose postwar status and income changed enormously thanks to a watershed 1949 deal between MCA and Universal Pictures for the services of James Stewart. Universal wanted the star but could not afford his usual rate of $200,000, so Wasserman and studio boss William Goetz worked out a two-picture arrangement (for *Harvey* and *Winchester '73*) whereby Stewart waived his salary in lieu of 50% of the films' profits. Profit-participation deals were scarcely new to Hollywood, but this level of participation was unprecedented, effectively making Stewart a partner with the studio on his pictures. Although other studio heads protested, Universal and Stewart reaped the benefits of the deal—the first of many such arrangements with Stewart and other stars throughout the 1950s. In fact, Stewart soon became the highest paid Hollywood actor and also one of the lowest taxed because he could sell his participation and be taxed on a capital gains basis rather than at a much higher salary-based rate.

The second strategy involved MCA's move into telefilm series production through its subsidiary, Revue Productions. This move was made possible by a 1952 agreement with the Screen Actors Guild (SAG) that granted MCA-Revue a "blanket waiver" to use SAG members in its productions, thus allowing MCA to both represent talent (as an agency) and also employ talent (as a producer). This exclusive deal was negotiated by Wasserman with SAG president (and MCA client) Ronald Reagan, absolving MCA of any conflict of interest and giving Revue an enormous advantage over competing telefilm producers. Revue was a resounding success and, by the late 1950s, was supplying the three TV networks with roughly 20% of their prime-time programs. MCA's third strategy involved TV syndication. In the early 1950s, the company began buying or leasing previously broadcast television series as well as feature films released before 1948. Given the uncertainty of market demand and audience taste at the time, MCA began this operation cautiously. Its first major movie syndication deal was with Republic Pictures for packages of Roy Rogers and Gene Autry westerns. But here, too, MCA's efforts were phenomenally successful—more so, in fact, than its highly profitable agency and TV production operations.

In the course of the 1950s, MCA devised ways to combine these diverse operations. Consider, for example, the case of Alfred Hitchcock. Early in the decade, Wasserman cut a lucrative deal with Paramount Pictures, giving Hitchcock a share of the profits and eventual ownership of his films (which included *To Catch a Thief, Rear Window, Vertigo,* and *Psycho*). In the process, Wasserman assembled a production unit around Hitchcock that ensured a certain consistency and stability in terms of production as well as additional income for MCA because most of the unit members were MCA clients.[1] With Hitchcock's film career set, Wasserman turned to television. He arranged with NBC to create a new series, *Alfred Hitchcock Presents,* to be produced by Revue. Here, too, Wasserman set up the deal so that ownership of the TV programs would revert to Hitchcock's company, Shamley Productions. As with the films, Hitchcock's TV shows were syndicated by MCA, which also developed various media tie-ins—a mystery magazine, multiple short-story anthologies, and so

on—that further expanded the Hitchcock franchise. In the early 1960s, Hitchcock sold his stake in all of these media products to MCA in exchange for stock, making him the company's third largest stockholder (behind Stein and Wasserman) and the wealthiest filmmaker in Hollywood.

In formal-aesthetic terms, Hitchcock's case is equally instructive of Hollywood's postwar transformation. By the 1950s, he had directed hits such as *Rebecca* (1940), *Suspicion* (1941), and *Notorious* (1946), and thus both the industry and the public were quite familiar with the nature and appeal of a "Hitchcock picture" from the "Master of Suspense." With Wasserman managing his career in the 1950s, Hitchcock was able to work with top stars (and MCA clients), such as Stewart, Cary Grant, and Grace Kelly, and to make "bigger" pictures in terms of budget and spectacle—films such as his 1959 hit, *North by Northwest,* a sophisticated geopolitical romance (and prototype for the upcoming Bond cycle) starring Grant and Eva Marie Saint, which was Hitchcock's most expensive and most commercially successful film to date. Hitchcock immediately followed that blockbuster hit with a low-budget exploitation film that he considered more of an experiment and a diversion than a major project. In fact, it was shot by Hitchcock's TV series crew for roughly one fifth the cost of *North by Northwest.* The film was *Psycho,* which radically undercut the classical Hollywood narrative (with its heroine murdered halfway through the film, its oddly sympathetic serial killer, etc.), reinvented the horror genre, confounded critics, and was by far Hitchcock's most popular and commercially successful film. And although films such as *Vertigo* and *Psycho* were exposing a much darker side of Hitchcock's trademark style, the hit TV series presented a purposefully toned-down version, suitably domesticated for family consumption and doled out in weekly, 30-minute doses.

With revenues from its agency, production company, and syndication arm flowing in, MCA raised its sights in the late 1950s. To accommodate Revue's growth, MCA purchased the Universal City studio lot in 1959. Then, in 1962, it dissolved its talent agency (at the behest of the Justice Department) and purchased Universal Pictures along with its parent company, Decca Records, thus becoming the first modern U.S. media conglomerate. MCA-Universal flourished during the 1960s due primarily to the fit between its film and television divisions and its unparalleled syndication operation. With its expanded resources, MCA pioneered the long-form TV series format (with *The Name of the Game, Columbo,* and others) as well as the "movie of the week" format.

Although MCA's TV operations flourished in the 1960s, Universal Pictures struggled—as did all of the Hollywood movie studios at the time. The relentless pursuit of blockbusters led to huge hits such as *The Sound of Music* (1965) but also huge misses such as *Cleopatra* (1963). By the late 1960s, even box-office successes such as *Hello, Dolly!* (1969) were losing money due to their enormous budgets, and costly flops such as *Dr. Doolittle* (1968) and *Tora! Tora! Tora!* (1970) threatened to bankrupt their studio-distributors. Meanwhile, low-budget "youth market" films such as *Bonnie and Clyde* (1967), *The Graduate* (1967), *2001* (1968), *Easy Rider* (1969), *Midnight Cowboy* (1969), and *M.A.S.H.* (1970) were doing solid business—albeit with a relatively limited, countercultural audience—and sowing the seeds of a New American cinema that was, in many ways, distinctly at odds with both classical Hollywood and the mainstream audience. Consequently, the movie industry found itself in a deep recession in 1969–1970, as movie studio stock values plummeted. The undervalued studios thus were prime takeover targets, resulting in a merger-and-acquisition wave that saw Gulf & Western acquire Paramount, Kinney National Services acquire Warner Bros., Transamerica acquire United Artists, and real estate magnate Kirk Kerkorian acquire MGM.

The studios began to rebound in 1972–1973, when *The Godfather, American Graffiti, The Sting,* and *The Exorcist* proved immensely popular with both the youth market and mainstream audiences. The turning point for the industry came with the 1975 release of *Jaws* by Universal, a watershed hit that pioneered the summer blockbuster and used a groundbreaking nationwide "saturation" marketing and release campaign.[2] Aesthetically, the film combined New American cinema stylistic techniques with classical Hollywood conventions. Complementing the film's wide release and extensive use of television advertising were marketable stars, a popular blend of genres, merchandising and marketing hooks, and striking visuals—all characteristics, according to Justin Wyatt (1994), of high-concept films. The $125 million-plus in North American rentals for *Jaws* reaffirmed more than just the effectiveness of blending cinematic styles and genres. In fact, it demonstrated that "high-concept" movies—movies that, according to Steven Spielberg, could be summed up in 25 words or less (and could be effectively marketed in 30-second TV ads)—were the most profitable and reliable business prospects for the studios. The explosive growth of shopping center multiplexes, combined with the studios' increasing expenditures on network TV advertising, further fueled the drive toward saturation marketing-release campaigns. Although marketing costs rose in the process, so did box-office returns, as one film after another began to hit the $100 million mark in domestic grosses during the late 1970s and early 1980s.

Films such as *Star Wars* (1977), *Superman* (1978), and *Raiders of the Lost Ark* (1981) not only brought in large profits for their studio-distributors but also launched lucrative multimedia "franchises"—entertainment product lines geared to a blockbuster movie hit. Along with the income generated by a widening array of product tie-ins, the studios also enjoyed additional revenues from the emerging video and cable markets.

The "home video revolution" started with the introduction of the Sony Betamax VCR in 1975, the same year that HBO introduced the pay-cable "movie channel." Basic cable was just beginning its ascent as well, and by the late 1970s, Ted Turner's Atlanta-based WTBS station would start the "superstation" trend with its then-novel combination of satellite with cable, providing still another significant new outlet for movies.

Cumulatively, these mid-1970s developments dramatically altered Hollywood's industrial practices as well as the aesthetics of its films, auguring a new era in media entertainment that was dubbed the "New Hollywood" by various critics and media scholars and that overwhelmed the New American cinema of the late 1960s and early 1970s. That earlier period of creative ferment had been heralded as a veritable Hollywood renaissance, due especially to the rise of a new breed of filmmakers such as Mike Nichols, Robert Altman, Arthur Penn, Martin Scorsese, and Hal Ashby. In the later 1970s, however, the complex interplay of economic, aesthetic, and technological forces sent the movie industry in a very different direction. As Anderson (1994), Balio (1996), Schatz (1993, 1997), and Wyatt (1994) all concur, the New Hollywood emerged via high-concept blockbusters that were financed and distributed by the major studios. The studios' power increased exponentially through the 1980s and 1990s with the stabilization of the blockbuster trend and the rise of an increasingly diversified, globalized "entertainment industry" in which motion picture operations represented only one component of the vast conglomerates that owned the studios. This New Hollywood, which still continues to evolve, consists of tightly diversified and horizontally integrated media companies focused on exploiting synergies between their various publishing, film, television, videogame, merchandising, and music divisions.

Indeed, we might view the 1980s and 1990s as a period when Hollywood's institutional structure fundamentally changed due to the combined forces of deregulation, conglomeration, and globalization. This began during the 1980s, when the corporate giants of the 1960s, such as Gulf & Western, Transamerica, and Kinney National, either got out of the entertainment business or reorganized their operations through a combination of downsizing, regrouping, and selling unprofitable divisions. Transamerica sold its controlling interest in United Artists, for example, whereas both Kinney (owner of Warner Bros.) and Gulf & Western (owner of Paramount) shed their nonentertainment divisions to focus on media-related ventures. Meanwhile, the quest for synergy across different "software" divisions intensified. Disney broke with its "family entertainment" tradition to create more "mature" films such as *Down and Out in Beverly Hills* and *Pretty Woman* through its new Touchstone division, for instance, and Warner Bros. moved into videogames through the purchase of Atari. Another tactic involved studio mergers with deep-pocketed conglomerates, which were motivated by the widening array of media technologies and "delivery systems" and facilitated by Reagan-era deregulation. In 1986, Rupert Murdoch's News Corporation purchased Twentieth Century Fox and, within months of the purchase, created a fourth U.S. broadcast television network. Later, two Japanese technology giants bought movie studios in an effort to wed a "software" producer to their established "hardware" divisions; Sony bought Columbia-TriStar in 1989, and Matsushita purchased MCA-Universal in 1990. The entry of Sony, Matsushita, and Australian-owned News Corp. also underscored the increasingly global stakes involved in the expanding entertainment industry and the eagerness of foreign investors to have a stake in Hollywood.

Of course, the "Hollywood" being invested in was not a Hollywood of film studios. In this Hollywood, television and motion picture divisions were fundamentally intertwined—a longstanding impulse that now, thanks to deregulation, had become a veritable requirement of industry survival. Though intended to benefit independent television producers by fostering a more competitive environment in television, the rolling back of media regulation ultimately benefited the studios (and their parent companies), which were better able to finance television productions and to exploit hit programs through their syndication divisions. In the emerging multichannel universe, ever-increasing profits could be generated from television production, but the established "Big Three" TV networks were unable to reap the full benefits. The launch of the Fox TV network also signaled a moment of crisis in the television industry, as all three TV networks changed ownership and management in 1985–1986 due in large part to these broad economic, technological, and regulatory changes. The churn in the television and cable industries steadily intensified, and the network upheaval that began in the mid-1980s reached a peak with the Telecommunications Act of 1996, which gave a broad-based federal sanction to the deregulatory trends of the previous decade. This act coincided—although it was hardly a coincidence—with yet another merger-and-acquisition wave in the mid-1990s involving various major players in the television arena. Disney purchased ABC, Viacom purchased CBS (along with Paramount, Blockbuster, MTV, and Nickelodeon), and Time-Warner purchased Turner Broadcasting. In addition, Warner Bros. and Paramount created two new "netlets"— cable networks—in the form of the WB channel and UPN (Aufderheide, 1999; Holt, 2003).

The dozens of new television channels put an increasing emphasis on narrowcasting and niche programming. Not only were shows increasingly targeted to specific demographic groups (Fox's *Martin* for African Americans, ABC's *Sabrina the Teenage Witch* for young adults), but entire cable channels were being developed for specific age groups, ethnicities, and lifestyles. Among the biggest success stories was Viacom's MTV, which turned several of its successful cable TV programs into hit feature films. The half-hour MTV animated cartoon/ music video hybrid *Beavis and Butthead* (1993–1997), for instance, generated the feature-length film, *Beavis and Butthead Do America* (1996), through another Viacom subsidiary, Paramount. Thus, the franchise mentality that pervaded film began to dominate the television environment as well, as entertainment conglomerates sought new ways to exploit popular products and create new "brands" across the company's various divisions.

Nowhere was this strategy more apparent than with the high-concept "event" film. From the release of *Jaws* to *Jurassic Park 3* (2001), the marketing and distribution strategies of the major studios evolved substantially. At the time of its release, the $12 million-budgeted *Jaws* opened on a record-setting 464 screens nationwide. By the time of *Jurassic Park 3*'s release a quarter century later, neither its $93 million budget nor 3,434-screen opening was out of the ordinary. Perhaps more striking about *Jurassic Park 3* was its absence of top talent either behind or in front of the camera—although Steven Spielberg's brand name was behind the film itself. The selling points for this film—along with so many other high-concept film and television products—were its spectacle, its special effects, and its "presold" status.

The rise of the big-budget blockbuster brought other important changes in Hollywood's market strategies and hence its motion picture output. As conglomerates continued to focus on franchise-scale films, their studio subsidiaries placed less emphasis on the standard star-genre fare that defined the classical Hollywood studio system. As the average motion picture budget approached $50 million by 2002, with an additional $30 million in marketing costs, the studios became less inclined to finance the kinds of "mainstream" comedies, mysteries, and romances that had been standard during the studio era. Occasional exceptions such as *Jerry Maguire* (1996) and *A Beautiful Mind* (2001) indicated that there was a strong market for more routine A-class star vehicles, as long as a star such as Tom Cruise or Russell Crowe was "attached." But the economics of the New Hollywood generally encourage either big-budget or low-budget production. Indeed, the industry has become increasingly bifurcated, with the majority of releases falling at either end of the budget spectrum.

This trend began in the late 1970s and early 1980s, when the studios' blockbuster impulse was countered by a number of companies that began to distribute low-budget films with smaller, character-driven stories targeted to specific niches such as African Americans, gays and lesbians, and art-cinema connoisseurs. Further fueling the trend were new avenues for film financing such as foreign presales, as well as additional avenues of distribution such as video and cable. Thus, as mogul-auteurs such as Spielberg and Lucas dominated high-end Hollywood, a new crop of indie-auteurs, including Jim Jarmusch, Spike Lee, John Sayles, Gus Van Sant, and Joel and Ethan Coen, staked out the low-budget independent realm. During the 1980s, independent filmmakers and distributors remained on the margins of the industry, as successful independent films such as the Coen brothers' *Blood Simple* and Sayles's *Brother From Another Planet* (both 1984) brought in a few million dollars at the box office, whereas most earned far less. Yet many films (and their directors) established themselves with a number of critics and moviegoers, particularly through film festivals, which were growing in number and attendance during this time.

The turning point for Hollywood's independent movement came in 1989. At the time, only a select few independent companies—notably New Line, Miramax, and Samuel Goldwyn—were faring well in the uncertain, marginal world of "indie" financing and distribution. A few films such as *Hairspray, Drugstore Cowboy,* and *Henry V* had done well in 1988–1989, but the real breakthrough film was Steven Soderbergh's *sex, lies and videotape,* a $1.1 million production that generated close to $25 million at the North American box office alone and took the festival circuit by storm. *sex, lies and videotape* demonstrated to many in the industry and the press that there was money to be made in the "quality" film business, particularly with the kind of skillful marketing that Miramax gave Soderbergh's film. The film's success put Miramax at the forefront of the American independent movement, a position it would maintain throughout the 1990s. Indeed, the fate of Hollywood's independent film world paralleled that of Miramax, which became the shaping force in the production, marketing, and distribution of low-budget films and filmmaking. Moreover, the string of subsequent Miramax hits, including *The Grifters* (1991), *Reservoir Dogs* (1992), *Passion Fish* (1992), and particularly *The Crying Game* (1992), led to another defining event in the New Hollywood's industrial and institutional development. In April 1993, Disney purchased Miramax. As an indie subsidiary, Miramax maintained its existing management while enjoying quasi-autonomy status and access to Disney's vast resources, financial and otherwise. And the deal gave Disney prestige at a relatively low cost, as well as additional product for its voracious pipeline.

The purchase of Miramax by Disney started a trend, and by the late 1990s, every studio had at least one niche division geared toward producing low-budget, "indie," or "art house" features. Generally speaking, these films were characterized by genre blending, a high degree of stylization, excessive sex or violence, an emphasis on dialogue and character development over plot, and name talent working "on the cheap." Landmark films of the era included *The Piano* (1993), *Pulp Fiction* (1994), *The Usual Suspects* (1995), *Boogie Nights* (1997), and *Good Will Hunting* (1997). Some studios had an additional division oriented toward low-budget "genre" fare, specifically horror films (*Scream*, 1996), urban comedies (*A Thin Line Between Love and Hate*, 1996), science fiction (*Mimic*, 1997), and teen romances (*She's All That*, 1999). Although some studio-based divisions such as Fox Searchlight, Paramount Classics, Miramax, and Fine Line readily exploited the label of "independence" for the purposes of marketing and publicity, others, such as Dimension, Screen Gems, and New Line, took a more aggressively commercial tack. And even as the term *indie* became synonymous with edgy, hip, and cutting-edge cinema, it lost much of its meaning as anything beyond a marketing tool.

Thus, by the early 2000s, the lines between art house and multiplex, alternative and commercial, independent and mainstream Hollywood were utterly blurred in both industry and press discourse. And despite the bifurcation of movie product between mass-marketed blockbusters and niche-marketed, low-budget films, the industry was more integrated and, in a sense, more "balanced" than it had been since the classical Hollywood era. This was a function of conglomerate control, however, which would cause as much concern and controversy for critics and scholars as the "studio system" had a half century earlier.

◆ Hollywood and Film Studies

Film studies as a distinct academic and scholarly discipline, especially in terms of autonomous departments and advanced degrees, is a relatively recent phenomenon, dating back to the 1960s and 1970s, although intellectuals and scholars from other disciplines have been teaching and writing about film—and specifically about Hollywood—since the early years of American cinema. The earliest writings of any real consequence about the cinema appeared in the mid-teens and focused primarily on the aesthetics of film as theorists and intellectuals debated its nature and status as an art form. The most significant of these was poet Vachel Lindsay's (1915) monograph, *The Art of the Moving Picture*, which staked a claim for cinema as a new and distinctly democratic art that combined traditional forms such as painting, sculpture, and architecture into a completely new form of expression. Another important early study, *The Photoplay: A Psychological Study*, was written by Hugo Munsterberg (1916), a professor of psychology at Harvard who saw film as a significant new form due to its unique capacity to "objectify mental processes" via camera work, cutting, and narrative construction. Manuals for screenplay construction also emerged at this same time, including *The Art of Photoplay Making* by Columbia literature professor Victor O. Freeberg (1918; see also Koszarski, 1990, pp. 95–97).

This debate about "film art" continued in the 1920s, as theorists and filmmakers from outside the United States began writing about cinema and specifically about Hollywood, including Sergei Eisenstein (1991) in a series of brilliant essays on "American montage." In the United States, business schools began to examine the cinema's industrial and economic aspects, most notably perhaps in a series of lectures organized at Harvard's MBA school, which resulted in a 1927 anthology, *The Story of the Films*, edited by the organizer of the lecture series, Joseph P. Kennedy (Boston banker and film financier, later cofounder of RKO Pictures, and father of JFK). In the 1930s, the academic discourse about Hollywood was dominated by sociologists and social scientists, who were increasingly concerned with the "effects" of movies on audiences, particularly children. Among the more notable assessments were two 1933 publications: the Payne Fund's *Motion Pictures and Youth* (Charters, 1933), a reasonable scholarly treatise based on a 5-year study by a group of respected researchers, and Henry James Forman's alarmist diatribe, *Our Movie-Made Children*, which held Hollywood responsible for a host of social woes.

A few years later, at the height of Hollywood's classical era, two cogent scholarly studies significantly advanced this social science approach. *Hollywood: The Movie Colony, the Movie Makers,* a 1941 best-seller, was sociologist (and later screenwriter) Leo Rosten's analysis of the mores, attitudes, and lifestyles of the film community. Mae D. Huettig's *Economic Control of the Motion Picture Industry,* published in 1944 (and based on her doctoral thesis at Pennsylvania University, funded by the Rockefeller Foundation), examined the institutional structure and economic practices of the Hollywood studio system. A much less sanguine industry analysis was written at about this time by Max Horkheimer and Theodor W. Adorno (1972), two German exiles residing in the L.A. environs, ironically enough. During the war, they composed their influential Marxist analysis of mass culture, *Dialectic of Enlightenment,* which included the groundbreaking essay, "The Culture Industry: Enlightenment as Mass Deception"—a savage critique of Hollywood movies and other forms of popular entertainment. This study helped spark the so-called "mass culture debates" that raged during the postwar era and engaged such leading U.S. intellectuals as Gilbert Seldes (1978), Dwight Macdonald (1961), and Robert Warshow (1962). In 1950, anthropologist and UCLA professor Hortense Powdermaker wrote *Hollywood: The Dream Factory,* a less pessimistic view of both the filmmaking process and films themselves as manifestations of contemporary social values and conditions. An even more adept analysis of Hollywood filmmaking was written at the same time by Lillian Ross (1952), whose book *Picture* (based on a series of *New Yorker* articles) traced the making of a single movie, *The Red Badge of Courage,* and provided a compelling inside look at MGM during Hollywood's panic-stricken postwar free fall.

The most significant writing about Hollywood during the 1950s came from Europe, particularly from a group of young critics in Paris writing for *Cahiers du Cinéma* under editor André Bazin (see Browne, 1990). This included François Truffaut, Jean-Luc Godard, and others who, as filmmakers a few years later, would create the French New Wave. The *Cahiers* critics formulated the *politique des auteurs,* a polemical view of commercial cinema— and most notably Hollywood—that posited the director as "author" of his or her films. The *Cahiers* critics also preferred the dynamic vitality of Hollywood genre films to the ponderous "quality" of literary adaptations and prestige pictures. Thus, John Ford was valued more highly for *Stagecoach* and *The Searchers* than for *The Grapes of Wrath* and *How Green Was My Valley.* More important, these critics championed as important *auteur* filmmakers such as Hitchcock and Howard Hawks, routinely dismissed by American critics as commercial hacks. Other European critics picked up the auteur chant, particularly the young Turks writing for *Movie* in Britain. Then, in 1962, American critic Andrew Sarris (1962–1963) wrote "Notes on the Auteur Theory in 1962" for the journal *Film Culture,* setting off a firestorm of critical and cultural debate. By decade's end, when he published *The American Cinema: Directors and Directions, 1929-1968* (1968), Sarris had transformed *auteurism* from a polemic to "a theory of film history" and had thoroughly won over the growing ranks of American cinephiles.

The auteur theory, especially as it was presented and promoted by Sarris, provided a conceptual schema and critical approach that rendered film studies safe for academia— and not just as a sidelight for scholars in other disciplines but as a field of study unto itself. Current changes in the film industry lent additional credence to this approach, notably the international art-cinema movement, with filmmakers Antonioni, Fellini, Bergman, Kurosawa, and Truffaut enjoying widespread success in the United States. By the late 1960s, as noted above, Hollywood was experiencing its own "new wave," as directors such as Arthur Penn, Mike Nichols, Paul Mazursky, and Robert Altman were heralded as auteurs in their own right, and "film schools" in New York and Los Angeles began producing a new generation of filmmakers such as Francis Ford Coppola, George Lucas, Brian DePalma, and Martin Scorsese, who were fiercely committed to an auteurist aesthetic.

A crucial complement to auteurism in the 1960s and 1970s was genre study. Indeed, the industrial and economic nature of Hollywood meant that the majority of its canonized auteurs were genre directors, and some of the most significant writing about Hollywood cinema at the time—Jim Kitses's (1970) *Horizons West,* for instance, and Peter Wollen's (1972) *Signs and Meaning in the Cinema*—focused on the interplay of authorship and genre. Although auteur-oriented genre studies often displayed a limiting literary and elitist bias, important intellectual movements in Europe promised to radically transform genre theory—and media studies generally. These centered on structuralism and semiotics—notably, the structural anthropology of Claude Lévi-Strauss (1963) and the theory of semiology (a "science of signs") proposed by Swiss linguist Ferdinand de Saussure (see Bally, Sechehaye, & Riedlinger, 1986). The two intellectual strains developed in tandem and posited a very different view of culture, language, the arts, mythology, and virtually all other forms of human communication. In essence, structuralism and semiotics viewed culture not, as Matthew Arnold (1993) and academic traditionalists would have it, as "the very best of what's been thought and said" but rather as "lived experience" itself, manifested in the myriad rituals, stories, social institutions, and other rule-bound (hence "structured") signifying systems that constitute everyday life. This view was refined by a cadre of European intellectuals, including Roland Barthes (1972), Louis Althusser (1984), Umberto Eco (1994), Jacques Lacan (1977), and Christian Metz (1974, 1982), who reconceptualized human

interaction and cultural expression with profound implications for the study of popular cinema.

Whereas early structuralism and semiotics tended to emphasize cinematic codes and conventions, later "poststructuralist" developments shifted the emphasis to both the process of interpretation ("decoding" films) and the "subject"—that is, the individual spectator. The feminist and civil rights movements were pertinent here, in their apt insistence that different cultural constituencies (different "reading formations" or "interpretive communities") tend to decode and deconstruct texts in very different ways—even Hollywood film texts designed to be read effortlessly and consistently by an undifferentiated mass audience. Perhaps the single most significant scholarly publication in this area was Laura Mulvey's "Visual Pleasure and Narrative Cinema," published in 1975 in the British film journal *Screen,* which combined feminist and psychoanalytic approaches to formulate an indictment of Hollywood cinema whose influence would be felt for years to come. Mulvey's argument, simply stated, focused on the narrative, stylistic, and technological practices through which Hollywood films systematically reinforced a sociocultural system wholly invested in patriarchal authority and phallocentric desire. Although Mulvey herself would later pull back from the somewhat strident claims of her groundbreaking essay, clearly she struck a chord with a wide range of film students and scholars, feminist or otherwise.[3]

With the growth of cultural studies and multiculturalism during the 1980s, Hollywood provided an endless supply of convenient targets for various minorities and marginalized groups, thanks to the fundamentally conservative (if not reactionary) ideology of many of its films. Douglas Kellner (1997), Michael Ryan and Kellner (1988), Susan Jeffords (1994), and Thomas Doherty (1988) were among the media analysts who employed a cultural studies perspective in their wide-ranging analyses of the 1980s Hollywood product, exploring the "dominant" Hollywood ideologies and also the means by which both media producers and audiences responded to these ideologies. Cultural studies seemed a useful analytical tool for many scholars in part because of its diverse theoretical and methodological approaches. From its initial formulation by Raymond Williams (1958), E. P. Thompson (1963), and Richard Hoggart (1957) in the 1950s and 1960s through its later development by the Birmingham Centre in the 1970s and 1980s, cultural studies was continually reinvented and reformulated, incorporating structuralism, feminism, race theory, postcolonial theory, poststructuralism, hegemony theory, discourse analysis, and postmodernist theory as necessary to suit the particular object of study. Similarly, the terrain of cultural studies proved malleable and fertile; industry, text, and audience were all viewed as viable subjects for the cultural studies scholar.

The unifying element across this diverse field of cultural studies was the belief that culture is a terrain of struggle and contestation, where battles over how society is defined and controlled are evident in the texts and practices of everyday life. Among the primary ways that cultural studies enriched media studies during the 1980s was through its analysis of the relations of power and the social and cultural contexts within which people view the "dominant" Hollywood product. In the Reagan-era Hollywood, during which cultural studies came of age in the United States, this perspective enabled scholars to interrogate the ideologies present in Hollywood films such as *First Blood* (1982), *Conan the Barbarian* (1982), and *Sudden Impact* (1983), which exemplified Hollywood's tendency to privilege a reactionary White male authority figure at the expense of less empowered groups.

Although a cultural studies framework was occasionally applied to analyses of the Hollywood mode of production during the 1980s (in Todd Gitlin's 1994 work on prime-time television production, for

example), more frequently the approach was used to explore consumption practices and text-reader relationships. The classic in this area was John Fiske's (1989) work, *Understanding Popular Culture,* which suggested ways that people exercised agency in their daily lives as they consumed Hollywood product. Although such "reader-oriented" perspectives were initially perceived as a crucial political move on the part of cultural studies scholars, soon the prevalence of such analyses—at the expense of exploring institutional agency and other industry-related topics—brought the field under attack both from those working within the cultural studies tradition (in Meaghan Morris's 1996 polemical essay "Banality in Cultural Studies," for example) and from those working outside a cultural studies framework.

Critical political economists actively countered the consumption-oriented cultural studies scholars during the 1980s by focusing on questions of institutional power rather than on popular responses to media texts. North American political economists such as Vincent Mosco (1996) and Robert McChesney (1993) and their European counterparts, including Nicholas Garnham (1995) and Peter Golding and Graham Murdock (1991), although differing on a number of key points, agreed that communication scholars had a responsibility to analyze and evaluate how specific modes of production and relations of power shape in determinate ways the terrain on which cultural practices take place (Kellner, 1997, p. 71). European critical political economists retained a more explicitly Marxist political orientation, arguing that viable solutions to social inequalities could not be found by working within the contemporary capitalist system; thus, the Hollywood film industry has not been central to their concerns about cultural production. North American political economists, on the other hand, took a slightly different tack that centered more directly on popular cinema, specifically on the Hollywood film industry. Although equally critical of capitalism, the latter group nonetheless accepted its continued existence and therefore sought reforms within the system. A primary goal of scholars such as Mosco (1996) and McChesney (1993), as well as Herbert Schiller (1989) and Noam Chomsky (see Peck, 1987), was to demonstrate how transnational media (which in their work were often synonymous with Hollywood) were exploitative and undemocratic (Mosco, 1996, p. 19). The standard remedy within this school of thought was the pursuit of public policy measures to facilitate the redistribution of resources.

There has been a general tendency among critical political economy scholars working with media to treat Hollywood as a monolithic (and fundamentally oppressive) entity. However, a number of scholars, including Janet Wasko, Eileen Meehan, and Thomas Guback, have retained their critical edge toward Hollywood while more closely and carefully interrogating the industry's processes and practices. For example, Wasko's (1994) book, *Hollywood in the Information Age,* was useful in exploring how Hollywood accommodated and incorporated new technologies into its production, distribution, and exhibition processes from the 1970s to the 1990s. Although coming from a critical political economy perspective, Wasko also incorporated ideas from media economics and cultural studies into her analysis. Media economics developed into a fruitful subdiscipline of political economy studies during the 1980s. As practiced by such individuals as Alan Albarran, Barry Litman, James Owers, and Alison Alexander, this field incorporates elements of micro- and macroeconomics and industrial organization theory into the study of entertainment practices (Albarran & Chan-Olmsted, 1998; Alexander, Owers, & Carveth, 1998; Litman, 1998). Since the 1980s, Douglas Gomery has been among the most prolific media economists writing about Hollywood. His work spans the whole history of Hollywood and covers the entire range of its industrial practices, from studio-era

production/distribution (*The Hollywood Studio System,* 1986) to the history of exhibition (*Shared Pleasures,* 1992) to broader institutional operations (*Who Owns the Media?* [Compaine & Gomery, 2000]).

The cumulative influence of cultural studies, critical political economy, and media economics has been considerable. From the 1970s to the present, the challenge for those working in film studies has been to incorporate and integrate these approaches into historical and critical analyses of contemporary media. The evolution of film studies in the past quarter century has been a bumpy one, as scholars have attempted to strike a balance between industrial/institutional analyses and textual/interpretive studies (and, by extension, between social scientific and humanistic theories and methodologies). The efforts of film studies scholars have been further complicated by developments both inside and outside the academy: From within, television studies has forced film studies to broaden its framework; from without, the emergence of new technologies, the integration of media industries, and the consolidation of (global) entertainment conglomerates have posed continued challenges to the field.

Film studies began this evolution in the mid-1970s with significant advances in film history, which until then was little more than a journalistic enterprise that chronicled Great Films by Great Men. Two books published in the mid-1970s, Garth Jowett's (1976) *Film: The Democratic Art* and Robert Sklar's (1994) *Movie-Made America,* propelled these advances not only in their integration of economic and industrial factors into the historical analysis but also in their efforts to situate Hollywood within the larger social and cultural context. A few years later, Robert C. Allen and Gomery's (1985) concise historiographic treatise, *Film History: Theory and Practice,* argued that the study of Hollywood should integrate aesthetic, economic, sociological, and technological research. Few historians have accomplished this, however—not even

Gomery himself in his invaluable (if limited) monograph, *The Hollywood Studio System* (1986), which surveyed the industrial, institutional, and economic landscape of American cinema in the 1930s and 1940s.

Another key contribution to film history in the mid-1980s was *The Classical Hollywood Cinema: Film Style and Mode of Production to 1960,* by Bordwell et al. (1985). At once a conservative and somewhat radical treatment of classical Hollywood, this book argues quite convincingly that the narrative and stylistic "paradigm" of classical American cinema was in place by the late teens—by 1917, to be precise—and only then did the studio system develop as a means to systematically reproduce the paradigm and also, crucially, to constrain innovation and variations on that model. These and other books moved well beyond the naive auteurism of the 1960s but without abandoning the concept of directorial authorship altogether. Indeed, they recognize that the director's personal style and vision are vital to the success of a film but that these elements must be factored into a highly complex equation when the collaborative complexities and institutional authority of Hollywood studios are involved.

These reassessments of Hollywood were written at the same time, interestingly enough, that the studios were returning to power (albeit as subsidiaries of massive conglomerates) and as new technologies such as cable and home video were delivering an ever-expanding array of classic films to an increasingly cine-literate audience—insistently reminding us, in other words, of the creative vitality and efficiency of classical Hollywood. Meanwhile, media conglomeration underscored the fundamental connectedness of various entertainment media, particularly film and television. And thus it is scarcely surprising that television studies rapidly emerged as a distinct discipline—or rather, as a subdiscipline of media studies alongside film studies—and that scholars began to examine the vital interdependence between the two, an interdependence that had eluded film historians for decades. Michele Hilmes's (1990) *Hollywood and Broadcasting* and Christopher Anderson's (1994) *Hollywood TV* were important, indeed imperative, interventions into both U.S. film history and also our basic conceptualization of "the media" as industrial, economic, and cultural forms in American life. Although conglomeration and globalization encouraged many scholars to regard contemporary media (and their products) as manifestations of the postmodern condition, Hilmes and Anderson suggested that this condition is as old as the media industries themselves.

Although some scholars attempted to make cultural studies more relevant by reconciling political economy and cultural studies approaches, others proposed a wholesale overhauling of cultural studies. In yet another effort to make cultural studies more engaged with regulatory and industrial issues, a group of Australian and British media scholars began to advance cultural policy studies in the late 1980s. As initially defined by Tony Bennett (1998) and Stuart Cunningham (1992), and later amended by Tom O'Regan (1992) and Toby Miller (1998), cultural policy studies raised a number of ideas, values, and analytical strategies that incorporated textual and institutional analysis into the study of media and provided a useful theoretical frame through a reinterpretation of Foucault's concept of governmentality. In addition, cultural policy studies enabled a way of visualizing the possibility for change "within the system" via a reformist politics that kept issues of power at the forefront of analysis. Cultural policy research also addressed ethical considerations concerning the roles and responsibilities of academics and media scholars.

Not until fairly recently has a cultural policy approach been taken up by North American scholars and applied to American media industries. A significant early effort appeared in 2002, in a collection of essays edited by Lewis and Miller (2002) under the title *Critical Cultural Policy Studies.* This publication signals the growing interest among U.S. media scholars in a policy-based approach, although this remains a remarkably difficult endeavor in an era of deregulation and conglomeration. The challenge for academics in the United States involves finding ways to develop cultural policy analysis within a context in which policy tends to be set internally by media conglomerates. American media scholars face an additional challenge as they attempt to become involved in media regulation because of the ways in which, historically, they have been marginalized in public policy discussions. This differs dramatically from Britain and Australia, where there is more direct interaction between government and industry and where the academy has a longstanding tradition of contributing to the public sphere.

◆ Conclusions: Industry Trends and Research Priorities

Despite the obvious applicability of both cultural policy and political economy analysis to Hollywood, particularly to the New Hollywood of the past two decades, American film scholars are just beginning to use these approaches effectively. Moreover, media scholars have yet to integrate these approaches into a coherent conceptual and analytical schema, which seems not only advisable but also absolutely essential in light of recent (and current) conditions. And despite qualifying both approaches with the term *critical,* neither devotes sufficient attention to the creation, composition, and meanings of media products themselves. If we define Hollywood, as suggested at the outset, as a synthesis of industrial, institutional, and formal-aesthetic forces, then in our view, the integration of political economy and cultural policy approaches, in a method that is in fact critical and is properly sensitive to the economic and regulatory environment, may well provide the tools necessary to examine and understand the New Hollywood. In

concluding this chapter, we briefly sketch out our rationale for such an assertion.

As mentioned above, a policy-oriented approach to contemporary Hollywood requires significant modification of the schema developed in Britain and Australia, given the twin forces (and governing ideologies) of media deregulation and free-market capitalism in the United States since the 1980s. U.S. media policy has been shaped primarily by the economic policies, market strategies, and corporate customs of the media industrialists themselves—with the implicit endorsement of the federal government. Thus, policy studies of Hollywood further require a political economy approach attuned not only to the patterns of ownership but also, crucially, to the complex and ever-shifting relations of power in the New Hollywood. The interrelated effects of deregulation, conglomeration, diversification, and globalization have transformed both the structure of the U.S. entertainment industry and the conduct of its dominant institutions.

As mentioned above, the studios are now subsidiaries of global media conglomerates, but they assume a privileged position vis-à-vis both the parent company and its other divisions due to the tremendous importance of blockbuster hits and movie-driven entertainment franchises, as well as the syndication value of filmed entertainment throughout the global media marketplace. And because TimeWarner, Sony, News Corp, Disney, Viacom, and the other media conglomerates are all configured somewhat differently, it is challenging indeed to gauge the position and relative importance of their Hollywood holdings—including the studios themselves and their various film-related subsidiaries. As of 2003, TimeWarner, for instance, included Warner Bros., the New Line and Fine Line indie subsidiaries, several Turner (TBS) television and cable channels, the WB cable channel, HBO, and still other operations (see Chapter 15, this volume).

Further complicating matters, particularly since the mid-1990s, has been the massive impact of digital technology, both actual and anticipated, on Hollywood—and on the U.S. economy in general. New technologies and "delivery systems" have been crucial throughout Hollywood's history, of course, and cable television and home video were key incentives in the merger-and-acquisition waves of the late 1980s and early 1990s. The ensuing digital revolution that accompanied the rapid emergence of the Internet, e-commerce, and the "new economy," along with the Holy Grail (for Hollywood) of media "convergence" and online delivery of filmed entertainment, led to further media industry realignments. The most notable of these was the merger of AOL (America Online) and Time-Warner in early 2000, whose initial $150 billion price tag well indicates both the overheated state of the new economy and the overinflated valuation of online delivery. The value of the merger would fall precipitously over the next several years with the collapse of the "new economy" and the general downturn of the U.S. economy. These developments brought new cries for regulation and dramatic shifts in the relations of power within the media industries.

This underscores, yet again, the need for an analytical approach to Hollywood—and to media in general—that integrates both a political economy and a cultural policy perspective. And because these industrial, institutional, technological, and economic factors dramatically affect media products, including Hollywood movies, this analytical approach also should entail a "critical" perspective that takes formal-aesthetic factors into account. Indeed, this dimension of film and media studies, particularly those addressing the New Hollywood, has been sorely lacking. Although scholars examining classical Hollywood have become increasingly adept at integrating these various factors into a coherent analysis of the industry and its products, remarkably few studies of postclassical Hollywood have done so. Christopher Anderson's (1994) *Hollywood TV* and Justin Wyatt's (1994) *High Concept* do indicate that such an approach is altogether possible, however, and that studies will be forthcoming of "film style and mode of production" (following Bordwell et al.'s 1985 analysis of classical cinema) within the New Hollywood's larger industrial and institutional context.

To be properly attuned to the structure of contemporary Hollywood and the nature of its products, analysts would do well to avoid reductive assumptions about studio production and the products themselves and to acknowledge the remarkable—and, in many ways, unprecedented—complexity of current media conditions. More specifically, analysts might note several interrelated paradoxes that pervade current media production and that effectively govern the New Hollywood. The first of these paradoxes involves the bifurcation of movie products between big-budget blockbusters designed for global consumption, on one hand, and the production of niche-market films for specialized and relatively sophisticated markets, on the other hand. This invokes a second paradox involving the concurrent expansion and fragmentation of media markets, as Hollywood designs products for both global and niche-market consumption. These markets involve actual consumers and active audiences, whose "citizenship" in a range of communities—global, regional, national, local, and so forth—is increasingly a function, for better or worse, of media consumption. This paradoxical role of citizen/consumer speaks to a related paradox involving Hollywood itself as both an international and a distinctly American phenomenon. Finally, we might note a more general paradox involving not only media products, markets, and consumers but the Hollywood studios and their parent conglomerates as well, and that has important implications regarding the political economy of the New Hollywood. That governing paradox is this: The increasing concentration of media ownership on a global scale has coincided with, and in fact has directly entailed, the increasing fragmentation of markets and audiences, the diversification of media products, and the demands for critical media consumption on the part of individuals.

Given these conditions, we might be thoroughly dismayed or somewhat encouraged about the prospects for Hollywood in the new millennium. But whatever one's general view, we cannot help but marvel at Hollywood's remarkable adaptability and at the persistence of the cinema as America's dominant culture industry and defining art form. This demands, however, that film scholars and media analysts be as adaptable as the culture industry we examine and that we develop "ways of seeing" the media and its products that discern both the complexity of the industry and the ongoing appeal of its products.

◆ Notes

1. The principal members of the Hitchcock unit were cinematographer Robert Burks, editor George Tomasini, composer Bernard Herrmann, costume designer Edith Head, assistant director (and later associate producer) Herbert Coleman, and writer John Michael Hayes.

2. *Jaws* exploited the saturation marketing tactics pioneered by such independent distributors as American National Enterprises (ANE) and Sunn Classics.

3. For the original article, see Mulvey (1975); for her later thoughts on the topic, see Mulvey (1989).

◆ References

Albarran, A., & Chan-Olmsted, S. (Eds.). (1998). *Global media economics: Commercialization, concentration, and integration of world media markets*. Ames: Iowa State University Press.

Alexander, A., Owers, J., & Carveth, R. (Eds.). (1998). *Media economics: Theory and practice*. Mahwah, NJ: Lawrence Erlbaum.

Allen, R., & Gomery, D. (1985). *Film history: Theory and practice*. New York: Knopf.

Althusser, L. (1984). *Essays in ideology*. London: Verso.

Anderson, C. (1994). *Hollywood TV: The studio system in the fifties*. Austin: University of Texas Press.

Arnold, M. (1993). *Culture and anarchy and other writings* (S. Collini, Ed.). New York: Cambridge University Press.

Aufderheide, P. (1999). *Communications policy and the public interest: The Telecommunications Act of 1996*. New York: Guilford.

Balio, T. (1985). *The American film industry*. Madison: University of Wisconsin Press.

Balio, T. (1996). Adjusting to the new global economy: Hollywood in the 1990s. In A. Moran (Ed.), *Film policy: International, national and regional perspectives* (pp. 23–38). London: Routledge.

Bally, C., Sechehaye, A., & Riedlinger, A. (Eds.). (1986). *Course in general linguistics by Ferdinand de Saussure*. LaSalle, IL: Open Court.

Barthes, R. (1972). *Critical essays* (R. Howard, Trans.). Evanston, IL: Northwestern University Press.

Bazin, A. (1999). The evolution of the language of cinema. In L. Braudy & M. Cohen (Eds.), *Film theory and criticism: Introductory readings* (pp. 43–56). New York: Oxford University Press. (Original work published 1968)

Bennett, T. (1998). *Culture: A reformer's science*. London: Sage.

Bordwell, D. (1986). Classical Hollywood cinema: Narrational principles and procedures. In P. Rosen (Ed.), *Narrative, apparatus, ideology* (pp. 3–17). New York: Columbia University Press.

Bordwell, D., Thompson, K., & Staiger, J. (1985). *The classical Hollywood cinema: Film style & mode of production to 1960*. New York: Columbia University Press.

Browne, N. (Ed.). (1990). *Cahiers du Cinéma 1969–1972: The politics of representation*. Cambridge, MA: Harvard University Press.

Charters, W. W. (Ed.). (1933). *Motion pictures and youth: A summary*. New York: Macmillan.

Compaine, B. M., & Gomery, D. (2000). *Who owns the media? Competition and concentration in the mass media.* Mahwah, NJ: Lawrence Erlbaum.

Cunningham, S. (1992). *Framing culture: Criticism and policy in Australia.* Sydney, Australia: Allen & Unwin.

Doherty, T. (1988). *Teenagers and teenpics: The juvenilization of American movies in the 1950s.* Boston: Unwin Hyman.

Eco, U. (1994). *The role of the reader: Explorations in the semiotics of texts.* Bloomington: Indiana University Press.

Eisenstein, S. (1991). *S. M. Eisenstein: Selected works: Vol. 2. Towards a theory of montage* (2nd ed., R. Taylor, Ed., & M. Glenny, Trans.). London: British Film Institute.

Finler, J. W. (1988). *The Hollywood story.* New York: Crown.

Fiske, J. (1989). *Understanding popular culture.* Boston: Unwin Hyman.

Forman, H. J. (1933). *Our movie-made children.* New York: Macmillan.

Freeburg, V. O. (1918). *Art of photoplay making.* New York: Macmillan.

Garnham, N. (1995). Political economy and cultural studies: Reconciliation or divorce. *Critical Studies in Mass Communication, 12*(1), 62–71.

Gitlin, T. (1994). *Inside prime time* (2nd ed.). New York: Routledge.

Golding, P., & Murdock, G. (1991). Culture, communication, and political economy. In J. Curran & M. Gurevitch (Eds.), *Mass media and society* (pp. 15–32). London: Edward Arnold.

Gomery, D. (1986). *The Hollywood studio system.* New York: St. Martin's.

Gomery, D. (1992). *Shared pleasures: A history of movie presentation in the United States.* Madison: University of Wisconsin Press.

Hilmes, M. (1990). *Hollywood and broadcasting: From radio to cable.* Urbana: University of Illinois Press.

Hoggart, R. (1957). *The uses of literacy: Aspects of working class life with special reference to publications and entertainments.* London: Chatto & Windus.

Holt, J. (2003). Vertical vision: Deregulation, industrial economy and prime time design. In M. Jancovich (Ed.), *Quality popular television: Cult TV, industry and fans* (pp. 11–31). London: British Film Institute.

Horkheimer, M., & Adorno, T. W. (1972). *Dialectic of enlightenment* (J. Cumming, Trans.). New York: Herder and Herder.

Huettig, M. D. (1944). *Economic control of the motion picture industry: A study in industrial organization.* Philadelphia: University of Pennsylvania Press.

Jeffords, S. (1994). *Hard bodies: Hollywood masculinity in the Reagan era.* New Brunswick, NJ: Rutgers University Press.

Jowett, G. (1976). *Film: The democratic art.* Boston: Little, Brown.

Kellner, D. (1997). Overcoming the divide: Cultural studies and political economy. In M. Ferguson & P. Golding (Eds.), *Cultural studies in question* (pp. 102–120). London: Sage.

Kennedy, J. P. (Ed.). (1927). *The story of the films as told by the leaders of industry to the students of the Graduate School of Business Administration.* Chicago: A. W. Shaw.

Kitses, J. (1970). *Horizons West; Anthony Mann; Budd Boetticher; Sam Peckinpah: Studies of authorship within the western.* Bloomington: Indiana University Press.

Koszarski, J. (1990). *An evening's entertainment: The age of the silent feature picture, 1915–1928* (Vol. 3). Berkeley: University of California Press.

Lacan, J. (1977). *Écrits: A selection* (A. Sheridan, Trans.). London: Tavistock.

Lévi-Strauss, C. (1963). *Structural anthropology* (C. Jacobson & B. Grundfest, Trans.). New York: Basic Books.

Lewis, J., & Miller, T. (Eds.). (2002). *Critical cultural policy studies: A reader.* London: Blackwell.

Lindsay, V. (1915). *The art of the moving picture.* New York: Macmillan.

Litman, B. R. (1998). *The motion picture megaindustry.* Boston: Allyn & Bacon.

Macdonald, D. (1961). *Masscult & midcult.* New York: Random House.

McChesney, R. W. (1993). *Telecommunications, mass media and democracy: The battle for the control of U.S. broadcasting.* New York: Oxford University Press.

Metz, C. (1974). *Film language: A semiotics of the cinema* (M. Taylor, Trans.). New York: Oxford University Press.

Metz, C. (1982). *The imaginary signifier: Psychoanalysis and the cinema* (C. Britton, A. Williams, & B. Brewster, Trans.). Bloomington: Indiana University Press.

Miller, T. (1998). *Technologies of truth: Cultural citizenship and the popular media.* Minneapolis: University of Minnesota Press.

Morris, M. (1996). Banality in cultural studies. In J. Storey (Ed.), *What is cultural studies? A reader* (pp. 147–167). London: Arnold.

Mosco, V. (1996). *The political economy of communication: Rethinking and renewal.* London: Sage.

Mulvey, L. (1975). Visual pleasure and narrative cinema. *Screen, 16*(3), 6–18.

Mulvey, L. (1989). *Visual and other pleasures.* New York: Macmillan.

Munsterberg, H. (1916). *The photoplay: A psychological study.* New York: Appleton.

O'Regan, T. (1992). (Mis)taking policy: Notes on the cultural policy debate. *Cultural Studies, 6*(3), 395–409.

Peck, J. (Ed.). (1987). *The Chomsky reader.* New York: Pantheon.

Powdermaker, H. (1950). *Hollywood: The dream factory.* Boston: Little, Brown.

Ross, L. (1952). *Picture.* New York: Rinehart.

Rosten, L. (1941). *Hollywood: The movie colony, the movie makers.* New York: Harcourt, Brace.

Ryan, M., & Kellner, D. (1988). *Camera politica: The politics and ideology of contemporary Hollywood film.* Bloomington: Indiana University Press.

Sarris, A. (1962–1963). Notes on the auteur theory in 1962. *Film Culture, 27,* 1–8.

Sarris, A. (1968). *The American cinema: Directors and directions, 1929–1968.* New York: Dutton.

Schatz, T. (1993). The new Hollywood. In J. Collins, H. Radner, & A. P. Collins (Eds.), *Film theory goes to the movies* (pp. 8–36). New York: Routledge.

Schatz, T. (1997). The return of the studio system. In E. Barnouw (Ed.), *Conglomerates and the media* (pp. 73–106). New York: New York Press.

Schiller, H. (1989). *Culture, Inc.: The corporate takeover of public expression.* New York: Oxford University Press.

Seldes, G. (1978). *Movies come from America, aspects of film.* New York: Ayer.

Sklar, R. (1994). *Movie-made America: A cultural history of American movies.* New York: Vintage.

Thompson, E. P. (1963). *The making of the English working class.* New York: Vintage.

Warshow, R. (1962). *The immediate experience: Movies, comics, theatre & other aspects of popular culture.* Garden City, NY: Doubleday.

Wasko, J. (1994). *Hollywood in the information age.* London: Polity.

Williams, R. (1958). *Culture and society, 1780–1950.* London: Chatto & Windus.

Wollen, P. (1972). *Signs and meaning in the cinema.* Bloomington: Indiana University Press.

Wyatt, J. (1994). *High concept: Movies and marketing in Hollywood.* Austin: University of Texas Press.

25

BOLLYWOOD AND INDIAN CINEMA

Changing Contexts and Articulations of National Cultural Desire

◆ Veena Naregal

One may justifiably regard the recent attention that Bollywood has evoked among distributors and audiences in the West as but the latest twist in a story where the first steps towards shaping a recognizably Indian cinema began just over a hundred years ago. The development of Indian cinema may most profitably be seen as part of creative struggles on the subcontinent to shape a cultural modernity through an engagement, firstly, with the agenda of the colonial state and, subsequently, with that of its postcolonial counterpart. In sketching the role of the commercial film industry in shaping distinctive cinematic institutions and practices, as well as cultural identities, this chapter points to several overlapping and often contradictory strands, whereby international trends have been simultaneously absorbed and resisted, even as the medium was used to reshape the patterns of cultural and linguistic diversity on the subcontinent into mass popular forms to reach new audiences.

As one of the most important sites through which the Indian experience of capitalistic modernity was mediated and a general public—beyond elitist, upper-caste reading audiences—was both constructed and contested, cinema occupies a unique position among Indian cultural institutions. And yet, on account of its "lowbrow" status—and its far-from-liminal presence notwithstanding—the commercial film industry has failed to win recognition from the Indian state or mainstream sectors of the economy until recently. This gulf between official discourse on cinema and the evident cinephilia of the moviegoing public affects all aspects of its production and consumption, including industrial organization, aesthetics, regulation, reception, and appreciation. Except for the interlude where a government-funded, neorealist "parallel" cinema movement was able to thrive between the 1970s and the mid-1980s, state patronage for the Indian media industries, up until the deregulation of the media sector in the 1990s, was directed mainly towards maintaining a monopoly over radio and television. Recent government moves to encourage financial institutions to invest in film production notwithstanding, and despite producing the largest number of films annually in the world, the Indian film industry has not been self-sustaining and remains dependent on informal sectors of the money market. The forms of mainstream, "parallel," "middle," and regional Indian cinemas and their consumption have been shaped not only by these political and industrial contexts but also by debates pertaining to patronage and other critical issues in the fields of theater, literature, and performance.

This account will focus mainly on cinematic developments in the second half of the 20th century but always with the implicit assumption that this narrative has been necessarily shaped by a larger temporal and spatial cultural dynamic.[1] Interestingly, despite their popular following, the realms of commercial cinema and popular music were dismissed with utter disdain until recently by the Indian English-language press and sections of the liberal-nationalist and left-oriented intelligentsia.[2] This attitude stemmed partly from bourgeois anxiety over the possible contamination of middle-class culture from contact with the "lowbrow," but it also illustrates the conceptual intricacies of what constitutes the "popular" in an intensely stratified and linguistically divided postcolonial society such as India's (Nandy, 1998a).

The subaltern studies project[3] did not explicitly address the making of modern audiences. Nevertheless, in problematizing the relationship between elite normative discourses and subaltern agency and consciousness, this body of work foregrounded how difficult it has been to thematize the disjunctures that define a colonial-modern popular culture. It also implicitly acknowledged that colonialism enduringly altered key parameters of subjectivity, social belonging, and cultural production. However, in trying to recover the voice of nonelite subjects from the historical record of colonialism and nationalism, the core work of subaltern studies largely discounted the dynamics of the cultural mainstream established through institutional shifts introduced during the colonial era. All the same, the subaltern studies analyses fed into the critique, emerging in the 1980s, of the nation-state and Third World nationalisms. They also underscored the questions postcolonial theory and cultural studies posed regarding the processes of cultural representation and co-option underlying national cultures and postcolonial/transnational flows.[4]

All these intellectual currents increasingly brought home the need to think about the nature of Indian middle-class dominance and its relation with lower-class/caste perspectives and the making of a national cultural mainstream.[5] Although the most influential work addressing such questions of culture and power focused mainly on print and the discourse of colonial/postcolonial intellectuals, the late 1980s saw the first serious attempts to engage with the codes and history of Indian commercial cinema as a significant cultural artifact, partly inspired by the "media revolution" taking place in India around the same time (Nandy, 1998a; Rajadhyaksha, 1986; Thomas, 1985; Vasudevan, 1989).[6] This led to further work analyzing the distinctive modes of address, narration, and reception of popular Indian cinema (Chakravarty, 1993; Nandy, 1998b, 1998b; Vasudevan, 1993, 2000a).[7] Not surprisingly, the only-too-obvious intersections between institutions of cinema and politics that have evolved in India—especially in the four southern states of Tamil Nadu, Andhra Pradesh, Karnataka, and Kerala[8]—also invited attention to the linkages between cinematic representation, ideology, and political power (Pandian, 1992, 1997, 2000). In surpassing the limited nature of print audiences, Indian cinema represented one of the most important sites where the experience of a general public was approximated and contested. More recent work has further probed the connections between large collectivities such as cinema audiences and debates about cultural values and political behavior (Prasad, 1999; Srinivas, 2000). With the erosion of middle-class support for secular nationalism since the late 1980s, the recent ideological shifts to redefine India as a Hindu nation have inspired a series of analyses on how these shifts are articulated and consumed through popular cinema (see Niranjana, 2000; Vasudevan, 2001).

And yet, despite this very rich and stimulating body of work, a number of important questions remain unaddressed about the structures of patronage, including the influences of the state and market forces mobilized in shaping the circuits of production and distribution of popular cultural products in postcolonial India. Most interestingly, as against the patronage available to print media from national and provincial business elites, as well as for broadcasting through state funds, commercial cinema has survived mainly through exploiting surplus merchant capital available through parallel money markets. Thus, quite uniquely perhaps, the links between mainstream and informal sectors of the economy have been integral to disseminating a "lowbrow" cultural mainstream, impinging thus in important ways on the public sphere. The implications of these connections between informal networks of finance and distribution and the contours of the public sphere within the scenario of Indian capitalistic modernity have seldom been analyzed,[9] and yet in the attempt to understand the *particular* trajectory of Indian modernity, the need cannot be overemphasized to address conceptually the role of such intersections in defining arenas of ideological/cultural production, distribution, and consumption, as well as the disjunctures between statist/elitist and mass/popular discourses. This chapter is an initial venture in that direction.[10]

◆ *Projecting Desire: History, Politics and Cinematic Form Through 1975*

This section of the analysis falls into three parts, focusing on the initial foundations of India's cinema, the implications of the shift to talkies, and the roles of cinema in the period between Independence in 1947 and the 18-month state of emergency imposed by Prime Minister Indira Gandhi[11] in 1975, which was a watershed moment in recent Indian history.

COMMERCIAL THEATER TO SILENT FILM

The antecedents of Hindi commercial cinema lie in the forms and circuits established through the Parsi theater, a genre named after the wealthy mercantile community of Persian origin settled in western India. As shipbuilders, brokers, financiers, and active collaborators in colonial trade, the Parsis emerged as one of the dominant groups to form the Indian bourgeoisie. An important marker of their cultural distinction was their patronage in establishing a colonial-hybrid urban theatrical practice in 19th-century Bombay. Backed by the popularity of itinerant Parsee theater companies, this served as the model for commercial showbiz traditions that emerged through the subcontinent. Most notably, these plays amalgamated a medley of influences, ranging from themes of heroism derived from Persian poetry, Elizabethan stage conventions, and spectacular effects picked up from European opera to indigenous courtly and folk musical forms. As these troupes flourished, forms such as the historical, the romantic melodrama, and the mythological, all replete with song and dance sequences and extravagant special effects, provided the bases for the transition to film.[12]

The foremost example of how Parsi capital, aided by its significant connections with international trade, played a leading role in establishing early film distribution infrastructure in India is provided by Jamshedji Framji Madan (1856–1923). Belonging to a family that combined entrepreneurial talents with an enthusiasm for the theater, Jamshedji Madan went on to found Madan Theatres, a joint-stock film-importing and production company and distribution empire, which, at its peak in the late 1920s, owned 172 theaters and controlled half the country's box office. Initially, Madan theaters mainly imported and exhibited British newsreels and silent films, but after World War I, they were increasingly importing Hollywood films. Soon spurred on to production by the success of indigenous silent films, including those by Dhundiram Phalke, Madan Theatres' first productions included filmed versions of their in-house theatrical successes, followed by a series of big-budget Indo-European collaborations, all presenting classical Hindu myths ("mythologicals") with interesting Orientalist overtones, such as *Nala Damayanti*[13] (1920, Eugenio De Liguoro), *Dhruva Charitra* (1921, Liguoro, *Triumph of Devotion*), and *Savitri Satyavan* (1923, Giorgio Mannini).

Born to a Brahmin family in Nasik, Maharashtra, and after his initial training at the colonial art schools in Bombay and Baroda, Phalke (1870–1944) worked as a portrait photographer, stage makeup artist, and magician. Seeing the film *Life of Christ* in a Bombay cinema in 1910 inspired Phalke to dedicate himself to harness cinema's resources to contribute to the anti-imperial *swadeshi*[14] movement by projecting Indian images for Indian audiences. Despite his modest background, Phalke's ambitions to found a modern filmmaking practice along industrial lines led him to England in 1912 and 1914 to learn the craft and procure equipment. Although only a small fraction of his work survives, Phalke is said to have made 44 silent features.[15] Clearly reveling in experimenting with cinematic effects and animation techniques, Phalke introduced the mythological genre, through which he was able to exploit traditional narratives to introduce obliquely coded anticolonial messages. Other significant initiatives of the silent era included the Kohinoor Film Company (*Telephone ni Taruni* [1926, Homi Master, *The Telephone Girl*]; *Bhaneli Bhamini* [1927, Homi Master, *Educated Wife*]; *GunSundari* [1927, Chandulal Shah, *Why Husbands Go Astray*]), established in 1919, which transformed production from Phalke's notion of a family-based cottage industry unit to one using methods resembling those of the Hollywood film factories. It also notably included the Imperial Films Company (*Mumbai Ni Biladi* [1927, Mohan Bhavnani, *Wildcat of Bombay*]; *Cinema Girl* [1930, B. P. Mishra]), set up after the decline of Kohinoor by Ardeshir Irani in 1926. This produced films in at least nine different languages—including Tamil, Telugu, Burmese, Malay, Pushtu, and Urdu—best known for their "socials" and historical costume-dramas, including *Alam Ara* (the heroine's name), the first Indian talkie, released in 1931.

◆ Talkies: Regional Cinemas and the Bombay "Social" Film

If the silent era saw film production assume its institutional and generic dimensions through its attempts to reach pan-Indian audiences, it also highlighted what has been an enduring and distinguishing characteristic—namely, that the unique popularity of India's commercial cinema has lain in its embeddedness in visual and cultural idioms largely outside the realm of the modern. The coming of sound rapidly curtailed Hollywood's share in the domestic market, allowing indigenous industry, especially the Hindi cinema emerging from Bombay, to enhance its claims to a national market, even as the new technology also created avenues for the birth of regional cinemas, especially in the larger linguistic zones of Bengali, Marathi, Tamil, and Telugu. Amidst much ferment and reorganization in

the industry, new studios were founded in Calcutta, Bombay, Pune, and Madras, which attracted talent from cultural elites and progressive voices, including a host of Hindi-Urdu writers,[16] starting with Munshi Premchand, K. A. Abbas, and Manto. If the social and literary reform movements had provided the core debates about Indian modernity in the 19th century,[17] typically from the 1940s onwards, the melodramatic mode emerged as the dominant channel through which these values and conflicts could attain their cinematic extension as popular discourse. The first decade after the talkies had seen the secular "social" film share its popularity with other genres such as "mythologicals," stunt films, and the "historical" or the devotional film, but the "social" melodrama emerged as the dominant commercial genre from the interwar years onwards. The imminence of Independence was undoubtedly a dynamic force field that drove the rearticulation of subjectivities and desire, and the film industry responded with generic narratives that attempted to meld together the promise of social transformation and nationalist aspirations with anxieties over modernization and cultural authenticity.[18]

And yet despite its evident keenness to lend itself to the task of modern nation building, given the socially and ideologically composite nature of Indian film audiences, this efflorescent cinematic activity only underscored how modes of address and viewing characteristics of the silent era would retain their relevance despite the advent of sound. These conditions of production and reception created idiosyncratic cinematic forms with a limited scope for linear narrative structures satisfying assumptions of "pure" realistic address directed towards the individual spectator. In contrast to the dominant mode of Hollywood cinema, the mode of address deployed by mainstream Indian cinema makes little attempt to subordinate spectacle and visceral effect to reinforce the realist illusion. Song and dance numbers, fight sequences, fantasy elements that include exotic costumes and settings, and direct frontal address into the camera that periodically ruptures the quasi-realistic plot all remain key elements in the aesthetic of what has been described as the typically disaggregated form of the Bollywood melodrama (Prasad, 1998).

Prominent among the new studios were New Theatres, Calcutta, Prabhat Studios, Kolhapur-Pune, and Bombay Talkies (see Bandyopadhyay, 1993). A major aim for B. N. Sircar in founding the impressively equipped New Theatres (1931–1955) was to create cinematic equivalents of acclaimed literary texts. The studio had several directors and stars on its payroll[19] and counted the populist devotional about *Chandidas* (1932), a medieval saint, and the Hindi and Bengali versions of *Devdas* (Barua, 1935) among its principal successes. Founded through a partnership between V. Shantaram, Vishnupant Damle, Fattelal, Dhaiber, and Baburao Pendharkar in Kolhapur, Prabhat Studios (1929–1953) moved to Pune in 1933 to produce several acclaimed films, some made simultaneously in separate Hindi and Marathi versions. Capitalizing on the talents of well-known figures of the popular Marathi stage,[20] Prabhat established its initial reputation through mythologicals and historicals, such as *Baji Prabhu* (1929), about an 18th-century historical figure, and *Ayodhyacha Raja* (1932, *The King of Ayodhya*). Prabhat also boasted of its excellent in-house facilities, and its later films included such "reformist"[21] classics as *Kunku/Duniya Na Mane* (1937, *Society Will Not Allow It*), *Manoos/Aadmi* (1939, *Man*), and *Shejari/Padosi* (1943, *Neighbour*).

Set up by Himanshu Rai, Bombay Talkies (1934–1955) probably holds a unique place in Indian film history in attracting the support of leading financial institutions in Bombay. Best known for its impressive array of European technicians,[22] Bombay Talkies launched the reputations of several leading stars, such as Ashok Kumar and Dilip Kumar, and directors such as N. R. Acharya (*Naya Sansar*, 1941, *New World*) and Gyan Mukherjee (*Kismet*, 1943, *Destiny*).

The conjunction of Independence and Partition in 1947 saw the film industry multiply its landmarks: The years 1945 to 1947 saw a threefold increase in the total number of films produced in the country, with the figure going from 99 to 280. And yet, interestingly, as Ashis Rajadhyaksha (1996, p. 29) has pointed out, despite this burgeoning output, Partition did not feature even once in the cinematic enterprise during the period when Indian commercial cinema forged its distinctive idioms.[23] Thus, although Bombay and other regional cinemas carry the definitive influence of Muslim talent and Islamic culture, it is striking that even as early as the 1940s, their emerging forms of address were marked in relation to an unnamed but implicitly Hindu, upper-caste, patriarchal identity, within which religious or ethnic minority characters typically figured as subordinate allies or antagonists of the hero.[24] "Muslim" themes and narratives could be significantly fore-grounded only through separate marginal genres—which, nevertheless, have supplied some of the biggest "evergreen" hits of Indian cinema—such as the "historical" courtly love dramas, featuring extravagant period costumes and sumptuous music and dance sequences, or the "Muslim social" that dealt with the Muslim North Indian middle class and its social problems, especially the need for education and reform, through narratives that were liberally laced with scintillating *ghazals* and *qawalis*.[25]

◆ From Independence to the 1975 National Emergency

Under Nehru, India embarked on a growth strategy built around state-led capitalistic growth, promotion of heavy industry, and a bureaucratized approach to issues of poverty. Hindi was recognized as one of India's official languages, along with Bengali, Marathi, Tamil, and more than 10 others. However, thanks to a largely economistic vision of progress during this period, the state seemed quite happy to relinquish any responsibility for all other cultural aspects of nation building to emergent forces or the market. This hands-off attitude towards cultural development policy partly stemmed from elitist/bourgeois anxieties about the contamination of respectable modern culture through contact with the "lowbrow." Such biases influenced official perceptions of the commercial film industry, which was largely viewed, at best, as a lucrative source of revenue and, at worst, as a source of moral corruption threatening "less enlightened" citizens and youth.[26] Left to grow largely outside of state support, Hindi cinema (and its regional counterparts) could not remain unaffected by these conservative strands within cultural policy thinking. As the film industry proceeded to produce spectacular, if bastardized, versions of the nation's "tryst with destiny" that approached the values of citizenship, industrial progress, and secular wisdom through the rhetoric of kinship and melodrama, commercial cinema seemed to uncannily foreshadow the increasingly populist directions that state policy itself was to take in the 1970s under Mrs. Gandhi's premiership.

The speculative economic boom at the end of World War II had brought new money into the film industry, leading to the rapid decline of old studios by the early 1950s and the emergence of new production banners such as Navketan, RK Films and Bimal Roy Productions, and many others that included the vast majority of freelance investors who saw the film industry as an avenue for quick returns. These developments only accentuated the gap between mass/popular and elitist/state-centered cultural agendas and perspectives. Consequently, one of the first policy initiatives vis-à-vis the film industry was the decision to raise the entertainment tax to 50% in Central Provinces and up to 75% in West Bengal, which led to nationwide protests from the industry. The comprehensive S. K. Patil Film Enquiry Committee Report, submitted in 1951—the same year as the First

Five-Year National Economic Plan was announced—only confirmed the mistrust with which the film industry was viewed in official circles and called for major state investment to produce a more salutary and "authentic" cinema. Similar elitist biases also led to an effective ban on film music on state-owned All-India Radio in 1952–1957. On its side, the Pakistani government responded with its own statist bigotry by officially banning the import of Indian films in 1952.

The core realistic melodramas produced by the three major filmmakers of the 1950s, Guru Dutt, Raj Kapoor, and Bimal Roy—which also mark IPTA's contribution to mainstream commercial cinema[27]—can be read as expressions of the shifts that nationalist utopias underwent as the Indian state attempted to assert its ascendancy as the arbiter of resources over the role of "high" culture and the economy.[28] Scripted by K. A. Abbas, Raj Kapoor's *Awaara* (Raj Kapoor, 1951, *The Vagabond*) and *Shri 420* (Raj Kapoor, 1955, *Mr. 420*) attempted to reconcile class divisions and the tensions of a transition to urban modernity through sentimental love stories, where the tramp-like hero acquires legitimacy and status via a narrative journey that marries capitalism and feudal paternalism, social justice and order, "authentic" tradition and urban modernity.

Guru Dutt's tragic classic, *Pyaasa* (Guru Dutt, 1957, *Eternal Thirst*), depicted the struggles of a romantic artist, Vijay, neglected by family and society, only to be acclaimed as a best-selling hero after he is thought dead. Making powerful use of brilliantly framed shots and intense lyrics, the film presented an anguished reflection on the state of the nation and the fate of those displaced by a corrupt commercialism. *Do Bigha Zamin* (Bimal Roy, 1953, *Two Acres of Land*) is the story of a small peasant, Shambhu, forced to go to the city to try and earn enough to redeem his small plot of land from the unscrupulous money lender, who has designs to sell it to urban brokers. Its more realistic elements clearly resonated with conflicts of the post-Independence period, but these were offset by its nostalgic evocations of rural "innocence" and sentimental depictions of urban working-class neighborhood solidarity.

More than any other, Mehboob's *Mother India* (1957) raised these motifs of an upright struggling peasant, a greedy money lender, and the long-suffering but strong Indian woman, who will sacrifice "everything" except her virtue to defend the honor of her family and kin, to the status of mythic stereotypes that endured throughout subsequent mainstream cinema. Equally, all these 1950s realist melodramas made available a lexicon of images representing rural and working-class lives as the mark of an "authentic" Indian-ness that the later, self-consciously neorealist "parallel" cinema movement also adopted.

In 1960, almost a decade after the S. K. Patil report, the government established the Film Finance Corporation and the Film Institute in Pune. Inspired in some measure by the success with both Western and Bengali audiences of world-renowned Bengali director Satyajit Ray's first film, *Pather Panchali* (1955, *Song of the Road*)—a project partly funded by the West Bengal State government—these twin initiatives aimed at fostering an "independent" cinema comprising realist films of so-called "good standard." Along with the two sequels (apparently made at Nehru's suggestion) that make up the Apu trilogy, Ray's early films embody an introspective, often nostalgic, depiction of the cultural moorings of the Bengali *bhadralok* (an often-used Bengali term for *cultural elite*). The evocation of Bengal's past through the internationalist idioms of cinematic realism expressed itself in Ray's work of this period, above all, through a focus on a highly elaborated atmospheric accuracy. This clearly marked a deliberate break with the less aestheticized depictions of the transition to modernization in the realist melodramas of Bombay's commercial cinema. Ray's cinematic aims resonated in interesting ways with the Nehruvian desire for coherent narratives of the past that implicitly

insinuate its movement towards the modern present while also simultaneously complementing and going beyond the propagandistic style of Films Division documentaries of this period.[29] In 1964, following this cultural policy logic, the Film Finance Corporation (FFC) was placed under the direct control of the Ministry of Information and Broadcasting.

In its first six years, the FFC gave out production loans for some 50 films, including Ray's *Charulata* (1964), *Nayak* (1966, *Actor*), and *Goopy Gyne Bagha Byne* (1968), followed by its support of the work of a generation of young filmmakers, including Mrinal Sen (*Bhuvan Shome*, 1969), Mani Kaul (*Uski Roti* [1969, *Bread*], *Ashaad ka Ek Din* [1971, *A Monsoon Day*], and *Duvidha* [1973, *In Two Minds*]), Kumar Shahani (*Maya Darpan* [1972, *Mirror of Illusion*]), and M. S. Sathyu (*Garam Hawa* [1972, *Hot Winds*]). In 1971, a ministry directive explicitly described the FFC's obligations as developing "film in India into an effective instrument for the promotion of national culture, education and healthy entertainment (through) loans for modest but off-beat films."

Significantly, these efforts to support a "high" cinematic aesthetic that was self-consciously Indian and yet did not interfere with the nation-state's rationalization of the cultural process went hand in hand with the government's emerging interest, beginning from 1959 and more rapidly from 1965 onwards, in establishing a nationwide television apparatus that could provide technological solutions to "cultural barriers," such as illiteracy and linguistic diversity, that were hindering national development processes.

Equally, these interventions on the part of the state also highlighted the film industry's continued inability to be financially self-sustaining and its dependence on outside sources for finance. The annual output of the Bombay industry would surpass the 1947 record figure of 183 Hindi films only in the year 1985. Nevertheless, by 1971, the Indian film industry's total output already made it the largest producer of films in the world. Taking advantage of a growing national market, the Bombay industry responded to the FFC program with an increasingly standardized "hold-all" entertainment formula that incorporated and subordinated elements of earlier indigenous genres into a narrative form designed to cut through regional and linguistic differences. Described as the "all-India film," this notion that the Hindi film has, by default, served a culturally integrative function has been high among the industry's claims about its own importance. Marking a partial shift since the days of the Patil report, the idea was also partly endorsed in official circles, implicitly acknowledging the limitations of the government's cultural policies and the increasing dependence of the state-run broadcasting sector on film music and other film-based formats to fill its own programming needs.

Indeed, this was a crucial period in Indian politics: Ruling ideologies came under increasing pressure as democratic processes brought new groups and regional elites into the political arena, accentuating regional, class, and rural-urban disparities. The late 1960s and 1970s marked the beginning of a protracted period of political discontent. Regional movements in Orissa, Maharashtra, and South India pressed for territorial reorganization according to linguistic boundaries. Around the same time, the initially peaceful peasant uprisings in West Bengal turned into violent insurrection directed against individual landowners, spreading first to other rural bases in the southern states of Andhra Pradesh, Kerala, and Tamil Nadu, and by 1970 had acquired the support of radical student groups in Calcutta. Indiscriminate police and military force was used to quell these upheavals, only to see the following years witness further mounting protests over inflation, food shortages, and labor unrest. Mrs. Gandhi's response to these challenges to the government's authority consisted of a series of populist and authoritarian initiatives that gave the state unprecedented centralized coercive powers. Simultaneously, she mobilized a highly emotive political rhetoric that sought support for government campaigns, such as her 20-point program, mainly by casting the state as the supreme victim of conspiracy by "antinational" forces.

The shrinking space in India for deliberation and dissent in addressing fundamental political problems found its reflection in the field of mass culture through three important films—*Sholay, Deewar,* and *Jai Santoshi Maa*—released in the same year as the declaration of National Emergency by Mrs. Gandhi in 1975. A huge box-office hit and revenge drama, *Sholay* (Ramesh Sippy, *Flames of the Sun*) revolves around Gabbar Singh, the dreaded rural bandit who is evil incarnate and strikes terror in the hearts of the innocent villagers of Rampur. Gabbar can only be subdued through extralegal means in the form of the ex-police officer, Thakur Baldev Singh, and with the help of two brave-hearted crooks, Jai and Veeru, played by Amitabh Bachchan and Dharmendra.

Deewar (Yash Chopra, *The Wall*) turned the conventional plot of two brothers, one of whom is a model cop and the other a gangster, into a powerful box-office hit that established Amitabh Bachchan in the persona of the melancholic, angry young man, who single-handedly seeks justice against a corrupt social order. The film reworks this customary pattern of mainstream cinema of a clash between the laws of kinship and state into a narrative that mobilizes sympathy for the working-class rebel, only to culminate in Vijay's death at his brother's hands, who is exhorted to perform his duty by the mother. Interwoven with several contemporary references—and made at a time when official rhetoric did not hesitate to paint Mrs. Gandhi as a benevolent mother-figure that the poor could look up to—the film's conclusion seemed to endorse the use of authoritarian means to overcome challenges to the power structure.

Another film to catch audience attention in a big way that year was *Jai Santoshi Maa*

(*Hail! Mother Santoshi*) (Lutgendorf, 2002). Reviving a genre that had not been used in Hindi cinema in nearly two decades, the film's success has been linked to its difference from earlier mythologicals in its being much closer to the mundane problems of Indian family life. The film turned a little-known mother-goddess, Santoshi Maa, into a deity with a huge following among urban working-class women.

The wave of peasant uprisings echoed by rising urban dissent brought home the urgent need to bridge the rural-urban divide. This political juncture coincided with a host of films aimed primarily at urban upper-middle-class audiences, taking rural life and/or social unrest as its themes, including Benegal's rural trilogy *Ankur* (1973, *Seedling*), *Nishant* (1975, *Night's End*), and *Manthan* (1976, *The Churning*); Karanth's *Chomana Dudi* (1975, *Choma's Drum*); and Karnad's *Kaadu* (1975, *The Forest*)—all of which were made under the auspices of the advertising industry or state funding.[30]

Simultaneously, in an effort to shore up the nation-space, the government embarked on a new phase of its mass communications policy. The early 1970s saw an expansion of terrestrial broadcasting beyond Delhi, the only city to have had a daily TV service since 1965. Bombay acquired its television center in 1971, a year after the second Indo-Pakistani War, followed in the next year by Srinagar, Kashmir's capital, and the northern city of Amritsar, ostensibly chosen on account of their proximity with the border with Pakistan. Similar efforts to induct the rural population at large into the national mainstream saw the launching of SITE (the Satellite Instructional Television Experiment), intended as a blueprint for the use of satellite technology for a nationwide network. Transmitted from Delhi and Ahmedabad, in its first phase, SITE beamed out educational programs about hygiene, health care, family planning, and the use of technology in agriculture to specially distributed community TV sets in about 2,500 villages spread across six states.

◆ Changing Institutional Contexts: Post-Emergency to 1992 and Beyond

The major forces that shaped media policy and distribution after 1975 were the expansion of the television sector, the arrival of video, the gradual dismantling of economic and industrial protectionism from the early 1980s onwards, and consequent shifts in the state's control from active participant to the new phase where its authority was asserted mainly as final arbitrator in the economic process. In addition, we will need to take into account the growth of an exclusivist Hindu nationalism symbolized by the 1992 destruction of the Babri Masjid mosque by a fundamentalist Hindu group and the terrible Bombay riots that ensued. The directions that film production took in the 1980s and 1990s need to be understood in light of the challenges and issues that the industry needed to contend with during this time.

Interestingly, some of the earliest evidence of the trend towards economic liberalization came in the wake of the government's space satellite program and the introduction of color television—the latter even being part of the Congress Party agenda for the 1980 elections, which saw Mrs. Gandhi return to power. Initially, incentives were offered to indigenous manufacturers of color TV sets, but soon major multinational electronic companies were given licenses to import unassembled TV kits. Furthermore, corresponding with India's largest loan hitherto of $5 billion from the International Monetary Fund (IMF), government cultural policy began to reflect a growing concern with India's image abroad, leading to the successfully mounted massive campaign to market Indian culture in Western capitals in the form of the Festivals of India, which featured India's best traditional and contemporary talent. Similarly, the hosting of the Ninth Asian Games was seen as an opportunity to showcase India's technological capabilities to the rest of the world, providing the context for the launching of a countrywide prime-time TV network for transmissions emanating from Delhi, as well as the introduction of color TV.

Color telecasting was inaugurated with Satyajit Ray's only Hindi films, *Sadgati* (*Deliverance*) and *Shatranj Ke Khilari* (*The Chess Players*) on April 25, 1982. Coinciding with a time when the size of Indian media audiences was accelerating significantly, thanks to the growing consumer base among the urban and semi-urban population, these developments gave the national government a magnified opportunity for a centralized and monopolistic dissemination of political images. One significant index of the growing audience size was the fact that in the 1980s, the circulation of regional-language newspapers surpassed that of the English-reading public for the very first time since Independence.[31] Not surprisingly, then, in light of the growing influence of market forces over state policy, one of the first major decisions of the new Rajiv Gandhi[32] government in 1984 was to do with the selling of prime-time slots to private advertisers and content producers, making Doordarshan, the national TV broadcaster, a fully commercial channel in 1985. *Hum Log* (*We, the People*)—aired over 1984–1985, modeled on Mexican "pro-development" soap-operas, and instrumental in making its sponsors, Nestlé Foods, a household name in India—was followed by several privately produced teleserials, leading to an approximately tenfold increase in TV set ownership just from 1984 to 1986.[33]

Simultaneously, video was emerging as another alternate delivery option. The size of the Indian video market was huge, relying as it did on the flourishing informal sector of the economy for its production and distribution circuits: By 1984, it was estimated that there were approximately 1 million VCRs in India and 30 million videotapes, pointing to a turnover of about 300 crore rupees (Rs 3 billion), already about one third the film industry's (Rajadhyaksha, 1990).

The industry had always felt that the treatment that it had been meted out by successive post-Independence governments had been far from sympathetic: For instance, in 1978, the industry had paid 187 crore rupees (Rs 1.87 billion) out of its declared turnover of 247 crore rupees (Rs 2.47 billion) as entertainment tax (Rajadhyaksha & Willemen, 1999, p. 27). The scarcity of distribution outlets in India has always been a bottleneck for the industry. In 1980, although the country had only 6,368 permanent and 4,024 touring movie theaters for a population of more than 800 million, government initiatives towards creating alternative cinema production through the FFC and the National Film Development Corporation (NFDC) did not include any serious interest in augmenting the distribution network.[34] But now, wedged between the state's centralized control over television production and the almost entirely illegal video market, the film industry found its territorial distribution arrangements, in place since the decline of the studios in the 1940s, being severely challenged. Moreover, the state was not averse to using the issue of antipiracy laws as a bargaining point to secure the industry's resources, personnel, and glamour to promote Doordarshan's expansion plans.

The impact of these changes on both mainstream and new Indian cinema was equally evident: The mid-1980s saw almost every single name associated with the "parallel" cinema movement, including such key figures as Satyajit Ray, Shyam Benegal, Govind Nihalini, Saaed Mirza, Ketan Mehta, and Vijaya Mehta, move into television production. Major commercial filmmakers, too, such as Ramanand Sagar and B. R. Chopra, followed suit in responding to what clearly was a significant juncture, with state and market pressures combining to produce major shifts in media production and policy.

Accentuated by expanding media audiences and new groups claiming access to the public sphere,[35] the protracted ideological crisis facing the Indian state took a fresh turn in 1986, when the Rajiv Gandhi government allowed the dispute between Hindus and Muslims over worship rights at the Babri Masjid mosque in Ayodhya to be reopened.[36] These decisions were echoed by major switches in television policy, which, despite recent changes, had been hitherto premised on the Nehruvian ideal of upholding the official neutrality of state institutions. Although it was true that since the 1950s, the playing of mostly Hindu devotional music on government-run radio had been justified as promoting "national integration" and/or "folk culture," nevertheless the decision to allow Ramanand Sagar's *Ramayana* to be aired on the national network, to a prime-time Sunday morning audience, marked a historic shift from prevailing norms and, arguably, a turning point in legitimizing the political ideology of *Hindutva*.[37]

Proposing that the *Ramayana* was at once "universal" but "essentially Hindu," the then Secretary for Information and Broadcasting, S. S. Gill, who showed a keen interest in telecasting the serial, justified the use of state media, arguing that the epic epitomized Mahatma Gandhi's own notion of *ram-rajya* (kingdom of Ram) as the exemplary indigenous model of the welfare state (Rajagopal, 2001, p. 85). Peak ratings showed viewer figures as high as 80% of TV households, and yet their implications were ominous. The same year saw massive protest demonstrations by Muslims, countered by rallies of militant Hindus determined to "reclaim" the Babri Masjid site. These were followed by the laying of the foundation stone for a temple at the disputed site in 1989 and culminated eventually in December 1992 with the attack on the Babri Masjid and bloody confrontations throughout the country.

The 1980s were therefore a challenging period for the film industry. The major big box-office draws in the early part of the decade included the big-budget Manmohan Desai films, which recycled the rebel-vigilante Amitabh-centered plots of the late 1970s into a series of semiparodic extravaganzas celebrating lumpen power (*Naseeb* [1981, *Fate*], *Coolie* [1983], *Mard* [1985, *Macho-Man*]).

However, soon interesting shifts emerged. The advertising potential of Doordarshan, backed by its several film-based programs featuring popular songs, had underscored the importance of catchy tunes and innovative music for the successful marketing of commercial cinema. Parallel to this, the audiocassette market had rapidly expanded since the late 1970s, and now the increasing profits to be made from the presale of music rights resulted in a growing integration between the music business and film production. The career of Gulshan Kumar, the self-proclaimed "audiocassette king," best illustrates these shifts: Starting off with an audiocassette repair shop in Delhi but sensing that the market was ripe for expansion, Kumar made huge profits initially through pirated versions of expensive HMV cassettes and, later, by issuing cheap remixed "cover versions" of old and new film songs. He eventually went on to head a business empire that spanned a range of products from soap and detergents, electronics, CDs, and video and film production.[38] These conditions brought back the genre of the teenage love story, replete with sentimental songs and shot in a glossy advertising style with "cutesy" visual effects made up of lush colors, brilliant contrasts, trendy costumes, and other objects of consumerist desire, including motorbikes, neon signs, fluffy toys, and the like. The biggest hit of 1988, *Qayamat se Qayamat Tak* (Mansoor Khan, 1988, *The Day of Judgement*), introduced this trend and was quickly followed by *Maine Pya Kiya* (Sooraj Barjatya, 1989, *In Love*). These two films launched two of the biggest stars to dominate Hindi cinema in the 1990s: Aamir Khan and Salman Khan, respectively.

In the 1990s, the work and career of the South Indian director Mani Ratnam perhaps best illustrates the changes under way. Ratnam first hit the national limelight with his Tamil film, *Nayakan* (1988, *Leader*), which refigured *The Godfather* to feature the Tamil mafia in Bombay. His next two films, *Agni Nakshtaram* (1989, *The Fire Constellation*) and *Anjali* (1990), saw him successfully exploit an MTV-inspired style making extensive use of back lighting, diffuse camera, flare filters, and songs with innovative rhythms and well-choreographed dance sequences. *Anjali* was an equally big hit in its dubbed Hindi version, clearly showing that Ratnam had tapped a nerve with respect to emerging audience tastes. Equally, his success on the national market showed the growing influence of the regional film industries in South India, whose total annual output had consistently surpassed the corresponding number of Hindi films produced each year since the late 1980s. Mani Ratnam's next film, the controversial and highly successful *Roja* (1993), once again released in Tamil and Hindi versions, was the story of a newly-wed Tamil hero who proves his patriotism by fighting antinational Islamic terrorists who kidnap him while he is on an assignment to assist the Indian army in Kashmir. With its demonization of Muslims as fanatical terrorists, an enemy and threat to the nation, in contrast to the benign cosmopolitanism of the Hindu hero and his bride, the film's politics echo the escalating majoritarian ideological backlash that has, since the 1990s, sought to claim India as a Hindu nation.

The contents and reception of his next film, *Bombay* (Tamil/Hindi, 1995), proved equally controversial. Bombay is a love story between a Hindu journalist, Shekhar, and a Muslim woman, Bano, that begins in a Tamil village but is played out against the rising tide of fanaticism in Bombay and the terrible riots that shook the city in the wake of the destruction of the Babri Masjid. In its bold use of documentary footage and direct references to contemporary events, *Bombay* marked a departure from the typical commercial film. However, both *Roja* and *Bombay* renormalized Hindu identity with modernity, patriotism, and the voice of reason. Furthermore, Mani Ratnam's claims to

neutrality were compromised when, fearing objections from the extremist Bombay-based pro-Hindu party, the Shiv Sena, over the film's alleged "concessions" towards Muslims, he sought and gained Shiv Sena leader Bal Thackeray's approval for the Hindi version before the film's release, mainly by agreeing to cuts the latter suggested.

The politics of these films resonates with a host of other recent mainstream offerings such as *Border* (J. P. Dutta, 1997) and *Gadar: Ek Prem Katha* (Anil Sharma, 2001, *Revolt: A Love Story*), which similarly fed off and into *Hindutva* sentiment through a hypermasculine and militantly espoused anti-Pakistani nationalism.[39]

◆ Expatriate Audiences, International Markets

If these attempts to mobilize a self-righteous, middle-class, ultra-patriotic address saw popular Hindi cinema turn its back on previous strands that had foregrounded issues of class and inequality (even if these themes had been delineated in ways that ultimately reinforced the status quo), these narrative changes were highlighted by other shifts indicating alterations in the composition and location of audiences for India's commercial cinema. By the early 1990s, the Bombay film industry had gained a degree of control over its losses from video piracy;[40] nevertheless, mounting pressures from the rise in raw film stock prices and the growth of cable and satellite television in the wake of economic reforms clearly made the industry eager to tap new markets.

In recent times, Indian film producers have found that international markets have proved a much more reliable source of revenue than the domestic circuit. Earnings from foreign markets still remain a small part of the film industry's revenues, but they have been increasingly attractive to filmmakers as well as to other parties with a stake in distribution revenues. The latter indeed was borne out by the shooting attack in late 2001 on film producer Raakesh Roshan, apparently over Bombay mafia demands for the international rights of his recent hit, *Kaho Na Pyaar Hai* (2001, *Say You Are in Love*) (see "Cash Boost for Bollywood," 2001). The current overseas interest has mainly been for the Bombay film; however, South Indian films have also proved a less important but still attractive export, with interest coming not just from émigré Tamil communities in Sri Lanka, Southeast Asia, and the West but also from mainstream or cult audiences in countries such as Japan and England.[41] In contrast to these moves to exploit foreign markets for Indian films, reports show that efforts by Hollywood companies to push dubbed versions of U.S. films in the Indian market or to collaborate with the Indian industry over investment and distribution deals, have met with only limited success (Rajadhyaksha, 1996, p. 28).

Such alertness to their changing constituencies has been the hallmark of India's commercial cinemas, which, as Ravi Vasudevan (2000b) points out, rather than address any fixed set of linguistic and cultural markers, have "from the period of sound cinema onwards, sought to fashion products which could move amongst a series of markets" (p. 120). In Britain, the first movie theaters catering to Asian audiences emerged in the 1970s: six in Birmingham, four each in Leicester and Bradford, and two in Derby (Tyrrell, 1998, p. 21). Video and, subsequently, the airing of Hindi films through Asian satellite TV channels, such as Zee and Sony, almost killed off this localized exhibition circuit. However, from 1993 onwards, commercial screenings through private hires of multiplexes by Asian entrepreneurs have been followed by the showing of Indian films in independent cinemas by non-Asian exhibitors.

With its successful marketing to Asian émigré audiences, Bollywood was bound to take notice. By the early 1990s, Bollywood narratives bore signs that the taste of expatriate Indian audiences for romance and family genres was influencing their choice of themes, characters, and settings. Several 1990s "super-hits," such as *Dilwale Dulhaniya Le Jayenge* (Aditya Chopra, 1995, *Brave of Heart Wins the Bride*) and *Pardes* (Subhash Ghai, 1997, *A Foreign Land*), often shot on location in England and/or continental Europe, have featured émigré Indians in search of their roots. They invited a familiar identification from the sizable viewer communities in the United Kingdom, Canada, and the United States, looking for ways to reinterpret their cultural heritage in the light of the opportunities and challenges of new lifestyles. As Patricia Uberoi has pointed out, such preferences of émigré audiences can coalesce in interesting ways with the aspirations and anxieties of the domestic Indian globalizing middle classes, who seek to legitimize their cultural desires by projecting them onto the figure of the expatriate, who has apparently "made it" (Uberoi, 1998).

The appeal of excessively sanitized family dramas such as the record-breaking *Hum Aapke Hain Koun* (Sooraj Barjatya, 1994, *Who Am I to You?*), *Kuch Kuch Hota Hai* (Karan Johar, 1998, *A Certain Feeling*), and *Kabhi Khushi Kabhi Gum* (Barjatya, 2001, *A Little Happiness, a Little Sorrow*) can be located in their successful peddling of consumerist utopias where all signs of poverty and oppression have been wished away through simple narrative choices that leave lives brimming with relentless happiness, wealth, and comfort. Along comparable lines, albeit with significant differences, the making and marketing of *Lagaan* (Gowariker, 2001, *Land-Tax*), using DTS technology to allow for easy dubbing into several languages, showed that the film was evidently made with an eye on international markets extending beyond the Indian diaspora. Launched with a massive promotional buildup, the film's premiere at Sun City, South Africa, in June 2001 was attended by the film's principal cast and production team and was followed by the film's simultaneous release in the United Kingdom, the

Hindi theater circuit in the United States, and throughout India. With its rerelease (after its nomination for an Academy Award) in most parts of Europe, Asia, and some mainstream theaters in the United States, perhaps *Lagaan* was Bollywood's first crossover hit.[42]

◆ *Conclusions*

With the television boom of the 1990s and the prospect of growing profits in international markets, there have been visible signs of corporatization of the Indian media scene, and yet these new patterns ultimately reflect the specific longer term constraints under which Indian film industries have developed. Entertainment conglomerates emerged during the postreforms period such as Zee Telefilms, UTV, Ramoji Films, and Balaji Telefilms, which variously combined interests in film production, distribution, television software, CD-ROMs, advertising, and event management, pointing to a new capital base, a visible nexus between cultural corporations and reputed directors, and the adoption of managerial techniques in media production (Prasad, 2000).

An interesting aspect of this trend has been the entry of several major Bollywood stars who have entered into film/media production in an attempt to cash in on the full commercial value of their image, exemplified by Amitabh Bachchan's controversial media conglomerate, ABCL (Amitabh Bachchan Corporation Limited), set up in 1995 to market a range of media products under the "Big-B" label,[43] and by Aamir Khan Productions, launched in 2000. Alongside, in a belated attempt to regularize financial flows into film production, these developments have been accompanied by the government's decision in 1998 to officially accord it the trade benefits of being an organized industry.

And yet despite these changes, Indian film production mostly remained characterized by the patterns of undercapitalization

and fragmentation delineated by Madhav Prasad (1998, pp. 40–41). Relying on renting all requisite technical resources, filmmakers remained dependent on surplus merchant capital and on a large number of independent producers, the latter often "one-time" film entrepreneurs hoping to capitalize on the availability of low-wage casual labor, evidenced in the enormous pay differences between stars, "character actors," and "extras" (Prasad, 1998). An industry report indicated that film financiers comprised mainly diamond merchants, brokers, builders, and other such individuals, with large amounts of liquid cash to spare, which they lent out at rates as high as 36% to 48% per annum ("Report on the Film Industry," 2001a). Furthermore, in a situation characterized by an acute scarcity of exhibition outlets,[44] where distribution and exhibition were seen as the most profitable aspects of the film business, the industry has long been seen as a distributors' market (Prasad, 1998; see also Barnouw & Krishnaswamy, 1980, pp. 137–139, 160–169). Commercial film finance came officially from distributors and, by the end of the 1990s, music companies—the main parties to profit from a film's success ("Report on the Film Industry," 2001a). Industry sources, however, claimed that, at a conservative estimate, approximately 30% to 35% of films were financed by underworld money (see "Film Production," 2001; "Role of the Dons," 2000). Besides, the presence of mafia money was useful in securing dates from top stars to keep production on schedule (see "Cleaning Up Bollywood," 2001). More recently, with growing international attention to Indian films, the Bombay mafia has shown a serious interest in securing control over overseas rights, mainly because of their potential for money laundering (Harding, 2001; "The Threat," 2001).

The recent enthusiasm for Bombay cinema among Western critics and mainstream audiences may signal a closer engagement between cultures promised by the experiments with the moving image that began almost simultaneously in different parts of the world just over a hundred years ago. Even Hollywood majors such as Columbia Tristar, Sony Pictures Entertainment, and Twentieth Century Fox have taken note of the emerging markets for Indian films.[45] And yet, at least within the United States, this interest comes at a time when the overall share of foreign cinema imports distributed in the domestic market has been diminishing.[46] Significantly, much of the interest has been in the area of distribution, rather than film production, propelled ostensibly less by cultural openness than by the quest for a share of easy profits in a lucrative market—objectives that indeed echo the ones that founded the distribution empire at the heart of the Madan media enterprise in the early years of the past century.

◆ Notes

1. As the language representing the largest linguistic zone in the country and understood by an estimated 400 million people, Hindi was designated the principal official language, with English being assigned associate official status. Effectively, English retains the status of "high" language as the predominant medium of higher education and the link language for official, intellectual, and business purposes. Historically, however, standardized Hindi developed in the latter half of the 19th century, through a bitterly waged struggle with Hindustani-Urdu, the language that emerged from the 17th century onwards as the effective lingua franca of much of the subcontinent for official, military, and trade purposes as well as among cultivated circles. Alongside the emergence of a mass-based national movement in the 1920s and 1930s led by the Indian National Congress, with Nehru and Gandhi at the helm, the rivalry between Hindi and Urdu came to be mapped on to the growing Hindu-Muslim divide. After Partition, Urdu, spoken by about 5% to 7% within Pakistan, became its official language. With its geographical spread and affinity with the Indo-Aryan group of languages spoken in North India, and as the erstwhile language of refined expression and the pan-Indian Parsi theater, it was quite befitting that the more broad-based Hindustani-Urdu emerged as the main language of the Indian film industry. However, outside of the emerging film culture, the space for Hindustani-Urdu was shrinking against the rapid Sanskritization of Hindi via official channels and at the hands of North Indian Hindu elites. Increasingly, the former was identified as marker of a Muslim identity. Yet it was no coincidence that Hindustani-Urdu culture supplied an overwhelming proportion of the talent flowing into the Bombay film industry, even as it definitively influenced the core literary, aesthetic, and visual conventions of Hindi commercial cinema. For an interesting account of the influence of Urdu culture on cinema, see Kesavan (1994).

2. For an interesting account of conventional middle-class viewpoints about commercial Indian cinema and its audience, see Vasudevan (1995). Interestingly, until the early 1990s, Western scholars interested in Indian cinema reserved their attention exclusively for the work of nonmainstream directors such as Satyajit Ray and Shyam Benegal (see, e.g., Armes, 1987).

3. Fuelled equally by dissatisfaction with existing assumptions of South Asian historiography and the need to theorize insurgency and postcolonial state power, the work of the subaltern studies project began in the early 1980s. Since then, the work of scholars associated with this loosely knit group has redefined the field of South Asian historiography; furthermore, it has generated important debates across disciplines such as politics, sociology, history, literature, and anthropology. A sampling of its earlier work can be found in Guha (1997).

4. For example, see Nairn (1981), Anderson (1983), Chatterjee (1986), Fanon (1961), Hall (1996), and Bhabha (1990).

5. For interesting work that addresses these questions, see Kaviraj (1992, 1997) and Chatterjee (1993).

6. For interesting studies of the significant expansion in Indian media audiences in the 1980s, see Jeffrey (2000) and Manuel (1993).

7. See also Notes 2 and 6.

8. "There are hardly any parallels elsewhere in the world for the way in which relations between the institutions of cinema and politics have evolved in post-Independence India. In two of the four South Indian states, film stars have launched their own political parties and achieved spectacular electoral victories. Even after their demise, the parties they have founded have retained a mass base and are in a position of strength vis-à-vis the national parties and other local rivals. In a third state, Karnataka, a star with an equally formidable following appeared for some time to be on the threshold of a political career" (Prasad, 1998, p. 37).

9. There is a notable paucity of work on the informal sector, the significant exception being Breman (1999). For a detailed study of the informal sector in agriculture, see Breman (1996).

10. For an analysis of the political implications of the limited size of colonial reading publics, see Naregal (2001, chap. 4); for a study of the links between media corporations and informal urban networks underlying the growth of cable and satellite television audiences, see Naregal (2000).

11. Mrs. Gandhi (1917–1984) was daughter of Jawaharlal Nehru and an important leader of the long-ruling Congress Party. She was prime minister from 1966 to 1977 and then again from 1980 until her assassination in October 1984.

12. For an interesting essay that traces the circulation and career of a text, the *Indar Sabha,* through print, theater, and eventually the early talkies era, see Hansen (2001).

13. Titles not translated in the text are proper nouns.

14. *Swadeshi* literally translates as "of one's own country." As an assertion of cultural and nationalist pride, it formed an important aspect of the anticolonial movement and involved a boycott of all foreign manufactured goods as well as titles and honors bestowed by the British. Besides attempts to foster native industry, it also involved efforts to reclaim indigenous traditions as way of unifying collective memories. As a technology with vast imaginative potential and reach, cinema seemed to offer especially fertile possibilities in this regard. For an account of Phalke as a Swadeshi filmmaker, see Shoesmith (1988).

15. The most significant of these being *Raja Harishchandra* (1914, remade 1917), *Lanka Dahan* (1918, *The Burning of Lanka*), *Shri Krishna Janam* (1919, *The Birth of Lord Krishna*), and *Kaliya Mardan* (1922, *The Slaying of Kaliya*).

16. For an explanation of the relationship between Hindi-Urdu and Bombay cinema, see Note 1.

17. Edward Said's (1979) *Orientalism* eloquently showed the discursive techniques through which colonial discourse sought to marginalize native cultures and assert its superiority and authority. In casting indigenous literary traditions and cultural practices as "low," "primitive," "uncivilized," and "degenerate," colonialism set up an enduring dynamic whereby native cultures, languages, and elites could upgrade their worth by submitting to a reform process that held up the hope of measuring up to the new norms through a borrowing of ideas, forms, and practices consonant with Enlightenment ideals. Typically, literature and the domestic sphere were the privileged sites on which the cultural and social domains were to be thus recrafted. More specifically, within both colonial and nationalist discourse, more than any other, gender remained the marked category that carried the burden of these overlapping struggles to define the boundaries between modernity and tradition, Western influence and indigenism, cultural imperialism and authenticity, and imperial and national identity. For an elaboration of historical-political contexts and implications of these debates and textual samples, see Sangari and Vaid (1989), Tharu and Lalitha (1993), and Chandra (1991).

18. For an excellent exegesis of the usefulness of melodrama in reconciling these divergent and contradictory impulses, see Thomas (1995) and Dissanayake (1993).

19. Some of the prominent names associated with New Theatres included Premankur Atorthy, Debaki Bose, Nitin Bose, P. C. Barua, Bimal Roy, and K. L. Saigal.

20. These included composers Govindrao Tembe and Keshavrao Bhosle and stars such as Keshavrao Date.

21. Colonialism did its cultural work by marginalizing native cultures and languages

through measuring them against norms derived from Western cultural history. However, native elites and traditions could hope to "improve" their worth by submitting to a "reform" process that basically entailed a copious borrowing of ideas, forms, and models from European intellectual and cultural traditions.

22. Including director Frantz Osten and glamorous star Devika Rani, who directed and acted in *Achyut Kanya*, (1936, *Untouchable Girl*), respectively.

23. For an innovative exploration of how mainstream Hindi cinema obliquely addressed the trauma and anxiety of partition, see Sarkar (1999).

24. For instance, many prominent Muslim actors and actresses, such as Dilip Kumar, Meena Kumari, Nimmi, and others, felt impelled to adopt more "neutral" Hindu names, although their real identity was widely known. For details of how the awareness of the dominant Hindu cultural referent colored publicity campaigns and controversies surrounding some popular films in the post-Independence period, see Vasudevan (1995, esp. 321–324).

25. The most celebrated instance of the courtly genre, of course, is *Mughal-e-Azam* (K. Asif, 1960, *The Grand Mughal*), which retells the well-known legend of love between the dancer Anarkali and Prince Salim, the son of the great Mughal emperor, Akbar. Echoing the theme of a patriarchal father opposed to the union of his son or daughter with a social inferior—one that crops up time and again in Indian popular cinema—the story of Salim and Anarkali has been committed to film several times in various Indian languages, most notably in its 1953 version as *Anarkali,* directed by Nandal Jaswantal. Significant examples of the "Muslim social" (which often shared elements of the setting, mood, and presentation of the "historical" film) would include *Elan* (1947, Mehboob, *Announcement*); *Chaudhvin ka Chand* (M. Sadiq, 1960, *Full Moon*); *Sahib, Bibi Aur Ghulam* (A. Alvi and Guru Dutt, 1962, *Master, Wife and Slave*); and *Mere Mehboob* (Harnam Singh Rawail, 1963, *My Beloved*). A nostalgic story of the tragedy of a courtesan, set against the decay of Muslim aristocratic culture in North India in the first half of the century,

Pakeezah (Kamal Amrohi, 1971, *The Pure One*), is often cited as the "farewell" of the "Muslim social."

26. For an account of the conflicts between the government and the Bombay film industry in the years following Independence, see Barnouw and Krishnaswamy (1980, esp. pp. 128–143). For a summary of entertainment tax and censorship policies, see also Pendakur (1990).

27. The Indian people's theater movement, the leftist, avant-garde movement, launched from Bombay in 1943, but also active in Bengal, Punjab, Kerala, Assam, and Andhra Pradesh. For more details, see Khan, Kabir, and Rajadhyaksha (1994) and Masud (1995).

28. To provide official patronage for music and theater, the Sangeet Natak Akademi had already been set up in 1953, and the National Gallery of Modern Art, Lalit Kala Akademi, and Sahitya Akademi, all launched in 1954, were similar initiatives in the visual arts and literature.

29. Set up in 1949 as the central film-producing organization responsible for the production and distribution of newsreels, documentaries, and other films required by the government of India for public information, education, and instructional and cultural purposes (UNESCO Report, 1973, quoted in Rajadhyaksha & Willemen, 1998, p. 96). The Films Division of India had a monopoly on documentary filmmaking until the period after the Emergency. Dubbed into 18 languages and compulsorily screened prior to every commercial screening in a permanent cinema house, until the expansion of Doordarshan, these films were the main visual channel through which the official promises of economic progress and development were disseminated.

30. For a good introduction to the Indian "parallel" cinema movement, see Reym-Binford (1987).

31. For an important analysis of post-Emergency changes in the structures of ownership and readership for the regional language press, see Jeffrey (2000).

32. Rajiv Gandhi (1944–1991), Indira Gandhi's eldest son and prime minister of India from 1984 to 1989. A professional pilot until his brother Sanjay died in 1981, he was drafted into politics by his mother. He was elected

to parliament, and when Mrs. Gandhi was assassinated in 1984, he led the Congress Party to a sweeping victory. His government encouraged foreign investment, and industry boomed with the loosening of business controls, but he had to resign as prime minister when the Congress Party lost its parliamentary majority. He was assassinated by Tamil separatists in 1991.

33. The increase is said to be from 2.7 million to 12.5 million in 1986 (see Rajadhyaksha & Willemen, 1999, p. 28).

34. The government-owned Akashvani auditorium and, subsequently, the Lotus cinema were the only outlets for nonmainstream films in Bombay, and even their availability has been fraught with bureaucratic difficulties.

35. By the mid-1980s, contrary to the expectations of liberal theory, representative democracy seemed to have accentuated the multiple axes of caste, language, regional identity, class, and community, along which difference and hierarchy can be plotted within Indian society. Through the 1970s, Mrs. Gandhi's legacy of political populism had created a heightened political momentum and expectations from the democratic process. This showed in large turnouts at the polls, but simultaneously, this increased participation saw the 1980s dominated by the subcontinent's version of identity politics as diverse upwardly mobile and aggrieved groups representing rural, urban, regional, tribal, religious, language, ethnic, and nativist interests sought to organize a public presence to claim their due, often resulting in open and even armed conflict with each other and the state. These pressures had been accentuated by the policy of "reservation" of government jobs and educational opportunities for the poorest and the most backward castes since the 1940s. Meant to address the need for social justice, such provisions had some unintended effects: By privileging a language of community rights, they encouraged demands for special dispensations for particular groups. Paradoxically, "backwardness" and a claim to exclusion became sought-after political goods for negotiating claims to state patronage and scarce opportunities. As low and backward caste groups got disillusioned with the Congress, the policy of reservation was a favored strategy of

non-Congress governments. In August 1990, V. P. Singh, heading the Janata Dal government, announced the decision to implement the Mandal Commission's recommendation to review prospects for backward classes and reserve 27% of state and central government jobs for them. The decision caused considerable unrest among upper castes, with several youths committing suicide by setting themselves on fire in protest against the announcement. For an introductory reading on the politics of caste, see Gupta (2000).

36. The city of Ayodhya in Uttar Pradesh is the presumed birthplace of Lord Ram. Staunch Hindu devotees assert that in the 16th century, the Mogul emperor Babur destroyed the temple marking the birthplace and constructed the Babri Masjid in its place. Muslims say the claim is spurious and lacks historical evidence. Until December 1992, the dispute had remained peaceful: A lawsuit brought by a Hindu priest in 1885 had been dismissed; in 1949, a statue of Ram was found in the mosque, but a court ordered the mosque locked, thus preventing both communities from squabbling over the site. However, in 1986, following another court ruling under Rajiv Gandhi's premiership, Hindus were allowed to access the site for worship, leading to large protests from Muslim groups. In 1989, efforts by the Vishwa Hindu Parishad and other Hindu revivalist groups to demolish the Babri Masjid, so as to assuage "injured Hindu pride" through the construction of a new temple of Ram, precipitated what was up to that time probably the most serious Hindu-Muslim rioting since partition in 1947. In 1990, to galvanize Hindu sentiment behind the Bharatiya Janta Party (BJP), party president L. K. Advani launched his *rath yatra* (chariot pilgrimage), a 10,000-kilometer journey in a van fashioned to look like a mythological chariot across India to Ayodhya to launch the construction of the new temple. Prime Minister V. P. Singh, invoking the principles of secularism, warned that the mosque would be protected "at all costs." As Advani and other BJP leaders approached Ayodhya, they were arrested. The BJP, in turn, withdrew its parliamentary support from the minority Singh government, and after a vote of no confidence, the prime minister submitted his resignation. On December 6, 1992,

with a Congress government under Narasimha Rao now in power in Delhi, Hindu-Muslim riots erupted throughout the country after the demolition of the Babri mosque in Ayodhya by Hindu militants and thousands of supporters. On the same day, the government dismissed the BJP-run state government of Uttar Pradesh and imposed direct presidential rule on the state. By December 12, 1992, the death toll from the religious clashes had climbed to 1,150. In January 1993, Hindu-Muslim riots broke out in Bombay, claiming some 560 lives in the first week.

37. Briefly, *Hindutva* is defined by its proponents as a revival of the "essence" of Hinduism. Such right-wing efforts to mobilize a majoritarian Hindu identity have successfully invoked many outmoded beliefs to feed a nostalgia for a golden past, allegedly destroyed by "foreign" invaders such as Muslim and the British, including the claim that present-day Hindus are lineal descendants of the Aryans (see Rajagopal, 2001).

38. Gulshan Kumar was one of the biggest names in the film and entertainment business when he was shot dead on August 12, 1997, allegedly because he failed to acquiesce to extortionist demands. He produced two major hits, including *Aashiqui* (1990, *Infatuation*), his first film, and *Bewaafa Sanam* (1995, *Unfaithful Lover*). Made with completely unknown faces and mediocre scripts, both films were packed with songs, sung by new entrants, but with tunes calculated to ensure that the film would do well.

39. The 1990s saw a spate of films that depicted a hero who was no longer railing at social injustice or corruption; instead, he was typically a valiant soldier or patriotic civilian, up in arms to rescue his country from the threat of 'evil' terrorists from across the border. *Gadar* was particularly significant in scaling new standards of jingoism by explicitly naming Pakistan as the "enemy" and the Other against which this neo-nationalism defined itself.

40. The release of *Hum Aapke Hain Koun* (1994) is a good example of how Rajashri Productions was able to control piracy by working closely with distributors. The number of copies being distributed was closely monitored: Initially, the film was released only at one cinema in Bombay, followed by 29 prints for India and 6

for the overseas market. It was announced that every legal print of the movie was being given a serial number, which would reproduce with any illegal copies (see Uberoi, 2001, p. 341).

41. In particular, the Tamil screen idol Rajnikant has gained a cult following among Japanese audiences. For details of a recent festival of South Indian cinema in Britain titled, "Imagine Asia," see Ramachandran and Kajendra (2002).

42. In recent years, Bollywood hits have frequently grossed higher box office collections than parallely released Hollywood blockbusters in North American and European markets. For figures, see Dodona Research (2001).

43. Amitabh's close connections with the Nehru-Gandhi family were quite well known. A schoolmate and close friend of Rajiv Gandhi, Amitabh contested the prestigious Lok Sabha seat from Allahabad on a Congress ticket in 1984 and won easily. Along with Rajiv Gandhi, Amitabh's name was drawn into the notorious Bofors case involving kickbacks over an arms deal. In 1994, the floating of Amitabh Bachchan Corporation Ltd. was announced with a great deal of media fanfare: Its goal was to corporatize Indian show-biz, and its ventures included the business of production and distribution of films and other entertainment shows, television software, music albums, and event and celebrity management. However, soon after the debacle of the 1996 Miss World Show in Bangalore, produced by ABCL, the company's losses and mismanagement surfaced. Court cases were filed against ABCL for bouncing of cheques and nonpayment of dues to United Television, Prasar Bharti (India's official broadcasting agency), and the public-sector Canara Bank, where the start-up loan for ABCL had come from. Almost all ABCL films failed at the box office. Finally, in March 1999, ABCL was put into receivership and referred to the Board for Industrial and Financial Reconstruction.

44. It is estimated that there are 12,548 theaters catering to a population of more than 1 billion in India, as against 31,000 in the United States, or 117 theaters per million versus 12.5 in India. See "Report on the Film Industry" (2001b).

45. Columbia Tristar was the distributor for *Monsoon Wedding* (Mira Nair, 2002) and *Bend*

It Like Beckham (Gurinder Chadha, 2002), and Sony Pictures has been involved in distributing English, Bengali, Hindi, and Punjabi films. See "Columbia, Fox Trot Into Masala Land" (2003).

46. One estimate puts the decline from 7% in the mid-1980s to 0.75% at present (see Miller, Govim, MacMurria, & Maxwell, 2001, p. 48).

◆ References

Anderson, B. (1983). *Imagined communities: Reflections on the origin and spread of nationalism.* London: Verso.

Armes, R. (1987). *Third World filmmaking and the West.* Berkeley: University of California Press.

Bandyopadhyay, S. (1993). *Indian cinema: Contemporary perceptions from the thirties.* Jamshedpur, India: Celluloid Chapter.

Barnouw, E., & Krishnaswamy, S. (1980). *Indian film* (2nd ed.). New York: Oxford University Press.

Bhabha, H. (1990). *Nation and narration.* New York: Routledge.

Breman, J. (1996). *Footloose labour: Working in India's informal economy.* Cambridge, UK: Cambridge University Press.

Breman, J. (1999). The study of industrial labour in post-colonial India: The informal sector: A concluding review. In J. Parry, J. Breman, & K. Kapadia (Eds.), *The worlds of Indian industrial labour.* New Delhi: Sage.

Cash boost for Bollywood. (2001, July 25). BBC News Online. Retrieved December 10, 2001, from URL:news.bbc.co.uk/hi/english/entertainment/film/newsid_1456000/1456962.stm

Chakravarty, S. S. (1993). *National identity in Indian popular cinema 1947–1987.* Austin: University of Texas Press.

Chandra, S. (1991). *The oppressive present: Literature and social consciousness in colonial India.* New Delhi: Oxford University Press.

Chatterjee, P. (1986). *Nationalist thought and the colonial world: A derivative discourse?* London: Zed.

Chatterjee, P. (1993). *The nation and its fragments: Colonial and postcolonial histories.* Princeton, NJ: Princeton University Press.

Cleaning up Bollywood. (2001, April 19). BBC News Online. Retrieved December 9, 2001, from http://news.bbc.co.uk/hi/english/audiovideo/programmes/crossing_continents/asia/newsid_1283000/1283350.stm

Columbia, Fox trot into masala land. (2003, June 30). *Economic Times.* Retrieved June 30, 2003, from http://economictimes.indiatimes.com/cms.dll/html/uncomp/articleshow?msid=44161846

Dissanayake, W. (Ed.). (1993). *Melodrama and Asian cinema.* Cambridge, UK: Cambridge University Press.

Dodona Research. (2001). *Bollywood: India's film industry.* Leicester, UK: Author.

Fanon, F. (1961). *The wretched of the earth* (C. Farrington, Trans.). New York: Grove.

Film production and film promotion. (2001). India Infoline Sector Reports. Retrieved December 9, 2001, from /www.indiainfoline.com/sect/mefi/ch04.html

Guha, R. (Ed.). (1997). *A subaltern studies reader, 1986–1995.* Minneapolis: University of Minnesota Press.

Gupta, D. (2000). *Interrogating caste: Understanding hierarchy and difference in Indian society.* New Delhi: Penguin.

Hall, S. (1996). The question of cultural identity in modernity. In S. Hall & P. du Gay (Eds.), *An introduction to modern societies.* Cambridge, MA: Blackwell.

Hansen, K. (2001). The Indar Sabha phenomenon: Public theatre and consumption in Greater India (1853–1956). In R. Dwyer & C. Pinney (Eds.), *Pleasure and the nation: The history, politics and consumption of public culture in India* (pp. 76–114). New Delhi: Oxford University Press.

Harding, L. (2001, January 15). Bollywood spins its own mobster yarn. *Guardian Online.* Retrieved December 10, 2001, from www.guardian.co.uk/elsewhere/journalist/story/0,7792,422515,00.html

Jeffrey, R. (2000). *India's newspaper revolution: Capitalism, politics, and the Indian-language press, 1977–99*. New Delhi: Oxford University Press.

Kaviraj, S. (1992). Writing, speaking, being: Language and the historical formation of identities in India. In D. Hellmann-Rajanayagam & D. Rothermund (Eds.), *Nationalstaat und Sprachkonflikte in Sud- und Sudostasien* (pp. 25–65). Stuttgart: Franz Steiner Verlag.

Kaviraj, S. (1997). A critique of the passive revolution. In P. Chatterjee (Ed.), *State and politics in India* (pp. 45–87). Delhi: Oxford University Press.

Kesavan, M. (1994). Urdu, Awadh and the Tawaif: The Islamicate roots of the Hindi cinema. In Z. Hasan (Ed.), *Forging identities: Gender, communities and the state* (pp. 244–258). New Delhi: Kali for Women.

Khan, P., Kabir, N., Kabir, M., & Ashis, R. (1994). The song picture man. *Sight and Sound, 4*(10), 26–28.

Lutgendorf, P. (2002, July/August). A "made to satisfaction goddess": Jai Santoshi revisited. *Manushi, 131*. Retrieved June 3, 2004, from http://free.freespeech.org/manushi/131/

Manuel, P. (1993). *Cassette culture: Popular music and technology in North India*. Chicago: University of Chicago Press.

Masud, Iqbal. (1995). The great four of the golden fifties. *Indian Horizons [India], 44*(1), 29–41.

Miller, T., Govim, N., MacMurria, J., & Maxwell, R. (2001). *Global Hollywood*. London: British Film Institute.

Nairn, T. (1981). *The break-up of Britain: Crisis and neo-nationalism*. London: New Left Books.

Nandy, A. (1998a). *The savage Freud and other essays on possible and retrievable selves*. New Delhi: Oxford University Press.

Nandy, A. (1998b). *The secret politics of our desires: Innocence, culpability and Indian popular cinema*. New Delhi: Oxford University Press.

Naregal, V. (2000). Integrating corporate interests, local and media networks: Cable operations in Bombay. *Contemporary South Asia Review, 9*(3), 289–314.

Naregal, V. (2001). *Language politics, elites and the public sphere: Western India*

under colonialism. New Delhi: Permanent Black.

Niranjana, T. (2000). Nationalism reconfigured: Contemporary South Indian cinema and the subject of feminism. In P. Chatterjee & P. Jeganathan (Eds.), *Community, gender and violence: Subaltern studies series XI* (pp. 138–166). New York: Columbia University Press.

Pandian, M. S. S. (1992). *The image trap: M. G. Ramachandran in film and politics*. New Delhi: Sage.

Pandian, M. S. S. (1997). Culture and subaltern consciousness: An aspect of MGR phenomenon. In P. Chatterjee & R. Bhargava (Eds.), *Readings on politics in India*. New Delhi: Oxford University Press.

Pandian, M. S. S. (2000). Parasakthi: Life and times of a DMK Film. In R. Vasudevan (Ed.), *Making meaning in Indian cinema*. New Delhi: Oxford University Press.

Pendakur, M. (1990). The Indian film industry. In J. Lent (Ed.), *The Asian film industry* (pp. 229–275). Austin: University of Texas Press.

Prasad, M. M. (1998). *Ideology of the Hindi film: A historical construction*. New Delhi: Oxford University Press.

Prasad, M. (1999, Autumn). Cine-politics: On the political significance of cinema in South India. *Journal of the Moving Image, 1*, 37–52.

Prasad, M. (2000). Signs of ideological re-form in two recent Hindi films: Towards real subsumption? In R. Vasudevan (Ed.), *Making meaning in Indian cinema* (pp. 145–167). New Delhi: Oxford University Press.

Rajadhyaksha, A. (1986). Neo-traditionalism: Film as popular art in India. *Framework, 32–33*, 20–67.

Rajadhyaksha, A. (1990). Beaming messages to the nation. *Journal of Arts and Ideas, 19*.

Rajadhyaksha, A. (1996). Strange attractions. *Sight and Sound, 6*(8), 28–31.

Rajadhyaksha, A., & Willemen, P. (Eds.). (1999). *Encyclopaedia of Indian cinema* (Rev. ed.). London: British Film Institute & Oxford University Press.

Rajagopal, A. (2001). *Politics after television: Hindu nationalism and the reshaping of the public in India*. New York: Cambridge University Press.

Ramachandran, N., & Kajendra, R. (2002). Going south. *Sight and Sound, 12*(5), 20–21.

Report on the film industry. (2001a). *India Infoline Sector Reports*. Retrieved December 12, 2001, from www.indiainfoline.com/sect/mefi/ch04.html

Report on the film industry. (2001b, August 31). *Screen*. Retrieved December 12, 2001, from www.screenindia.com/20010831/freport.html

Reym-Binford, M. (1987). The two cinemas of India. In J. D. H. Downing (Ed.), *Film and politics in the Third World* (pp. 145–165). New York: Autonomedia.

Role of the dons. (2000, December 10). *The Week*. Retrieved December 10, 2001, from www.the-week.com/20dec10/enter.htm

Said, E. (1979). *Orientalism*. New York: Vintage.

Sangari, K., & Vaid, S. (Eds.). (1989). *Recasting women: Essays in Indian colonial history*. New Delhi: Kali for Women.

Sarkar, B. (1999). *Allegories of dispersal: Nation and participation in Indian cinema, 1947–1977*. Unpublished doctoral dissertation, University of Southern California.

Shoesmith, B. (1988). Swadeshi cinema: Cinema politics and culture: The writings of D. G. Phalke. *Continuum, 2*(1), 44–73.

Srinivas, S. V. (2000). Is there a public in the cinema hall? *Framework, 42*. Retrieved June 9, 2004, from www.frameworkonline.com/ 42svs.htm

Tharu, S., & Lalitha, K. (1993). *Women writing in India: From 600 BC to the present* (Vols. 1–2). New Delhi: Oxford University Press.

Thomas, R. (1985). Indian cinema: Pleasures and popularity. *Screen, 26*(3–4), 116–131.

Thomas, R. (1995). Melodrama and the negotiation of morality in mainstream Hindi cinema. In C. Breckenridge (Ed.), *Consuming modernity: Public culture in a South Asian world* (pp. 157–182). Minneapolis: University of Minnesota Press.

The threat from the underworld continues. (2001, November 5). Rediff.com. Retrieved December 10, 2001, from www.rediff.com/entertai/2001/nov/05mafia.htm

Tyrrell, H. (1998). Bollywood in Britain. *Sight and Sound, 8*(8), 20–22.

Uberoi, P. (1998). The diaspora comes home: Disciplining desire in Dilwale Dulhaniya Le Jayenge. *Contributions to Indian Sociology, 32*(3), 305–336.

Uberoi, P. (2001). Imagining the family: An ethnography of viewing HAHK. In R. Dwyer & C. Pinney (Eds.), *Pleasure and the nation: The history, politics and consumption of public culture in India* (pp. 309–351). New Delhi: Oxford University Press.

Vasudevan, R. (1989). The melodramatic mode and the commercial Hindi cinema: Notes on film history, narrative and performance in the 1950s. *Screen, 30*(3), 29–50.

Vasudevan, R. (1993). Shifting codes, dissolving identities: The Hindi social film of the 1950s as popular culture. *Journal of Arts and Ideas, 23*(4), 51–85.

Vasudevan, R. (1995). Addressing the spectator of a "Third World" national cinema: The Bombay "social" film of the 1940s and 1950s. *Screen, 36*(4), 305–324.

Vasudevan, R. (Ed.). (2000a). *Making meaning in Indian cinema*. New Delhi: Oxford University Press.

Vasudevan, R. (2000b). National pasts and futures: Indian cinema. *Screen, 41*(1), 119–125.

Vasudevan, R. (2001). Bombay and its public. In R. Dwyer & C. Pinney (Eds.), *Pleasure and the nation: The history, politics, and consumption of public culture in India* (pp. 186–211). New Delhi: Oxford University Press.

26

MEDIA VIOLENCE AND SEX

What Are the Concerns,
Issues, and Effects?

◆ Stacy L. Smith, Emily Moyer-Gusé,
and Edward Donnerstein

P ublic concern over children's exposure to violence and sex in the media is not new. During the early 1900s (Lowery & DeFleur, 1988), parents, educators, and policymakers expressed worry that depictions of crime, sex, and love in major motion pictures were having detrimental effects on youth. Yet nearly a hundred years later, the same concern is on the mind of many child advocates in the United States (Steyer, 2002), especially given the increasingly graphic and explicit forms of media violence and sex available to today's youth. As the president of the Parents Television Council recently wrote,

> On broadcast television, the medium with the widest reach, sexual references and depictions are far more common than all the punches, kicks, and shootings put together—and though there could never be a spectacular, dramatic sexual equivalent of Littleton, the impact of media-promoted promiscuity is no less real, or less devastating, than the impact of media-glamorized violence. (Bozell, 1999, p. 2)

The purpose of this chapter is to examine whether such concerns are warranted. To this end, it is subdivided into six sections. We first examine the amount and context of violence in three popular media: television, music videos, and video games. Next, we review "effects" literature on the impact of media violence on aggression, fear, and desensitization. Within each of these outcomes, the research, theorizing, and moderating variables will be explicated. The third section focuses on content patterns surrounding media sex. Much attention is devoted to portrayals of sex across the overall landscape of television programming, as well as its presence in specific genres and day parts. In the fourth section, the handful of studies examining the impact of televised portrayals of sex on youth is summarized. Although the previous sections in this chapter treat media sex and violence separately, the fifth section examines the theorizing and harmful effects associated with exposure to the juxtaposition of these two content features. In the final section, we offer some possible solutions to the negative effects associated with exposure to media sex and violence.

◆ Media Violence

How much exposure does the American child have to media violence? Many content analyses have been conducted to answer this very question, especially with regards to television (see Gerbner & Gross, 1976; Greenberg, Edison, Korzenny, Fernandez-Collado, & Atkin, 1980; Lichter & Amundson, 1992, 1994; Potter et al., 1995; Potter & Ware, 1987). However, Wilson and her colleagues completed recently the largest and most comprehensive investigation for the National Television Violence Study (NTVS; see Smith et al., 1998; Wilson et al., 1997, 1998). Funded by the National Cable Television Association, the NTVS researchers were commissioned to monitor violence during the 1994–1995, 1995–1996, and 1996–1997 television viewing seasons.

Before presenting the results, three unique aspects of the NTVS project are worth noting. First, the scholars crafted a highly conservative definition of violence. Only intentional acts of force attempting to physically harm an animate being were included in the definition. Second, the

NTVS researchers randomly sampled and assembled a composite week of television content each year across 23 popular broadcast, independent, and cable channels. The sample was created across 9 months (i.e., October to June) each year and included programs airing from early in the morning (6:00 a.m.) to late at night (11:00 p.m.). As such, the biases that may result from using an intact week or a single day cannot be leveled against the NTVS sampling plan. Third, the NTVS researchers focused on coding the context of violence, rather than amount. Summarizing all of the effects literature to date (Wilson et al., 1997, p. 22), Table 26.1 illustrates the impact that different contextual features have on three harmful outcomes associated with exposure to media violence. Using this table, the NTVS researchers crafted a coding scheme uniquely sensitive to capturing the context of violence on American television.

Across 3 years, the results from the NTVS data reveal that there are five general trends in the presentation of violence. First, violence is pervasive on television. Well over half of all programs (58%–61%) on television feature one or more instances of violence. Approximately 17,000 different

Table 26.1 The Impact of Media Violence by Context Factor

	Outcome Variables		
	Learning Aggression	*Emotional Desensitization*	*Fear*
Attractive perpetrators	↗		
Attractive victims			↗
Weapons	↗		
Extensiveness	↗	↗	↗
Graphicness		↗	
Justification	↗		
Rewards	↗		
Punishments	↘		
Realism	↗	↗	
Humor	↗		↗

Source: Smith et al. (1998). Adapted with permission.

NOTE. ↗ An increase of a particular outcome variable. ↘ A decrease of a particular outcome variable.

violent exchanges are presented per week. Furthermore, the results show that there are about 6 different violent incidents shown per hour. Using this finding, 2- to 11-year-olds who watch on average almost 3 hours of television programming per day (Nielsen Media Research, 2000) are being exposed to roughly 126 incidents of violence per week or more than 6,500 incidents per year.

The second trend is that violence on television is likely to be glamorized. More than a third of all interactions feature attractive perpetrators (37%–40%), and roughly a quarter show violence as justified or socially sanctioned. Third, violence on television is sanitized. Despite the fact that many violent incidents on television involve a gun (23%–26%) and a majority would result in moderate or extreme harm in the real world (52%–54%), the bulk of aggressive exchanges are devoid of pain. For example, roughly 55% of all violent incidents involve absolutely no pain to the victim, and less than 20% of all violent programs feature the long-term physical, emotional, financial, or societal effects of aggression. As little as 14% to 15% of all violent scenes feature some blood or gore.

The fourth trend is that violence on television is not chastised. Roughly 40% of all violent shows with bad characters show them getting away with their violent actions. Looking at violent scenes, approximately three fourths show violence without any verbal or nonverbal remorse, criticism, or penalty (71%–75%). Fifth, violence is often trivialized. In roughly 40% of all violent scenes, humor is juxtaposed with aggressive acts.

Although these are overall trends, it is worth noting that genre may exert a considerable influence on these patterns. Perhaps the two "worst offenders" are movies and children's shows. Movies, which are primarily shown on the premium outlets, are the most likely genre to feature violence. Almost 90% depict one or more acts of aggression, and roughly 60% of violent films feature 9 or more violent exchanges (Smith et al., 1998). Movie violence also is more likely to be realistic and graphic, thereby potentially heightening a desensitization effect. Children's shows are also problematic, with roughly 13 violent incidents per hour (Smith et al., 1998), which is substantially higher than all other genres. Violence in children's series is likely to also be devoid of the long-term repercussions of aggression, presented in humorous contexts, and filled with incidents involving unrealistically low levels of harm.

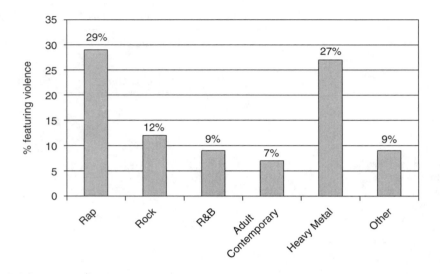

Figure 26.1 Proportion of Music Videos With Violence by Genre

Despite the fact that children spend a great deal of time with television, other forms of media consumption may also routinely feature violent messages. Music is important, especially among young adolescents and teens. The Kaiser Family Foundation (1999, p. 20) nationwide survey reveals that 14- to 18-year-olds spend 2 hours and 34 minutes per day listening to the radio, CDs, and/or tapes, and 8- to 13-year-olds spend 1 hour and 22 minutes. Among those 7th to 12th graders who listened to music on one of these sources the day before being interviewed, the three most frequently mentioned types of music consumed were rap/hip-hop, alternative rock, and heavy metal. These three types of genres sometimes feature music videos with violence (see Figure 26.1), especially rap songs (DuRant et al., 1997; Smith & Boyson, 2002). Although a great deal of public concern has generated over the violent, sexual, and drug-laden lyrics in rock and rap (American Academy of Child and Adolescent Psychiatry, 2000; American Academy of Pediatrics, 1997), we have little systematic evidence to date regarding the prevalence of aggression or others forms of antisocial conduct in words associated with such music.

Video games also are popular among youth. According to the nationwide Kaiser survey (Kaiser Family Foundation, 1999), 8- to 18-year-old boys spend roughly 41 minutes per day playing video games, whereas girls spend only 12. There is much concern surrounding the increasingly realistic, graphic, and explicit violent content in interactive games (Parvaz, 1999) such as *Grand Theft Auto, Carmageddon,* or *Kingpin: Life of Crime.* However, only a handful of content studies have examined violence in video games (Braun & Giroux, 1989; Dietz, 1998; Thompson & Haninger, 2001). Using the NTVS coding scheme, Smith, Lachlan, and Tamborini (2000) assessed the amount and nature of violence in 60 of the most popular games across three platforms: Nintendo 64, Sony Playstation, and Sega Dreamcast. Based on ratings by the Entertainment Software Review Board (ESRB), comparisons were made regarding violence between those games rated for all players (i.e., "K-A" or "E") and those rated for teen/adult players (i.e., "T" and "M").

The results revealed substantial differences in the prevalence and context of violence (see Figure 26.2). Games for older children and adults feature four times as

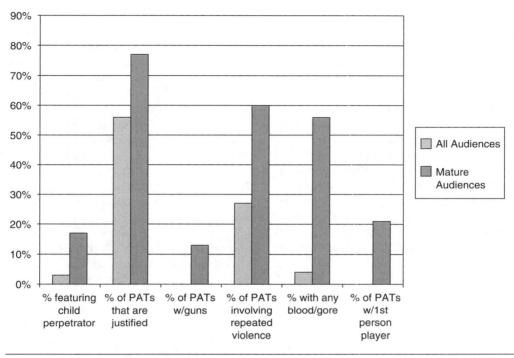

Figure 26.2   Amount and Context of Violence by Video Game Rating

many violent interactions per minute than do those general-audience games (e.g., 4.59 incidents per minute vs. 1.17 per minute). Thus, the average boy playing mature video games is exposed to roughly 188 violent exchanges per day, 1,300 per week, or 5,200 in 1 month. Furthermore, the violence in games rated "T" or "M" is more likely than games rated "K-A" or "E" to feature perpetrators engaging in repeated acts of justified violence involving weapons that result in some bloodshed.

Clearly, the research presented above reveals that violence is a staple in most American children's media diets. Whether they are watching broadcast television or playing games on their new X-box video game platform, youngsters are being bombarded with messages involving carnage and cruelty. Given this, the next question we have to ask is what impact does media violence have on children's and adolescents' socioemotional development. The answer to this question is in the next section.

◆ *Effects of Media Violence*

Perhaps no other feature of media content has attracted so much empirical attention as violence. Over the past 40 years, innumerable investigations have been conducted to examine the impact of television violence on individuals' thoughts, attitudes, and behaviors (for review, see National Institute of Mental Health, 1982; Paik & Comstock, 1994). We consider the effect of exposure to media violence on three harmful outcomes below.

AGGRESSION

One of the early psychologists to examine the relationship between exposure to television violence and subsequent aggression was Albert Bandura. Using the infamous "Bobo" doll paradigm (Bandura, 1965), children would view a model aggressing against an inflated doll with a variety of toys and inanimate objects. Immediately after, children saw the model either being rewarded for his aggressive acts, punished, or receiving no reinforcements. The children were then given the opportunity to play with toys and objects, some of which were similar to those seen in the short film and others were not. The results revealed that children exposed to the conditions where the model was rewarded or not punished for his actions were significantly more aggressive than were those exposed to the model punished (Bandura, 1965). The results from this experiment and others reveal that mediated depictions may not only be teaching children how to behave violently but that reinforcements may also moderate performance effects.

The laboratory early research of Bandura and others (Bandura, Ross, & Ross, 1963a, 1963b; Berkowitz & Geen, 1966; Hicks, 1965) was criticized for its low external validity (Freedman, 1984). Yet a number of scholars also have examined the relationship between viewing TV violence and aggression with survey methodology (for review, see Comstock & Scharrer, 1999). For example, McLeod, Atkin, and Chaffee (1972) found that violence viewing was a significant and positive predictor of adolescents' aggressiveness, even when multiple controls are taken into account. Other surveys have found a similar relationship (McIntyre & Teevan, 1972; Robinson & Bachman, 1972). Despite these findings, the survey research is not without its limitations. One criticism is that some uncontrolled third variable may be driving the correlation between violence viewing and aggression. Another criticism is that the causal direction between violence viewing and aggression is not clear. It could be the case that exposure to TV violence leads to aggression, whereas it is equally plausible that aggressive children seek out violent content.

To tease out the directionality issue, Leonard Eron and Rowell Huesmann conducted a series of longitudinal investigations (Lefkowitz, Eron, Walder, & Huesmann, 1972). They found that early exposure to television violence at age 8 was a significant but weak predictor of adult criminality 22 years later, despite controls for social class, intellectual functioning, and parenting variables (see Huesmann & Miller, 1994, p. 168). Although this relation only held for boys, other investigations have demonstrated a longitudinal effect between early violence viewing and later aggression for girls as well (Huesmann, Lagerspetz, & Eron, 1984; Huesmann, Moise, Podolski, & Eron, 1998). This later finding is presumably due to the increase in aggressive females on television over the past few decades.

In sum, research reveals that exposure to television violence contributes to aggressive behavior. This conclusion has been reached by virtually every professional organization looking into the issue, such as the U.S. Surgeon General (Surgeon General's Scientific Advisory Committee, 1972), the American Psychological Association (1993), and even the American Medical Association (1996). Now that we know television violence can increase aggressiveness, it becomes important to examine the *size* or *magnitude* of this effect. Based on the most recent and comprehensive meta-analysis incorporating 217 published and unpublished studies, Paik and Comstock (1994) found an overall effect size of $r = .31$, which is moderate using Cohen's (1988) rule of thumb. Put another way, TV violence can explain 10% of the variability in viewer aggressiveness.

What theoretical mechanisms can be used to account for the impact of television violence on viewer aggression? Early research in the media violence arena relied heavily on Bandura's (1971) social learning theory. According to this perspective, individuals learn new behaviors by observing live or vicarious models such as those depicted in the mass media. This perspective further illustrates that reinforcements delivered to models can influence performance effects. In the 1980s, Bandura revised his theory to account for cognitive (e.g., attention, retention), motivation (e.g., vicarious, direct reinforcements), and performance factors as well as observer characteristics that may influence the media violence-aggression relationship, either through learning or disinhibition. His reformulation, social cognitive theory (Bandura, 1986), proposes one of several cognitive mechanisms heavily relied on by researchers to explain and predict the effect of media violence on viewer aggression.

Other cognitive models have also been advanced. Berkowitz (see Jo & Berkowitz, 1994) has offered a "priming" effects explanation for the short-term effects of media violence on aggression. Using cognitive models from psychology, Berkowitz (see Jo & Berkowitz, 1994, p. 45) argues that memory is a collection of networks that store in nodes previous thoughts, feelings, and action tendencies. This perspective further assumes that stimuli can "prime" other semantically related concepts in memory, thereby heightening the probability that similar thoughts, feelings, and action tendencies with the same meaning will come to mind (p. 46). Based on this approach, Jo and Berkowitz (1994, p. 46) argue that exposure to media violence may, for a short time, (a) prime hostile thoughts in viewers, thereby altering their evaluations of others; (b) cause viewers to perceive violent actions as justified and resulting in positive outcomes; and (c) increase resultant aggression.

Research has investigated the impact of media violence on priming aggressive thoughts (Bushman & Geen, 1990). For example, Bushman (1998) found that participants exposed to a short violent film clip were more likely to list aggressive associations when presented with a list of homonyms than were those exposed to an equally exciting short nonviolent film. Arguing that priming effects occur rather automatically and involuntarily, Bushman conducted a second experiment to assess whether viewing violent content activates and increases the accessibility of aggressive thoughts from memory. Using a lexical decision task, he found that individuals exposed to a violent film clip recognized aggressive words significantly faster than did those exposed to a nonviolent film clip.

Although these findings reveal a priming effect, they do not demonstrate whether activating aggressive thoughts is the cognitive mediator between exposure to violence and antisocial behavior. Research has offered priming as the causal explanation for increases in subsequent aggression after exposure to media violence (Jo & Berkowitz, 1994; Josephson, 1987), but we could only find one study that has tested the relationship more directly. Anderson and Dill (2000) found that undergraduates playing a violent video game had more aggressive thoughts immediately after as well as retaliatory aggressive behavior (i.e., noise blasts delivered to opponent) than did those playing an equally arousing and enjoyable but nonviolent video game. These results are consistent with other social psychological research demonstrating priming effects on aggression with nonmedia stimuli (Carver, Ganellen, Froming, & Chambers, 1983).

Berkowitz's priming perspective focuses on explaining transient effects, whereas Huesmann (1988) presents an information-processing model designed to explicate both the short- and long-term impact of consuming media violence on aggression. Huesmann argues that scripts or cognitive maps guide social problem solving. Scripts can be formed by direct experience or vicariously through observation of media models (p. 15). Through repeated viewing of media violence, children may develop and reinforce aggressive scripts for dealing with interpersonal conflict (Huesmann et al., 1984).

Encoding of violent acts seen in the media will be contingent on a variety of factors, however. As noted below, the realism of the portrayal and identification with violent characters should facilitate encoding effects. Also, Huesmann (1988) argues that emotional state (e.g., anger, arousal) should also play a role in the encoding process. Not only must violent acts be encoded, but they must also be retained in memory. Mental rehearsal, fantasizing about aggression, and cognitive rumination should all strengthen storage of aggressive content in long-term memory.

In addition to encoding and storage, media violence may also trigger the retrieval of aggressive scripts for social problem solving. Cues present in the natural environment that are similar to those when the script was encoded can facilitate retrieval (Huesmann, 1988, p. 21). Huesmann (1988, p. 21) also argues, however, that other "aggressive" stimuli (e.g., guns or knives) can activate violent scripts from memory, even if they were not present when the script was encoded. As a result, this perspective can also account for the short-term priming effect that exposure to media violence may have on viewer aggression.

The impact of media violence on aggression will undoubtedly be moderated by a variety of factors. In terms of message features, evidence suggests that violence on television that is enacted by attractive perpetrators (Bandura, 1986), realistic (Atkin, 1983; Berkowitz & Alioto, 1973), gun laden (Berkowitz & LePage, 1967; Leyens & Parke, 1974), extensive (Huesmann et al., 1984; Huesmann et al., 1998), devoid of consequences (Baron, 1971a, 1971b), rewarded or not punished (Bandura, 1965; Bandura et al., 1963b), and humorous in nature (Berkowitz, 1970) can all increase the probability of resultant aggression in both children and adults.

Viewer variables can also ameliorate or exacerbate the effects of exposure to media violence on aggression. Research reveals that younger children (Paik & Comstock, 1994), the socially unpopular (Huesmann, 1986), low intellectual achievers (Huesmann, 1986), the characteristically aggressive (Bushman, 1995; Josephson, 1987), high identifiers with characters on TV (Huesmann & Eron, 1986; Huesmann et al., 1984), and those who believe TV is realistic (Huesmann et al., 1984) are more at risk of learning and/or enacting aggression after exposure to media violence.

FEAR

Another potential harmful effect associated with exposure to media violence is fear. There are two types of fear effects: short-term responses and long-term alteration of beliefs about the world in which we live. Research in each of these areas will be reviewed below.

Most of the research on children's fear responses to media content has been conducted by Joanne Cantor and her graduate students at the University of Wisconsin, Madison (for review, see Cantor, 1994, 2002). Research reveals that most children are frightened by mass media fare over the course of development. To illustrate, Wilson, Hoffner, and Cantor (1987, p. 42) asked preschool and elementary school age children if they had ever been scared by something on TV or film. Roughly 75% of the children in two separate studies responded affirmatively. More recently, Cantor and Nathanson (1996, p. 145) found that 43% of randomly sampled parents of kindergarten and second, fourth, and sixth graders said that their children had been frightened by something on TV. These latter findings are consistent with other research revealing that parents often underestimate children's fright reactions to media content (Cantor & Reilly, 1982).

Not only are children being aroused by scary images on television, but some of these reactions can persist over time in the form of behavioral and emotional upset (Hoekstra, Harris, & Helmick, 1999). For example, Harrison and Cantor (1999) asked undergraduates if they had ever been frightened by a TV show or movie and experienced lingering upset. A full 90% responded that they had, and nearly half (44%) indicated that the recalled incident occurred before the age of 13. More than half of the undergraduates stated experiencing disturbances in behaviors such as eating or sleeping patterns, and 35.5% indicated that they avoided or dreaded the depicted situation (p. 105). Roughly a quarter of those experiencing lingering fright indicated that the upset lasted more than a year and that they were still being affected at the time they filled out the survey.

Cantor (2002, p. 291) explains the impact of the mass media on fear by using a stimulus generalization perspective. She argues that there are certain conditioned/unconditioned stimuli that evoke fear responses. When these stimuli are shown in the mass media, they evoke a similar—but less—intense arousal response. Cantor has shown from research that three types of depictions may evoke fear: dangers and injuries, deformities and distortions, and/or characters' expressions of fear or depictions of endangerment (p. 291). Each of these types of portrayals is relatively common in violent media content.

Empirical research also reveals that not all types of viewers will be affected by these types of depictions. Age or level of cognitive development moderates how children make sense of and respond to different types of mass media fare (see Wilson & Smith, 1998). In general, preschool and younger elementary school age children interpret television programming differently than do their older elementary school age counterparts. At least two skills influence the types of images younger and older children perceive as scary.

The first skill is the ability to attend to perceptual versus conceptual information. Given their focus on appearance or perceptual cues (Flavell, 1977), younger children attend to those striking visual or audio components presented in media fare (Hoffner & Cantor, 1985). Older children, on the other hand, are able to discount striking appearances and instead focus on conceptual or behavioral information that is relevant to character evaluations or the plot (Hoffner & Cantor, 1985). The second skill is the ability to differentiate between fantasy and reality. Younger children are more likely than their older counterparts to believe that what they see on TV is real (Hawkins, 1977). With age and maturity, children begin to evaluate television characters, settings, and events based on whether

they are possible or probable in the real world (Dorr, 1983; Morison, Kelly, & Gardner, 1981).

Because of differences in skills, younger and older children respond to different types of media depictions with fear. For example, a younger child is more likely to be frightened by concrete dangers that "look" scary but actually pose no threat of real world harm, such as monsters and witches (Cantor & Sparks, 1984; Sparks, 1986). Older children are more likely to fear abstract threats that are possible or probable in the real world such as depictions of terrorism, nuclear war, and stranger violence (Cantor, Wilson, & Hoffner, 1986; Cantor & Nathanson, 1996; Smith, Moyer, Boyson, & Pieper, 2002).

In addition to age, at least a few other variables may moderate fright effects. One variable is gender. Females are typically more scared by dangers and threats depicted in the mass media than are males (Peck, 2000; Smith & Wilson, 2002; Wright, Kunkel, Pinon, & Huston, 1989). Usually, these differences are explained in terms of sex role socialization, with girls being taught that expressing their emotions is more normative or socially appropriate than boys. Another factor is dispositional empathy. Highly empathic children may be more likely to respond with fear when individuals in the media are shown falling prey to violence than their less empathic peers. Indeed, Hoffner and Haefner (1993) found that empathy was a positive and significant predictor of negative affect and enduring upset in response to the Gulf War news footage. Hoekstra et al. (1999) found that fantasy empathy and, to a lesser degree, perspective taking predicted undergraduates' fear responses to scary mass media fare as children or adolescents.

In sum, research reveals that a fair number of children report being frightened by the mass media and that some effects endure well beyond the viewing situation. These fear effects may be moderated by age, gender, and other dispositional attributes such as empathy. Another line of inquiry has investigated the long-term impact of exposure to television violence on "cultivating" beliefs that the world is a mean and scary place. Leading this research program back in the 1970s was George Gerbner and his research team at the University of Pennsylvania (see Gerbner, Gross, Morgan, & Signorielli, 1994). The concept of cultivation refers to television's influence on shaping individuals' perceptions of social reality in a way that mirrors the world seen on television (Gerbner et al., 1994).

This idea was first tested in terms of entertainment messages about violence. Because violent messages permeate television programming, heavy viewers should see the world as a more violent and scary place than light viewers. In fact, a large body of evidence shows that when compared to light viewers, heavy viewers tend to (a) view society as more violent; (b) perceive a greater danger walking alone at night in a city; (c) purchase protective devices such as dogs, locks, or guns; and (d) have more overall fear of crime (Gerbner & Gross, 1976; Gerbner, Gross, Jackson-Beck, Jeffries-Fox, & Signorielli, 1978; Gerbner, Gross, Signorielli, Morgan, & Jackson-Beck, 1979). Many of these results have been obtained with both adult and child samples (for comprehensive review, see Hawkins & Pingree, 1982).

Despite these findings, cultivation theory has been criticized over the past few decades (Hawkins & Pingree, 1982; Potter, 1994). One criticism is that much of the research documenting cultivation effects is based on cross-sectional surveys, making the direction of causality between exposure and social reality beliefs impossible to ascertain. Yet experimental research shows that repeated viewing of violence can also elicit increases in fear amongst viewers (Bryant, Carveth, & Brown, 1981; Ogles & Hoffner, 1987). Thus, there seems to be a correlational and causal relationship between repeated viewing of television and distorted beliefs about social reality.

Conceptually, cultivation theory has been criticized for not explicating the

psychological processes responsible for the relationship between heavy viewing and distorted perceptions of social reality (Hawkins & Pingree, 1982). However, Shrum (1995, 2002) has explained this relationship in terms of heuristic processing. According to research on the availability heuristic, individuals' estimations or "set size" judgments are a function of the ease with which relevant information is available or accessible in memory (Tversky & Kahneman, 1973). The more easily that information about a particular construct is recalled, the higher are individuals' probability or frequency estimates of a given class of events. Based on this reasoning, heavy consumers of violent content should have in memory numerous exemplars pertaining to violent crime that are readily accessible, thereby explaining their increased or distorted estimates of violent activity in the world.

Scholars have also argued that the effects of heavy viewing on perceptions of social reality may be moderated by several content and viewer variables. In terms of content, Gerbner et al. (1994) argues, "Exposure to the total pattern rather than only to specific genres or programs is what accounts for . . . the cultivation of shared conceptions of reality among otherwise diverse publics" (p. 18). Yet researchers have argued (Gunter, 1994) and studies show that heavy viewing of specific types of programming content (e.g., crime dramas, cartoons, news) is positively associated with distorted perceptions of violence in society, even after controlling for total television viewing and/or exposure to different genres (Hawkins & Pingree, 1982; Smith & Wilson, 2002).

It has been argued that viewer variables may also influence the impact of exposure to television on social reality perceptions. For example, studies show that perceived realism (Potter, 1986), experience with crime (O'Keefe, 1984), cognitive abilities (Van Evra, 1990), and family communication/ peer integration (Rothschild, 1984) may all moderate cultivation effects.

DESENSITIZATION

A final harmful effect associated with exposure to television violence is desensitization. Desensitization refers to "an attempt to create conditions whereby information about a fear stimulus is encoded in the absence of fear responses" (Foa & Kozak, 1986, p. 27). Systematic desensitization procedures were used originally to treat individuals suffering from phobic responses to different types of threatening stimuli such as blood, bodily mutilation, or insects. Scholars have argued that the same process can occur with exposure to television violence. Through repeated exposure to violence, viewers become "desensitized," or less aroused by, more accepting of, and less sensitive to televised aggression. These effects, as will be demonstrated below, can also "spill over" and have serious social consequences.

Some of the early work on systematic desensitization explored the impact of televised violence on individuals' physiological responsivity (Thomas, 1982). Cline, Croft, and Courrier (1973) found that heavy viewers of television were significantly less aroused by a violent film clip than were light viewers of television. Although these data suggest an over-time effect, other studies reveal that physiological desensitization to violence can occur rather quickly. Thomas, Horton, Lippencott, and Drabman (1977) found that men exposed to a short violent film clip subsequently were less aroused by a portrayal of real-life violence (18-minute riot film) than were men exposed to a short sports clip. Similar findings were obtained with a sample of children (Thomas et al., 1977).

Although this research demonstrates the impact of television violence on arousal, it does not reveal whether individuals' attitudes towards violence are affected. That is, does exposure to television violence influence viewers' attitudes or evaluations towards aggression? Research suggests that it can. In one study, Thomas and Drabman (1978) found that children exposed to a short aggressive film were more likely to

indicate that aggression is a normative response to social conflict than were those exposed to a short neutral film. Thus, viewing television violence can influence both arousal responses and attitudes towards aggression.

Tolerance of real-life violence can also be affected by exposure to TV violence. Drabman and Thomas (1974) exposed children to either a short violent film or nothing. Immediately after exposure, the children were asked to "babysit" two younger children by watching them on a videotape monitor ostensibly broadcast from another location. The measure of aggression tolerance was the amount of time it took for participants to seek the experimenter for help when a fight broke out between the younger children on the tape. The results revealed that children exposed to the violent clip took significantly longer to seek help when a staged physical altercation occurred than did those who did not see any violent content. Similar findings have been obtained with other samples of children (Hirsch & Molitor, 1994; Thomas & Drabman, 1975), even when incorporating viewing control groups and using more contemporary depictions of violence.

Overall, the results from the desensitization literature suggest that media violence can affect viewers' arousal responses, attitudes, and tolerance of real-life aggression. It must be mentioned, however, that most of the evidence above relied on fairly benign depictions of violence from shows and films popular in the 1960 and 1970s (e.g., *Mannix, Hopalong Cassidy, The Champion*). Because media content is more graphic and shocking today, the impact of exposure to such explicit aggression on desensitization is likely to be even more pronounced.

◆ Media Sex

How much sex is on American television? Kunkel and his colleagues have been doing research at the University of California, Santa Barbara to answer this very question (Kunkel, Cope, Farinola, Biely, & Donnerstein, 1998; Kunkel, Cope-Farrar, Biely, Farinola, & Donnerstein, 2001). Commissioned by the Kaiser Family Foundation, Kunkel and his research team have been biennially assessing the frequency and context of sexual talk and behavior on television. Sampling across 10 broadcast and cable channels, the researchers compiled a composite week for each programming source from early in the morning to late at night. Yearly, the researchers evaluate roughly 1,100 programs for sexual content (Kunkel et al., 2001).

The results reveal four main conclusions. First, sex on television is on the rise. A full 68% of all programs in the sample contained some form of sex talk or behavior, as compared to 56% two years earlier. Second, portrayals of teenagers engaging in sex have become more frequent. From 1998 to 2000, representations of teenagers tripled from 3% to 9% of all characters engaging in sex. This figure goes up to 32% when teens are combined with young people ages 18 to 24. Portrayals of young characters pose a potentially greater risk for imitation because young viewers are likely to identify with similar, attractive characters (Bandura, 1986).

Third, safe sex messages are extremely rare on television. Of all scenes with sexual content, only 2% featured any mention of precaution. A similarly low proportion of scenes depicted the realistic consequences of sex (2%), which is unfortunate because portrayals featuring the negative reinforcements of unprotected sex may inhibit such risky behavior (Bandura, 1986). Fourth, sex on television is frequently combined with humor, which may trivialize the seriousness of such mature behavior. The overwhelming majority of sitcoms contain sex (84%), at an average rate of 7.5 scenes per hour. This is especially important when considering that sitcoms are the genre of choice among 8- to 18-year-olds (Kaiser Family Foundation, 1999).

Although the above trends focus on the overall landscape of television programming, certain time periods may feature more or less sexual content. Given that prime time is the most popular viewing time across all segments of the population (Nielsen Media Research, 2000), many researchers have quantified the presence of sex during this day part (Cope-Farrar & Kunkel, 2002; Franzblau, Sprafkin, & Rubinstein, 1977; Greenberg, Stanley, et al., 1993; Lowry & Shidler, 1993; Lowry & Towles, 1993; Sapolsky, 1982; Sapolsky & Tabarlet, 1991; Ward, 1995). Studies have shown that sexual behavior and references occur in 75% of all prime-time network shows (Kunkel et al., 2001).

What about those prime-time programs most viewed by young people? In a recent study of the top 15 programs viewed among 12- to 17-year-olds, 82% of the episodes featured sex at an average rate of 11 sexual interactions per hour (Cope-Farrar & Kunkel, 2002). This figure is significantly higher than the amount (68%) and frequency (4 scenes per hour) of sex across the entire landscape of television programming (Kunkel et al., 2001). Unlike the previous analyses of prime-time television (Kunkel et al., 2001), teens' favorite shows were equally likely to portray sexual behaviors and sexual talk (62% vs. 67%, respectively) (Cope-Farrar & Kunkel, 2002). Furthermore, 75% of the characters involved in sexual behavior faced no clear consequences for their sexual behavior. However, when consequences were portrayed in teens' favorite prime-time shows, they were overwhelmingly positive in nature.

In addition to prime time, another factor that may influence the presentation of sex is genres. One type of genre that contains a great deal of sex is soap operas. Many content analyses have focused on soap operas because of their popularity among young girls (Greenberg & Busselle, 1994; Greenberg & D'Alessio, 1985; Greenberg, Stanley, et al., 1993; Heintz-Knowles, 1996). To sum across studies, sex is prevalent on soaps and is most likely to occur between unmarried characters. In the Kunkel et al. (2001) content analysis, 80% of soap operas portrayed some sexual content. A recent study of 97 hours of soap operas revealed that verbal and/or visual messages about sex occurred more than 6 times per hour (Heintz-Knowles, 1996). This finding is relatively consistent with other soap studies documenting between 6.64 and 3.67 sexual incidents per hour, respectively (Greenberg & Busselle, 1994; Greenberg, Stanley, et al., 1993).

Not only is sex common on soap operas, but precautionary messages are extremely rare. In a study by Greenberg and Busselle (1994), 50 different episodes of soap operas were examined; only 3 contained a discussion of safe sex or contraception, and only 1 mentioned the risk of sexually transmitted diseases (STDs). Similarly, a recent study (Heintz-Knowles, 1996) found that only 8% of all sexual acts featured the positive or negative consequences of such intimate behavior. Thus, the template for sex on soaps seems to be unmarried characters engaging in or talking about sex with very little consequence.

Another genre that garners a great deal of research is music videos. Several analyses of music videos generally and MTV specifically also have been undertaken (Baxter, DeRiemer, Landini, Leslie, & Singletary, 1985; Greeson & Williams, 1987). The content of music videos is particularly important because of their popularity among adolescents, especially girls. Among 11- to 19-year-old females, the more frequently watched network is MTV (*Media Use*, 2000). More generally, 75% of 9- to 12-year-olds and 80% of 12- to 14-year-olds watch music videos. As the number of TV channels featuring music videos continues to grow with the advent of new outlets such as MTV2, MuchMusic, and VH1-Classics, quantifying the amount of sexual content within this genre becomes even more important. Current studies suggest that sexual content is prevalent in music videos, with 47% to 60% of music videos

containing sexual references (Baxter et al., 1985; Greeson & Williams, 1987). Independent of music videos, song lyrics have been analyzed for their sexual content. One study found that the top five songs listed in *Billboard* magazine from 1950 to 1980 have shifted over time from focusing on romantic/emotional love to an emphasis on sexual behavior.

In addition to television, movies are extremely pervasive in young people's lives. Roughly 60% of 9- to 17-year-olds find it important to see the latest movies (*Media Use*, 2000). Furthermore, renting movies is now America's number one favorite leisure activity (*Media Use*, 2000). As technology increases, people are faced with more options for seeing movies than ever before. Video rentals, pay-per-view channels, and the availability of more movie channels on cable outlets may make it increasingly difficult for parents to monitor the movies their children are viewing. Going to movies at the theater is also a popular activity among adolescents, with 90% reporting that they go to the movies "frequently" or "occasionally" (*Media Use*, 2000).

When it comes to the content of movies, sex sells. In a recent study, college students read descriptions of movies that either did or did not include sex. Participants expressed preference for those movies that mentioned sex in the description (Bahk, 1998). Because the movie industry is driven by consumer demand and moviegoers prefer sex, sex is prevalent in movies. A recent analysis of the 50 most profitable films of 1996 found that 40% of the movies featured at least some sex. As expected, R-rated movies were more likely to feature sex than PG- or PG-13-rated movies (Bufkin & Eschholz, 2000).

In addition to the popularity of movies among young people, some specific movies gain extreme popularity among teen audiences. In this way, moviegoing is considered an "in" activity among 92% of teens (*Media Use*, 2000). Sex appears to be even more present in those movies most favored by teens. One study analyzed 16 R-rated movies popular among teens (Greenberg, Siemicki, et al., 1993). All 16 of these films contained at least 1 sex act, and the average was nearly 11 sex acts per hour. The representation of sex in movies also tends to ignore risk and responsibility messages. Sexual precaution is portrayed even less in the movies than on television. Of the top-grossing movies of 1996, only 1 of 36 movies depicting sex acknowledged protection or birth control (Bufkin & Eschholz, 2000).

The Internet is another medium that has received attention and concern regarding its sexual content. One in five parents of 2- to 17-year-olds cite the Internet as the media influence of greatest concern in raising their children, second only to TV (Annenberg Public Policy Center, 1999). Basic experience with the Internet suggests that such concern may be warranted, in that sexual and pornographic content seems quite common. In fact, a recent study examined the 10 most popular search engines and revealed that the most popular term that Internet users search for online is *sex* (Pastore, 2001). *Sex* was used as a search term more often online than *games, music, travel, cars, jobs, health,* and *weather* combined.

Although sexual content seems to be abundant online, conducting a comprehensive content analysis of sex on the Internet may be difficult if not impossible due to the vast amount and constantly changing nature of online information.

Despite these limitations, a recent study examined the content of Web sites that were accessed when different terms were typed into Excite and Web Crawler search engines (Smith, Gertz, Alvarez, & Lurie, 2000). The researchers typed in five different key words: *sexual health, sex education, sexual intercourse, teen sex,* and *sex advice for teens.* The results showed the following:

The keyword search yielded a total of 5,952,130 web pages. It was impractical to sort through all of these pages to identify duplicates. Four percent of web pages with compatibility scores greater than or equal to 70% were classified as sex education pages and 1% were position statements, for a total of 41 relevant pages. Sixty-three percent of the pages were classified as pornography. (Smith et al., 2000, p. 5)

Overall, the purpose of this section was to examine the prevalence of sex in the media. Much like media violence, sex saturates many entertainment messages independent of medium. We now turn to examine what impact exposure to such depictions may have on viewers, especially children and adolescents.

◆ Effects of Media Sex

Although a number of factors contribute to adolescents' sexual behavior, the media have been accused of playing a central role in shaping their behaviors (Kaiser Family Foundation, 1996). In a recent survey, 53% of teens said that they use TV and movies as a source of information about sex and birth control (Kaiser Family Foundation, 1996). This source of sexual learning may be problematic, especially because television often depicts sex as glamorized with attractive characters engaging in such mature behavior without precaution or consequence. Given this skewed source of sexual information, it becomes important to examine the impact of sexual portrayals on youngsters' sexual socialization.

Significantly fewer studies have been conducted on the impact of sex in comparison to violence. This is probably due to the fact that there are inherent difficulties in conducting experiments with young people when the topic of sex is involved (see Greenberg, Perry, & Covert, 1983). Despite this fact, a handful of studies have been conducted, and we review those in detail below.

LEARNING

To begin with, two studies have looked at young viewers' ability to learn sexual information from television. Results from one study show that 5th and 6th graders who viewed a sex education program scored significantly higher on a subsequent questionnaire about sexual facts than did those who did not (Greenberg et al., 1983). This revealed that television is capable of teaching sexual information, at least when programs are designed specifically for that purpose. Because most TV programming that adolescents view is designed for enjoyment rather than education, a more recent study examined learning from entertainment shows (Greenberg, Linsangan, & Soderman, 1993). In this study, 9th- and 10th-grade participants were exposed to scenes featuring various types of sexual content such as prostitution, married sex, homosexuality, and unmarried sex. Those participants exposed to three of the four sexual topic areas learned significantly more in the way of sexual terms than did those not exposed.

ATTITUDES

Aside from learning information, televised portrayals of sex may also influence viewers' attitudes towards such intimate behavior (Calfin, Carroll, & Schmidt, 1993; Greeson & Williams, 1986; Strouse & Buerkel-Rothfuss, 1993). In particular, Greeson and Williams (1986) assessed the effects of music videos on adolescents' attitudes and values about sex. To this end, 7th and 10th graders were randomly assigned to watch a series of videos that previously aired on MTV. The results on a single-item measure of acceptability of premarital sex revealed that viewers were more likely to approve of such behavior after exposure to the music videos.

Although the last study suggests that a single exposure may influence attitudes, the next question to ask is the following: What impact does heavy viewing of sexual content have on young viewers? Bryant and Rockwell (1994) attempted to address this by examining how massive exposure to sexual depictions influence adolescents' moral evaluations. For 3 hours on 5 consecutive nights, 13- to 14-year-olds were randomly assigned to watch programs featuring (a) sex between unmarried couples, (b) sex between married couples, or (c) programs that feature no sexual content. No more than a week after exposure, the adolescents returned to view 14 short excerpts from broadcast TV featuring both sexual indiscretions (i.e., extramarital affairs) and nonsexual transgressions. The results revealed that adolescents massively exposed to sex between unmarried characters rated the sexual indiscretions as "less bad" than did those in the other two conditions. Similar findings were obtained in a follow-up experiment when using a nonviewing control group.

BEHAVIOR

To date, only two studies have examined the relationship between exposure to sexual content on television and adolescents' early initiation of intercourse. These studies yield a mixed set of results. Peterson, Moore, and Furstenberg (1991) examined the relationship between sexual behavior and television exposure in a two-wave panel study. In 1976, parents of 7- to 11-year-olds filled out measures assessing their children's patterns of exposure to TV, and children indicated whether there were any rules about TV viewing in the home. Five years later, the same participants were resurveyed. At Time 2, the 11- to 16-year-olds were asked to estimate their exposure to television and to report on their own as well as their friends' sexual experiences. Early exposure to television at Time 1 was not correlated with later sexual activity. However, the authors caution against making any definitive conclusions on the basis of these data alone, due to methodological limitations of the study (i.e., imprecise exposure measurement).

A second study has also looked at the relationship between TV viewing and adolescents' sexual behavior (Brown & Newcomer, 1991). A total of 391 adolescents ages 10 to 15 were surveyed in 1978, 1979, and finally in 1981. Each time, participants responded to questions about their (a) overall exposure to TV, (b) exposure to 67 predetermined "sexy" prime-time shows, and (c) own sexual behavior. At Time 3 only, the results show a significant relationship between sexual behavior and the proportion of "sexy" television programming watched relative to total viewing. That is, nonvirgins reported viewing a higher proportion of sexy television than did virgins, despite controls for social class, pubertal development, or friends' encouragement about sex.

Overall, the research revealed above suggested that youngsters are learning information about sex from television and that exposure is affecting their attitudes and moral evaluations. The effect of viewing TV sex on behavior is less clear. However, theories suggest that television may play a key role in shaping adolescents' thoughts, attitudes, and beliefs about romantic relationships, intimacy, and even sexual behavior. For instance, a cultivation approach may argue that viewing repeated messages regarding sex on television may be teaching viewers that sex is to be taken lightly, without much thought, precaution, or consequence. With heavy viewing, young viewers may cultivate unrealistic attitudes and beliefs about negative consequences of sex or the importance of practicing safe sex.

The theory of reasoned action (Ajzen & Fishbein, 1980) specifies more precisely the impact of television sex on shaping adolescents' attitudes and behaviors. According to this approach, intentions and behaviors are determined by the combined influence of attitudes and subjective norms surrounding the behavior. Attitudes are composed of perceived positive and negative consequences of a behavior, whereas subjective norms are made up of perceptions of what important others think about engaging in the behavior. Using this model, television's sanitized view of sex and its consequences may contribute to young viewers developing positive attitudes towards risky sexual behaviors (e.g., not practicing safe sex). Because televised portrayals of teen sex are on the rise, adolescent viewers may also perceive that engaging in such mature behavior is important or even normative in romantic relationships.

A script perspective may suggest a different course of events. Children who are biologically predisposed to early intercourse (i.e., hormonal, genetic predispositions) may be particularly attentive to and encode depictions about sex on TV. Such active involvement may lead to the development of sexual scripts that influence adolescents' perceptions and expectations about romantic relationships. Repeated exposure to sexual scenes on television may frequently prime such scripts, thereby increasing their chronic accessibility and use to guide sexual decision making.

Similar to media violence, the impact of media sex should be moderated by a variety of factors. Age is important because many of the sexual phrases and terms used on television will be inaccessible to children due to a lack of understanding (Silverman-Watkins & Sprafkin, 1983). Thus, televised "sex talk" should have very little impact on younger children. Another important intervening variable is gender. It has been demonstrated that girls enjoy sexual depictions on broadcast TV more than do boys (Greenberg, Stanley, et al., 1993). In addition to greater reported enjoyment, girls may look to the media as a source of social information about sex. In fact, one study found that after exposure to a music video about teen pregnancy, girls reflected more about the content than did boys (Thompson, Walsh-Childers, & Brown, 1993). Some studies have shown that children from families where parents are not very involved, are more likely to engage in sex at an early age (Peterson et al., 1991). Communication and active coviewing can actually help to protect young viewers from the effects of exposure to sexual content (Bryant & Rockwell, 1994; Strouse, Buerkel-Rothfuss, & Long, 1995).

SEX AND VIOLENCE

Although the previous sections focused on sex and violence in isolation, this section examines the effects of juxtaposing these two explicit content features on viewers. This pairing is often found in particular R-rated "slasher" films that feature graphic violence, often in a sexualized context (Yang & Linz, 1990). For example, films from the *Halloween, Friday the 13th,* and *Nightmare on Elm Street* series are quintessential examples of slasher content. Such films are often popular among teen audiences. A study revealed that nearly 70% of college students reported at least some exposure to slasher films on video and at the movie theater (Buerkel-Rothfuss, Strouse, Pettey, & Shatzer, 1993).

Given their popularity, it becomes important to examine the impact that viewing such explicit content may be having on teens. Research in this area has demonstrated that exposure to R-rated, sexually violent slasher films can lead to a desensitization effect, such that viewers experience less negative emotional arousal (e.g., anxiety) with heavy viewing (Linz, Donnerstein, & Adams, 1989; Linz, Donnerstein, & Penrod, 1984, 1988). This effect has been demonstrated using self-report as well as physiological measures of arousal.

One particular study (Linz et al., 1984) looked at the impact of repeated exposure to full-length slasher films on men over 5 consecutive days. Measures were taken after exposure each day. When compared to evaluations on Day 1, the men rated the films on Day 5 as less violent and less degrading to women, and they reported fewer negative reactions to the content. In a similar study,

participants were exposed to either two or five films, one every other day. Again, increased exposure was negatively correlated with negative affect (Linz et al., 1988).

These studies also went a step further by investigating how exposure to sexually violent films may "spill over" and affect evaluations of violence in "real life." To accomplish this, after exposure to the slasher films, participants viewed a rape trial and were asked to evaluate the victim and the defendant on several variables. Compared to a nonviewing control group, male participants exposed to massive doses of sexually explicit content judged a female rape victim as significantly less injured (Linz et al., 1984; Linz et al., 1989) and less worthy, and they tended to perceive her as being more responsible for what happened and as making less of an attempt to resist assault (Linz et al., 1984). Participants also had less sympathy for the victim (Linz et al., 1984; Linz et al., 1988), even when the measures were taken as much as 2 days after the last violent exposure. Although all of the research above has involved all males, heavy viewing of sexually explicit and graphically violent stimuli has been found to affect females' perceptions of the victims of violence as well (Krafka, Linz, Donnerstein, & Penrod, 1997).

Linz et al. (1984) have suggested that repeated viewing of slasher content systematically desensitizes viewers to violence and its real-world consequences (Foa & Kozak, 1986). In explanation, heavy viewers become increasingly comfortable with anxiety-provoking situations in the films. They also assert that this self-awareness of anxiety reduction is paramount in the formation of other perceptions and attitudes about violence portrayed in the films that are then carried over to other contexts. This idea is based on notions of exposure therapy to treat pathological fears. Research reveals that simply showing a phobic a feared stimulus will significantly reduce anxiety once evoked by the object or situation (Foa & Kozak, 1986).

Does exposure to the admixture of sex and violence influence aggression? The answer to this question has been sharply disputed in the social sciences. For obvious ethical reasons, most of the research in this area has focused on *adults'* aggressive reactions to violent sexually explicit content. As a result, we will only briefly mention it here. Studies in this domain usually occur in the laboratory, where male participants are either angered or not and then exposed to videos featuring (a) explicit sex, (b) violence plus explicit sex, or (c) neutral content. After exposure, the participant is given an opportunity to aggress against the confederate, usually by means of electric shock. Using this general procedure, several studies have demonstrated that exposure to violent pornography can increase aggressive behavior among male viewers (Donnerstein, 1980; Donnerstein & Barrett, 1978; Donnerstein & Berkowitz, 1981). Typically, these findings have been explained in terms of excitation transfer (Zillmann, 1991) or a social learning perspective (Bandura, 1971).

In fact, a meta-analysis of pornographic effects (Allen, D'Allessio, & Brezgel, 1995) has demonstrated that exposure to sexually explicit violence is a small to moderate predictor of aggressive behavior ($r = .217$, $k = 7$, $n = 353$). Such effects may be moderated by the sex of the confederate (Donnerstein, 1980; Donnerstein & Berkowitz, 1981) as well as the presence of anger manipulation prior to exposure (Allen et al., 1995; Donnerstein, 1980; Donnerstein & Berkowitz, 1981). Taken together, these studies indicate that participants previously angered by a female confederate are most likely to act aggressively after exposure to violent sexually explicit content.

SOLUTIONS TO HARMFUL EFFECTS

We have discussed throughout this chapter the potential harmful influences of exposure to specific media depictions of sex and violence. One should not assume, however, that these effects cannot be mitigated. Thus, we would like to conclude this chapter by reviewing the potential solutions to these concerns and addressing which ones are considered to be the most viable and why.

Media Literacy and Critical Viewing

A large number of organizations concerned with the well-being of children and families have recommended that professionals take a more active role in reducing the impact of violent media (e.g., American Medical Association, American Psychological Association). Research on intervention programs has indicated that we can reduce some of the impact of media violence by "empowering" parents in their roles as monitors of children's television viewing (e.g., Singer & Singer, 1998). Potentially effective strategies for parents to use to reduce the impact of viewing television violence have been summarized elsewhere (Comstock & Paik, 1991).

Another strategy has been to provide child viewers themselves with the cognitive tools necessary to resist the influence of television violence. For example, Huesmann, Eron, Klein, Brice, and Fischer (1983) attempted to motivate children not to encode and later enact aggressive behaviors they observed on television. They designed their intervention to take advantage of ideas from counterattitudinal advocacy research found effective in producing enduring behavioral changes in other domains. Specifically, the intervention was predicated on a notion contained in both dissonance and attribution theory—when a person finds himself or herself advocating a point of view that is either unfamiliar or even counter to an original belief, he or she is motivated to shift attitudes into line with what is being advocated. Children in the Huesmann et al. experimental group were first credited with the antiviolence attitudes that the experimenters wished them to adopt and then asked to make videotapes for other children who had been "fooled" by television and "got into trouble by imitating it," even though they themselves knew better. The children composed persuasive essays explaining how television is not like real life and why it would be harmful for other children to watch too much television and imitate the violent characters. A videotape of each child reading his or her essay was then played before the entire group. This gave the child an opportunity to see himself or herself advocate an antiviolence position and also made the child's position public. The intervention was successful both in changing children's attitudes about television violence and in modifying aggressive behavior. Four months after the intervention, there was a significant decline for the experimental group in peer-nominated aggression and attitudes about the acceptability of television violence.

Some of the techniques based on the cognitive consistency approach discussed above have been applied to interventions designed to mitigate the impact of exposure to mass media sexual violence (i.e., Linz, Arluk, & Donnerstein, 1990; Linz & Donnerstein, 1989). As one example, Linz et al. (1990) tested the effectiveness of an intervention designed to modify reactions to sexually violent films, decrease rape myth acceptance, and sensitize viewers to the plight of a rape victim presented in a videotaped legal trial.

Male college students were brought into the laboratory and shown a documentary on the psychological impact of sexually violent films (an ABC *20/20* presentation in which the first author, film producers, and adolescents discussed the impact of such films on viewers and society). They then watched the two rape education films. After viewing, participants were assigned to one of three experimental conditions: a "cognitive consistency" condition in which the men wrote essays about myths of sexual violence, videotaped these essays, and watched a videotape playback of themselves and others advocating their antirape position; a "no-playback" condition in which the men wrote the same essays and

read them to the camera but exchanged their essays with others instead of seeing themselves advocate their position; or a "traditional persuasion" condition in which they wrote neutral essays about media use and watched a playback of these. Two additional control conditions—one in which men watched a film documentary on television news, rather than the rape and sexually violent film documentaries, and a no-intervention condition in which the men participated in the final phase of the research only—were also included in the design. A few weeks later, the men were contacted and asked to participate in a film-viewing study, in which they watched clips from sexually violent films and a videotaped reenactment of a rape trial, and then evaluated both.

The results indicated that levels of rape myth acceptance were lowest for those men who had participated in either the cognitive consistency or the no-playback conditions. Participants in these groups reported being more depressed in response to the violent films, were more sympathetic to the victim portrayed in the rape trial, and were more likely to perceive the victim as less responsible for her own rape than were participants in other conditions.

Linz, Wilson, and Donnerstein (1992) have suggested that a systematic program of research be undertaken, with the goal to develop a formal, easily administered educational program concerning media sexual violence. The program should be suitable for high school educators. To create such a program, research is needed to examine what types of information would be most powerful in changing adolescents' attitudes about mass media sexual violence, the optimal format for adolescents to learn and incorporate these messages into their repertoire of values, the most effective communication source for conveying this educational information, and whether social psychological factors, such as a critical viewing companion, facilitate immediate and long-term changes in beliefs and attitudes about sexual violence. We believe that educational interventions will be effective to the extent that they are formed and administered on the basis of systematic research into each of these questions.

Another educational resource is the mass media themselves. Professionally produced educational movies about violence, which are also designed to be entertaining, have great potential for informing the public and, under some conditions, might even change antisocial attitudes about violence. An example in this area is provided by an NBC made-for-television movie. In September 1990, NBC aired a made-for-TV movie about the trauma and aftermath of acquaintance rape. This program, titled *She Said No,* was featured during prime-time hours and attracted a large audience. *She Said No* also received critical acclaim, winning an award from American Women in Radio and Television for its realistic portrayal of the plight of a rape victim. An evaluation of the effectiveness of this movie was undertaken by Wilson, Linz, Donnerstein, and Stipp (1992). The study measured whether exposure to this movie would decrease acceptance of rape myths and/or increase awareness of date rape as a serious social problem.

The study employed a total of 1,038 adults, randomly selected from four locations in the United States who were assigned to view or not to view *She Said No* over a closed-circuit channel, prior to the network broadcast of the film. Individuals from this representative sample were randomly assigned to view or not view the made-for-TV movie in their own home—a more naturalistic viewing environment than is achieved in most media experiments. The viewers and nonviewers were contacted the next day and asked about acceptance of rape myths and perceptions of rape as a social problem.

The results of this study indicated that the television movie was a useful tool in educating and altering perceptions about date rape. Specifically, exposure to the movie increased awareness of date rape as a social problem across all viewers, independent of gender or age. The movie also had

a prosocial effect on older females who were less likely after exposure to attribute blame to women in date rape situations, as compared to older women who did not view the movie.

The above strategies have focused primarily on traditional media such as TV and film. We know, however, that children and adolescents spend more time currently with the Internet, which presents its own problems with regard to exposure. In thinking about solutions to children's and adolescents' access to inappropriate Internet content, there are additional approaches that could be considered, although not considered all that effective. The first is government regulation, restricting the content. The second is technology, including blocking software and some form of rating system.

Government Regulation

Within the United States, the First Amendment protects offensive speech from censorship, including sexually explicit materials. In general, the U.S. courts have struck down most content restrictions on books, magazines, and films. There are, of course, exceptions such as "obscenity," child pornography, and certain types of indecent material, depending on the time, place, and manner of the presentation. In 1996, Congress passed a bill to deal specifically with Internet content regulation primarily in the area of pornography.

The bill took as its premise a number of questions that are to be considered with regard to the issue of the protection of children. First, is access to pornography *easy* for children? The answer is probably yes, if the individual has some computer savvy. As we discussed earlier, sophisticated search engines make the search rapid and extensive. Second, is access to pornography *accidental*? Except for the typing errors, the answer is probably no. Finally, is access to this type of material *harmful*? This is difficult to assess and depends on many factors, as we discussed above. Nevertheless, most of us would agree that we should certainly monitor and protect children from these unwanted sites.

The Supreme Court of the United States ruled on the Communications Decency Act in 1998 and, as expected, held it to be unconstitutional and an infringement on freedom of speech. Likewise, other courts have noted that service providers, such as America Online, could not be held liable for the sending of pornographic materials over the Internet. More recently, the courts have upheld the First Amendment rights of virtual child pornography. It is obvious that the courts are well aware that government regulation in this area would be difficult or near impossible, given not only the vastness of materials available but also the global scope of the Internet.

Blocking Technology

One solution has been the development of software that is designed to block unwanted sites. This blocking software can block known adult sites, for instance, or any site containing predetermined words such as *sex* and *gambling,* as well as other unwanted content. There are a number of these types of software available that perform these and other functions.

But none of these blocking systems is completely effective. The Web changes quite rapidly, and software designed for today may not be entirely appropriate tomorrow. In one test of the effectiveness of blocking adult sites (Consumer Reports, 1999), it was found that one program was able to block out 18 of 22 selected sites. Other programs were able to block about half the adult sites, and one of the tested programs did not block any of the sites. Furthermore, those blocking e-mail or chat group communications were often defeated by either transposing letters or renaming the Web browser on the hard disk.

In a more recent test of these products by Consumer Reports (2001), there was some improvement in the ability of this type of software to block objectionable materials that contain sexually explicit content or

violently graphic images or that promote drugs, tobacco, crime, or bigotry. Far more troubling, however, was the finding that a filter appeared to block legitimate sites based on moral or political value judgments. Given their blocking of certain word strings or known sites, highly educational Web pages are also blocked. As the report rightfully concludes, filtering software is no substitute for parental supervision.

◆ References

Ajzen, I., & Fishbein, M. (1980). *Understanding attitudes and predicting social behavior.* Englewood Cliffs, NJ: Prentice Hall.

Allen, M., D'Allessio, D., & Brezgel, K. (1995). A meta-analysis summarizing the effects of pornography II: Aggression after exposure. *Human Communication Research, 22*(2), 258–283.

American Academy of Child and Adolescent Psychiatry. (2000). *The influence of music and music videos.* Retrieved June 24, 2002, from www.aacap.org/publications/facts-fam/musicvid.htm

American Academy of Pediatrics. (1997). *Testimony of the American Academy of Pediatrics on the social impact of music violence before the Senate Subcommittee on Oversight of Government Management, Restructuring, and the District of Columbia.* Retrieved June 24, 2002, from www.aap.org/advocacy/washing/t1106.htm

American Medical Association. (1996). *Physician guide to media violence.* Chicago: Author.

American Psychological Association. (1993). *Violence and youth: Psychology's response.* Washington, DC: Author.

Anderson, C. A., & Dill, K. E. (2000). Video games and aggressive thoughts, feelings, and behavior in the laboratory and in life. *Journal of Personality and Social Psychology, 78*(4), 772–790.

Annenberg Public Policy Center. (1999). Media in the home. In *Fourth Annual Survey of Parents and Children.* Philadelphia: Author.

Atkin, C. (1983). Effects of realistic TV violence vs. fictional violence on aggression. *Journalism Quarterly, 60,* 615–621.

Bahk, C. (1998). Descriptions of sexual content and ratings of movie preference. *Psychological Reports, 82*(2), 367–370.

Bandura, A. (1971). *Social learning theory.* New York: General Learning Press.

Bandura, A. (1965). Influence of models' reinforcement contingencies on the acquisition of imitative responses. *Journal of Personality and Social Psychology, 1*(6), 589–595.

Bandura, A. (1986). *Social foundations of thought and action: A social cognitive theory.* Englewood Cliffs, NJ: Prentice Hall.

Bandura, A., Ross, D., & Ross, S. A. (1963a). Imitation of film-mediated aggressive models. *Journal of Abnormal and Social Psychology, 66*(1), 3–11.

Bandura, A., Ross, D., & Ross, S. A. (1963b). Vicarious reinforcement and imitative learning. *Journal of Abnormal and Social Psychology, 67*(6), 601–607.

Baron, R. A. (1971a). Aggression as a function of magnitude of victim's pain cues, level of prior anger arousal, and aggressor-victim similarity. *Journal of Personality and Social Psychology, 18*(1), 48–54.

Baron, R. A. (1971b). Magnitude of victim's pain cues and level of prior anger arousal as determinants of adult aggressive behavior. *Journal of Personality and Social Psychology, 17*(3), 236–243.

Baxter, R., DeRiemer, C., Landini, A., Leslie, L., & Singletary, M. (1985). A content analysis of music videos. *Journal of Broadcasting & Electronic Media, 29*(3), 333–340.

Berkowitz, L. (1970). Aggressive humor as a stimulus to aggressive responses. *Journal of Personality and Social Psychology, 16*(4), 710–717.

Berkowitz, L., & Alioto, J. T. (1973). The meaning of an observed event as a determinant of its aggressive consequences. *Journal of Personality and Social Psychology, 28*(2), 206–217.

Berkowitz, L., & Geen, R. G. (1966). Film violence and the cue properties of available targets. *Journal of Personality and Social Psychology, 3*(5), 525–530.

Berkowitz, L., & LePage, A. (1967). Weapons as aggression-eliciting stimuli. *Journal of Personality and Social Psychology, 7*(2), 202–207.

Bozell, B. (1999). *Media influence: The rest of the story.* Retrieved from www.parentstv.org/PTC/publications/lbbcolumns/1999/col19990518.asp

Braun, C. M. J., & Giroux, J. (1989). Arcade video games: Proxemic, cognitive, and content analyses. *Journal of Leisure Research, 21,* 92–105.

Brown, J., & Newcomer, S. (1991). Television viewing and adolescents' sexual behavior. *Journal of Homosexuality, 21,* 77–91.

Bryant, J., Carveth, R. A., & Brown, D. (1981). Television viewing and anxiety: An experimental examination. *Journal of Communication, 31*(1), 106–119.

Bryant, J., & Rockwell, S. (1994). Effects of massive exposure to sexually oriented prime-time television programming on adolescents moral judgment. In D. Zillmann, J. Bryant, & A. Huston (Eds.), *Media, children, and the family* (pp. 183–195). Hillsdale, NJ: Lawrence Erlbaum.

Buerkel-Rothfuss, N. L., Strouse, J. S., Pettey, G., & Shatzer, M. (1993). Adolescents' and young adults' exposure to sexually oriented and sexually explicit media. In B. S. Greenberg, J. D. Brown, & N. L. Buerkel-Rothfuss (Eds.), *Media, sex, and the adolescent* (pp. 99–113). Cresskill, NJ: Hampton.

Bufkin, J., & Eschholz, S. (2000). Images of sex and rape: A content analysis of popular Film. *Violence Against Women, 6*(12), 1317–1344.

Bushman, B. J. (1995). Moderating role of trait aggressiveness in the effects of violent media on aggression. *Journal of Personality and Social Psychology, 69,* 950–960.

Bushman, B. J. (1998). Priming effects of violent media on aggressive thoughts. *Personality and Social Psychology Bulletin, 24*(5), 537–545.

Bushman, B. J., & Geen, R. G. (1990). Role of cognitive-emotional mediators and individual differences in the effects of media violence on aggression. *Journal of Personality and Social Psychology, 58*(1), 156–163.

Calfin, M., Carroll, J., & Schmidt, J. (1993). Viewing music-videotapes before taking a test of premarital sexual attitudes. *Psychological Reports, 72,* 475–481.

Cantor, J. (1994). Fright reactions to mass media. In J. Bryant & D. Zillmann (Eds.), *Media effects: Advances in theory & research* (pp. 213–245). Hillsdale, NJ: Lawrence Erlbaum.

Cantor, J. (2002). Fright reactions to mass media. In J. Bryant & D. Zillmann (Eds.), *Media effects: Advances in theory & research* (2nd ed., pp. 287–306). Mahwah, NJ: Lawrence Erlbaum.

Cantor, J., & Nathanson, A. (1996). Children's fright reactions to television news. *Journal of Communication, 46*(4), 139–152.

Cantor, J., & Reilly, S. (1982). Adolescents' fright reactions to television and films. *Journal of Communication, 32*(1), 87–99.

Cantor, J., & Sparks, G. (1984). Children's fear responses to mass media: Testing some Piagetian predictions. *Journal of Communication, 34*(2), 90–103.

Cantor, J., Wilson, B. J., & Hoffner, C. (1986). Emotional responses to a televised nuclear holocaust film. *Communication Research, 13,* 257–277.

Carver, C. S., Ganellen, R. J., Froming, W. J., & Chambers, W. (1983). Modeling: An analysis in terms of category accessibility. *Journal of Experimental Social Psychology, 19,* 403–421.

Cline, V. B., Croft, R. G., & Courrier, S. (1973). Desensitization of children to televised violence. *Journal of Personality and Social Psychology, 27*(3), 360–365.

Cohen, J. (1988). *Statistical power analysis for the behavioral sciences* (2nd ed.). Hillsdale, NJ: Lawrence Erlbaum.

Comstock, G., & Paik, H. (1991). *Television and the American child.* New York: Academic Press.

Comstock, G., & Scharrer, E. (1999). *Television: What's on, who's watching, and what it means.* San Diego: Academic Press.

Consumer Reports. (1999). *Internet blocking software.* Yonkers, NY: Consumer Union of the United States.

Consumer Reports. (2001). *Digital chaperones for kids.* Yonkers, NY: Consumer Union of the United States.

Cope-Farrar, K., & Kunkel, D. (2002). Sexual messages in teens' favorite prime-time television programs. In J. Brown, J. Steele, & K. Walsh-Childers (Eds.), *Sexual teens, sexual media* (pp. 59–78). Mahwah, NJ: Lawrence Erlbaum.

Dietz, T. (1998). An examination of violence and gender role portrayals in video games: Implications for gender socialization and aggressive behavior. *Sex Roles, 38,* 425–442.

Donnerstein, E. (1980). Aggressive erotica and violence against women. *Journal of Personality and Social Psychology, 39*(2), 269–277.

Donnerstein, E., & Barrett, G. (1978). Effects of erotic stimuli on male aggression toward females. *Journal of Personality and Social Psychology, 36*(2), 180–188.

Donnerstein, E., & Berkowitz, L. (1981). Victim reactions in aggressive erotic films as a factor in violence against women. *Journal of Personality and Social Psychology, 41*(4), 710–724.

Dorr, A. (1983). No shortcuts to judging reality. In J. Bryant & D. R. Anderson (Eds.), *Children's understanding of television* (pp. 199–220). New York: Academic Press.

Drabman, R. S., & Thomas, M. H. (1974). Does media violence increase children's tolerance for real life aggression? *Developmental Psychology, 10,* 418–421.

DuRant, R. H., Rich, M., Emans, S. J., Rome, E. S., Allred, E., & Woods, E. R. (1997). Violence and weapon carrying in music videos: A content analysis. *Archives of Pediatrics and Adolescent Medicine, 151,* 443–448.

Flavell, J. H. (1977). *Cognitive development.* Englewood Cliffs, NJ: Prentice Hall.

Foa, E. B., & Kozak, M. J. (1986). Emotional processing of fear: Exposure to corrective information. *Psychological Bulletin, 99,* 20–35.

Franzblau, S., Sprafkin, J., & Rubinstein, E. (1977). Sex on TV: A content analysis. *Journal of Communication, 27*(2), 164–170.

Freedman, J. L. (1984). Effect of television violence on aggressiveness. *Psychological Bulletin, 96*(2), 227–246.

Gerbner, G., & Gross, L. (1976). Living with television: The violence profile. *Journal of Communication, 26*(2), 173–199.

Gerbner, G., Gross, L., Jackson-Beeck, M., Jeffries-Fox, S., & Signorielli, N. (1978). Cultural indicators: Violence profile no. 9. *Journal of Communication, 28,* 176–207.

Gerbner, G., Gross, L., Morgan, M., & Signorielli, N. (1994). Growing up with television: The cultivation perspective. In J. Bryant & D. Zillmann (Eds.), *Media effects* (pp. 17–42). Mahwah, NJ: Lawrence Erlbaum.

Gerbner, G., Gross, L., Signorielli, N., Morgan, M., & Jackson-Beeck, M. (1979). The demonstration of power: Violence profile no. 10. *Journal of Communication, 29,* 177–196.

Greenberg, B., & Busselle, R. (1994). *Soap operas and sexual activity.* Report prepared for the Kaiser Family Foundation, Menlo Park, CA.

Greenberg, B., & D'Alessio, D. (1985). Quantity and quality of sex in the soaps. *Journal of Broadcasting & Electronic Media, 29*(3), 309–321.

Greenberg, B., Linsangan, R., & Soderman, A. (1993). Adolescents' reactions to television sex. In B. S. Greenberg, J. D. Brown, & N. L. Buerkel-Rothfuss (Eds.), *Media, sex, and the adolescent* (pp. 196–224). Cresskill, NJ: Hampton.

Greenberg, B., Perry, K., & Covert, A. (1983). The body human: Sex education, politics and television. *Family Relations: Journal of Applied Family & Child Studies, 32*(3), 419–425.

Greenberg, B. S., Siemicki, M., Dorfman, S., Heeter, C., Stanley, C., & Soderman, A. (1993). Sex content in R-rated films viewed by adolescents. In B. S. Greenberg, J. D. Brown, & N. L. Buerkel-Rothfuss (Eds.), *Media, sex, and the adolescent* (pp. 45–58). Cresskill, NJ: Hampton.

Greenberg, B., Stanley, C., Siemicki, M., Heeter, C., Soderman, A., & Linsangan, R. (1993). Sex content on soaps and prime-time television series most viewed by adolescents. In B. S. Greenberg, J. D. Brown, & N. L. Buerkel-Rothfuss (Eds.), *Media, sex, and the adolescent* (pp. 29–44). Cresskill, NJ: Hampton.

Greenberg, B. S., Edison, N., Korzenny, F., Fernandez-Collado, C., & Atkin, C. K. (1980). *Life on television: A content analysis of U.S. TV drama.* Norwood, NJ: Ablex.

Greeson, L., & Williams, R. (1987). Social implications of music videos for youth: An analysis of the content and effects of MTV. *Youth & Society, 18*(2), 177–189.

Gunter, B. (1994). The question of media violence. In J. Bryant & D. Zillmann (Eds.), *Media effects: Advances in theory & research* (pp. 163–211). Hillsdale, NJ: Lawrence Erlbaum.

Harrison, K., & Cantor, J. (1999). Tales from the screen: Enduring fright reactions to scary media. *Media Psychology, 1*(2), 97–116.

Hawkins, R. P. (1977). The dimensional structure of children's perceptions of television reality. *Communication Research, 7,* 193–226.

Hawkins, R. P., & Pingree, S. (1982). Television's influence on social reality. In D. Pearl, L. Bouthilet, & J. Lazar (Eds.), *Television and behavior: Ten years of scientific progress and implications for the eighties* (Vol. 2). Rockville, MD: U.S. Department of Health and Human Services.

Heintz-Knowles, K. (1996). *Sexual activity on daytime soap operas: A content analysis of five weeks of television programming.* A report to the Kaiser Family Foundation, Menlo Park, CA.

Hicks, D. J. (1965). Imitation and retention of film-mediated aggressive peer and adult models. *Journal of Personality and Social Psychology, 2*(1), 97–100.

Hirsch, K., & Molitor, F. (1994). Children's toleration of real-life aggression after exposure to media violence: A replication of the Drabman and Thomas studies. *Child Study Journal, 24*(3), 191–207.

Hoekstra, S. J., Harris, R. J., & Helmick, A. L. (1999). Autobiographical memories about the experience of seeing frightening movies in childhood. *Media Psychology, 1*(2), 117–140.

Hoffner, C., & Cantor, J. (1985). Developmental differences in responses to a television character's appearance and behavior. *Developmental Psychology, 21*(6), 1065– 1074.

Hoffner, C., & Haefner, M. J. (1993). Children's strategies for coping with news coverage of the Gulf War. *Communication Research Reports, 2*(10), 171–180.

Huesmann, L. R. (1986). Psychological processes promoting the relation between exposure to media violence and aggressive behavior by the viewer. *Journal of Social Issues, 42*(3), 125–140.

Huesmann, L. R. (1988). An information-processing model for the development of aggression. *Aggressive Behavior, 14,* 13–24.

Huesmann, L. R., & Eron, L. D. (Eds.). (1986). *Television and the aggressive child: A cross-national comparison.* Hillsdale, NJ: Lawrence Erlbaum.

Huesmann, L. R., Eron, L. D., Klein, A., Brice, P., & Fischer, P. (1983). Mitigating the imitation of aggressive behaviors by changing children's attitudes about media violence. *Journal of Personality and Social Psychology, 44,* 899–910.

Huesmann, L. R., Lagerspetz, K., & Eron, L. D. (1984). Intervening variables in the television violence-aggression relation: Evidence from two countries. *Developmental Psychology, 20*(5), 746–775.

Huesmann, L. R., & Miller, L. S. (1994). Long-term effects of repeated exposure to media violence in childhood. In L. R. Huesmann (Ed.), *Aggressive behavior: Current perspectives* (pp. 153–186). New York: Plenum.

Huesmann, R., Moise, J., Podolski, C. L., & Eron, L. (1998). Longitudinal relations between children's exposure to television violence and their later aggressive and violent behavior in young adulthood: 1977–1992. *Journal of the American Medical Association, 39*(2), 201–221.

Jo, E., & Berkowitz, L. (1994). A priming effects analysis of media influences: An update. In J. Bryant & D. Zillmann (Eds.), *Media effects: Advances in theory & research* (pp. 43–60). Mahwah, NJ: Lawrence Erlbaum.

Josephson, W. L. (1987). Television violence and children's aggression: Testing the priming, social script, and disinhibition predictions. *Journal of Personality and Social Psychology, 53*(5), 882–890.

Kaiser Family Foundation. (1996). *The entertainment media as "sex educators?" and, other ways teens learn about sex, contraception, STDs and AIDS.* A report to the Kaiser Family Foundation, Menlo Park, CA.

Kaiser Family Foundation. (1999). *Kids & media @ the new millennium.* Menlo Park, CA: Author.

Krafka, C., Linz, D., Donnerstein, E., & Penrod, S. (1997). Women's reactions to sexually aggressive mass media depictions. *Violence Against Women, 3,* 149–181.

Kunkel, D., Cope, K., Farinola, W., Biely, E., & Donnerstein, E. (1998). *Sex on TV: A biennial report to the Kaiser Family Foundation.* Menlo Park, CA: Kaiser Family Foundation.

Kunkel, D., Cope-Farrar, K., Biely, E., Farinola, W., & Donnerstein, E. (2001). *Sex on TV (2): A biennial report to the Kaiser Family Foundation.* Menlo Park, CA: Kaiser Family Foundation.

Lefkowitz, M. M., Eron, L. D., Walder, L. O., & Huesmann, L. R. (1972). Television violence and child aggression: A follow up study. In G. A. Comstock & E. A. Rubinstein (Eds.), *Television and social behavior: Television and adolescent aggressiveness* (Vol. 3, pp. 35–135). Washington, DC: Government Printing Office.

Leyens, J. P., & Parke, R. D. (1974). Aggressive slides can induce a weapons effect. *European Journal of Social Psychology, 5*(2), 229–236.

Lichter, S. R., & Amundson, D. (1992). *A day of television violence.* (Available from the Center for Media and Public Affairs, 2101 L Street, Suite 405, Washington, DC, 20037)

Lichter, S. R., & Amundson, D. (1994). *Violence in prime time television: 1992–1993.* (Available from the Center for Media and Public Affairs, 2101 L Street, Suite 405, Washington, DC, 20037)

Linz, D., Arluk, I. H., & Donnerstein, E. (1990). Mitigating the negative effects of sexually violent mass media through pre-exposure briefings. *Communication Research, 17,* 641–674.

Linz, D., & Donnerstein, E. (1989). The effects of counter-information on the acceptance of rape myths. In D. Zillmann & J. Bryant (Eds.), *Pornography: Research advances and policy considerations* (pp. 259–288). Hillsdale, NJ: Lawrence Erlbaum.

Linz, D., Donnerstein, E., & Adams, S. (1989). Physiological desensitization and judgments about female victims of violence. *Human Communication Research, 15*(4), 509–522.

Linz, D., Donnerstein, E., & Penrod, S. (1984). The effects of multiple exposures to filmed violence against women. *Journal of Communication, 34*(3), 130–147.

Linz, D., Wilson, B., & Donnerstein, E. (1992). Sexual violence in the mass media: Legal solutions, warnings, and mitigation through education. *Journal of Social Issues, 48,* 145–171.

Linz, D. G., Donnerstein, E., & Penrod, S. (1988). Effects of long-term exposure to violent and sexually degrading depictions of women. *Journal of Personality and Social Psychology, 55*(5), 758–768.

Lowery, S. A., & DeFleur, M. L. (1988). *Milestones in mass communication research* (2nd ed.). White Plains, NY: Longman.

Lowry, D., & Shidler, J. (1993). Prime-time TV portrayals of sex, "safe" sex, and AIDS: A longitudinal analysis. *Journalism Quarterly, 70,* 628–637.

Lowry, D., & Towles, D. (1993). Prime time TV portrayals of sex, contraception and venereal diseases. *Journalism Quarterly, 70*(3), 628–637.

McIntyre, J. J., & Teevan, J. J., Jr. (1972). Television violence and deviant behavior. In G. A. Comstock & E. A. Rubinstein (Eds.), *Television and social behavior: Television and adolescent aggressiveness* (Vol. 3, pp. 383–435). Washington, DC: Government Printing Office.

McLeod, J. M., Atkin, C. K., & Chaffee, S. (1972). Adolescents, parents, and television use: Adolescent self report measures from Maryland and Wisconsin samples. In G. A. Comstock & E. A. Rubinstein (Eds.), *Television and social behavior: Television and adolescent aggressiveness* (Vol. 3, pp. 173–238). Washington, DC: Government Printing Office.

Media use in America. (2000). Mediascope Issue Briefs. Retrieved from www.mediascope.org/pubs/ibriefs/mua.htm

Morison, P., Kelly, H., & Gardner, H. (1981). Reasoning about the realities of television: A developmental study. *Journal of Broadcasting, 25,* 229–242.

National Institute of Mental Health. (1982). *Television and behavior: Ten years of scientific progress and implications for the eighties: Vol. 2. Technical reports.* Rockville, MD: U.S. Department of Health and Human Services.

Nielson Media Research. (2000). *2000 report on television.* New York: Author.

Ogles, R. M., & Hoffner, C. (1987). Film violence and perceptions of crime: The cultivation effect. In M. L. McLaughlin (Ed.), *Communication yearbook 10* (pp. 384–394). Newbury Park, CA: Sage.

O'Keefe, G. J. (1984). Public views on crime: Television exposure and media credibility. In R. N. Bostrom (Ed.), *Communication yearbook 8* (pp. 514–535). Beverly Hills, CA: Sage.

Paik, H., & Comstock, G. (1994). The effects of television violence on antisocial behavior: A meta-analysis. *Communication Research, 21*(4), 516–546.

Parvaz, D. (1999). *Murder, pimping, drugs: Subjects guarantee concern.* Retrieved October 4, 2002, from http://seattlepi.nwsource.com/videogameviolence/game14.shtml

Pastore, M. (2001). *Search engines, browsers still confusing many Web users.* Retrieved March 22, 2002, from http://cyberatlas.internet.com/big_picture/traffic_patterns/article/0" 5931_588851,00.html

Peck, E. (2000). Gender differences in film-induced fear as a function of type of emotion measure and stimulus content: A meta-analysis (Doctoral dissertation, University of Wisconsin, Madison, 2000).

Dissertation Abstracts International, 61(1–A), 17.

Peterson, J., Moore, K., & Furstenberg, F. (1991). Television viewing and early initiation of sexual intercourse: Is there a link? *Journal of Homosexuality, 21,* 93–118.

Potter, W. J. (1986). Perceived reality and the cultivation hypothesis. *Journal of Broadcasting & Electronic Media, 30,* 159–174.

Potter, W. J. (1994). Cultivation theory and research: A methodological critique. *Journalism Monographs, 147,* 1–34.

Potter, W. J., Vaughan, M. W., Warren, R., Howley, K., Land, A., & Hagemeyer, J. C. (1995). How real is the portrayal of aggression in television entertainment programming? *Journal of Broadcasting & Electronic Media, 39,* 496–516.

Potter, W. J., & Ware, W. (1987). An analysis of the contexts of antisocial acts on prime time television. *Communication Research, 14,* 664–686.

Robinson, J. P., & Bachman, J. G. (1972). Television viewing habits and aggression. In G. A. Comstock, & E. A. Rubinstein (Eds.), *Television and social behavior: Television and adolescent aggressiveness* (Vol. 3, pp. 372–382). Washington, DC: Government Printing Office.

Rothschild, N. (1984). Small group affiliation as a mediating factor in the cultivation process. In G. Melischek, K. E. Rosengren, & J. Strappers (Eds.), *Cultural indicators: An international symposium* (pp. 377–387). Vienna, Austria: Verlag der Osterreichischen Akademie der Wissenschaften.

Sapolsky, B. (1982). Sexual acts and references on prime-time TV: A two-year look. *Southern Speech Communication Journal, 47,* 212–226.

Sapolsky, B., & Tabarlet, J. (1991). Sex in primetime television: 1979 versus 1989. *Journal of Broadcasting & Electronic Media, 35*(4), 505–516.

Shrum, L. J. (1995). Assessing the social influence of television: A social cognition perspective on cultivation effects. *Communication Research,* 22(4), 402–429.

Shrum, L. J. (2002). Media consumption and perceptions of social realty: Effects and underlying processes. In B. Jennings (Ed.), *Media effects: Advances in theory and research* (2nd ed., pp. 69–95). Mahwah, NJ: Lawrence Erlbaum.

Silverman-Watkins, L. T., & Sprafkin, J. N. (1983). Adolescents' comprehension of televised sexual innuendos. *Journal of Applied Developmental Psychology, 4,* 359–369.

Singer, D. G., & Singer, J. L. (1998). Developing critical viewing skills and media literacy in children. *Annals of the American Academy of Political & Social Sciences, 557,* 164–179.

Smith, M., Gertz, E., Alvarez, S., & Lurie, P. (2000). The content and accessibility of sex education information on the Internet. *Health Education and Behavior, 27*(6), 684–694.

Smith, S. L., & Boyson, A. (2002). Violence in music videos. *Journal of Communication, 52*(1), 61–83.

Smith, S. L., Lachlan, K., & Tamborini, R. (2000, November). *Popular video games: Quantifying the amount and context of violence.* Paper presented at the annual conference of the National Communication Association in Atlanta, GA.

Smith, S. L., Moyer, E. J., Boyson, A. R., & Pieper, K. M. (2002). Parents' perceptions of their child's fear reactions to TV news coverage of the terrorists' attacks. In B. S. Greenberg (Ed.), *Communication and terrorism: Public and media responses to 9/11* (pp. 193–209). Cresskill, NJ: Hampton.

Smith, S. L., & Wilson, B. J. (2002). Children's exposure to, comprehension of, and fear reactions to television news. *Media Psychology, 4,* 1–26.

Smith, S. L., Wilson, B. J., Kunkel, D., Linz, D., Potter, W. J., Colvin, C. M., et al. (1998). Violence in television programming overall: University of California, Santa Barbara study. In *National Television Violence Study* (Vol. 3, pp. 5–220). Thousand Oaks, CA: Sage.

Sparks, G. G. (1986). Developmental differences in children's reports of fear induced by the mass media. *Child Study Journal, 16,* 55–66.

Steyer, J. P. (2002). *The other parent.* New York: Pocket Books.

Strouse, J., & Buerkel-Rothfuss, N. (1993). Media exposure and the sexual attitudes and behaviors of college students. In B. S. Greenberg, J. D. Brown, & N. L. Buerkel-Rothfuss (Eds.), *Media, sex, and the adolescent* (pp. 277–292). Cresskill, NJ: Hampton.

Strouse, J., Buerkel-Rothfuss, N., & Long, E. (1995). Gender and family as moderators of the relationship between music video exposure and adolescent sexual permissiveness. *Adolescence, 30*(119), 505–521.

Surgeon General's Scientific Advisory Committee on Television and Social Behavior. (1972). *Television and growing up: The impact of televised violence.* Washington, DC: Government Printing Office.

Thomas, M. H. (1982). Physiological arousal, exposure to a relatively lengthy aggressive film, and aggressive behavior. *Journal of Research in Personality, 16,* 72–81.

Thomas, M. H., & Drabman, R. S. (1975). Toleration of real life aggression as a function of exposure to television violence. *Journal of Personality and Social Psychology, 35,* 450–458.

Thomas, M. H., & Drabman, R. S. (1978). Effects of television violence on expectations of other's aggression. *Personality & Social Psychology Bulletin, 4*(1), 73–76.

Thomas, M. H., Horton, R. W., Lippencott, E. C., & Drabman, R. S. (1977). Desensitization to portrayals of real-life aggression as a function of exposure to television violence. *Journal of Personality and Social Psychology, 35,* 450–458.

Thompson, K. M., & Haninger, K. (2001). Violence in E-rated video games. *Journal of American Medical Association, 286*(5), 591–598.

Thompson, M., Walsh-Childers, K., & Brown, J. D. (1993). The influence of family communication patterns and sexual experience on processing of a movie video. In B. S. Greenberg, J. D. Brown, & N. L. Buerkel-Rothfuss (Eds.), *Media, sex, and the adolescent* (pp. 248–263). Cresskill, NJ: Hampton.

Tversky, A., & Kahneman, D. (1973). Availability: A heuristic for judging frequency and probability. *Cognitive Psychology, 5,* 207–232.

Van Evra, J. (1990). *Television and child development.* Hillsdale, NJ: Lawrence Erlbaum.

Ward, M. (1995). Talking about sex: Common themes about sexuality in the prime-time television programs children and adolescents view most. *Journal of Youth and Adolescence, 24*(5), 595–615.

Wilson, B., Linz, D., Donnerstein, E., & Stipp, H. (1992). The impact of social issue television programming on attitudes toward rape. *Human Communication Research, 19,* 179–208.

Wilson, B. J., Hoffner, C., & Cantor, J. (1987). Children's perceptions of the effectiveness of techniques to reduce fear from mass media. *Journal of Applied Developmental Psychology, 8,* 39–52.

Wilson, B. J., Kunkel, D., Linz, D., Potter, J., Donnerstein, E., Smith, S. L., et al. (1997). Violence in television programming overall: University of California, Santa Barbara. In *National Television Violence Study* (Vol. 1, pp. 3–268). Thousand Oaks, CA: Sage.

Wilson, B. J., Kunkel, D., Linz, D., Potter, W. J., Donnerstein, E., Smith, S. L., et al. (1998). Violence in television programming overall: University of California, Santa Barbara. In *National Television Violence Study* (Vol. 2, pp. 3–204). Thousand Oaks, CA: Sage.

Wilson, B. J., & Smith, S. L. (1998). Children's responses to emotional portrayals on television. In P. Andersen & L. Guerrero (Eds.), *Handbook of communication and emotion: Theory, application, and contexts* (pp. 533–569). San Diego: Academic Press.

Wright, J. C., Kunkel, D., Pinon, M., & Huston, A. C. (1989). How children reacted to televised coverage of the space shuttle disaster. *Journal of Communication, 39*(2), 27–45.

Yang, N., & Linz, D. (1990). Movie ratings and the content of adult videos: The sex violence ratio. *Journal of Communication, 40*(2), 28–42.

Zillmann, B. (1991). Empathy: Affect from bearing witness to the emotions of others. In J. Bryant & D. Zillmann (Eds.), *Responding to the screen* (pp. 135–167). Hillsdale, NJ: Lawrence Erlbaum.

AUTHOR INDEX

SUBJECT INDEX

global impact of satellite television,
489–491
move from cable to satellite, 487–489
Brooker, W., 173
Brunsdon, Charlotte, 252–253, 254, 267
Bryant, J., 203
BSB (British Sky Broadcasting), 490
BSkyB, 490
Buenos Aires, alternative media in, 52–53
Bull, Michael, 434
Bullet (hypodermic needle) theory of
media, 469n14
Burgelman, J.-C., 321
Burundi, alternative media in, 47
Bushman, B., 211, 547
Busterna, J. C., 295
Butsch, R., 228–229
Byars, J., 324

Cable News Network (CNN), 70, 78,
117, 300, 315, 488, 490–491
Cable television, 281, 485–489, 490
deregulation of, 490
pay-per-view program, 159, 296, 553
Calabrese, A., 321
Caldwell, John T., 426–427
Call-and-response, 437–438
Campbell, R. B., 456
Canada
cable television in, 487, 489
early radio in, 480
satellite television in, 490
Canal Plus, 70, 490
Cantor, Joanne, 195, 205, 206, 207–208,
548–549
Cantril, Hadley, 187, 188
Capitalism
advertising relationship to, 449, 452,
456, 467
cultural, 315
disorganized, 68
global, 254
growth of print, 85
monopoly, 280
neoliberal, 282
political economics and, 309–310,
317, 321–322
role in nation building of, 377
social-democratic, 449
structural change within, 439
utilitarianism and, 21
Carey, James, 267
Caribbean media, advertising/gender in,
24–25

Cartoon Network, 315, 491
Cartoons, 207, 214, 504
Carveth, R., 322
Castells, Manuel, 231, 233
Catharsis hypothesis, 191, 203, 206
Catholic Church, 126
CBC (Christian Broadcasting
Company), 488
CBS (Columbia Broadcasting Service),
69, 70, 298, 480, 483, 504
CBS Records, 69
CCCS (Birmingham Centre of
Contemporary Cultural Studies),
254, 256, 257, 440, 509
CCITT (Consultative Committee for
International Telephony and
Telegraphy), 133
CDA (critical discourse analysis), 108, 109
Celebratory media economics, 322
Cellular phone, 150, 152, 155–156,
160, 489
Censure/sensure, 340
Centerwall, B. S., 191
Central America, news media/political
power in, 351
Central Intelligence Agency (CIA), 127,
482, 491
Chaffee, S. H., 190, 194
Chamberlin, Edward H., 293
Chambers, T., 296
Chan, J., 281, 403
Chandler, Alfred Jr., 125
Channel Four (Britain), 99
Chat room, 207, 243
Chatman, Seymour, 415
Chauvinistic media patriotism, 388–389
Chen, Kuan Hsing, 276
Child
attention to media by, 213–215
cognitive development of, 212–213
comprehension, of media by, 215–216
passive *vs.* active viewer debate, 214
See also Violence/sex, in media
Child pornography, 95, 561
Chile, alternative media in, 54, 58
China
early radio in, 480
film music in, 438
nationalism and, 385
news media/political power in, 352
satellite television in, 491
See also East Asian media/cultural
studies
Chouliaraki, L., 110

Miron, D., 210
Misattribution theory of humor, 203–204
Mita, M., 278
Mobile computing, 150, 151 (fig), 156
Mobile phone, 155
Mobile telephony, merge with computing,
    155–156
Modem, 150, 298
Modern, beginnings of, 277
Moeran, B., 453, 465–466
Molotch, H., 404
Monopolistic competition, 293
Montage, 215
Montgomery, M., 323
Mood management theory,
    204, 207–208
Moore, K., 555–556
Moral panic, 95, 102n11, 232, 235, 259,
    340, 388–389
Morgan, M., 192
Mori, Y., 273
Morley, David, 171, 176, 267, 273, 282
Morris-Suzuki, T., 320
Mosco, Vincent, 310–311, 313, 314, 318,
    321–322, 324, 325n3, 509, 510
Moslem fundamentalist, 96
Mother India (Film), 524
Mothers Against Drunk Driving, 355
Mothers of the Plaza de Mayo, 52–53
Motion Picture Association of America
    (MPAA), 320
Motion Picture Research Council, 186
Move from cable to satellite, 487–489
The Movie Channel, 488
Moy, P., 356
MPAA film classification system, 92
MTV, 438, 488, 504, 553, 555
MUD (multiuser dungeon/domain),
    151–152, 156
Multilateral communication, 147
Multilevel analysis, 354–355
Multiuser dungeon/domain (MUD),
    151–152, 156
Mulvey, Laura, 508
Mumford, Lewis, 137
Mundy, John, 437
Munsterberg, Hugo, 185, 196n2, 506
Murdoch, Rupert, 69, 70, 87, 88,
    319–320, 325n5, 490, 503
Murdock, Graham, 311, 312, 313, 317,
    321, 323–324, 405, 448, 509
Murray, J. P., 218
Music Corporation of America (MCA),
    500–502

Music culture/media
    conclusions to, 441–442
    disciplining music studies
    cultural studies/popular
        culture, 431
    ethnomusicology, 430–431
    introduction to, 429
    musicology, 429–430
    popular music studies, 431–432
    sociology, 430
    mediation in popular music studies,
        432–433
    social life of music technologies
        overview of, 433–434
    technological mediation/musical
        authenticity, 434–435
    technologies/musicianship
        identity politics, 440–441
        Internet music, 438–439
        music industries/work/political
            economy of music, 439–440
        overview of, 435–436
        role of technologies in identity,
            436–437
        spaces/places, 441
        visual economy of music, 437–438
Music industry, global, 382–383
Music television, 438
Music video, 438, 544 (fig), 553
Musicology, 429–430
Muslims, 99, 113, 247n5,
    535n36–536n36
Mutually dependent technological
    system, 125
Mutz, D. C., 355, 356
Mythologies (Barthes), 415

NAACP (National Association for the
    Advancement of Colored People), 299
NAAWP (National Association for the
    Advancement of White People), 31
Naficy, H., 241–242
NAFTA (North American Free Trade
    Agreement), 78, 134
NAMAC (National Association of Media
    Arts and Culture), 140n4
Namibia, alternative media in, 57
Napoli, P., 93
Napster, 245
Narrative theory, 400
Narrative/genre
    genre, 423–426
    film, 424–425
    television, 423, 424, 425–426

ABOUT THE EDITORS

John D. H. Downing is Director of the Global Media Research Center in the College of Mass Communication and Media Arts at Southern Illinois University. From 1990-2003, he was John T. Jones, Jr., Centennial Professor of Communication at the University of Texas at Austin. His published books include *The Media Machine* (1980), *Radical Media* (1984/2001), *Film and Politics in the Third World* (1987), *Questioning the Media* (co-editor, 1990/1995), *Internationalizing Media Theory* (1996), and *Representing "Race"* (with Charles Husband, 2004). He is a member of the editorial team of the new journal *Global Media and Communication* and editor of the forthcoming Sage Encyclopedia of Alternative Media.

Denis McQuail is Emeritus Professor at the School of Communication Research, University of Amsterdam, and Visiting Professor, University of Southampton, England. He graduated in modern history at the University of Oxford and took his Ph.D. at the University of Leeds, where he worked in the Granada Television Research Unit. Subsequently he taught sociology at the University of Southampton before taking the Chair in Mass Communication at the University of Amsterdam. He has researched and written on a range of media-related topics, especially political communication, audiences, standards of press performance, media policy, and communication theory. He has held a variety of visiting posts at a number of universities including the University of Pennsylvania, Columbia, Harvard, and the universities of Tampere, Moscow, Minho (Portugal), the Catholic University of Portugal, Seijo (Tokyo), and Doshisha (Kyoto). He received an honorary doctorate from the University of Gent. His publications include *Television in Politics* (with Jay Blumler, 1968), *Communication Models* (with Sven Windahl, 1981/93), *Mass Communication Theory* (several editions, 1983-2005), *Media Performance* (1992), *Audience Analysis* (1997), and *Media Accountability and Freedom of Publication* (2003). A number of these have been translated into several languages. He is currently an editor of the *European Journal of Communication* and board member of *Political Communication* and *Gazette*.

Philip Schlesinger is Professor of Film and Media Studies at the University of Stirling, where he is Director of Stirling Media Research Institute. He has been a visiting Professor of Media and Communication at the University of Oslo, has held the Queen Victoria Eugenia chair at the Complutense University of Madrid, and was a Jean Monnet Fellow at the European University Institute. He is a Fellow both of the Royal Society of Edinburgh and the Royal Society of Arts and an Academician of the UK's Academy of Social Sciences. A long-standing editor of *Media, Culture & Society* journal, he has written extensively on media, communications, and cultural questions and his work has been widely translated. His current research focuses on European communicative space, cultural creativity, and the representation of exile. His most recent, co-authored, books, are *Open Scotland?* (2001) and *Mediated Access* (2003).

Ellen A. Wartella was appointed Executive Vice Chancellor and Provost of the University of California, Riverside, after serving as Dean of the College of Communication at the University of Texas, the largest and most comprehensive communication college in the country. Dr. Wartella earned her Ph.D. in Mass Communication from the University of Minnesota in 1977 and completed her postdoctoral research in development psychology in 1981 at the University of Kansas. An active scholar whose research focuses on the effects of media on child development; she held the Walter Cronkite Regents Chair in Communication, Mrs. Mary Gibbs Jones Centennial Chair in Communication, UNESCO Chair in Communication, and Professor of Radio-Television-Film at the University of Texas. She has written and edited several books and has published numerous book chapters and journal articles on mass media and communications. Dr. Wartella is co-principal investigator on the Children's Research Initiative, a five-year, multisite research project funded by NSF. She serves on several national boards including the Decade of Behavior National Advisory Committee; The National Academies of Sciences Board on Children, Youth, and Families; The Sesame Workshop; Kraft Foods Global Health and Wellness Advisory Council; and The National Educational Advisory Board for the Council of Better Business Bureaus.

ABOUT THE CONTRIBUTORS

Alan B. Albarran is Professor and Chair of the Department of Radio, Television and Film at the University of North Texas, Denton, and Editor of the *Journal of Media Economics*. He holds B.A. and M.A. degrees from Marshall University and a Ph.D. from the Ohio State University. His publications range from articles in scholarly journals, edited volumes, and six books, including *Time and Media Markets* (2003); *Media Economics: Understanding Markets, Industries and Concepts* (2nd ed., 2002); *Management of Electronic Media* (2nd ed., 2002); and *Understanding the Web: Social, Political, and Economic Dimensions of the Internet* (2000). He is Editor for a new *Handbook of Media Management and Economics* to be published in 2005. He has lectured in several countries, including Spain, France, Germany, Sweden, Great Britain, Italy, Finland, Switzerland, and Mexico. He will present a workshop on media economics in China in 2005.

Sandra Braman is a Professor of Communication at the University of Wisconsin–Milwaukee and Chair of the Communication Law and Policy of the International Communication Association. Her current work includes *Change of State: An Introduction to Information Policy* (in press) and the edited volume *Communication Researchers and Policy-makers* (2003), *The Emergent Global Information Policy Regime* (2004), and *The Meta-technologies of Information: Biotechnology and Communication* (2004). With Ford Foundation and Rockefeller Foundation support, she has been working on problems associated with the effort to bring the research and communication policy communities more closely together. She earned her Ph.D. from the University of Minnesota in 1988 and previously served as Reese Phifer Professor at the University of Alabama, Henry Rutgers Research Fellow at Rutgers University, and Research Assistant Professor at the University of Illinois-Urbana.

Brigitta Busch, Ph.D., is a Senior Research Fellow in the Department of Applied Linguistics, University of Vienna. Between 1999 and 2003, she was the head of the Centre for Intercultural Studies at the University of Klagenfurt. During her work as an expert for the Council of Europe's Confidence-Building Measures Programme, she was involved in a number of intercultural projects in Eastern and Southeastern Europe. Her main research interests focus on sociolinguistics (multilingualism), discourse analysis, media policies, and intercultural communication. Recent publications include the following: *Sprachen im Disput. Medien und Öffentlichkeit in multilingualen Gesellschaften* (2004); *Bewegte Identitäten. Medien in transkulturellen Kontexten* (with B. Hipfl and K. Robins, 2001); and *Language, Discourse and Borders: Current Issues in Language and Society* (coedited with H. Kelly-Holmes).

Clifford Christians is a Research Professor of Communications, Professor of Journalism, and Professor of Media Studies at the Institute of Communications Research, University of Illinois–Urbana. He has published widely in media ethics and is the author or coauthor of *Responsibility in Mass Communication* (with William Rivers and Wilbur Schramm, 3rd ed., 1980), *Jacques Ellul: Interpretive Essays* (with Jay Van Hook, 1981), *Media Ethics: Cases and Moral Reasoning* (with Mark Fackler, Kim Rotzoll, and Kathy McKee, six editions, 1938–2000), *Communication Ethics and Universal Values* (with Michael Traber, 1997), and *Moral Engagement in Public Life: Theorists for Contemporary Ethics* (with Sharon Bracci, 2002). His research and teaching interests include the philosophy of technology, communication theory, and professional ethics. He has won five University of Illinois teaching awards.

Alfonso Gumucio Dagron is a development communication specialist with experience in Africa, Asia, the South Pacific, Latin America, and the Caribbean. Before becoming the Managing Director of the Communication for Social Change Consortium, he worked 7 years with UNICEF in Nigeria and Haiti and served as international communication specialist for FAO, UNDP, and UNESCO, among other United Nations agencies. He is familiar with issues of communication for child rights, indigenous populations, arts and culture, human rights, community organization, health, and sustainable development. His major country experience also includes Burkina Faso, Bangladesh, Ethiopia, Nicaragua, Costa Rica, Colombia, Papua New Guinea, Mozambique, Mexico, Guatemala, and Bolivia, his home country. He is the author of various studies on communication and has also published several books of his poetry and narrative. As a filmmaker, he directed documentaries on cultural and social issues.

Edward Donnerstein is a Professor of Communication and Dean of the College of Social and Behavioral Sciences at the University of Arizona. Prior to his appointment at Arizona in 2002, he was the Rupe Chair in the Social Effects of Mass Communication and Dean of Social Sciences at the University of California, Santa Barbara. A social psychologist, he received his Ph.D. in psychology and held appointments at the University of Wisconsin, as well as visiting positions at the University of Lethbridge and Beijing University, China. His major research interests are in mass media violence and mass media policy. He has published more than 200 scientific articles in these general areas and serves on the editorial boards of academic journals in both psychology and communication. He has testified at numerous governmental hearings both in the United States and abroad regarding the effects and policy implications surrounding mass media violence and pornography, including testimony before the U.S. Senate on TV violence.

Joke Hermes teaches television studies in the Department of Media Studies (Faculty of the Humanities), University of Amsterdam. Her research interests focus on questions of genre and gender in popular culture and cultural citizenship. She is coeditor and founder of the *European Journal of Cultural Studies*. Her publications include *Reading Women's Magazines* (1995), *The Media in Question* (1998), and *Rereading Popular Culture* (2005), in addition to articles on gender and media in edited collections, as well as popular television from the perspective of audiences in journals.

Michele Hilmes is a Professor of Media and Cultural Studies and Director of the Wisconsin Center for Film and Theater Research at the University of Wisconsin–Madison. She is the author or editor of several books on broadcasting history, including *The Television History Book, Radio Voices: American Broadcasting 1922–1952, Only Connect: A Cultural History of Broadcasting in the United States,* and *The Radio Reader: Essays in the Cultural History of Broadcasting.*

Todd Joseph Miles Holden is a Professor of Mediated Sociology and Chair of the Department of Multi-Cultural Societies in the Graduate School of International Cultural Studies (GSICS) at Tohoku University, Sendai, Japan. He has written extensively on the themes of globalization, identity, gender, political values, and societal development in a number of cultural contexts, including Japan, Malaysia, and the United States. The media he has assayed include television, advertisements, cell phones, the Internet, novels, and film. His recent works include *Globalization, Culture and Inequality in Asia* (2003), coedited with Tim Scrase and Scott Baum, and *medi@sia: Communication and Society In and Out of Global Cultural Context* (forthcoming). He writes a regular column for the e-zine *PopMatters*, earnestly dabbles in philosophical fiction, and has created and maintains a number of institutional and personal Web sites.

Myungkoo Kang is a Professor of Communication Studies at Seoul National University. His publications include books and articles on discourse politics of modernization and politics of journalism in South Korea. In 2002, he edited a special issue on the Korean economic crisis in *Inter-Asia Cultural Studies: Movement* as a forum for critical intellectuals and social activists in the Asian region. Currently, he is working on a book on the cultural history of consumption in South Korea, focusing on the material and cultural conditions of modern life. He has been involved in various kinds of social activism since the late 1980s, including media reform movements and community access media movements. In February 2003, he finished the report "Building a Participatory Community Access Media: Toward an Expressive Public Sphere."

Jenny Kitzinger is a Professor of Communication and Media Studies at Cardiff University. Her work examines power struggles in media production processes and is particularly concerned with questions of media influence and audience reception. She has also written extensively about focus group research methods. Her empirical research projects (funded by major awards from bodies such as the ESRC, the Wellcome Trust, and the NHS executive) have focused on two main areas: (a) sexual violence and (b) risk, health, and science controversies. She has published more than 100 articles and chapters on these issues. Recent books include *Framing Abuse: How the Media Influence Us; The Circuit of Mass Communication: Media Strategies, Representation and Audience Reception in the AIDS Crisis; Developing Focus Group Research: Politics, Theory and Practice;* and *Mass Media and Power in Modern Britain.*

Tannis M. MacBeth (formerly Tannis MacBeth Williams) is a developmental psychologist in the Department of Psychology at the University of British Columbia in Vancouver, B.C., Canada, where she has contributed to the development of women's studies undergraduate and graduate degree programs as well as the university's Centre for Research in Women's Studies and Gender Relations. The common thread underlying her research has been her focus on social issues. Her interest in media content and effects began with her discovery in 1973 of a town without television; that research was published as Williams, T. M. (Ed.), *The Impact of Television: A Natural Experiment in Three Communities.* Her current teaching and research continue to reflect her media and feminist interests. She also studies the role of stereotypes for beliefs about the menstrual, lunar, and day-of-week cycles, as well as the attachment styles of adult twins.

Daniel G. McDonald is currently Professor of Communication at Ohio State University, where he is also Chair of the Graduate Studies Committee. He received his Ph.D. from the University of Wisconsin in 1983. His research focuses on social-psychological aspects of audience uses of the media. Most recently, he has been concerned with intra-audience effects—the effects of audience members on each other through their reactions to media content. His work has been published in a number of journals in the field, including *Communication Research, Journal of Broadcasting & Electronic Media,* and the *Journal of Communication.*

Emily Moyer-Gusé is currently a graduate student in the Communication Department at the University of California, Santa Barbara. She received her M.A. in communication at Michigan State University. Her research interests center on children's understanding and processing of media as well as mass media effects on children and adolescents.

Veena Naregal (Ph.D., University of London) is Reader at the Institute of Economic Growth, Delhi. Her research and teaching interests include South Asian cultural and political history, globalisation and media, and Asian cinemas. She is currently working on two projects: one on comparative media histories in Asia, and another on political patronage and vernacular culture in Western India. She is author of *Language Politics, Elites and the Public Sphere: Western India Under Colonialism.*

Erik Neveu is a Professor of Political Science at the University of Rennes 1 (France). He belongs to the editorial board of *Réseaux* and to the Centre de Recherche sur l'Action Politique en Europe, one of the major French political science research teams. His research interest targets journalism and the public sphere, social movements, cultural studies, and gender studies. He recently published *Sociologie du journalisme* (2001); *Political Journalism, New Practices, New Challenges* (coedited with R. Kuhn, 2002); *Introduction aux Cultural Studies* (with A. Mattelart, 2003); and *Bourdieu and the Journalistic Field* (coedited with R. Benson, 2004). He is currently developing, with Annie Collovald, a reception study among the French readers of detective novels, questioning the linkages between these reading habits and their biographies.

Horace Newcomb is the Director of the George Foster Peabody Awards Program and holds the Lambdin Kay Chair for the Peabody Awards in the Grady College of Journalism and Mass Communication at the University of Georgia. He received a B.A. from Mississippi College and M.A. and Ph.D. degrees from the University of Chicago. He is the author of *TV: The Most Popular Art* (1974), coauthor of *The Producer's Medium* (1983), and editor of six editions of *Television: The Critical View* (1976–2000). In 1973–1974, while teaching full-time, he was also the daily television columnist for the *Baltimore Morning Sun.* He is the editor of *The Museum of Broadcast Communications Encyclopedia of Television,* a three-volume reference work containing more than 1,200 entries on major people, programs, and topics related to television in the United States, the United Kingdom, Canada, and Australia.

Virginia Nightingale is an Associate Professor in the School of Communication, Design and Media at the University of Western Sydney, Australia. Her scholarly writing has focused on the theories and practice of audience research. Her research activities address the impact of mass media on children's culture. This research has included work on television advertising and children, children's understanding of the concept of media harm, and children's understanding of violence in media images. Earlier research focused on cross-cultural studies of audiences. She is the author of *Studying Audiences: The Shock of the Real* (1996). With Karen Ross, she is coauthor of *Media and Audiences: New Perspectives* (2003) and coeditor of *Critical Readings: Media and Audiences* (2003).

Alisa Perren is a doctoral candidate in the Department of Radio-Television-Film at the University of Texas, Austin. Her primary research interests are in media industry studies, American film and television history, and the development of niche markets in contemporary Hollywood. She has published articles on Miramax's marketing and distribution practices as well as on the development of new U.S. broadcast and cable networks in the 1990s.

Tom Schatz is Warner Regents Professor (and former Chairman) of the Radio-Television-Film Department at the University of Texas, where he is currently the Executive Director of the UT Film Institute. He has written four books about Hollywood films and filmmaking, including *Hollywood Genres, The Genius of the System*, and, most recently, *Boom and Bust: American Cinema in the 1940s*. His writing on film also has appeared in numerous magazines, newspapers, and journals, including the *New York Times*, the *Los Angeles Times*, *Premiere, The Nation, Film Comment*, and *Cineaste*. He is currently writing a book on MCA-Universal with Thom Mount, former president of Universal Pictures. As Executive Director of the newly created Film Institute at the University of Texas, Schatz oversees the development of a program devoted to training students in narrative and digital filmmaking, as well as the actual production of feature-length commercial films (in partnership with its commercial counterpart, Burnt Orange Productions).

Holli A. Semetko is Vice Provost of International Affairs and Director of the Claus M. Halle Institute for Global Learning and Professor of Political Science at Emory University. Her research interests include media effects on political attitudes, the role and influence of media in elections and politics, European politics and public opinion, and cross-national comparative research. She has lived and worked in Britain, Germany, the Netherlands, and the United States. She is also an Adjunct Professor at the Amsterdam School of Communications Research at the University of Amsterdam, where she held the chair of audience and public opinion research from 1995 to 2003. She received her Ph.D. in political science from the London School of Economics & Political Science in 1987.

John Sinclair is a Professor in the School of Communication, Culture and Languages at Victoria University of Technology, Melbourne, Australia. He has been researching the globalization of media for more than 20 years, with special reference to the internationalization of the advertising and commercial television industries, particularly in developing regions such as Latin America and India. His published work includes *Images Incorporated: Advertising as Industry and Ideology*, *Latin American Television: A Global View*, and the coedited works *New Patterns in Global Television: Peripheral Vision* (with Liz Jacka and Stuart Cunningham) and *Floating Lives: The Media and Asian Diasporas* (with Stuart Cunningham). He has held visiting professorships at the University of California, San Diego, and the University of Texas at Austin, and he has been UNESCO Visiting Professor of Communication at the Universidad Autónoma de Barcelona. He is on the International Council of the International Association for Media and Communication Research.

Stacy L. Smith is an Assistant Professor in Media Entertainment at the Annenberg School for Communication at the University of Southern California. She received her Ph.D. in communication with an emphasis on human development in 1999 from the University of California, Santa Barbara. Before joining USC, she was a faculty member in the Department of Communication at Michigan State University. Her area of expertise is in children's cognitive and affective reactions to entertainment violence, with an emphasis on the news. She is a coauthor of three book volumes of the *National Television Violence Study* (1997–1998) and has coauthored approximately two dozen book chapters on children's responses to the media in areas such as violence, sex, and advertising. Her work has appeared in journals such as *Journal of Broadcasting and Electronic Media*, *Journal of Communication*, *Media Psychology*, and *Communication Research*.

Annabelle Sreberny is currently a Visiting Professor of Global Media and Communication Studies in the new Media and Film Studies Programme at SOAS, University of London. She was educated at Cambridge and Columbia, has held academic posts in Iran and the United States, and was Director of the Centre for Mass Communication Research at the University of Leicester from 1992 to 1999. Major book titles include *Rethinking International News for the New Millennium* (with C. Paterson, 2004); *Gender, Politics and Communication* (2000); *Media in a Global Context* (1997); *Globalization, Communication and Transnational Civil Society* (1996); *Questioning the Media* (1995); and *Small Media, Big Revolution: Communications and Culture in the Iranian Revolution* (1985). She is at work on a book on media and globalization.

Randall S. Sumpter is an Associate Professor of Communication and Coordinator of journalism education at Texas A&M University, College Station. His research concentration is media history, particularly the development of news work routines, and media sociology. His research has been published in *Journalism & Mass Communication Quarterly, American Journalist, Communication Law & Policy, Journalism History, Newspaper Research Journal,* and *Critical Studies in Mass Communication.* He teaches media history, editing for the mass media, and a graduate-level research methods course. After a 16-year career as a reporter and editor, he earned his M.A. in mass communication from the University of Florida and a Ph.D. from the University of Texas, Austin.

Jan A. G. M. van Dijk is full Professor of Communication Science at the University of Twente, the Netherlands, Department of Communication. His teaching chair is called *The Sociology of the Information Society.* He has been investigating the social aspects of information and communication technology since 1984. His research specializes in social, cultural, and political/policy issues. Key publications in English are *The Network Society* (1999), translated and published in several other languages; *Digital Democracy* (2000), coedited with Ken Hacker; and *The Deepening Divide: Inequality in the Information Society* (forthcoming).

Silvio Waisbord is Senior Program Officer at the Academy for Educational Development in Washington, D.C. His current interests are communication, health, and development. He was Associate Professor of Journalism and Media Studies at Rutgers University. He is the author of *Watchdog Journalism in South America* and coeditor of *Latin Politics, Global Media.*

Janet Wasko (Ph.D., University of Illinois) is a Knight Professor of Communication Research in the School of Journalism and Communication at the University of Oregon. She has authored several works, including *Movies & Money: Financing the American Film Industry* (1982), *Hollywood in the Information Age* (1995); *Understanding Disney: The Manufacture of Fantasy* (2001); and *How Hollywood Works* (2003). She has been coeditor of other volumes on issues in political economy of communications and democratic communications.

D. Charles Whitney is a Professor of Sociology and of Creative Writing at the University of California, Riverside. He had been a professor at the University of Texas, Austin, in the School of Journalism since 1993, where he also held an appointment as Professor of Radio-TV-Film. His Ph.D. is in mass communication from the University of Minnesota, and his research specialties are in the sociology of mass media communicators and in political communication and public opinion. He is coauthor or editor of five books: *MediaMaking: The Mass Media in a Popular Culture* (1998; 2nd ed., 2004), *AudienceMaking: How the Media Create the Audience* (1994), *Mass Communication Review Yearbook* (Vol. 3, 1982) and (Vol. 4, 1983), and *Individuals in Mass Media Organizations: Creativity and*

Constraint (1982). He is the author of more than 75 book chapters, journal articles, reports, and papers.

Ruth Wodak is a Professor of Applied Linguistics and Discourse Analysis at the University of Vienna. Besides various other prizes, she was awarded the Wittgenstein Prize for Elite Researchers in 1996 and is head of the Wittgenstein Research Centre's "Discourse, Politics, Identity." Her current research projects include, amongst others, "The Discursive Construction of History," "Communication in Institutions" (research on EU organizations), "Research on European Identities," and "Political Language, Political Discourses." Her research interests focus on discourse analysis, gender studies, language and politics, prejudice, and discrimination. She is a member of the editorial board of a range of linguistic journals and coeditor of the journals *Discourse and Society* and *Language and Politics.* She has held visiting professorships at Uppsala, Stanford University, University Minnesota, and Georgetown University.

Nabeel Zuberi is a Senior Lecturer in Film, Television and Media Studies at the University of Auckland. He is the author of *Sounds English: Transnational Popular Music* (2001) and coeditor (with Luke Goode) of *Media Studies in Aotearoa/New Zealand* (2004), and he has published other articles and book chapters. He is currently working on a book about the impact of digital technologies on popular music studies. His other research interests include a project on South Asian diaspora media and popular culture. He is a member of the editorial board for the forthcoming *Encyclopedia of Alternative Media and Communication.*